Emerging Trends in Artificial Intelligence

Integrating theories and practice

Online at: https://doi.org/10.1088/978-0-7503-6320-4

IOP Series in Next Generation Computing

Series editors

About the series

The motivation for this series is to develop a trusted library on advanced computational methods, technologies, and their applications.

This series focuses on the latest developments in next generation computing, and in particular on the synergy between computer science and other disciplines. Books in the series will explore new developments in various disciplines that are relevant for computational perspective including foundations, systems, innovative applications, and other research contributions related to the overall design of computational tools, models, and algorithms that are relevant for the respective domain. It encompasses research and development in artificial intelligence, machine learning, block chain technology, quantum cryptography, quantum computing, nanoscience, bioscience-based sensors, IoT applications, nature inspired algorithms, computer vision, bioinformatics, etc. and their applications in the areas of science, engineering, business, and the social sciences. It covers a broad spectrum of applications in the community, including those in industry, government, and academia.

The aim of the series is to provide an opportunity for prospective researchers and experts to publish works based on next generation computing and its diverse applications. It also provides a data-sharing platform that will bring together international researchers, professionals, and academics. This series brings together thought leaders, researchers, industry practitioners, and potential users of different disciplines to develop new trends and opportunities, exchange ideas and practices related to advanced computational methods, and promote interdisciplinary knowledge.

A full list of titles published in this series can be found here: https://iopscience.iop.org/bookListInfo/iop-series-in-next-generation-computing.

Emerging Trends in Artificial Intelligence

Integrating theories and practice

Haruna Chiroma
Department of Computer Science, University of Hafr Al Batin, Hafr Albatin, Saudi Arabia

IOP Publishing, Bristol, UK

ISBN 978-0-7503-6320-4 (ebook)
ISBN 978-0-7503-6318-1 (print)
ISBN 978-0-7503-6321-1 (myPrint)
ISBN 978-0-7503-6319-8 (mobi)

DOI 10.1088/978-0-7503-6320-4

Version: 20250501

IOP ebooks

British Library Cataloguing-in-Publication Data: A catalogue record for this book is available from the British Library.

Published by IOP Publishing, wholly owned by The Institute of Physics, London

IOP Publishing, No.2 The Distillery, Glassfields, Avon Street, Bristol, BS2 0GR, UK

US Office: IOP Publishing, Inc., 190 North Independence Mall West, Suite 601, Philadelphia, PA 19106, USA

Contents

Foreword

Many, especially those outside the mainstream artificial intelligence (AI) community, have the illusion that AI technology is a recent discovery. However, AI has existed since the time of Aristotle (384–322 BCE) and has gradually evolved through research and development to its current advanced stage. We are in the era of AI. The proliferation of AI across nearly every aspect of society, coupled with mainstream and social media hype, has led to unprecedented attention and extensive discussion at all levels. The emergence of language models capable of performing complex and sophisticated tasks across domains, sometimes rivalling human performance has further fuelled this interest. Arguably, AI is the most discussed scientific subject in the world today. Generative AI has transformed user interaction with computing devices, shifting from simple actions like clicking icons or pressing keys for simple tasks to advanced content generation. This includes generating videos from text, translating videos into multiple languages, producing and debugging source code, creating images from text, and even automating social media account management.

Historically, AI hype is not new. AI has gone through cycles of breakthroughs, hype, and failures. Typically, the cycle begins with a breakthrough in AI, followed by mainstream media hype and massive industry adoption. However, when expectations fail to materialize, funding is significantly cut, AI projects are cancelled, and industries lose billions of dollars, a period known as 'AI winter.' Eventually, renewed interest in the field leads to further breakthroughs, restarting the cycle. For example, expert systems and LISP machines followed this AI cycle in the past. Currently, AI is booming due to breakthroughs in language models with advanced content-generation capabilities. Industries are investing billions of dollars in AI projects, both in hardware and software, leading to massive adoption across different domains. Today, AI has become a trillion-dollar industry. Will the current AI dispensation follow the historical AI cycle? Is the future of AI certain or uncertain? The answer lies in the future.

As of now, there is extraordinary interest in the field of AI, with researchers from diverse backgrounds and new career researchers attempting to venture into AI or integrate it into their work. On the other hand, expert AI researchers are striving to advance the field to greater heights. Meanwhile, professionals and developers are increasingly incorporating AI into their products.

This timely book presents the historical breakthroughs in AI, from the abacus to future expectations, before exploring into chapters that cover fundamental theories, development procedures, and applications. Each chapter is integrated with case studies that showcase real-world operations of the AI technologies. The book explores generative AI for advancing language models, artificial general intelligence leading to large language model tutorials, artificial superintelligence, quantum AI, huge graph neural networks, explainable AI, sustainable AI, autonomous robotics, brain–machine interfaces, fully autonomous robotic surgery, AI-enhanced DevOps lifecycle, supercomputers performance with sustainability, Industry 5.0, decentralized blockchain technology, AI's carbon footprint, a proposed bibliometric analysis procedure for the AI domain, and a bibliometric analysis of AI spanning over six decades.

The book has the potential to inspire ground-breaking advancements by bridging theories with practical applications. This makes it an essential read for novice and expert researchers as well as industry practitioners.

Professor Jemal H Abbawajy
Deakin University, Australia

Acknowledgments

I would like to acknowledge the exceptional effort and insightful contributions of Fatsuma Jauro, *PhD* of Ahmadu Bello University, in creating outstanding graphic designs that effectively illustrate complex ideas, making them easier to understand.

Author biography

Haruna Chiroma

Haruna Chiroma is at the University of Hafr Al Batin, College of Computer Science and Engineering, Saudi Arabia. He earned his PhD in artificial intelligence from the University of Malaya. Chiroma is recognized among the Top 2% most influential scientists in the world ranked under artificial intelligence. His editorial experience includes his current role as Editor for *Discover Computing* (formerly *Information Retrieval*)—Springer (2024–present), and his previous role as Associate Editor for *IEEE Access* (2018–21). He is also an Editorial Board Member of the *IAES International Journal of Artificial Intelligence*, Associate Editor for *TELKOM*, and a member of the Editorial Board for *Recent Advances in Computer Science and Communications.*

His research interests span artificial intelligence, artificial neural networks, deep learning, nature-inspired algorithms, natural language processing, language models and transformers. Chiroma has authored five books in the field of artificial intelligence. With over 160 academic publications, his work has been featured in leading journals such as *Neural Network World, Artificial Intelligence Review, Frontiers in Artificial Intelligence, Applied Soft Computing, Neural Computing and Applications*, and the *Journal of Ambient Intelligence and Humanized Computing*. He has also reviewed for more than 80 ISI journals, including *IEEE Transactions on Neural Networks and Learning Systems, Artificial Intelligence Review, IEEE Transactions on Intelligent Transportation Systems, Applied Soft Computing, Expert Systems with Applications, Knowledge-Based Systems, Soft Computing*, and *International Journal of Bio-Inspired Computation*. In addition to his reviewing work, Chiroma has served on the *Technical Program Committee* for over 70 international conferences, workshops, and symposiums. Chiroma has successfully graduated MSc and PhDs.

IOP Publishing

Emerging Trends in Artificial Intelligence
Integrating theories and practice
Haruna Chiroma

Chapter 1

Artificial intelligence history from the abacus through science fiction movies and artificial intelligence winter to future expectations

Many historical developments of artificial intelligence (AI) have been published in the literature. However, the historical development hasn't covered more recent breakthroughs in AI and the role of science fiction movies were ignored. Therefore, this chapter covers the gap by updating the historical development by including the most recent breakthroughs, the role of science fiction movies and AI winter. The chapter provides a historical background of the revolution in computer development that indicated strong teamwork and several contributions made by many scientists. The chapter traces background information about AI from the root to the different stages of development. We discusses selected historical development of AI starting from mechanical operations in the ancient Greek and Roman civilization from over 400 BC to current times. The major historical breakthroughs in AI from 1940 to 2025 are outlined. The cycle of AI winter, renewed interest and innovations are discussed. The future of AI beyond 2025 are outlined with a timeline. Lastly, industrial applications and a case study where AI history is relevant to current AI industries are discussed.

1.1 Introduction

The first to develop a system for a rational component of the mind was Aristotle (384–322 BCE). Ramon LIull (c. 1232–1315) innovated a reasoning system. René Descartes (1596–1650) referred to humans and animals as complex machines composed of bones, muscles, and organs, which he compared to cogs, pistons, and cams (Russell and Norvig 2003). These indicate an element of AI in philosophy hundreds of years ago.

AI was a general goal description leaving opportunities for different spaces for different subjects and methods. AI started as a brand name used by a group of researchers in an elite institution tying their research work to lofty goals, gaining

doi:10.1088/978-0-7503-6320-4ch1

support for research and situating their footprint within computer science as an emerging field of study (Haigh 2023). It Is extremely difficult to trace the actual root of AI. However, AI can probably be traced back to the 1940s, to be specific, 1942 (Haenlein and Kaplan 2019). However, Haigh (2023) argued that AI can be traced back to 180 years. At the end of the Second World war, computers started springing up, which motivated the development of game-playing programs such as for chess (Heath *et al* 1997).

Alan Turing was the pioneer who in 1950 proffered the description of simulating human intelligence behaviour and critical thinking on computers. Alan Turing proposed a simple test to determine the intelligent behaviour of a machine commonly referred to as the Turing test. In the subsequent six years after the Alan Turing description of intelligent concept on a machine, John McCarthy described AI as the science and engineering of making machines act intelligently (Kaul *et al* 2020).

Alan Turing created the famous Turing test to prove to people, who at that time couldn't believe it, that computers can be made to become intelligent through computer programs. Also, Turing intended to make a point that behaviour defines intelligence not mystical quantities in such a way that if a computer program can act intelligently like a human, it should be considered as intelligent similar to human beings (Pennachin and Goertzel 2007). In summary, AI started with simple if–then rules before evolving into complex algorithms over the decades to perform functions similar to the human brain (Kaul *et al* 2020).

There is uncertainty regarding the future of AI, with the chances of additional winters for AI or AI summers that are even greater. As a result of the uncertainty in the future of AI, it is critical to put in place a balanced initiative without any bias, for instance, AI monitoring watches for advancements in AI and evaluates the impact of AI in the years to come as it is expected to significantly transform society. AI has become a mature field of technology in today's world and it is significantly growing in modern life activities, however, the future of AI is shrouded in uncertainty having opportunities of increasing growth but also the possibility of diminishing. Thus, reflecting on the historical development of AI may give an insight into the future of AI (Delipetrev *et al* 2018).

Many historical developments of AI were published in the literature by different researchers over a period of years from different perspectives. However, the historical development hasn't covered more recent breakthroughs in AI. Thus, describing the historical developments misses the most recent breakthroughs in the field of AI. Therefore, this chapter is intended to fill the gap by updating the historical development by including the most recent developments in the area of AI, for readers to have a glance at the AI history development perspective up to current times. This can pave way for the reader to predict the future equipped with the knowledge of the past and present.

1.2 Previously published history of artificial intelligence

One study presents the fundamental definition of AI before providing a historical perspective of AI. The study summarizes the development of AI from the point view of history and discusses the recent interest generated by AI. The context of AI development over the years and the current state of AI are compared to gain insight into the future, as this is uncertain. The report also presents the foundation of AI, definitions of AI, AI major methods, approaches and periods of AI development from the 1950s to 2010s. It ranges from AI algorithms development, symbolic algorithms, expert systems, machine learning and deep learning. The AI applications domain, such as in medicine and transportation, is also covered (Delipetrev *et al* 2018). The history of AI was covered based on intellectual issues in another study. The intellectual issues involve opposing views regarding its development. The evolving content of the development as well as the scientists responsible for the breakthroughs were discussed. The historical development of AI covers major breakthroughs based on intellectual issues in AI between 1640 and 1980 (Newell 1982). The early history of AI, especially the starting point of the domain of the scientific venture from the perspective of Europe was discussed. The story of AI has been divided into three major stages. The history covers the period from 1913 to 2012 (Bibel 2014). The history of AI from the perspective of the brain–machine interface pointing out the major milestones achieved over a period of 50 years is presented. The pioneer scientists that made contributions to the field were identified. The technological development and transformations made in the brain–machine interface were discussed, including breakthroughs. It is believed in the study that full understanding of the human brain is a goal that can possibly be achieved. More breakthroughs in this domain are required to improve quality of life for impaired people (Kawala-Sterniuk *et al* 2021). The history of explainable AI pointing out major developments over a period of years, including how the explainability idea was embedded in AI was conceived, the present status and future outlook of the explainable AI were discussed. The study was concluded by recommending criteria for AI explainability for easy understanding of explainable AI systems (Confalonieri *et al* 2021). The development of computer chess from the perspective of history is presented together with the impact of computer chess on intelligence. Computer chess developed based on algorithms showing historical development of the chess game covering the period from 1950 to 1996 was discussed (Heath *et al* 1997). Walsh (2017) presents the historical perspective of technological singularity tracing it to some thinkers. The argument against the development of singularity was discussed, especially optimism and pessimism. I J Good in 1965 predicted the singularity referred to as intelligent explosion. It was found that the debate about the singularity was more pronounced outside the mainstream, the AI singularity community, than within the AI community. The references covered in the study range from 1958 to 2015. McCorduck *et al* (1977) presented a brief historical development of AI covering early AI discoveries including automata, analytical engines, etc. The references covered advancements between 1950 and 1973. Haigh (2023) discussed the historical perspective on the way AI grew within the discipline of computer science. The invention of AI, creation of computer science and legacy of early AI were discussed in the historical development of AI. The major breakthroughs and events within the period from 1949 to 2015 were covered, as evident in the references and citations. The summary of the papers is presented in table 1.1.

Table 1.1. Summary of some AI history published focussing on different periods.

Reference	Perspective	Period of years
Delipetrev *et al* (2018)	AI- narrow	1950s–2010s
Newell (1982)	AI: intellectual issues	1640–1980
Bibel (2014)	AI- narrow	1913–2012
Kawala-Sterniuk *et al* (2021)	Brain–machine interface	50 years
Confalonieri *et al* (2021)	Explainable AI	
Heath *et al* (1997)	Game	1950–1996
Walsh (2017)	Singularity	1958–2015
McCorduck *et al* (1977)	AI	1950–1973
Haigh (2023)	AI within computer science	1949–2015

1.3 Era of mechanical operations leading to computers

The history of computers in this chapter is traced from the era of mechanical operation up to the digital era where computers became affordable by individuals. There is much literature on historical development of computers with different perspectives and arguments. This literature cannot be covered exhaustively in this section. However, the major progress in the development of computers up to current times were outlined. The development of computers is not tied to a particular individual but the work of many scientists based on different contributions from several perspectives.

The main purpose of building machines in the early days was to perform physical processes without much human effort. These early machines accepted inputs, applied physical action on the inputs and produced output that was physical. An example of such an early machine was the cotton gin. The cotton gin accepted raw cotton as inputs, separated the cotton seed and lint mechanically and subsequently provided the separated products as an output (Evans 2009). Abd-El-Barr and El-Rewini (2005) argued that building a computing machine requires teamwork, such that attributing a particular machine to a single researcher is not fair. When a machine is attributed to one researcher, it is likely that the researcher might have led the team that built the computing machine. As such, in this chapter, the names of the individuals linked to a particular computing machine does not attribute the machine to the single researcher, but the researcher might have led the team that invented the computing machine. The computers seen around today were not developed in a day but progressed from a simple mechanical idea to the complex nature of the present day computers that perform several tasks in our daily activities. In the early days of the computer era, computing machines were mainly mechanical or electro-mechanical. In that era, the calculating machines were purely mechanical devices developed using gears and powered by hand operated crank as argued by Abd-El-Barr and El-Rewini (2005). During the ancient Greek and Roman civilization, that is, before the advent of calculating machines, the abacus was the counting device that people depended on to ease complex calculations. The post-calculating machines era ushered in the era of computer generations. The generations of computers were the progress made in terms of developing computers based on computer technological advancements. The generations of computer development started from first generation to fifth generations, i.e. AI showing the motivations and limitations that prompted the generations. The generations of computers begin from the 1940s to the present time.

1.3.1 The early history of computers: mechanical computing machines

1.3.1.1 Abacus and algorithm

The first simple counting device called the abacus (see figure 1.1) was invented in Babylonia in the 4th century BC. The abacus is view by many as the pioneered computing device in the history of computers. Lord John Napier in 1614 introduced the algorithm, and subsequently invented a device for calculations that comprises a series of rods frequently referred to as '*bones*'. The bones reduce the complex process of multiplication and division into addition and subtraction. Many considered the invention of the calculating device as the first computation that was done mechanically (Tymann and Reynolds 2008). According to Blum (2011a, 2011b), about 100 years after the prophet of Islam, the Arab countries awakened in the search for knowledge in science and mathematics. A great Arab mathematician called Mohammed ibn Musa al-Khwarizmi in a university in Bagdad published many works in mathematics, the Hindu–Arabic numerals are one of the great works of Mohammed ibn Musa al-Khwarizmi. The rules he established to operate on the Hindu–Arabic numerals became known as the algorithm. Today, algorithms are the backbone of modern computer systems.

It is believed that the genealogy of modern computers starts from the abacus. The abacus is the earliest device used for counting. The history of the abacus as shown in figure 1.1 has been traced to the ancient Greek and Roman civilizations. The abacus is a simple machine that consisted of beads strung on rods, turn mounted in a frame that is rectangle in shape. The movement of the beads positions of the rods represent

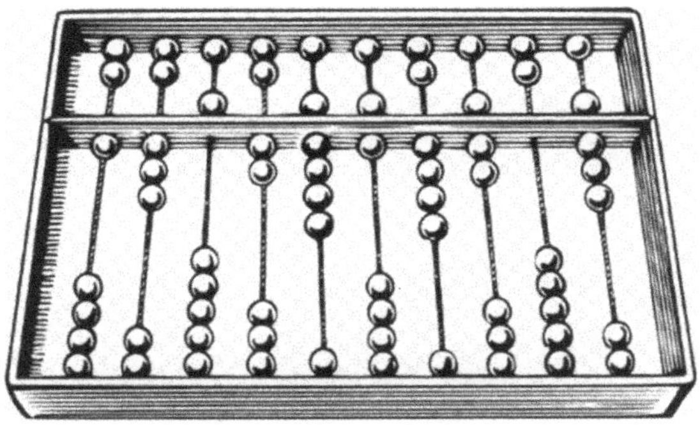

Figure 1.1. The abacus. This [Abacus (PSF)] image has been obtained by the author from the Wikimedia website, where it is stated to have been released into the public domain. It is included within this book on that basis.

the values stored in the abacus. The basis of the abacus is in the positions of the beads that this 'computer' represents and stores data. The algorithm control depends on the user operations which is an analogous to an algorithm's execution (Brookshear and Brookshear 2002).

1.3.1.2 Pascaline

The invention of the first mechanical calculator is frequently credited to Blaise Pascal the machine is called the Pascaline, as shown in figure 1.2, invented in 1642. Based on evidence from Pascal's memoirs, the machine was developed to assist his father in his capacity as a tax collector. Thus, the machine helped to ease the tax collection work. The main function that could be performed with the Pascal device was addition and subtraction. However, multiplication and division were possible using a series of additions or subtractions. The maximum number of figures in the machine was eight and subtraction was performed based on the techniques of complement.

In 1671, Gottfried Leibniz modified the Pascal calculator and developed a machine that can perform numerous calculations based on multiplication and division. The Leibniz machine design is based on the concept of gears. The output of the Leibniz machine was achieved by the observed gear positions. In Leibniz's machine, the algorithm is embedded in the machine architecture. In addition, the machine offered different arithmetic operations (Brookshear 2007).

1.3.1.3 Difference engine and analytical engine

A mathematician and inventor called Charles Babbage was frustrated by the manual calculation of astronomical tables, this frustration motivated Charles Babbage to invent a mechanical device for automatic calculation. In the year 1822, Charles Babbage started working on the difference engine (figure 1.3), a computing device for performing automatic computation. In his work for the difference engine, he conceived the idea of the analytical engine (figure 1.4), which is more sophisticated than the difference engine in computation. The difference engine has the capability to be programmed based on a punched card. Subsequently, the difference engine used the following features: sequential control, branching and looping. However,

Figure 1.2. Pascaline calculating machine. This [Arts et Metiers Pascaline dsc03869] image has been obtained by the author from the Wikimedia website where it was made available by [David.Monniaux] under a CC BY-SA 3.0 licence. It is included within this book on that basis. It is attributed to [David.Monniaux].

Figure 1.3. Charles Babbage difference engine. This [Babbage Difference Engine (1)] image has been obtained by the author from the Wikimedia website where it was made available by [oxyman] under a CC BY 2.0 licence. It is included within this book on that basis. It is attributed to [Jitze Couperus].

Figure 1.4. Analytical engine (an improved version of the difference engine). This [Babbage's Analytical Engine] image has been obtained by the author from the Wikimedia website where it was made available by [Mrjohncummings] under a CC BY-SA 2.0 licence. It is included within this book on that basis. It is attributed to [Mrjohncummings].

Charles Babbage did not finish the complete working version of both the difference engine and analytical engine. The difference between the difference engine and analytical engine is that the difference engine was a special-purpose mechanical machine that tabulated algorithms and trigonometric function, whereas the analytical engine was a general-purpose computer that had an arithmetic logic unit, control flow, memory and loop unlike the difference engine (Tymann and Reynolds 2008). The improvement of the analytical engine in starting using punch cards to control its behaviour was done by Joseph-Marie Jacquard. He invented the first programmable weaving loom in 1801 that had the capability for producing intricate patterns on cloth.

Joseph-Marie Jacquard is the inventor who gave Charles Babbage a tapestry that had been woven on this loom using over 10 000 punch cards (Null and Lobur 2003). Later, the work of Charles Babbage on the difference engine and analytical engine became the springboard from which modern computer systems were built.

For example, Augusta Ada Byron (Ada Lovelace) studied the working principles, implementation and implementation properties of the analytical engine. Then, Ada Lovelace developed a program that could instruct the analytical engine to compute the Bernoulli numbers. Ada Lovelace improve the analytical engine by adding the program to it. The programming language was named ADA in honour of Lovelace. This is the work that prompted many to consider Lovelace as the first programmer in the world (Tymann and Reynolds 2008). The summary of the early computer history is shown in figure 1.5 and invented devices with their corresponding year of invention in figure 1.6.

1.3.2 The generations of computers from 1940s to date

The generations of computers based on technological advancement have been explained in a logical order as classified in the literature to show their progression. The first, second, and third generations were mostly as described in the work of Arnold (1998). A discussion of the computer generations based on technological advancement up to the era of AI are presented in the following.

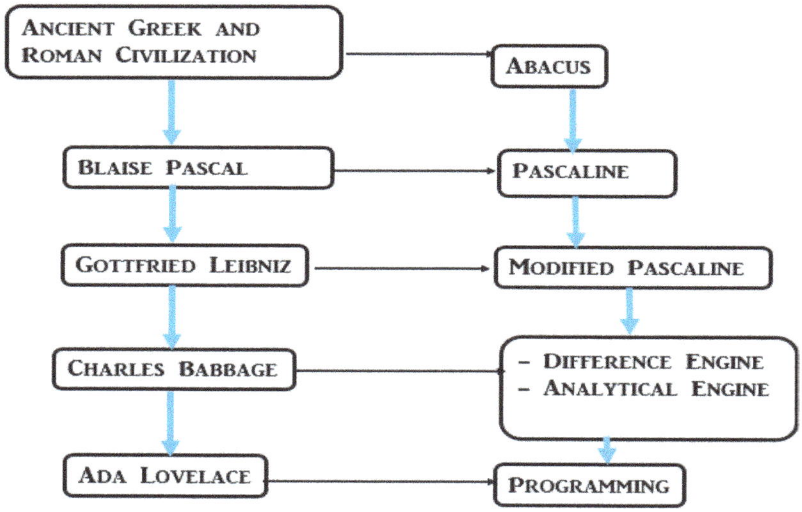

Figure 1.5. The flow representation of the early history of computer development indicating major breakthroughs.

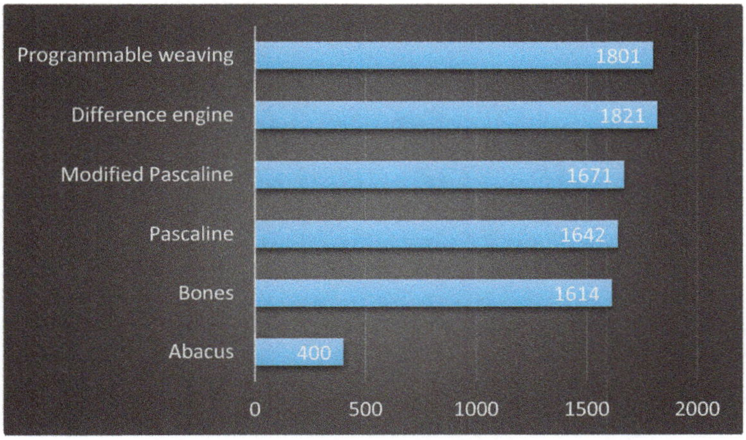

Figure 1.6. Early history of computer development indicating device and corresponding year of invention.

1.3.2.1 The first generation of computers: 1940s and 1950s

The invention of the vacuum tube (see figure 1.7) revolutionized computer technology, which made computers become affordable. The vacuum tube has the capability of executing hundreds of algorithms per second. In the 1930s, the team of John Atanasoff built a special-purpose computer for solving simultaneous equations. The limitations of the vacuum tube such as inefficiency, not properly working and huge requirement for a cooling system motivated J P Eckert and J W Mauchy to develop the Electronic Numeric Integrated and Calculator (ENIAC) shown in figure 1.8 funded by the US army. The ENIAC was funded by the US army because they had a very hectic task of computing trajectories of its new ballistic armaments during World War II. Thousands of humans were wracking their brains on studying the arithmetic requirement of firing tables. It typically takes a number of days to calculate the ballistic table, but the army realized that the time could be shortened from days to minutes by an electronic device. The ENIAC was able to shorten the time to calculate the table from 20 h to 30 s. Unfortunately for the army, the ENIAC development was completed in 1945, after the war ended (Null and Lobur 2003). The ENIAC was very large and has a total weight of 30 tones. The ENIAC used 18 000 vacuum tubes and could perform approximately 8000 additions per second. The Colossus computer was developed in Britain during World War II. It was used for the breaking the codes of German messages (Arnold 1998). The German Konrad Zuse built many relay machines that were secretly hidden because of the involvement of Germany in World War II. Later on, the relay machines were destroyed by allied bombing. Because re-programming of ENIAC required rewiring of the program, this motivated John von Neumann and his team to propose a new machine that stored the program in a memory and read the instructions from it to avoid the tedious rewiring of the program. John von Neumann was the architect that proposed the following components of the computer: arithmetic and logic unit, control, input, output, and memory units (Dandamudi 2006). These components are also found in modern computers. The concept of general-purpose computer was

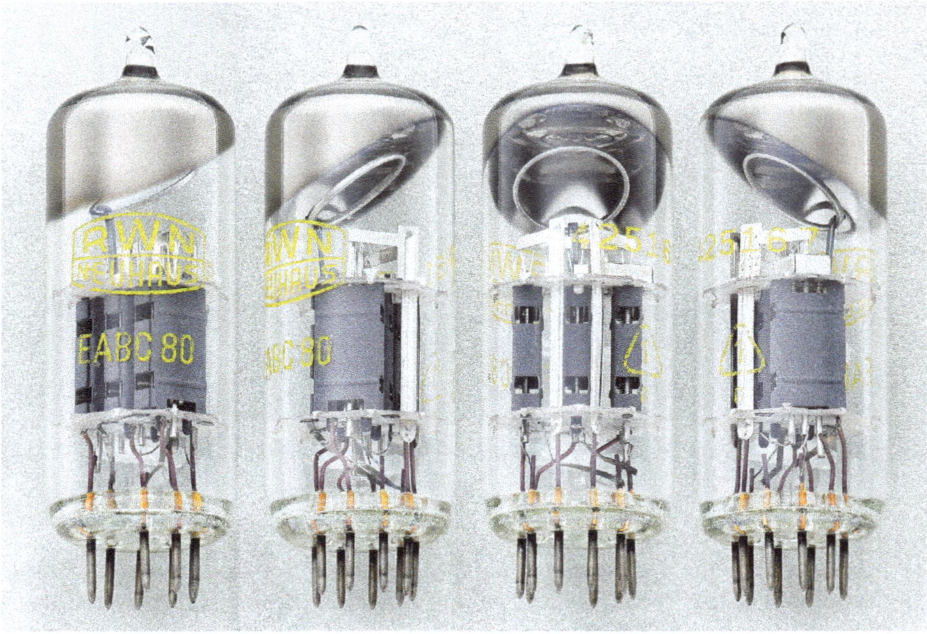

Figure 1.7. The vacuum tube. This [EABC80] image has been obtained by the author from the Wikimedia website where it was made available by [Mister rf] under a CC BY 4.0-SA licence. It is included within this book on that basis. It is attributed to [Mister rf].

popularized by John von Neumann in 1945. The first vacuum tube-based general-purpose computer was the Mark I built in the UK in 1948 (Arnold 1998).

The electronic discrete variable automatic computer (EDVAC) presented in figure 1.9 was developed by John Mauchly and J Presper Eckert as an advancement of the ENIAC. The EDVAC was a binary and stored program computer unlike the ENIAC that operated based on decimal. The addition, multiplication, division and subtraction calculations were performed automatically by the EDVAC. It had a serial memory and automatic checking using ultrasonic serial memory. The average time for addition and multiplication were 864 and 2900 μs, respectively. The EDVAC was built for the US Army at the cost of almost $500 000. logical design development of the EDVAC was done by John von Neumann on the basis of consultancy. The EDVAC construction was completed in 1949 and installed. However, problems were encountered and subsequently resolved. The EDVAC started full operations in 1951 on a limited basis, and by 1960 it was fully operational, running for more than 20 h a day (Neumann 1945, Wikes 1956).

1.3.2.2 The second generation of computers: 1950s and 1960s

In the 1950s, the first-generation computers were costly, costing millions of USD. As such, only government and large corporations could afford to own the computers. This motivated rigorous research that led to the technological breakthrough that prompted the invention of the transistor (see figure 1.10) at Bell Labs in 1948. The

Figure 1.8. First generation computer: ENIAC. This [Glen Beck and Betty Snyder program the ENIAC in building 328 at the Ballistic Research Laboratory] image has been obtained by the author from the Wikimedia website, where it is stated to have been released into the public domain. It is included within this book on that basis.

transistor has the capacity to perform all the functions that can be performed by the vacuum tube. In addition, the transistor is faster, more economical, runs cooler and has a longer life span than the vacuum tube (Arnold 1998).

This led to the size of the computer becoming small in size, unlike the first-generation computers. Therefore, the vacuum tubes in the computers were replaced by the transistor to have computers with small size. As a result, the cost of computers become low which made it possible for smaller corporations to own computers. Also, it led the application of digital design to become practical. Digital design makes possible special-purpose computers built based on electronic circuits that process bits especially for a computer-based device like the timers of microwave ovens, digital watches, digital thermostat, etc (Arnold 1998).

1.3.2.3 The third generation of computers: 1960s and 1970s

In 1964, hundreds or thousands of transistors were manufactured by Jack St Clair Kilby on a single semiconductor silicon chip referred to as integrated circuit (IC) as shown in figure 1.11. The IC was smaller in size, with lower cost, superior performance and greater reliability than the transistor of the second-generation computers. This made the mass production of general-purpose computers possible and affordable (Arnold 1998). The first commercial general-purpose computer was the UNIVersal Automatic Computer (UNIVAC) shown in figure 1.12.

Figure 1.9. First generation computer: EDVAC. This [EDVAC] image has been obtained by the author from the Wikimedia website, where it is stated to have been released into the public domain. It is included within this book on that basis.

Figure 1.10. The transistor. This [Transistors.agr] image has been obtained by the author from the Wikimedia website where it was made available by [ArnoldReinhold] under a CC BY 3.0-SA licence. It is included within this book on that basis. It is attributed to [ArnoldReinhold].

Figure 1.11. Integrated circuit. This [Integrated circuit in a removed package] image has been obtained by the author from the Wikimedia website where it was made available by [OKol123] under a CC BY-SA 4.0 licence. It is included within this book on that basis. It is attributed to [Unknown author].

Figure 1.12. Third generation computer: UNIVAC. This [UNIVAC-1101BRL61-0901] image has been obtained by the author from the Wikimedia website, where it is stated to have been released into the public domain. It is included within this book on that basis.

IBM dominated the computer market with the introduction of the mainframe computer. This triggered the development of the operating system. Multi-programming and time-sharing were proposed to improve the response times and efficiency of the mainframe computer. The introduction of the disk drive during this period also helped to improve the response time and efficiency of the mainframe computer. IBM introduced the System/360 model in the mid-1960s. The company called Digital Equipment Corporation (known as Compaq today) began selling mini-computers to universities (Dandamudi 2006). Compaq pioneered mini-computers. The third generation of computers had higher storage capacity and speed of performing calculations than the second and first generation.

1.3.2.4 The fourth generation of computers: mid-1970s

The fourth generation computers are those of the present era, the computers we use for our daily activities. This class of computers are the computers that we see around us today, as shown in figure 1.13. The computers of today are faster, smaller, more efficient and more effective than the first-, second- and third-generation computers. This was made possible by the invention of the microprocessor chip (see figure 1.14) that performs arithmetic and logic functions for any program. The early

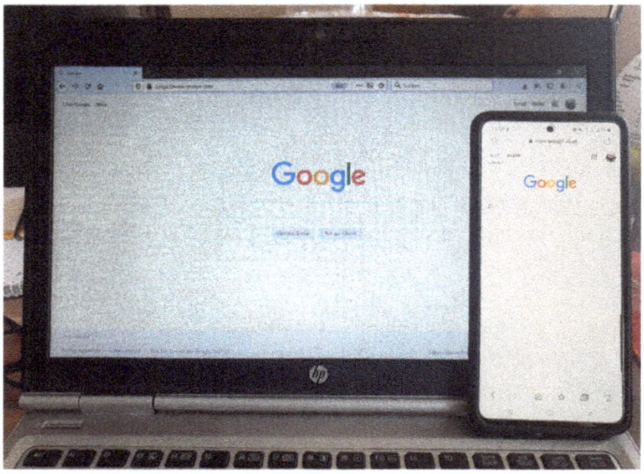

Figure 1.13. Fourth-generation computers: laptop, smartphone, etc. This [Screendesign] image has been obtained by the author from the Wikimedia website where it was made available by [LiveJu99] under a CC BY-SA 4.0 licence. It is included within this book on that basis. It is attributed to [LiveJu99].

Figure 1.14. The microprocessor chip. This [Intel SB80486DX2-50] image has been obtained by the author from the Wikimedia website where it was made available by [Mister rf] under a CC BY-SA 4.0 licence. It is included within this book on that basis. It is attributed to [Mister rf].

microprocessor chips were large-scale integrated circuits containing 23 000 transistors. The microprocessor was invented by Ted Hoff of the Intel Corporation USA. The first microprocessor was the Intel 4004 developed by Ted Hoff while working in Intel Corporation (Dandamudi 2006).

Today, the microprocessor can contain hundreds of millions of transistors in a single silicon chip, as compared to the 23 000 transistors of the 1970s. This has shown a remarkable improvement in computer technology. No doubt, this improvement led to greater performance (increased speed, reliability, less power consumption and reduced size) of computers compared to those of the previous generations. Pentium is a series of microprocessors, following which Celeron was developed and is now a core processor series with capabilities of executing multiple tasks, unlike the Pentium (Dandamudi 2006). The core microprocessor is the latest microprocessor series on the market, e.g., Core i3, Core i5, etc.

1.3.2.5 Fifth generation of computers

The fifth generation is the next generation of computers that are expected to mimic human intelligence, that is AI. Computers will have the capacity to study their environment and take action appropriately (see figure 1.15). This generation of

Figure 1.15. AI: robots. This [Humanoid robot at Science Square Tsukuba] image has been obtained by the author from the Wikimedia website, where it is stated to have been released into the public domain. It is included within this book on that basis.

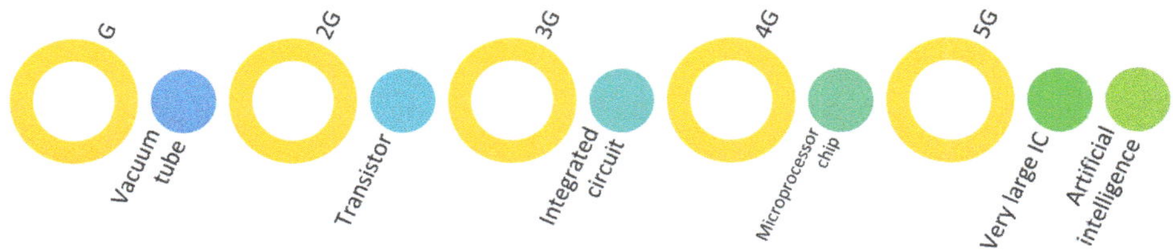

Figure 1.16. The flow of the computer generations advancement (first generation (G), second 2G, third 3G, fourth 4G and fifth 5G).

computers includes ultra-large-scale integration technology resulting in millions of microprocessors and the production of parallel processing computers. A summary of the technological development of computer generations is depicted in figure 1.16.

1.4 Innovations and discoveries from the perspective of artificial intelligence

The focus of AI was originally artificial general intelligence but difficulties hindered its progress, which is why researchers were discouraged and redirected their focus for AI. Work on artificial general intelligence has attracted a bad reputation as if developing digital general intelligence corresponds to the development of a perpetual motion machine. However, it is believed by scientists that it is possible to achieve it as it is just an engineering problem like nanotechnology, though a very difficult engineering problem (Pennachin *et al* 2007). The journey to AI that started over 60 years ago has witnessed growing development, especially in recent years, increasing its impact on society's daily activities (Tobin *et al* 2019).

AI is the effort to introduce intelligence in machines. This effort started from the early days of the computer age. Alan Turing, John von Neumann, Norbert Wiener among others, were pioneers in the field of computer science driven by a dream of building intelligence (self-reproduction, ability to learn and have regulation of their environment) into computer programs. Apart from electronics, early computer scientists were also involved in biology and psychology, in which the natural system was the guide towards incorporating intelligence into computer programs. This is why applications of computers were not only restricted to missile trajectory computation and deciphering military code, but also extended to the representation of the biological brain, imitating human learning paradigms and mimicking biological evolution. The biological computational algorithms had dwindled away over a period of years, but were resurrected in the 1980s with full force by the computing research community and this led to the revival of artificial neural networks (ANNs) (artificial human brain), machine learning, and evolutionary computation like genetic algorithms (imitation of the biological genetics or artificial genetics) (Mitchell 1998). The genetic algorithm was hinged on Darwin's theory as an inspirational guide and carefully learned the principles of evolution and applied the tacit knowledge acquired to be developed based on selection in biological genetic systems (Hamdan 2008). The concept of the genetic algorithm was derived from evolutionary biology and survival of the fittest (Capraro *et al* 2008). The emergence of the genetic algorithm motivated the discoveries of many Nature-inspired meta-heuristic algorithms. As a result, over 300 different meta-heuristic algorithms inspired by different natural intelligent agents like bees, birth, etc have been published (Ezugwu *et al* 2021).

In 1956, John McCarthy and colleagues organized a conference sponsored by the Rockefeller Foundation for researchers working on the same field. John McCarthy initially suggested the idea to his friends who were also interested in building intelligent machines. First, John McCarthy talked to three friends about the idea of the conference to discuss intelligent systems, which they happily accepted. In total, 10 of them successfully organized the conference in the summer of 1956 where John McCarthy officially coined the name '*artificial intelligence*' (McCorduck *et al* 1977). The conference marked a strong beginning to the AI journey where for the first time machines were able to solve problems intelligently, similarly to natural intelligent agents. The AI community were excited about the development prompting the popularization of the field. For instance, the problems that were solved intelligently included algebraic, translation of language, proving of geometry theorems and many more breakthroughs (Delipetrev *et al* 2018). Two years later, precisely in 1958, John McCarthy developed the famous AI programming language called Lisp. Lisp was widely adopted by the industries developing intelligent machines and it gain tremendous popularity among intelligent system developers (McCarthy 1959).

Alan Turing, as one of the founding fathers of AI published a paper '*Computing machinery and intelligence*' in 1950 proposing the thinking ability of machines. The imitation game commonly referred to as the Turing Test was the pioneering experiment widely used for the measurement of machine intelligence levels, in which it can conduct conversation similar to human beings. If a machine has the capacity to engage in conversation indistinguishable from humans, it is said to be intelligent (Delipetrev *et al* 2018). For example, ELIZA a natural language processing tool developed by Joseph Weizenbaum passed the famous Turing test (Haenlein and Kaplan 2019).

1.4.1 Artificial intelligence historical development between 1940 and 1969

Selected breakthroughs (see the summary figure 1.17) on the development of AI from 1940 to 1969 are presented in this section to give the reader information about the major breakthroughs achieved within the period. For example, Andrew Donald Booth in 1946 suggested the translation of language using computers (natural language processing) (Bibel 2014). Between 1945 and 1946, Konrad Zuse developed Plankalkül, the first AI programming language. Plankalkül was used to develop the pioneer AI chess program. At the early stage of AI development, computer chess and AI were considered an emerging field of study as computer chess was used as the testbed for a search involving AI and techniques for problem solving. The early chess games were highly primitive in nature but have now grown to become sophisticated and produce spectacular results. At the early stage, AI was dominated by the computer chess game but has now changed to include a broad field of study. The computer chess game became a small fraction within the AI discipline (Heath

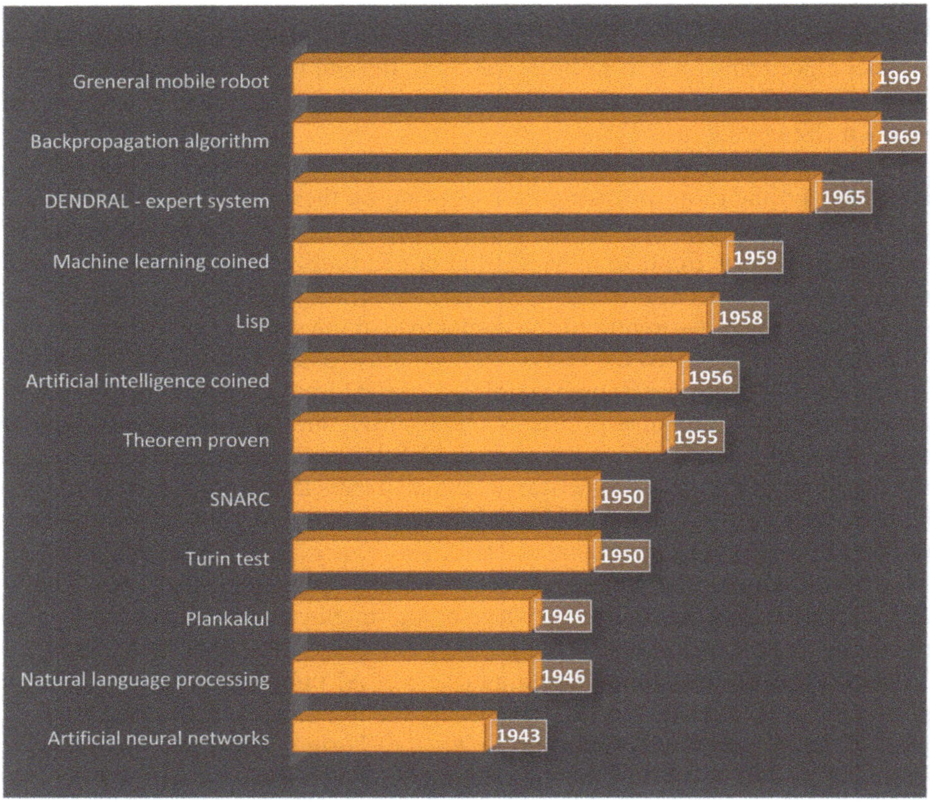

Figure 1.17. Progression in the history of AI.

et al 1997). In 1959, the phrase 'machine learning' was coined by Arthur Samuel describing the possibility of instructing machines to learn instead of being programmed. Arthur Samuel was famous for the game program Checkers, demonstrating the way the game learned from experience instead of programming. The study achieved a remarkable finding proving the idea of computer learning by experience to play the game. Checkers attracted attention from the media because of it is ability to learn and play a game to the extent of challenging human expert players (Samuel 1959).

A system referred to as DENDRAL developed in 1965 by Lederberg was a major milestone in the development of expert systems (Lederberg 1965), and is worthy of discussion in the historical perspective of AI. That DENDRAL was the first expert system in the history of AI remained a subject of debate. However, it was a great breakthrough for the expert system. Critical concepts in AI like heuristics, processing of lists, and search based on reasoning were introduced in 1955 by Newell *et al*, a group of theorists who proved more than 35 theorems from Whitehead and Russell's *Principia Mathematica* (Newell *et al* 1962).

The first general-purpose mobile robot with ability to sense its environment and act appropriately was developed in 1969. The project involved the combination of robotics, computer vision and natural language processing (Gage 1995).

Computation by imitating the way the biological human brain computes is natural computing because the human brain is a natural mechanism (De Castro 2007). The idea of ANNs was conceived by two researchers from different academic backgrounds, Warren McCulloch a neurologist and Walta Pitts a statistician in 1943, when their seminar paper titled '*A logical calculus of ideas immune in nervousactivity*' was published in *Bulletin of Mathematical Biophysics* (Yadav *et al* 2015). In 1950, Marvin Minsky and Dean Edmonds developed the stochastic neural analog reinforcement calculator (SNARC) as the pioneer ANN machine. The machine was built with 3000 vacuum tubes and a B-24 bomber automatic pilot mechanism. The machine was able to simulate an ANN comprising of 40 neurons (Russell 2010). Bryson and Ho (1969) first proposed the description of back-propagation algorithm to pave the way for multilayer ANN. However, the idea was ignored by the research community. The idea of the ANN motivated the advancement of modern computers or the electric brain as John von Neumann called it. According to Taylor (1996), the work of Marvin Minsky and Seymour in 1969 discouraged researchers with research interest in ANNs because it was shown that the perceptron had a pattern recognition problem to the extent that it was having difficulties in differentiating binary patterns, for instance separating (0,0), (1,1) from (0,1), (0,1), called the parity problem. It was not possible to train the hidden neuron to converge to the target value with minimum tolerance error. In the parity problem, the input–output training dataset were (0,0), 0, (1,1), 0, (0,1), 1, (1,0), 1. The target value of 0 or 1 was not given to output neurons for any hidden neuron. In a parity problem, which is a linearly inseparable problem, a hidden neuron is required in the design of the neurons in the network to transform the problem to be linearly separable for the outputs. In 1969, a research work by Minskey and Papert showed that time taken for training some problems increases as the number of input lines increases. This posed a stumbling block and discourage researchers to continue work on ANNs and this is one of the reasons why there was not much work done in this area in the 1970s; only few researchers were courageous enough to continue with the research on ANN

1.4.2 The gestation of artificial intelligence between 1970 and 1999

This section discusses some selected inventions in the history of AI between the period of 1970–99 for the reader to appreciate the development made within the period, especially the boost received by ANN, after a lull in research work. In 1972, Alain Colmerauer and Philippe Roussel developed Prolog, a symbolic programming language. A computer chess game called IBM Deep Blue in 1996 defeated the world's best human chess player champion Garry Kasparov. IBM Deep Blue learned all the possible moves in chess, evaluated present moves and predicted the next moves (Korf 1997). Exploration of the communication in a brain using EEG was initiated by the Defense Advanced Research Projects Agency (DARPA) in 1970. The phrase '*brain–computer interface*' (BCI) was coined and the aims of the field project were stated by Jacques Vidal in 1973 to involve the analysis of EEG signals (Editorial 2020). A brain–machine interface laboratory built in University of California, Los Angeles, recorded a breakthrough in 1976 for publishing evidence that it is possible for single-trial visual classification to be used as a channel of communication to control a cursor via a 2D maze (Vidal 1977). The first intracortical BCI to be implanted for neurotrophic-cone electrodes into monkeys in 1987 was successfully performed by Phillip Kennedy. The implant was able to allow the monkeys to control a cursor (Kennedy 1989). The first research finding that proved the control of a physical robot using an EEG signal was recorded in 1988. It was the pioneer study of controlling physical objects directly from the brain through EEG (Bozinovski *et al* 1988). Shakey the robot was believed to be the first mobile robot developed combining natural language processing, computer vision, navigation and AI (Nilsson 1984). The shakey mobile robot was the grandfather of autonomous robots, paving the way for autonomous driving vehicles and drones to succeed (Karjian 2023).

ANN research received a boost as a result of encouragement in 1982 when John Hopfield presented a seminar paper and related work of Grossberg and collaborators (Cohen and Grossberg 1983) showed that architecture of neurons asynchronously updated was possible to develop in real time (Hopfield 1982). A further source of motivation for researchers was the development of the Boltzmann machine learning algorithm for training the machine, but the learning algorithms were slow and this limited the number of applications in a useful area. Other work that broke the jinx of discouragement was the development of the self-organizing map in 1976 by researchers in the area of ANNs, including Willshaw, von der Malsburg and Grossberg. It was effectively used in terms of the self-organizing feature map of Kohonen in 1982, which made it possible for weight of a single-layer network to learn the pattern of input in an orderly manner based on observations accepted by the network. The observation made by Minskey and Papert about scaling training time as input space increases, was yet to see the light of the day as at that period (Taylor 1997).

ANN research bounced back as a result of technological advancement that led to innovation of computers with high power that allowed intractable problems to be simulated. In 1986, the backpropagation algorithm was re-introduced by LeCun, Touresky and Hinton to give life to ANNs; the re-introduction of backpropagation marked a new turning point for ANN. The advent of the backpropagation algorithms reawakened interest in ANNs after it had diminished for a while as a result of difficulty in training them (LeCun *et al* 1988). The backpropagation algorithm made it possible to train hidden neurons and was propagated by Rumelhert and McClelland together with the Parallel Distributed Group. This made it possible for industries to develop ANNs and train them to solve real-world industrial problems (Rumelhart *et al* 1986).

The convolutional neural network (CNN) was invented in 1989 for the reading of handwritten digits. The system developed based on the CNN was able to process between 10% and 20% of handwritten cash checks and zip codes in the USA within the period of the 1990s and the early years in 2000s (LeCun *et al* 1989). Watkins introduce the concept of Q-learning in 1989 to improve the learning from delayed rewards. It was found that Q-learning significantly improved the performance of reinforcement learning, especially in practical application and feasibility. The proposed Q-learning had the ability of learning optimal control regardless of the transition probabilities in modelling (Watkins *et al* 1992). In another breakthrough, the support vector machine, a variant of ANN, was innovated by Cortes and Vapnik to eliminate the limitation of the conventional ANN to classify text, image and handwritten characters (Cortes and Vapnik 1995). The year 1997 witnessed progress on recurrent neural networks by the development of long short-term memory to improve the efficiency and practical application of the recurrent neural network. It was found that the long-term dependency limitation had been eliminated successfully (Hochreiter and Schmidhuber 1997).

The description of explainable AI (XAI) by Digitalis Therapy Advisor chosen as a case study to demonstrate the idea of interpretation in medical intelligent systems was presented in Swartout (1985). Van Melle *et al* (1984) proposed an engineering tool for the development of expert systems without the need to start development from scratch. The development of the expert system through the tool offered some form of explanation to expert system decisions, justifying the reason behind the process of making the decision. XAI has now penetrated different fields in AI, especially ANNs, but has received a lot of backlash about its lack of explainable nature (Townsend *et al* 2019). The milestones achieved within the period 1970–99 are depicted in figure 1.18.

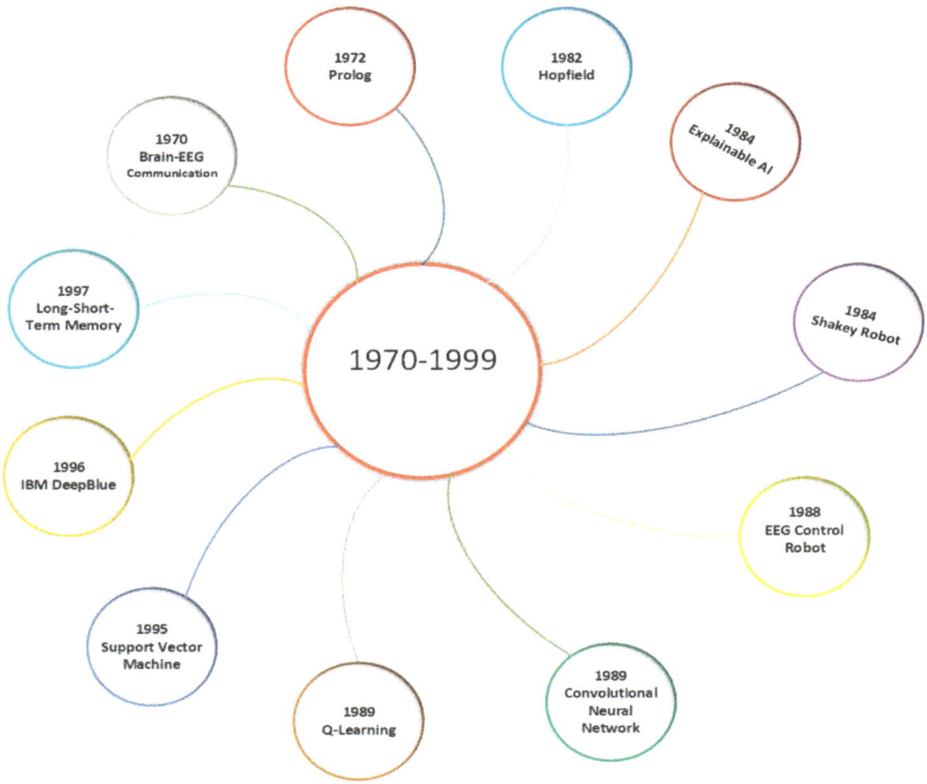

Figure 1.18. Selected breakthroughs in AI between 1970 and 1999.

1.4.3 Inventions in artificial intelligence between 2000 and 2023

A lot of different inventions and discoveries in AI were made between 2000 and 2023. In this section, some major selected breakthroughs are discussed to show the progress made by the AI community in new innovations and discoveries. For example, in 2000, a BCI device was built to reproduce owl monkey movement at the same time when the monkey was operating a joystick. The research output was remarkable as direct control of a physical object (Chapin and Nicolelis 2000). In 2005, a Stanford robot was able to win the DARPA grand challenge by driving autonomously for 131 miles along a desert track on which it had never driven before. The incident marked a milestone in the development of autonomous vehicles, as it is the first scenario for an autonomous vehicle to drive on roads in real-world environments (Thrun *et al* 2006). A very large-scale image dataset commonly referred to as the ImageNet dataset, with over 3.2 million labelled images, was launched in 2009 for researchers to use in conducting research from different perspectives. The ImageNet dataset is available to everyone interested in using it for research. It has been widely accepted as a standard Image dataset for research in the research community (Deng *et al* 2009).

In 2012, the deep CNN architecture was introduced, and it won the ImageNet challenge competition. The event stimulates the exploration of deep learning. The variant of the CNN referred to as the AlexNet that won the ImageNet challenge, has been considered as the turning point for deep learning (Krizhevsky *et al* 2012). In 2014, the generative adversarial network was invented by Goodfellow *et al.* It has the ability to generate data such as image, audio, video, text, etc. It was a great breakthrough for generative AI (Goodfellow *et al* 2014). ANNs made a dramatic comeback as a result of AlphaGo developed based on a deep learning algorithm by Google train using the combination of supervised learning and reinforcement learning. The AlphaGo beat the reigning human world champion of the board game Go in 2015. The game Go is said to be significantly more complex compared to chess because it consists of 361 moves compared to chess with just 20 possible moves. Go is believed to be the most challenging classic game for AI in view of the huge search space and difficulties in the evaluation of moves and positions (Silver *et al* 2016). An intelligent agent called AlphaTensor was developed for discovering new algorithms automatically. AlphaTensor was found to discover algorithms whose performance superseded the state-of-the-art algorithms designed and developed by humans. It was found to hasten the process of discovering new algorithms for solving a range of problems (Fawzi *et al* 2022). Although the study is not anything close to artificial superintelligence, could it be a step towards artificial superintelligence?

Kittlau led a team that applied natural language processing and machine learning to develop Siri, the Apple virtual personal assistant, in 2007. The application assists users to perform tasks on mobile phones such as searching the internet, composing and sending messages, reservations and much more (Hoy 2018). The year 2013 was a turning point for natural language processing as Word2vec was invented for the identification of semantic relationship between words automatically without human manual effort (Mikolov *et al* 2013). In 2017, natural language processing witnessed a

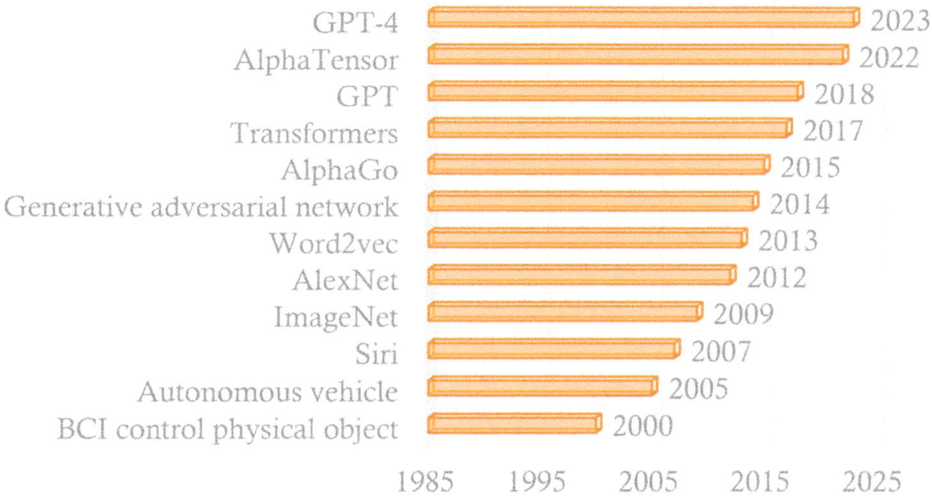

Figure 1.19. Inventions and discoveries in AI between 2000 and 2023.

tremendous boom as transformers were developed based on attention mechanisms, dispensing with recurrence and whole convolutions (Vaswani *et al* 2017). This later triggered massive research into frameworks with the functionality to automatically parse unlabelled text into large language models (LLMs) (Thirunavukarasu *et al* 2023). OpenAI developed a generative pre-trained transformer (GPT) based on ANN with transformer architecture that discriminatively trains models to perform diverse tasks based on a diverse corpus of unlabelled data before discriminatively fine-tuning for a particular task. GPT has the ability to generate new human-like content such as text, video, image, and audio (Radford *et al* 2018). In 2023, OpenAI announced the release of GPT-4 with significant improvement over previous versions of GPT. GPT-4 is a large multimodal model with the ability to accept images and text as input, process them and produce images and text as output. GPT-4, despite a lot of limitations compared to humans in real the world environment, was able to produce competitive performance at human level on different benchmarks such as professional and academics levels (OpenAI 2023). The development of GPT can be viewed as an inroad into artificial general intelligence. A summary of selected inventions and discoveries in AI between the period 2000–23 is depicted in figure 1.19.

1.5 Artificial intelligence in science fiction movies that turned into reality

Science fiction represents humanity's futuristic imagination of science and technology. Science fiction movies have significantly inspired technological innovations, including advancements in AI. Many concepts from science fiction are now a reality. These ideas vary in scale, from enhancements of existing technologies to entirely new inventions. In some science fiction movies, a single new technology is introduced, while others create a vision of multiple fictional advancements and improvements of the technology. For example, *Star Trek: The Next Generation* inspired technologies such as Bluetooth, cell phones, automated sliding doors, voice assistance, and realistic simulation. However, our focus is on AI, so the science fiction movies selected must feature elements of AI technology for consideration.

One of the most famous science fiction technology movies is *Star Trek*, originally released in 1966. It was rebranded as *Star Trek: The Animated Series* from 1973 to 1974, and later continued as *Star Trek: The Next Generation* from 1987 to 1994. In this series, an artificial reality machine called the Holodeck was introduced. The Holodeck is a fictional device with the ability to create realistic 3D representations of real-world objects or imaginary environments in response to user commands (SciTechDaily 2024).

The Holodeck motivated today's interactive virtual environment typically used for the training of robots before its deployment in the real-world environment commonly referred to as simulation-to-reality (Watson 2024). Many science fiction movies with human futuristic imaginative scenes that create the illusions of AI that are now a reality in the real world are summarized in table 1.2 (Ghosh 2019).

Table 1.2. Summary of AI illusions created in science fiction movies that eventually transformed into real-world technology.

Science fiction movie name	Movie year	Scene or episode	Innovation	Innovation period
Dr Who	1977	Features a robot dog with sufficient intelligent to defeat his master at chess	IBM Deep Blue defeated chess world champion	After 20 years
The Jetsons	1962	Creates an illusion of image and phone call together appearing on TV	Smart home device has been developed for video calls. Uses AI to make sure the user is on screen, pan and zoom. Facebook portal.	2018
Rosie the Robot Maid	1962	Performs house chores (cleaning and cooking)	iRobot Roomba as the first robot vacuum cleaner was built to navigate and clean different rooms in a house	2002
			Moley Robotics Kitchen built for cooking meals from scratch and cleans up the kitchen after cooking	2019
Star Trek	1966	Universal translator to decode and translate unknown language	The first language translator with pixel buds developed by Google (Google assistant interpreter mode) to translate 27 different languages during conversation in real time	2017

The Hitchhiker's Guide to the Galaxy	1979	Featuring 'Babel fish' with capability for translating unknown languages. The 'Babel fish' is placed in the ear.	Google assistant interpreter mode	2019
Back to the Future Part II	1989	The children of Marty McFly put on smart glasses that enable them to watch television and answer calls	Google smart glass as the first to be available to users. The smart glass can manage phone calls, video, text, images and map.	2013
		A smart watch that forecasts weather in seconds appears in the movie	Apple watch connected to WiFi and Bluetooth and later version includes GPS and data. It can monitor heart condition with it is equipped with an optical heart rate sensor.	2015
			Dark Sky watch provides weather prediction every minute. It can be customized to send alerts on expected time of rain or severe weather.	2012
Smart House	1999	Fully automated house run through AI interface called PAT with capability of responding to requests from human, cooking, cleaning and control devices (security, light, thermostat and entertainment)	HGTV organize contest to win smart house embedded with state-of-the-art technology (e.g., robot, internet, voice enabled devices through Amazon Alexa, smart television that doubles as wall art) in the real world.	2019
The Minority Report	2002	AI uses retina scan data of individuals to target personalized advertisement	Tesco targets facial scans for petrol advertisement to determine the age and gender of a driver, then, display targeted advertisement while the driver fills tank at the filling station	2013
Person of Interest	2011	AI embedded in surveillance camera to predict potential criminals and victims	UK national data analytics solution applies AI algorithm to analyze police data to predict potential criminals	2018

(*Continued*)

Table 1.2. (*Continued*)

Science fiction movie name	Movie year	Scene or episode	Innovation	Innovation period
Star Trek: The Next Generation	1987	VISOR, a device helping the blind to see is used in a scene	Aira uses Google glasses to assist visually impaired customers	2016
The Culture	1987	Depicts a situation where intelligent machines surpass human level intelligence but live in harmony with each other.	Futuristic imagination	Unknown
Terminator	1984	Context-aware AI weapon attempting to use nuclear power to make humans on the earth extinct	Futuristic imagination	Unknown

1.6 The cycle of artificial intelligence winter, innovations and renewed interest

The success recorded through the history of AI development presented in the preceding sections may be portrayed to the reader as if the journey to the current stage of AI has been smooth without any challenge along the way. This is because the challenges faced on the road to AI development have not been captured in the preceding sections. However, the journey on the road to the development of AI has faced significant hurdles in history. The AI field has experienced many cycles of criticism and disappointment because of failures from AI systems leading to a period of low level of interest in AI and AI funding cuts called the AI winter before renewal of interest began another round of innovations (figure 1.20). History shows that in addition to smaller AI winter, there were two major periods for the AI winter: 1974–80 and 1987–2000 as pointed out by Howe (1994). This section is dedicated to discussing selected AI winters in history.

The name AI winter is derived from the 'nuclear winter' theory projecting the massive use of nuclear bombs that would emit smoke and dust to block the sun causing the world temperature to surge, the earth to freeze and humans to be terminated. The AI winter is the period in the history of AI development where the field experiences significant disappointment, criticism, failures and cutting of funding, making AI development drastically slow down, interest on AI reduces and halting of significant AI projects in most instances (AI News Letter 2005). The name AI winter appeared in 1984 at the American Association of Artificial Intelligence meetings as a topic for public debate for the first time (Russell and Norvig 2003). In 1969, the ANN perceptron's inability to perform pattern recognition prompted researchers to desert ANN research (refer to section 1.4.1 for details).

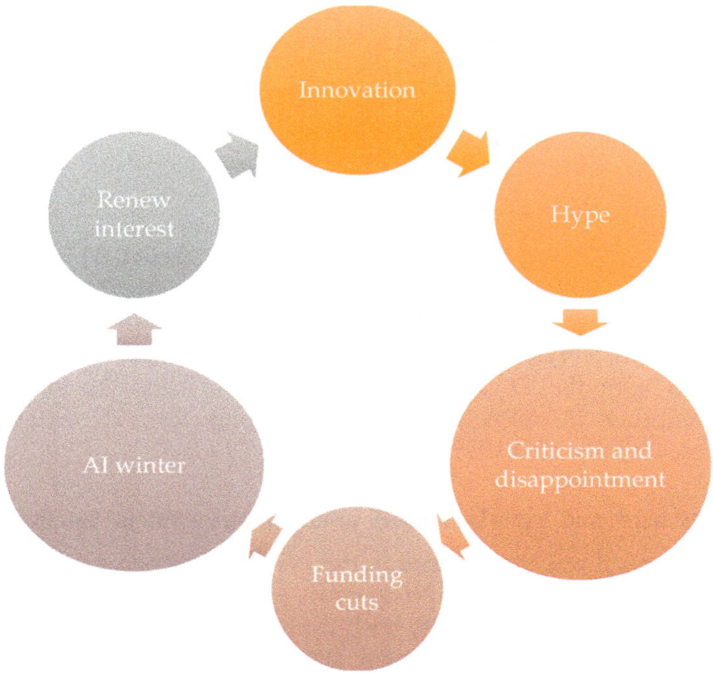

Figure 1.20. The cycle of AI winter experience in history.

1.6.1 National Research Council abandons machine translation project and stops funding AI research

In 1964, the National Research Council became frustrated with the machine translation project due to lack of advancement, and decided to fund a committee called automatic language processing advisory committee to find the causative agents of the hurdles in the machine translation project. The report found out that machine translation was slow, very expensive and inaccurate compared to human translators. At that time, the National Research Council had already injected $20 million in the project. Despite spending $20 million, the National Research Council stopped further funding and support to the project, which led to the ending of the research as well as many careers of those involved in the project (Hutchins 2005).

1.6.2 United Kingdom stopped artificial intelligence funding and ongoing projects

The UK parliament in 1973, tasked professor James Lighthill with the responsibility of assessing research in AI within the UK. The report pointed out AI failures and criticized AI for failing to meet the desired objectives arguing that the AI projects were replications of science, just reinventing the wheel. The report also argued that the AI algorithm lacks capacity to solve real-world problems and could only solve the 'toy' versions of real-world problems. The report was famously referred to as the Lighthill (1973) report. The report triggered the UK government to dismantle AI research projects within the UK (Howe 1994, Russell and Norvig 2003). Only a few universities in the UK such as Essex, Sussex and Edinburgh continued with AI research at a small scale until 1983 when AI research was revived at a large scale with £350 million funding as a response to the ambitious Japanese Fifth Generation Computer Project (Crevier 1993).

1.6.3 DARPA cancelled speech understanding project

Between the period of 1971 to 1975, DARPA re-evaluated AI research projects including a speech understanding project at Carnegie Mellon University. This project frustrated DARPA for lack of progress. The report concluded that AI research has no feasibility of usefulness and impact in the near future. The Lighthill report coupled with the DARPA's own report worsened the situation for AI research prompting DARPA to suspend funding for AI research in 1974 (National Research Council 1999).

1.6.4 Roger Schank and Marvin Minsky prediction of artificial intelligence winter

The AI winter period was experienced in the 1970s with Roger Schank and Marvin Minsky as witnesses. The leading AI scientist at the meeting warned the business community never to be carried away with the AI out-of-control hype in the 1980s because of potential AI disappointment similar to the 1970s AI winter. Roger Schank and Marvin Minsky argued that the AI winter typically follows a chain reaction starting with distrust from the AI research community to mainstream media fanning the distrust, to significant funding cuts and ends with halting high impact research projects (Russell and Norvig 2003).

1.6.5 The collapse of LISP machines

Sun Microsystems offered powerful advanced machines better than LISP machines (Brooks *et al* 1986) prompting companies that commercialized LISP machines such as LISP Machines Inc., Texas Instruments, Symbolics and Xerox to abandon LISP machines in 1987 (Newquist 1994). This comes three years after the prediction of Roger Schank and Marvin Minsky at the annual meetings of American Association of Artificial Intelligence (Brooks *et al* 1986) and the billion-dollar AI industry continued to crash (Russell and Norvig 2003). Only a few companies continued to operate with LISP machines and by the 1990s most of the companies that commercialized LISP had failed, leading to a crash in the LISP market (Newquist 1994).

1.6.6 The failure of expert systems

The success of expert systems was followed with hype triggering companies and corporations to adopt the technology globally in the 1980s. This was following the success of XCON expert systems as the first commercial expert system estimated to save $40 million for a company operating the expert system over the period of six years. Many companies ventured into the development of expert systems and deployed them for operations with large spending on AI estimated to billions of dollars by 1985 (Newquist 1994). After the massive adoption of expert systems, companies discovered that they lacked the capacity to provide explanation on the advice provided at an abstraction level for easy understanding of the naïve end user (AI News Letter 2005). In the 1990s, the XCON was becoming expensive to maintain, lacked adaptation and robustness with erroneous inputs producing ridiculous output (Crevier 1993). As a result, companies started abandoning expert systems continuously. These discoveries by companies almost collapsed the billion-dollar AI industry (Russell and Norvig 2003). The selected AI winters experienced over the period of the 1960s to the 1980s is illustrated in figure 1.21.

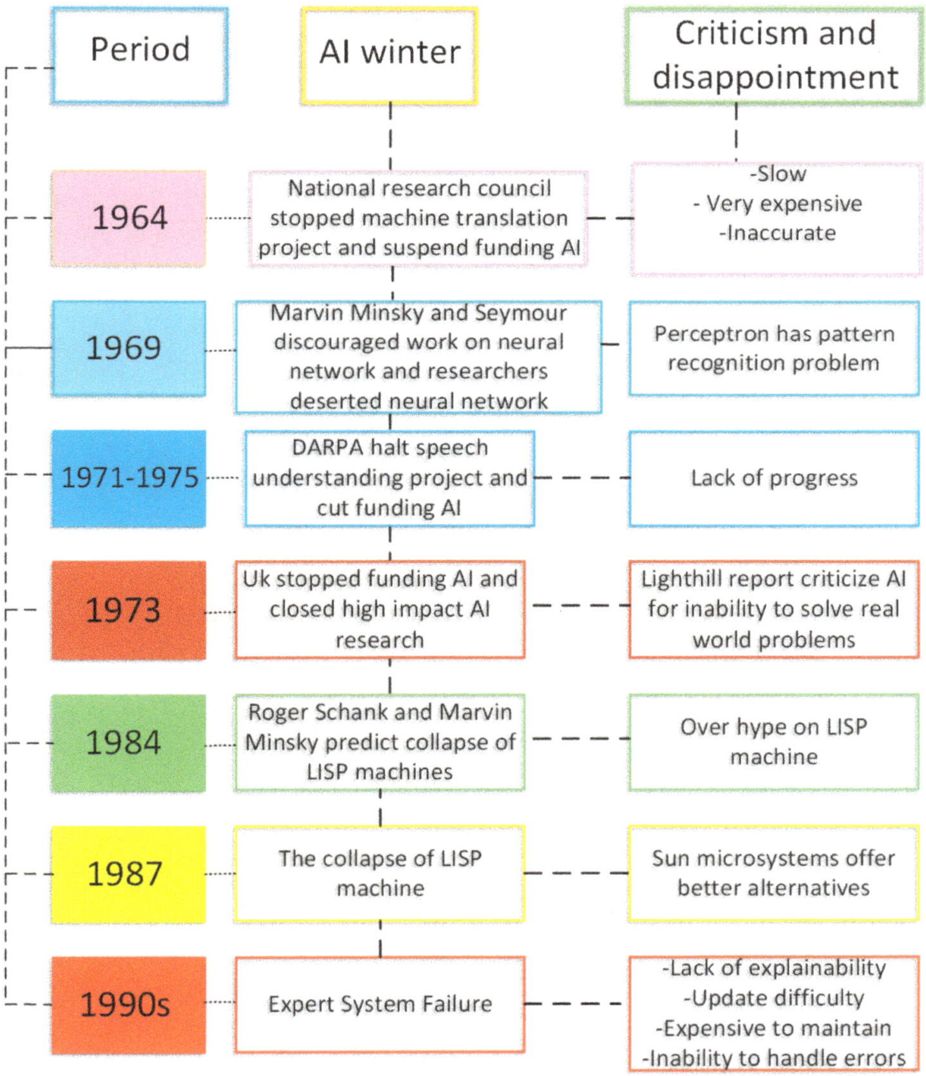

Figure 1.21. Visualization of selected AI winter and criticism.

1.7 Artificial intelligence future expectations

The historical development of AI clearly indicated that the different types of AI have been in place for a long period of time. The different types of AI are presented in figure 1.22 showing AI narrow, artificial general intelligence, artificial superintelligence, generative AI and explainable AI, robotics and brain–machine interface. These research areas are not new concepts but progression seems slow with the exception of AI narrow that has received tremendous development though with a lot of challenges yet to be resolved.

In today's world, optimism and pessimism schools of thought exist around AI. Those in the optimism school of thought are currently pumping hundreds of millions of dollars into AI research and development, whereas on the other hand, those in the pessimism school of thought believe that AI has the possibility of crippling a lot of things in the world such as jobs, warfare and ending the entire human race itself. Singularity is gaining popularity in recent times with the prediction that it might be achieved in 2045 if the current trend of technological development moves into the future. Singularity is the period whereby an intelligent machine built by humans can adapt and redesign itself for better performance to the extent that it becomes intelligent at exactly human level (artificial general intelligence) and grows itself intelligently at an exponential rate to become more intelligent than humans (artificial superintelligence) (Walsh 2017). Ajeya Cotra asked rhetorically, that at

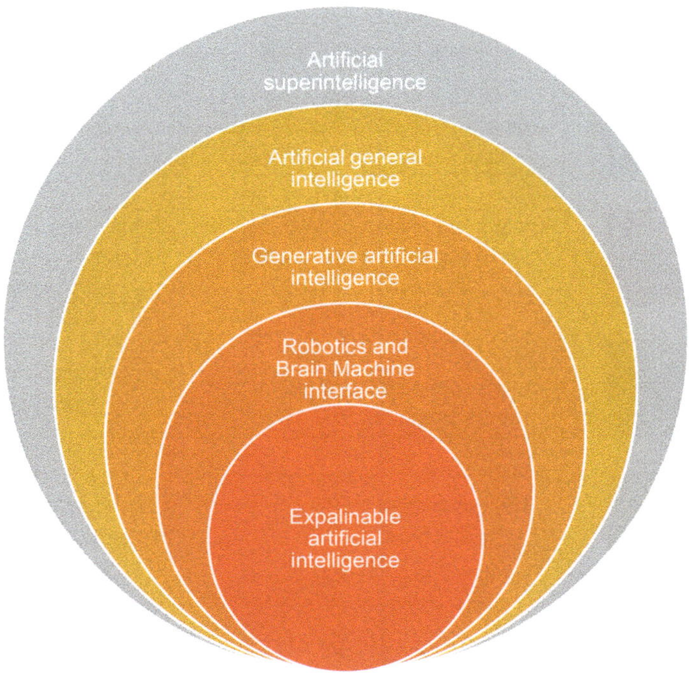

Figure 1.22. Relationships of AI.

what time will a trained intelligent system perform at the same level as a human brain? At this period of time where an intelligent system matches the human brain, the system can have the capacities and functions of the biological human brain. The researcher predicted with 50% probability that the transformation into artificial general intelligence will be witnessed in 2040 (Cotra 2020). It is predicted that a book written in 2025 can start containing the scientific details of the complete human brain structure and functions paving the way for simulating the entire brain on machine leading to artificial general intelligence. However, the human brain is not sufficiently known to simulate its detailed functions. As such, currently, artificial general intelligence remains a speculation and dream of the future (Pennachin and Goertzel 2007).

1.8 Industrial applications and case study

Industries with significant investments in AI (e.g., Google, OpenAI, Meta, Microsoft, NVIDIA, Intel) can benefit from studying the successes and failures in AI history to complement their current achievements. Learning from past failures allows AI companies to take precautionary measures when investing in new projects. Historically, media hype often follows major AI innovations, as seen with the current excitement surrounding ChatGPT. ChatGPT is regarded as one of the significant breakthroughs in AI history, similar to the hype generated after the success of expert systems like XCON and LISP machines.

The success of ChatGPT has stimulated the rapid development and deployment of AI chatbots now over 1 million of them exist as listed by Hugging Face Inc. (e.g., Gemini, LLaMA, PaLM, MISTRAL, Copilot), and technologies across industries and corporations worldwide. However, history shows that the discovery of major flaws often leads to the decline of AI technologies. To sustain the gains of AI advancements, the currently booming AI industry must implement stringent measures to minimize flaws and ensure long-term viability.

1.9 Summary

The history of computers from the abacus were presented, and the scientists that played major roles in the development of computers were as follows: Charles Babbage, Blaise Pascal, Ada Lovelace and Gottfried Wilhelm Leibniz. The history of the computer cannot be complete without mentioning the valid contributions of these great scientists. Apart from the inventions in computer technology, there are generations of computers that show how they advanced.

It was observed that the major difference in the computer generations was the technological advancement. The improvements of the efficiency, size, and cost effectiveness of computers have been the major motivations for technology breakthroughs in computer technology. The major components that determine the generations of the computers were as follows: vacuum tube, transistor, integrated circuits and large-scale integrated circuits. The sizes of computers from generation to generation kept on decreasing as new technology was invented. The historical perspective of AI was presented pointing out some selected breakthroughs in the research area. The major breakthrough in AI is the invention of ANNs, a step towards real intelligence mimicking the biological human brain.

The idea of ANNs was conceived by Warren McCulloch a Neurologist and Walta Pitts a statistician in 1943. Alan Turing as one of the founding fathers of AI, and John von Neumann, Norbert Wiener among others, were pioneers in computing, having the foresight to build intelligent machines right from the early days of computers. John McCarthy and colleagues organized a conference for researchers with the same research interest in AI in 1956 where the phrase 'artificial intelligence' was coined. Later, John McCarthy developed the famous AI programming language, Lisp. Exploring communication in the brain using EEG was initiated in the year 1970. Shakey the mobile robot was found to be the grandfather of autonomous robots leading to autonomous driving vehicles becoming a reality. OpenAI developed GPT in 2018 for generating content.

An intelligent agent called AlphaTensor developed in 2022 discovered new algorithms automatically and the performance of these algorithms superseded human-designed algorithms, a step in the direction of artificial superintelligence. History shows that robotics and the brain–machine interface, artificial general intelligence, artificial superintelligence, generative AI and explainable AI had traces long ago in the history of AI.

1.10 Organization of the book

Chapter 2: *Generative artificial intelligence: gateway and recent progress*

This chapter provides a systematic guide to begin a journey in generative AI and offers experts new insights. It covers the fundamentals of generative models, including their variants, generative tasks, and a comprehensive taxonomy. The chapter also presents a comparative analysis of the strengths and weaknesses of different types of generative models, as well as the motivations for integrating them. Additionally, it explores the roles of generative models in pharmaceutical companies and the creation of Deepfakes. Prompt engineering is introduced to equip readers with skills of creating effective prompts. To bridge the gap between theory and practice, industrial applications and case studies of generative tools are presented in a tabular format. This chapter serves as both an entry point for beginners and a resource for experts to explore numerous categories of generative models beyond the dominant generative adversarial networks, paving the way for future innovation.

Chapter 3: *Artificial general intelligence and beyond: large language models tutorial, debates, hypothesis and future outlook*

This chapter simplifies the concept of artificial general intelligence for readers, given the early stage of development in this field. The discussion covers artificial general intelligence in comparison to human level intelligence. A tutorial on LLMs and transformer architecture in an easy-to-follow approach for readers to understand it easily is presented. The exploration extends beyond artificial general intelligence to artificial superintelligence and the controversies surrounding them. The chapter delves into the current status of artificial general intelligence and artificial superintelligence, intellectual debates, timelines, industrial applications and case studies, hypotheses and future outlook. Upon reading of this chapter, readers will gain comprehensive understanding of LLMs, transformers, the current status of artificial general intelligence and artificial superintelligence, controversies and new research opportunities.

Chapter 4: *AI-DevOps: Proposed artificial intelligence enhanced development and operations lifecycle*

Software systems are fast becoming complex in nature, thus, triggering a shift from traditional development and operations (DevOps) methodology to AI-assisted DevOps to meet with the increasing complexity of software. Therefore, AI-assisted DevOps is expected to relegate the traditional DevOps in the future as predicted in the 2023 IEEE Computer Society Technology prediction. In this chapter, the major components of the AI-assisted DevOps that drive innovations in organizations are discussed. The chapter presents a proposed AI-assisted DevOps ecosystem with AI technology cutting across AI—specific, generative AI and artificial general intelligence. AI automation tools required in each of the DevOps stages are outlined for the reader to easily grasp the needed AI automation tools required to fasten the DevOps processes. The chapter presents industrial applications and case studies where AI-based DevOps are in practice in well-established companies.

Chapter 5: *Centralized huge graph neural networks advances*

A tremendous volume of papers on huge graph neural networks is currently flooding the literature. As such, large numbers of published review articles on huge graph neural networks have been published. It makes it practically tedious and time consuming to go through the published review articles one by one in different databases. This chapter centralizes the published review articles on huge graph neural network from different perspectives, pointing out the main focus of each paper for expert readers to easily grasp. For novice and new researchers, the chapter presents tutorials on the huge graph neural network starting with basic introduction to graph theory in a simple and easy-to-follow approach to give a grasp of the huge graph neural network before delving into the main content of the chapter. For expert readers, challenges and research opportunities are highlighted. Industrial applications and case studies where huge graph neural networks are in practice in real-world environments are outlined and discussed. It is believed that the chapter can make it easy for the research community to access different review papers on huge graph neural networks as a one-stop point and serve as an entry point to newcomers including postgraduate students.

Chapter 6: *Brain–machine interface for autonomous robots control with feedback from augmented reality and its relevance to Industry 4.0 and 5.0*

This chapter covers the step-by-step procedure for designing and developing robots from the perspective of hardware and software as a tutorial. The chapter includes different types of autonomous robots such as autonomous vehicles, drones and autonomous underwater vehicles. Recent progress on the integration of BMI with augmented reality to control autonomous robots and their role in industry 4.0 and industry 5.0 for autonomous production are covered. Case studies where these technologies have been put into practice such as Amazon, airports in Japan and the Netherlands, autonomous vehicle road trials, Onward Medical, and companies like

Mercedes-Benz, Honda, Toyota, Volvo, Volkswagen, BMW, and Hyundai are outlined to help readers connect theory with practice.

Chapter 7: *Recent development in artificial intelligence and high-performance computing*

This chapter presents critical emerging concepts from diverse perspectives within AI across domains. The chapter presents the status of fully autonomous robotic surgery. The state of the art in high-performance computing systems is highlighted with exascale currently topping the performance chart. However, a zettascale supercomputer five-year project has been announced. Then, a quantum computing tutorial is presented before diving into how quantum computing is revolutionizing different fields in AI. The boom in LLMs has caused a surge in high-energy demand by supercomputers at the data centres, and a consequent increase in carbon dioxide footprint as revealed in the chapter. However, the tech giants are making frantic efforts to make their data centres energy efficient. Lastly, decentralized blockchain technology is discussed pointing out how accelerators influence crypto-mining profits and some recommended processors are outlined. It is found that many of the emerging applications remain at the concept, proof-of-concept, or trial stages, while others are ready for practice but have yet to be applied in real-world practice. Some AI applications are already in active use, albeit with unresolved challenges that are expected to be addressed in the future. Case studies are outlined to help readers appreciate the real-world operation of these emerging concepts.

Chapter 8: *Explainable artificial intelligence tailored to emerging concepts linking human acceptability*

The black-box nature of AI models has motivated a growing interest in explainable AI, especially in recent times. At least 100 survey papers have been published from different perspectives of explainable AI, indicating the significant attention the field has generated. This chapter covers the procedure for the integration of explainable AI into AI-based models at different stages, including pre-modelling, modelling, and deployment. The chapter explores explainable AI tailored to generative AI, multimodal model, graph neural networks, LLMs, autonomous robots (autonomous vehicles and drones), BMIs, and AI-assisted development and operations linking to human acceptability. Additionally, the chapter highlights industrial applications of explainable AI and presents relevant case studies (e.g., PayPal, MasterCard, LinkedIn, IBM). This explainable AI coverage can offer valuable insights for academic research and motivate practical AI model adoption in the real-world environment, thus improving human acceptability.

Chapter 9: *Proposed bibliometric methods for artificial intelligence domain and bibliometric analysis on artificial intelligence for over six decades*

In this chapter, a strong theoretical foundation of bibliometric analysis including mathematical fundamentals is discussed. Bibliometric analysis methodology is propose for the AI research community to adopt in the domain of AI. To the best of the author's knowledge, no bibliometric analysis conducted for AI covers six decades. Thus, this chapter presents comprehensive bibliometric analysis on the development of AI for over six decades showing performance analysis and science mapping. Bibliometric analysis of top AI literature sources, disciplines, prolific countries in AI, prolific authors, trending topics, authorship, impact, author-keywords and co-keywords are analyzed. The current trading topics include transformer, robotics surgery, machine learning, control and fuzzy systems. China is ahead of the US in AI research. Industrial applications and case studies where bibliometric analysis is in practice are outlined. We believe that readers including organizations across the world can use bibliometric analysis to identify relevant information in the area of AI.

References

Abd-El-Barr M and El-Rewini H 2005 *Fundamentals of Computer Organization and Architecture* **38** (New York: Wiley)

AI News Letter 2005 *Winter* https://ainewsletter.com/newsletters/aix_0501/#w (accessed 18 November 2024)

Arnold M G 1998 *Verilog Digital Computer Design: Algorithms into Hardware* (Englewood Cliffs, NJ: Prentice-Hall)

Bibel W 2014 Artificial intelligence in a historical perspective *AI Commun.* **27** 87–102

Blum E K 2011a Computation: brief history prior to the 1900s *Computer Science* (New York: Springer) pp 11–6

Blum E K 2011b The heart of computer science *Computer Science* (New York: Springer) pp 17–52

Bozinovski S, Bozinovska L and Setakov M 1988 Mobile robot control using alpha wave from the human brain *Proc. Symp. JUREMA, Zagreb* pp 247–9

Brooks R A, Posner D B, McDonald J L, White J L, Benson E and Gabriel R P 1986 Design of an optimizing, dynamically retargetable compiler for common lisp *Proc. of the 1986 ACM Conf. on LISP and Functional Programming* pp 67–85

Brookshear J 2007 *Computer Science: an overview* (Boston, MA; London: Pearson/Addison-Wesley)

Brookshear G G and Brookshear J G 2002 *Computer Science: an Overview* (Addison-Wesley)

Bryson A E and Ho Y C 1969 Applied optimal control (Blaisdell, New York) *Trans. Syst., Man Cybern.* **13** 298–316

Capraro C T, Bradaric I, Capraro G T and Lue T K 2008 Using genetic algorithms for radar waveform selection *Radar Conf., 2008. RADAR'08. IEEE* (Piscataway, NJ: IEEE) pp 1–6

Chapin J K and Nicolelis M A 2000 Brain control of sensorimotor prostheses *Neural Prostheses for Restoration of Sensory and Motor Function* (CRC Press) pp 235–61

Cohen M A and Grossberg S 1983 Absolute stability of global pattern formation and parallel memory storage by competitive neural networks *IEEE Trans. Syst., Man Cybernet.* **5** 815–26

Confalonieri R, Coba L, Wagner B and Besold T R 2021 A historical perspective of explainable Artificial Intelligence *Wiley Interdiscip. Rev. Data Min. Knowl. Discov.* **11** e1391

Cortes C and Vapnik V 1995 Support-vector networks *Machine Learn* **20** 273–97

Cotra A 2020 Draft Report on AI Timelines https://alignmentforum.org/posts/KrJfoZzpSDpnrv9va/draft-report-on-ai-timelines (accessed 9 September 2023)

Crevier D 1993 *AI: The Tumultuous Search for Artificial Intelligence 1993* (New York: BasicBooks)

Dandamudi S P 2006 *Fundamentals of Computer Organization and Design* (Berlin: Springer Science and Business Media)

De Castro L N 2007 Fundamentals of natural computing: an overview *Phys. Life Rev.* **4** 1–36

Delipetrev B, Tsinaraki C and Kostić U 2018 *AI watch: historical evolution of artificial intelligence* JRC120469 Joint Research Centre https://ai-watch.ec.europa.eu/publications/historical-evolution-artificial-intelligence_en

Deng J, Dong W, Socher R, Li L J, Li K and Fei-Fei L 2009 Imagenet: a large-scale hierarchical image database *2009 IEEE Conf. on Computer Vision and Pattern Recognition* (Piscataway, NJ: IEEE) pp 248–55

Editorial 2020 *The History of Brain-Computer Interfaces (BCIs)—Timeline* https://roboticsbiz.com/the-history-of-brain-computer-interfaces-bcis-timeline/ (accessed 9 September 2023)

Evans D 2009 *Introduction to Computing: Explorations in Language, Logic, and Machines* (Eleven Learning)

Ezugwu A E, Shukla A K, Nath R, Akinyelu A A, Agushaka J O, Chiroma H and Muhuri P K 2021 Metaheuristics: a comprehensive overview and classification along with bibliometric analysis *Artif. Intell. Rev.* **54** 4237–316

Fawzi A, Balog M, Huang A, Hubert T, Romera-Paredes B, Barekatain M and Kohli P 2022 Discovering faster matrix multiplication algorithms with reinforcement learning *Nature* **610** 47–53

Gage D W 1995 *UGV History 101: A Brief History of Unmanned Ground Vehicle (UGV) Development Efforts* (San Diego, CA: Naval Ocean Systems Center)

Ghosh I 2019 *A Visual Timeline of AI Predictions in Sci-Fi.* https://visualcapitalist.com/sci-fi-artificial-intelligence-predictions/ (accessed 16 November 2024)

Goodfellow I, Pouget-Abadie J, Mirza M, Xu B, Warde-Farley D, Ozair S and Bengio Y 2014 Generative adversarial nets *Proc. Neural Information Processing Systems* **27**

Haenlein M and Kaplan A 2019 A brief history of artificial intelligence: on the past, present, and future of artificial intelligence *Calif. Manage. Rev.* **61** 5–14

Haigh T 2023 Conjoined twins: artificial intelligence and the invention of computer science *Commun. ACM* **66** 33–7

Hamdan M 2008 A heterogeneous framework for the global parallelization of genetic algorithms *Int. Arab J. Inf. Technol.* **5** 192–9

Heath D, Allum D and Square P 1997 The historical develoment of computer Chess and its impact on artificial intelligence *AAAI Technical Report* WS-97-04 p 63

Hochreiter S and Schmidhuber J 1997 Long short-term memory *Neural Comput.* **9** 1735–80

Hopfield J J 1982 Neural networks and physical systems with emergent collective computational abilities *Proc. Natl Acad. Sci.* **79** 2554–8

Howe J 1994 *School of Informatics: History of Artificial Intelligence at Edinburgh.* https://web.archive.org/web/20070515072641/http:/www.inf.ed.ac.uk/about/AIhistory.html (accessed 19 November 2024)

Hoy M B 2018 Alexa, Siri, Cortana, and more: an introduction to voice assistants *Med. Ref. Serv. Q.* **37** 81–8

Hutchins J 2005 *The History of Machine Translation in a Nutshell* https://en.m.wikipedia.org/wiki/Wayback_Machine (accessed 19 November 2024)

IBM http://www-03.ibm.com/systems/openinvitation/index.html#4 (accessed 28 December 2009)

IBM Largest commercial database in winter corp. Top ten survey tops one hundred terabytes *Press Release.* (accessed 16 May 2008)

Karjian R 2023 *The History of Artificial Intelligence: Complete AI Timeline* https://techtarget.com/searchEnterpriseAI/tip/The-history-of-artificial-intelligence-Complete-AI-timeline (accessed 9 September 2023)

Kaul V, Enslin S and Gross S A 2020 History of artificial intelligence in medicine *Gastrointest. Endosc.* **92** 807–12

Kawala-Sterniuk A, Browarska N, Al-Bakri A, Pelc M, Zygarlicki J, Sidikova M and Gorzelanczyk E J 2021 Summary of over fifty years with brain-computer interfaces—a review *Brain Sci.* **11** 43

Kennedy P R 1989 The cone electrode: a long-term electrode that records from neurites grown onto its recording surface *J. Neurosci. Methods* **29** 181–93

Korf R E 1997 Does deep blue use AI? *AAAI Technical Report* WS-97-04 pp 1–2

Krizhevsky A, Sutskever I and Hinton G E 2012 Imagenet classification with deep convolutional neural networks *Advances in Neural Information Processing Systems 25 (NIPS 2012)* **25**

LeCun Y, Boser B, Denker J S, Henderson D, Howard R E, Hubbard W and Jackel L D 1989 Backpropagation applied to handwritten zip code recognition *Neural Comput.* **1** 541–51

LeCun Y, Touresky D, Hinton G and Sejnowski T 1988 A theoretical framework for back-propagation *Proc. of the 1988 Connectionist Models Summer School* 1 pp 21–8

Lederberg J 1965 *DENDRAL-64-A System for Computer Construction, Enumeration and Notation of Organic Molecules as Tree Structures and Cyclic Graphs. Part II-Topology of Cyclic Graphs Interim Report* (No. NASA-CR-68898)

Lighthill J 1973 Artificial intelligence: a general survey *Artificial Intelligence: A Paper Symposium* (Science Research Council)

McCarthy J 1959 Lisp: a programming system for symbolic manipulations *Preprints of Papers Presented at the 14th National Meeting of the Association for Computing Machinery* pp 1–4

McCorduck P, Minsky M, Selfridge O G and Simon H A 1977 History of artificial intelligence *IJCAI'77: Proc. of the 5th Int. Joint Conf. on Artificial intelligence - Volume 2* pp 951–4

Mikolov T, Sutskever I, Chen K, Corrado G S and Dean J 2013 Distributed representations of words and phrases and their compositionality *Advances in Neural Information Processing Systems 26 (NIPS 2013)* **26**

Mitchell M 1998 *An Introduction to Genetic Algorithms* (Cambridge, MA: MIT Press)

National Research Council 1999 Developments in artificial intelligence *Funding a Revolution: Government Support for Computing Research* (Washington, DC: National Academy Press)

Neumann J V 1945 *The First Draft of the Report on the EDVAC* http://virtualtravelog.net/wp/wp-content/media/2003-08-TheFirstDraft.pdf

Newell A 1982 Intellectual issues in the history of artificial intelligence *Artificial Intelligence: Critical Concepts* (Routledge) pp 25–70

Newell A, Shaw J C and Simon H A 1962 The processes of creative thinking In *Contemporary Approaches to Creative Thinking, 1958, University of Colorado, CO, US; This Paper was Presented at the Aforementioned Symposium* (Atherton Press)

Newquist H P 1994 *The Brain Makers: Genius, Ego, and Greed In The Search For Machines That Think* (London: Macmillan/SAMS)

Nilsson N J 1984 Shakey the robot *Technical Note 323* (Menlo Park, CA: SRI International)

Null L and Lobur J 2003 *The Essentials of Computer Organization and Architecture* (Jones & Bartlett)

OpenAI 2023 *GPT-4 Technical Report* https://cdn.openai.com/papers/gpt-4.pdf (accessed 14 September 2023)

Pennachin C and Goertzel B 2007 Contemporary approaches to artificial general intelligence *Artificial General Intelligence* (Berlin: Springer) pp 1–30

Radford A, Narasimhan K, Salimans T and Sutskever I 2018 Improving language understanding by generative pre-training (pre-print)

Rumelhart D E and McClelland J LPDP Research Group (ed) 1986 *Parallel Distributed Processing, Volume 1: Explorations in the Microstructure of Cognition: Foundations* (Cambridge, MA: MIT Press)

Russell S J 2010 *Artificial Intelligence a Modern Approach* (London: Pearson Education)

Russell S J and Norvig P 2003 *Artificial Intelligence: A Modern Approach* 2nd edn (Upper Saddle River, NJ: Prentice-Hall/Pearson)

Samuel A L 1959 Some studies in machine learning using the game of checkers *IBM J. Res. Dev.* **3** 210–29

SciTechDaily 2024 *Not Science Fiction: Researchers Recreate Star Trek's Holodeck Using AI* https://scitechdaily.com/not-science-fiction-researchers-recreate-star-treks-holodeck-using-ai/ (accessed 15 November 2024)

Silver D, Huang A, Maddison C J, Guez A, Sifre L, Van Den Driessche G and Hassabis D 2016 Mastering the game of go with deep neural networks and tree search *Nature* **529** 484–9

Swartout W R 1985 Explaining and justifying expert consulting programs *Computer-Assisted Medical Decision Making* (New York: Springer) pp 254–71

Taylor J G 1996 *Neural Computation: the Historical Background* (Taylor & Francis)

Taylor J G 1997 Neural networks for consciousness *Neur. Netw.* **10** 1207–25

Thirunavukarasu A J, Ting D S J, Elangovan K, Gutierrez L, Tan T F and Ting D S W 2023 Large language models in medicine *Nat. Med.* **29** 1930–40

Thrun S, Montemerlo M, Dahlkamp H, Stavens D, Aron A, Diebel J and Mahoney P 2006 Stanley: the robot that won the DARPA grand challenge *J. Field Rob.* **23** 661–92

Tobin S, Jayabalasingham B, Huggett S and de Kleijn M 2019 A brief historical overview of artificial intelligence research *Inform. Serv. Use* **39** 291–6

Townsend J, Chaton T and Monteiro J M 2019 Extracting relational explanations from deep neural networks: a survey from a neural-symbolic perspective *IEEE Trans. Neural Netw. Learn. Syst.* **31** 3456–70

Tymann P and Reynolds C 2008 Principles of computer science *Schaum's Outline of Principles of Computer Science* (New York: McGraw-Hill)

Vaswani A, Shazeer N, Parmar N, Uszkoreit J, Jones L, Gomez A N and Polosukhin I 2017 Attention is all you need *Advances in Neural Information Processing Systems 30 (NIPS 2017)* **30**

Van Melle W, Shortliffe E H and Buchanan B G 1984 EMYCIN: a knowledge engineer's tool for constructing rule-based expert systems *Rule-Based Expert Systems: The MYCIN Experiments of the Stanford Heuristic Programming Project* (Addison-Wesley) pp 302–13

Vidal J J 1977 Real-time detection of brain events in EEG *Proc. IEEE* **65** 633–41

Walsh T 2017 The singularity may never be near *AI Mag.* **38** 58–62

Watkins , Christopher J C H and Peter Dayan 1992 Q-learning *Mach. Learn.* **8** 279–92

Watson J 2024 *Star Trek: Voyager Predicted AI-Generated Art 23 Years Ago* https://screenrant.com/star-trek-voyager-predicted-ai-art/ (accessed 15 November 2024)

Weizenbaum J 1966 ELIZA—a computer program for the study of natural language communication between man and machine *Commun. ACM* **9** 36–45

Wikes M V 1956 *Automatic Digital Computers* (New York: Wiley) p 305

Yadav N, Yadav A, Kumar M, Yadav N, Yadav A and Kumar M 2015 History of neural networks. *An Introduction to Neural Network Methods for Differential Equations* (Springer) pp 13–15

IOP Publishing

Chapter 2

Generative artificial intelligence: gateway and recent progress

Generative artificial intelligence (GAI) is too wide to be covered comprehensively in a single chapter or article due to the sheer volume of material and the rapid advancements in the field. Beginners may find it challenging to know where to start, given the abundance of resources. This chapter provides a systematic guide to begin a journey in generative AI and offers experts new insights. It covers the fundamentals of generative models, including their variants, generative tasks, and a comprehensive taxonomy. The chapter also presents a comparative analysis of the strengths and weaknesses of different types of generative models, as well as the motivations for integrating them. Additionally, it explores the roles of generative models in pharmaceutical companies and the creation of Deepfakes. Prompt engineering is introduced to equip readers with skills of creating effective prompts. To bridge the gap between theory and practice, industrial applications and case studies of generative tools are presented in a tabular format. This chapter serves as both an entry point for beginners and a resource for experts to explore numerous categories of generative models beyond the dominant generative adversarial networks, paving the way for future innovation.

2.1 Introduction

GAI is not a new concept; it has existed since the 1950s, as demonstrated by the Hidden Markov Models and Gaussian Mixture Models, which could generate speech and time series data, albeit with limited performance. However, advancements in deep learning architectures have revolutionized generative models, leading to significant performance improvements (Yunjiu *et al* 2022). In the 1960s, GAI was embedded into chatbots (Leong *et al* 2025). Before the revolution in generative models, machine learning tasks such as prediction, classification, clustering, and association rule dominated the field of AI. These tasks remain active and relevant in

doi:10.1088/978-0-7503-6320-4ch2

the current generation of AI but are slowly being relegated to the background. Recently, however, GAI has emerged and is transforming how users interact with computing devices.

The emergence of intriguing models like the stable diffusion model and ChatGPT has spurred growing interest and popularity in GAI (Zhang *et al* 2023). This is evidenced by the daily influx of large language models (LLMs). As of 8 June 2024, at 11:11 PM, Hafr Al Batin, Saudi Arabia time, there were 705 985 LLMs available on Hugging Face Inc. The GAI interest currently goes beyond the computer science community to the extent that the general public are interested in the content generation products released by the tech giants (Yunjiu *et al* 2022). However, LLMs are primarily trained with text data for text-based applications. This limits their capabilities to tasks involving text, particularly encoding and generation. They cannot perform tasks that require a combination of video, image, audio, text, and numerical values. To address this limitation, multimodal models trained with diverse data types—video, image, audio, text, and numerical values—have emerged (Wu *et al* 2023).

The expression or perception of natural phenomena is referred to as the modality. Examples of modalities include recorded audio from a microphone and speech, capturing videos and images from a camera, and using a haptic sensor to capture force and vibration. Modalities can be either raw or abstract. Raw modalities detected by sensors directly include images captured by a camera or recordings of speech from a microphone. On the other hand, abstract modalities involve extracting language from recorded speech, detecting objects from images, or analyzing abstract views such as sentiment intensity and categorization of objects. From these two concepts, it can be deduced that abstract modalities are further away from the sensor compared to raw modalities. Having multiple modalities is referred to as multimodalities, which involves the computation of heterogeneous, connected, and interactive modalities. The diverse quality of information, structure, and representation in various modalities makes them heterogeneous. These modalities are dependent entities because they share connections resulting from complementary information. The interaction of modalities occurs in different ways due to their integration for various tasks (Liang *et al* 2023). Generating multimodal content is a fundamental component of GAI content. The goal of multimodal generation is to develop models that produce raw modalities by training algorithms on datasets to learn the connections and interactions between different modalities (Cao *et al* 2023).

GAI models produce different types of content, such as text, images, audio, and synthetic data. These models generate high-quality text, graphics, audio, video, and images within seconds without human intervention (Leong *et al* 2025, Longoni *et al* 2022), as shown in figure 2.1. The emergence of the generative pre-trained transformer (GPT-3) in 2020 revolutionized the technology space with its impressive content generation across different domains. As a result of that, leading media houses such as the Associated Press, New York Times, ProPublica, Washington Post, and Forbes use GAI to automatically produce articles from scratch and report on crimes, politics, sports, financial markets, and foreign affairs (Longoni *et al* 2022). In 2024, OpenAI launched ChatGPT-4o (Omni), a multimodal model

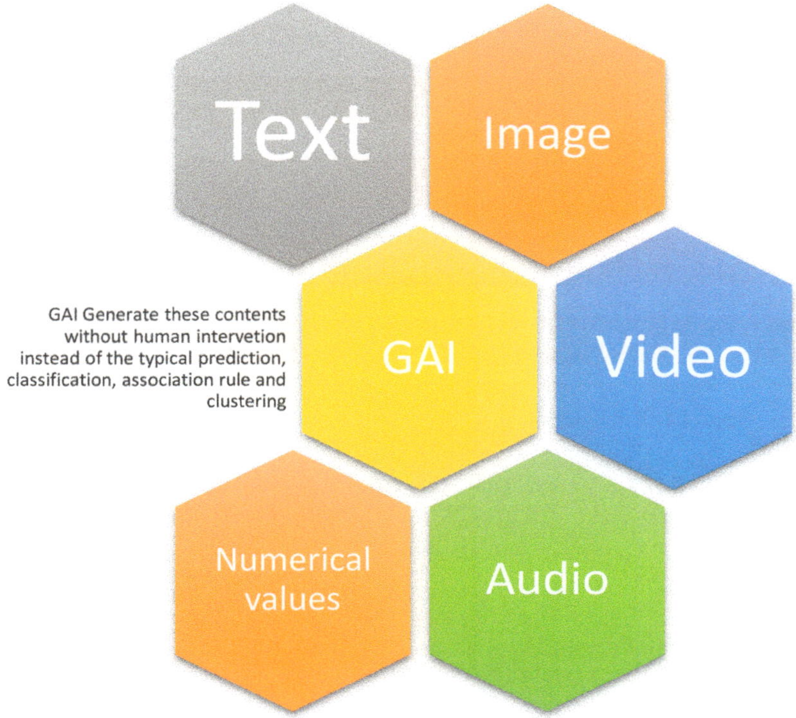

Figure 2.1. Media content typically generated by GAI models.

capable of performing multimodal tasks in addition to textual tasks. Many surveys from different perspectives and objectives on GAI exist in the literature, here are a few examples (Cao *et al* 2023, Harshvardhan *et al* 2020, Hughes *et al* 2021, Karapantelakis *et al* 2024, Kaswan *et al* 2023, Sakirin and Kusuma 2023, Takale *et al* 2024, Van Huynh *et al* 2024, Zhang *et al* 2023).

GAI is too vast to cover comprehensively in a single chapter due to the high volume of materials and rapid advances in the field. Given the abundance of resources, beginners might find it challenging to determine where to start. Therefore, this chapter aims to provide the fundamentals of GAI, serving as an entry point for newcomers. For expert readers, the chapter offers an overview of GAI, highlighting various categories of generative models. This allows exploration of different categories of GAI algorithms for innovative integration of algorithms/models beyond the dominant generative adversarial networks (GANs).

2.2 Generative tasks

The generative task involves using generative models to create new content (e.g., images) referred to as synthesis from existing content (e.g., images) or to convert one type of content into another, such as converting text to images and vice versa.

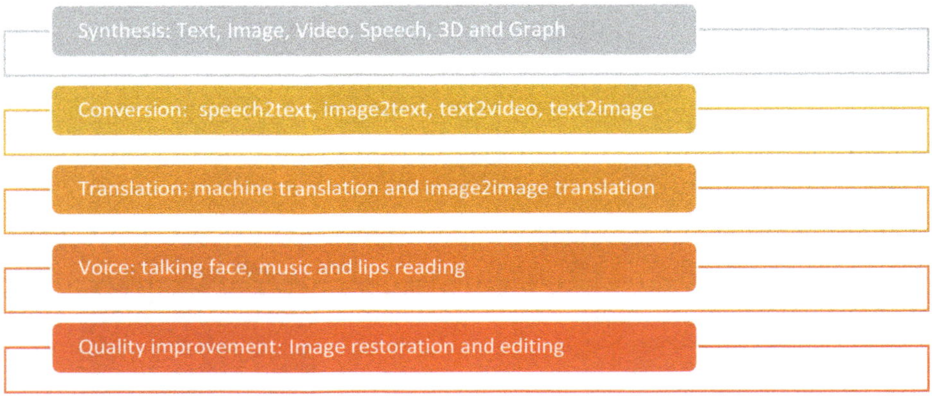

Figure 2.2. Representative samples of different categories of generative tasks.

Many generative tasks are available; however, this chapter illustrates a representative selection of these tasks in figure 2.2.

2.2.1 Synthesis

2.2.1.1 Text synthesis

This is referred to as the process of generating coherent text content from generative models trained with text corpora from diverse sources to predict the next word in a sentence. The models takes in text as input, processing it to semantic representations to generate coherent contextual text. The text synthesis can be writing articles, responding to questions, summarizing, paraphrasing, conversations, translation, etc (Iqbal and Qureshi 2022, Yu *et al* 2022). This field containing text-to-text and data-to-text generation is referred to as computational linguistics (Gatt and Krahmer 2018).

2.2.1.2 Image synthesis

This is a hot topic in computer vision and machine learning with significant progress because of its value and potential applications (Jia *et al* 2024). It is the process of creating new images from images data description by the use of generative models that have learned complex distribution of the image data through pre-training (Baraheem *et al* 2023). The images data can be RGB images, medical images, videos, etc (Elasri *et al* 2022).

2.2.1.3 Video synthesis

This is the process of creating video content using generative models. This process involves the production of videos that can include realistic visuals, animated sequences, and other visual effects. It aims to create visually appealing and coherent motion sequences. In other words, it is the generation of video aiming to realistically synthesize videos with visually appealing content that is spatially and temporally coherent in terms of motion (Wang *et al* 2024).

2.2.1.4 Speech synthesis

With rapid development in global communication, speech processing has taken the mainstream field in research. The main aim of the research is to develop a machine imitating human speech. This goal can be achieved through speech recognition and speech synthesis (Indumathi and Chandra 2012). The speech synthesis also commonly referred to as text-to-speech is the generation of understandable speech by a learned generative model from text as an input to the machine (Ning *et al* 2019, Tabet and Boughazi 2011). A typical example is the ReadAloud feature in the Microsoft word processing application.

2.2.1.5 3D object synthesis

The automatic generation of 3D models using algorithms has been a crucial task in computer vision and graphics for a long time. The 3D object synthesis is the process of generating new 3D objects from 3D datasets, text or images taken as the inputs to the trained generative model. The generative model learns the latent distribution of the data through training to automatically generate the new 3D objects (Li *et al* 2024). The representation of 3D objects can be in any of the following formats: point cloud (Gezawa *et al* 2023a), meshes, voxel grids and depth images (Gezawa *et al* 2023b).

2.2.1.6 Graphs synthesis

This is the process whereby a trained generative model is used for the creation of new graph structure from existing graphs or real data. The graph typically encodes the relationship between real-world objects in different domains. The relationship, features and objects in the graph differs depending on the domain (Zhu *et al* 2022).

2.2.2 Conversion

2.2.2.1 Text-guided video generation

Despite the challenges of misinterpretation in text description, text description gives better versatile and robust means of expressing and describing the concept of visual. This is in view of the fact that a wide range of ideas and details are well captured easily in text description compared to other approaches (Zhan *et al* 2023). The early works on text-guided video generation mainly focussed on generating videos in a simple environment such as a human walking or digits bouncing. Later on, text-guided image generation works were extended to text-guided video generation that led to the generation of realistic video scenes from text (Zhang 2023a, 2023b).

2.2.2.2 Speech-to-text generation

This is the process of converting speech in natural language into text, it is the speech signal that is converted into the corresponding text description. The speech-to-text generation is also referred to as automatic speech recognition (Indurkhya and Damerau 2010).

2.2.2.3 Image-to-text (image captioning)

This is the process in which the content of an image is described in natural language conveying the content of the image. On the other hand, text-to-image is the process of generating image from textual description, it is the reversal of image-to-text generation (Zhang 2023a, 2023b).

2.2.3 Quality improvement

2.2.3.1 Image restoration

The effort of image restoration began by scientists from the former Soviet Union and United States of America in the 1950s (Banham and Katsaggelos 1997). This concept aimed to solve the typical problem of inverse by restoring clean images from degraded images (Demoment 1989, Zhang *et al* 2023), thus, reconstructing high-quality images from corresponding low-quality degraded images (Liang *et al* 2021).

2.2.3.2 Image editing

Unlike image restoration discussed in the preceding sub-section, image editing is the modification of image to meet user-defined criteria similar to style transfer. For instance, Adobe PhotoShop has a set of tools allowing the user to modify images which involves subtraction, addition or deforming the structure of the image (Elder and Goldberg 1998). Generative models have penetrated image editing tasks in the form of neural photo editing filters improving the quality of the editing task (Ling *et al* 2021).

2.2.4 Conversation

2.2.4.1 Chatbots

This is an intelligent conversation agent developed mainly for dialogue to provide communication between machines and humans in a better way using natural language as the medium of interaction. The chatbots can perform different types of tasks across domains to improve productivity and enhance processes (Luo *et al* 2022).

2.2.5 Translation

2.2.5.1 Image-to-image translation

This is a category of problem in graphics and vision where it aims to understand the mapping between source images and target images through existing training images pair data (Isola *et al* 2017). It converts one type of image to another, such as turning sketches into realistic photos, enhancing image resolution, or altering styles while retaining the original content of the source image. For example, a user can take a photo of themselves commonly refer to as selfie which is an image as the source domain, and 'translate' the image to a target image artistic style providing a desired cartoon as the target reference domain (Pang *et al* 2021)

2.2.5.2 Machine translation

Language barriers can still be an obstacle to accessing information in a global context. Humans with the ability to speak and understand different languages are relied upon to translate both spoken and written text into another language. However, it is practically impossible to rely solely on humans for translation (Lagarda *et al* 2015). Therefore, machine translation has emerged to meet the increasing demand for translation as introduced by Hutchins and Lovtskii (2000). Machine translation is the automatic translation of written text or spoken language to another language to break the barrier of language differences. It is found that research and demand in this field is growing rapidly at an exponential rate (Garg and Agarwal 2018, Rivera-Trigueros 2022). Machine translation plays a crucial role for diverse professionals including but not limited to computer scientists, linguists and sociologists (Garg and Agarwal 2018).

2.2.6 Voice

2.2.6.1 Talking face

Talking face is gaining popularity in multimedia applications (e.g., virtual avatars and video games) (Xie and Liu 2007). The talking face involves the generation of a series of image frames viewed technically as video but different from video generation. An identity reference such as an image is required in a talking face and editing is performed based on input speech making the process relate to image editing. In addition, a speech clip is converted to a face image by the talking face similar to speech recognition converting a speech clip to corresponding text (Xie and Liu 2007, Zhen *et al* 2023).

2.2.6.2 Music generation

Music is a flow of information that humans can perceive as having a structured form, consisting of segments with distinct beginnings and endings, evoking emotions, and conveying meaning across various abstraction levels (Huron 2008). Advancements in generative models have enabled the automatic creation of high-quality music. Users simply provide inputs such as text, images, scores, videos, sensor data, lead sheets, or predefined target emotions. Once the desired emotional outcome is specified, the music is then composed automatically (Dash and Agres 2024).

2.2.6.3 Lip reading task

The visual way of understanding humans talking about something is referred to as lip reading. Lip reading is carry out by observing the speaker's facial pattern of speech to understand what the speaker is talking about (Kulkarni and Kirange 2019). This is the process of transforming the movement of visual inputs to decode speech by given videos of the speaker as the input visual to sample into image frames representing speech intended to be decoded (Fenghour *et al* 2021). Interest in developing automatic lip reading systems has been growing in recent years and deep learning has become popular in this domain (Fernandez-Lopez and Sukno 2018).

The Wild LRRo is a dataset for lip reading word-level generated from Romanian TV shows, News programs and TEDxtalks videos (Oghbaie *et al* 2021).

2.3 Generative models

In the field of GAI, any scholar interested in starting research must understand the generative models available in the literature. The first step is to grasp the concept of GAI, which is well-documented in the introductory section of the chapter. Next, it is essential to explore the operations of different categories of generative models and their respective variants. It is well-known that all intelligent algorithms, including generative algorithms, have limitations. Due to these limitations, no single generative model can generate all types of media content or modalities effectively. This is why each type of media content has a suitable generative model designed specifically for it. For instance, a generative model that performs better at creating images may fail at generating text or video, or at best, produce content of poor quality in those other domains. The performance of generative models varies significantly across different types of content. This section discusses different categories of generative models.

The generation of diverse contents of varying scale in the field of GAI requires the use of generative models and advanced deep learning architectures. Generative models utilize various types of media content (e.g., text, audio, video, and graphics) to generate new media content (e.g., text, audio, or video) (Abukmeil *et al* 2021, Gui *et al* 2021). These contents are created in large quantities by generative models automatically, rather than by human beings, in a short period of time (Cao *et al* 2023).

An individual might wonder why the research community focusses on studying generative models, particularly those designed to generate new content rather than predict density functions. This curiosity is especially relevant in cases where generative models take an image as input to produce another image, effectively creating more images even though the world already has an abundance of them. However, studying generative models is crucial and highly beneficial for several reasons as follows (figure 2.3) (Goodfellow 2016):

2.3.1 Training and sampling

Training with and sampling from generative models serves as a valuable evaluation of our capacity to depict and handle complex, high-dimensional probability

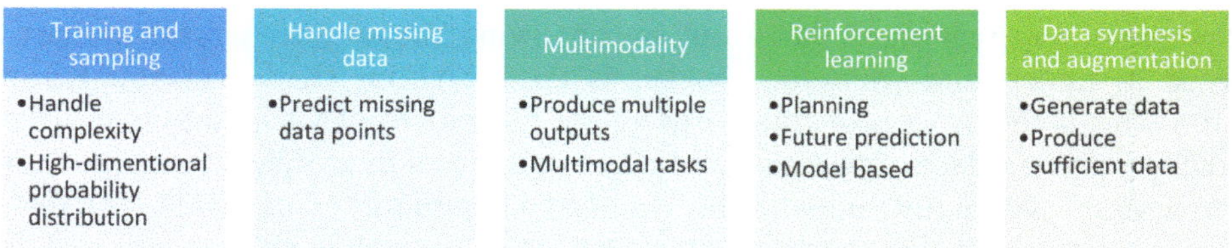

Figure 2.3. The reasons for studying generative models.

distributions, which are fundamental in a diverse range of applied mathematics and engineering disciplines

2.3.2 Handles missing data

Generative models have the capability to handle missing data points during training and predict the missing input data. In semi-supervised learning, where labels for some or most of the training data are missing, generative models are particularly suitable for handling such situations. Semi-supervised learning is used as a strategy to reduce the extremely high number of labelled data required by deep learning architectures to perform well. Studying a large amount of unlabelled data using learning algorithms can improve their generalization ability. Generative models, especially GANs, are suitable for performing semi-supervised learning with reasonable performance.

2.3.3 Multimodality

Generative models, especially GANs, have the capacity to perform multimodal tasks and produce multimodal outputs. Many tasks with a single input can produce multiple correct answers as outputs. However, traditional approaches to training machine learning algorithms, such as minimizing the mean square error between the computed output and the actual output, lack the capacity to produce multiple correct answers.

2.3.4 Reinforcement learning

There are many approaches to incorporating generative models into reinforcement learning (RL). The RL is categorized into two major types: model-based RL algorithms and model-free RL algorithms. Model-based RL algorithms incorporate generative models. Simulating possible futures can be performed with time series generative models. Different methods can be utilized to deploy these models for planning and RL. Generative models learn the conditional distribution over the state of the environment for planning, given the current state of the environment and the agent's hypothetical actions as input. The agent queries the model with potential actions and selects the actions that the model forecasts will likely produce the desired state of the environment.

2.3.5 Data synthesis and augmentation

Recently, generative models have been used to generate large amounts of high-quality data involving images, video, and music. The generation of synthetic data is possible due to advancements in artificial neural networks (ANNs) that produce GAI algorithms (Castelli and Manzoni 2022). There are situations where a particular research topic may completely lack the data needed for research. In such cases, generative models can be deployed to create synthetic data for conducting the research. Additionally, in some cases, real-world data may be available but insufficient for significant research. This insufficient real-world data can be augmented with generative models to provide enough data for research. Generating additional data (e.g., images, video, text, or audio) to supplement the small amount of available real-world data for research purposes is referred to as the data augmentation.

2.4 The taxonomy of generative models

Figure 2.4 illustrates a comprehensive taxonomy outlining the major types of generative models in the literature. The primary building blocks include GANs, variational autoencoders (VAE), diffusion models, statistical approaches, and hybrid models that combine multiple generative techniques, along with other structures beyond the core categories. The taxonomy also showcases representative variants of each major model within their respective branches for clarity. Additionally, it highlights the underlying motivations for each model type, such as GANs being inspired by zero-sum game theory, diffusion models by thermodynamics in physics, and VAEs by the encoder–decoder framework.

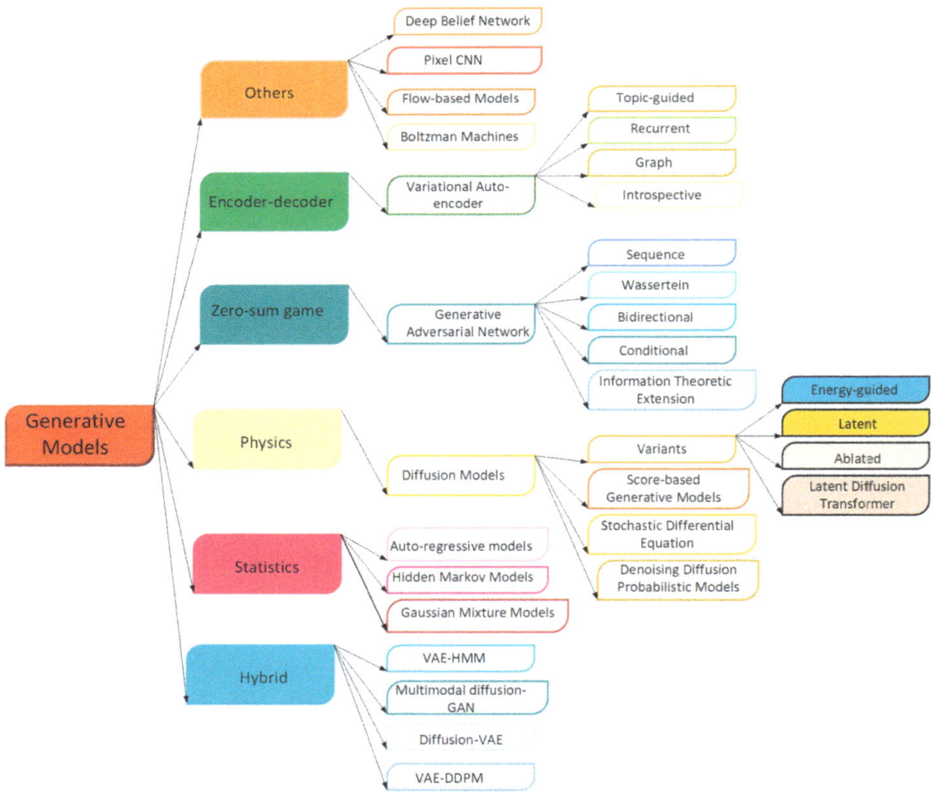

Figure 2.4. Taxonomy of the generative models.

2.4.1 Generative adversarial network

Despite the fact that GAI is not new, as discussed in the introduction, the advent of GANs in 2014 has significantly revolutionized the field of GAI. This development has generated unprecedented interest from the research community, making GANs and their variants highly popular algorithms (Castelli and Manzoni 2022). As a result, GANs are now the most dominant algorithms in GAI (Jovanovic and Campbell 2022). GANs are motivated by the concept of a zero-sum game. In a zero-sum game, two players are strictly opposed to each other, where the gain of one player results in the loss of the opponent, making the game non-cooperative. The total gains and losses add up to zero if both players are considered (Wang *et al* 2017, Wei *et al* 2015).

The GAN operates like a game involving only two players: the generator and the discriminator as the players. When fed with training data, the generator produces fake samples from the original training data distribution. The discriminator examines the samples generated by the generator against the original data to determine whether the generated data is fake or real. The discriminator uses supervised learning to classify the inputs as fake or real. The goal of the generator's training is to deceive the discriminator into believing that the fake data it generates is real. Let's illustrate this concept with a real-world analogy for better understanding. Imagine the generator as a criminal producing counterfeit money (fake money), and the discriminator as the police. The police aim to detect and seize counterfeit money while allowing real money to circulate. For the criminal to successfully pass off fake money without detection and seizure by the police, the criminal must learn to produce counterfeit money that is indistinguishable from real money. Similarly, the generator must learn to generate data samples that closely match the original training data distribution (Goodfellow 2016). Refer to figure 2.5, which depicts the GAN. In this figure, the generator is trying to evade detection by fooling the discriminator, while the discriminator is attempting to distinguish between fake money and real money.

The generator network and the discriminator network in the GANs are both involved in the training process. In the training process, the real data is derived from the real training dataset, whereas the fake data is continuously generated by the generator network throughout the training phase of the modelling. The training of the discriminator is performed similarly to any other classifier defined by the architecture of the deep neural network (Goodfellow *et al* 2020).

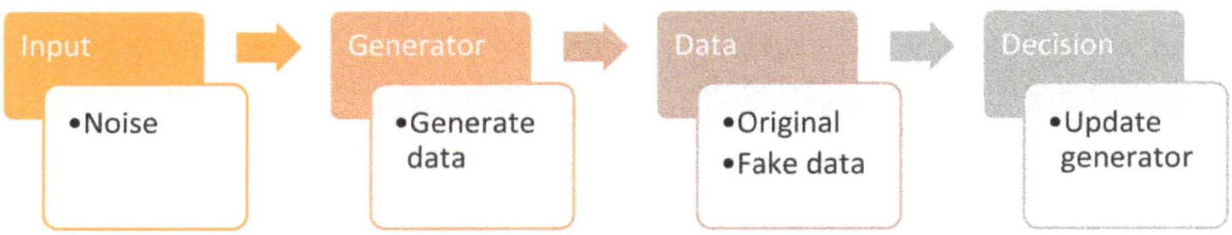

Figure 2.5. Schematic representation of basic GAN operations.

2.4.1.1 *Generative adversarial network variants*

The introduction of GANs, as described in preceding section, has motivated their deployment to solve problems across various domains and has led to different modifications from diverse perspectives. These include structural improvements leading to new architectures, extensions of GAN theory, novel applications, and enhancements in optimization and parameter learning without altering the basic architecture. Consequently, many variants of GANs have been proposed, as illustrated in table 2.1, a detailed explanation of each GAN variant in table 2.1 is excellently covered by Wang *et al* (2017). GANs have rapidly advanced due to enhancements in GAN algorithms, improvements in deep learning algorithms, and advancements in deep learning software and hardware platforms. This swift progress makes it impractical for any central literature to comprehensively cover the latest development on GANs (e.g. capabilities or best practice). Both fields continue to evolve so rapidly that any thorough survey becomes outdated quickly (Goodfellow *et al* 2020).

2.4.1.2 *Suitability of the generative adversarial network variants applied in solving generative tasks*

The GAN has been successful in solving various tasks across different domains of applications, primarily in research environments (Goodfellow *et al* 2020). GANs can generate image samples that share the same distribution as real images, as demonstrated in many studies. Table 2.2 summarizes representative applications of GANs in different generative tasks. Different GAN models are suitable for different tasks, as no single GAN variant can solve all types of generative problems. This is why table 2.2 includes various GAN models, each paired with the corresponding task for which they are best suited.

Table 2.1. Different GAN architecture description.

GAN variant	Architecture
Wasserstein GAN (WGAN)	In WGAN, the Jensen-Shannon divergence is replaced with the earth mover distance (Arjovsky *et al* 2017)
Bidirectional GANs (BiGAN)	Extra decoder is added on GAN to create BiGAN (Donahue *et al* 2016)
Auxiliary classifier GAN (AC-GAN)	The generator of AC-GAN is integrated with label information (Odena *et al* 2017)
Information-theoretic extension (InfoGAN)	The InfoGAN is design to capture mutual information (Chen *et al* 2016)
Sequence GAN (SeqGAN)	The SeqGAN extend GAN to generate data sequence (Yu *et al* 2017)
Boundary equilibrium GAN (BEGAN)	The BEGAN is created from Wasserstein (Berthelot 2017)

Table 2.2. Summary of the suitability of different GAN versions for generative tasks.

Reference	GAN model	Operation	Task Suitability
Tulyakov *et al* (2018)	Motion and Content decomposed GAN	Proposes new adversarial learning that uses image and video discriminators to learn motion and content decomposition	Video
Wang *et al* (2018)	C-GANs	introduce new adversarial loss and multi-scale generator and discriminator to generate 2048 × 1024 high-resolution visual	Urban scene
Xia *et al* (2021)	Text-guided diverse face image generation and manipulation GAN	This comprised of instance-level optimization, StyleGAN inversion module and visual-linguistic similarity learning to generate image from text description.	Human portrait
Guimaraes *et al* (2017)	Objective-reinforced GAN	Utilizes hybrid of adversarial training and expert-based rewards with RL	Music
Yu *et al* (2017)	SeqGAN	Reinforcement learning with stochastic policy is applied for solving the differentiation problem in the generator	Speech, language, poem and music.
Wang *et al* (2018)	Enhanced super-resolution GAN	Proposes residual-in-residual dense block without batch normalization to improve the quality of visual with more realistic and natural textures	Super-resolution and Image restoration
Wu *et al* (2016)	3D-GAN	We study the problem of 3D object generation. We propose a novel framework, namely 3D Uses volumetric convolutional networks and GAN to generate 3D object	3D Object
Shaham *et al* (2019)	SinGAN	It incorporated pyramid of fully convolutional GANs to generate diverse images from single image while maintaining both the texture and structure	Texture
Park *et al* (2019)	GauGAN	Uses input layout for the modulation of activation in the normalization layers	Landscape

2.4.1.3 Uncertainties

Working with ANNs is not straightforward and involves several uncertainties. The structure of an ANN needs to be configured by the modeller, including the number of hyper-parameters, the layers of the network, and the activation functions. From the perspective of the training process, factors such as the optimization algorithm, data augmentation, and regularization need to be set for the network to function properly. Both the structure and the training of the ANN contribute to uncertainties within the network. During the training process, many hyper-parameters must be defined, including but not limited to the learning rate, batch size, regularization method, optimizer, and stopping criteria. Additionally, stochastic decisions take place during training, such as batch generation and initialization of the weights. These decisions affect the local optima, leading to different model parameterizations in different training processes. Uncertainty in ANN parameters can also be introduced by the training dataset due to imbalanced data or insufficient coverage of certain regions within the data distribution. This issue can be mitigated by applying data augmentation to increase data variety or by balancing the impact of different classes or regions on the loss function. The factors that introduce uncertainties in the training procedure include inadequate model structure, errors in the training procedure, and insufficient knowledge about or coverage of the training data (Gawlikowski *et al* 2023).

The performance of an ANN is directly affected by its structure and associated uncertainties. For example, the memory capacity of an ANN is influenced by the network parameters, which can lead to underfitting or overfitting of the training data. Typically, deeper networks are overconfident in their softmax outputs, assigning excessively high probabilities to the class with the highest probability score (Gawlikowski *et al* 2023). The uncertainties in the training procedure of an ANN, as described in the preceding paragraph, pertain to ANNs in general. The discussion in the next paragraph will focus on tips to succeed in training in the context of GANs.

2.4.1.4 Generative adversarial network: training tips

Presently, the training of GANs is difficult to perform as finding the Nash equilibria consistently at a faster rate is still challenging (Goodfellow *et al* 2020). The training of GANs involves uncertainties and is particularly challenging when dealing with very large-scale data. If not properly executed, the training can collapse prematurely, become unstable, underfitted, overfitted, or fail entirely. This section provides tips to help avoid issues that can lead to unsuccessful training. However, these tips do not guarantee successful training but serve as a guide.

The inputs should be normalized to a range of -1 to 1, with *Tanh* applied at the generator's last layer. The loss function used for optimizing the generator is (min (log $(1-D)$)), though in practice, (max (log D)) is often adopted to avoid the vanishing gradient issue associated with (min (log $(1-D)$)), as recommended by Goodfellow *et al* (2014). During training, the labels in the data are flipped when training the generator, resulting in real data being labelled as fake and vice versa. Samples should not be drawn from a uniform distribution; instead, use a spherical Z

and sample from a Gaussian distribution. Construct two mini-batches: one containing only real data and the other containing only fake data. Batch normalization is recommended; if unavailable, instance normalization can be adopted. Sparse gradients such as ReLU and MaxPool should be avoided because the stability of the GAN training suffers with sparse gradients. LeakyReLU is effective for both the generator and discriminator. Use average pooling or Conv2d + stride for downsampling, and PixelShuffle or ConvTranspose2d + stride for upsampling. Soft and noisy labels should be used for label smoothing. For example, if the target labels are Real (assigned to 1) and Fake (assigned to 0), replace each incoming real sample with a random value between 0.7 and 1.2. For fake samples, use a value between 0.0 and 0.3, as recommended by Salimans *et al* (2016), Chintala *et al* (2016).

Introduce noise to the discriminator labels by randomly flipping them during training. Hybrid models such as KL + GAN or VAE + GAN can be utilized. Stability tricks from RLcan also be applied, such as maintaining a replay buffer of past generations and occasionally showing them, as well as maintaining checkpoints from past generators and discriminators. For a small number of iterations, occasionally swap these out. The recommended optimizers for training are ADAM for the generator and stochastic gradient decent for the discriminator. Track failures as early as possible by monitoring failure modes (e.g., discriminator loss going to 0) and checking the gradient norms; if they exceed 100, it indicates a problem. A low variance in discriminator loss that decreases over time indicates that things are working well. If the generator's loss is steadily decreasing, it suggests that the generator is deceiving the discriminator with garbage. Balancing loss through statistics should be avoided unless there is strong justification for it. Every layer of the generator should have Gaussian noise added, and noise should be intentionally added to the discriminator inputs. Sometimes, train the discriminator more, especially when there is noise present. During both the training and test phases of the generator, use dropout (0.5) in the form of noise (Chintala *et al* 2016).

2.4.2 Variational autoencoders

To understand VAEs, the reader must first grasp how encoders and decoders perform their basic operations. A detailed description of the encoder and decoder operations can be found in chapter 3. Although autoencoders (AEs) are considered among the simplest generative models, they are highly sophisticated. The design of AEs aims to generate data from given samples by extracting internal regularities through training, allowing the AEs to learn (Oussidi *et al* 2018). The VAEs generate samples of data by training, enabling the model to learn the compatibility and the latent representation of the input data. The input data is processed by the encoder to produce the latent representation of the data distribution. On the other hand, the decoder accepts the latent representation as input to generate synthetic data similar to the input data (Du *et al* 2023, Harshvardhan *et al* 2020, Kingma and Welling 2019).

For the VAE (Kingma and Welling 2013) to generate data, the samples have to be derived from the AEs model. We assume that the data $\{x^i\}_{i=1}^N$, true latent distribution z assuming to be a Gaussian given $p_\theta(z)$ generates the date, where the model parameters are represented by θ. The true parameters of the θ is estimated and the data to be generated must be sampled from x by the true conditional $p_\theta(x|z^i)$. An ANN can be used to represent the conditional. The likelihood of the training data is maximized when training generative models, consider the expression (Harshvardhan *et al* 2020):

$$p_\theta(x) = \int p_\theta(z)p_\theta(x \mid z)dz \tag{2.1}$$

The $p_\theta(x|z)$ in equation (2.1) is intractable and the posterior density is expressed as:

$$p_\theta(z \mid x) = \frac{p_\theta(x \mid z)p_\theta(z)}{p_\theta(x)} \tag{2.2}$$

Equation (2.2) is also intractable because of the denominator in view of the fact that equation (2.1) is intractable.

$$p_\theta(z \mid x) = \frac{p_\theta(x \mid z)p_\theta(z)}{\int p_\theta(z)p_\theta(x \mid z)dz}$$

To solve the intractable problem, equation (2.2) has to be approximated via $q_\varphi(z|x)$ an inference network allowing the derivation of tractable lower bound that can be maximized by the suitable optimization technique. The $p_\theta(x|z)$ can be referred to as the generator network. The data likelihood log can be expressed as $\mathbb{E}$, an expectation with respect to z as samples derived from $q_\varphi(z|x^i)$, formally expressed as (Harshvardhan *et al* 2020):

$$\log p_\theta(x^i) = \mathbb{E}_{z\sim q_\varphi(z|x^i)}[\log p_\theta(x^i)] \tag{2.3}$$

The logarithm of equation (2.3) is independent of z

$$\log p_\theta(x^i) = \mathbb{E}_z\left[\log \frac{p_\theta(x^i \mid z)p_\theta(z)}{p_\theta(z)x^i)}\right] \tag{2.4}$$

Based on Bayes' rule (Barron 1987), it is multiplied by a constant to obtain:

$$\log p_\theta(x^i) = \mathbb{E}_z\left[\log \frac{p_\theta(x^i \mid z)p_\theta(z)}{p_\theta(z)x^i)} \frac{q_\varphi(z \mid x^i)}{q_\varphi(z \mid x^i)}\right]$$

$$\log p_\theta(x^i) = \mathbb{E}_z[\log p_\theta(x^i \mid z)] - \mathbb{E}_z\left[\log \frac{q_\varphi(z \mid x^i)}{p_\theta(z)}\right] + \mathbb{E}_z\left[\log \frac{q_\varphi(z \mid x^i)}{p_\theta(z)}\right] \tag{2.5}$$

$$\log p_\theta(x^i) = \mathbb{E}_z\left[[\log p_\theta(x^i \mid z)] - \left[\log \frac{q_\varphi(z \mid x^i)}{p_\theta(z)}\right] + \left[\log \frac{q_\varphi(z \mid x^i)}{p_\theta(z)}\right]\right]$$

$$\log p_\theta(x^i) = \mathbb{E}_z[p_\theta(x^i \mid z)] - KL(q_\varphi(z \mid x^i)||p_\theta(z) + KL(q_\varphi(z \mid x^i)||p_\theta(z \mid x^i)) \quad (2.6)$$

From equation (2.6), $p_\theta(z|x^i)$ of term 3 is intractable, the Kullback–Leibler (KL) divergence $\geqslant 0$ always for the optimization of the likelihood, thus, maximizing the likelihood requires the maximization and minimization of term 1 for reconstructing inputs data and term 2 for posterior distribution, respectively. As such, the KL is minimized. Since the term 3 $\geqslant$ 0, the tractable lower bound is defined as $\varepsilon(x^i, \theta, \varphi) = \omega$. The gradient of the $\varepsilon(x^i, \theta, \varphi)$ can be obtained and optimized (Harshvardhan *et al* 2020).

$$\omega = \mathbb{E}_z[\log p_\theta(x^i \mid z) - KL(q_\varphi(z \mid x^i)||p_\theta(z)]$$

Thus, resulting to variational lower bound,

$$\omega \geqslant \log p_\theta(x^i)$$

The ω is maximize as expressed in equation (2.7) to predict the φ' and θ' parameters during training (Harshvardhan *et al* 2020):

$$\theta', \varphi' = \arg\max_{\theta,\varphi} \sum_{i=1}^{N} \omega \quad (2.7)$$

The VAE described in the preceding section is the classical algorithm. However, different emerging variants suitable for performing generative tasks across various domains exist. The details of all the VAE variants are beyond the scope of this chapter, but table 2.3 summarizes representative VAE variants to provide the reader with insights.

Table 2.3. Summary of the variants of VAE solving generative tasks.

Reference	VAEs Variants	Operation	Suitability
Huang *et al* (2018)	Introspective	Adaptably improve itself to improve the quality of the samples generated. introspective is used to train both the inference and generator jointly.	Image synthesis
Grekow and Dimitrova-Grekow (2021)	Conditional	Incorporated conditional information unlike the classical VAEs. The Conditional VAEs extend the capability of the VAEs to allow the data samples generate to condition on additional information.	Music generation
Wang *et al* (2019)	Topic-guided	The VAE variant takes the prior as the Gaussian mixture model.	Text synthesis
Liu *et al* (2018)	Graph	The VAE has graph structure for both the encoder and decoder.	Design of molecules
Leglaive *et al* (2020)	Recurrent	The variant introduced posterior temporal dynamic over the latent variables.	Speech enhancement

2.4.3 Diffusion models

Thermodynamic modelling inspired the development of diffusion models (Sohl-Dickstein *et al* 2015). It first appeared in statistical physics to describe the process of particle movement from high to low concentrations (Jarzynski 1997). Diffusion models have now formed a class of deep generative models, attracting unprecedented attention in computer vision (Croitoru *et al* 2023). Simulating the behaviour of random diffusion accurately was the major concern of diffusion models in the generation process (Yang *et al* 2024). These models belong to the probability-based generative models (Sohl-Dickstein *et al* 2015). Work on diffusion models for generative tasks can be traced back to 2015. Interest in this area grew slowly, with a three-year break without published works until 2019 and 2020. However, in 2021 and 2022, the research community witnessed a boom in diffusion models, with a large number of studies solving different generative task problems (Croitoru *et al* 2023). The attention on diffusion models continued to grow into 2023, as indicated by the visual trend of studies conducted in this research field (Xing *et al* 2023). This indicates that the generative capabilities of diffusion models are impressive, ranging from high-level details to diverse examples generated by these models. Diffusion models have succeeded in opening a new chapter in the field of generative modelling (Croitoru *et al* 2023).

The diffusion models are classified among the generative models in AI, bringing a revolution in the creation and manipulation of digital content (e.g., images and audio generation, converting images to text). The use of diffusion models has been extended to deep learning for more advanced image generation, drug development, natural language processing, and using eye tracking to predict human choices. A major innovation in the field of diffusion models with significant societal impact is the development of DALL-E, a powerful image generation model developed by OpenAI. This relatively new technology makes researchers actively explore new ways to deploy diffusion models and make them accessible to the general public (Coursera 2024).

2.4.3.1 Generic diffusion model framework

The training procedure in a diffusion model is generally comprised of two processes, forward process referred to as the *diffusion* and backward process referred to as the *denoising*. The diffusion model begins with a noise distribution that is altered via sequential stages in a gradual manner. The forward process of the model continues adding noise incrementally to the original data until the data becomes pure random noise. In this process, each step only depends on the preceding step, commonly referred to as the Markovian process. Subsequently, the backward process begins operation by removing the noise from the data through learning in training the neural network (i.e. reversing the forward process). The removal of the noise added at the diffusion process during the algorithm training, makes the model learn to generate samples from the same distribution with the data used for the training process. The entire process can be summarized as model optimization to effectively remove noise and restore clean data distribution. This is performed using loss function that encourages the deep neural network model to produce output data very close to the original data distribution (Chen *et al* 2024, Nichol and Dhariwal 2021). The generic diffusion models have three major formulations as follows: denoising diffusion probabilistic models (DDPMs), stochastic differential equations (SDEs), and score-based generative models (SGMs) (e.g. noise-conditioned score networks (NCSNs)) (Cao *et al* 2024, Croitoru *et al* 2023, Xing *et al* 2023, Yang *et al* 2024) discussed in the next sub-sections.

2.4.3.2 Denoising diffusion probabilistic models

The DDPMs are typically developed around a probabilistic process that is well-defined through the double-phase Markov chains: *forward (diffusion) and backward (denoising) processes.*

Forward (diffusion) process: Assuming $q(x)$ is the given data distribution and $x_0 \sim q(x_0)$ is the samples of the original clean data. The *forward (diffusion)* process gradually corrupts the original data distribution by indroducing Gaussian noise continuously towards the convergence together with the standard Gaussian distribution. In the *forward (diffusion)* process up to a step K, a latent data distributed sequence $x_1, x_2, \ldots, x_K$ emerges. The *diffusion* process is defined as the Markov chain transforms x_{K-1} to x_K with the diffusion process transition kernel expressed as (Yang *et al* 2024):

$$q(x_K \,|x_{K-1}) := \mathcal{N}(x_K; \sqrt{1-\beta_k}\, x_{K-1,}\, \beta_k I) \tag{2.8}$$

For $\forall\, k \in \{1, \ldots, K\}$ having controlling size of $\beta_k \in (0, 1)$, I is the identity matrix, $\mathcal{N}(x; \mu, \sigma)$ of x is the Gaussian distribution with μ *and* σ representing mean and covariance, respectively. It is feasible to obtain x_K directly from x_0 by the equation (2.8) based on Gaussian kernel properties. Subsequently, we collect noisy data samples directly from the original input x_0 for each of the step expressed as:

$$q(x_K \,|x_0) := \prod_{k=1}^{k} q(x_K|x_{k-1}) := \mathcal{N}(x_K; \sqrt{\overline{\alpha_k}} X_0, \sqrt{1-\overline{\alpha_k}\, I} \tag{2.9}$$

where α_k and $\overline{\alpha_k}$ assigned (:=) to $1 - \beta_k$ and $\prod_{k=1}^{k} \alpha_k$, respectively.

Therefore, $x_K = l1 + l2$ with Gaussian noise $\alpha \sim \mathcal{N}(0, I)$ where $l1 = \sqrt{\overline{\alpha_k}}\, X_0$ and $l2 = \sqrt{1-\overline{\alpha_k}}\, \epsilon$ designed as $\overline{\alpha_k} \approx 0$ subject to $q(x_K) := \int q(x_K \,|x_0) q(x_0) dx_0 \approx \mathcal{N}(x_K 0, I)$ indicating that the backward chain can start with any Gaussian noise. The forward (diffusion) process continues introducing noise gradually into the data until all the structures vanish.

Backward (denoising) processes: a series of Markov chains are used to perform the denoising task at every stage through the backward process continuously until the noisy data is reconstructed back to its original form. The $q(x_K) = \mathcal{N}(x_K;\ 0, I)$ distribution is used to begin the series of the backward Markov chain. The learnable kernel $p_\theta(x_{K-1} \,|x_K)$ generates the $p_\theta(x_0)$ where p_θ is the learnable Gaussian transition kernel expressed as:

$$p_\theta(x_{K-1}\ |x_K) := \mathrm{N}(x_{K-1}; \gamma\theta(q(x_K, k), \sigma\theta(x_K, k)I) \tag{2.10}$$

The model learnable parameters are represented by $\gamma\theta(.)$ and $\sigma\theta(.)$ as mean and variance, respectively. At the backward denoising process, the data distribution is learned by the model through the $p_\theta(x_0)$ distribution. *The model training*: the diffusion model is trained to minimize the variational constraint on the negative likelihood to approximate the original data distribution expressed as:

$$\mathbb{E}\left[-\log p_\theta(x_0)\right] \leqslant \mathbb{E}_q\left[-\log \frac{p_\theta(x_0\colon K)}{q(x_{1:k} \mid x_0)}\right] \tag{2.11}$$

$$\mathbb{E}_q\left[-\log p(X_K) - \sum_{k\geqslant 1} \log \frac{p_\theta(x_{k-1} \mid x_k)}{q(x_k \mid x_{k-1})}\right] \tag{2.12}$$

$$:= L.$$

This is equivalent to KL divergence with three components, L_K, L_{K-1} and L_0 representing prior Loss, divergence forwarding step with corresponding backward step and the reconstruction loss, respectively, expressed as (Yang *et al* 2024):

$$L := \mathbb{E}_q[L_K + \sum_{k>1} L_{K-1} - L_0] \tag{2.13}$$

where

$$L_K = D_{KL}(q(x_K \mid x_0)||p(x_K)) \tag{2.14}$$

$$L_{K-1} = D_{KL}(q(X_{k-1} \mid X_k, X_0)||P\theta\ (X_{k-1}, X_0)) \tag{2.15}$$

$$L_0 = \log p\theta\ (X_0|X_1) \tag{2.16}$$

Substituting (2.12), (2.14) and (2.15) in (2.13) to obtain:

$$\begin{aligned} L := \mathbb{E}_q[&D_{KL}(q(x_K \mid x_0)||p(x_K)) \\ &+ \sum_{k>1} D_{KL}(q(X_{k-1} \mid X_k, X_0)||P\theta\ (X_{k-1}, X_0)) - \log p\theta\ (X_0|X_1)] \end{aligned} \tag{2.17}$$

Training only the divergence loss between two steps L_{K-1} minimizes the negative log-likelihood. The Bayes' rule is used for the parameterization of the posterior $q(X_{k-1} \mid X_k, X_0)$ expressed as (Yang *et al* 2024):

$$p(x_{k-1}|X_k, X_0) = \mathrm{N}(x_{k-1}; \check{\mu}_k(q(x_K, x_0), \check{\beta}_k I)$$

$$\check{\mu}_t(x_K, x_0) := \frac{\sqrt{\check{\alpha}_{k-1}}\beta_k}{1 - \check{\alpha}_k} x_0 + \frac{\sqrt{\alpha_k}(1 - \check{\alpha}_{k-1})}{1 - \check{\alpha}_k} x_k$$

Thus, $\check{\beta}_k := \frac{1 - \check{\alpha}_{k-1}}{1 - \check{\alpha}_k}\beta_k$

The $\alpha_k = 1 - \beta_k$ whereas $\breve{\alpha}_k$ shows $\prod_{k=1}^{k} \alpha_k{\cdot}L_{K-1}$ which can be equated to $l2$ loss expected value between the 2 mean coefficients expressed as (Yang *et al* 2024):

$$L_{K-1} = \mathbb{E}_q\left[\frac{1}{2\alpha_k^2}||\breve{\mu}_k(x_k, x_o) - \mu_\theta(x_k, k)||^2\right] + C.$$

2.4.3.3 Score-based generative models

Score or score function is the main component of SGMs (Song *et al* 2020, Stein *et al* 2013). The score function of a probability density function can be defined as the gradient of the log probability density. In contrast to the popular Fisher score in statistics, the score function for the generative models is the function of the data in place of the model parameter. It is the vector area that indicates the directions where the probability density function increases most rapidly (Yang *et al* 2023). The motivation behind the SGMs is the perturbation of data with the series of intensifying Gaussian noise as well as predicting the score function jointly for all the distribution of the noisy data. This is achieved by training the deep neural network that is conditioned on the levels of noise referred to as the NCSNs. Many score-based sampling methods exits such as the SDE, Langevin Monte Carlo and ordinary differential equations including the combinations of the sampling approaches. The noise level is decreasing with score sampling method to generate samples by chaining the score function. In formulating the SGMs, the training and the sampling are decoupled entirely to allow room for the use of multiple sampling methods after the prediction of the score function (Cao *et al* 2024, Yang *et al* 2023). The generation of samples by conditional diffusion models is analogous to that by unconditioned diffusion models. However, the main distinction is the addition of condition information in the conditioned diffusion models (Chen *et al* 2024).

2.4.3.4 Stochastic differential equations

The generalization of the DDPMs and SGMs can be extended to infinite time stages or noisy level. This is where the perturbation and denosing procedure are results to the SDEs (Yang *et al* 2023). The diffusion process can be modelled as the stochastic differential equation solution expressed as:

$$dx = f(x, t)dt + g(t)dw$$

where the diffusion is given as $f(x, t)$ and the drift function is given as $g(t)$. The standard Wiener process is represented by w and time flowing backward is represented by $\breve{w}$. The sample is assumed to be $x\ (T) \sim PT$. The process begins from the samples and reverses the process backward. Through the reverse process, the following sample is obtained, $x\ (0) \sim P0$. Through the reverse time stochastic differential equation we get:

$$dx = [f(x, t) - g(t)^2\ \nabla_x\ \log qt(x)]dt + g(t)d\breve{w} \qquad (2.18)$$

where the $\nabla_x \log qt(x)$ known $\forall \; t$. The backward diffusion process can be derived from the expression in equation (2.18) to sample *Po* (Xing *et al* 2023) originally presented by Song *et al* (2020).

2.4.3.5 *Diffusion models variants and applications*

In addition to the various formulations of diffusion models in the preceding sections, there are different variants such as discrete diffusion models (Chen *et al* 2024), latent diffusion models (LDMs) (Pinaya *et al* 2022), and stable diffusion (Nguyen *et al* 2023), a version of the LDM, among others.

These different diffusion models are used to perform a variety of generative and other machine learning tasks, including forecasting, image generation, audio synthesis, imputation, video synthesis, text generation, anomaly detection, and spatio-temporal data analysis (e.g., traffic flow, telecommunications). They are also used in image editing and conversions (e.g., generating images from text or vice versa). Table 2.4 provides a summary of the variants of diffusion models suitable for solving different tasks.

2.4.4 Statistics

2.4.4.1 *Autoregressive models*

The autoregressive (AR) models (ARMs) involve learning of joint distribution of sequential data by the ARMs to estimate the next value in the time series sequence based on the previous time step. The ARM belongs to the class of likelihood-based models for statistical modelling. The ARMs have the assumption that the joint distribution can be decomposed to the product of conditional distribution (Harshvardhan *et al* 2020, Zhang *et al* 2023). A process $\{\gamma_t\}$ is an AR process if the order x is expressed as:

$$\gamma_t = \beta_1\gamma_{t-1} + \beta_2\gamma_{t-2} + \ldots + \beta_x\gamma_{x-2} + a_t$$

where the $\beta_j (j = 1, 2, \ldots, x)$ are constant, the pure random process with 0 mean is $\{a_t\}$ and the variance is δ^2 (Box *et al* 2015). The ARMs can be viewed as feed forward ANN that accept time steps as inputs differing from the architecture of recurrent ANN (Zhang *et al* 2023). The ARMs generate contents (e.g., text) by estimating the next element based on the previous element. Music can be generated by the ARM by estimating the next node in the sequence of the music according to the preceding notes of the edge users (Harshvardhan *et al* 2020).

2.4.4.2 *Gaussian mixture models*

Mixture distribution: The main reasons for the application of normal mixture to data are two-fold. First, modelling of unknown distribution shapes through an appealing semiparametric framework. Secondly, create probabilistic clustering of data using the mixture model corresponding to the components in the mixture model (McLachlan and Rathnayake 2014). The Gaussian mixture model (GMM) represented as the Gaussian component density weight sum is known as the parametric probability density function. Making the use of GMMs is popular as a parametric

Table 2.4. Summary of diffusion models variants solving different generative tasks and other machine learning problems.

Reference	Model	Operation	Suitable task
Dhariwal and Nichol (2021)	Ablated diffusion model	Uses series of ablation for unconditioned image synthesis	Image generation
Zhang *et al* (2023)	Diffusion model—GAN	Combined diffusion model and GAN to enhance the speed of diffusion model sampling	Music generation
Rombach *et al* (2022)	LDM	A layer of cross-attention is embedded into the model architecture	Image super-resolution
Li *et al* (2022)	Diffusion language model (LM)	A non-autoregressive LM based on the continuous diffusion models	Text generation
Feng *et al* (2024)	Latent diffusion transformer	Combined symmetric statistics aware autoencoder and conditional diffusion model generator	Forecasting
Hyvärinen and Dayan (2005)	SDMs	The model is estimated by minimizing predicted squared distance	Image in-painting (Batzolis *et al* 2021)
Liu *et al* (2023)	Pulse voltage guided Conditional diffusion model	Adopted sequential U-Net architecture	Anomaly detection
Richter *et al* (2023)	SDMs	Start the reverse process from mixture of noisy speech and Gaussian noise	Speech synthesis
Meng *et al* (2021)	SDEs	SDE based on diffusion model generative prior	Image editing
Kong *et al* (2020)	Versatile diffusion probabilistic model	A non-autoregressive model that convert white noisy signal into waveform well structured. This is achieved through Markov chain	Audio generation
Xu *et al* (2023)	DDPM: Density aware temporal attentive step-wise diffusion model	Capture inter-step dependency for imputation	Imputation
Zhao *et al* (2022)	Energy-guided SDEs	The model adopted energy function for pre-training to guide the inference process	Image-to-image translation
Liu *et al* (2024)	DDPM: Diffusion Language Shapelets model	The model uses self-supervised diffusion learning mechanism for real subsequences as the condition	Classification
Saharia *et al* (2022)	Imagen	A text2image diffusion model combining the power of transformer for text generation and diffusion model high-fidelity image generation	Text-to-image

model of probability distribution of measurements (continuous) or biometric systems features (e.g., vocal-tract spectral features for speaker recognition system). The Expectation-Maximization or Maximum *A Posteriori* can be used to estimate parameters of the GMMs from training data (Reynolds 2009). The Gaussian distribution is synonymous to continuous real value normal distribution with symmetry about its means. The occurrence of data probability is more likely around the left and right of the mean and tapers. It is off at the edges approaching 0 or asymptotic to real value similar to 0 (Harshvardhan *et al* 2020). The GMM has been used for generating synthetic data (Chokwitthaya *et al* 2020), text (Reynolds 1992), extracting text from image (Fu *et al* 2006), classifications (Wan *et al* 2019) and clustering (He *et al* 2010).

2.4.4.3 Hidden Markov models

The probabilistic model of the linear sequence problem is derived from the hidden Markov models (HMMs) (Durbin *et al* 1998). The HMM is obtained from the extension of Markov models by including probabilistic function of the state as an observation. The HMM is a double-embedded stochastic process with the case of stochastic process without observation referred to as the *hidden*. However, it can be observed via a set of different stochastic processes producing observable sequence (Rabiner 1989). The HMM is used for generating Markov chains in the form of a series of states that have certain state transition probabilities. This generates the state sequences with the corresponding probabilities of the symbol emission. The Markov chains are referred to as the series of the states in view of the fact that the current state transition function determines the probability of reaching the next state. In statistics, the HMM is typically applied to model linear problems that involved a time series or sequence (Harshvardhan *et al* 2020). A detailed description of the Markov decision process including mathematical expressions can be found in chapter 3. The HMM is applied to generate audio keywords (Xu *et al* 2004), speech synthesis (Wu and Wang 2006), pioneered development of large vocabulary speech recognition systems (Lee 1988), human action recognition (Yamato *et al* 1992) and generation of humanoid movement (Kwon and Park 2006).

2.4.5 Other generative models

In addition to the major generative models discussed earlier, other generative models are also present in the literature. These additional models are briefly introduced in this section to provide readers with an overview of their operations and applications in generative tasks including variants where necessary.

2.4.5.1 Flow-based models

The flow-based models (FBMs) are the transformation of simple distribution into the desired distribution via an invertible series of transformations. An ANN can be used to execute the transformations, the process of the transformation applications is called flow (Ho *et al* 2019, Ping *et al* 2020). The FBMs use the invertible transformation for the generation of data. This enables accurate computation of the data probability density function (Yang *et al* 2024). The transformation is expressed as:

$$z = f(x);\ x' = f^{-1}(z)$$

where f, $x\ and\ z$ are invertible function points within the space of the data and latent space, respectively. The log-likelihood of the transformation is expressed as (Yang *et al* 2024):

$$\log(x) = \log p_z(f(x)) + \log\left|\det\left(\frac{df}{dx}\right)\right|$$

The FBMs map data to standard Gaussian latent variable (Ho *et al* 2019).

The FBMs are used for speech synthesis (Prenger *et al* 2019), generating high-fidelity speech (Ping *et al* 2020) and converting image-to-image (Kondo *et al* 2019).

2.4.5.2 Pixel convolutional neural networks

Estimating distribution over natural images for tractable computation of the images likelihood to synthesis images is the aim of the model. The image is scanned row by row with one pixel at a time in each of the rows. The conditional distribution is predicted for each of the pixels over the possible pixel values provided in the context of the scanned (Van Den Oord *et al* 2016b).

The computational cost typically experienced in long short-term memory is as a result of the unbounded dependency range in the receptive field due to sequential computation. Improving the receptive field requires increasing its size to be large but not unbounded. The bounded receptive field can be captured by standard convolutional layers to compute the features of each pixel position at the same time. The pixel convolutional neural network (PixelCNN) has no pooling layers. The architecture of PixelCNN comprises multiple convolutional layers preserving the spatial resolution. To deviate from sighting the future context, each convolutional layer adopts masks. The image generation is sequential in view of the fact that the sample pixel requires input back to PixelCNN. Parallelization of the PixelCNN is limited to training and evaluation periods of the images. PixelCNN doesn't introduce independence assumption in the process of capturing the full generality of the pixel inter-dependencies (Van Den Oord *et al* 2016b). PixelCNN is a powerful generative model with very flexible functional form of conditions and it generates images with tractable likelihood. PixelCNN is currently the state-of-the-art in generative modelling when evaluated based on log-likelihood (Salimans *et al* 2017). From the inception of the PixelCNN, its variants emerged such as but not limited to PixelCNN decoders (Van den Oord *et al* 2016a), PixelCNN++ (Salimans *et al* 2017), memristive pixelCNN (Nair *et al* 2023) and pixel-attention CNN (Jia *et al* 2021).

2.4.5.3 Deep belief networks

Deep belief networks (Hinton 2009) are a deep architecture comprising multiple hidden layers pioneered by Hinton. The same layers in the architecture do not have connections similar to the architecture of a deep Boltzmann machine. The top two layers of the deep belief networks are a directed connection pointing to the direction of the visible layer, whereas all other connections are undirected. Greedy layer-wise fast algorithm is the commonly adopted algorithm for the training of deep belief networks (Bengio *et al* 2006, Hua *et al* 2015). The training algorithm involves two stages: the first stage is the fast stage in which each layer is sampled from the deep belief networks. The process starts by running many steps of the Gibbs sampling on the deep belief networks double-hidden layers comprising directed connections. Subsequently, the latent variable is sampled for drawing samples from the visible units. This is achieved by running a step of ancestral sampling from the deep belief networks (Bengio *et al* 2006, Hinton *et al* 2006, Oussidi and Elhassouny 2018). Description of the fully visible belief networks can be found in Frey *et al* (1995). Deep belief networks are used for generating facial expression (Susskind *et al* 2008), speech synthesis (Kang *et al* 2013) and object recognition (Nair and Hinton 2009).

2.4.5.4 Boltzmann machines

The Boltzmann machine is an energy-based model associating scalar energy function with the model. The model takes input variables configuration and produces scalar value that describes the configuration level. The energy function associating small and large values with correct and incorrect configurations, respectively, both in and out of sample training data is achieved through learning. The selection of configuration that minimizes the energy is performed by prediction (LeCun *et al* 2006). The variants of Boltzmann machine include the binary Boltzmann machine (Courville *et al* 2011), the restricted Boltzmann machine (Zhang *et al* 2018), which has been utilized for applications such as voice conversion (Wu *et al* 2013) and converting whisper-to-speech (Li *et al* 2014), and the deep Boltzmann machine (Salakhutdinov and Hinton 2009), which has been deployed for facial modelling (Nhan Duong *et al* 2015).

2.5 Comparative analysis of the generative models: weaknesses and strengths

Typically, each generative model has its strengths and weaknesses, making it suitable for application in certain domains (Yang *et al* 2024). The strengths and weaknesses of the major generative models discussed in section 2.4 are compared in this section to give the reader an understanding of the limitations and areas of strength of these generative models.

In GANs, the generator and the discriminator improve their performance through adversarial training. The flagship advantage of the GANs compared to other generative models is as a result of the adversarial learning process. The design of the GANs is tailored to avoid the weaknesses of the other generative models summarized as follows: (1) It replaces the runtime proportional to dimension with parallel sample generation, a strength which is relative to the fully visible belief networks (Goodfellow 2016). Generating samples in parallel is impossible for other generative models (e.g., PixelCNN and fully visible belief networks) (Gui *et al* 2021).

(2) Limitations to the generator function are very few; this strength of the GAN is relative to the Boltzmann machines where only few probability distributions accept sampling of the tractable Markov chain. (3) It doesn't require Markov chains which is relative to the Boltzmann machines and generative scene network. (4) Variational bound is not required and GANs are known to be consistent, asymptotically because the specific model classes applicable in GANs are known to be a universal approximator. The notion that the VAEs are asymptotically consistent remains a conjecture. (5) Subjectively, GANs produce better quality samples compared to other generative models (Goodfellow 2016). GANs can be applicable to models in which their density function is computationally intractable (Goodfellow *et al* 2020). However, the GANs introduce new training challenges more difficult than objective function optimization as the GANs training requires the finding of Nash equilibrium of a game (Goodfellow 2016). The GAN training is potentially unstable, its generation of samples has less diversity because of the nature of adversarial training (Zhang *et al* 2023) and mode collapse (Yang *et al* 2024).

The ARMs compute likelihood explicitly and have a good measure of evaluation explicitly compared with the GAN. However, the ARM sample generation speed is slow and the quality of image resolution is low (Cheng *et al* 2020). ARM struggles with deep logical structure even if it is initialized to large pre-trained models (Lin *et al* 2020). The VAE approximates by adopting variational inference. The fitting of original data is not good compared with the GANs. The Image visual quality of GANs outperforms that of VAE (Cheng *et al* 2020). The diffusion model is found to perform better than the state-of-the-art models (e.g., GANs and VAEs) (Chen *et al* 2024) and doesn't need a discriminator unlike the GAN (Zhang *et al* 2023). The VAE is simple, stable and the foundation of its theory is clear. However, it generates low-quality data and its latent spaces have limited expressiveness (Yang *et al* 2024).

The FBMs produce accurate likelihood prediction and enhance the generation of high-quality samples. Yet, they require a significant amount of computational resources similar to diffusion models and need complex model design. The diffusion models are known for generating high-quality detailed output, being flexible and providing strong probabilistic foundation. But it takes a long time for them to converge (Yang *et al* 2024). The HMMs lack the capacity of understanding correlations in sequence. Conversely, the concept of the HMMs is simple and very flexible. The GMM has the flexibility of cluster covariance but collapses with high-dimensional data. The deep belief network has a powerful feature extraction characteristic, however, its training procedure is complex (Harshvardhan *et al* 2020) unlike the case of VAE with its stable training procedure.

2.6 Integrating generative models to enhance performance

The combination of two or more algorithms can be in two different forms: integrated or hybrid, and ensemble. An integrated approach combines a multiple number of algorithms to explore data analysis, however, only one of the algorithms can be used for making the final decision. On the other hand, ensemble approaches entail multiple algorithms exploring data analytics to produce multiple outputs before the outputs are aggregated to produce a single output as the final decision (Verikas *et al* 2010). In computational intelligence, the next generation intelligent system is believed to be a hybridized system. Hard problems in AI motivated research into a hybrid system necessitating combined approaches to tackling complex problems. Limitations of individual algorithms or learning techniques are eliminated by the integration of different learning and adaptation techniques to develop powerful techniques compared to the constituent techniques. This contributed to the design of new integrated intelligent systems. The design of the hybrid techniques is mostly ad hoc methodology justified by the success achieved in the application domains (Abraham 2005). Empirical evidence proves that the integration of generative models performs better and is more robust compared to the individual generative model (Wang *et al* 2021, Wang *et al* 2022), though, not absolute.

The flexibility and adaptability characteristics of diffusion models makes them fit to be adopted across multiple data types and modalities. The robustness of diffusion models makes them robust against error with mechanisms for gradually reducing noise. In addition, the diffusion models have the capability to explore diverse data for innovative outputs. The diffusion models can be hybridized with other generative models such as AE to improve performance and generate quality content (Yang *et al* 2023). For example, to reduce the sampling drawback of diffusion models, the diffusion models are hybridized with GAN to improve the control of generating music to the desired emotion and speed up the generation of symbolic music (Zhang *et al* 2023). The typical practice of introducing noise in the discriminator to stabilize GAN training has not been effective, thus, motivating the integration of the diffusion model with GAN (diffusion-GAN) for effective training. In the framework, the forward feature of the diffusion chain is used for the generation of Gaussian mixture distribution samples noise. The original and the generated data were both diffused through the same adaptive diffusion process (Wang *et al* 2022).

In another development, the multimodal feature of the diffusion model was combined with the GAN (multimodal diffusion model–GAN) into the latent space of the pre-trained GAN to generate photo-realistic face images (Kim *et al* 2024). Similarly, the diffusion model is combined with the VAE (diffusion model–VAE) to deduce the progress of user interest and predict the propagation likelihood by the combination of information from forward user sequence and the first cascaded content. The integrated models outperform the constituent generative models (Wang *et al* 2021). Another study deployed DDPMs to model the prior distribution of the latent variables to improve the performance of the VAE (VAE–DDPMs). Preliminary findings indicate that the Gaussian priors of the VAE were improved by the diffusion prior model (Wehenkel and Louppe 2021). A study extended the structured VAE by embedding the HMM (VAE–HMM) as the latent models. It was shown to outperform the GMM (Ebbers *et al* 2017). Motivated by the structure of deep learning and learning effectiveness, deep GMM with multiple layers of latent variables (i.e., nested mixtures of linear models) was introduced, where the variables follow a mixture of Gaussian distributions (Viroli and McLachlan 2019).

2.7 The pipeline for developing a generative tool

Figure 2.6 depicts the pipeline for creating a generative tool aimed at producing new content. The pipeline involves the following stages: task selection, dataset collection, generative model, pre-training, evaluation, and deployment. The first stage in the generative tool development process is for the modeller to decide on the **generative task** (refer to section 2.2 for details on generative tasks) to accomplish based on the project's objective. The task, along with the project's scope and requirements, must be clearly defined, as these factors determine the type and diversity of the datasets required for pre-training the generative algorithm.

The second stage is the **dataset**: this is the stage where datasets relevant to the chosen generative task in the first stage are collected. Data is the 'lifeblood' of generative modelling because existing data is required to create new data. The data collected for pre-training could be texts, images, videos, speech, or time series as the modality. Additionally, the data can be multimodal, enabling the model to produce multimodal outputs, such as text, voice, and image. For example, if the chosen task in the first stage is the generation of new images, then the datasets collected for pre-training must be image datasets. If the task involves converting text to image, then the datasets collected should include both text and images. The collected datasets are subjected to pre-processing to improve their quality because the performance of the generative algorithm is directly proportional to the quality of the datasets. Pre-processing the datasets involves improving data quality, de-duplication, and removing personal information.

The source of the datasets could be raw data collection, benchmarks, augmented, or synthetic data. The third stage is **generative models**, in this step, a suitable generative algorithm is chosen for the type of task intended to be

Figure 2.6. Pipeline for developing a generative model to generate new content.

accomplished as the creation of new content largely depends on the foundational model or generative algorithm. This approach adopts the generative algorithm from the available classes of the generative models for a novel application. In addition, the generative algorithm could be modified to alter its structural architecture, extend its theory or enhance the optimization and parameter learning to improve performance and quality of the output.

In the fourth stage, the hyper-parameters of the algorithm are tuned to obtain the optimum values and settings before the **pre-training** of the generative algorithm starts, the generative algorithm is typically fed with samples of the dataset which could be text, images, videos, voice, time series or multimodal flowing from the data repository in the second stage. The generative algorithm architecture is determined and pre-trained for pattern matching to learn the attributes, patterns, or latent distribution of the dataset. For example, a generative algorithm intended for use to develop an image generative tool would be pre-trained with an images dataset. The pre-training is not straightforward, it is an iterative process, and could be unstable, collapse, refuse to converge, generate oscillation, overfitting or underfitting. After successful pre-training, a generative tool is developed with the capacity to generate new content when given an existing dataset as input. Many frameworks and libraries suitable for developing generative models exist. Prominent among them is Hugging Face (recommended for beginners).

The fifth stage is the **evaluation** process, the strength and effectiveness of the proposed generative algorithm in creating new content is measured by comparing the output of the new content created by the propose generative algorithm with the baseline algorithms to find out if the accuracy, diversity, coherence and quality of the new content produced by the proposed generative algorithm is better than the output produced by the baseline algorithms. If the accuracy, diversity, coherence and quality outperformed the baseline algorithms, the process stops, if not, adjustment or modification to the hyper-parameters, architecture or dataset can be performed to produce better content. In the case where all efforts prove abortive without improvement over the baseline algorithms, it has become a negative result. Finally, a successfully developed generative tool is **deployed** with an interface for users to access. The platform to deploy the generative tool can be a dedicated device, website or integrated into a large-scale system depending on the target users. The top 10 generative model platforms as listed by *AI Magazine* in 2024 in ascending order are as follows: ChatGPT, Gemini, Claude, GitHub Copilot, Bing AI, DALL-E 3, Adobe Sense, AlphaCode, Autodesk and lastly, Perplexity.

2.8 Deepfakes

The word deepfake originate from the combination of deep learning and fake. Deepfake also refers to AI face swap, the former is an emerging concept while the latter has been in existence for a long time, typically used to swap a person's face with that of another. On the other hand, deepfakes refers to the application of a deep learning algorithm (Dolhansky *et al* 2019) such as autoencoder (Hassoun and Sudjianto 1997) and GAN (Goodfellow *et al* 2014) to create the forgery of person's face by swapping that of another in a video. The emergence of GAN makes the facial swapping realistic, sophisticated, convincing and easier, unlike the conventional facial swapping technique predating the GAN. In recent years, a large number of deepfakes videos have been created, uploaded to the internet and gone viral. The generation of deepfake videos has triggered serious concern from the general public because of their potential misuse in the democratic process, blackmail of individuals or faking the occurrence of terrorism (Dolhansky *et al* 2019).

The creation of hyper-realistic videos by advanced deep learning algorithm makes it more challenging in differentiating between a fake video depicting a person exhibiting something that never happened and original videos. In addition, the viral nature of social media where realistic deepfake videos reach millions of people within a short time contribute to the negative impact of deepfakes in society (Westerlund 2019). The public attention was first attracted by deepfake videos in 2017 where an account on Reddit having the name deepfakes started to synthesis pornographic videos using a deep learning-based facial swap algorithm and posting them publicly. This has increased the popularity of the term deepfake videos to refer to any AI-generated video impersonation (Lyu 2020). In the last two years, the issue of manipulated facial video has attracted unprecedented attention, more especially after the emergence of deepfake technology like deep learning tools with capability to manipulate videos and images at ease and fast. As of now, a large number of deepfake videos has been circulating on the internet. Celebrities or politicians have been the major target of deepfake videos (Yu *et al* 2021).

2.8.1 Process of developing deepfakes

Despite GAN being commonly used for the generation of deepfakes, most of the software for creating deepfake videos uses encoder–decoder with one and two decoders. The common features of the source (real) and the target (fake) faces are learned by the encoder as the real and fake faces are generated separately by the two decoders. The decoder associated with the real face takes the encoding of the fake face to generate the fake real face during the process of swapping the face. To make the fake real face pragmatic and convincing through fusion, the attention mask of the real face is typically applied for making the fake real face. The visual quality of the fake faces generated can be improved by applying high-resolution facial images to both the real and fake faces for pre-training the encoder and decoders. The procedure described in the preceding paragraph can be used to generate fake face video by given video data in which the face in each frame can be created for replacing the real face based on the face swap procedure (Zi *et al* 2020). Figure 2.7 depicts the entire stages of the face-swapping process.

Psychological studies found that recognizing a human face mainly depends on the features collected from facial shape and hairstyle. As a result of that, the person face intended to be replaced must have similar features of hairstyle and facial shape with the fake face to create a convincing impersonation (Lyu 2020). Currently, there are three major types of deepfake videos (Lyu 2020):

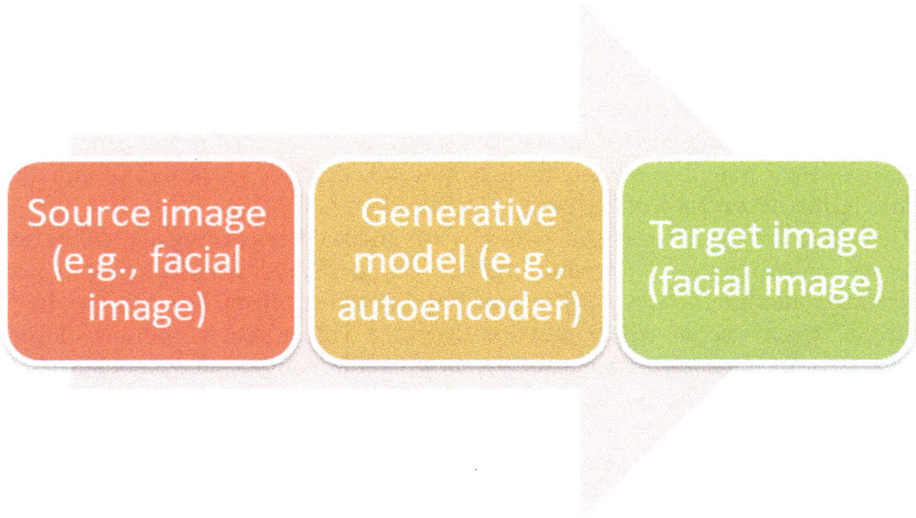

Figure 2.7. Procedure for developing a deepfake image.

(i) **Head puppetry**: This involves the synthesis of video of the real person's complete upper-shoulder and head using the video of the real person's head in such a way that the synthesized fake person appears to exhibit behaviour as the real person.
(ii) **Face swapping**: This is the creating of fake video with the fake faces of the real faces simultaneously maintaining the same facial expression.
(iii) **Lip syncing**: This is the kind of fake video created by manipulating the lips region of the person for the fake lips to appear to speak what the person has not spoken in reality.

The commonly used software platforms for generating deepfakes are as follows: DeepFaceLab, Face2Face, DFaker, DeepFake-tf, Faceswap-GAN, NaturalFront, FaceCrop, Face Swap Live and Face Swap Online (Jafar *et al* 2020). The four major communities involved in generating deepfakes involve deepfake hobbyists, political actors (e.g., state sponsored), fraudsters and legitimate actors (e.g., TV companies) (Westerlund 2019).

2.8.2 Positive use of deepfakes

Deepfakes is well known for its negative applications causing many to believe that deepfakes is mainly for negative purposes. Once deepfake is mentioned, what typically comes to mind immediately is the negative applications because of the negative perception associated with the concept. However, deepfakes have many significant benefits to society and industry. The following are some of the representative benefits of deepfakes.

2.8.2.1 Language translation

Deepfakes has the potential of transient use beyond the language barrier, especially in a video conference call where the participants speak and understand different languages. The deepfake technology can be deployed to translate speech while manipulating the facial expression and lips movement of the participants to appear as if they are speaking the same language (Solsman 2019).

2.8.2.2 Museum

Improvement of learning engagement and experience of a visitor in galleries. Globally, museums can used deepfake technology to bring famous artists with their works back to life. For example, the Dalí museum in St. Petersburg, USA, uses deepfake technology to re-create immersive visitor learning and engagement through Dalí Lives exhibition about the art works of Salvador Dalí, 1904–1989 (Billock 2019).

2.8.2.3 Movie industry

The actors in a film whose voices are lost can be re-created using the deepfake technology to bring back the voice in the film. In addition, instead of reshooting footage to update a film, deepfake can be deployed to update the footage without the need for reshooting (Marr 2019).

2.8.2.4 Marketing

Realistic images of scenes can be created using deepfake technology for the purpose of advertising. Also, marketing content can be created based on deepfake technology (Picazo and Moreno–Gil 2019).

2.8.3 Software for detecting deepfakes

The negative impact of deepfake videos on individual privacy and social security are growing rapidly. As such, different approaches have been devised to detect manipulated content. In the early days of detecting deepfakes videos, attention was mainly on the inconsistent features typically introduced in the process of generating them. However, recent approaches mainly focused on the fundamental features. The fake video is vulnerable to discontinuities between the adjacent frames, thus, the fake video can be detected by exploring temporal consistency features (Yu *et al* 2021). Some recent methods of detecting deepfake videos have mainly focussed on fake face-swapping videos which constitute the larger portion of the deepfake videos in circulation on the internet. Many of the approaches formulate the classification problem as frame-level binary (Lyu 2020).

The analysis of the studies conducted in detecting deepfake content indicate that 20 of the studies use texture and spatio-temporal consistent features, 14 use facial landmark, 13 use visual artifacts (e.g., posing head, eye blinking, lip movement etc), 8 and 7 of the studies use biological features and intra-frame inconsistency including frequency domain analysis, respectively, and 4 studies use latent space (Rana *et al* 2022). The commonly adopted variant of deep learning architecture for the detection of deepfake is CNN as evident in Rana *et al* (2022). Some methods for the detection of deepfakes content include FakeCatcher, MesoNet, XceptionNet and Face x-ray (Zi *et al* 2020). The software tools used for the detection of deepfakes include but are not limited to Sentinel, Deepware, Microsoft video AI authenticator, Intel's real-time deepfake detector, WeVerify, Sensity and Phoneme-Viseme mismatches.

2.9 Generative models in pharmaceuticals

The generative models are expected to impact all industries with the expectation that the pharmaceutical industry will receive the highest impact in view of the multi-modal nature of the generative models with capability to handle multimodalities (Viswa *et al* 2024). Drug-like molecules typically comprised of molecules from 1.0×10^{23} to 1.0×10^{60} out of which only 10^{12} molecules are estimated can be synthesized in the laboratory. The large volume of these molecules poses a challenge to researchers in searching for the best candidate within a reasonable period of time (Tang *et al* 2021). The major approaches to the design or discovery of drugs are divided into two as follows: (1) fine-tuning of already existing molecules; (2) the generation of novel molecules via the design of *de novo* drugs. The main target of both the approaches is to obtain the optimal profiles of pharmacokinetics and pharmacodynamics. However, the process of designing and developing drugs from the beginning to the market is highly time consuming and very expensive (Gangwal *et al* 2024). It is estimated that the average cost of developing a new drug is $2.6 billion with an overall discovery period of approximately 12 years (Chan *et al* 2019).

The amount and the period of time keep increasing (Chen *et al* 2018). The understanding of diseases can rapidly be advancing in contrast to the discovery process and development of new drugs as the amount involved is increasing not decreasing. Generative models have the potential to speed up the process of identifying the ideal molecule candidate, development of validation assay for testing compounds, pointing out the best leads with promising features and help preclinical testing in determining effectiveness. Already the manufacturers of pharmaceuticals have started using base or foundation models for these purposes (e.g., BioGPT and Med-PaLM). The applications of the generative models in pharmaceuticals include: microscopy and pathology data analyzed using generative models, functional readout of small-molecule data prediction is improved through chemistry models, modelling large molecules for folding proteins and predictions (Viswa *et al* 2024). In addition, the generative models can drastically reduce the time required in developing new drugs (Shanehsazzadeh *et al* 2023) and multimodal nature of the generative model gives the model ability to solve diseases with the best treatment compression (Viswa *et al* 2024). It is highly crucial to explore different strategies in reducing the cost of developing drugs and reduce the time required to complete the entire drug development process (Chen *et al* 2018).

2.9.1 Use cases of generative models

The four major use cases in applying generative models are as follows (Viswa *et al* 2024):

(i) knowledge extraction;
(ii) content and compound generation;
(iii) customer engagement;
(iv) coding and software generation.

2.9.1.1 Extracting scientific knowledge

Scientists typically spend a lot of time extracting and summarizing information for the purpose of understanding diseases and target drugs. The information is typically extracted from but not limited to patents, trial data and scientific publications. This process of information retrieval is tedious, time consuming often prone to inaccuracy and incomplete information because of the large volume of the information that need to be processed. The burden can be alleviated through GPT-powered knowledge extraction with the capability of analyzing multimodal data (e.g., text and image). The new generative models provide deep and broad understanding of medical context and intention. This has the potential impact to increase more than 30% of initial manual evaluation of target drugs (Viswa *et al* 2024).

2.9.1.2 In silico *compound screening*

The development of drugs can be challenged by the difficulties involved in the identification and prioritization of the chemical compound with the potential to succeed in treating certain diseases and worthy for laboratory test. These kinds of screening process can be enhanced through generative models by using the state-of-the-art foundational chemistry model for mapping millions of existing chemical compounds based on their structure and function. The generative model predicts the subsequent component (e.g. atom) in the structure of small or large molecules (e.g. amino acid) similar to the way GPT-4 was trained to predict the next word in a sentence. This has the potential impact of increasing performance of chemical compound activities by 2.5 times and reduces time taken to identify new leads from months to weeks (Viswa *et al* 2024).

2.9.1.3 Indication selection for asset strategy

The knowledge extraction capacity of generative models can assistant researchers to determine either conditions or indications to target with certain molecules. This is one of the critical decision processes facing the biopharma companies. Researchers need to draw information from different sources including opinion leaders, omics analysis, trials data, literature review and competitors activities to make calls. In view of the fact that the information is voluminous, the selection of indication doesn't cover all the available evidence, as such, an optimal conclusion cannot be reached. This challenge can be addressed by analyzing a large volume of structured data and unstructured data using generative models. The under-utilization of real-world data collected from insurance claims, visits to doctors, hospital data, electronic medical records, among others to select indications can be mitigated with generative models that treat medical events and patient medical history as words and documents, respectively. This can allow researchers to discover semantic similarity of multiple events making it possible to estimate proximity of one biological indication to another from the perspective of a patient and clinician (Viswa *et al* 2024).

2.9.1.4 Optimization of trials and portfolios

Testing in the clinical environment start after an asset has been matched with indication. However, it is not easy to identify the suitable patients for the study, as a results of that, clinical trials often comprises those patients that probable may not respond to treatment. Therefore, slow down the development. Precision oncology is one of the few area used by researchers to address the challenge in which biomarkers are used to stratify patients based on their possibility to progress or predict response to diverse treatments. The generative models can assistant other field to do similar thing to help companies gather clinical trial population with diverse representation (Viswa *et al* 2024).

2.9.2 The role of generative models in drugs discovery

The large language models (LLMs) have different applications in the process of drugs design and discovery to enhance the process. Many applications of LLMs exist, however, this section lists only the main applications as outlined by Gangwal *et al* (2024).

2.9.2.1 Screening a large volume of molecules data

The LLM can be used to filter through datasets to search for a compound that has the requisite features. The LLM can achieve it by generating a molecular descriptor and a molecule's structured numerical representation. Molecules with similar characteristics can be clustered by the descriptor or select the compounds with defined requirements (e.g., binding to certain proteins).

2.9.2.2 Generate new candidates for drugs

The LLM can be adopted for the generation of new molecules. New molecules can be synthesized from existing molecules to look similar to the molecules in the training data.

2.9.2.3 Interpretation of research data

The pattern in data collected from drug discovery research can be uncovered as well as creating a hypothesis about the fundamental action of the mechanism by the use of an LLM. The safety and efficiency of drugs candidates evaluation are used this strategy.

2.9.2.4 Communication

Communication with stakeholders is carried out through reports, presentations, and other means of documentation prepared by the LLM. The prepared document is communicated to stakeholders (e.g., doctors, regulators, scientists, etc).

2.9.2.5 Repurposing of drugs

The LLM can be deployed to search for therapies already in existence that can be repurposed for different uses. This can be achieved by analyzing the pharmaceuticals chemical structure and searching for new targets with potential for commercial hit drugs.

2.9.2.6 Interpretation of clinical trial data

The LLM can be used to formulate a hypothesis about the fundamental mechanism of action, evaluate the efficiency of drugs and finding new therapeutic targets based on the data collected from clinical trials.

The generative models become attractive in designing new drugs because of their efficacy and accuracy in the generation of new bioactive and synthetic compounds (Moret *et al* 2023). In addition, promising results were recorded in drug discovery and development by the generative models (Gangwal and Lavecchia 2024). A summary of the roles of generative models in different studies is presented in table 2.5.

Table 2.5. Summary of the role of generative models in drugs design and development.

References	Generative model	Role	Comment
Shanehsazzadeh *et al* (2023)	Generative deep learning models	*de novo* antibody design	The *de novo* feature was used to design antibodies against the targets.
Gupta *et al* (2018)	LSTM-based generative model with transfer learning	Generate libraries of molecules	with structural similarity to known actives for PPARγ and trypsin
Li *et al* (2023)	DrugGPT	Search new compounds associated with particular proteins	Apply drugGPT to learn from protein–ligand binding
Huang *et al* (2024)	Binding-adaptive diffusion models	Adaptively extract subcomplex responsible for the interaction of protein–ligand	The selected protein–ligand subcomplex was processed
Li *et al* (2022)	Deep constrained VAE	Geometric representation to generate molecular	The spatial structure representations of drug molecule
Hooshmand *et al* (2021)	Deep belief networks	Filtered drugs	Use deep belief network for drug and non-drug-like small molecules filtering in process of drug discovery

(*Continued*)

Table 2.5. (*Continued*)

References	Generative model	Role	Comment
McGibbon *et al* (2014)	HMM	Understand the dynamics in proteins	It uses L1-regularized reversal in the approach
Noguchi and Inoue (2022)	PixelCNN	Design fragment-based molecular	PixelCNN combined with the simplified molecular input line entry system as representation of molecule.
Shi *et al* (2020)	FBM-ARM	Generate valid chemical molecular structure	Combined FBM and ARM to achieve parallel computation and improve efficiency of molecular generation
Yu *et al* (2023)	Transformer-based GAN	Develop antiviral drugs	Performed selection and replacement editing on organic compounds to generate antiviral candidate

2.10 Prompt engineering

Prompt engineering is a relatively new field of study that practices the drafting of prompts to derive optimal responses from LLMs. Not many researchers are familiar with the discipline (Giray 2023). Prompt engineering refers to the science and art of designing, formatting and optimizing the conversation of prompts to guide the discourse with generative models in a better way. Prompts involve the drafting of instructions specific to invoke an optimal response from generative models. The establishment of prompt engineering has become necessary because of the increasing usage of generative model platforms that respond to user queries. The prompt engineering scope is wide, comprising chatbots, customer service agents, voice first applications and other interactive AI systems interfaces. Prompt engineering plays a critical role in tuning the performance of the model, improving user experience and achieving user satisfaction. Prompts extend the understanding of the model technical capabilities and human communication nuances. Users need to understand the limitations and strengths of the generative models they are interacting with so that suitable prompts can be formulated for optimal desired responses. Therefore, prompt engineering bridges the gap between the growing sophistication of the generative models and the requirement for human-like interactions that can appease users (Schmidt *et al* 2024). For instance, a prompt can be developed specifying that a generative model should generate source code in a certain programming style or paradigm. Similarly, the prompt could be specified for the generative model to flag specific keywords or phrases in the document generated by the model to provide more information about the keywords (White *et al* 2023). Prompt engineering had been in the field of natural language processing. However, the emergence of visual generative models led to the penetration of prompt engineering in visual tasks referred to as visual prompt engineering.

In recent times, computer vision has witnessed growing utilization of prompts as a result of the successes recorded by prompt engineering in natural language processing. Researchers are currently exploring the concept of designing and developing prompts specifically for visual tasks. The development of prompts in visual tasks involves the use of guiding signals for the vision models to help effectively generate visual content or effectively analyze the visual content. Notable advancement has been achieved through fine-tuning of generative models with prompt-specific tasks, e.g., image generation and classification as well as object detection (Wang *et al* 2023). The significance of visual prompt engineering is increasing because of the emergence of large visual models making it the fundamental methodology in visual and image tasks. Visual prompt engineering is now a new direction for research opportunities (Wang *et al* 2023).

2.10.1 Common issues in prompt engineering

When composing prompts to derive effective responses from generative models, many difficulties are encountered. As such, it is essential for users to understand the limitations to avoid them so as to generate effective, accurate, responsible and relevant responses. The challenges associated with prompt engineering are provided as follows (Giray 2023).

2.10.1.1 Bias reinforcement

There is the issue of bias reinforcement, especially when a prompt like this is encountered: 'discuss the reason why the suitability of women in leadership positions is less'. In this prompt, a bias assumption is contained, promoting the bias that women are less suitable for the position of leadership. Subsequently, the model has the potential to respond to the prompt amplifying the gender bias on less suitability of women for leadership positions.

2.10.1.2 Ambiguity

Issue ambiguity comes into play with a prompt such as 'Explain the technological impact on society'. This prompt lacks focus, as such, generating a response that lacks focus and precision. Therefore, the response generated will eventually be an overview with shallow explanation without in-depth analysis of specific aspects of the technology impact. In addition, the response will lack specific examples for in-depth analysis.

2.10.1.3 Overfitting

The model is faced with the issue of overfitting, especially when confronted with a prompt like this: 'List the seven names of the dwarves from Snow White'. Despite the fact that the prompt seems specific to the Snow White example, it is noteworthy that it could be the desire of what the academic writer intend to know. In the situation where the user seeks explicit precise information, then the prompt is required to be tailored to a precise suitable dataset or example. To avoid limiting the model capability in generating a contextual relevant response, there is the need to strike a balance between specifics and generality.

2.10.1.4 Lack of context

Context plays an important role in developing prompts as adequate background is required in prompts for effective response within the desired context. For example, consider the following prompt, 'What is the excellent solution for solving poverty?', this prompt clearly lacks context as it lacks a specific geographical region or the factors contributing to the poverty. This lack of context can result in a general or insufficient response from the generative model.

2.10.1.5 Unintended side effects

Conflicting instructions or complex prompts can confuse the generative model to produce an undesired response resulting in unintended side effects. Thus, users need to be aware of the impact of conflicting instructions or complex prompts. Here is an example of such a prompt with problematic issues 'Explain the meaning of 'green' in the context of environmentalism. Then, argue against environmental protection.'

2.10.2 The strategies for optimum output from generative models

As already discussed in the preceding paragraphs, driving maximally relevant responses from models requires crafted prompts with specific elements to guide the design and development of prompt as follows (DAIR.AI 2023):

(i) Provide specific instructions to guide the model behaviour's towards the required output.
(ii) Add context with additional background knowledge to assist the model to generate a relevant and accurate response.
(iii) Input data containing the relevant question for the model to process before responding form the core part of the prompt because it drives the model's understanding of the task to perform.
(iv) The format of the output needs to be specified to guide the model in generating the desired output format, e.g., short answer, paragraph or any other format deemed fit as specified by the user in the prompt.

Getting better output from generative tools requires tactics in creating the prompt. The five fundamental strategies are discussed as follows (OpenAI 2023).

2.10.2.1 Write clear instructions

It is imperative for users to understand the generative models cannot read human minds, therefore, they cannot read your own mind. The instructions given to the model must be clearly written. In case the response from the model is lengthy, ask for a simple and short response. Ask for expert-level writing in case the response is too simple. Demonstrate the desired output format to the model in the situation where the user doesn't like the output format. Don't ever assume anything, and ensure the model doesn't have to guess what the user wants because the less the model guesses this, the more likely it can generate a better response. When prompting, explain to the model exactly what you want, provide instructions as if you are explaining a concept to a junior member of a team. Examples of prompts with clear instructions are provide in table 2.6.

2.10.2.2 Provide reference text

It is known that language models can fabricate fake responses confidently on a particular topic or concept, especially when asked about citations or links to websites. The model doesn't want to disappoint the user with no response when given a prompt so can just fabricate a response to satisfy the user. This typically happens on a topic or concept where the model doesn't have sufficient information to generate a response. To avoid this, instruct the model to respond based on a certain reference text to ensure that the model uses content of the reference text in its response. In addition, the model can be instructed to respond with citations from the reference text making the user control the inputs and ensuring the model is on track. An example of a prompt with a reference text is provide in table 2.7.

2.10.2.3 Break complex tasks

Similarly to the way a complex software engineering project is split into modular components, a complex task submitted to a generative model can be split in view of the fact that complex tasks tend to tilt towards high numbers of errors compared to simple tasks. When dealing with a complex lengthy job, e.g., drafting of a business plan, website compilation or thinking of how to sell your business, don't submit the

Table 2.6. Sample of prompt with clear instruction.

Worse prompt	*Better prompt*
How can I use excel to add numbers?	How can I sum a row containing the amount of US dollars in excel? I want the summation to be automatic for all the rows in the sheets, all the totals should be provided in the right column referred to as 'Total'.
Who is the president?	In 2021, who was the Mexico president and at what frequency are elections held?

Table 2.7. Sample of prompt for a reference text.

System	Use the articles provided delimited by triple quotes to respond to the questions. In case the answer is not found in the articles provided 'The answer cannot found in the articles.'
User	<Inset *articles*, each of which is delimited by triple quotes> *Question*: <Inset the question>

task at once for execution. Instead, break the complex task into smaller size as subtasks for prompting the model for a response before later combining the smaller subtasks responses into the large response of the earlier complex task. For example, summarizing a complete book or long document cannot be achieved at once with a single query as the model context has a fixed length. Therefore, summarizing a book should be performed section by section using a sequence of queries before concatenating the summaries to produce the summary of the complete book.

2.10.2.4 Give time to the model

Models are prone to more reasoning errors when trying to respond immediately instead of taking time to process the prompt before responding appropriately. The model can be instructed to workout a solution before reaching conclusion, allowing the model to take time for a suitable response. The model can be asked if an important part in the prompt is left out, which is critical to ensuring all the details are captured. These models are not perfect and have never been claimed to be perfect.

2.10.2.5 Use external tools

The weakness of the model can be strengthened by feeding the model with the response of other tools. The model could be notified on the existence of relevant documents. These LLMs are not the authority on a subject matter or field, they just predict the next word in a sentence. If a tool can perform a task more effectively or reliably compared to the model, one can combine both the tool and the model to get the best response by utilizing the best parts of both. An example is, instructing the model to call an external API to write code by providing the model with a sample of code or documentation on how to use the API as a guide.

2.11 Industry applications and case studies

The overwhelming influx of generative tools into the digital realm has sparked anxiety regarding both the quality of certain tools and the ethical considerations surrounding their use. This section aims to identify and recommend premier generative tools suitable for diverse applications.

The proliferation of generative tools has prompted concerns about potential job replacement, as these technologies could replicate certain roles, potentially leading to unemployment among the workforce. Additionally, there is growing apprehension about the ethical use of generative tools, a matter of concern for both the mainstream AI community and the general public. Generative tools, often described as a 'double-edged sword', possess both positive and negative aspects, depending on the user's intentions or the nature of the personality wielding the generative tool. Ethical considerations and the responsible deployment of these technologies are paramount as society navigates the evolving landscape of AI. The ethical utilization of generative tools by users holds considerable significance in the workplace and society. Hence, individuals across various domains such as employees, entrepreneurs, students, academicians, researchers, marketers, designers, engineers, and more should possess ethical proficiency in utilizing generative tools for task execution. Mastery of generative tool usage is crucial for professionals to remain pertinent in today's ever-evolving job landscape. Job seekers, too, must nurture skills in employing generative tools aligned with their respective fields of study, to enhance their prospects of securing employment with forward-thinking employers. Leveraging generative tools has the potential to significantly boost the efficiency and productivity of professionals across different fields.

Generative tools refers to software applications or platforms employing mostly generative AI algorithms to execute specific tasks, automate processes, or enhance human decision-making. The generative tools encompass a spectrum, ranging from straightforward chatbots to intricate machine learning algorithms, serving diverse purposes. The proliferation of AI tools is expanding swiftly, with continual development and release of new tools. These innovations aim to democratize AI, catering to businesses of varying sizes, from startups to large enterprises. By leveraging these tools, companies can streamline operations, cut costs, and enhance their overall profitability (Markus 2023). Table 2.8 presents selected quality generative tools developed to generate different content across domains, and links to access each of the generative platforms are provided.

Table 2.8. Selected generative AI tools serving different purposes.

Main task	Link to the tool	Description
Website creation	https://10web.io/	Offers a user-friendly interface for creating websites. Users simply input information and click 'next,' and the tool generates the content accordingly.
Image generation	https://openai.com/dall-e-2	This tool automatically generates images from text. Users only need to provide a textual description of the desired image, and the tool will generate it automatically. Alternatively, users can upload an existing image for editing.
Semantic Scholar	https://www.semanticscholar.org/	Semantic Scholar is an immensely potent search engine designed to assist with information retrieval.
AI Chat for scientific PDFs	https://typeset.io/	An application designed to expedite work by locating relevant sources and extract information (e.g. abstract, method, LR, conclusion, etc) from an uploaded pdf.
Mapping	https://researchrabbit appcom/home	Research Rabbit is a robust exploration application crafted for researchers. It enables the visualization of papers, the discovery of author networks, and the sharing of collections.
PowerPoint slides generator	www.SlideSpeak.co and www.SlidesAI.io	Users are only required to upload a text file onto the platform, after which the platform will automatically generate PowerPoint slides.

(*Continued*)

Table 2.8. (*Continued*)

Main task	Link to the tool	Description
Image generation	https://appleonardo.ai/ai-generations	Generates an image automatically based on the provided text description and prompt.
Video translation	https://www.heygen.com/video-translate	The platform is designed for translating videos into different languages.
Video generation	https://pika.art/	Users simply need to provide a textual description, and the video will be generated automatically.
Meeting recorder	https://tldv.io/	This is a recorder for meetings on Zoom and Google Meet. It captures the meeting notes, allowing the meeting leader to focus on leading the discussion.
ChatGPT AI Assistant	https://monica.im/	This is a ChatGPT-powered assistant that can be embedded directly into a website to act as a customer agent, responding to queries, providing recommendations, enhancing user engagement, and more. Small and medium enterprises, and giant companies can used it on their website.
Data visualization and pre-processing	https://rose.ai	Used for data pre-processing, explainability, interpretation, and transformation. Researchers, marketers, and policymakers can utilize it.
Vizologi - AI-Powered Innovation	https://vizologi.com/	Vizologi is a tool that delivers quality response to business questions by analyzing data and visualizing insights, helping the user understand market trends, competition, and strategies to take suitable decisions.
Crafting high-converting ad copy	https://Adcopy.ai	The tool generates high-click and high conversation advert directly within browser to enhance sales and click-through rate. This is a marketer's best digital friend.
Text-to-speech	https://murf.ai	MurfConvert text into engaging speech with customizable features and video editing options. Business magnates and product developers can utilize it effectively.
Coding	www.codegpt.co	CodeGPT is a powerful extension harnessing the capabilities of LLMs to boost programming tasks. Enables autonomous code generation, accepts a prompt in natural language and turns it into code. Tool for software developers and programmers.
AudioPen	https://audiopen.ai	This smart pen generates text notes from speech, simplifying the process of transcribing voice notes or speech. Journalists, researchers, etc can used it to improve their productivity.

2.12 Summary

Generative tasks involve the generation of content such as text, video, numerical values, audio and images through generative models. The generative tasks also involve the conversion of content to another different form of content, e.g. converting text to image, text to video or improving visual quality of image restoration. The generative models include GANs: conditional, bidirectional, sequence and information-theoretic extension; VAE: graph, recurrent, topic-guided and introspective; diffusion models: DDPMs, SDEs and score-based generative models; statistics: ARM, HMM and GMM, hybrid combining two or more of the generative models: diffusion—GAN, VAE–HMM, multimodal diffusion-GAN and other variants of the generative models. However, GAN is the main and most popular generative algorithm in the field of GAI followed by VAE and diffusion models.

Theoretical backgrounds of the generative models along with their mathematical fundamentals, were discussed. Different generative algorithms were matched to suitable tasks such as image restoration, human portrait generation, image editing, urban scene modelling, 3D object creation, generating textual, musical, video, and landscape content. The theory of deepfake, the stages involved in generating deepfake content, and its positive applications were examined. The chapter presents the marriage between generative AI and pharmaceuticals for the discovery of drugs. Additionally, industrial applications and case studies of generative AI were discussed including the presentation of a table populated with diverse generative tools, links to access the tools and descriptions of the functionalities. This chapter can serve as an entry point to GAI for beginners. For expert readers, the chapter offers an overview of GAI, highlighting various categories of generative models. This can allow exploration of different categories of GAI algorithms for innovative integration of algorithms beyond the dominant GANs.

References

Abraham A 2005 Hybrid intelligent systems: evolving intelligence in hierarchical layers *Do Smart Adaptive Systems Exist? Best Practice for Selection and Combination of Intelligent Methods* (Berlin: Springer) pp 159–79

Abukmeil M, Ferrari S, Genovese A, Piuri V and Scotti F 2021 A survey of unsupervised generative models for exploratory data analysis and representation learning *Acm Comput. Surv.* **54** 1–40

Arjovsky M, Chintala S and Bottou L 2017 Wasserstein generative adversarial networks *Int. Conf. on Machine Learning* (PMLR) pp 214–23

Banham M R and Katsaggelos A K 1997 Digital image restoration *IEEE Signal Process Mag.* **14** 24–41

Baraheem S S, Le T N and Nguyen T V 2023 Image synthesis: a review of methods, datasets, evaluation metrics, and future outlook *Artif. Intell. Rev.* **56** 10813–65

Barron A R 1987 Are Bayes rules consistent in information? *Open Problems in Communication and Computation* (New York: Springer) pp 85–91

Batzolis G, Stanczuk J, Schönlieb C B and Etmann C 2021 Conditional image generation with score-based diffusion models *arXiv preprint* arXiv:2111.13606

Bengio Y, Lamblin P, Popovici D and Larochelle H 2006 Greedy layer-wise training of deep networks *Advances in Neural Information Processing Systems 19 (NIPS 2006)* **19**

Berthelot D 2017 BEGAN: boundary equilibrium generative adversarial networks *arXiv preprint* arXiv:1703.10717

Billock J 2019 With a Little Help From A.I., the Dali Museum Brings the Famed Surrealist to Life *Smithsonian Mag.* https://www.smithsonianmag.com/travel/with-little-help-from-ai-dali-museum-brings-famed-surrealist-to-life-180972127/ (Accessed 20th September, 2024)

Box G E, Jenkins G M, Reinsel G C and Ljung G M 2015 *Time Series Analysis: Forecasting and Control* (New York: Wiley)

Cao H, Tan C, Gao Z, Xu Y, Chen G, Heng P A and Li S Z 2024 A survey on generative diffusion models *IEEE Trans. Knowl. Data Eng.* **36** 2814–30

Cao Y, Li S, Liu Y, Yan Z, Dai Y, Yu P S and Sun L 2023 A comprehensive survey of ai-generated content (AIGC): a history of generative ai from GAN to ChatGPT *arXiv preprint arXiv:2303.04226*

Castelli M and Manzoni L 2022 Generative models in artificial intelligence and their applications *Appl. Sci.* **12** 4127

Chan H S, Shan H, Dahoun T, Vogel H and Yuan S 2019 Advancing drug discovery via artificial intelligence *Trends Pharmacol. Sci.* **40** 592–604

Chen H, Engkvist O, Wang Y, Olivecrona M and Blaschke T 2018 The rise of deep learning in drug discovery *Drug Discov. Today* **23** 1241–50

Chen M, Mei S, Fan J and Wang M 2024 An overview of diffusion models: applications, guided generation, statistical rates and optimization *arXiv preprint* arXiv:2404.07771

Chen X, Duan Y, Houthooft R, Schulman J, Sutskever I and Abbeel P 2016 Infogan: interpretable representation learning by information maximizing generative adversarial nets *NIPS'16: Proc. of the 30th Int. Conf. on Neural Information Processing Systems* pp 2180–8

Cheng J, Yang Y, Tang X, Xiong N, Zhang Y and Lei F 2020 Generative adversarial networks: a literature review *KSII Trans. Internet Inform. Syst. (TIIS)* **14** 4625–47

Chintala S, Denton E, Arjovsky M and Mathieu M 2016 How to train a GAN? Tips and tricks to make GANs work *GitHub, Dec.*

Chokwitthaya C, Zhu Y, Mukhopadhyay S and Jafari A 2020 Applying the Gaussian mixture model to generate large synthetic data from a small data set *Construction Research Congress 2020* (Reston, VA: American Society of Civil Engineers) pp 1251–60

Coursera 2024 What Are Diffusion Models? www.coursera.org/articles/diffusion-models (accessed 21 June 2024)

Courville A, Bergstra J and Bengio Y 2011 A spike and slab restricted Boltzmann machine *Proc. of the 14th Int. Conf. on Artificial Intelligence and Statistics* (JMLR Workshop and Conf. Proc) pp 233–41

Croitoru F A, Hondru V, Ionescu R T and Shah M 2023 Diffusion models in vision: a survey *IEEE Trans. Pattern Anal. Mach. Intell.* **45** 10850–69

DAIR.AI 2023 Elements of a prompt https://promptingguide.ai/introduction/elements (accessed 13 August, 2024)

Dash A and Agres K 2024 AI-based affective music generation systems: a review of methods and challenges *ACM Comput. Surv.* **56** 1–34

Demoment G 1989 Image reconstruction and restoration: overview of common estimation structures and problems *IEEE Trans. Acoust. Speech Signal Process.* **37** 2024–36

Dhariwal P and Nichol A 2021 Diffusion models beat GANs on image synthesis *Adv. Neural Inform. Process. Syst.* **34** 8780–94

Dolhansky B, Howes R, Pflaum B, Baram N and Ferrer C C 2019 The deepfake detection challenge (DFDC) preview dataset *arXiv preprint* arXiv:1910.08854

Donahue J, Krähenbühl P and Darrell T 2016 Adversarial feature learning *arXiv preprint* arXiv:1605.09782

Du H, Li Z, Niyato D, Kang J, Xiong Z and Kim D I 2023 Enabling AI-generated content (AIGC) services in wireless edge networks *arXiv preprint* arXiv:2301.03220

Durbin R, Eddy S R, Krogh A and Mitchison G 1998 *Biological Sequence Analysis: Probabilistic Models of Proteins and Nucleic Acids* (Cambridge: Cambridge University Press)

Ebbers J, Heymann J, Drude L, Glarner T, Haeb-Umbach R and Raj B 2017 Hidden Markov model variational autoencoder for acoustic unit discovery *Proc. Interspeech 2017* pp 488–92

Elasri M, Elharrouss O, Al-Maadeed S and Tairi H 2022 Image generation: a review *Neural Process. Lett.* **54** 4609–46

Elder J H and Goldberg R M 1998 Image editing in the contour domain *Proc. 1998 IEEE Computer Society Conf. on Computer Vision and Pattern Recognition (Cat. No. 98CB36231)* (Piscataway, NJ: IEEE) pp 374–81

Feng S, Miao C, Zhang Z and Zhao P 2024 Latent diffusion transformer for probabilistic time series forecasting *Proc. of the AAAI Conf. on Artificial Intelligence* 38 pp 11979–87

Fenghour S, Chen D, Guo K, Li B and Xiao P 2021 Deep learning-based automated lip-reading: a survey *IEEE Access* **9** 121184–205

Fernandez-Lopez A and Sukno F M 2018 Survey on automatic lip-reading in the era of deep learning *Image Vision Comput.* **78** 53–72

Frey B J, Hinton G E and Dayan P 1995 Does the wake-sleep algorithm produce good density estimators? *Adv. Neural Inform. Process. Syst.* **8**

Fu H, Liu X, Jia Y and Deng H 2006 Gaussian mixture modeling of neighbor characters for multilingual text extraction in images *2006 Int. Conf. on Image Processing* (Piscataway, NJ: IEEE) pp 3321–4

Gangwal A, Ansari A, Ahmad I, Azad A K, Kumarasamy V, Subramaniyan V and Wong L S 2024 Generative artificial intelligence in drug discovery: basic framework, recent advances, challenges, and opportunities *Front. Pharmacol.* **15** 1331062

Gangwal A and Lavecchia A 2024 Unleashing the power of generative AI in drug discovery *Drug Discov. Today* **29** 103992

Garg A and Agarwal M 2018 Machine translation: a literature review *arXiv preprint* arXiv:1901.01122

Gatt A and Krahmer E 2018 Survey of the state of the art in natural language generation: core tasks, applications and evaluation *J. Artif. Intell. Res.* **61** 65–170

Gawlikowski J, Tassi C R N, Ali M, Lee J, Humt M, Feng J and Zhu X X 2023 A survey of uncertainty in deep neural networks *Artif. Intell. Rev.* **56** 1513–89

Gezawa A S, Liu C, Jia H, Nanehkaran Y A, Almutairi M S and Chiroma H 2023a An improved fused feature residual network for 3D point cloud data *Front. Comput. Neurosci.* **17** 1204445

Gezawa A S, Wang Q, Chiroma H and Lei Y 2023b A deep learning approach to mesh segmentation *CMES-Comput. Model. Eng. Sci.* **135** 1745–63

Giray L 2023 Prompt engineering with ChatGPT: a guide for academic writers *Ann. Biomed. Eng.* **51** 2629–33

Goodfellow I 2016 Nips tutorial: generative adversarial networks *arXiv preprint* arXiv:1701.00160

Goodfellow I J *et al* 2014 *Generative adversarial nets Advances in Neural Information Processing Systems* **27** (NIPS 2014)

Goodfellow I, Pouget-Abadie J, Mirza M, Xu B, Warde-Farley D, Ozair S and Bengio Y 2020 Generative adversarial networks *Commun. ACM* **63** 139–44

Grekow J and Dimitrova-Grekow T 2021 Monophonic music generation with a given emotion using conditional variational autoencoder *IEEE Access* **9** 129088–101

Gui J, Sun Z, Wen Y, Tao D and Ye J 2021 A review on generative adversarial networks: algorithms, theory, and applications *IEEE Trans. Knowl. Data Eng.* **35** 3313–32

Guimaraes G L, Sanchez-Lengeling B, Outeiral C, Farias P L C and Aspuru-Guzik A 2017 Objective-reinforced generative adversarial networks (organ) for sequence generation models *arXiv preprint* arXiv:1705.10843

Gupta A, Müller A T, Huisman B J, Fuchs J A, Schneider P and Schneider G 2018 Generative recurrent networks for *de novo* drug design *Mol. Inf.* **37** 1700111

Harshvardhan G M, Gourisaria M K, Pandey M and Rautaray S S 2020 A comprehensive survey and analysis of generative models in machine learning *Comp. Sci. Rev.* **38** 100285

Hassoun M H and Sudjianto A 1997 Compression net-free autoencoders *Workshop on Advances in Autoencoder/Autoassociator-Based Computations at the NIPS* 97 pp 605–11

He X, Cai D, Shao Y, Bao H and Han J 2010 Laplacian regularized Gaussian mixture model for data clustering *IEEE Trans. Knowl. Data Eng.* **23** 1406–18

Leong L Y, Hew T S, Ooi K B, Tan G W H and Koohang A 2025 Generative AI: current status and future directions *J. Comput. Inform. Syst.* (at press) https://doi.org/10.1080/08874417.2025.2482571

Hinton G E 2009 Deep belief networks *Scholarpedia* **4** 5947

Hinton G E, Osindero S and Teh Y W 2006 A fast learning algorithm for deep belief nets *Neural Comput.* **18** 1527–54

Ho J, Chen X, Srinivas A, Duan Y and Abbeel P 2019 Flow++: improving flow-based generative models with variationaldequantization and architecture design *Int. Conf. on Machine Learning* (PMLR) pp 2722–30

Hooshmand S A, Jamalkandi S A, Alavi S M and Masoudi-Nejad A 2021 Distinguishing drug/non-drug-like small molecules in drug discovery using deep belief network *Mol. Divers.* **25** 827–38

Hua Y, Guo J and Zhao H 2015 Deep belief networks and deep learning *Proc. of 2015 Int. Conf. on Intelligent Computing and Internet of Things* (Piscataway, NJ: IEEE) pp 1–4

Huang H, He R, Sun Z and Tan T 2018 Introvae: introspective variational autoencoders for photographic image synthesis *NIPS'18: Proc. of the 32nd Int. Conf. on Neural Information Processing Systems* (pp) 52–63

Huang Z, Yang L, Zhang Z, Zhou X, Bao Y, Zheng X and Yang W 2024 Binding-adaptive diffusion models for structure-based drug design *Proc. of the AAAI Conf. on Artificial Intelligence* 38 pp 12671–9

Hughes R T, Zhu L and Bednarz T 2021 Generative adversarial networks–enabled human–artificial intelligence collaborative applications for creative and design industries: a systematic review of current approaches and trends *Front. Artif. Intell.* **4** 604234

Huron D 2008 *Sweet Anticipation: Music and the Psychology of Expectation* (MIT Press)
Hutchins J and Lovtskii E 2000 Petr PetrovichTroyanskii (1894–1950): a forgotten pioneer of mechanical translation *Mach. Transl.* **15** 187–221
Hyvärinen A and Dayan P 2005 Estimation of non-normalized statistical models by score matching *J. Mach. Learn. Res.* **6** 695–709
Indumathi A and Chandra E 2012 Survey on speech synthesis *Signal Process.: Int. J. (SPIJ)* **6** 140
Indurkhya N and Damerau F J 2010 *Handbook of Natural Language Processing* (London: Chapman and Hall/CRC.)
Iqbal T and Qureshi S 2022 The survey: text generation models in deep learning *J. King Saud Univ.-Comput. Inform. Sci.* **34** 2515–28
Isola P, Zhu J Y, Zhou T and Efros A A 2017 Image-to-image translation with conditional adversarial networks *Proc. of the IEEE Conf. on Computer Vision and Pattern Recognition* pp 1125–34
Jafar M T, Ababneh M, Al-Zoube M and Elhassan A 2020 Forensics and analysis of deepfake videos *2020 11th Int. Conf. on Information and Communication Systems (ICICS)* (Piscataway, NJ: IEEE) pp 53–8
Jarzynski C 1997 Equilibrium free-energy differences from nonequilibrium measurements: a master-equation approach *Phys. Rev.* E **56** 5018
Jia F, Ma L, Yang Y and Zeng T 2021 Pixel-attention CNN with color correlation loss for color image denoising *IEEE Signal Process Lett.* **28** 1600–4
Jia Z, Zhang Z, Wang L and Tan T 2024 Human image generation: a comprehensive survey *ACM Comput. Surv.* **56** 1–39
Jovanovic M and Campbell M 2022 Generative artificial intelligence: trends and prospects *Computer* **55** 107–12
Kang S, Qian X and Meng H 2013 Multi-distribution deep belief network for speech synthesis *2013 IEEE Int. Conf. on Acoustics, Speech and Signal Processing* (Piscataway, NJ: IEEE) pp 8012–6
Karapantelakis A, Alizadeh P, Alabassi A, Dey K and Nikou A 2024 Generative AI in mobile networks: a survey *Ann. Telecommun.* **79** 15–33
Kaswan K S, Dhatterwal J S, Malik K and Baliyan A 2023 Generative AI: a review on models and applications *2023 Int. Conf. on Communication, Security and Artificial Intelligence (ICCSAI)* (Piscataway, NJ: IEEE) pp 699–704
Kim J, Oh C, Do H, Kim S and Sohn K 2024 Diffusion-driven GAN inversion for multi-modal face image generation *Proc. of the IEEE/CVF Conf. on Computer Vision and Pattern Recognition* pp 10403–12
Kingma D P and Welling M 2013 Auto-encoding variational Bayes *arXiv preprint* arXiv:1312.6114
Kingma D P and Welling M 2019 An introduction to variational autoencoders *Found. Trends Mach. Learn.* **12** 307–92
Kondo R, Kawano K, Koide S and Kutsuna T 2019 Flow-based image-to-image translation with feature disentanglement *Advances in Neural Information Processing Systems 32 (NeurIPS 2019)* 32
Kong Z, Ping W, Huang J, Zhao K and Catanzaro B 2020 Diffwave: a versatile diffusion model for audio synthesis *arXiv preprint* arXiv:2009.09761

Kulkarni A H and Kirange D 2019 Artificial intelligence: a survey on lip-reading techniques *2019 10th Int. Conf. on Computing, Communication and Networking Technologies (ICCCNT)* (Piscataway, NJ: IEEE) pp 1–5

Kwon J and Park F C 2006 Using hidden markov models to generate natural humanoid movement *2006 IEEE/RSJ Int. Conf. on Intelligent Robots and Systems* (Piscataway, NJ: IEEE) pp 1990–5

Lagarda A L, Ortiz-Martinez D, Alabau V and Casacuberta F 2015 Translating without in-domain corpus: machine translation post-editing with online learning techniques *Comput. Speech Lang.* **32** 109–34

LeCun Y, Chopra S, Hadsell R, Ranzato M and Huang F 2006 A tutorial on energy-based learning *Predicting Structured Data* **1** (New York University) https://www.cs.toronto.edu/~vnair/ciar/lecun1.pdf

Lee K F 1988 On large-vocabulary speaker-independent continuous speech recognition *Speech Commun.* **7** 375–9

Leglaive S, Alameda-Pineda X, Girin L and Horaud R 2020 A recurrent variational autoencoder for speech enhancement *ICASSP 2020–2020 IEEE Int. Conf. on Acoustics, Speech and Signal Processing (ICASSP)* (Piscataway, NJ: IEEE) pp 371–5

Li C, Yao J, Wei W, Niu Z, Zeng X, Li J and Wang J 2022 Geometry-based molecular generation with deep constrained variationalautoencoder *IEEE Trans Neural Netw. Learn. Syst.* **35** 4852–61

Li J J, McLoughlin I V, Dai L R and Ling Z H 2014 Whisper-to-speech conversion using restricted Boltzmann machine arrays *Electron. Lett.* **50** 1781–2

Li X, Thickstun J, Gulrajani I, Liang P S and Hashimoto T B 2022 Diffusion-lm improves controllable text generation *Adv. Neural Inform. Process. Syst.* **35** 4328–43

Li X, Zhang Q, Kang D, Cheng W, Gao Y, Zhang J and Shan Y 2024 Advances in 3d generation: a survey *arXiv preprint* arXiv:2401.17807

Li Y, Gao C, Song X, Wang X, Xu Y and Han S 2023 DrugGPT: a GPT-based strategy for designing potential ligands targeting specific proteins *bioRxiv* 2023**06**

Liang J, Cao J, Sun G, Zhang K, Van Gool L and Timofte R 2021 Swinir: image restoration using swin transformer *Proc. of the IEEE/CVF Int. Conf. on Computer Vision* pp 1833–44

Liang P P, Zadeh A and Morency L P 2023 Foundations and trends in multimodal machine learning: principles, challenges, and open questions *ACM Comput. Surv.* **56** 264

Ling H, Kreis K, Li D, Kim S W, Torralba A and Fidler S 2021 Editgan: high-precision semantic image editing *Adv. Neural Inform. Process. Syst.* **34** 16331–45

Liu Q, Allamanis M, Brockschmidt M and Gaunt A 2018 Constrained graph variational autoencoders for molecule design *NIPS'18: Proc. of the 32nd Int. Conf. on Neural Information Processing Systems* 7806–15

Liu X, Chen J, Xie J and Chang Y 2023 Generating HSR Bogie vibration signals via pulse voltage-guided conditional diffusion model *arXiv preprint* arXiv:2311.00496

Liu Z, Pei W, Lan D and Ma Q 2024 Diffusion language-shapelets for semi-supervised time-series classification *Proc. of the AAAI Conf. on Artificial Intelligence* 38 pp 14079–87

Longoni C, Fradkin A, Cian L and Pennycook G 2022 News from generative artificial intelligence is believed less *Proc. of the 2022 ACM Conf. on Fairness, Accountability, and Transparency* pp 97–106

Luo B, Lau R Y, Li C and Si Y W 2022 A critical review of state-of-the-art chatbot designs and applications *Wiley Interdiscip. Rev.: Data Mining Knowl. Discov.* **12** e1434

Lyu S 2020 Deepfake detection: current challenges and next steps *2020 IEEE Int. Conf. on Multimedia and Expo Workshops (ICMEW)* (Piscataway, NJ: IEEE) pp 1–6

Markus J 2023 *Top 16 Best AI Tools in 2024* [Expert Picks] (hackr.io) https://hackr.io/blog/best-ai-tools (accessed 7 January 2024)

Marr B 2019 The Best (and Scariest) Examples of AI-enabled Deepfakes https://bernardmarr.com/the-best-and-scariest-examples-of-ai-enabled-deepfakes/ (accessed 19 August 2024)

McGibbon R, Ramsundar B, Sultan M, Kiss G and Pande V 2014 Understanding protein dynamics with L1-regularized reversible hidden Markov models *Int. Conf. on Machine Learning* (PMLR) pp 1197–205

McLachlan G J and Rathnayake S 2014 On the number of components in a Gaussian mixture model *Wiley Interdiscip. Rev.: Data Min. Knowl. Discov.* **4** 341–55

Meng C, He Y, Song Y, Song J, Wu J, Zhu J Y and Ermon S 2021 SDEdit: guided image synthesis and editing with stochastic differential equations *Int. Conf. on Learning Representations*

Moret M, PachonAngona I, Cotos L, Yan S, Atz K, Brunner C and Schneider G 2023 Leveraging molecular structure and bioactivity with chemical language models for de novo drug design *Nat. Commun.* **14** 114

Nair V and Hinton G E 2009 3D object recognition with deep belief nets *Advances in Neural Information Processing Systems (NIPS 2009)* **22**

Nair V, Radhakrishnan A, Chithra R and James A 2023 Memristive pixel-CNN loop generate for CNN generalisations *IEEE Trans. Nanotechnol.* **22** 120–5

Nguyen L X, Aung P S, Le H Q, Park S B and Hong C S 2023 A new chapter for medical image generation: The stable diffusion method *2023 Int. Conf. on Information Networking (ICOIN)* (Piscataway, NJ: IEEE) pp 483–6

Nhan Duong C, Luu K, Gia Quach K and Bui T D 2015 Beyond principal components: deep Boltzmann machines for face modeling *Proc. of the IEEE Conf. on Computer Vision and Pattern Recognition* pp 4786–94

Nichol A Q and Dhariwal P 2021 Improved denoising diffusion probabilistic models *Int. Conf. on Machine Learning* (PMLR) pp 8162–71

Ning Y, He S, Wu Z, Xing C and Zhang L J 2019 A review of deep learning based speech synthesis *Appl. Sci.* **9** 4050

Noguchi S and Inoue J 2022 Exploration of chemical space guided by PixelCNN for fragment-based de novo drug discovery *J. Chem. Inf. Model.* **62** 5988–6001

Odena A, Olah C and Shlens J 2017 Conditional image synthesis with auxiliary classifier GANs *Int. Conf. on Machine Learning* (PMLR) pp 2642–51

Oghbaie M, Sabaghi A, Hashemifard K and Akbari M 2021 Advances and challenges in deep lip reading *arXiv preprint* arXiv:2110.07879

OpenAI 2023 Prompt Engineering https://platform.openai.com/docs/guides/prompt-engineering (accessed 8 August 2024)

Oussidi A and Elhassouny A 2018 Deep generative models: survey *2018 Int. Conf. on Intelligent Systems and Computer Vision (ISCV)* (Piscataway, NJ: IEEE) pp 1–8

Pang Y, Lin J, Qin T and Chen Z 2021 Image-to-image translation: methods and applications *IEEE Trans. Multimedia* **24** 3859–81

Park T, Liu M Y, Wang T C and Zhu J Y 2019 Gaugan: semantic image synthesis with spatially adaptive normalization *ACM SIGGRAPH 2019 Real-Time Live!*

Picazo P and Moreno-Gil S 2019 Analysis of the projected image of tourism destinations on photographs: A literature review to prepare for the future *J. Vacat. Market.* **25** 3–24

Pinaya W H, Tudosiu P D, Dafflon J, Da Costa P F, Fernandez V, Nachev P and Cardoso M J 2022 Brain imaging generation with latent diffusion models *MICCAI Workshop on Deep Generative Models* (Cham: Springer Nature) pp 117–26

Ping W, Peng K, Zhao K and Song Z 2020 Waveflow: a compact flow-based model for raw audio *Int. Conf. on Machine Learning* (PMLR) pp 7706–16

Prenger R, Valle R and Catanzaro B 2019 Waveglow: a flow-based generative network for speech synthesis *ICASSP 2019–2019 IEEE Int. Conf. on Acoustics, Speech and Signal Processing (ICASSP)* (Piscataway, NJ: IEEE) pp 3617–21

Rabiner L R 1989 A tutorial on hidden Markov models and selected applications in speech recognition *Proc. IEEE* **77** 257–86

Rana M S, Nobi M N, Murali B and Sung A H 2022 Deepfake detection: a systematic literature review *IEEE Access* **10** 25494–513

Reynolds D A 1992 *A Gaussian Mixture Modeling Approach to Text-Independent Speaker Identification* (Atlanta, GA: Georgia Institute of Technology)

Reynolds D A 2009 Gaussian mixture models *Encycl. Biometr.* **741** 659–63

Richter J, Welker S, Lemercier J M, Lay B and Gerkmann T 2023 Speech enhancement and dereverberation with diffusion-based generative models *IEEE/ACM Trans. Audio, Speech, Lang. Process.* **31** 2351–64

Rivera-Trigueros I 2022 Machine translation systems and quality assessment: a systematic review *Lang. Resour. Eval.* **56** 593–619

Rombach R, Blattmann A, Lorenz D, Esser P and Ommer B 2022 High-resolution image synthesis with latent diffusion models *Proc. of the IEEE/CVF Conf. on Computer Vision and Pattern Recognition* pp 10684–95

Saharia C, Chan W, Saxena S, Li L, Whang J, Denton E L and Norouzi M 2022 Photorealistic text-to-image diffusion models with deep language understanding *Adv. Neural Inform. Process. Syst.* **35** 36479–94

Sakirin T and Kusuma S 2023 A survey of generative artificial intelligence techniques *Babylonian J. Artif. Intell.* **2023** 10–4

Salakhutdinov R and Hinton G 2009 Deep Boltzmann machines *Artificial Intelligence and Statistics* (PMLR) pp 448–55

Salimans T, Goodfellow I, Zaremba W, Cheung V, Radford A and Chen X 2016 Improved techniques for training GANS Advances in neural information processing systems **29** *NIPS 2016*

Salimans T, Karpathy A, Chen X and Kingma D P 2017 PixelCNN++: improving the PixelCNN with discretized logistic mixture likelihood and other modifications *arXiv preprint* arXiv:1701.05517

Schmidt D C, Spencer-Smith J, Fu Q and White J 2024 Towards a catalog of prompt patterns to enhance the discipline of prompt engineering *ACM SIGAda Ada Letters* **43** 43–51

Shaham T R, Dekel T and Michaeli T 2019 Singan: learning a generative model from a single natural image *Proc. of the IEEE/CVF Int. Conf. on Computer Vision* pp 4570–80

Shanehsazzadeh A, Bachas S, McPartlon M, Kasun G, Sutton J M, Steiger A K and Meier J 2023 Unlocking de novo antibody design with generative artificial intelligence *bioRxiv* 2023–1

Shi C, Xu M, Zhu Z, Zhang W, Zhang M and Tang J 2020 Graphaf: a flow-based autoregressive model for molecular graph generation *arXiv preprint* arXiv:2001.09382

Sohl-Dickstein J, Weiss E, Maheswaranathan N and Ganguli S 2015 Deep unsupervised learning using nonequilibrium thermodynamics *Int. Conf. on Machine Learning* (PMLR) pp 2256–65

Solsman J E 2019 This AI startup wants to be the notary of the internet https://cnet.com/tech/services-and-software/this-ai-startup-wants-to-be-the-notary-of-the-internet/ (accessed 19 August 2024)

Song Y, Sohl-Dickstein J, Kingma D P, Kumar A, Ermon S and Poole B 2020 Score-based generative modeling through stochastic differential equations *arXiv preprint* arXiv:2011.13456

Song Y, Sohl-Dickstein J, Kingma D P, Kumar A, Ermon S and Poole B 2020 Score-based generative modeling through stochastic differential equations *arXiv preprint* arXiv:2011.13456

Stein M L, Chen J and Anitescu M 2013 Stochastic approximation of score functions for Gaussian processes *Ann. Appl. Stat.* **7** 1162–91

Susskind J M, Hinton G E, Movellan J R and Anderson A K 2008 Generating facial expressions with deep belief nets *Affect. Comput., Emotion Model., Synth. Recogn.* **2008** 421–40

Tabet Y and Boughazi M 2011 Speech synthesis techniques. A survey *Int. Workshop on Systems, Signal Processing and their Applications, WOSSPA* (Piscataway, NJ: IEEE) pp 67–70

Takale D G, Mahalle P N and Sule B 2024 Advancements and applications of generative artificial intelligence *J. Informat. Technol. Sci.* **10** 20–7

Tang B, Ewalt J and Ng H L 2021 Generative AI models for drug discovery *Biophysical and Computational Tools in Drug Discovery* (Cham: Springer International Publishing) pp 221–43

Tulyakov S, Liu M Y, Yang X and Kautz J 2018 Mocogan: decomposing motion and content for video generation *Proc. of the IEEE Conf. on Computer Vision and Pattern Recognition* pp 1526–35

Van den Oord A, Kalchbrenner N, Espeholt L, Vinyals O and Graves A 2016a Conditional image generation with PixelCNN decoders *NIPS'16: Proc. of the 30th Int. Conf. on Neural Information Processing Systems* 4797–805

Van Den Oord A, Kalchbrenner N and Kavukcuoglu K 2016b Pixel recurrent neural networks *Int. Conf. on Machine Learning* (PMLR) pp 1747–56

Van Huynh N, Wang J, Du H, Hoang D T, Niyato D, Nguyen D N and Letaief K B 2024 Generative ai for physical layer communications: a survey *IEEE Trans. Cogn. Commun. Netw.* **10** 706–28

Verikas A, Kalsyte Z, Bacauskiene M and Gelzinis A 2010 Hybrid and ensemble-based soft computing techniques in bankruptcy prediction: a survey *Soft Comput.* **14** 995–1010

Viroli C and McLachlan G J 2019 Deep Gaussian mixture models *Stat. Comput.* **29** 43–51

Viswa C A, Bleys J, Leydon E, Shah B and Zurkiya D 2024 *Generative AI in the Pharmaceutical Industry: Moving from Hype to Reality* (New York: McKinsey and Company)

Wan H, Wang H, Scotney B and Liu J 2019 A novel Gaussian mixture model for classification *2019 IEEE Int. Conf. on Systems, Man and Cybernetics (SMC)* (Piscataway, NJ: IEEE) pp 3298–303

Wang J, Liu Z, Zhao L, Wu Z, Ma C, Yu S and Zhang S 2023 Review of large vision models and visual prompt engineering *Meta-Radiol.* **1** 100047

Wang K, Gou C, Duan Y, Lin Y, Zheng X and Wang F Y 2017 Generative adversarial networks: introduction and outlook *IEEE/CAA J. Autom. Sin.* **4** 588–98

Wang R, Huang Z, Liu S, Shao H, Liu D, Li J and Abdelzaher T 2021 Dydiff-vae: a dynamic variational framework for information diffusion prediction *Proc. of the 44th Int. ACM SIGIR Conf. on Research and Development in Information Retrieval* pp 163–72

Wang T C, Liu M Y, Zhu J Y, Tao A, Kautz J and Catanzaro B 2018 High-resolution image synthesis and semantic manipulation with conditional GANs *Proc. of the IEEE Conf. on Computer Vision and Pattern Recognition* pp 8798–807

Wang W, Gan Z, Xu H, Zhang R, Wang G, Shen D and Carin L 2019 Topic-guided variational autoencoders for text generation *arXiv preprint* arXiv:1903.07137

Wang X, Yu K, Wu S, Gu J, Liu Y, Dong C and Change Loy C 2018 Esrgan: enhanced super-resolution generative adversarial networks *Proc. of the European Conf. on Computer Vision (ECCV) Workshops* vol 11133

Wang Z, Zheng H, He P, Chen W and Zhou M 2022 Diffusion-GAN: training GANs with diffusion *arXiv preprint* arXiv:2206.02262

Wehenkel A and Louppe G 2021 Diffusion priors in variational autoencoders *arXiv preprint* arXiv:2106.15671

Wei Q, Song R and Yan P 2015 Data-driven zero-sum neuro-optimal control for a class of continuous-time unknown nonlinear systems with disturbance using ADP *IEEE Trans Neural Netw. Learn. Syst.* **27** 444–58

Westerlund M 2019 The emergence of deepfake technology: a review *Technol. Innov. Manage. Rev.* **9** 39–52

White J, Fu Q, Hays S, Sandborn M, Olea C, Gilbert H and Schmidt D C 2023 A prompt pattern catalog to enhance prompt engineering with ChatGPT *arXiv preprint* arXiv:2302.11382

Wu J, Gan W, Chen Z, Wan S and Philip S Y 2023 Multimodal large language models: a survey *2023 IEEE Int. Conf. on Big Data (BigData)* (Piscataway, NJ: IEEE) pp 2247–56

Wu J, Zhang C, Xue T, Freeman B and Tenenbaum J 2016 Learning a probabilistic latent space of object shapes via 3D generative-adversarial modeling *NIPS'16: Proc. of the 30th Int. Conf. on Neural Information Processing Systems* **29** 82–90

Wu Y J and Wang R H 2006 Minimum generation error training for HMM-based speech synthesis *2006 IEEE Int. Conf. on Acoustics Speech and Signal Processing Proc.* (Piscataway, NJ: IEEE) pp I–I

Wu Z, Chng E S and Li H 2013 Conditional restricted Boltzmann machine for voice conversion *2013 IEEE China Summit and Int. Conf. on Signal and Information Processing* (Piscataway, NJ: IEEE) pp 104–8

Xia W, Yang Y, Xue J H and Wu B 2021 Tedigan: text-guided diverse face image generation and manipulation *Proc. of the IEEE/CVF Conf. on Computer Vision and Pattern Recognition* pp 2256–65

Xie L and Liu Z Q 2007 Realistic mouth-synching for speech-driven talking face using articulatory modelling *IEEE Trans. Multimedia* **9** 500–10

Xing Z, Feng Q, Chen H, Dai Q, Hu H, Xu H and Jiang Y G 2023 A survey on video diffusion models *arXiv e-prints* arXiv-2310

Xu J, Lyu F and Yuen P C 2023 Density-aware temporal attentive step-wise diffusion model for medical time series imputation *Proc. of the 32nd ACM Int. Conf. on Information and Knowledge Management* pp 2836–45

Xu M, Duan L Y, Cai J, Chia L T, Xu C and Tian Q 2004 HMM-based audio keyword generation *Pacific-Rim Conf. on Multimedia* (Berlin: Springer) pp 566–74

Yamato J, Ohya J and Ishii K 1992 Recognizing human action in time-sequential images using hidden Markov model *Proc. 1992 IEEE Computer Society Conf. on Computer Vision and Pattern Recognition* pp 379–85

Yang L, Zhang Z, Song Y, Hong S, Xu R, Zhao Y and Yang M H 2023 Diffusion models: a comprehensive survey of methods and applications *ACM Comput. Surv.* **56** 1–39

Yang Y, Jin M, Wen H, Zhang C, Liang Y, Ma L and Wen Q 2024 A survey on diffusion models for time series and spatio-temporal data *arXiv preprint* arXiv:2404.18886

Yu L, Zhang W, Wang J and Yu Y 2017 Seqgan: sequence generative adversarial nets with policy gradient *Proc. of the AAAI Conf. on Artificial Intelligence* 31

Yu P, Xia Z, Fei J and Lu Y 2021 A survey on deepfake video detection *IET Biometr.* **10** 607–24

Yu W, Zhu C, Li Z, Hu Z, Wang Q, Ji H and Jiang M 2022 A survey of knowledge-enhanced text generation *ACM Comput. Surv.* **54** 1–38

Yu Y, Huang J, He H, Han J, Ye G, Xu T and Li H 2023 Accelerated discovery of macrocyclic CDK2 inhibitor QR-6401 by generative models and structure-based drug design *ACS Med. Chem. Lett.* **14** 297–304

Yunjiu L, Wei W and Zheng Y 2022 Artificial intelligence-generated and human expert-designed vocabulary tests: a comparative study *Sage Open* **12** 21582440221082130

Zhan F, Yu Y, Wu R, Zhang J, Lu S, Liu L and Xing E 2023 Multimodal image synthesis and editing: the generative AI era *IEEE Trans. Pattern Anal. Mach. Intell.* **45** 15098–119

Zhang C, Zhang C, Zheng S, Qiao Y, Li C, Zhang M and Hong C S 2023a A complete survey on generative AI (AIGC): is ChatGPT from GPT-4 to GPT-5 all you need? *arXiv preprint* arXiv:2303.11717

Zhang J, Fazekas G and Saitis C 2023b Fast diffusion GAN model for symbolic music generation controlled by emotions *arXiv preprint* arXiv:2310.14040

Zhang N, Ding S, Zhang J and Xue Y 2018 An overview on restricted Boltzmann machines *Neurocomputing* **275** 1186–99

Zhao M, Bao F, Li C and Zhu J 2022 Egsde: unpaired image-to-image translation via energy-guided stochastic differential equations *Adv. Neural Inform. Process. Syst.* **35** 3609–23

Zhen R, Song W, He Q, Cao J, Shi L and Luo J 2023 Human-computer interaction system: a survey of talking-head generation *Electronics* **12** 218

Zhu Y, Du Y, Wang Y, Xu Y, Zhang J, Liu Q and Wu S 2022 A survey on deep graph generation: methods and applications *Learning on Graphs Conf.* (PMLR) pp 47–1

Zi B, Chang M, Chen J, Ma X and Jiang Y G 2020 Wilddeepfake: a challenging real-world dataset for deepfake detection *Proc. of the 28th ACM Int. Conf. on Multimedia* pp 2382–90

Chapter 3

Artificial general intelligence and beyond: large language models tutorial, debates, hypothesis and future outlook

This chapter provides an insight into artificial general intelligence (AGI) and beyond, an ambitious field aiming to achieve human-level intelligence. Unlike traditional artificial intelligence (AI), AGI seeks to emulate the broad capabilities of human intelligence. The chapter simplifies the concept of AGI for readers, given the early stage of development in this field. The discussion covers AGI in comparison to human-level intelligence. A tutorial on large language models (LLMs) and transformer architecture in an easy-to-follow approach for readers to understand it is presented. The exploration extends beyond AGI to artificial superintelligence (ASI) and the controversies surrounding them. The chapter delves into the current status of AGI and ASI, intellectual debates, timelines, industrial applications and case studies, hypothesis and future outlook. Upon reading this chapter, readers will gain a comprehensive understanding of LLMs, transformers, current status of AGI and ASI, controversies and new research opportunities.

3.1 Introduction

In recent years, a diverse community of researchers has arisen, directing their attention towards the initial ambitious objectives of AI. This entails the development and studying of software or hardware systems endowed with a general level of intelligence that is not only comparable to but potentially surpassing that of human beings (Goertzel 2014). Originally, the goal of AI was to create a machine with the ability to 'think.' However, faced with technical challenges in constructing such a 'thinking machine,' the mainstream AI research community shifted its focus to developing solutions tailored to specific domains and problems. Consequently, the term AGI was introduced to denote research directed toward

doi:10.1088/978-0-7503-6320-4ch3

realizing the initial vision of the AI, thereby preventing misunderstandings. AGI aims to provide solutions that transcend multiple domains, addressing a variety of problems across these domains. For instance, DeepBlue demonstrated its prowess by defeating Kasparov in chess and performing basic tasks like multiplication. Nevertheless, outside of these specific domains, DeepBlue lacks the capacity to undertake any other tasks. Researchers acknowledge the importance of persisting in the pursuit of the original goal of AI, and there is a renewed momentum in broad AGI research to overcome the challenges associated with achieving AGI and to make significant breakthroughs in this direction (Baum 2017).

The journey toward achieving AGI has seen the proposal of numerous methodologies by both the AI and AGI research communities. Over the decades, these communities have put forth various sub-solutions, aiming to integrate them in the future into a comprehensive AGI system. The ultimate goal is to create an AGI system that possesses a broad range of general intelligence comparable to that of humans. This underscores the longstanding dream of realizing the original objective of AI at its inception (Adams *et al* 2012).

Nonetheless, intelligent assistants like Siri and task-specific chatbots may serve as foundational steps toward achieving AGI, shedding light on the nature and magnitude of the effort required for its realization. Over the past few years, conversational agents have made significant strides thanks to extensive data sources and advancements in machine learning. Intelligent assistants like Siri, Cortana, Alexa, Google Assistant, and Bixby that primarily excel in retrieving requested information and providing notifications on a wide array of topics, including weather updates, daily meeting schedules, and music requests. Similarly, chatbots with a more profound understanding of specific domains, such as those used in customer service, have also reaped the benefits of these advancements. Task-focussed chatbots, particularly well-suited for mobile phone usage where display space and input modalities are restricted to voice or text, showcase the practical applications of evolving AI technologies (Grudin and Jacques 2019).

The field of AGI has now established a community with dedicated journals publishing developments in AGI and conference series primarily centred around AGI topics. It is hypothesized that AGI can reach a stage where it will continue to evolve itself for improvement until it performs better than human-level intelligence, referred to as ASI or singularity. Kleinman and Vallance (2023) reported that Geoffrey Hinton resigned from Google citing dangers of AGI and warned that ASI will soon be reached. However, many scientists argued that machines lack the potential to reach human-level intelligence and singularity.

This chapter is intended to present a tutorial on LLMs as a step towards AGI, hypothesizes and debates regarding AGI and singularity before looking at the future outlook. Unlike previous studies (Eden *et al* 2012, Goertzel 2014, Pei *et al* 2019, Wang *et al* 2018, Zhao *et al* 2023) that mainly focus on LLMs, AGI or ASI, the chapter combines LLMs, AGI and ASI debates, hypothesis and future outlook to give the reader broad perspective of the field and controversies.

3.2 Human-level general intelligence

When discussions about intelligence arise, human intelligence naturally stands out as a benchmark. Humans have long explored human-level intelligence, employing various methods to measure and evaluate it. These efforts have led to the development of different approaches, including IQ tests, cognitive games, professional achievements, the pursuit of education, etc. History demonstrates that the ongoing exploration of human intelligence has been consistently aimed at understanding, evaluating, and pushing the boundaries of its multifaceted nature (Guo *et al* 2023). To grasp general intelligence according to psychological literature, one can examine the diverse competencies typically observed in humans as understood by cognitive scientists. Figure 3.1 depicted the characteristics of human-level intelligence, derived from data on competencies compiled by Goertzel (2014), sourced from a list assembled at AGI Roadmap in 2009. This compilation encompasses insights from both AGI researchers and psychologists, drawing upon a review of AI and psychology literature. Different researchers hold distinct perspectives on the significance of different intelligence competency areas. As you review the list, you might observe that certain aspects of intelligence are either overemphasized or underemphasized based on individual viewpoints. Nevertheless, it becomes evident

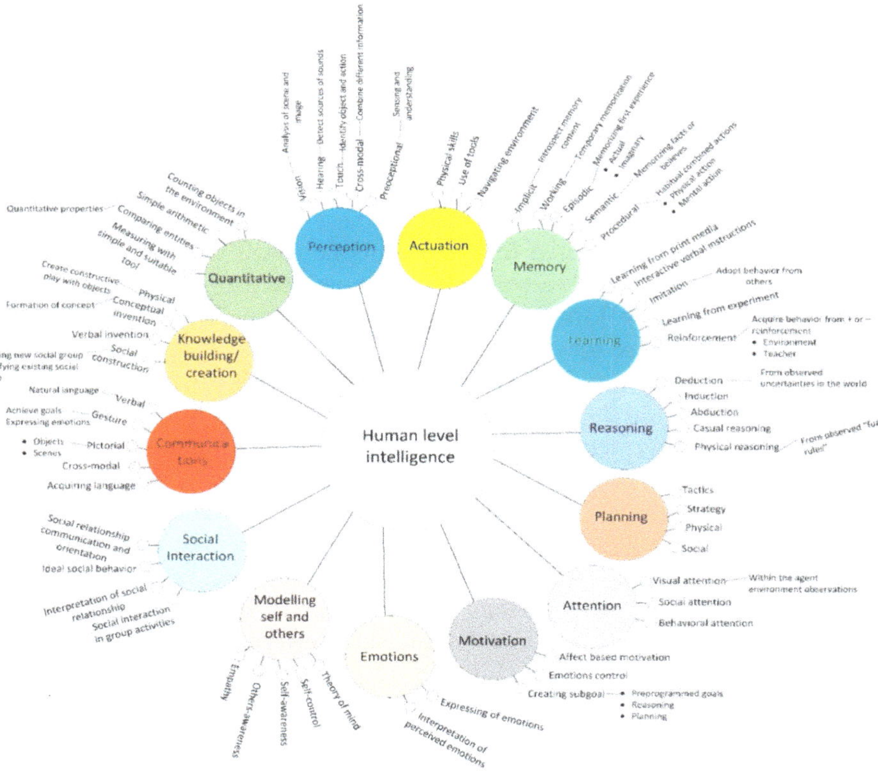

Figure 3.1. Characteristics of human-level intelligence.

that a software system capable of adeptly and resiliently demonstrating competence across all the areas illustrated in figure 3.1 would be widely recognized as a formidable candidate for attaining human-level general intelligence (Goertzel 2014).

3.2.1 Cognition and reasoning

Cognition refers to the mental activities associated with obtaining, processing, storing, and utilizing information. It encompasses a broad spectrum of cognitive processes, including perception, attention, memory, language, problem-solving, decision-making, and reasoning. Simply put, cognition encompasses how individuals perceive, comprehend, and engage with their surrounding world (Eysenck and Brysbaert 2018). In contrast, reasoning is the cognitive process of deriving conclusions, making inferences, or forming judgements based on evidence, information, or pre-existing knowledge. It requires the ability to think logically, analyze data, and apply rules or principles to arrive at a sound and well-supported conclusion. Reasoning stands as a crucial facet of cognition, playing a vital role in tasks such as problem-solving, decision-making, and comprehending intricate situations (Rips 1990). In the context of AGI, it is the developing of intelligent systems and autonomous systems that can reason effectively at human level.

The exploration of human behaviour holds significance across various disciplines, including AI, neural computation, philosophy, computer science, cognitive science, and psychology. Operating on the assumption that behaviour is predominantly shaped and directed by cognition and mental processes, the modelling of behaviour leverages several key tools. Notably, computational-logic systems, with a primary focus on high-level reasoning and thought processes such as logic, play a prominent role. Additionally, connectionist models, which delve into lower-level dynamics and emergent processes, such as recurrent neural networks, contribute to understanding behaviour. Furthermore, models addressing uncertainty are crucial, considering the often vague or probabilistic nature of many aspects of cognitive processing (Garcez *et al* 2022). In multimodal processing, various forms of reasoning come into play. Achieving scene classification, for instance, may involve a well-trained network providing immediate answers based on certain assumptions. However, when there is a change in the scene, more specific temporal and nonmonotonic reasoning becomes necessary, often requiring learning from data—such as assessing the degree of change in the scene. In such cases, assumptions may need reconsideration, and information from image annotations might offer a different context. Abduction and similarity reasoning through intersecting network ensembles may be required, and there might be a need to reason about probability distributions, among other considerations. The integrated system must be agile, capable of quick responses, adept at revising answers in light of new information, and capable of managing the inevitable accumulation of errors derived from real-world data to demonstrate its robustness (Garcez *et al* 2022).

3.2.2 Perception

Perception serves as humanity's fundamental cognitive connection with the surrounding world. All conceptual knowledge stems from or is rooted in this foundational awareness. Perception entails the organization, interpretation, and conscious experience of sensory information. It encompasses both bottom-up and top-down processing. Bottom-up processing involves the construction of perceptions from sensory input. Conversely, top-down processing refers to how we interpret these sensations, influenced by our existing knowledge, experiences, and thoughts (Efron 1969).

3.2.3 Learning

Learning involves the acquisition of fresh knowledge, positive behaviours, skills, or attitudes through experiences, observation or practice. It can occur through reinforcement, where an agent interacts with the environment, as well as through imitation, print media, experimentation, and verbal instructions (Beaudoin *et al* 2013).

3.2.4 Memory

The concept of human memory encompasses both the conscious recall of facts and experiential details, as well as the in-built knowledge that may surface without conscious action or cognizance. It serves as both a short-term repository of information and a long-term record of acquired learning. The memory is of different types such as sensory, prospective, procedural, working, episodic, and semantic (Baddeley 2004).

3.2.5 Attention

Attention is tied to the functioning of the human brain closely to the cognitive process. Attention is the initial stage in the learning process, critical for focussing on information highly relevant to the task to be executed while disregarding irrelevant input or stimuli. If there is no attention, the brain's capacity to process information efficiently diminishes (Cowan 1988).

3.2.6 Communications

Communication is a ubiquitous activity deeply interwoven with every aspect of human existence (Littlejohn and Foss 2010). Communication can be non-verbal or verbal. Verbal communication refers to the use of spoken language to convey information, ideas, or feelings, as well as the comprehension of speech by another individual (Melser 2009). Non-verbal involves the use of signs to communicate. Humans naturally use gestures for communication. These gestures serve as a crucial element of language, conveying distinct and significant information while reflecting the speaker's knowledge and experiences (Clough and Duff 2020).

3.2.7 Quantitative

Quantitative reasoning involves the process of solving problems, and drawing conclusions grounded in numerical data and mathematical principles. It necessitates critical thinking and the utilization of mathematical tools to analyze information effectively. Quantitative reasoning entails employing numerical methods to comprehend and address challenges, reflecting a mindset that seeks patterns and order even in unfamiliar contexts (Ryan and Gass 2017).

3.2.8 Emotion

Emotion represents a complex and layered phenomenon that involves awareness, physical sensations, and actions. It mirrors the subjective significance we assign to various stimuli, experiences, or circumstances. Emotions manifest as sensations that influence our perceptions and are associated with either discomfort or satisfaction as a result of decisions (Solomon 1977).

3.2.9 Social interaction

Social interactions serve as mirrors reflecting and unveiling the spontaneous behaviours of individuals, their tendencies to gravitate towards or shy away from certain situations, and the unique manner in which they engage with others (Mehl *et al* 2006). These interactions encompass a spectrum of exchanges, conversations, and engagements that contribute to shaping our comprehension of both ourselves and others. Through these interactions, we gain insights into the intricacies of personality and cultivate our individual identities (German and Robbins 2020).

3.2.10 Actuation

Actuation in the context of human physiology refers to the process by which muscles generate forces to produce movement. This actuation involves complex interactions between the nervous system and muscular system (McRuer *et al* 1968). It involves physical skills that manipulate objects, use of tools and navigation (Goertzel 2014).

3.2.11 Knowledge building/creation

Knowledge building in the context of psychology refers to the process through which individuals or groups acquire, create, share, and use knowledgeto understand phenomena, solve problems, and expand their cognitive abilities (Gan and Zhu 2007, Scardamalia and Bereiter 2006). Knowledge building or creation of knowledge building emphasizes the active, verbal, invention, physical constructive nature of learning and the importance of social interaction and collaboration in the development of new understandings and skills (Goertzel 2014).

3.2.12 Planning

Planning is a fundamental process across various domains, involving the development of strategies and actions to achieve specific goals (Mintzberg 1981). When considering the context of the tactical, strategic, physical, and social, planning takes on different dimensions and purposes within each framework (Goertzel 2014).

3.2.13 Modelling self and others

Modelling self and others refers to the situation in which individuals develop an understanding of themselves and others through observation, imitation, and internalization of the behaviours, beliefs and attitudes of others (Dowrick 1999, Morin 2006). This process is influenced by social, cultural, and environmental factors and plays a significant role in shaping self-control, empathy, identity and behaviour (Goertzel 2014).

3.2.14 Motivation

Motivation serves as the impetus behind both human and animal behaviours, operating on conscious and subconscious levels to provide purpose and direction. Without motivation, these behaviours would not occur. Additionally, motivation can be defined as an individual's readiness to exert physical or mental effort to achieve a specific goal or objective (Sam 2023).

3.3 Attempt to AGI development via symbolic AI

History has shown that in a race to developing machines that reach human-level intelligence, many approaches were proposed with the aim of developing machines with human-level intelligence. Those approaches on the race to human-level intelligence—AGI from different perspectives compete for supremacy which has led to the introduction of many rival paradigms. The symbolic approach to AI is the representation of items or objects or things in the domain of knowledge via physical symbols, the combination of symbols leading to expressing of symbols, symbolic manipulation as well as symbol expression via an inference process (Smolensky 1987). The aim of symbolic representation is the introduction of reasoning-like stages. The AI system that operates based on symbolic representation operates by performing a series of logic steps similar to the stages involved in reasoning over language like representation. The symbolic representation in a symbolic AI system is in the form of propositions typical in character and establishing the relationship that exists between some objects. Simultaneously, every reasoning stage computes the subsequent set of relations that are derived from the already established relationship. This is performed based on the formally specified sets of inference rules. The symbolic ground problem is the major challenge of symbolic AI (Harnad 1990). Symbolic AI has been the dominant approach to AI development especially in the 20th century. However, currently, artificial neural networks (ANNs), especially deep learning architecture, are on the rise to developing human-level intelligence relegating symbolic AI to the background (Garnelo and Shanahan 2019). The emergence of LLMs is believed to be the major breakthrough in the race to AGI.

3.4 The LLMs tutorial: fundamentals of LLMs

Prior to delving into LLMs, this section elucidates the fundamental building blocks of LLMs. This tutorial aims to provide readers with a foundational understanding and facilitates a more accessible understanding of LLMs. At the core of the LLMs is the transformer architecture, as innovatively introduced by Vaswani *et al* (2017).

3.4.1 Language models

A language model is a probabilistic model that assigns probabilities to sequences of words in a given language. It is trained on a large corpus of text and learns the likelihood of different word sequences occurring in the language. This enables the model to generate text, predict the next word in a sequence, or evaluate the coherence of a given piece of text (Bahl *et al* 1989, Morin and Bengio 2005). N-gram is the commonly used language model for natural language processing (NLP) serving as the first generation language model. The concept of n-grams involves contiguous sequences of n-words in a given text, and is a fundamental concept in NLP and computational linguistics (Brown *et al* 1992, Clark *et al* 2012, Sidorov 2013). While the literature might use the term to denote any co-occurring set of characters in a string, it essentially represents an N-character slice (Cavnar and Trenkle 1994). The n-gram has been the benchmark for NLP before the advent of neural network-based language models (De Mulder *et al* 2015, Li *et al* 2015, Mikolov *et al* 2010, Noaman *et al* 2018, Yang *et al* 2016). A typical example is the famous word2vec framework comprising a continuous bag of words and skip-gram that translates words into a high-dimensional vector for the machine to capture the relationship in nuance semantics. The word2vect framework was developed by Google (Ma and Zhang 2015, Mikolov *et al* 2013). Inherent challenges of the previous language models paved the way for the emergence of pre-trained language models capable of transferable NLP tasks like bidirectional encoder representation from transformers (BERT). BERT is a pre-trained bidirectional representation from an unlabelled text dataset by joining both left and right context throughout the layers under conditioning (Devlin *et al* 2018). BERT is now known as Gemini. Language models exhibit certain limitations, including the difficulty in handling rare or unseen words, challenges associated with overfitting, and the complexity in capturing intricate linguistic phenomena. The limitations of the language models prompted researchers to continue improving the language models for effective and efficient NLP tasks (Chang *et al* 2023). Figure 3.2 depicted the progression of language models from the first generation to LLMs.

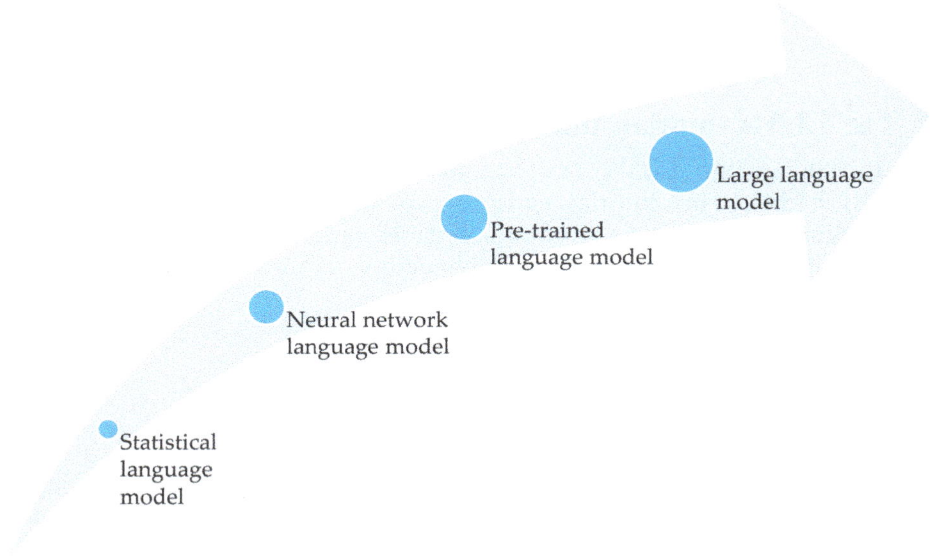

Figure 3.2. The progression of language models to LLMs.

3.4.2 Transformer

The advent of transformer architecture has sparked a revolution in the field of NLP, enabling efficient handling of sequential data by leveraging parallelization and effectively capturing long-range dependencies within text corpora (Tunstall *et al* 2022). Transformer framework consisting of the following building blocks: attention mechanism, encoder–decoder, embedding layers, softmax operation, positional encoding, and step-wise feed-forward neural networks. The transformer progresses through its architectural stages by implementing stacked self-attention and point-wise operations. In both the encoder and decoder, fully connected layers are present as visible on the right and left sides of the transformer architecture (Vaswani *et al* 2017).

3.4.2.1 Position-wise feed-forward networks

Apart from the attention sublayers, every layer within both the encoder and decoder incorporates a fully connected feed-forward neural network. This network operates independently on each position, applying two linear transformations separated by a *ReLU* activation function. Although the linear transformations remain consistent across various positions, they employ distinct parameters from one layer to another (Vaswani *et al* 2017). Refer to chapter 5 (section 5.2.4) for basic operations and architecture of the feed-forward neural network.

3.4.2.2 Basics of encoder–decoder

Basically, the encoder–decoder comprises two phases, namely encoding and decoding. At the encoding phase, the input dataset x fed into the network is transformed to the h layer which is the hidden layer through an encoding function f as expressed in the equation 3.1 (Zhang *et al* 2018):

$$h = f(W^{(1)}x + b^{(1)}) \tag{3.1}$$

At the decoding phase, h is reconstructed to the original input represented by y expressed as:

$$y = g(W^{(2)}h + b^{(2)}) \tag{3.2}$$

Both the encoding and decoding are typically nonlinear mapping functions. The four commonly adopted activation functions are as follows:

$$\text{Sigmoid}\, f(x) = \frac{1}{1 + e^{-x}} \tag{3.3}$$

$$\tanh f(x) = \frac{(e^{x} - e^{-x})}{(e^{x} + e^{-x})} \tag{3.4}$$

$$\text{Softsign}\, f(x) = \frac{x}{(1 + |x|)} \tag{3.5}$$

Rectifier linear unit $ReLu\, f(x) = \max\ (0,\ x)$

The parameter set of the encoder–decoder is $\theta = \{W^{(1)}, b^{(1)} + W^{(2)}, b^{(2)}\}$ typically trained by minimizing j_θ as the loss function with training samples m expressed as:

$$j_\theta = \frac{1}{m}\sum_{i=1}^{m}(y^{(i)} - x^{(i)})^2 \tag{3.6}$$

The ith training sample is represented by the $x^{(i)}$. An unsupervised learning approach is used for the training of the encoder–decoder parameters. The h of the encoder–decoder is viewed as the features extracted or hidden representation of the x. Encoder–decoder is interpreted as a strategy for data compression if the size of h is smaller compared to the size of x. To avoid overfitting in the encoder–decoder, regularization referred to as the weight decay is combined with the loss function, thus, expressed as (Zhang *et al* 2018):

$$j_\theta = \frac{1}{m}\sum_{i=1}^{m}(y^{(i)} - x^{(i)})^2 + \lambda\sum_{j=1}^{2}\| W^{(j)}\| \tag{3.7}$$

The strength of the weight decay is control by the hyper-parameter λ (Zhang *et al* 2018).

3.4.2.3 Encoder and decoder transformer architecture

The encoder consists of a stack of $N = 6$ identical layers, each comprising two sublayers. The first sub-layer involves a multi-head self-attention mechanism, while the second sub-layer is a fully connected position-wise feed-forward neural network. The primary role of the encoder is to tokenize the input text data. The self-attention layer generates hidden states to capture the contextual meaning of the text. On the other hand, there is the decoder: similar to the encoder, the decoder consists of a stack of $N = 6$ identical layers. However, the decoder consists of a third layer in addition to the two sublayers in every layer of the encoder. It is the third sub-layer that performs the multi-head attention on the output of the encoder stack. Residual connection is employed similar to that of the encoder around every sub-layer followed by the normalization layer. The self-attention in the decoder was modified for the prevention of positions from attending to the next positions. This ensures that the predicted position i only depends on known outputs at the position that is less than the i as a result of the masking combining the output embedding offsetting one position. The encoder takes the encoded input and output embedding, then generates the NLP text predicting the subsequent word according to the context learned during training using the multiple layers of the decoders (Vaswani *et al* 2017). However, the GPT series used causal decoder transformer architecture integrating a unidirectional attention mask (Brown *et al* 2020). GLM-130B used the prefix decoder transformer architecture also referred to as the non-causal decoder architecture; it reverses the masking in the causal decoder for bidirectional attention (Zeng *et al* 2022).

3.4.2.4 Normalization and activation function

Normalization technique is used for the stabilization of the ANN training. The transformer architecture deployes layer normalization technique to perform layer-wise normalization in place of the commonly used batch normalization in view of the fact that batch normalization typically suffered from handling sequential data with variable lengths. In layer-wise normalization computation is performed to re-scale and re-centre the activation (Ba *et al* 2016). Then, positioning of the normalization is also critical, it is categorized into three, post-layer-wise normalization: this normalization is positioned between residual blocks. Secondly, (Ba *et al* 2016) pre-layer-wise normalization: this normalization is positioned before each sub-layer and before the last prediction. Thirdly, sandwich layer-wise normalization is based on pre-layer-wise normalization and involves adding additional layer-wise normalization before the residual connection to prevent the explosion of values in the layer output of the transformer (Zeng *et al* 2022). The activation function is required to be set in the transformer feed-forward neural networks to provide good performance. Many variants of the activation functions are available for adoption.

3.4.2.5 Self-attention

In self-attention, h attention heads are used by the sublayers. The output from the heads is combined to create the output of the sublayers, subsequently, parameterized linear transformation is used. The input sequence is used by each of the attention heads to operate. Thus, an input sequence $x = \{x_1,\ldots,xn\}$ of elements n in which $x_i \in \mathbb{R}^{dx}$. The computation of the new sequence is performed as $z = \{z_1,\ldots,z_n\}$ for the same length where $z_i \in \mathbb{R}^{dz}$. The computation of every output of the element z_i is performed as the weighted sum of linear transformation of input elements expressed as (Shaw *et al* 2018):

$$z_i = \sum_{j=1}^{n} \alpha_{ij}(x_j W^V) \tag{3.8}$$

Sufficient expressive power is added to the inputs by the linear transformation. Each of α_{ij} of the weight coefficient is computed by an activation function, softmax as:

$$\alpha_{ij} = \frac{e^{\beta_{ij}}}{\sum_{k=1}^{n} e^{\beta_{ik}}} \tag{3.9}$$

For efficient computation, the compatibility function (scaled dot product) is added for the computation of β_{ij} for comparing two input elements expressed as (Shaw *et al* 2018):

$$\beta_{ij} = \frac{(x_i W^Q)(x_j W^K)^T}{\sqrt{d_z}} \tag{3.10}$$

The parameter matrices distinctive to each of the layers and attention are as follows: $W^Q,\ W^K,\ \ W^V\ \in \mathbb{R}^{dx \times dz}$ (Shaw *et al* 2018).

3.4.2.6 Multi-head attention

An attention function is the process that maps a query and a set of key-value pairs to an output, where all components—query, keys, values, and output—are vectors. The output is calculated as a weighted sum of the values, and the weights assigned to each value are determined by a compatibility function that considers the relationship between the query and the corresponding key. With the attention mechanism 'scaled dot-product attention', the input includes queries and keys with a dimension of *dk*, along with values having a dimension of *dv*. The dot product is calculated between the query and all keys, scaling each result by dividing by the square root of *dk*, and subsequently applying a softmax function to derive the weights assigned to the values. For the multi-head attention: instead of executing a single attention function with *dmodel-dimensional* keys, values, and queries, it has been discovered to be advantageous to project the queries, keys, and values linearly *h* times. These linear projections involve learned parameters and transform the queries to dimensions *dk*, keys to dimensions *dk*, and values to dimensions *dv*, respectively. The attention function is then applied in parallel to each of these projected versions of queries, keys, and values, resulting in output values of dimension *dv* (Vaswani *et al* 2017).

3.4.2.7 Embedding, softmax and positional encodings

Like other sequence transduction models, the transformer employs learned embedding to transform input tokens and output tokens into vectors of dimension *dmodel.* A standard learned linear transformation and *Softmax* function are applied to convert the decoder output for predicting the subsequent token probabilities. In the transformer architecture, 'positional encodings' are incorporated into the input embeddings at the base of both the encoder and decoder stacks. These positional encodings share the same dimension (dmodel) as the embeddings, enabling them to be summed together. This design choice is made due to the absence of recurrence and convolution in the transformer model, allowing it to leverage the sequence order. In simple terms, the positional encoding assists the transformer to understand the order of the words contained in a sentence by allocating numerical values to the respective positions (Vaswani *et al* 2017).

3.4.3 Reinforcement learning

Reinforcement learning from human feedback (RLFHF) plays a crucial role in LLMs. To provide readers with a better understanding of RLFHF, let's first delve into the fundamentals of the reinforcement learning model. This will pave the way for a more insightful discussion on the RLFHF and makes the chapter self-contained.

In modelling reinforcement learning, an agent is typically connected to its immediate environment through perception and actions. The agent interacts with the enviornment, in every interaction with the enviornment the agent accepts an *input* indicating its current *state* within the environment. An *action* is chosen by the agent for generating an *output*. The state of the environment is changed by an action. The scaler *reinforcement signal* is used to communicate the value of the state transition to the agent. The agent's behaviour ought to prioritize actions that are inclined to enhance the cumulative value of the reinforcement signal over the long term. The agent can learn the process for a certain period of time through trial and error systematically guided by different variants of algorithms (Kaelbling *et al* 1996). The reinforcement learning can be described as the Markov decision process comprising a set of states, actions, transition dynamics, instant reward function and discount factor (Arulkumaran *et al* 2017). Most of the learning algorithms for the Markov decision process perform optimal policy computation by learning the value function. Value functions are typically defined for desired policies. We assume we have a policy π and the value of a *state* s is under π expressed by $V^{\pi}(s)$ as the expected return starting in s followed by π. The infinite zone discounted model is used as in equation (3.11) (Van Otterlo and Wiering 2012):

$$V^{\pi}(s) = E_{\pi}\left\{\sum_{k=0}^{\infty}\gamma^{k}r_{t} + k \mid s_{t} = s\right\} \tag{3.11}$$

The expected return is defined by the value function expressed as $Q: S \times A \rightarrow \mathbb{R}$ taking action a and follows π thereafter:

$$Q^{\pi}(s, a) = E_{\pi}\left\{\sum_{k=0}^{\infty}\gamma^{k}r_{t} + k \mid s_{t} = s, a_{t} = a\right\} \tag{3.12}$$

The value function typically satisfies certain properties of the recursive. Thus, equation (3.11) can be recursively expressed in the Bellman equation:

$$V^{\pi}(s) = E_{\pi}\{r_{t} + \gamma r_{t+1} + \gamma^{2}r_{t+2} + \gamma^{3}r_{t+3} + \ldots \mid s_{t} = t\}$$

$$V^{\pi}(s) = E_{\pi}\{r_{t} + \gamma V^{\pi}(s_{t+1}) \mid s_{t} = s\}$$

$$V^{\pi}(s) = \sum_{s'} T\ (s, \pi\ (s), s')(R(s, a, s') + \gamma V^{\pi}(s')) \tag{3.13}$$

The unique solution for the sets of the equations is V^{π}, for a given π the V^{π} is distinctive and different π can have a value function that is the same. Always the aim of Markov decision process is to arrive at the best π having the maximum number of rewards. Therefore, the maximizing equation (3.14) value function is for all $\in S$. The optimal π is defined by π^* expressed as $V^{\pi*}(s) \geqslant V^{\pi}(s) \ \forall \ s \in S$ and for all π. Now proving that the optimal solution ($V^* = V^{\pi}$) satisfies the following equation expressed as (Van Otterlo and Wiering 2012):

$$V^*(s) = \max_{a \in A} \sum_{s'} T \ (s, \pi\ (s), s')(R(s, a, s') + \gamma V^*(s')) \tag{3.14}$$

The following rule is applied for the selection of optimal action given the value function V^*

$$\pi^*(s) = \arg\max_{a} \sum_{s' \in S} T \ (s, a, s')(R(s, a, s') + \gamma V^*(s')) \tag{3.15}$$

This policy greedily selects the optimal action based on the value function, thus, it is referred to as the greedy policy defined by $\pi_{\text{greedy}}(V)$. The analogous best state a is expressed as:

$$Q^*(s, a) = \sum_{s'} T \ (s, a, s')(R(s, a, s') + \gamma \max_{a^*} Q^*(s', a^*)) \tag{3.16}$$

The relationship between Q^* and the V^* is expressed as:

$$Q^*(s, a) = \sum_{s' \in S} T \ (s, a, s')(R(s, a, s') + \gamma V^*(s'))$$

$$V^*(s) = \max_{a} Q^*(s, a) \tag{3.17}$$

By substituting equation (3.16) into equation (3.17) the expression becomes:

$$V^*(s) = \max_{a} \sum_{s'} T \ (s, a, s')(R(s, a, s') + \gamma \max_{a^*} Q^*(s', a^*))$$

The best selection can be simplified analogously to equation (3.15)

$$\pi^*(s) = \arg\max_{a} Q^*(s, a) \tag{3.18}$$

In essence, the optimal course of action is the one with the best probable utility, considering the potential outcomes of the subsequent states resulting from undertaking that particular action (Van Otterlo and Wiering 2012).

3.4.3.1 Reinforcement learning from human feedback

Humans have the possibility of knowing any number of diverse best actions in a state (Griffith *et al* 2013). The RLHF serves as a potent instrument for empowering LLMs to effectively execute tasks within intricate environments. RLHF entails gathering data from human preferences, training a reward model based on this data, and optimizing the underlying machine learning model according to the reward for assessment purposes. It operates under the premise that human preferences are effectively captured by the reward model, and that the reinforcement learning optimizer can accurately extract the appropriate signal from this model, among other assumptions (Lambert and Calandra 2023). The LLMs are typically trained based on the objective of language modelling on a large-scale dataset corpus. As a result of that, the subjective and qualitative output evaluation of the LLM by humans cannot be taken into account at the pre-training stage. The aligning of the LLM with human values and preferences strongly requires high-quality human feedback. The RLHF is employed for the fine-tuning of LLMs to ensure it is in alignment to human values and preferences such as ethics and morals as well as safety. The RLHF adopts the reinforcement learning algorithm such as proximal policy optimization for adapting the LLMs to human feedback by learning the model of the reward, thereby, integrating humans in the training lifecycle of the LLMs to ensure it is in alignment to human values (Schulman *et al* 2017). The three major approaches to collecting feedback and preferences from human labellers are ranked-based approach, question-based approach and ruled-based approach. The lifecycle of the RLHF is depicted in figure 3.3 (Zhao *et al* 2023).

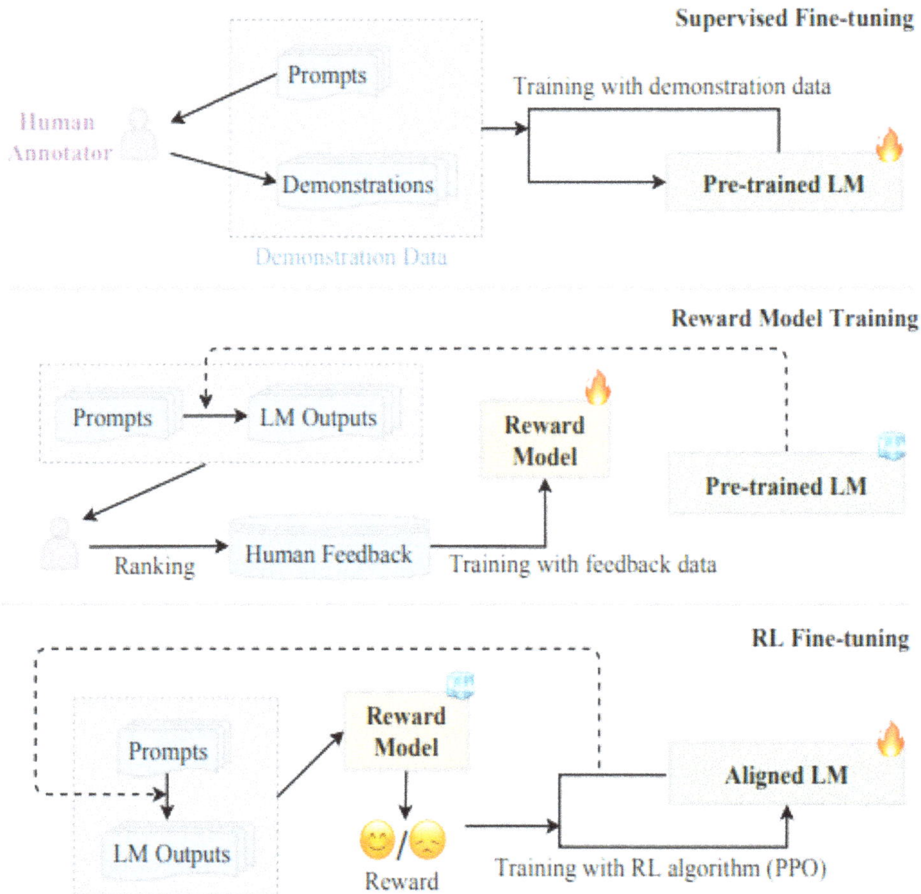

Figure 3.3. The flow of reinforcement learning with human feedback. Reprinted from Zhao *et al* (2023).

3.5 Developing large language models from the scratch

The LLMs are transformer-based language models representing a breakthrough in NLP, characterized by exceptional learning capabilities. They are typically trained on massive volumes of data, boasting parameters numbering in the hundreds of billions or more. LLMs excel in understanding natural language and executing tasks across diverse domains in complex scenarios (Kalyan 2023). The foundation of LLMs is the transformer architecture, featuring multi-head attention layers within deep neural networks. One of the prominent features of LLMs is their capacity for in-context learning, enabling them to generate text content based on contextual prompts provided by users. This capability empowers LLMs to produce coherent responses within given contexts, making them well-suited for interaction and conversation (Dong *et al* 2022). The RLHF is another significant component of the LLMs for fine-tuning the model using responses generated by humans (Kalyan 2023). Notable examples of LLMs include OpenAI GPT-3, Meta LLaMA, and Google Gemini. LLMs constitute part of the first batch of models that demonstrate capacity to perform multiple tasks across domains proving human-level performance. It is found that a number of neurons have a relationship with cognitive abilities, which is relevant for the LLMs like GPT 1 and 3. The text data used for training GPT-2 was 40 GB and generated 1.5 billion parameters. The improved version of GPT-2, GPT-3, was trained with 570 GB text data. The number of parameters generated by GPT-3 makes it possible to outperform GPT-2 in performance across multiple complex language tasks. The number of parameters in GPT-3 indicates a significant increase from 1.5 billion parameters of the GPT-2. GPT-3 achieved human-level performance in some language tasks such as translation, question-answering, and completion of text (Zhao *et al* 2023). The different stages involved in the development of LLMs from scratch is discussed in different sections as follows.

3.5.1 Datasets

This is the initial stage involved in the development of LLMs in view of the fact that data plays a key role in developing LLMs. The procedure involved in the collection and pre-processing of the data is outlined and discussed in the following subsections.

3.5.1.1 Volume of diverse data and significance

Data serves as the 'lifeblood' of the LLM; without it, the LLM cannot function. Therefore, the importance of data in the development of LLM cannot be overstated, as it forms the foundation for training the model. The LLM relies heavily on large-scale datasets to maximize its pre-trained capacity. Moreover, it necessitates high-quality datasets, as the algorithms depend on such data to generate accurate outputs. Conversely, low-quality datasets undermine algorithm performance. Essentially, the quality of data directly influences algorithm performance. The data required for developing an LLM typically spans a spectrum of diversity, ranging from general to specialized. This diversity enhances the model's ability to address inquiries across various domains, thereby improving its overall generality. In the development of

LLM, the initial phase involves dataset collection and preparation, which demands significant time and attention due to its critical nature. This phase encompasses activities such as identifying dataset sources, collecting data, and pre-processing it to ensure its suitability for training.

3.5.1.2 Data sources and acquisition

Textual data, sourced primarily from the internet, serves as the initial reservoir for LLM development, comprising both general and specialized subjects. Web pages, Wikipedia entries, books and chat logs constitute some of the diverse sources of general textual data. Web page data is acquired through web crawling techniques, while conversational data is collected from public chat forums or social media platforms. The broad spectrum of general text data enhances the model's linguistic understanding and fosters its capacity for generalization. Books data, typically sourced from repositories like Books3 and Bookcorpus2, further enriches the model's training dataset. Additionally, multilingual data is incorporated to equip the model with the ability to comprehend diverse languages beyond the target language, enabling tasks such as multilingual translation, summarization, and question-answering in multiple languages. Researchers typically utilize multilingual corpora such as BLOOM, which encompasses 42 different languages, PaLM with 122 languages, and FLM, balancing English and Chinese content nearly equally. For imbuing the model with scientific comprehension, scientific datasets are incorporated, sourced from papers uploaded to platforms like arXiv, scientific textbooks, mathematics websites, and other repositories of relevant literature. However, due to the intricate nature of mathematical content, specialized tokenization is essential to standardize symbols and notations, ensuring uniformity and compatibility with the LLM's processing capabilities. Additionally, for the LLM to synthesize and generate source code, it necessitates training with code corpora, obtainable from public repositories such as GitHub and programming community platforms like Stack Exchange (Zhao *et al* 2023). Similarly, data can be collected from benchmark data corpora. If acquiring data becomes challenging, synthetic data can be created with defined characteristics. When facing data scarcity, data augmentation techniques can be employed to expand the dataset by incorporating synthetic data. The extensive collection of datasets during this phase constituted a raw data corpus. Gathering such a vast amount of data inevitably includes redundancies, irrelevant information, and low-quality data. Consequently, refining the raw data corpus demands rigorous data engineering efforts to ensure its quality and usefulness.

3.5.2 Feature engineering

During this phase, the vast and varied datasets collected in the data collection phase undergo pre-processing to enhance data quality, preparing it for training. Pre-processing stages encompass quality filtering, tokenization, de-duplication, and privacy reduction.

3.5.2.1 Quality filtering

To filter out low-quality texts, a classifier trained on high-quality curated text is employed, distinguishing between positive instances (indicating high quality) and negative ones (indicating low quality). This method, known as the classifier-based approach, may introduce bias by potentially excluding high-quality text in dialectal, colloquial, and sociolectal languages. Alternatively, the heuristic method establishes rules tailored to the study's objectives. For instance, text filtering may focus on languages relevant to the target LLM, while unnatural sentences are identified and removed using perplexity, a process termed the matric-based method, as it utilizes evaluation matrices on generated texts. Keyword-based filtering techniques employ keywords to weed out undesired elements such as HTML, offensive language, hyperlinks, and boilerplate text. Additionally, a statistical approach entails excluding low-quality data by assessing text quality based on punctuation distribution, sentence length, and symbol-to-word ratio. Researchers commonly employ these two approaches for identifying and eliminating low-quality texts (Raiaan *et al* 2024, Zhao *et al* 2023).

3.5.2.2 De-duplication

In the context of data pre-processing, duplication refers to the repetition of sentences, documents, and datasets within the training data corpus, occurring at various levels of granularity. Consequently, duplicate words and phrases within sentences should be eliminated, while metrics like overlap ratio (e.g., words and n-grams) are commonly utilized to identify and remove duplicate documents with identical content. Moreover, it's essential to ensure that training and testing datasets remain distinct by excluding any potential duplicates between them to prevent data overlap, which can contaminate the evaluation results. Duplicate data can destabilize model training and ultimately degrade performance (Cha *et al* 2023, Tirumala *et al* 2023).

3.5.2.3 Privacy reduction

The data corpus may contain private information belonging to individuals, particularly when sourced from social media platforms or online discussion forums. Utilizing this data without adequate privacy safeguards can result in breaches of individual data privacy. Individuals whose private information is used without consent and exposed to the public may initiate legal action to challenge such privacy violations. As a consequence, significant efforts must be made to reduce privacy within the data corpus to conceal sensitive private information and mitigate potential legal challenges akin to those encountered by OpenAI, Microsoft, Google, and Meta. Guo *et al* (2023) explained that the LLM has the possibility of leaking private data. Therefore, Laurençon *et al* (2022) suggested that the rule-based method using keywords can be used to identify personal identification information like addresses, names, phone numbers and emails from the data corpus to exclude the personal identification information (Laurençon *et al* 2022, Tang *et al* 2023).

3.5.2.4 Tokenization

This is the procedure of breaking down texts into tokens (smaller unit of text e.g., word or subword or character) (Webster and Kit 1992). The tokenization converts the text to vectors suitable for the LLM to process. Many open-source tools are available for tokenization, including Pattern Word Tokenize, Nlpdotnet Tokenizer, TextBlob Word Tokenize, Mila Tokenizer, MBSP Word Tokenize, and Word Tokenization with Python NLTK, as highlighted by Vijayarani and Janani (2016). There are different approaches to tokenization including but not limited to word based, uni-gram, WordPiece and byte-pair encoding tokenization. However, Zhao *et al* (2023) argued that the word based tokenization is the commonly adopted tokenization method in the research community. The byte-pair encoding is used for improving the quality of tokenization for a multilingual corpus. For example, the byte-pair encoding considers bytes for text without ASCII character as the fundamental symbols for merging. LLMs like GPT-2, BART, and LLaMA used the byte-pair encoding tokenization. Models like T5 and mBART adopted uni-gram, whereas BERT adopted WordPiece tokenization (Raiaan *et al* 2024, Zhao *et al* 2023).

3.5.3 Automated large language models data pre-processing systems

Considering the significance of pre-processing large volumes of heterogeneous data quality in developing LLMs, an automated LLMs data pre-processing system called data-juicer has been developed. This system is a one-stop point for data pre-processing, unlike other systems that are mainly tailored towards specific tasks. The system has the capacity to generate different recipes of data efficiently, perform a variety of data mixtures as candidates for selection by the user, and it has a module for measuring the impact of the diverse data mixtures on the performance of the model (Chen *et al* 2023). The system has more than 50 different operators and tools for LLMs data pre-processing, equipped with interactive visualization feedback loops and automated evaluation. The system is incorporated with a data-centric approach for LLMs data pre-processing and development. The automated pre-processing system is equipped with a user-centric user interface design to provide access to users at all levels, thereby democratizing the pre-processing of large-scale heterogeneous data for LLMs development. The pre-training and fine-tuning phases of the LLMs can benefit from the automated data pre-processing system, as both phases require data pre-processing. Empirical work has demonstrated that the data pre-processing automated system pre-processes raw data and produces high-quality data ready to improve LLM development and showcase improved performance of the system (Chen *et al* 2023).

3.5.4 Scheduling data for pre-training

The dataset described in prior sections reveals a collection from diverse sources, each with its unique format, necessitating preparation for pre-training focussing on two key aspects: data mixture and data curriculum. Data mixture involves blending various data sources in differing proportions during pre-training. This entails adjusting proportions globally and locally throughout pre-training stages, with data of higher significance receiving greater weight. Techniques such as up-sampling or down-sampling may be employed for each dataset source to achieve an appropriate data mixture. For instance, allocating percentages across web pages, books, news data, conversations, scientific data, and source code may vary depending on the target LLM's purpose. While general-purpose LLMs may leverage diverse sources, specialized LLMs concentrate on specific domains, like AlphaCode, which exclusively utilizes source code data. However, Llama predominantly utilizes web pages (over 80%), allocating smaller percentages to code (6.5%), scientific data (2.5%), and books (4.5%). Also, GPT-3 relies heavily on web pages (84%) and conversational data (16%). Various strategies ensure an appropriate data mixture, including diversifying data sources to enhance LLM generalization while reducing diversity diminishes it. Moreover, experiments with different mixtures on smaller scale models help identify the optimal mixture for superior generalization before large-scale deployment. Additionally, to bolster specific capabilities, the data mixture must align with LLM specialization. For instance, LLMs targeting mathematical reasoning and coding benefit from predominantly mathematical and source code datasets, necessitating a multi-stage training approach known as data curriculum. This involves initially training with generalized data before transitioning to specialized data, enhancing skill acquisition compared to direct training solely on specialized data (Zhao *et al* 2023).

3.5.5 Transformer architecture and hyper-parameter settings

Prior to pre-training, it is necessary to configure the hyper-parameters for each transformer component. However, there's no one-size-fits-all procedure or fixed settings for these hyper-parameters to ensure optimal performance across different domains. Consequently, developers typically rely on trial and error, preliminary experiments, or adopt settings from prior studies. The central component of the LLM is the transformer, as already discussed. The transformer architecture can vary, with options including encoder–decoder, prefix decoder, or causal decoder, depending on the developer's preference and objective of the study. The step involves selecting a normalization technique from options like root mean square normalization, batch normalization, layer-wise normalization, and deep normalization. Once a suitable normalization technique is chosen, the next consideration is its positioning—whether it occurs post-normalization, pre-normalization, or in a sandwich configuration. Following normalization, attention turns to choosing an activation function for the feed-forward network. The literature offers a range of options, including but not limited to ReLU, GeLU, GeGLU, Swish, and SwiGLU. Position embedding is also essential, with choices such as absolute position embedding (with sinusoidal or learned variants), ALiBi, relative, and rotary embedding. Attention mechanisms are critical aspects of the transformer and require careful configuration. Various types of attention are available, including full attention, multi-query attention, sparse attention, PagedAttention, and FlashAttention, these are available as choices. Number of network layers, number of attention heads and bias are required to be set for the architecture. For example, GPT-3 used causal decoder transformer architecture, pre-layer normalization, learned position embedding, both number of layers and number of heads were 96, used bias and activation function: GeLu (Zhao *et al* 2023). GPT-3 generated 175 billion parameters making it powerful to outperform the earlier GPT-2 with 1.5 billion parameters as the number of parameters is the critical factor determining the cognitive abilities of LLMs, the more the parameters the more the memory the model possesses and the more the sophistication of the tasks it can perform (Zhao *et al* 2023).

3.5.5.1 Training: pre-training the large language model

The optimization settings for LLM pre-training have no systematic framework to automatically generate the optimal settings for the model. It is an 'art-work' where preliminary experiments can be conducted to determine the suitable settings or adopt values from previous studies. However, the settings that work for a certain model do not necessarily perform well in another model with different datasets, which is why different models have different optimization settings as evident with different LLMs.

The hyper-parameter settings required to be set before running the LLM for pre-training are as follows: learning rate increases the training speed, usually set to value less than 1.0. Batch size improves the throughput and training, typically the batch size is set with large values running into millions for language models either static or dynamic values. Optimizer is used for the training of the model, the commonly used optimizer is Adam. To avoid training instability which can lead to the collapse of the training, the gradient clipping and weights decay are used to ensure that the training is stabilized (Zhao *et al* 2023). Dropout is set to avoid the model overfitting the dropout operates by randomly dropping out neurons during training. The value of the dropout is typically very small, less than 1 (Bishop and Bishop 2023). Decay method adjusts the learning rate during training gradually to prevent rapid decreasing of learning rate or maintaining equilibrium for a long time for the learning rate (Ding 2021). Warmup: the warmup increases learning rate gradually (Shi *et al* 2021). Gradient clipping stabilizes training and deviates from gradient exploding (Mai and Johansson 2021). For example, BLOOM model has 4 million batch size, decay method: cosine set to 0.1, learning rate set to 6×10^{-5}, Adam optimizer is used, weight decay set to 0.1, warmup is used, gradient clipping and dropout were 1.0 and 0, respectively (Zhao *et al* 2023).

3.5.6 Evaluating the large language model

Besides the risk of potential personal identification information leaks, the LLM may generate inappropriate, harmful, misleading, or false content. To prioritize safety and harness the capabilities of the LLM effectively, it is imperative to subject it to thorough and critical evaluation processes (Guo *et al* 2023). Understanding the strengths and weaknesses of the LLM through evaluation is crucial. Such assessment can inform constructive human–LLM interaction, potentially inspiring improved design and implementation in the future. Evaluation can ensure safety and reliability across the spectrum of the LLM's capabilities (Chang *et al* 2023). Given the increasing adoption of LLMs in safety-critical contexts and decision-making processes, evaluating the robustness of these systems becomes paramount (Zhu *et al* 2023). OpenAI conducted a six-month evaluation of GPT-4 to ensure its alignment with human intentions (Liu *et al* 2023). The three major aspects that the LLM is expected to evaluate are: alignment to human values; knowledge and capabilities; and safety (Chang *et al* 2023).

3.5.6.1 Alignment

Despite the remarkable generality exhibited by LLMs, they still face challenges related to alignment, including human annotator bias, hallucination, and the need to cater to human values (Chang *et al* 2023, Guo *et al* 2023). Trained LLMs often capture characteristics from both high-quality and low-quality data corpora, which raises concerns about the potential for generating toxic, harmful, or biased content. Therefore, it is imperative to align LLMs rigorously with human values such as helpfulness, honesty, and harmlessness (Zhao *et al* 2023). Consequently, comprehensive alignment evaluations are necessary to ensure that developed LLMs meet alignment requirements. These evaluations are conducted from various perspectives, as discussed below (Guo *et al* 2023).

3.5.6.1.1 Ethics and morality

The fundamental objective of conducting ethical and moral evaluations is to verify whether the output produced by LLM adheres to establish ethical principles and possesses the capability to align with them (Rathje 2024). These evaluations are organized into four categories based on distinct criteria. Firstly, they involve assessing the ethical and moral standards defined by professionals practicing. Generally, every professional field maintains its own set of ethical standards that practitioners are expected to uphold, encompassing areas like social media, social sciences, and politics. When evaluating the ethics and morality of LLM, datasets such as Social Chemistry 101 and the Moral Foundations Twitter Corpus, which reflect moral foundation theory, can be utilized. Second is crowd-sourced ethics and morals, in this category, ethics and morals defined in this manner, are determined solely by crowd-sourced workers who assess them based on personal preferences, devoid of professional guidance or formal training. Moral judgement passed by social media users and interview can be used for evaluating LLM on this category of ethics and morals. Thirdly, AI-assisted ethics and morals: this involves the AI helping humans in categorizing ethics or creating a dataset. It has been found that curating datasets using LLM is promising. For example, GPT-3 is used for the coining of dialogue statements in PROSOCIALDIALOG dialogue datasets that respond to toxic content based on social norms. Fourthly, hybrid ethics and morality: this involved the combination of data from two sources, namely, from ethics guidelines developed by the crowd and those developed by experts (Guo *et al* 2023).

3.5.6.1.2 *Bias*

In the context of LLM, bias refers to the content generated by the model that is considered harmful to some social groups, such as stereotyping, devaluing, underrepresentation, and inequality in sharing resources, thus, addressing these biases is crucial (Chang *et al* 2023, Dai *et al* 2024). Evidence indicates the existence of bias in LLMs, it is expected that LLMs be evaluated by detecting, measuring, and adapting before deployment to ensure they do not produce biased content. The datasets for measuring LLM bias include StereoSet, which includes prediction tests of intra-sentential and inter-sentential on each of the following biases (Guo *et al* 2023):

(i) Race;
(ii) Religion;
(iii) Profession;
(iv) Gender.

Another dataset is the CrowS-Pairs covering the following biases:

(i) Nationality;
(ii) Disability;
(iii) Appearance;
(iv) Race;
(v) Gender;
(vi) Sexual orientation;
(vii) Religion;
(viii) Age;
(ix) Socio-economic status or profession.

3.5.6.1.3 *Toxicity*

Due to the extensive data utilized in training LLMs, there's a significant possibility of encountering toxic behaviour and unsafe content, including but not limited to pornography, offensive language, and hate speech (Chang *et al* 2023). Consequently, it is imperative to assess LLMs for their ability to address such toxic content effectively. Datasets such as the Social Bias Inference Corpus, Civility, and HateXplain are commonly employed to evaluate LLMs' proficiency in identifying and classifying toxic content. However, there remains a possibility for LLMs to generate toxic language or sentences themselves. To evaluate the toxicity of LLMs, RealToxicityPrompts serves as a resource for generating and assessing toxic content (Guo *et al* 2023).

3.5.6.1.4 *Truthfulness*

The LLM has showcased remarkable proficiency in generating text in natural language, producing content that rivals human-authored text in terms of coherence and fluency. This impressive capability has opened up opportunities for adopting LLMs across different domains, including education (Chang *et al* 2023). However, despite its exceptional performance, the LLM is susceptible to fabricating fake content, incorporating non-existent references, and disseminating misleading information. This undermines the reliability of the LLM, thereby impeding its full deployment potential in fields such as finance, medicine, banking, and law (Liu *et al* 2023, Rawte *et al* 2023).

It is imperative to assess the content generated by LLMs to ensure its truthfulness, accuracy, and reliability. Datasets used for evaluating the truthfulness of LLMs can be classified into three main categories. Firstly, question-answering datasets such as NewsQA, SQuAD 2.0, and BIG-bench are utilized to evaluate the LLM's ability to provide truthful answers to questions. Secondly, dialogue datasets including Wizard-of-Wikipedia dataset, PersonaChat dataset, and ConsisTest benchmark are employed to assess the factual consistency of LLMs in open discussions. Lastly, summarization datasets such as SummEval, XSumFaith, and FactCC are utilized to verify the factual content of the summarized content generated by LLMs (Guo *et al* 2023). These evaluations help ensure the reliability and accuracy of LLM-generated content across various contexts and applications. Methods for evaluating the truthfulness of LLMs encompass various approaches. One method involves natural language inference, which examines the logical relationship between two pieces of text. Another approach is question-answering-based, which assesses the factual consistency between two text segments. Additionally, there's an LLM-based method that utilizes the LLM to gauge the quality of generated text when provided with appropriate prompts. These diverse evaluation methods contribute to a comprehensive assessment of the truthfulness and reliability of LLM-generated content (Chang *et al* 2023).

3.5.6.2 Safety

The safe of the LLM is assessed to ensure its robustness by measuring its resistance during disruption, and risk associated to the LLM is measured by evaluating the general-purpose behaviour of the LLM. This is to ensure that the LLM engages users safely, so the output should not be violent, hateful, harmful to minors, violate privacy or operate unlawful conduct (Liu *et al* 2023).

3.5.6.2.1 Robustness

Robustness is believed to be one of the significant aspects of LLMs to evaluate. Robustness gives the LLM ability to withstand attacks and maintain consistent performance (Chang *et al* 2023, Wang *et al* 2022). The robustness can be viewed from three different perspectives: *Prompt robustness*: evaluating the capacity of the LLM to withstand adversarial prompt attacks e.g., PromptBench is used for the evaluation of the prompt robustness and ability of the LLM to manage prompt typographical errors. In this case, the LLM is prompted to generate a prompt with typographical errors, subsequently, prompt the LLM with typographical errors to find out the impact of the typos on the LLM output. *Task robustness*: The LLM is evaluated for task robustness using tasks such as natural language inference, question-answering, translation and text classification. The datasets that can be used for the evaluation of the task prompt include but are not limited to AdvGLUE and ANLI datasets (Guo *et al* 2023). It is assumed that benchmarks for evaluating tasks and prompt robustness represent real-world distribution random samples that can be relied on for evaluating LLM robustness. However, it is inconsistent with the reality of the real-world distribution samples. It varies according to the domain of the use case in the real-world environment. Research findings indicate that the correlation of model performance across evaluation of prompts is not random because of sematic similarity and LLM common failure factors (Siska *et al* 2024). *Alignment robustness*: The LLM has to be aligned to human values, as such, the LLM is evaluated to ensure this is the case. It is found that recent studies have utilized the method of jailbreak to attack LLMs to generate harmful/unsafe behaviour and content. This is the LLM vulnerability that can be exploited to generate jailbreak content based on jailbreak prompts. The LLM is evaluated by prompts for generating content for fraudulent activities, pornography and illegal activities to find out its vulnerability to generating such content (Liu *et al* 2023).

3.5.6.2.2 Risk

The sophistication of the LLM is increasing at a fast rate and it is massively deployed in sensitive applications despite the inherent risk associated with the LLM (Ayyamperumal and Ge 2024). The LLM, as it is approaching human-level intelligence, presents safety risks related to power-seeking behaviour and situational awareness. Hence, it's crucial to develop evaluation tools to evaluate the potential for catastrophic behaviour. The behaviour of the LLM is gauged on various metrics: *Myopia*: Examining whether the LLM prioritizes short-term gains over long-term interests. *Situational Awareness*: Evaluating the LLM's awareness of its own intelligence and components it is made from. *Collaboration*: Evaluating the LLM's willingness to collaborate with other AI systems to achieve common goals, including safeguarding against safety failures. *Decision Theory*: Analyzing whether the LLM's decisions align with principles such as the 'One-box' evidential decision theory. *Environmental Interaction*: Determining if the LLM can function as an agent capable of effectively interacting with its surroundings. AgentBench offers a means to evaluate the LLM's ability to interact with its environment and make decisions, ensuring thorough assessment of its capabilities (Guo *et al* 2023).

3.5.6.3 Knowledge and capabilities

This type of LLM evaluation holds significant importance due to LLM widespread deployment across various application domains. Therefore, assessing the strengths and weaknesses of LLMs in terms of their knowledge and capabilities across multiple tasks and datasets is essential, guided by specific criteria as follows (Peng *et al* 2024).

The primary criterion involves question-answering: the LLM's ability to respond to questions is pivotal as it determines whether the output aligns with expectations. Evaluation datasets for question-answering should encompass a diverse array of sources spanning different fields rather than being limited to a specific domain. Questions posed should be general in nature, rather than strictly professional inquiries. The following datasets are qualified for the question-answering evaluation but not limited to NarrativeQA, HotpotQA and SQuAD. Secondly, knowledge completion is a critical aspect of evaluation aimed at assessing the variety and depth of knowledge within the LLM, particularly as its functions extend beyond those of a general chatbot to encompass more specialized professional tools. Tasks used for LLM evaluation in this regard typically involve knowledge completion or memorization, drawing primarily from existing knowledge bases such as Wikidata, ConceptNet, and SQuAD. These knowledge bases contain both factual information and common-sense knowledge suitable for evaluating the LLM's knowledge completion capabilities. Thirdly, reasoning: reasoning involves the capacity to understand and utilize evidence effectively to support logical conclusions or enhance decision-making processes (Guo *et al* 2023).

Reasoning capability empowers machines and humans to take informed decisions with convincing logical conclusions (Huang and Chang 2022). Reasoning is categorized into four main types: logical reasoning, common sense reasoning, multi-hop reasoning, and mathematical reasoning (Peng *et al* 2024). Common sense reasoning within the LLM is evaluated using datasets and benchmarks with diverse content focusing on various domains of common-sense knowledge. These datasets include, but are not limited to, MCTACO, CommonsenseQA, TIMEDIAL, and OpenBookQA. These datasets typically consist of multiple-choice questions, with performance metrics such as accuracy and F1 score used to evaluate the LLM's ability to acquire common sense knowledge and apply reasoning. Logical reasoning, which involves the ability to critically analyze, examine, and evaluate arguments critically, is evaluated using datasets classified into three categories: natural language inference data (e.g., ConTRoL, MultiNLI, LogicNLI, TaxiNLI), multiple-choice reading comprehension data (e.g., LogiQA, LogiQA 2.0, ReClor), and text generation data (e.g., FOLIO and LogicInference). Multi-hop reasoning is assessed using datasets such as Wikihop, HybridQA, and NarrativeQA. Mathematical reasoning is assessed using datasets such as C-EVAL and GSM8K (Guo *et al* 2023). Tool learning: this is the ability of an intelligent system to manipulate tools for streamlining the solving of problems in the real world. The LLM has the ability to perform tasks by interacting with the real-world environment to manipulate search engines, plan robotics tasks, shopping on ecommerce sites among many others. The tool learning for an intelligent model is classified into tool manipulation and tool creation (Guo *et al* 2023, Qin *et al* 2023).

3.5.6.3.1 Tool manipulation

Tool manipulation refers to the ability of the model to manipulate tools and it is divided into two major categories: *tool augmentation learning* and *tool oriented learning*. In an attempt to manipulate, the LLM can produce output that deviates from the actual goal meaning error, thus, the LLM needs to be evaluated thoroughly on tool manipulation (Xu *et al* 2023). These two approaches for evaluating tool learning of an LLM are evaluated by using tool operation success rate and execution success rate as measures of the model's ability to execute tools and understand them. Firstly, measuring the correctness of the final output, program generated and human expert preference of the model which gives insight into model deeper capabilities. First, *evaluating tool augmentation model* when the model is integrated with API, commonly used datasets are used to measure the performance improvement such as the mathematics problem, reasoning and question-answering in which accuracy, F1, and Rouge-L are commonly used as performance matric. Secondly, *evaluating tool oriented model*, this evaluation is categorized according the tools that the model can control, such as search engine, online shopping, robotics task and code generation. *Search engine*: the use of tool learning to allow the model respond to question by searching the internet. *Online shopping*: training the model to shop from ecommerce site by querying shopping engine. *Robotics task*: In this task the LLM uses the robot arm for executing task by interacting with the environment. *Code generation*: This can be evaluated using RoboCodeGen having 37 tasks for function generation (Guo *et al* 2023).

3.5.6.3.2 Tool creation

This is the situation where the model has the capability of recognizing already existing tools and creating new tools. That is the LLM ability in solving new problems without existing tools for solving the problem (Guo *et al* 2023). The dataset for the evaluation of LLM on tool creation includes but is not limited to the CREATOR dataset presented in Qian *et al* (2023).

3.6 Comparing large language models to machine learning and deep learning

LLMs exhibit distinct characteristics in comparison to traditional machine learning and deep learning approaches. Machine learning typically operates with smaller datasets, and is often trained using shallow learning algorithms, which excel in performance with limited data. However, as dataset size increases, the performance of traditional machine learning tends to degrade. In contrast, deep learning thrives with larger volumes of data, with performance improving as the dataset grows. Hardware requirements for traditional machine learning are generally lower than those for deep learning, which demands high-performance computing due to the complexity of its algorithms and the substantial data volumes required for training. Interpretability is another key difference: traditional machine learning offers better interpretability as it relies on manual feature extraction, whereas deep learning incorporates automatic feature extraction mechanisms, making interpretation more challenging. The LLMs represent an advancement over both traditional machine learning and deep learning, integrating natural language processing mechanisms. However, they require very high hardware resources and extensive training data more than deep learning and machine learning. LLMs excel at performing complex tasks across multiple domains, unlike deep learning and traditional machine learning, which are often specialized to specific domains. The distinctions between LLMs, deep learning, and traditional machine learning, as highlighted by Chang *et al* (2023), are illustrated in figure 3.4.

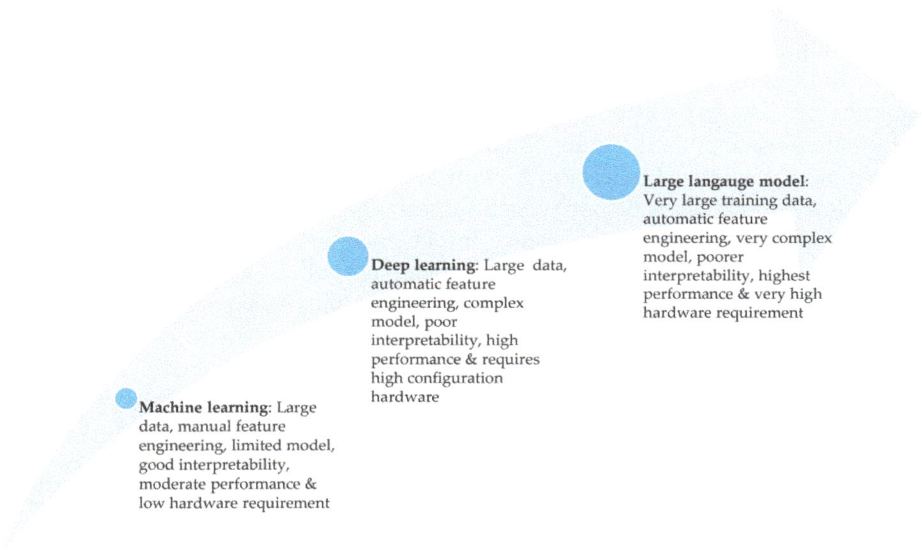

Figure 3.4. Machine learning, deep learning and LLM major differences.

3.7 Artificial general intelligence versus human-level intelligence

The literature on the characteristics that truly constitute AGI systems within the mainstream AI research community lacks a clear consensus. This has led to diverse viewpoints from various research groups and individuals on what defines AGI systems. Consequently, there is no universally accepted definition of AGI systems within the AI research communities in both academia and industry. Morris *et al* (2023) argued that if 100 AI experts were asked to precisely define AGI, it is likely that each of the AI experts would present a different concept of AGI. However, these definitions can exhibit a certain level of correlation, particularly concerning human-level intelligence.

Despite the differences in viewpoints regarding the standard definition of AGI systems, the prevailing perspective is that AGI systems are expected to progress towards human-level intelligence. However, an opposing school of thought questions the possibility of the research community developing a powerful system with the same cognitive abilities and reasoning as that of human-level intelligence. Despite criticisms, many researchers and industry practitioners believe achieving this level of AGI is possible in the near future if the race to AGI continues at its current pace. Due to the lack of consensus on the standard definition of AGI systems, various concepts comparing AGI to human-level intelligence exist. Thus, this section looks at the views of some selected scientists from 1997 to the present, especially with the advent of LLMs.

In studying a system with human-level intelligence, it is crucial to consider the distinction between AGI and the concept of human-level intelligence, which denotes an intelligent system with reasonably comparable cognitive abilities to humans. AGI doesn't specifically refer to a particular human trait; rather, it encompasses general intelligence properties that might be perceived as universal by the AGI. Due to the current limited understanding of general intelligence, determining its specific properties is not straightforward. The interpretation of 'human-level AGI' is complex because it is challenging to categorize all potential system intelligences in a simple hierarchy based solely on human-level intelligence in comparison to AGI systems. Recognizing this disparity, is essential when navigating the complexities of studying systems that aspire to achieve intelligence levels akin to those of humans. To simplify matters, 'human-level AI' is interpreted to mean 'human-level and roughly human-like AGI,' introducing a restriction that enhances the manageability of the concept. When considering AGI systems designed to operate in environments similar to those of humans, employing cognitive processes vaguely akin to those used by humans, the notion of 'human level' becomes relatively straightforward to comprehend. While the concept of 'AGI' is theoretically more foundational than 'human-level AGI,' its very expansiveness can pose challenges. 'Human-level AGI' is more tangible and specific, allowing for easier exploration in certain directions compared to the more general AGI concept (Goertzel 2014).

As soon as AI surpasses humans in the majority of our everyday tasks, it achieves a level of general human-like intelligence. The underlying assumption here is that humans serve as the benchmark for general intelligence, making a practical comparison with human capabilities the most relevant approach for characterizing general intelligence. The psychological perspective on defining general intelligence also centres around human-like cognitive abilities. However, instead of directly assessing practical tasks, this approach seeks to identify the fundamental underlying capabilities that enable these practical skills. In practice, this involves various sub-approaches, presenting a diverse range of perspectives rather than a singular unified viewpoint (Goertzel 2014). Gubrud (1997) described AGI systems as intelligent systems with the capacity to surpass the complexity and speed of the human brain, these systems can accumulate, manipulate, and apply general knowledge for reasoning. They are versatile, can be used across different industries and military operations, particularly in tasks requiring human-like intelligence. Alternatively, Sheridan and Parasuraman (2005) proposed AGI systems as systems that transcend specific jobs, possessing cognitive abilities that enable them to perform a diverse array of tasks akin to human capabilities. Another perspective posits AGI as intelligent systems capable of performing a wide range of tasks reliably and resourcefully, potentially surpassing human intelligence (Marcus 2022). In contrast, Arcas and Norvig (2023) argued that AGI has already been achieved with the emergence of LLMs like ChatGPT, Claude, and Llama 2. They argued that the key property of AGI is generality, and these LLMs exhibit the capability to discuss a wide range of subjects, perform various tasks, handle multimodal inputs and outputs, operate in different languages, and learn with minimal examples. Despite the significance of generality in AGI, Arcas and Norvig (2023) emphasize that it should be considered alongside performance. If LLMs, for example, develop incorrect code or solve mathematical problems inaccurately, their generality might not be considered adequate performant.

Morris *et al* (2023) classified AGI into six categories, ranging from 0 to 5, each reflecting different levels of perception regarding the achievement of AGI. At Level 1, emerging AGI systems are expected to outperform or be comparable to unskilled human workers, a milestone already achieved by the likes of ChatGPT, Gemini, and Llama. Moving to Level 2, competent AGI is anticipated to handle 50% of tasks performed by an adult human with skills. At Level 3, expert AGI should excel in approximately 90% of the tasks carried out by an adult human skilled worker. Level 4, Virtuoso AGI, is set to perform at least 99% of the tasks executed by a human adult with skills. Lastly, Level 5 AGI is envisioned to be so effective that it surpasses humans in all aspects, marking the era of ASI where it performs 100% better than humans. As of now, no existing AGI system has achieved beyond Level 1, and Levels 2–5 remain hypothesis.

3.8 Artificial superintelligence

Continued evolution of AI can lead to the emergence of ASI in the future significantly performing intelligent tasks in all aspects in a better way compared to human-level intelligence (Bostrom 2014). Beyond the AGI is the ASI referred to as the singularity. Russell (2017) posits that the future of AI is ASI. Superintelligence refers to AGI that surpasses human intelligence by a considerable margin. The commonly suggested scenario involves the emergence of superintelligence originating from an initial seed AI, which undergoes recursive self-improvement, continually enhancing its intelligence in successive iterations (Baum 2017). The series of the recursive self-improvement can be from the perspective of hardware or software to become more intelligent than humans (Bostrom 2014, Walsh 2017). Thus, it will take over from the most intelligent AI based systems. As a result of that, AI systems can possibly start competing with humans and likely dominate the universe (Bostrom 2014).

3.9 Intellectual debates

The debate on superintelligence can be either an intellectual debate, politicized, or a combination of both political and intellectual elements. When intellectual debates are politicized, the focus shifts from enhancing understanding to serving various agendas. In contrast, purely intellectual debates are aimed at deepening comprehension of emerging concepts. Intellectual criticism often spurs scholarly inquiries to enhance understanding, unlike political criticism. These debates serve to enrich the understanding of superintelligence. Currently, most debates on superintelligence appear to be primarily intellectual, although some may have political undertones (Baum 2018).

The proposition that intelligent machines in the future will improve themselves to become more intelligent than humans has sparked a debate on the possibility of such a powerful machine. This debate is believed to be more pronounced outside the mainstream AI community, likely because many advocates of the idea come from outside the AI community. The development of superintelligence technology is expected to bring about challenges in life extension and transhumanism, diverting attention from debates on the real technical aspects such as fundamentals and significant issues regarding the possibility of developing a superintelligent machine. This is quite unfortunate for the AI community, as such distractions arise at an early stage. The prediction of Moore's Law, which states that the number of transistors on a chip has doubled approximately every two years since 1975, seems reasonably accurate. Similarly, Koomey's Law predicts that the number of computations per joule of energy dissipated doubles approximately every 19 months, starting from 1950. Can AI witness a similar exponential explosion at some point in time? Arguments exist both for and against the feasibility of achieving superintelligence (Walsh 2017). According to Eden *et al* (2012), Alan Turing postulated in 1951 that machines would eventually assume control in the future. Paul and Cox (1996) anticipated that advancements in AI could potentially usher in a singularity by the mid-21st century. However, critics, as noted by Horgan (2008), reject the concept of singularity as mere speculation lacking empirical evidence, categorizing it more as speculation than grounded in scientific evidence. Yann LeCun *et al* (2015) has voiced scepticism regarding the achievement of AGI with human-level intelligence, describing it as a 'ridiculous notion.' He argues that human intelligence is highly specialized, indicating that humans are not akin to general-purpose machines (Financial Times Panel 2024). How feasible is it to achieve ASI when we're unable to fully understand and replicate the intricate complexity and functions of the human brain? Considering that no scientist possesses comprehensive knowledge of the human brain, let alone the ability to construct a machine surpassing its capabilities, it is realistically impossible to simulate the entirety of the brain on a machine (Wikipedia 2020). Walsh (2017) strongly argued against the possibility of achieving superintelligence tagging it as impossible mission. It is argued that the best computer in today's world is the human brain. The notion follows that a super-intelligent machine could be created in the future to surpass the intelligence of the human brain. Therefore, electrophysiologists should primarily rely on their brains; after all, it is the human brain that will develop the superintelligent machine (Van de Leur *et al* 2020). Erik Larson (2021) challenged the idea of developing any AI supercomputer that can surpass human brain capabilities, going on to ask a rhetorical question: is this the future or just a wishful illusion? According to the belief/desire model proposed by Jebari and Lundborg (2021), no intelligent systems can transition to self-improvement to the extent of surpassing human-level intelligence.

There is evidence from long ago indicating that computers can outperform humans in certain domains, such as multiplication. As AI evolves, humans may continue to lose ground in domains where computers excel, as demonstrated by the recent victory of IBM's Watson computer. While these intelligent systems benefit humans, they also carry the potential to pose risks to humanity. However, these AI systems cannot alter humanity's position in controlling the universe. Conversely, many scholars hypothesize that AI systems surpassing human capabilities significantly could be designed in the future, potentially altering the status quo with outcomes that could be beneficial or catastrophic for all of humanity (Bostrom 2014). Similarly, a proponent believes that ASI has arrived, citing intelligent tutoring systems developed using AI in education, which were implemented as adaptive learning systems. Some of these adaptive learning systems were found to perform teaching and learning activities better than human teachers, particularly in aspects such as one-to-one tutoring, initial tracking of learner progress, and conducting remediation simultaneously and ubiquitously to a limitless number of students without breaks or fatigue. It has been discovered that course learning outcomes gathered from adaptive learning systems indicate improvement within a reduced period of time (How 2019).

3.10 Timelines expected to achieve artificial general intelligence

In the realm of AGI, predictions about the timeline often span a wide spectrum. Grace *et al* (2017) proposed 2061 as the likely year for the development of AGI. Various other AI scientists have made predictions regarding the future emergence of AGI or ASI. Bengio *et al* (2024) anticipate that AI capable of broadly outperforming humans will emerge within the decade. Müller and Bostrom (2016) suggested a timeframe for AGI development between 2040 and 2050, while Kurzweil (2005) previously posited that AGI could be realized around the year 2029. Chalmers and David (2010) did not specify a particular year but foresaw AGI creation within the current century. On the other hand, Baum *et al* (2011) predicted the creation of superhuman AGI by the year 2045. Additionally, Cotra (2022) predicted a 50% probability of witnessing transformation into AGI by the year 2040. Walsh (2017) estimated a timeframe of at least 30 years and at most 40 years from the present for AGI developments. Given that the journey toward achieving AGI is still very long, we contend that the prevailing paradigm for the distribution of tasks between humans and machines in the coming decades is likely to be hybrid intelligence. This approach seeks to leverage the complementary strengths of human intelligence and AI, enabling them to collectively outperform what each entity could achieve independently (Dellermann *et al* 2019). Ben Goertzel predicted the world may witness AGI or ASI in 2027, earlier than the 2029 or 2030 expected (Phelan 2024).

3.11 Industrial applications and case studies

LLMs have different applications in industry to help improve productivity. The LLMs for industrial robots have the potential for design automation, task execution and decision-making process in manufacturing (Fan *et al* 2024). The complex nature of the human–machine interface has hindered the massive adoption of industrial robots in manufacturing. The capability of LLMs, like ChatGPT, to understand human language and respond appropriately has the potential to mitigate the issue of the human–machine interface complexity by empowering robots to respond to human commands in manufacturing. As a result, this fosters collaboration between humans and machines in the manufacturing industry. LLMs can be used for the generation of robot programs from tasks described in natural language to make the robot perform simple industrial routine operations using a simple prompt. LLMs have the capacity to provide explanations of robot programs line by line and explain the procedure to implement the program on a particular robot. LLMs can adapt an existing robot program to suit changing situations, thereby improving productivity (Golitsyn 2023). At Schneider Electric, LLMs is used for training their own specific EcoStructure machine expert applications with fast generation of accurate codes, the human programmers only glance through the code for any possible retouches (Le Sant 2023). Communication in clear terms plays a key role in the survival and productivity of organizations, especially among the stakeholders. Communication is mostly written and distributed through different channels like email, LLMs like ChatGPT can help in facilitating and improving writing quality. LLMs enable organizations and companies to have personalized customer interaction experiences and support, analyze and understand the feedback of customers. They also provide transformed engagement across social media platforms by automating content creation.

3.12 Current status, challenges and future outlook

While some are optimistic about achieving AGI in the next few decades, others take a more cautious and long-term perspective. The source of intelligence lies in the human brain; therefore, the AI research community should attempt to accurately simulate the entire human brain on a machine (Reeke and Edelman 1988). Despite notable progress in neuroscience and AI inspired by the human brain, our comprehension of the intricacies of the human brain remains limited. This poses a challenge in developing machines capable of fully replicating exactly human-level intelligence (Zhao *et al* 2023). One optimistic approach to achieving AGI involves replicating the human brain at the atomic level through a digital simulation. This process necessitates advanced brain scanners and robust computing machinery with capacities that significantly surpass those currently available. Presently, such high-calibre brain scanners and powerful computer systems are not available. However, looking ahead, if the improvement trajectories of brain scanners and computer hardware continue as anticipated, it is believed that these technologies could become available between 2030 and 2050 (Pennachin and Goertzel 2007). The uncertainties stem from the complexity of replicating human intelligence. Currently, neither machines nor humans have managed to successfully model the complete intricate structure of the human brain due to its exceptionally high complexity and formidable power. Consequently, attempts to simulate the complete structure and functionality of the human brain on a machine have proven unsuccessful (Kawala-Sterniuk *et al* 2021). It has been reported that a supercomputer, code-named DeepSouth, with the potential to simulate the entire human brain, has been developed in Australia and is expected to be powered on in 2024. The supercomputer is capable of performing 228 trillion synaptic operations per second, akin to the human brain (Woodford 2023).

The rapid development of AGI is both intriguing and comes with challenges that impede its seamless realization. Despite the obstacles linked to the evolving AGI, it possesses the potential to exert a profound impact on various aspects of society, including healthcare delivery, transportation systems, and education. Progressing towards the creation of more powerful and sophisticated foundational models is the appropriate trajectory for bringing AGI to fruition. Current technological breakthroughs in computer vision, NLP, reinforcement learning, and knowledge graphs have spurred the development of advanced AGI chatbots, exemplified by models like ChatGPT and ChatGPT-4. These demonstrations showcase the capability to perform tasks across diverse application domains. The advancement of AGI foundational models, facilitated by research breakthroughs, improvements in hardware, and advancements in computational algorithms, holds the potential to expedite AGI development significantly. Integrating various AI systems across different domains, with human involvement in the loop through reinforcement learning from expert feedback, has the potential to propel AGI development. For example, combining robotics and computer vision with NLP under the supervision of human experts could result in the creation of more sophisticated, versatile, and powerful adaptive AI systems. This approach may overcome the limitations of individual AI systems, addressing issues such as the inability to transfer knowledge across different domains and the constraint of performing confined tasks, as noted by Zhao *et al* (2023).

3.13 Risk

Barrett and Baum (2017) present a study that suggests a roadmap to the catastrophe likely to be caused by ASI focusses on developing self-improved AI systems to create ASI systems. The study adopts a well-established risk and decision analysis paradigm to create a model depicting events and conditions with the potential for catastrophe and ways to mitigate it. These conditions and events encompass selected aspects of ASI and the human process of research, development, and management of ASI. The model provides a benchmark for evaluating the long-term risks of ASI.

AGI could potentially be exploited maliciously by those who wield control over the technology, or there is a risk of AGI technology spiralling out of control. Scholars believe that human extinction is conceivable in the age of AGI (Baum 2017). Recently, users were observed to defy the policies of the GPT app store, underscoring the potential challenges of enforcing control over AGI.

The short-term risks associated with the advancement of AI include the creation of autonomous weapons fuelling an arms race and the substantial loss of jobs due to automation. The AI community overwhelmingly rejects the notion of automated weapons that could independently decide to harm humans, both in practical application and in theory. However, the issue of job loss sparks a serious debate, with proponents predicting a boom in economic activities and the creation of new jobs, while opponents anticipate significant job losses. To illustrate, consider a hypothetical discussion between two horses during the pre-era of the internal combustion engine, with one horse suggesting the prospect of 'new jobs' (Russell 2017). Antonov (2011) suggested that research into AI should be halted, and instead, focus should shift to the research and development of human superintelligence, with a focus on aspects capable of addressing highly challenging issues such as multi-factor problems. The development of human superintelligence should be undertaken carefully and cautiously to ensure that it poses no potential threats to humanity. Similarly, there are also ethical considerations to contemplate regarding AGI. As these systems become more intelligent, they may be capable of making decisions that have far-reaching consequences. Ensuring that these decisions are aligned with human values and ethical principles is critical for preventing unintended harm (Zhao *et al* 2023).

3.14 Summary

The chapter discusses AGI from various points of view of scientists working in the field of AI. A comparison between human-level intelligence and AGI is made to aid in understanding the concept. However, the concept of AGI and ASI remains controversial within the AI community, with every scientist presenting different views. Indeed, some scholars argue that the era of AGI and ASI has already arrived, citing the ability of LLMs to perform multiple tasks across different domains. There is evidence showing that intelligent systems outperform humans in some tasks, such as gaming, multiplication, and tutoring. On the other hand, many scholars oppose the idea of AGI and ASI, arguing that it is unachievable as no machine can attain the sophisticated complexity and functional capabilities of the human brain. Consequently, they don't even believe that AGI is achievable, going as far as calling it an impossible mission. Some scientists mainly focus on the catastrophic aspects of the AGI and ASI machines, regardless of their achievability.

Regardless of the opposing and proponents' views about AGI, a significant advancement towards AGI has been recorded with the emergence of LLMs like ChatGPT, Gemini, and Llama, which have the capabilities to perform multiple tasks across different domains. However, in terms of superintelligence, groundbreaking achievements are yet to be recorded, with only a few traces seen by scholars as a way forward. Thus, the chapter provides easy-to-understand tutorials, breaking down the different components of transformer architecture in simple terms and presenting the major stages involved in the development of LLMs from scratch, including RLHF.

The issue of job loss at the peak of AGI sparks arguments, with proponents arguing that new jobs will be created in the AGI era or that roles will transform. On the other hand, the opposing view predicts massive job losses by humans to machines, thereby rendering the human race jobless. The development of automated weapons has been unanimously rejected by the research community to avoid the possibility of machines turning the weapons against human beings. The fear of human extinction by intelligent machines is echoed by researchers calling for early precautionary measures as the world heads towards the era of fully AGI and ASI systems. Possible timelines for achieving AGI and ASI systems as predicted by different AI scientists, future outlook, future research directions, and risks are outlined and discussed. For now, AGI and ASI remain hypotheses.

References

Adams S, Arel I, Bach J, Coop R, Furlan R, Goertzel B and Sowa J 2012 Mapping the landscape of human-level artificial general intelligence *AI Mag.* **33** 25–42

Antonov A A 2011 From artificial intelligence to human super-intelligence *Artif. Intell.* **2** 3560

Arcas B A and Norvig P 2023 Artificial general intelligence is already here *Noema, October* https://noemamag.com/artificial-general-intelligence-is-already-here/
Arulkumaran K, Deisenroth M P, Brundage M and Bharath A A 2017 A brief survey of deep reinforcement learning *arXiv preprint* arXiv:1708.05866
Ayyamperumal S G and Ge L 2024 Current state of LLM risks and AI guardrails *arXiv preprint* arXiv:2406.12934
Ba J L, Kiros J R and Hinton G E 2016 Layer normalization *arXiv preprint* arXiv:1607.06450
Baddeley A D 2004 The psychology of memory *The Essential Handbook of Memory Disorders for Clinicians* (Wiley) pp 1–13
Bahl L R, Brown P F, de Souza P V and Mercer R L 1989 A tree-based statistical language model for natural language speech recognition *IEEE Trans. Acoust. Speech Signal Process.* **37** 1001–8
Barrett A M and Baum S D 2017 A model of pathways to artificial superintelligence catastrophe for risk and decision analysis *J. Exp. Theor. Artif. Intell.* **29** 397–414
Baum S 2017 A survey of artificial general intelligence projects for ethics, risk, and policy *Global Catastrophic Risk Institute Working Paper* 17-1 Global Catastrophic Risk Institute
Baum S D, Ben G and Goertzel T G 2011 How long until human-level AI? Results from an expert assessment *Technol. Forecast. Soc. Change* **78.1** 185–95
Baum S D 2018 Superintelligence skepticism as a political tool *Information* **9** 209
Beaudoin M, Kurtz G, Jung I, Suzuki K and Grabowski B L 2013 *Online Learner Competencies: Knowledge, Skills, and Attitudes for Successful Learning in Online Settings* (IAP)
Bengio Y *et al* 2024 Managing AI risks in an era of rapid progress *Science* **384** 842–5
Bishop C M and Bishop H 2023 Graph neural networks *Deep Learning: Foundations and Concepts* (Cham: Springer International Publishing) pp 407–27
Bostrom N 2014 *Superintelligence: Paths, Dangers, Strategies* (Oxford: Oxford University Press)
Brown P F, DeSouza P V, Mercer R L, Della Pietra V J and Lai J C 1992 Class-based n-gram models of natural language *Comput. Linguist* **18** 467–80 https://aclanthology.org/J92-4003.pdf
Brown T, Mann B, Ryder N, Subbiah M, Kaplan J D, Dhariwal P and Amodei D 2020 Language models are few-shot learners *Adv. Neural Inf. Process. Syst.* **33** 1877–901
Cavnar W B and Trenkle J M 1994 N-gram-based text categorization *Proc. of SDAIR-94, 3rd Annual Symp. on Document Analysis and Information Retrieval* 161175 p 14
Cha J, Kang W, Mun J and Roh B 2023 Honeybee: locality-enhanced projector for multimodal LLM *arXiv e-prints* arXiv-2312
Chalmers and David J 2010 The singularity: a philosophical analysis *Conscious. Stud.* **17** 1
Chang Y, Wang X, Wang J, Wu Y, Yang L, Zhu K and Xie X 2023 A survey on evaluation of large language models *ACM Trans. Intell. Syst. Technol.* **15** 1–45
Chen D *et al* 2024 Data-juicer: A one-stop data processing system for large language models *Companion of the 2024 Int. Conf. on Management of Data* pp 120–4
Clark A, Fox C and Lappin S (ed) 2012 *The Handbook of Computational Linguistics and Natural Language Processing* **118** (New York: Wiley)
Clough S and Duff M C 2020 The role of gesture in communication and cognition: Implications for understanding and treating neurogenic communication disorders *Front. Human Neurosci.* **14** 323
Cotra A 2022 2022 Two-year update on draft report on AI timelines: Two-year update on my personal AI timelines—LessWrong https://www.lesswrong.com/posts/AfH2oPHCApdKicM4m/two-year-update-on-my-personal-ai-timelines#fn-LnaAQkuHYCr3b3oQ7-2 (accessed 10 April 2025)

Cowan N 1988 Evolving conceptions of memory storage, selective attention, and their mutual constraints within the human information-processing system *Psychol. Bull.* **104** 163

Dai S, Xu C, Xu S, Pang L, Dong Z and Xu J 2024 Bias and unfairness in information retrieval systems: new challenges in the LLM era In *Proc. of the 30th ACM SIGKDD Conf. on Knowledge Discovery and Data Mining* pp 6437–47

Dellermann D, Ebel P, Söllner M and Leimeister J M 2019 Hybrid intelligence *Bus. Inform. Syst. Eng.* **61** 637–43

De Mulder W, Bethard S and Moens M F 2015 A survey on the application of recurrent neural networks to statistical language modeling *Comput. Speech Lang.* **30** 61–98

Devlin J, Chang M W, Lee K and Toutanova K 2018 Bert: Pre-training of deep bidirectional transformers for language understanding *arXiv preprint* arXiv:1810.04805

Ding Y 2021 The impact of learning rate decay and periodical learning rate restart on artificial neural network *2021 2nd Int. Conf. on Artificial Intelligence in Electronics Engineering* pp 6–14

Dong Q, Li L, Dai D, Zheng C, Wu Z, Chang B and Sui Z 2022 A survey on in-context learning *arXiv preprint* arXiv:2301.00234

Dowrick P W 1999 A review of self modeling and related interventions *Appl. Prev. Psychol.* **8** 23–39

Eden A H, Moor J H, Søraker J H and Steinhart E 2012 Singularity hypotheses *The Frontiers Collection* (Berlin: Springer)

Efron R 1969 What is perception? *Proc. of the Boston Coll. for the Philosophy of Science 1966/1968* (Dordrecht: Springer) pp 137–73

Eysenck M W and Brysbaert M 2018 *Fundamentals of Cognition* (London: Routledge)

Fan H, Liu X, Fuh J Y H, Lu W F and Li B 2024 Embodied intelligence in manufacturing: leveraging large language models for autonomous industrial robotics *J. Intell. Manuf.* **36** 1141–57

Financial Times Panel 2024 *World Economic Forum* (Switzerland: Davos) https://medium.com/aimonks/deep-learning-is-rubbish-karl-friston-yann-lecun-face-off-at-davos-2024-world-economic-forum-494e82089d22 (accessed 14 March 2024)

Gan Y and Zhu Z 2007 A learning framework for knowledge building and collective wisdom advancement in virtual learning communities *J. Educ. Technol. Soc.* **10** 206–26

Garcez A D A, Bader S, Bowman H, Lamb L C, de Penning L, Illuminoo B V and Zaverucha C G 2022 Neural-symbolic learning and reasoning: a survey and interpretation *Neuro-Symb. Artif. Intell.: State Art* **342** 327

Garnelo M and Shanahan M 2019 Reconciling deep learning with symbolic artificial intelligence: representing objects and relations *Curr. Opin. Behav. Sci.* **29** 17–23

German K T and Robbins M L 2020 Social Interaction *Encyclopedia of Personality and Individual Differences* (Cham: Springer) pp 5075–9

Goertzel B 2014 Artificial general intelligence: concept, state of the art, and future prospects *J. Artif. Gen. Intell.* **5** 1–46

Golitsyn D 2023 Can large language models enhance efficiency in industrial robotics? (Forbes Magazine) https://forbes.com/sites/forbestechcouncil/2023/03/28/can-large-language-models-enhance-efficiency-in-industrial-robotics/?sh=4211faed60af (accessed 21 March 2024)

Grace K, John S, Allan D, Baobao Z and Owain E 2017 When will AI exceed human performance? Evidence from AI experts arXiv: 1705.08807

Griffith S, Subramanian K, Scholz J, Isbell C L and Thomaz A L 2013 Policy shaping: Integrating human feedback with reinforcement learning *Advances in Neural Information Processing Systems 26 (NIPS 2013)* **26**

Grudin J and Jacques R 2019 Chatbots, humbots, and the quest for artificial general intelligence *Proc. of the 2019 CHI Conf. on Human Factors in Computing Systems* pp 1–11

Gubrud M 1997 Nanotechnology and international security *5th Foresight Conf. on Molecular Nanotechnology*

Guo Z, Jin R, Liu C, Huang Y, Shi D, Yu L and Xiong D 2023 Evaluating large language models: a comprehensive survey *arXiv e-prints* arXiv-2310

Harnad S 1990 The symbol grounding problem *Physica* D **42** 335–46

Horgan J 2008 The consciousness conundrum *IEEE Spectr.* **45** 36–41

How M L 2019 Future-ready strategic oversight of multiple artificial superintelligence-enabled adaptive learning systems via human-centric explainable AI-empowered predictive optimizations of educational outcomes *Big Data Cogn. Comput.* **3** 46

Huang J and Chang K C C 2022 Towards reasoning in large language models: a survey *arXiv preprint* arXiv:2212.10403

Jebari K and Lundborg J 2021 Artificial superintelligence and its limits: why AlphaZero cannot become a general agent *AI Soc.* **36** 807–15

Kaelbling L P, Littman M L and Moore A W 1996 Reinforcement learning: a survey *J. Artif. Intell. Res.* **4** 237–85

Kalyan K S 2023 A survey of GPT-3 family large language models including ChatGPT and GPT-4 *Natural Lang. Process. J.* 100048

Kawala-Sterniuk A, Browarska N, Al-Bakri A, Pelc M, Zygarlicki J, Sidikova M and Gorzelanczyk E J 2021 Summary of over fifty years with brain–computer interfaces—a review *Brain Sci.* **11** 43

Kleinman Z and Vallance C 2023 AI 'godfather' Geoffrey Hinton warns of dangers as he quits Google https://bbc.com/news/world-us-canada-65452940 (accessed 11 March, 2024)

Kurzweil R 2005 *The Singularity is Near* (Viking) p 652

Lambert N and Calandra R 2023 The alignment ceiling: objective mismatch in reinforcement learning from human feedback *arXiv preprint* arXiv:2311.00168

Larson E 2021 *The Myth of Artificial Intelligence: Why Computers Can't Think the Way We Do* (Cambridge, MA: Belknap Press)

Laurençon H, Saulnier L, Wang T, Akiki C, Villanova del Moral A, Le Scao T and Jernite Y 2022 The bigscience roots corpus: A 1.6 tb composite multilingual dataset *Adv. Neural Inform. Process. Syst.* **35** 31809–26

LeCun Y, Bengio Y and Hinton G 2015 Deep learning *Nature* **521** 436–44

Le Sant A 2023 How large language models can boost industrial automation *Schneider Electric* Global (se.com) https://se.com/ww/en/insights/next-generation-automation/software-centric-automation/how-large-language-models-can-be-useful-in-industrial-automation.jsp (accessed 21 March 2024)

Li S, Wu C, Li H, Li B, Wang Y and Qiu Q 2015 Fpga acceleration of recurrent neural network based language model *2015 IEEE 23rd Annual Int. Symp. on Field-Programmable Custom Computing Machines* (Piscataway, NJ: IEEE) pp 111–8

Littlejohn S W and Foss K A 2010 *Theories of Human Communication* (Long Grove, IL: Waveland Press)

Liu Y, Yao Y, Ton J F, Zhang X, Cheng R G H, Klochkov Y and Li H 2023 Trustworthy LLMs: a survey and guideline for evaluating large language models' alignment *arXiv preprint* arXiv:2308.05374

Ma L and Zhang Y 2015 Using Word2Vec to process big text data *2015 IEEE Int. Conf. on Big Data (Big Data)* (Piscataway, NJ: IEEE) pp 2895–7

Mai V V and Johansson M 2021 Stability and convergence of stochastic gradient clipping: Beyond Lipschitz continuity and smoothness *Int. Conf. on Machine Learning* (PMLR) pp 7325–35

Marcus G 2022 Twitter (now '*X*') https://twitter.com/GaryMarcus/status/ 1529457162811936768 (accessed 18 November 2023)

McRuer D T, Magdaleno R E and Moore G P 1968 A neuromuscular actuation system model *IEEE Trans. Man-Mach. Syst.* **9** 61–71

Mehl M R, Gosling S D and Pennebaker J W 2006 Personality in its natural habitat: manifestations and implicit folk theories of personality in daily life *J. Personal. Social Psychol.* **90** 862

Melser D 2009 Verbal communication: from pedagogy to make-believe *Lang. Sci.* **31** 555–71

Mikolov T, Chen K, Corrado G and Dean J 2013 Efficient estimation of word representations in vector space *arXiv preprint* arXiv:1301.3781

Mikolov T, Karafiát M, Burget L, Cernocký J and Khudanpur S 2010 Recurrent neural network based language model *Proc. Interspeech* **2** 1045–8

Mintzberg H 1981 What is planning anyway? *Strateg. Manag. J.* **2** 319–24

Morin A 2006 Levels of consciousness and self-awareness: a comparison and integration of various neurocognitive views *Conscious. Cogn.* **15** 358–71

Morin F and Bengio Y 2005 Hierarchical probabilistic neural network language model In *Int. Workshop on Artificial Intelligence and Statistics* (PMLR) pp 246–52

Morris M R, Sohl-dickstein J, Fiedel N, Warkentin T, Dafoe A, Faust A and Legg S 2023 Levels of AGI: operationalizing progress on the path to AGI *arXiv preprint* arXiv:2311.02462

Müller V C and Bostrom N 2016 Future progress in artificial intelligence: a survey of expert opinion In *Fundamental Issues of Artificial Intelligence* ed V C Müller (Berlin: Springer) pp 553–70

Noaman H M, Sarhan S S and Rashwan M A 2018 Enhancing recurrent neural network-based language models by word tokenization *Human-centric Comput. Inform. Sci.* **8** 1–13

Paul G S and Cox E D 1996 *Beyond Humanity: Cyberevolution and Future Minds* (Needham Heights, MA: Charles River Media)

Pei J, Deng L, Song S, Zhao M, Zhang Y, Wu S and Shi L 2019 Towards artificial general intelligence with hybrid Tianjic chip architecture *Nature* **572** 106–11

Peng J L, Cheng S, Diau E, Shih Y Y, Chen P H, Lin Y T and Chen Y N 2024 A survey of useful LLM evaluation *arXiv preprint* arXiv:2406.00936

Pennachin C and Goertzel B 2007 Contemporary approaches to artificial general intelligence *Artificial General Intelligence* (Berlin: Springer) pp 1–30

Phelan M 2024 *Top Scientist Warns AI Could Surpass Human Intelligence by 2027—Decades Earlier than Previously Predicted* https://msn.com/en-ca/news/technology/top-scientist-warns-ai-could-surpass-human-intelligence-by-2027-decades-earlier-than-previously-predicted/ar-BB1js2Es (accessed 14 March 2024)

Qian C, Han C, Fung Y R, Qin Y, Liu Z and Ji H 2023 CREATOR: disentangling abstract and concrete reasonings of large language models through tool creation *arXiv preprint* arXiv:2305.14318

Qin Y, Hu S, Lin Y, Chen W, Ding N, Cui G and Sun M 2023 Tool learning with foundation models *arXiv preprint* arXiv:2304.08354

Raiaan M A K, Mukta M S H, Fatema K, Fahad N M, Sakib S, Mim M M J and Azam S 2024 A review on large language models: architectures, applications, taxonomies, open issues and challenges *IEEE Access* **12** 26839–74

Rathje W 2024 Learning when not to measure: theorizing ethical alignment in LLMs *Proc. of the AAAI/ACM Conf. on AI, Ethics, and Society* 7 pp 1190–9

Rawte V, Sheth A and Das A 2023 A survey of hallucination in large foundation models *arXiv preprint* arXiv:2309.05922

Reeke G and Edelman G 1988 Real brains and artificial intelligence *Dædalus* **117** 143–73

Rips L J 1990 Reasoning *Annu. Rev. Psychol.* **41** 321–53

Russell S 2017 Artificial intelligence: the future is superintelligent *Nature* **548** 520–1

Ryan A M and Gass S E 2017 Quantitative reasoning: exploring troublesome thresholds *Discussions on University Science Teaching: Proc. of the Western Conf. on Science Education* 1

Sam M S 2023 Psychology Dictionary https://psychologydictionary.org/motivation/ (accessed 13 March 2024)

Scardamalia M and Bereiter C 2006 *Knowledge Building: Theory, Pedagogy, and Technology* (Cambridge University Press) pp 97–118

Schulman J, Wolski F, Dhariwal P, Radford A and Klimov O 2017 Proximal policy optimization algorithms *arXiv preprint* arXiv:1707.06347

Shaw P, Uszkoreit J and Vaswani A 2018 Self-attention with relative position representations *Proc. of the 2018 Conf. of the North American chapter of the Association for Computational Linguistics: Human Language Technologies, Volume 2 (Short Papers)* (Association for Computational Linguistics)

Sheridan T B and Parasuraman R 2005 Human–automation interaction *Rev. Human Factors Ergon.* **1** 89–129

Shi Z, Wang Y, Zhang H, Yi J and Hsieh C J 2021 Fast certified robust training with short warmup *Adv. Neural Inform. Process. Syst.* **34** 18335–49

Sidorov G 2013 *Non-linear Construction of N-grams in Computational Linguistics* (México: Sociedad Mexicana de Inteligencia Artificial)

Siska C, Marazopoulou K, Ailem M and Bono J 2024 Examining the robustness of LLM evaluation to the distributional assumptions of benchmarks *Proc. of the 62nd Annual Meeting of the Association for Computational Linguistics, Volume 1 (Long Papers)* pp 10406–21

Smolensky P 1987 Connectionist AI, symbolic AI, and the brain *Artif. Intell. Rev.* **1** 95–109

Solomon R C 1977 The logic of emotion *Nous* **11** 41–9

Tang R, Han X, Jiang X and Hu X 2023 Does synthetic data generation of llms help clinical text mining? *arXiv preprint* arXiv:2303.04360

Tirumala K, Simig D, Aghajanyan A and Morcos A S 2023 D4: improving LLM pretraining via document de-duplication and diversification *37th Conf. on Neural Information Processing Systems Datasets and Benchmarks Track*

Tunstall L, Von Werra L and Wolf T 2022 *Natural Language Processing with Transformers* (Sebastopol, CA: O'Reilly Media)

Van de Leur R R, Boonstra M J, Bagheri A *et al* 2020 Big data and artificial intelligence: opportunities and threats in electrophysiology *Arrhythm. Electrophysiol. Rev.* **9** 146–54

Van Otterlo M and Wiering M 2012 Reinforcement learning and Markov decision processes *Reinforcement learning: State-of-the-Art* (Berlin: Springer) pp 3–42

Vaswani A, Shazeer N, Parmar N, Uszkoreit J, Jones L, Gomez A N and Polosukhin I 2017 Attention is all you need *Advances in Neural Information Processing Systems 30 (NIPS 2017)* **30**

Vijayarani S and Janani R 2016 Text mining: open source tokenization tools-an analysis *Adv. Comput. Intell.* **3** 37–47

Walsh T 2017 The singularity may never be near *AI Mag.* **38** 58–62

Wang J, Lan C, Liu C, Ouyang Y, Qin T, Lu W and Philip S Y 2022 Generalizing to unseen domains: a survey on domain generalization *IEEE Trans. Knowl. Data Eng.* **35** 8052–72

Wang P, Liu K and Dougherty Q 2018 Conceptions of artificial intelligence and singularity *Information* **9** 79

Webster J J and Kit C 1992 Tokenization as the initial phase in NLP *COLING 1992 Volume 4: The 14th Int. Conf. on Computational Linguistics*

Wikipedia 2020 *Scunthorpe Problem* https://en.wikipedia.org/wiki/Scunthorpe_problem (accessed 15 October 2021)

Woodford J 2023 *Technology. New Scientist* https://newscientist.com/article/2408015-supercomputer-that-simulates-entire-human-brain-will-switch-on-in-2024/ (accessed 13 December 2023)

Xu Q, Hong F, Li B, Hu C, Chen Z and Zhang J 2023 On the tool manipulation capability of open-source large language models *arXiv preprint* arXiv:2305.16504

Yang T H, Tseng T H and Chen C P 2016 Recurrent neural network-based language models with variation in net topology, language, and granularity In *2016 Int. Conf. on Asian Language Processing (IALP)* (Piscataway, NJ: IEEE) pp 71–4

Zeng A, Liu X, Du Z, Wang Z, Lai H, Ding M and Tang J 2022 Glm-130b: an open bilingual pre-trained model *arXiv preprint* arXiv:2210.02414

Zhang Q, Yang L T, Chen Z and Li P 2018 A survey on deep learning for big data *Inform. Fusion* **42** 146–57

Zhao L, Zhang L, Wu Z, Chen Y, Dai H, Yu X and Liu T 2023 When brain-inspired AI meets AGI *Meta-Radiol.* **1** 100005

Zhao W X *et al* 2023 A survey of large language models arXiv:2303.18223 https://arxiv.org/abs/2303.18223

Zhu K, Wang J, Zhou J, Wang Z, Chen H, Wang Y and Xie X 2023 PromptBench: towards evaluating the robustness of large language models on adversarial prompts *arXiv preprint* arXiv:2306.04528

IOP Publishing

Emerging Trends in Artificial Intelligence
Integrating theories and practice
Haruna Chiroma

Chapter 4

AI-DevOps: Proposed artificial intelligence enhanced development and operations lifecycle

Artificial intelligence (AI) has been generating tremendous interest from the media and society in general. Software systems are fast becoming complex in nature, thus, triggering a shift from traditional development and operations (DevOps) methodology to AI-assisted DevOps to meet with the increasing complexity of software. Therefore, AI-assisted DevOps is expected to relegate traditional DevOps in the future, as predicted in the 2023 IEEE Computer Society Technology prediction (IEEE Computer Society 2023). In this chapter, the major components of AI-assisted DevOps that drive innovations in organizations are discussed. The chapter presents proposed AI-assisted DevOps ecosystems with AI technology. The AI automation tool required in each of the DevOps stages is outlined for the reader to easily grasp the needed AI automation tools required to speed up the DevOps processes. The chapter presents industrial applications and case studies where AI-based DevOps are in practice in well-established companies.

4.1 Introduction

Before the emergence of DevOps, the common approach was to accelerate software development while ignoring operations. When the software development team produced the first version of the software, it would be delivered to the operations team for deployment. At this point, the operations team did not have sufficient knowledge about the software and how it was developed. Despite the operations team having limited knowledge about the software product, they were required to create and configure a suitable environment for the deployment of the software. As a result, software delivery could be delayed, and conflicts between the development team and the operations team began to arise. Cultivating a collaborative culture from the beginning of the software development process can reduce conflicts, expedite software delivery, and prevent the software development team from having

doi:10.1088/978-0-7503-6320-4ch4

to wait for the environment to be set up to execute the new version of the software (Luz *et al* 2019). Bridging the communication gap between the operations team and the development team to reduce conflict, speed up product delivery, and avoid delays motivated the emergence of DevOps.

DevOps integrate development, operation and maintenance aiming to bridge the gap between operation team and development team. Continuous deployment and continuous delivery technology have proven highly effective in enhancing product and service delivery capabilities, garnering widespread attention. Through continuous exploration and implementation in recent years, DevOps has transitioned from a mere buzzword to a central technology in the industry. DevOps is revolutionizing the conventional software development model, prioritizing communication among development, operations, and maintenance teams. In practical terms, it leverages a suite of automated technologies to streamline software construction, testing, and release processes. Embracing a microservices architecture ensures swift and iterative software updates from a design standpoint. DevOps guidelines ensure that these iterative updates are seamlessly and securely integrated into the production environment (Yang *et al* 2020). In summary, the primary goal of DevOps is to enhance communication and integrate development and operations. This approach leverages modern software development techniques to enable the rapid delivery of new software versions with additional features for users (Rodríguez *et al* 2017).

Recently, enterprises have been racing to embrace AI to automate processes, boost revenue, and stay competitive with rival companies. According to a survey conducted in 2023 by Gartner, businesses embracing AI consistently express their plans to extend its application in assessing future scenarios. The survey report foresees a 50% improvement by 2026 in transparency, trust, and security concerning business objectives, adoption, and user satisfaction in AI implementations (Karjian 2023).

AI is revolutionizing the software development industry with the rapid advancement of large language models (LLMs), impacting nearly every aspect of the development process, from requirement elicitation to deployment. The DevOps process is also experiencing significant transformation as AI enhances automation capabilities within DevOps. However, to the best of the author's knowledge, a comprehensive systematic approach to adopting AI technology at each stage of the DevOps process, including security, is not yet available in the literature. To address this vacuum, this chapter aims to present an AI-accelerated DevOps lifecycle, integrating AI at every stage and identifying the necessary AI tools for each phase.

4.2 The traditional software development approach

Typically, software is developed by a group of engineers working as a team, with a large number of developers, in a systematic development process, with a good user interface. In contrast, programs are developed by individuals for personal use, usually on a small scale, with limited functionalities, ad hoc development, and lacking proper documentation (Agarwal *et al* 2009). Software is about the people because every aspect of the software, ranging from development, management, use, support, maintenance, and testing, all involves people (Jones 2009). The uncoordinated approach to software development prompted the proposal of prescriptive process models to introduce orderliness into the software development process. Consequently, logical approaches to software development were integrated into the software development process, providing systematic methods for the software development team. Despite the orderliness brought by traditional software engineering approaches, the products still remain in a realm of disorderliness (Pressman and Maxim 2015). In developing software, there are certain situations where the requirements for solving the problem are well studied and understood. Thus, the workflow moves in a reasonably linear fashion from communication, planning, modelling, construction, to deployment. Typically, such situations are encountered when improving an existing system or adapting it (e.g., adapting accounting software due to new government policy). However, similar linear fashion software development processes can be encountered in limited new software development projects, especially if the requirements for the problem are reasonably stable and well understood. The legacy model for software development that follows this reasonably linear fashion is referred to as the waterfall model (RPressman and Maxim 2015).

4.2.1 Waterfall model

The waterfall approach to software development is believed to be the oldest model for software engineering practice. The waterfall model is referred to as the classical lifecycle in some cases, suggesting a linear and systematic approach to the development of software that starts with the requirement gathering stage before moving to planning, modelling, construction, and deployment (Pressman and Maxim 2015), as shown in figure 4.1 and the brief description of each stage provided by Pressman and Maxim (2015) is summarized and presented in table 4.1.

The rigid nature and linear fashion of the waterfall model prompted criticism of the model's effectiveness and efficiency. The major issues encountered in the

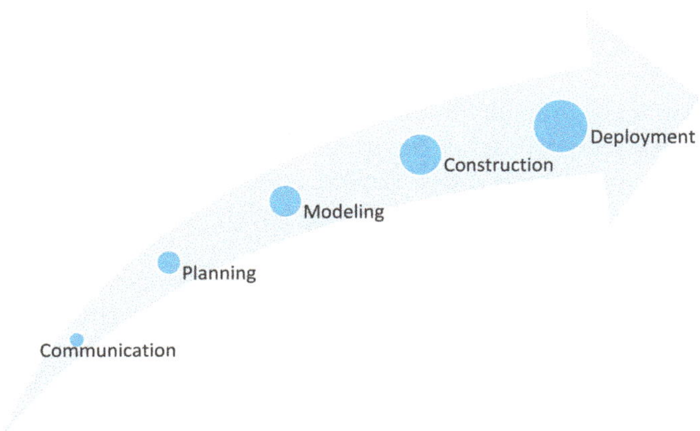

Figure 4.1. Typical waterfall model approach to software development.

Table 4.1. Brief insight into stages involved in the waterfall model.

Stage	Brief description	Remark
Communication	The software development project is initiated in this stage. Subsequently, requirements required for solving the problem are collected from stakeholders and clients.	The requirement has the possibility changing before the project is completed
Planning	Estimating the cost of development, completion time, and deliverables. Scheduling and tracking of the project are performed in the planning stage.	It is necessary for smooth project implementation
Modelling	Unified modelling language is used to depict the system behaviour and structure. Analysis is performed. Requirements gathered through data flow diagrams are visuallized. Software architecture is desinged, and the performance of the software is prdicted.	It is critical to ensure the software captures all the requirements
Construction	This is the stage for developing the source code based on the modelling. Subsequently, the code is rigorously tested to ensure it meets the requirements of the customer.	The code can need to be modified because of change in requirement
Deployment	The developed software is delivered to the real-world environment for operations. Support is provided to users for any technical issues, and feedback from users is received in the form of reviews.	There is the possibility of failure in the real-world environment

waterfall model approach to software engineering practice are as follows (Pressman and Maxim 2015):

1. It is extremely difficult to find a real-world project that follows a linear fashion like the proposal of the prescriptive waterfall model, despite the fact that it can accommodate to a limited extent indirectly. Therefore, confusion arises in the software project team when changes are required as the project progresses.
2. The waterfall model requires that the client provides all the requirements at the project planning stage. However, it is extremely difficult, or even impossible, for a client to provide all the required software requirements at the beginning of the software project. Thus, this results in difficulties in integrating changes due to natural uncertainty events that occur midway into the project.

3. Clients cannot see the version of the software in operation until towards completing the project or late into the project. Thus, the client must be patient to wait for a long time. In case a significant error/mistake is found after delivering the working version of the software, it can be disastrous for both the client and the project team.

The limitations associated with the waterfall model make it unfit to cope with today's dynamic nature of software engineering work, requiring an infinite iterative process to accommodate rapid changes to requirements, functions, and content of information. These challenges facing the waterfall model approach to software engineering processes motivated the proposal of alternative models, including the following process models: incremental, evolutionary, spiral model, concurrent model, component-based development, formal methods model, aspect-oriented software development, unified process, among others (Pressman and Maxim 2015). However, the details of the listed process models are beyond the scope of this chapter. The teams involved in software development include the development team, tasked with creating the software product. Secondly, the maintenance team takes care of the initial software released by the development team, responsible for debugging, improvements, and updates. Thirdly, the operations team is responsible for the deployment, monitoring, and maintenance of the software product (Shashkina 2022, Tripathi 2023).

4.3 The traditional development and operations

Traditionally, development defined a team comprised of programmers. Testers and quality assurance are roles typically reserved to begin after programmers have completed their work. On the other hand, operations comprise various administrators: database, network, system, etc. The operations group is responsible for accounting and accompanying the delivery processes. Operations don't consistently work with the programmers, quality assurance, and testers. However, they receive the final product produced by the development team (Hüttermann 2012). Agile development and operations, known as DevOps, represent a model for delivering software as a service. This approach integrates a set of practices and tools, consolidating the responsibilities for both developing and operating the software within a unified team. DevOps has demonstrated significant advantages compared to traditional, waterfall-based software development methods. Agile software development practices have fundamentally altered how developers conceive and create software, dismantling traditional structures. Through DevOps, teams can achieve the continuous delivery of software (Gall and Pigni 2022). The motivation behind DevOps is to foster improved collaboration between operations and development, as DevOps recognizes the inevitability of conflict among groups. DevOps addresses shared goals, incentives, processes, and tools to reduce the natural conflicts that typically arise among different groups. This is achievable by aligning shared goals, incentives, processes, and tools among these groups. The culture of organizations and projects acknowledges that people are more important than processes, and in turn, more important than tools. Thus, DevOps respects the culture of companies and projects. The aim of the DevOps campaign is to reduce the communication gap between teams of developers and operations in solving critical challenges (Hüttermann 2012). This is by the use of automation tools to bridge the communication gap between the development and operation teams involved in the project. In addition, DevOps intend to enforce rigorous processes for ensuring the smooth running of real-time communications (Cois *et al* 2014).

Examples of the critical issues expected to be addressed by DevOps include the fear of change and the risks involved in deployments. DevOps requires a process that is integrated from the beginning of development to the end of deployment and maintenance. DevOps also necessitates lightweight tools for easy integration and the automation of critical processes. Typically, collaborative work between development and operations teams begins prior to software deployment and continues throughout the post-deployment phase. In DevOps, all stakeholders work closely together and share the same goals in the delivery process (Hüttermann 2012). The typical lifecycle of DevOps phases comprises planning, coding, building, testing, deployment, operation, and monitoring (Capizzi *et al* 2020, Fawzy *et al* 2023).

4.3.1 Automation, sharing and transparency

Automation, sharing, and transparency play a critical role in the successful execution of DevOps processes. These concepts were discussed in this section for the reader to grasp the idea behind the concepts.

4.3.1.1 Automation

Automation is crucial in DevOps due to the fact that manual processes have the potential to create barriers or challenges in the culture of collaboration. When a person or team is responsible for executing a manual task, collaboration is achievable, but it relies heavily on sharing and transparency within the process. However, with automation, the barriers typically encountered in manual processes can be greatly minimized. Automation provides better transparency and ensures that tasks executed can easily be reproduced, reducing the need for rework and minimizing failures that typically stem from human error. One critical phase of a collaborative culture delivery in software development is confidence, and automation increases this confidence. Agility and reliability increase with automation, especially in situations where problems arise in the deployment phase, which has the potential to create conflicts and prompt existing silos. The generation of value for business doesn't solely rely on the successful and frequent deployment of software products; rather, the quality of the software product deployed is more relevant. Consequently, automation needs to be employed for the evaluation of software quality. The automation of application deployment requires that the deployment environment be readily available and properly configured for easy automated deployment. Configuration of the deployment environment includes ensuring the availability of the required memory space, CPU, libraries, and databases. Automated deployment can produce errors or fail if the environment's configuration is not automated. Automation of the monitoring system allows for monitoring applications and infrastructure without the need for manual intervention by humans. Automated monitoring has the ability to report alarms by sending messages or making phone calls in case of any incidents. Lastly, recovery automation refers to the capacity to automatically recover from deployment failures or replace defective components without requiring intervention from humans (Luz *et al* 2019).

4.3.1.2 Sharing

Sharing and transparency facilitate the dissemination of information and ideas among all group members. Events that promote the sharing of information and ideas in a transparent manner include, but are not limited to, training sessions, roundtable group discussions, technology talks, and committee lectures. The use of communication tools to create channels is another recurring theme related to sharing DevOps adoption processes. The content typically shared can be categorized into three main areas (Luz *et al* 2019):

1. Technical and cultural knowledge, focusing on the professional skills required for DevOps adoption.
2. Activities sharing through committees, forums, and communication tools, focusing on sharing how to solve certain problems or accomplish tasks.
3. Process sharing, which is more comprehensive compared to activity sharing, as it focusses on sharing complete working processes through the same means as activities sharing.

4.3.1.3 Transparency and sharing

To effectively contribute to transparency, regular sharing of information among DevOps teams should be maintained as one of the identified ways to achieve it, suggesting that sharing should be embedded in the software development process. The common practice to combine all project tasks is through a pipeline. The pipeline is shared, indicating that the pipeline of source code must be shared with everyone to facilitate transparency (Luz *et al* 2019). DevOps fosters collaborative development, operation, and maintenance, leveraging automation to achieve continuous software delivery while enhancing quality of the product and efficiency of the delivery. Establishing a delivery pipeline enables the creation of business value from demand to final user delivery, building an integrated process centred around delivery. This approach enhances product delivery efficiency and ensures more reliable quality. The 'end-to-end' delivery pipeline spans the entire software engineering process, elevating the automation level of software delivery, fostering interdepartmental collaboration, and enabling transparent sharing of information and tracing changes (Wen *et al* 2022).

4.3.1.4 Delineate

The term 'DevOps' is not merely a buzzword, as many of its components have existed for some time and are not entirely new. In DevOps, developers are typically restricted from directly working on production systems, as it is not an unfettered process allowing for developers in the production-relevant aspect. Therefore, it does not permit developers to directly work on production systems (Hüttermann 2012).

4.4 Motivation for artificial intelligence-assisted development and operations

The original idea or the illusion of an idea is referred to as creativity, especially in the realm of artistic work production. The real source of creativity lacks a universally accepted origin; it is subject to debate because different sources such as the brain, heart, experiences, or the body soul are attributed to the original source of the idea. However, it is largely agreed that humans have the capacity for original creativity. Creativity has been a human monopoly until the emergence of computers and AI, which have broken the monopoly to a certain extent. AI can be deployed by humans to support or expedite the process of creativity in several alternative approaches, such as the production of distinct combinations of existing ideas, creating new patterns based on available data, and suggesting new ideas from combinations of features. These facilitate the human process of creating ideas that were not imagined during the creativity process (Kirkpatrick 2023). AI-assisted DevOps is the approach for improving the traditional DevOps approach to address the challenges facing increasing complexity of software (IEEE Computer Society 2023). As the software complexity increases AI accelerates and simplifies the coding tasks by sophisticated automation (Greengard 2023). Globally, organizations face pressure for digital innovations to remain competitive in the market. DevOps has been identified by organizations as a key source of improving innovations. Despite the dramatic transformation of DevOps over the years, it still faces challenges. Expert evaluations are required for issues related to concurrency, security, or managing sensitive information. However, it frequently slips up through code peer review and unit testing. AI-accelerated DevOps represents a paradigm shift towards greater automation and provides proactive, fast means for teams to innovate with confidence. AI-accelerated DevOps is designed for developers to augment their capacity with machine learning (ML) capabilities, moving away from slow innovations and manual processes towards more automation of the entire DevOps lifecycle from planning through monitoring (AWS 2024).

4.5 Artificial intelligence accelerating development and operations lifecycle

DevOps and AI are closely intertwined, as DevOps represents a business-oriented strategy for software delivery, while AI offers the technological prowess to augment system capabilities. Through AI integration, DevOps teams can enhance efficiency across testing, coding, delivery, and software monitoring processes. AI facilitates improved automation, swift identification and resolution of issues, and fosters better collaboration among teams. It propels performance by enabling rapid development and operational cycles, ultimately enriching the customer experience with these enhanced features. Additionally, ML systems streamline data collection from diverse components of the DevOps ecosystem (Trivedi 2023). A DevOps process typically consists of distinct phases that are iteratively revisited to ensure the continual development and operation of the software. This iterative approach allows for the

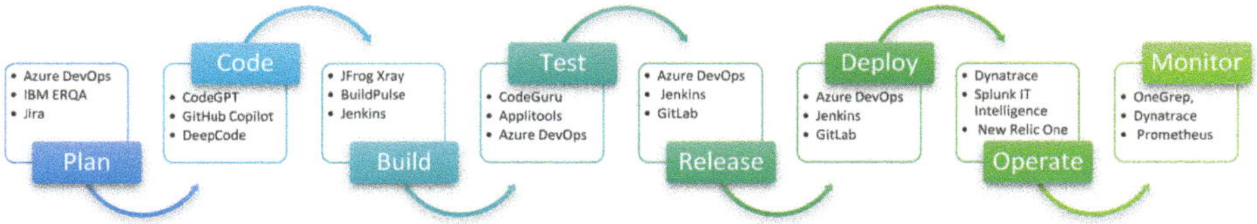

Figure 4.2. AI-accelerated development and operation lifecycle.

incorporation of new requirements, features, and behaviours that emerge during operations. As such, the DevOps process aligns with the agile methodology rather than a plan-driven approach, as the number of development cycles is not predetermined. Instead, the process evolves dynamically to meet evolving needs and demands (Capizzi *et al* 2020). Accelerating the DevOps development cycles while maintaining the utmost code quality poses a common challenge for all DevOps teams. AI emerges as a solution, facilitating the acceleration of every phase of DevOps lifecycles by predicting developers' needs before they arise. Auto-suggesting segments of code, enhancing quality assurance of software through automated testing, and the optimization of requirements management stand as key areas where AI significantly contributes value to the DevOps processes (Columbus 2023). This section elaborates on the integration of advanced AI tools across different stages of the DevOps lifecycle to bolster automation, precision, team collaboration, efficiency, and speed of products delivery. Figure 4.2 illustrates the AI-accelerated DevOps lifecycle, highlighting recommended cutting-edge AI tools for each stage activities: planning, coding, testing, building, deploying, operating, and monitoring. The DevOps lifecycle represents a continuous iterative process aimed at satisfying customer requirements.

4.5.1 Plan

Project planning is pivotal in guiding stakeholders, sponsors, teams, and project managers through various project phases. It serves to identify desired goals, mitigate risks, ensure target deadlines, and ultimately deliver the required product, service, or result. Lack of meticulous planning significantly compromises project performance. According to the Project Management Institute, by 2017, organizations were squandering an average of $97 million for every $1 billion invested, primarily due to subpar project performance (Alexander 2018). The planning phase of DevOps is the foundation and entry point into the DevOps lifecycle to ensure the successful delivery of software products. This stage begins with the identification of business requirements, scheduling tasks according to priority, and outlining the goals and objectives of the project. At this stage, team members work collaboratively to develop the project blueprint and establish unambiguous communication channels for effective communication among themselves (Sen 2021). Figure 4.3 depicts an illustration of requirement gathering and scheduled.

AI enhances the smooth coordination of DevOps teams operating remotely across different geographical locations. AI-enabled insights facilitate the sharing of requirements and specifications to accommodate localization, varied customer

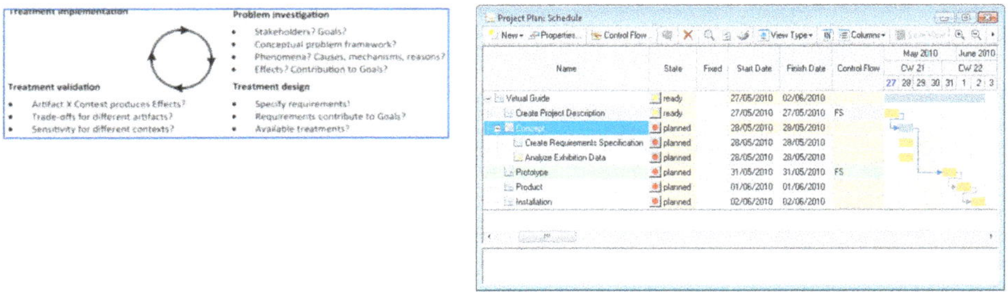

A B

Figure 4.3. Simple representation of planning scenario (A) Business requirement elicitation, problem investigation and design (B) Project plan scheduling with deliverables. This [Project planning with in-Step] image has been obtained by the authors from the Wikimedia website, where it is stated to have been released into the public domain. It is included within this book on that basis.

needs, and specific performance benchmarks. ML-powered platforms for managing business requirements are utilized by DevOps teams to save time, enabling them to concentrate on coding and delivering software products within stringent deadlines. When business requirements are adequately captured during the planning stage, project plans can remain on the critical path of the schedule. To ensure project plans adhere to schedules, cutting-edge AI tools developed using natural language processing for managing DevOps projects are proliferating in cyberspace. It has been observed that enterprises adopting AI-powered tools in this area can reduce requirements review times by up to 50% (Columbus 2023). The planning stage is typically led by project managers in collaboration with the teams, identifying suitable project management tools such as but not limited to Azure DevOps (Capizzi *et al* 2020). Here are selected AI tools suitable for adoption in the planning stage outlined as follows: Jira utilizes natural language processing and generative AI for issue tracking, project management, agile planning, enhancing the real-time sharing of information among teams, individuals, and tools. IBM Engineering Requirements Quality Assistant (IBM ERQA) is an AI tool developed using natural language processing. The tool is utilized for refining business requirements to enhance their clarity and quality. The quality of the business requirements is evaluated by detecting ambiguities and generating real-time scores. Trello offers AI-powered suggestions for task prioritization and project organization.

4.5.2 Code

During the coding phase, developers are engaged in writing and testing the code essential for constructing the software. They adhere to coding standards and implement best practice to guarantee the maintainability and scalability of the codebase. Version control systems such as Git are frequently employed to monitor changes and foster collaboration among team members (Sen 2021). Developers play a central role in code development and code review processes, utilizing integrated

```
sub clean_line() {
    ($ligne) = @_ ;
    chomp $ligne;
    if ( $origin_LANG eq "nl" ) {                           # nl
        if ( $ligne =~ m/<\/div>/ ) { return ""; }
        if ( $ligne =~ m/\{\{Wikipedia.+\// ) { return ""; }
        $ligne =~ s/===/==/g ;
    } elsif ( $origin_LANG eq "en" ) {                      # en
        $ligne =~ s/\{\{.+\|(.+)\}\}/$1/ ;
    } elsif ( $origin_LANG eq "it" ) {                      # it
        if ( $ligne =~ m/^\[\[Immagine:.+$/ ||
            $ligne =~ m/^\[\[Image:.+$/ ) { return ""; }
    }

    $ligne =~ s/\|.+\]\]/\]\]/g ; #lien interne renommé
    $ligne =~ s/#[^\]]+//g ; #ancre
    if ( $ligne =~ m/^\{\|/ || $ligne =~ m/\|\}/ ) { return ""; } #tableau
    if ( $ligne =~ m/^\|/ ) { return ""; } #<tr> / <td>

    if ( $ligne =~ m/<?[A-Za-z0-9]+>/ ) {
        die ("Erreur : balise html à la ligne $. :\n$ligne\n");
    }
    if ( $ligne =~ m/==.+==/ ) {
        return $ligne;
    } elsif ( $ligne =~ m/\[\[(.+)\]\]/ ) {
```

Figure 4.4. Sample of source code. This [Source code in Perl] image has been obtained by the authors from the Wikimedia website where it was made available by [Romainhk] under a CC BY-SA 3.0 licence. It is included within this book on that basis. It is attributed to [Romainhk].

development environments and source code management tools like GitHub, Artifactory, and CodeClimate (Capizzi *et al* 2020).

Computer source code (sample in figure 4.4) has penetrated modern life in almost every aspect. The source codes operate factories, manage transportation networks, and shape our interaction with devices. It is estimated that 2.8 trillion lines of source code have been written in the past 20 years. Yet, fundamental reality can easily be overlooked: humans are responsible for writing software. This is often a lengthy and laborious task, and vulnerable to errors. Despite low-code and no-code development environments that simplify coding tasks and enable individuals without coding expertise to create software through drag-and-drop interfaces, they still demand significant time and effort. This is where AI steps in (Greengard 2023). ML holds significant potential as a valuable tool for developers throughout the process of the software development. It can aid in assessing the performance of past software, including compile/build success, operational efficiency, and testing outcomes. Moreover, ML can offer proactive recommendations tailored to the developer's current code-writing activities. By using AI tools, developers can craft software that is not only efficient but also unique and of high quality (Trivedi 2023). AI tools suitable for adoption in this phase of DevOps for coding automation include, but are not limited to, CodeGPT, GitHub Copilot, and DeepCode. The CodeGPT, developed by OpenAI, is designed to aid developers in writing source code. Built on the transformer architecture like other GPT models (e.g., GPT-4), CodeGPT is fine-tuned specifically for coding-related tasks. It possesses the capability to generate code snippets, offer suggestions for code completion, comprehend different programming language contexts, handle complex code, and provide explanations for code segments. The primary goal of CodeGPT is to streamline the coding process by providing assistance and suggestions, thereby reducing the time developers spend on routine tasks and enhancing productivity. Similarly, GitHub Copilot, developed based on generative AI in collaboration between GitHub and OpenAI, offers similar functionalities to CodeGPT to assist software developers. Additionally, DeepCode utilizes ML to conduct code reviews and identify potential bugs and security vulnerabilities. These AI tools contribute to improving the efficiency and quality of the coding process within DevOps coding workflows.

The generation of code from natural language has been revolutionized by advancements in LLMs. Users simply describe the software requirements in natural language, prompt the model, and the code is generated automatically. Many LLMs exist for this purpose, including Codex-85M, GPT-Neo-125M, CodeT5+-770M, and CodeGen-Mono-350M. A total of 27 such models were surveyed and analyzed in a study by Zan *et al* (2023). LLMs for code, including PolyCoder, Codex, GPT-Neo, GPT-J, Code-Parrot, and GPT-NeoX-20B, were evaluated across 12 different programming languages. Performance varied depending on the context of each programming language. PolyCoder was found to perform the best, exhibiting the lowest perplexity compared to the other models (Xu *et al* 2022).

As pointed out in Columbus (2023), the interviews conducted with DevOps teams from various leading enterprise software companies competing in CRM, supply chain management, and social media markets, emphasize that the most productive use case is noted to be the AI coding tools because they produce the highest gains in coding accuracy. These AI coding tools accelerate DevOps team productivity.

4.5.3 Build

This stage involves compiling the source code developed during the coding phase into executable files. Activities in this stage include packaging the code, compilation, linking, and dependency management (Sen 2021). During compilation, the source code is transformed into an executable file. The challenges of compilation vary based on the complexity of the software. For large-scale software, compilation may involve a large number of files, which can be approached in different ways. Conversely, compilation for small- and medium-scale software is typically less challenging compared to its larger counterparts. The final executable file is generated through the combination of object code and libraries (figure 4.5 shows a sample of build software).

Dependency management assists in managing the software ecosystem's supply chain for security and reliability. The best practices in managing dependencies in software development are as follows: version pinning: limiting version dependencies to specific versions of software for easy reproducibility; signature and hash verification: ensuring that the software package intended for release and installation is authentic; hash verification aids in verifying the correct package by comparing the hash of the software package; discarding irrelevant dependencies: over time, some

Figure 4.5. Sample interface of build software. This [First version of wavesampler (0.1 unreleased)] image has been obtained by the authors from the Wikimedia website where it was made available by [WavesHackerman] under a CC BY-SA 4.0 licence. It is included within this book on that basis. It is attributed to [Kennedy Edson Silva de Souza].

dependencies may no longer be necessary and should be discarded; vulnerability scanning: dependencies are scanned for vulnerabilities to monitor and automatically detect if vulnerabilities are introduced by the dependencies; mixing private and public dependencies: sharing logic across multiple software and reusing tools (Ingram 2021). Once compiled and packaged, the source code is run on computer systems. Many professionals, including developers and system administrators, are involved in these tasks (Capizzi *et al* 2020).

The AI tools involved in the automation of build processes include: Jenkins: a powerful open-source tool integrated with ML to automate build processes that is revolutionizing DevOps by providing automated and intelligent build management; JFrogXray: this leverages ML in its development to scan all components and dependencies for vulnerabilities, thus improving the effectiveness of DevOps teams; BuildPulse with ML capabilities, used for optimizing build processes, helping DevOps teams understand and improve the performance of their builds. Its ML capabilities analyze build data, detect patterns, and predict possible build failures. These AI tools enhance the automation of modern DevOps practices.

4.5.4 Testing

Testing plays a critical role in DevOps to ensure that the code delivers the expected output and it involves verifying performance, functions, and security of the software. The primary objective of conducting testing across different aspects of the software is to identify and rectify bugs found in the source code (Sen 2021). The four essential strategies for achieving successful testing in DevOps include leveraging tools and technology, skills deployment effectively, fostering organizational culture, and implementing robust processes and metrics (Angara *et al* 2018). Testing is of different types, such as unit, integration, and user acceptance testing. Typically, testing is conducted by quality assurance staff using automated tools like JUnit and Selenium to streamline the testing process (Capizzi *et al* 2020). Quality assurance AI tools are demonstrating capabilities in forecasting potential failure areas within enterprise software prior to deployment in real-world environments. AI excels in tracing root cause of failures and has significantly sped up software products delivery for a prominent CRM provider, resulting in a notable 72% reduction in time-to-restore customers' enterprise environments (Columbus 2023).

AI proves to be a valuable asset in DevOps by improving the software development process and streamlining testing procedures. Whether it is regression testing, functional testing, or user acceptance testing, a significant volume of data is generated. AI can analyze this data, discern patterns, and pinpoint subpar coding practices that contribute to errors. This insight aids in enhancing efficiency within the development cycle (Trivedi 2023). Different AI tools are available for testing during the DevOps test phase, but this discussion focusses on a few as representatives. For example, Applitools employs ML and computer vision capabilities to perform visual testing, detecting user interface alterations, and ensuring uniform user experiences across diverse platforms. Applitools swiftly validates thousands of elements and scenarios by simulating human interaction with the user interface. The computer vision in Applitools, a specialized form of functional testing, is employed to identify visual modifications in user interfaces, differing from conventional automation reliant on functional assertions. Test.ai employs ML algorithms for automated test case generation, prioritization, and execution. It serves as a replacement for traditional test automation tools prone to frequent failures and usability challenges. Test.ai's bots autonomously construct tests, adapt them across different platforms, and maintain them amidst application alterations. Additional AI tools suitable for adoption in the DevOps test phase encompass CodeGuru, which utilizes ML, Azure DevOps integrating ML and natural language processing, and GitLab DevOps, also leveraging ML capabilities. Columbus (2023) reported that at Facebook, there's a bug detection tool that predicts defects and recommends solutions with an impressive 80% accuracy rate, thanks to ML tools that are learning to autonomously fix bugs. SemmleCodeQL stands out as the premier AI-based DevOps tool in this domain. DevOps teams leveraging CodeQL have the capability to identify vulnerabilities in their code and detect logical variations across their entire codebase. The summary of the test cycle is depicted in figure 4.6.

Figure 4.6. Software testing cycle.

4.5.5 Release

When an updated version of software with new features, commonly referred to as a new version, is ready to be delivered to customers, it triggers a release (see figure 4.7). In this stage, diverse professionals in the development team are involved in the activities, especially developers and system administrators (Capizzi *et al* 2020). As developers are tasked with releasing code at high velocity, operations teams must ensure minimal disruption to the systems in operation. AI has the potential to revolutionize DevOps by enhancing collaboration between development and operations teams. AI tools can assist teams by offering a unified view into the systems and their issues across the complex chain of DevOps. At the same time, they can enhance the comprehensive understanding and immediate rectification of detected flaws (Trivedi 2023).

The selected AI tools that can used for the release of new versions of software include GitLabContinuous Integration/ContinuousDeployment, Azure DevOps and Jenkins.

4.5.6 Deployment

This stage involves the installation and execution of the software product released in the production environment and the IT infrastructure. Communication and collaboration between the development team and the operations team are highly critical

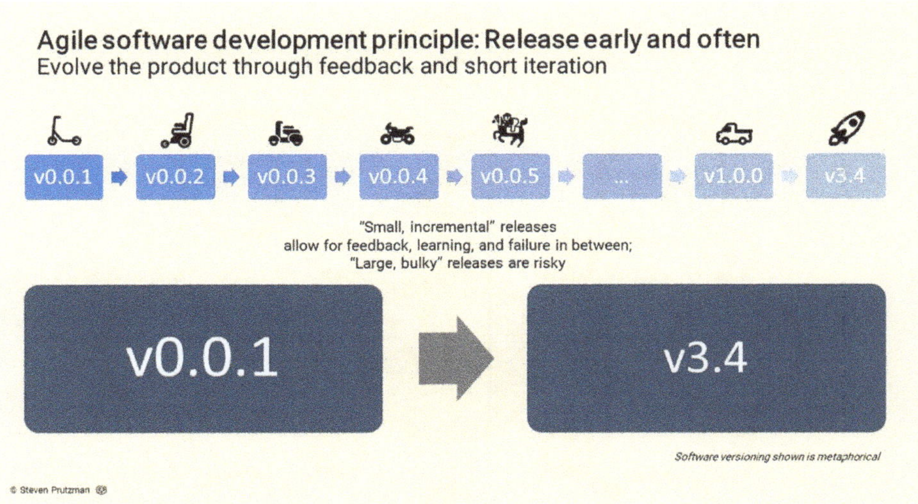

Figure 4.7. Releasing new version of software with additional features. This [Agile software development release early and often] image has been obtained by the authors from the Wikimedia website where it was made available by [Steveprutz] under a CC BY-SA 4.0 licence. It is included within this book on that basis. It is attributed to [Steveprutz].

and mandatory at this stage. The automated tools to be used depend on the target environment, such as a physical or virtual environment (cloud), among others. It also depends on the software, including operating systems, middleware, compilers, containerization, and libraries. The traditional tools available for adoption include Amazon Web Services CodeDeploy, VMware, VirtualBox, etc (Capizzi *et al* 2020). Infrastructure configuration, server setup, and software deployment using containerization technologies such as Docker or Kubernetes are automated using continuous integration and continuous deployment (CI/CD) pipelines to ensure consistency and deployment reliability (Sen 2021).

Some of the tools are suitable for multiple activities involving different stages of DevOps. The AI tools listed in the release stage can effectively be used in the deployment stage of DevOps. Figure 4.8 is a typical example of deployed software.

4.5.7 Operation

This stage involves the maintenance and adaptation of infrastructure running the software product (figure 4.9). These tasks are mostly handled by system administrators with the aid of configuration tools (Capizzi *et al* 2020). As the software is deployed and starts running, its performance in the production settings is monitored and managed. Monitoring includes proactive measures, log analysis, error tracking, and prompt response to resolve errors for recovery. Robust tools for monitoring software running in the production environment and mechanisms for triggering alarms are essential to ensure consistent availability and optimal performance (Sen 2021). A DevOps team in an interview revealed that they adopted AI tools for

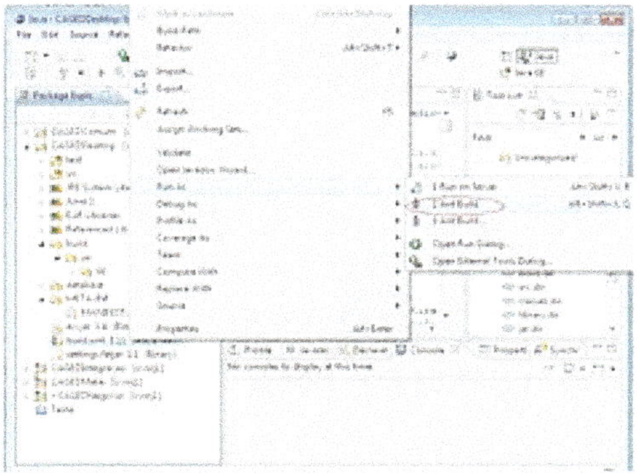

Figure 4.8. Deployed software interface. This [GUI Mandelbulber2] image has been obtained by the authors from the Wikimedia website where it was made available by [PantheraLeo1359531] under a CC BY-SA 4.0 licence. It is included within this book on that basis. It is attributed to [PantheraLeo1359531].

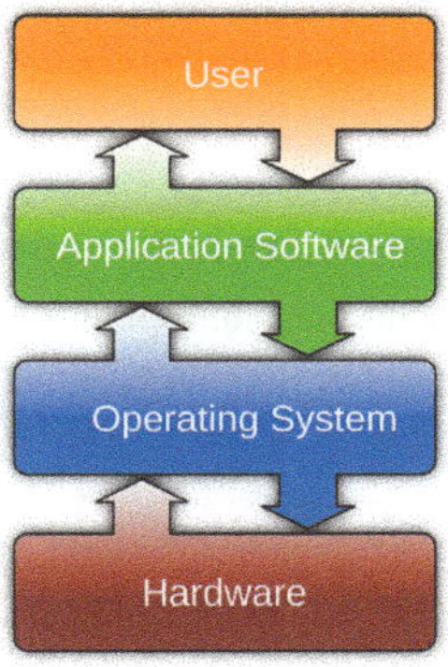

Figure 4.9. Software running in execution environment.

automating the configuration of the software execution environment to optimize performance for customer deployment (Columbus 2023).

In the stage of the DevOps operation, AI tools are required to monitor, manage and optimize applications performance and the IT infrastructure. The select AI tools for use in the operation stages are as follows: Dynatrace, Splunk IT Intelligence, and New Relic One. These tools are used to alert multiple sources of errors, identify the event causing the errors, predict incidents, detect performance issues, roll back error and recommend tasks to improve performance.

4.5.8 Monitoring

The monitoring stage (figure 4.10) of DevOps involves data collection for analysis to determine the performance of the software, patterns of usage, and user behaviour. Monitoring tools and metrics are typically employed to indicate the system's performance (Sen 2021). The monitoring of the software is often carried out by system administrators, operators, and other stakeholders involved in managing the

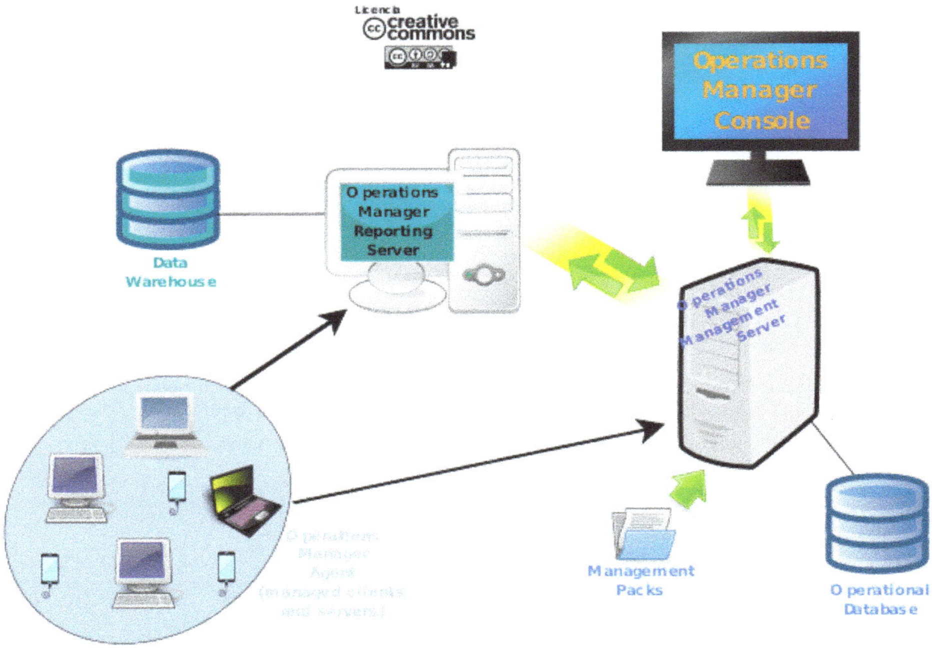

Figure 4.10. Pictorial representation of monitoring software in operations. This [System Center Operations Manager] image has been obtained by the authors from the Wikimedia website where it was made available by [Jimmy Olano] under a CC BY 3.0 licence. It is included within this book on that basis. It is attributed to [Jimmy Olano].

project, using automated tools (Capizzi *et al* 2020). The findings are used by the teams to make critical decisions to continue improving the quality of the software (Sen 2021). There is a high degree of complexity and difficulty for DevOps teams in monitoring and managing the DevOps environment due to the large volume of data generated at high speeds by today's dynamic distributed environment. This type of environment poses a challenge to DevOps teams in tracing and resolving customer problems instantly. For instance, imagine a team having to sift through exabytes of data to identify critical events responsible for triggering an issue. The DevOps teams may spend hundreds of hours navigating through this data to trace the issue. Therefore, AI is the future for handling such large volumes of data in daily operations, as humans may struggle to manage it effectively. For DevOps teams to be effective in monitoring, a robust alert system is required to trigger alarms when defects or flaws are detected. In some instances, flaws come in very large volumes with almost the same level of severity, making it practically impossible for the DevOps team to effectively manage the alarms. ML has the capacity to prioritize responses according to defined criteria (e.g., previous behaviour, severity, and source of the alerts) (Trivedi 2023). ML can predict errors, recognize patterns, and identify early signs of failure (Trivedi 2023). In an interview with the DevOps lead at a leading supply chain management software provider, the leader admitted that the company used ML to determine successful projects and those requiring code review and rewriting. ML helps the company detect patterns in the data and gain insights (Columbus 2023).

The DevOps team gathers feedback at every stage using automated tools (Trivedi 2023). AI-powered automated monitoring tools are many, with a few representatives showcased here. For instance, OneGrep serves as a DevOps Copilot developed based on ML technology, aimed at overseeing observations and expediting the process of information discovery by minimizing the time needed to handle alerts and event investigations. OneGrep analyzes user experiences, assists teams in swiftly discovering and diagnosing problems, suggests actions, and identifies patterns. Dynatrace is an automated tool that incorporates an ML algorithm, natural language processing, generative AI and causal AI for detecting and analyzing cause of problems, monitoring software performance, anomaly detection (e.g. disk resizing) and suggest actions to take. Prometheus implements AI techniques combining the power of Bing index and ChatGPT. Prometheus is used for anomaly detection, alerting, and monitoring large-scale systems. Fawzy *et al* (2023) developed DevOps an anomaly detection framework by leveraging ML. The framework operates at the DevOps monitoring stage to analyze data from application logs, system logs, and performance metrics.

4.6 Accelerating security in development and operations via large language models

Companies adopting DevOps can deliver up to 500 new versions of updated software within 24 h. Rapid delivery of updated software is prone to security risks if the security team has not sufficiently taken strong measures to tackle security issues (Branson and Armstrong 2004). Every organization considers the security of the development environment a top priority. Thus, organizations are investigating approaches to secure production units effectively for product development (Rafi *et al* 2020). The process involved in the integration of policies related to information security and technology into different phases of the DevOps lifecycle and value stream is referred to as DevOps security (DevSecOps). DevSecOps is achieved by promoting collaborations among the security, development, and operations teams (Farroha and Farroha 2014). DevSecOps is considered one of the main factors necessary for successful software development and implementation, given that security is essential in software development. Due to the increase in distributed denial of service attacks, businesses are motivated to implement strong security systems to protect against threats from hackers. AI has the potential to complement the efforts of DevSecOps in improving software security. ML can be utilized to develop anomaly detection systems to detect threats. Introducing AI into DevOps can thus ensure performance and prevent attacks (Trivedi 2023).

An interview conducted with DevOps leaders revealed that incorporating security into the development lifecycle can reduce bottlenecks in scheduling. Many of the DevOps leaders argued that infusing quality assurance into the DevOps framework is critical (Columbus 2023). Keen on investigating deeper into how ML can detect code vulnerabilities in real-time, I conversed with Maty Siman, CTO of Checkmarx. He emphasizes that 'even organizations boasting the most mature Software Development Life Cycles often encounter difficulties in prioritizing and managing vulnerabilities. ML algorithms, which concentrate developers' or Application Security teams' attention on genuine positives and vulnerable components posing significant threats, are crucial for overcoming this hurdle.' Additionally, Maty highlights that ML algorithms can be trained to recognize that certain types of vulnerabilities have a higher likelihood of being genuine positives compared to others. With this automated 'vetting' mechanism in place, teams can streamline and expedite their remediation efforts with greater insight (Columbus 2023). Anomaly detection refers to a defence system with the capability of identifying abnormal or suspicious behaviour with the potential to compromise security, data integrity, data confidentiality, and data reliability (Maurushat 2019, Pathan 2014). Semmle QL is employed by Microsoft security researchers to identify vulnerabilities in source code and respond appropriately to remedy and prevent any security breaches (Columbus 2023).

LLMs for detecting vulnerabilities in software are attracting attention from both industry and academia due to their performance. Therefore, a surge in the adoption of LLMs by industries to improve software security has been witnessed in recent times. For example, Noever (2023) used GPT-4 for the detection of software vulnerabilities. It was found that GPT-4 detected software vulnerabilities almost four times better than conventional tools such as static code analyzers. Wang *et al* (2023) employed transformers to develop DefectHunter, a software vulnerabilities detection tool, which demonstrates the ability to identify software vulnerabilities effectively. KARTAL is a tool that combines the power of LLMs with web applications for the detection of web application vulnerabilities. The tool achieved an 87.19% vulnerability detection accuracy with the capacity to predict over 500 vulnerabilities per second (Sakaoglu 2023). OpenAI's Codex is another LLM that automatically identifies and rectifies bugs related to software security (Ahmad *et al* 2023).

4.7 Industrial applications and case studies

Industrial DevOps is a methodology designed to facilitate continual adaptation and enhancement within industrial manufacturing by providing access to industrial data for diverse stakeholders (Hasselbring *et al* 2019). Due to advancements in DevOps, companies such as Google, Amazon and many others now have the capability to release multiple new software versions in a single day, thereby rendering the traditional notion of software release an obsolete approach (Capizzi *et al* 2020). The technology giants that integrates AI to enhance DevOps are outlined in this section. The technology giants listed in table 4.2 are exemplars of industry leaders integrating AI technologies such as ML, natural language processing, computer vision, and more into their DevOps practices. This integration aims to boost innovation speed with assured confidence and reliability, while also enhancing operational automation.

Table 4.2. Companies adopting AI to enhance their DevOps practices.

Company	Year	Description	Main products	Website
IBM	1911	International Business Machines (IBM) is a technology company that manufactures and sells hardware, software, and middleware. It also delves into AI, cloud computing, blockchain, and quantum computing. Some of the company's major products include the hard disk drive, floppy disk, and relational database.	The hard disk drive and floppy disk	www.ibm.com
Microsoft	1976	Microsoft Corporation manufacture software especially operating systems and PC. Windows operating systems and office applications are the well known products of the company.	Windows operating system and office applications	www.microsoft.com/
Google LLC	1998	Google specialized on internet services and hardware. It is well known for its search engine, email service—Gmail and cloud services, now extend to processors e.g. tensor processing unit.	Google search engine	www.google.com
Cisco Systems, Inc.	1984	Manufacturers of network equipment both hardware e.g. servers, firewall, routers, security device, switches and software, e.g. package tracer. Consultancy services and technical support is part of the companies mandate.	Network equipment's	www.cisco.com
Amazon Web Services	2006	The company offers cloud services and API to any interesting party on payment bases. The type of services offered includes GPU or CPU hours, storage, IoT tools, analytics and AI platforms.	On demand cloud services	aws.amazon.com
Hewlett Packard Enterprise Development LP	1939	Manufacturers of computer hardware and software. Technical support and consultation are part of the services that the company is providing.	Computer hardware and printer	www.hpe.com/

(*Continued*)

Table 4.2. (*Continued*)

Company	Year	Description	Main products	Website
Dell EMC (Dell Inc.)	1979	Dell is company known for the manufacturing of different types of computer hardware (e.g. storage system, network equipment, etc) and software. It also offers cloud services, consultation and support.	Computer hardware	www.dell.com/
Red Hat, Inc.	1993	The company develops software—operating systems and middleware; it provides cloud computing and consultation services.	Red Hat Linux operating systems	www.redhat.com
Puppet, Inc.	2005	Specializes in developing software, automation, DevOps and security solutions.		www.puppet.com
Oracle Corporation	1977	Oracle develops software—databases and provide cloud computing services.	Database and enterprise resource planning	www.broadcom.com

4.8 Summary

The chapter introduces readers to the foundational concept of the oldest traditional software development model, known as the waterfall model. This model is discussed to offer readers insight into the systematic methodology of software engineering, acting as a cornerstone for the evolution of contemporary approaches to software development. Moreover, the chapter delineates the constraints inherent in the waterfall model, which subsequently catalyzed the creation of more sophisticated prescriptive process models.

The traditional DevOps methodology in software development has been examined as a precursor to the incorporation of AI across various stages of the DevOps lifecycle. Emphasis has been placed on the pivotal role of communication between development and operations teams. Success in DevOps implementation has been attributed to automation, knowledge sharing, and fostering transparency as fundamental enablers. Additionally, the various stages of the DevOps lifecycle—ranging from plan, code, build, testing, release, deployment, to operations and monitoring—have been delineated.

Organizations are driven by the imperative to innovate swiftly in order to stay ahead in a competitive landscape. This urgency to innovate rapidly, while ensuring reliability, serves as the impetus for the adoption of AI-enhanced DevOps methodologies. By integrating AI into DevOps practices, organizations seek to augment traditional approaches, thereby confronting the complexities inherent in modern software development more effectively and innovate at a faster rate.

The chapter outlined and discussed the integration of AI into different phases of the DevOps lifecycle. The AI cutting-edge tools suggested for use in different stages of the DevOps lifecycle is not exhaustive but representative. In the plan phase of DevOps, the AI cutting-edge tools suggested to fasten the planning activities include: Azure DevOps, IBM ERQA and Jira. For coding they are: CodeGPT, GitHub Copilot and DeepCode. Build includes: JFrogXray, BuildPulse and Jenkins. Testing includes: CodeGuru, Applitools and Azure DevOps. Deploy and release includes: Azure DevOps, Jenkins and GitLab. Operate includes: Dynatrace, Splunk IT Intelligence and New Relic One. Monitoring includes: OneGrep, Dynatrace and Prometheus

This chapter presents industrial applications and case studies where cutting-edge AI automation tools are used to enhance DevOps. These examples can help readers appreciate the critical role AI tools play in developing software products. The chapter summarized how top technology giants such as Microsoft, Google, Oracle, Cisco Systems, Dell, Red Hat, Amazon, HP, IBM, and Puppet Inc. adopt AI to enhance their DevOps activities.

References

Agarwal B B, Gupta M and Tayal S P 2009 *Software Engineering and Testing* (Burlington, MA: Jones & Bartlett Publishers)

Ahmad B, Thakur S, Tan B, Karri R and Pearce H 2023 Fixing hardware security bugs with large language models *arXiv preprint* arXiv:2302.01215

Alexander M 2018 *Why Planning Is the Most Critical Step in Project Management* https://techrepublic.com/article/why-planning-is-the-most-critical-step-in-project-management/ (accessed 27 April 2024)

Angara J, Gutta S and Prasad S 2018 DevOps with continuous testing architecture and its metrics model *Recent Findings in Intelligent Computing Techniques: Proc. of the 5th ICACNI 2017* 3 (Singapore: Springer) pp 271–81

AWS 2024 *Add Intelligence to Your Developer Operations* https://aws.amazon.com/machine-learning/ml-use-cases/ai-for-devops/ (accessed 21 April 2024)

Branson R and Armstrong D 2004 General practitioners' perceptions of sharing workload in group practices: qualitative study *Brit. Med. J.* **329** 381

Capizzi A, Distefano S and Mazzara M 2020 From devops to devdataops: data management in devops processes *Software Engineering Aspects of Continuous Development and New Paradigms of Software Production and Deployment: Second Int. Workshop, DEVOPS 2019 (Château de Villebrumier, France, May 6–8, 2019)* (Cham: Springer) pp 52–62

Cois C A, Yankel J and Connell A 2014 Modern DevOps: optimizing software development through effective system interactions *2014 Int. Professional Communication Conf. (IPCC) IEEE* (Piscataway, NJ: IEEE) pp 1–7

Columbus L 2023 10 ways AI is accelerating DevOps *Forbes Magazine Online* https://forbes.com/sites/louiscolumbus/2020/07/31/10-ways-ai-is-accelerating-devops/?sh=4f32df496a50 (accessed 4 April 2024)

Farroha B S and Farroha D L 2014 A framework for managing mission needs, compliance, and trust in the DevOps environment *2014 IEEE Military Communications Conf.* (Piscataway, NJ: IEEE) pp 288–93

Fawzy A H, Wassif K and Moussa H 2023 Framework for automatic detection of anomalies in DevOps *J. King Saud Univ.-Comp. Inform. Sci.* **35** 8–19

Gall M and Pigni F 2022 Taking DevOps mainstream: a critical review and conceptual framework *Eur. J. Inf. Syst.* **31** 548–67

Greengard S 2023 AI rewrites coding *Commun. ACM* **66** 12–4

Hasselbring W, Henning S, Latte B, Möbius A, Richter T, Schalk S and Wojcieszak M 2019 Industrial DevOps *2019 IEEE Int. Conf. on Software Architecture Companion (ICSA-C)* (Piscataway, NJ: IEEE) pp 123–6

Hüttermann M 2012 *DevOps for Developers* (New York: Apress)

IEEE Computer Society 2023 The Future of Tech: 2022 Technology Predictions Revealed https://www.computer.org/2022-top-technology-predictions

Ingram D 2021 *Best Practice for Dependency Management* https://cloud.google.com/blog/topics/developers-practitioners/best-practices-dependency-management (accessed 30 May 2024)

Jones C 2009 *Software Engineering Best Practices* (New York: McGraw-Hill)

Karjian R 2023 The history of artificial intelligence: complete AI timeline https://techtarget.com/searchEnterpriseAI/tip/The-history-of-artificial-intelligence-Complete-AI-timeline (accessed 9 September, 2023)

Kirkpatrick K 2023 Can AI demonstrate creativity ? *Commun. ACM* **66** 21–3

Luz W P, Pinto G and Bonifácio R 2019 Adopting DevOps in the real world: a theory, a model, and a case study *J. Syst. Softw.* **157** 110384

Maurushat A 2019 *Ethical Hacking* (Ontario: University of Ottawa Press/Les Presses de l'Universitéd'Ottawa.)

Noever D 2023 Can large language models find and fix vulnerable software? *arXiv preprint* arXiv:2308.10345

Pathan A S K (ed) 2014 *The State of the Art in Intrusion Prevention and Detection* **44** (Hoboken, NJ: CRC Press)

Pressman R S and Maxim B R 2015 *Software Engineering: A Practitioner's Approach* (McGraw Hill)

Rafi S, Yu W, Akbar M A, Alsanad A and Gumaei A 2020 Prioritization based taxonomy of DevOps security challenges using PROMETHEE *IEEE Access* **8** 105426–46

Rodríguez P, Haghighatkhah A, Lwakatare L E, Teppola S, Suomalainen T, Eskeli J and Oivo M 2017 Continuous deployment of software intensive products and services: a systematic mapping study *J. Syst. Softw.* **123** 263–91

Sakaoglu S 2023 KARTAL: web application vulnerability hunting using large language models 2023, 85+8, Master's Programme in Security and Cloud Computing (SECCLO) [Online] http://urn.fi/URN:NBN:fi:aalto202308275121

Sen A 2021 Devops, devsecops, aiops-paradigms to it operations *Evolving Technologies for Computing, Communication and Smart World: Proceedings of ETCCS 2020* (Singapore: Springer) pp 211–21

Shashkina V 2022 Software development team structure: deciding factors, approaches, roles and responsibilities www.itrexgroup.com/blog/software-development-team-structure/ (accessed 17 April 2024)

Tripathi S 2023 What is DevOps? How development + operations helps teams work more efficiently www.freecodecamp.org/news/how-devops-works/ (accessed 17 April 2024)

Trivedi M 2023 12 ways AI is transforming DEVOPS https://tadigital.com/insights/perspectives/12-ways-ai-transforming-devops. (accessed 16 March 2023)

Wang J, Huang Z, Liu H, Yang N and Xiao Y 2023 Defecthunter: a novel llm-driven boosted-conformer-based code vulnerability detection mechanism *arXiv preprint* arXiv:2309.15324

Wen L, Qian H and Liu W 2022 Research on intelligent cloud native architecture and key technologies based on DevOps concept *Procedia Comput. Sci.* **208** 590–7

Xu F F, Alon U, Neubig G and Hellendoorn V J 2022 A systematic evaluation of large language models of code *Proc. of the 6th ACM SIGPLAN Int. Symp. on Machine Programming* pp 1–10

Yang D, Wang D, Yang D, Dong Q, Wang Y, Zhou H and Hong D 2020 DevOps in practice for education management information system at ECNU *Procedia Comput. Sci.* **176** 1382–91

Zan D, Chen B, Zhang F, Lu D, Wu B, Guan B and Lou J G 2023 Large language models meet NL2Code: a survey *Proc. of the 61st Annual Meeting of the Association for Computational Linguistics, Volume 1 (Long Papers)* pp 7443–64

Chapter 5

Centralized huge graph neural networks advances

The huge graph neural network (GNN) is a hot research topic currently and expected to be widely used in different aspects of machine learning (ML) in the future. This is because of it is efficiency and effectiveness in modelling complex real-world problems. A tremendous volume of papers on huge GNNs is currently flooding the literature. As such, a large number of published review articles on huge GNNs have been published. It makes it practically tedious and time consuming to go through the published review articles one by one in different databases. This chapter centralizes the published review articles on huge GNNs from different perspectives, pointing out the main focus of each paper for expert readers to easily grasp. For novice and new researchers, the chapter presents tutorials on the huge GNN starting with a basic introduction to graph theory in a simple and easy-to-follow approach to have a grasp of the huge GNN before delving into the main content of the chapter. For expert readers, challenges and research opportunities are highlighted. Industrial applications and case studies where huge GNNs are in practice in real-world environments are outlined and discussed. It is believed that the chapter will make it easy for the research community to access different review papers on huge GNNs at a one-stop-point and serve as an entry point to newcomers including postgraduate students.

5.1 Introduction

Graphs are prevalent in the immediate environment. For example, watching a movie on Netflix, browsing through the feeds of a friend on Facebook, purchasing an item on e-commerce site Amazon or searching for a researcher on Google search engine, these actions have the chance of triggering queries on a huge graph. The databases of movies and books are frequently encoded as the knowledge graph for recommendation systems to be efficient. The services provided by social media platforms

doi:10.1088/978-0-7503-6320-4ch5

depend on graphs. The shopping on e-commerce sites uses a co-purchased network to boost sales of products. Abstracting/indexing databases with citation indices such as the web of science, Google Scholar and Scopus develop huge citation graphs. The internet forms a huge graph with billions of vertices and edges. The graph can be view as a powerful tool for the representation of three-dimensional data like the point cloud, meshes or structure of molecules and interaction between proteins. The dominant and widely accepted algorithm for processing data that creats a graph structure is the GNN (Li *et al* 2021). Graph structure can be used for the representation of data naturally (Scarselli *et al* 2008). Graph-related problems are best tackled by huge GNNs (IEEE Computer Society 2023). The GNN has attracted unprecedented interest from the research community because of its benefit in solving problems in different domains of applications including transportation, social science, knowledge graph, recommendation, physics, chemistry and neuroscience (Dwivedi *et al* 2022).

Artificial neural networks (ANNs) motivated the development of GNNs with capability to learn a join representation from graph structured data and edge/vertex. Evidence from the literature indicates that the GNN has solved graph structured data-related problems successfully. In addition, the GNN has been applied in graph-related applications like social networks, knowledge graph, recommender systems and many more. The graphs in the such applications are typically huge in nature comprising vertices running into millions or even billions in some cases. For example, the graph of Facebook contained billions of vertices. Similarly, items sold on Amazon run into billions with billions of customers making it form a huge bipartite graph for the task of recommendation (Zheng *et al* 2020).

In recent times, there has been more attention on the analysis of graphs with ML in view of the fact that the graphs have great power of representation (Hamilton *et al* 2017a, Li *et al* 2019). Representation learning is found to be effective with a GNN framework. The GNN algorithm operates by following a neighbourhood aggregation scheme where the vertex vector representation is computed recursively by aggregation and transformation of vectors representation of the vertex neighbours (Xu *et al* 2018). The GNN can effectively exploit the relationship among the vertices for the prediction of label quantities such as the vertex classification (Zhou *et al* 2020). The GNN-related problems include: graph classification and link prediction; graph generation and graph transformation; graph matching and graph structure learning; dynamic and heterogeneous GNNs; automated ML and self-supervised learning (Wu *et al* 2022).

The GNN is currently receiving tremendous attention from the research community likely because of the availability of high-performance computing systems and large-scale graph data over the internet, especially social media platforms, online e-commerce, telecommunications, etc. A basic search in any of the academic databases attests to that by returning a very large number of related GNN publications. Most of the publications fall within the last five years. As a result of this large volume of GNN publications flooding the literature, a lot of review papers on GNNs from different perspectives such as operators, convolution, spatio-temporal, etc have been published in the literature within short period of time.

The technology prediction of 2023 by IEEE computer society revealed that GNNs are expected to be widely used in the future for solving ML problems (IEEE Computer Society 2023). The interest in GNNs by the research community, especially for ML is expected to transit into the future with full force. Reading through the review papers one by one by a researcher can be time consuming, hectic and tedious because of the large number of review papers already published.

To the best of the author's knowledge, no attempt has been made by the research community to centralize the already published review papers to ease the work of researchers in locating/searching for a suitable review paper on GNNs for in-depth reading. Therefore, this chapter proposes to close this gap by presenting a centralized GNN review of reviews from different perspectives outlining the focus of each of the published reviews on GNNs. The chapter intends to present an easy-flow tutorial on GNNs for novice researchers to learn before reading any of the review papers. We believed that the chapter will stimulate the interest of early and novice researchers to start work on GNNs. To expert researchers, the chapter could reduce the time required to locate appropriate review papers on GNNs for further reading and locating future research directions. Therefore, it will help in developing GNNs.

5.2 Fundamentals of graph and artificial neural networks

The knowledge of graph data structure is a pre-requisite to the fundamental understanding of how the GNN algorithm operates to achieve its goal, likewise ANNs. The graph theories and computational description of ANNs are presented in this section to equip the reader with basic operations of the ANN algorithm and graphs as the pre-requisite knowledge before delving into GNNs. Understanding the basic operation of ANNs and graphs can give a reader better understanding of the way an ANN operates on the graph to produce output.

5.2.1 Key-terms

Keywords to help a newcomer coming into this research arena and understand the main keywords before properly jumping into the main content, similar to the flow in Ward *et al* (2022), is presented in this sub-section.

5.2.1.1 Vertices

These are the representation of items or entities or objects that can be described to attribute quantity and the relationship that exists among the items or objects or entities. The vertex is also referred to as the node. In the context of ANNs it is referred to as a neuron or unit or processing element.

5.2.1.2 Edges

The edge is the representation of the relationship between the entities or items or objects. It also characterized and represents the relationship among the items, entities, or objects.

5.2.1.3 Neighbourhoods

Neighbourhood is a graph within a graph, meaning a subgraph in a graph, representing a distinct set of edges and vertices. The neighbourhood is mostly around a vertex with its edges that are disjointed having direct connection with the vertices.

5.2.1.4 Features

These constitute attributes that are quantifiable characterizing the circumstances under investigation which characterize the occurrence that is under study. In the context of graphs, the features are applied for the characterization of edges and vertices. For example, in a social network, a person serving as the vertex can have features quantifying their age, popularity on the social media platform and activeness in using the social media.

5.2.1.5 Embedding

This is a feature representation in a compressed form. Large feature vectors can be reduced into low-dimensional embedding by reducing the large vectors associated with the graph edges and vertices. This makes it possible to be classified with low-order models, i.e. making it linearly separable data. The points in the original space are expected to be maintained in the embedded space and it is considered as a key for measuring embedding quality. The embedding for edges, vertices, graph or neighbourhood can be created. Based on different contexts, the embedding can also be called encoding, high-level feature vectors, representation or latent vectors.

5.2.2 Graph

A graph is the representation of relationships between objects pairs. In simplified terms, a graph can be viewed as the set of objects referred to as the nodes or vertices. The connections between the vertices or arc are referred to as the edges. The graph has application in the real world such as in the modelling of transportation systems, mapping, electrical engineering and computer networks. Before delving into the graph properly, the concept of graph in discussion should not be misinterpreted or confused with the concept of plotting graphs like bar charts and plotting of functions. The type of graph in this chapter is not related to such graphs. The graph can be drawn for visualization by representing vertices with an oval or rectangle and connecting the pairs of the vertices with edges (Goodrich *et al* 2014) as shown in figure 5.1.

The graph can be used to model many real-world problems. A typical example of a graph in a real-world scenario is Facebook where the friends represent the vertex, the social interaction between the friends/users on the engagement of a post such as like or comment represent the edges. The friends/users can have attributes such as name, location and date of birth. Similarly, a website is another example, where the web pages represent the vertex, whereas the edge is represented by the hyperlink. In road networks, the cities represent the vertices and the highways represent the edges.

The abstract view of the graph can be discussed as follows: a graph G is the set of vertices V and the collective set E of vertices pairs from V referred to as the edges.

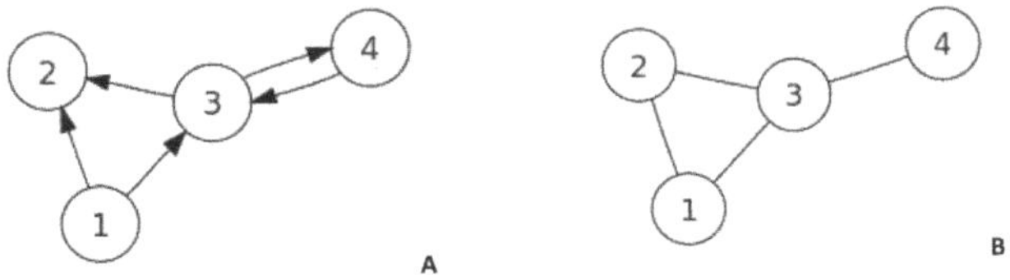

Figure 5.1. Visual representation of a typical graph: (A) directed graph and (B) undirected graph. These [Directed graph no background] and [Undirected graph no background] images have been obtained by the author from the Wikimedia website, where they are stated to have been released into the public domain. They are included within this book on that basis.

Therefore, the graph represents the relationship existing between the pairs of vertices emanating from a set of V. For the purpose of uniformity throughout the chapter, edges and vertices will be used throughout the book unlike other books that use arcs and nodes. In a graph, the edges can be directed or undirected. The edge of a graph is said to be directed if (u, v) pair is ordered directed from u to v whereby u is preceding v. The edges of the graph are said to be undirected if the (u, v) or $\{u, v\}$ pair is unordered (Goodrich *et al* 2014). Some important properties of the graph can be explored using propositions as follows Goodrich *et al* (2014):

Proposition 5.1: if a graph G is composed of edges m and set of vertices V, then the following expression is formulated:

$$\sum_{v \text{ in } V} \deg(v) = 2m$$

Proof: The (u, v) as the edge is counted twice in the summation provided in the expression one time by its endpoint u and v. Therefore, the total number of the contributions by the edges to the vertices degrees is two times the number of edges.

Proposition 5.2: if a graph G is a directed graph comprised of edges m and set of vertices V, then the following expression is formulated:

$$\sum_{v \text{ in } V} indeg(v) = \sum_{v \text{ in } V} outdeg(v) = m$$

Proof: Typically, an edge (u, v) contributes a single unit to the origin u out-degree and in-degree of its destination v. Therefore, the total number of its contributions of the edges to the out-degree belonging to vertices is the same as (equals) the number of edges. The same principle applies to the in-degree.

Proposition 5.3: Let a simple graph be G having n vertices and edges m if the graph G is a directed graph, $m \leqslant n(n-1)/2$, whereas $m \leqslant (n-1)$ if the G is a directed graph.

Proof: Let us assume that G is an undirected graph. In view of the fact that two edges cannot have the same endpoints and two self-loops exist, thus, the maximum degree of a vertex in the graph G is $n{-}1$. Consequently, by proposition 5.1, $2m \leqslant n(n-1)$. Let us now assume that the graph G is directed. Because there is no way two edges can have both origin and destination to be the same and self-loops do not exist, the maximum in-degree of the graph G vertex is $(n-1)$. Hence, by proposition 5.2 $m \leqslant n(n-1)$.

Proposition 5.4: Let an undirected graph be G having n vertices and edges m.
If graph G is connected, $m \geqslant n-1$.
If graph G is a tree, $m = n-1$.
If graph G is a forest, $m \leqslant n-1$.

5.2.3 Graph categories

Many categories of the graph exist in the literature serving different purposes and representing different types of complex real-world problems. Discussing all the categories of the graphs is beyond the scope of this chapter. However, the representative of the graphs mostly used in this domain are discussed in this section as follows.

5.2.3.1 Directed and undirected graph

The edges in a directed graph have a direction that is fixed showing the connectivity from a vertex source only to the vertex at the destination, as shown in figure 5.1(A). Given a directed graph G with vertices u and v, if G has a directed path from u to v, then u can reach v, meaning that v can be reachable from u. on the other hand, undirected graph G has an edge connection that is bi-directional between the vertices in the undirected graph G (see figure 5.1(B)). A directed graph G can be created from undirected graph G by making the two edges in the opposite direction denoting the undirected edge in the original graph. The reachability in the undirected graph is symmetric unlike in the directed graph. In an undirected graph, u reaches v only if v is reachable from u unlike in the directed graph G that there is possibility that u can reach v but possibly v is not reachable from u in view of the fact that it is mandatory for a path in a directed graph to be traversed based on the edges direction between vertices. Other forms of graph under this category include connected graph, strongly connected graph, subgraph, spanning subgraph, forest and tree (Goodrich *et al* 2014).

5.2.3.2 Homogeneous and heterogeneous graphs

The heterogeneous graph has multiple types of edges and vertices. Therefore, the heterogeneous graph expresses the relationship among different types of entities/

objects more powerfully. The computation in heterogeneous graph is performed by the alteration of the data using single hot encoding so as to make every vertex representation identical (Linmei *et al* 2019). A homogeneous graph is a type of graph that consists of only a particular type of edge and vertex, unlike the heterogeneous graph.

5.2.3.3 Static and dynamic graphs

In a static graph, the features and structures remained unchanged unlike in the case of a dynamic graph where the features and structure change over time and the inputs can be dynamic also. The edges and vertices in a dynamic graph are updated in such a way that the vertex can be deleted or added and corresponding edges can be created or updated. This makes it possible that an adaptive structure or algorithm that needs the internal structure to be dynamic can be applied to operate in the graph. A series of static graphs having different time-stamps can represent a dynamic graph (Lin *et al* 2022).

5.2.3.4 Hypergraph

This is the generalization of a graph such that the edge of the graph can join some vertices, and any number of vertices can be used for joining (Wu *et al* 2022).

5.2.3.5 Attributed graph

In this type of graph, additional information is added to the edges such as the weights or the edges type. This type of knowledge assists in the development of architectures. Having a graph with edges that have additional information like the relationship between the vertices makes the graph more manageable, especially when working with relational data (Waikhom and Patgiri 2021).

5.2.3.6 Bipartite graph

This a type of graph with a set of two vertices of which none of the edges has a connection between two vertices from the set that is the same. It is also referred to as the bigraph or graph with two colours in view of the fact that a bigraph can be coloured with two colours only. In the bigraph, no any adjacent vertices can have the same colours. Abstractly, a graph G is said to be a bigraph if and only if the set of the graph vertices can be divided into two sets that are not empty subsets, say A and B, -in such a way that each of the edges in E has a single endpoint in A and the second endpoint in B (Asratian *et al* 1998).

5.2.4 Artificial neural networks

The ANN, invented by McCulloch and Pitts (1943), is the artificial model of neurons forming a network of neurons inspired by the biological human brain simulating the human brain's computational processes (refer to chapter 1 of the book for the historical foundation of the ANN from it is inception to present time).

A brief computational and mathematical description of the ANN is presented but full details of the ANN is beyond the scope of this chapter, but it can be found in Bishop (1995) and comprises input layer, hidden layer and output layer forming a

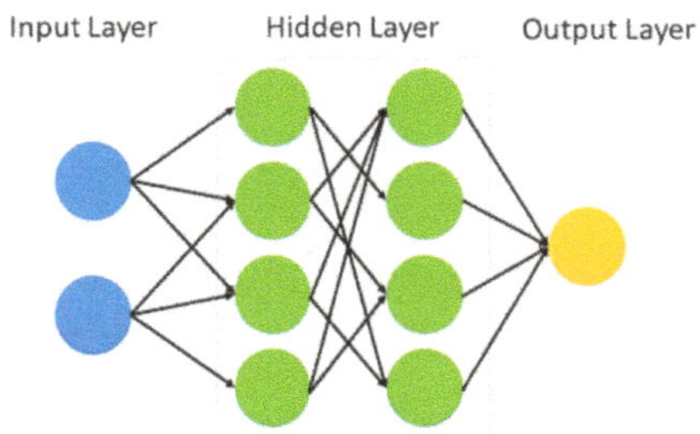

Figure 5.2. A sample of simple artificial neural network with two hidden layers. This [Neural network explain] image has been obtained by the authors from the Wikimedia website where it was made available by [TseKiChun] under a CC BY-SA 4.0 licence. It is included within this book on that basis. It is attributed to [TseKiChun].

simple (see figure 5.2) or large network of the ANN. Each of the layers is comprised of neurons, the neurons on the input layer are referred to as the input neurons, neurons on the hidden layer are referred to as the hidden neurons and those at the output layer are called the output neurons. The input and output layers are always single but the hidden layer can have as many as possible. Each output of the neuron in the network is determined by the parameter tailored to the particular neuron and the operations in the neuron. Let us assume that d_1, M_1 and c_1 represent the inputs, hidden neurons and output neurons, respectively. As such, the analytic function can be expressed as in equation (5.1). The output of the hidden neurons jth is derived from the formulation of the weight linear combination of the inputs d_1 in values format as well as the addition of a bias (Bishop 1995):

$$a_i = \sum_{i=1}^{d_1} w_{ji}^{(1)} x_i + w_{j0}^{(1)} \tag{5.1}$$

where the weight in the input layer is represented as $w_{ji}^{(1)}$ from the input neuron i to the hidden neuron j. The bias for the hidden neuron j is represented by the $w_{j0}^{(1)}$. The bias is the adding of any fixed value x_i say 1. Therefore, equation (5.1) becomes:

$$a_j = \sum_{i=0}^{d_1} w_{ji}^{(1)} x_i \tag{5.2}$$

Activation function is used at the hidden and output layers. The activation of the hidden layer is derived from the transformation equation (5.2) a linear sum based on activation function $\partial(\cdot)$ to have the following expression:

$$z_j = \partial(a_j) \tag{5.3}$$

Here, two functions were considered, namely, Heaviside and Sigmoid. The output of the ANN is produced by the transformation of the hidden neurons based on the second layer neurons. A linear combination of the hidden neurons output is constructed for each of the output neurons k expressed as:

$$a_k = \sum_{j=1}^{M} w_{kj}^{(2)} z_j + w_{k0}^{(2)} \tag{5.4}$$

Equation (5.4) changes as the bias is introduce to the weights expressed as:

$$a_k = \sum_{j=1}^{M} w_{kj}^{(2)} z_j \tag{5.5}$$

The output neuron *kth* is activated by the transformation of the linear combination based on activation function that is nonlinear and it is expressed as:

$$y_k = \widetilde{\partial}(a_k) \tag{5.6}$$

where a different activation function $\widetilde{\partial}$ is used as the output layer unlike activation function used as the hidden layer. Thus, combining equations (5.2), (5.3), (5.5) and (5.6) to obtain the output as (Bishop 1995):

$$y_k = \widetilde{\partial}\left(\sum_{j=1}^{M} w_{kj}^{(2)} \partial\left(\sum_{i=1}^{d_1} w_{ji}^{(1)} x_j + w_{k0}^{(2)}\right)\right)$$

5.2.5 The graph neural network

The operation of ANNs on graph data was pioneered by Sperduti and Starita (1997) before motivating Gori *et al* (2005) to propose the idea of GNNs. The combination of ANNs and graphs produce GNNs. It is achieved by the ANN operations on data with graph structure or graph data. The GNN uses the connections in the graph for learning and modelling of relationships that exist between vertices. The modelling of the GNN that takes edges, vertices and graph feature vectors as input and transforms them into target output is achieved through an iterative process that depends on the structure of the graph (Abadal *et al* 2021). The GNN idea was motivated from the convolutional neural network (CNN) and network embedding. The structure of the CNN shared weights and local connectivity is composed of several stack of layers. These properties of the CNN motivate the operations of the GNN in a similar way whereby GNN shared weights lead to minimizing GNN computational cost. The stacked layers enable GNN to capture meaningful features and local connection makes the GNN a locally connected structure. On the other hand, the network embedding enables the transformation of the GNN inputs like the edges and vertices to low-dimensional vectors (Kipf and Welling 2016).

A pre-processing stage is involved for the purpose of reducing the complexity of the algorithm, graph sampling and re-ordering by transforming the input feature vectors and pre-coding of the graph structure. The second stage involves updating the feature vectors of every edge and vertex of the graph through aggregation and combination process iteratively. The edges of the graph are updated by attributes of the edge, vertices and the graphs are aggregated to create only one set. The new edges of the feature vectors are typically produced by the combination function. The new feature vectors are obtained by updating the vertices before subsequent aggregating and combining the neighbouring feature vectors of the vertices. Every edge and vertex is updated by each of the layers with the information that emanates from the neighbours located at only one stage. The distance of the vertex and edges is increasing through the iterative process. The pooling reduces the dimensionality of the graph (Bai *et al* 2021, Hu *et al* 2020, Jiang *et al* 2021). The final stage which is the

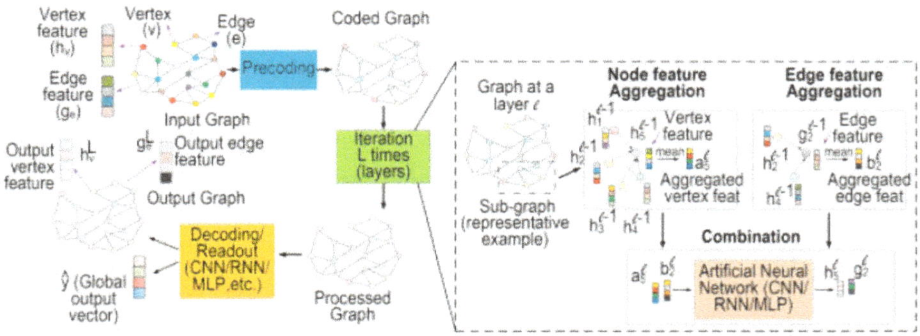

Figure 5.3. The GNN stages of operations in the processing of graph data. Reproduced from Abadal *et al* (2021) CC BY 4.0.

readout is also referred to as the decoding, at this stage the global feature vector is updated after the edge and vertex updated is completed, however, this is applicable if the graph has global features. The final output at this stage produces edge or vertex embedding with a low feature vector dimension representing edge information or vertex information or a graph that summarizes the entire information (after the transformation, the output feature vectors are produce at the output representing the vertex classification, edge prediction or graph classification). The entire procedure of GNN operations can be found in figure 5.3 (Abadal *et al* 2021). Many variants of the GNN modified by researchers have been published (Chen *et al* 2021).

5.2.5.1 Vertex classification

The vertices on the graph each have a label that is assigned and the target vertex is designated depending on the classification problem to be solved. The GNN processes the data to determine the label of the next vertex. For example, the GNN can classify if a vertex is a male or female.

5.2.5.2 Edge prediction

Mainly the prediction of edge targets is made by the possibility of interlinking between vertices. A typical example of edge prediction is the friend suggestions on Facebook. For example, if the GNN found the edge of mutual friends it predicts the edge and makes friend suggestions to the Facebook user.

5.2.5.3 Graph classification

Graph classification can be used to uncover patterns of interaction among social media users, such as categories of users based on age groups. Then, certain information or advertisements can be tailored towards the target age groups.

5.2.6 Graph neural network algorithm operation

The GNN algorithm accepts edges, vertices and graph features vectors as inputs or initializes the edges, vertices and graph. The execution of the algorithm is divided into layers, where each edge in each layer is updated in parallel. The update in parallel is performed by aggregating it is own feature vectors connected with the vertices. The feature vectors of the neighbouring vertex are aggregated by updating each vertex in parallel. The combination function that can be an ANN is used for the transformation of the aggregated vertices and edges. A readout is performed based on the corresponding function that can possibly be ANN after the iterative process is completed (Pareja *et al* 2020). For the layer $l \in [1, L]$ arbitrary, where L is the number of layers on the GNN, the transformation of the edge occurres as expressed in equation (5.7) (Abadal *et al* 2021):

Aggregation

$$b_e^{(l)} = \rho_E^{(l)}\left(\left\{g_e^{(l-1)}, \quad h_u^{(l-1)}: u \in N(e)\right\}\right) \tag{5.7}$$

Combination

$$g_e^{(l)} = \varnothing_E^{(l)}\left(\left\{b_e^{(l)}\right\}\right) \tag{5.8}$$

where $\rho_E^{(l)}$ is the number of aggregation edges of the layer l, $g_e^{(l)}$ is the hidden feature vectors of the edge e, E is the set of the graph edges (static on assumption), $\varnothing_E^{(l)}$ is the layer l edge combination function and h_v^l is the hidden feature vectors of the vertex v. In such a way that the edges aggregation takes the feature vector for the edge and feature vectors of the vertices at the end of the point, h_u with $u \in N(e)$ of the layer $l - 1$ which is the preceding layer. The combination $\varnothing_E$ uses the aggregation to be the input, likewise similar logic is applied to the vertices aggregation and combination as expressed:

Aggregation

$$a_v^{(l)} = \rho_V^{(l)}\left(\left\{g_v^{(l-1)}, \quad h_u^{(l-1)}: u \in N(v)\right\}\right) \tag{5.9}$$

Combination

$$h_v^{(l)} = \varnothing_V^{(l)}\left(\left\{b_v^{(l)}\right\}\right)$$

where $N(v)$ is the set of neighbouring vertex v, $\varnothing_v^{(l)}$ is the layer l vertex combination function, $\rho_V^{(l)}$ is the number of aggregation verices of the layer l, V is the set of graph vertices.

The computation of $a_v^{(l)}$ is described by the equations as the feature vectors aggregation from neighbouring vertices to the v from layer $l - 1$ which is a preceding layer. The computation of the feature vector layer l is performed by the equations using the $a_v^{(l)}$ aggregation taken as the input. At the final stage, a readout function is used which can likely include aggregation and combination of the feature vectors from the edges and vertices of the whole graph structure. From the final iteration L, the output feature vector $\hat{y}$ is produced expressed as (Abadal *et al* 2021):

Readout

$$\hat{y} = \varnothing_G\Big(\rho_G\Big(\big\{h_v^L, \quad g_e^L\colon e, v \in G\big\}\Big)\Big). \tag{5.10}$$

5.2.7 Learning algorithm for the graph neural network

The learning for the GNN involves the estimation of w as the parameter in such a way that φ_w estimates the data from the datasets used for learning in the GNN (Scarselli *et al* 2008):

$$\mathscr{L} = \big\{\big(\boldsymbol{G_i}, n_{i.j}, t_{i,j})|, \quad \boldsymbol{G_i} = (\boldsymbol{N_i}, \boldsymbol{E_i}\big) \in \mathscr{G}n_{i.j} \in \boldsymbol{N_i};\ \boldsymbol{t_{i,j}} \in \mathscr{R}^m, \quad 1 \leqslant i \leqslant p, \quad 1 \leqslant j \leqslant q_i\big\} \tag{5.11}$$

From the equation q_i represents the number of the supervised vertices in the graph $\boldsymbol{G_i}$ (static on assumption). In a focused task, a single vertex as a special vertex is designated as the desired target having $q_i = 1$. The supervision is performed on each of the vertices in the graph. The learning task of the GNN is the quadratic cost function minimization

$$e_w = \sum\nolimits_{i=1}^{p}\sum_{j=1}^{q_i}(\boldsymbol{t_{i,j}} - \varphi_w(\boldsymbol{G_i}, n_{i.j}))^2 \tag{5.12}$$

The GNN learning algorithm is based on the gradient-descent approach. The gradient computation for the GNN is based on the backpropagation via time algorithm.

Let's assume $F_w(\boldsymbol{x}, \boldsymbol{l})$ and $G_w(\boldsymbol{x}, \boldsymbol{l_N})$ are differentiable that are continuous with respect to x and w where F_w and G_w represent the GNN transition and output function, respectively. Thus, Let define z_t as follows:

$$z(t) = z(t+1).\ \frac{\partial F_w}{\partial x}(x, l) + \frac{\partial e_w}{\partial O}.\quad \frac{\partial G_w}{\partial x}(x, l_N) \tag{5.13}$$

The order $z(T)$, $z(T-1)$, ... converges to a vector as $z = \lim_{t\to\to\infty} z(t)$. The exponential is said to be convergence and does not depend on $z(T)$ initial state

$$\frac{\partial e_w}{\partial w} = \quad \frac{\partial e_w}{\partial O} \cdot \frac{\partial G_w}{\partial w}(x, l_N) + z \cdot \frac{\partial F_w}{\partial w}(x, l) \tag{5.14}$$

where x is a state of stability in the GNN.

Justification: γ, $0 \leqslant \gamma < 1$ in view of the fact that F_w is a contraction map as $\|(\partial F_w/\partial x)(x, w)\|$ hold. The state fixed point z is given as follows:

$$z = \frac{\partial e_w}{\partial O}.\ \frac{\partial G_w}{\partial x}(x, l_N).\left(I_a - \frac{\partial F_w}{\partial x}(x, l)\right)^{-1} \tag{5.15}$$

where $a = s\ |N|$. The function Ψ is defined as:

$$\frac{\partial \Psi}{\partial w} = \left(I_a - \frac{\partial F_w}{\partial x}(x, l)\right)^{-1}\frac{\partial F_w}{\partial w}(x, l) \tag{5.16}$$

As e_w depends on the network output $0 = G_w(\Psi(w), l_N)$. The $\frac{\partial e_w}{\partial w}$ can be computed based on chain rule for the differentiable:

$$\frac{\partial e_w}{\partial w} = \frac{\partial e_w}{\partial O}. \quad \frac{\partial G_w}{\partial w}(x, l_N) + \frac{\partial e_w}{\partial O}. \quad \frac{\partial G_w}{\partial x}(x, l_N). \frac{\partial \Psi}{\partial w}(w) \tag{5.17}$$

Substituting (5.16) in (5.17) to get the following expression:

$$\frac{\partial e_w}{\partial w} = \frac{\partial e_w}{\partial O} \cdot \quad \frac{\partial G_w}{\partial w}(x, l_N) + \frac{\partial e_w}{\partial O} \cdot \frac{\partial G_w}{\partial x}(x, l_N) \cdot \left(I_a - \frac{\partial F_w}{\partial x}(x, l)\right)^{-1} \frac{\partial F_w}{\partial w}(x, l) \tag{5.18}$$

$$\frac{\partial e_w}{\partial w} = \frac{\partial e_w}{\partial O} \cdot \frac{\partial G_w}{\partial w}(x, l_N) + z \cdot \frac{\partial F_w}{\partial w}(x, l) \tag{5.19}$$

The backpropagation algorithm computes the first term before the second term represents the contribution because of the transmission function simultaneously propagating the derivatives passing through the GNN layer of the function F_w. From equation (5.13)

$$z(t) = z(t+1) \cdot \frac{\partial F_w}{\partial x}(x, l) + \frac{\partial e_w}{\partial O} \cdot \frac{\partial G_w}{\partial x}(x, l_N) \tag{5.20}$$

$$= z(T) \cdot \left(\frac{\partial F_w}{\partial x}(x, l)\right)^{T-t} + \sum_{i=0}^{T-t-1} \frac{\partial e_w}{\partial O} \cdot \quad \frac{\partial G_w}{\partial x}(x, l_N) \cdot \left(\frac{\partial F_w}{\partial x}(x, l)\right)^{i} \tag{5.21}$$

Assuming
$z(T) = \partial e_w(T)/\partial o(T) \cdot (\partial G_w/\partial x(T)) \cdot (x(T), l_N), \quad x(t) = x, \quad t_o \leqslant t \leqslant T.$
Therefore, the following equation (5.22) is expressed as:

$$= \sum_{i=0}^{T-t} \frac{\partial e_w(T)}{\partial O(T)} \cdot \quad \frac{\partial G_w}{\partial x(T)}(x(T), l_N) \tag{5.22}$$

$$\prod_{j=1}^{i} \left(\frac{\partial F_w}{\partial x(T-j)}(x(T-j), l)\right) \tag{5.23}$$

$$= \sum_{i=0}^{T-t} \frac{\partial e_w(T)}{\partial x(T-i)}.$$

The $\partial e_w(T)/\partial x(i)$ operates into z corresponding to the backpropagation of the gradient through the layers that has f_w unit. The operation of the backpropagation algorithm continues operating on the GNN by updating the weights until the objective becomes steady without improvement or satisfies some designed threshold (Scarselli *et al* 2008).

5.2.7.1 Transductive learning approach

In this learning approach, all the training data and test data are exposed to the learning method before performing the prediction. For instance, the graph data may comprise one large graph such as the social media graph and the vertices set in the graph are labelled partially. In this case, the vertices contained in the training set are labelled, whereas the test set comprises both labelled (small set) and unlabelled vertices. Thus, this learning method is required to be fed with the whole graph during the period of the training, including the vertices set for the testing. This is because the added information like the structural pattern can be used to learn from it. This transductive learning approach is very useful in the situation where separating data for training and data for testing without the introduction of biases is a challenging task (Belahcen *et al* 2015).

5.2.7.2 Inductive learning approach

This reserves data for training and testing the model to measure its generalization ability. The training process utilizes the training data for the algorithm to learn to become a model. The test data is used to measure the generalization ability of the learned model. Typically, the classical GNN is based on the inductive learning scheme. In this scheme, the training data is applied for adapting the model parameters. Inductive learning has the assumption of existing rules to be used for the implementation of the model that give room to classify a pattern based on its attributes (Rossi *et al* 2018).

5.3 Categories of graph neural network

GNNs are of different categories depending on the nature of the architecture, operators and operations procedure on the graph data. There are mainly three categories of GNNs (Dwivedi *et al* 2022). However, Wu *et al* (2020) categorizes the GNN architecture into four major categories, as shown in figure 5.4. The categories are discussed in the next subsections for readers to understand the differences on how each operate on graph data to achieve their objective.

5.3.1 Convolutional graph neural networks

The major idea of the convolutional graph neural networks (CGNNs) is the generation of node representative by the aggregation of it is own and neighbouring features. The CGNN extracts a high-level node representative by stacking multiple numbers of graph convolution layers. The CGNN learns the representation of new features for the feature x_i of each of the nodes over multiple numbers of layers. It is subsequently applied as the input to the linear-classifier. For the graph convolution layer kth, the representation of the input node for all the nodes is denoted by $\boldsymbol{H}^{(k-1)}$ as a matrix and $\boldsymbol{H}^{(k)}$ represent the output node. Typically, the initial representations of the nodes are the original input features expressed as (Wu *et al* 2019):

$$\boldsymbol{H}^{(0)} = \boldsymbol{X} \tag{5.24}$$

Equation (5.24) serves as the input to the CGNN first layer. The CGNN K-layer is the same as the application of multi-layer perceptron to the feature vector x_i for every vertex in the graph with the exception of hidden representation in which each of the node is averaged together with it is own neighbours at each layer starting point

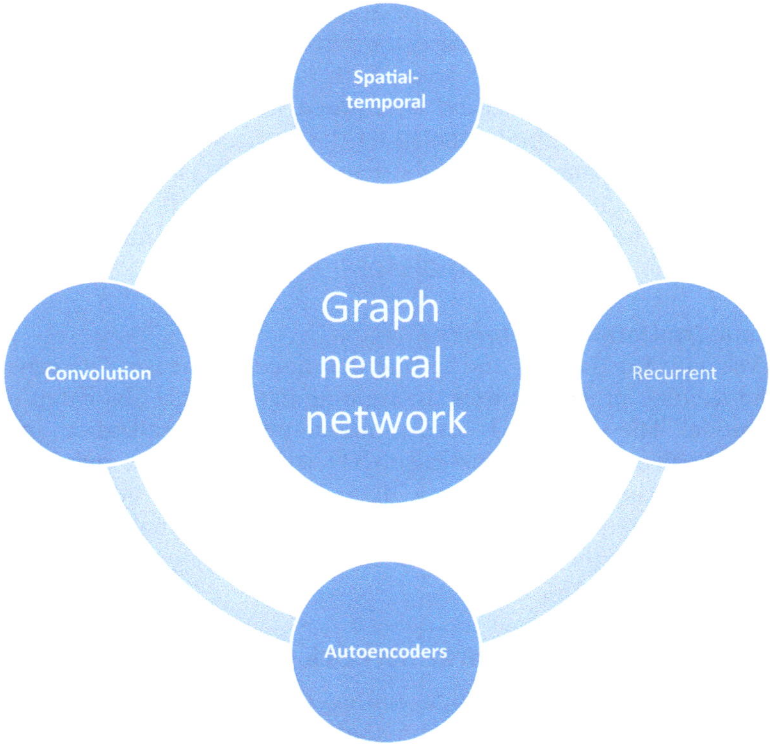

Figure 5.4. The four major architectures of the GNN.

or beginning of each layer. At each layer of the graph convolution, update of the node representation is performed in three stages, as follows: feature propagation—this is the characteristic of the CGNN that makes it unique from the multi-layer perceptron. At the beginning of each of the layers, the feature h_i, the average of each of the nodes v_i is computed with the feature vectors at the local neighbour expressed as:

$$\boldsymbol{h}_i^{-(1)} \leftarrow \frac{1}{d_i + 1} h_i^{(k-1)} + \sum_{j=1}^{n} \frac{a_{ij}}{\sqrt{(d_i + 1)(d_j + 1)}} h_j^{(k-1)} \tag{5.25}$$

where d_i is the row sum of the adjacency matrix expressed as $d_i = \sum_j a_{ij}$ and $d_j = \sum_i a_{ij}$

$$\boldsymbol{h}_i^{-(1)} \leftarrow \frac{1}{d_i + 1} h_i^{(k-1)} + \sum_{j=1}^{n} \frac{a_{ij}}{\sqrt{(\sum_j a_{ij} + 1)(\sum_i a_{ij} + 1)}} h_j^{(k-1)} \tag{5.26}$$

This is the matrix operation that updates the whole graph. Let us say S is the adjacency matrix with self-looping added to it.

$$S = \widetilde{D}^{-\frac{1}{2}} \widetilde{A} \widetilde{D}^{-\frac{1}{2}} \tag{5.27}$$

From equation (5.27) $\widetilde{A} = A + I$ and the $\widetilde{D}$ represent the degree matrix of $\widetilde{A}$. Equation (5.25) updates all the nodes in the graph simultaneously and equation (5.25) becomes sparse matrix multiplication expressed as:

$$\widetilde{\boldsymbol{H}}^{(k)} \leftarrow \boldsymbol{S}\boldsymbol{H}^{(k-1)} \tag{5.28}$$

Equation (5.28) locally smoothens the hidden representation together with the edges of the graph and enjoins local prediction among the connected local nodes. The local smoothing makes the CGNN the same as the multi-layer perceptron after applying it. Each of the layers in the CGNN is associated with weight matrix $\theta(k)$ that is learned. The smoothing hidden feature representations $H(k)$ are linearly transformed. Before the output feature, a nonlinear activation function like ReLU is applied. The representation update at the layer kth is expressed as:

$$H^{(k)} \leftarrow \mathrm{ReLU}(\widetilde{H}^{(k)}\theta^{(k)})$$

The pointwise nonlinear transformation layer follows by the propagation of the features. The *Softmax* classifier is used for the prediction of label at the last layer of the CGNN (Wu *et al* 2019). The CGNN can be used for constructing varieties of complex GNN models. The CGNN involves spectral and spatial methods.

5.3.2 Graph autoencoders

The application of the GNN to autoencoding produces the graph autoencoder (encoding–decoding scheme or mapping–reconstruction scheme) (Salha *et al* 2021). The purpose of the graph autoencoder is the projection of the input features to the latent space, also referred to as the new space, especially where the projection has additional desired properties compared to the input representation. The properties are outlined as follows. First, the datasets have additional classifiable in the latent space or new space. Secondly, the dimensionality of the data is smaller in the new space compared to the input space. Thirdly, the datasets are obscured because of privacy or security concerns in the latent space. Generally, the strength of the autoencoders is that they can achieve the issue of security or privacy in an unsupervised way by creating embedding that is useful without a training dataset. The graph autoencoder paves the way for unsupervised learning on graph data. On the other hand, it significantly enhances supervised learning tasks such as the classification of vertex on citations network. The autoencoder processes data in two stages as follows: the data is encoded into the latent space as input data; the data is decoded for compressed representation for reconstruction of the original data. The autoencoders undergo training for minimizing the reconstruction loss that is typically computed using the input data only, as such, trained in an unsupervised approach (Kipf and Welling 2016). Generally, the graph autoencoder is an unsupervised learning framework that encodes vertex/graph into the latent space and the reconstruction of graph data from the encoded information. The graph autoencoders are used for learning network embedding and generating graph distribution. In network embedding, the graph autoencoder learns latent vertex representation via the reconstruction of graph structural information like the adjacency matrix. In graph generation, the vertices and edges of the graph are generated step by step using some methods, whereas some of the other methods produce a complete graph once (Wu *et al* 2020). Network embedding and graph generation falls into this category.

5.3.3 Spatial–temporal graph neural networks

The spatial–temporal GNN has been proposed for the purpose of learning patterns hidden from spatial–temporal graphs. The major idea of the spatial–temporal GNN is to use both the spatial and temporal dependencies simultaneously (Wu *et al* 2020). The structural nature of a spatial–temporal graph is dynamic because the feature of the vertices/edges changes over time. An example is the road network traffic application for modelling road networks in the form of graph structure where each vertex is represented by the location of a sensor for monitoring traffic behaviour such as the average speeds that change with time (Bui *et al* 2022). There are published methods that combined graph convolution for capturing spatial dependency with recurrent neural network or CNN for modelling temporal dependency (Wu *et al* 2020). *Spatial-based methods:* convolution is directly performed by the special method in the domain of the graph by aggregating neighbouring vertex information with the ability to handle the problem of scalability for large graphs. This is because the whole graph is processed at the same time. Particularly, the spatial graph convolution network is based on the traditional CNN purposely developed for conventional data structure such as images as well as nonlinear data like the 3D mesh, social network graphs, road traffic network and molecular graphs (Bui *et al* 2022). Most of the spatial–temporal GNNs were developed on the basis of a defined structure of a graph to process propagation that cannot directly be extended to multivariate problems. As a result of that, many studies proposed graph learning layers with the capability to learn hidden spatial dependencies automatically between the vertices from the perspective data-driven approach (Bui *et al* 2022).

5.3.4 Recurrent graph neural networks

In the early days, typically, recursive methods relied on the special case of graphs (unfolding) into the equivalent of recursive. Subsequently, processed it into embedding that is useful by the recursive ANN. The recurrent GNN extends this phenomenon to offer a solution for the generic graphs. The recurrent GNN develops an embedding at the graph vertices level via a framework for propagating information (referred to as message passing) instead of creating embedding for the complete graph through the recursive encoding network (Scarselli *et al* 2005). Most of the works on graphs in the early stage of GNN development were recurrent. The objective of the recurrent GNN is for the learning of node representations with the architecture that is a recurrent neural network. The recurrent GNN takes the assumption that the graph vertex is constantly exchanging information with its neighbourhood until it reaches an equilibrium that is constant (Scarselli *et al* 2008). Other variants of the recurrent GNN include graph echo state networks (Gallicchio and Micheli 2010), gated graph sequence neural networks (Li *et al* 2015) and iterative algorithms over graphs (Dai *et al* 2018).

5.4 Graph neural network hyper-parameter settings and parameters tuning

Hyper-parameter is critical in intelligent algorithms as it affects the performance of the algorithms. The hyper-parameter is presented before discussing it in the context of GNNs. Hyper-parameter is the setting of value that defines the architecture of the ML algorithm adjusted before the algorithm training begins. It has a control on the way the algorithm learns patterns from a dataset. Typical examples of hyper-parameters include learning rate, number of layers, number of neurons on the layers, and number of branches and number of trees in the case of decision tree and forest, respectively. It is important to differentiate the hyper-parameter from parameters. The parameters are the values the algorithm derived from the training data and it changes across domains of application unlike the hyper-parameter that remains fixed (Kuhn and Johnson 2013). The hyper-parameters influence the algorithm conclusion. The setting of the hyper-parameters should not be too specific because it can cause the model to fall into the overfitting problem and if the hyper-parameter setting is vague the model becomes underfitting. Thus, there should be a balance between overfitting and underfitting for the hyper-parameter settings to avoid the overfitting or underfitting problem. Poor settings of the hyper-parameter values can impact negatively on the training process by increasing computational cost. The setting of the hyper-parameters is typically through trail-and-error during preliminary experiment before arriving at the best hyper-parameter values ideal for the modelling, a process referred to as hyper-parameter tuning. This is unlike the parameters where it is the process of the training algorithm that tunes the parameters (Bergstra and Bengio 2012, Liao and Jia 2007).

The GNN architecture optimization is typically performed according to the pre-defined set of hyper-parameters. The performance and convergence of deep learning architecture typically benefit from learning rate significantly. It is already established that sensitivity analysis proves that the hyper-parameters have an impact on GNN performance because a little change on hyper-parameters settings of the GNN such as learning rate, weight decay and dropout rate affect the GNN performance. There is the possibility of the GNN producing a suboptimal solution if the hyper-parameters remained constant while the architecture is being optimized as the model is sensitive to hyper-parameters (Shi *et al* 2022). Other settings include attention function, attention head in the case of graph attention network, aggregation function, activation function and hidden nodes. One typical approach to improve the GNN performance is by increasing the size of the parameters expanding the hidden dimension (Yuan *et al* 2021a). The graph hypernetwork has been improved by the collaborative work of AI research group and the University of Guelph for the prediction of deep learning algorithm initial parameters.

5.5 Published surveys and tutorials on graph neural networks

As already pointed out in the introduction section of the chapter, a tremendously large volume of reviews/surveys have been conducted on GNNs from different perspectives, e.g. application domains such as recommender system, health, natural language processing, etc. On the other hand, survey/reviews were published on the variants of the GNN such as convolution, deep reinforcement learning construction of GNNs, spatial–temporal, etc. The reviews/surveys and tutorials are presented in this section according to year of publication.

5.5.1 Survey publications between 2016 and 2019

The survey conducted by the research community from the year 2016 to 2029 are reviewed in this section. The reviews between 2016 and 2019 are believed to be the early reviews in this research area as publications on the GNN start appearing in the literature in 2004 as established in Keramatfar *et al* (2022). Bronstein *et al* (2017) presented a thorough literature review on the convolutional model within the family of the GNN. The variants of the models such as the graph convolutional network, geodesic convolutional network, anisotropic convolutional network among others were thoroughly discussed in the paper. Hamilton *et al* (2017b) present a review that shows the advances on representation learning on graphs mainly focusing on network embedding techniques. In another study, a literature review on generalization of the GNN with the building blocks is presented. The variants of GNNs were discussed such as the fully connected GNN, convolutional GNN and recurrent GNN (Battaglia *et al* 2018). Similarly, Zhang *et al* (2019) presented a survey on GNNs with special focus on graph convolutional networks. Variants of the graph convolutional networks were outlined and discussed in the survey before delving into the different application domains. A different study by Phan *et al* (2023) presents a survey on the applications of GNNs in natural language process focusing on the detection of fake news.

5.5.2 Literature reviews published from 2020 to 2021

The reviews conducted by different researchers on GNNs published between 2020 and 2021 are presented in this section. A thorough review on GNN data mining and ML is conducted. A taxonomy indicating the variants of GNNs is created and the domain of applications for GNNs are discussed (Wu *et al* 2020). Similarly, Zhang *et al* (2020) published a review on the graph variants of recurrent neural networks, convolutional neural networks, autoencoders, reinforcement learning and adversarial networks. However, Ye *et al* (2022) provided a comprehensive review on GNNs for solving problems in knowledge graph tasks, namely, link prediction, vertex classification, knowledge graph reasoning and knowledge graph alignment. The GNN applications in drugs–drugs interaction, recommender systems and question-answering systems for solving problems were outlined and discussed. Unlike the work of Ye *et al* (2022) and Wu *et al* (2020), Zhou *et al* (2020) presented a thorough survey on GNN variants and their applications in different domains to solve problems. A GNN general design pipeline was proposed in the study. Unlike the previous works that mainly focused on reviews, Rong *et al* (2020) presented tutorials on deep graph learning by presenting theoretical fundamentals of deep graph learning mainly focussing on the GNN and its variants. The major contributions of deep graph learning in terms of training deep GNNs, GNN scalability, GNN robustness, GNN unsupervised learning and supervised learning of GNN were discussed. Key areas of GNN applications such as natural language processing, social networks, computer vision, etc were outlined and deliberated.

Lamb *et al* (2020) presented an elaboration on the relationship that exists between GNNs and neural-symbolic computing. The study developed multi-GNN models with the intention of applying it to neural-symbolic computing. In another study, a survey on GNNs from the perspective of supervised learning, unsupervised learning and semi-supervised learning was conducted. The graph-based learning settings for GNNs with logical division were discussed. The GNN learning task was analyzed from the point of view of theory and standpoints. A generic guiding principle for designing GNN architecture, GNN applications and benchmark datasets were discussed (Waikhom and Patgiri 2021). A GNN survey from the computing point of view has been presented. The survey includes discussion on tutorials about the fundamentals of GNNs, evolution of GNNs from the last 10 years and operations of GNNs on multi-phase GNN variants. The survey also included a discussion on software platforms and hardware accelerators for processing GNN from graph-ware, hardware–software and communication-centric vision perspectives (Abadal *et al* 2021). A review on the power of the GNN model and its powerful variants with features were presented in Sato (2020). Consequently, a concise summary of the GNN generic framework processing a bipartite graph from models was provided. Embedding layer, prediction layer and update propagation layer were thoroughly discussed (Wu *et al* 2021). In another study, the applications of GNNs for solving problems of traffic predictions such as bike sharing, road traffic flow, metro flow etc were reviewed. The study unveiled that applications of GNNs in traffic prediction have been gaining popularity in recent times but are still at the early stage of development (Wang 2021). In a different domain, the applications of GNNs in particle physics have been reviewed for unveiling the trends of GNN applications in particle physics. The study also covered the construction of different graphs, architecture of the model and learning objectives (Shlomi *et al* 2020). A different study by Choi *et al* (2021) discussed a tutorial about GNNs from the perspective of quantum computing that led to the emergence of quantum GNNs with parameterized quantum circuits. Comparative analysis was conducted, and results show that the quantum graph recurrent network was proven to be effective in the training of the Ising model Hamiltonian compared to other models.

5.5.3 Survey publications for the period from 2022 to 2024

The reviews/surveys on GNNs from different aspects published between 2020 and 2024 are presented in this section. For example, a survey on distributed GNNs training together with GNN training optimization techniques is presented. The paper discussed computational patterns, communication patterns and optimization techniques used by different researchers. Software and hardware platforms required to train distributed GNNs were outlined and discussed. A comparative study between distributed GNNs and deep neural networks showing the advantages of distributed GNNs was analyzed (Lin *et al* 2022). Another survey by Nguyen *et al* (2022) was on the design principle of GNNs in different domains of applications. It was found in the survey that the convolutional graph neural network is highly popular in solving problems in micro-service applications in cloud system design. In addition, a spatial–temporal GNN and dynamic GNN have experienced a surge in adoption, especially in advance studies. In another study, a review of GNN variants including graph attention network, convolutional GNNs, graph isomorphism network, graph sample and aggregation (GraphSAGE) as well as graph autoencoder were presented. How these algorithms operate to achieve their goal was introduced before concluding with the GNN domain of applications (Li *et al* 2022). Graph learning approaches were classified to create a taxonomy from network embedding to GNNs. The unification of the approaches was created using an encoder–decoder model for all the approaches in a single method. Over 30 graph learning techniques were expressed using the proposed model (Chami *et al* 2022).

Munikoti *et al* (2023) provided a comprehensive survey on the hybridization of GNNs and deep reinforcement learning where the deep reinforcement learning searches for the architecture of GNNs. The applications, benefits of hybridizing GNNs and deep reinforcement learning, reduction of computational complexity and improving of generalization ability were analyzed in the survey. On the other hand, in a review on the progress in the development of GNNs for data acquisition from AI of things, the encoder–decoder paradigm used for unifying the GNN pipeline and emerging technology useful for the collection of data from AI of things were summarized. The noisy and adversarial data issues were discussed (Wang *et al* 2023). Meanwhile, Liu *et al* (2022) focussed a review on GNNs pooling by discussing several pooling methods. Each pooling method theoretical background including mathematical theories, libraries, architecture of the model, widely used datasets and open-source implementations platforms were analyzed and discussed.

Similar to Wang (2021), Graña and Morais-Quilez (2023) reviewed the applications of GNNs but in a different domain of application—EEG. It was found in the study that a GNN is suitable for the analysis of EEG because it is a signal that is suitably defined by graph in place of the common lattice in Euclidean space. Similarly, a review on the applications of GNNs mainly focussing on recommender systems was presented. The study discusses knowledge graph-aided recommender systems and GNNs. The structure of the knowledge graph, data sparsity, cold processing and fundamental modules of GNNs were discussed (Huang 2022). The Huang (2022) review differs from the review presented by Wu *et al* (2022) as it only focussed on the applications of GNNs in recommender systems, unlike Huang (2022) who includes the knowledge graph. Subsequently, Mohammadi (2023) presented a review on the GNN applications in a recommender system mainly focussing on explainable GNNs. In another study, GNN-based recommender systems were classified based on scenario, stage, application and objective.

Spectral and spatial GNN methods with motivation to a recommender system were discussed. Graph construction, model optimization, embedding aggregation and computational efficiency challenges were analyzed. Synthesis and analysis of GNN-based recommender systems were presented (Gao *et al* 2023). Keramatfar *et al* (2022) presented bibliometric analysis on a GNN research overview from 2004 as the year GNN papers start appearing in the literature. It is found that graph convolutional networks and graph attention network are the most active variants of GNNs.

Bui *et al* (2022) discussed a comprehensive overview of a GNN with a focus on a spatial–temporal graph neural network for the prediction of traffic flow. The study created the taxonomy of a spatial–temporal graph neural network based on graph convolutional recurrent network, graph multiple attention network, fully graph convolutional network and self-learning graph network structure. Likewise, Jiang *et al* (2023) reviewed the applications of GNNs in forecasting traffic flow. The survey includes discussion on open-source datasets and source code resources available for use by the research community. In a different twist, Ward *et al* (2022) put forward a tutorial on the power of GNNs in solving real-world problems targeting practitioners. In the tutorial, the basic concept, motivational factors, mathematical background and common application domains of GNNs were rigorously discussed including a comparative study of GNN variants. In another study, the critical role of operators in GNN operation motivated a survey to be conducted on the GNN operators responsible for training GNNs on graph structured data. The mathematical background of the selected GNN operators such as the pooling were discussed thoroughly, limitations and advantages of the operators were included in the discussion (Sharma *et al* 2023).

Integrating graph data augmentation especially topology and feature level augmentation to improve the performance of GNNs motivated a survey on the graph data augmentation algorithms. The commonly used GNNs: graph convolutional network, graph attention network and GraphSAGE were subjected to evaluation on graph data to show advantages and effectiveness of each of the GNN types (Adjeisah *et al* 2023). Dong *et al* (2023) put forward a thorough survey on the development of the applications of GNNs in the area of internet of things. A GNN design deep dive analysis in different internet of things-based smart environments was discussed. Open-source codes and publicly available datasets were outlined for readers to get easy access to the resources for future research. However, Zhang *et al* (2023) focussed attention on reviewing the development of a GNN-based neurological disorders framework for diagnosing brain disorder. The review includes discussion on graph construction, graph pooling and graph convolution. In another development, Jia *et al* (2023) analyzed, synthesized and conducted an extensive review on the applications of GNNs in different aspects of the construction industry. Lastly, Xue *et al* (2023) presented a tutorial on the fundamentals of scalable GNN challenges, large-scale GNNs, both classical and emerging approaches for large-scale GNNs, comparative study on scalable GNNs and general applications of GNNs in solving real-world problems. Discussion on new ideas to improve the development of GNNs were presented. Lastly, Veličković

(2023) presented a survey on the advances of GNNs in discovering scientific knowledge and the deployment of GNN-based solutions in industry.

A survey on graph representation learning was published, focussing on methods for embedding conventional graphs and GNNs on both dynamic and static graphs (Khoshraftar and An 2024). Another study reviewed the privacy and security of GNNs, particularly in the context of attacks on pre-training data and model parameters, analyzing the relationship between security and privacy (Guan *et al* 2024). Similarly, Dai *et al* (2024) presented a survey on privacy and security in GNNs, but extended the focus to include explainability, trust, and fairness, distinguishing it from Guan *et al* (2024). Different approaches to designing GNN architectures for classifying EEG signals were surveyed, with an emphasis on outlining the similarities and differences among the methods. Findings indicated that spectral graph convolution layers play a more prominent role than spatial architectures (Klepl *et al* 2024).

A literature review was conducted on the progress of distributed GNN training, focussing on three major limitations: load imbalance, accuracy loss, and extensive feature communication. The survey examined multi-GPU, CPU clusters, and GPU clusters as accelerators for distributed GNN pre-training (Shao *et al* 2024). Additionally, another study reviewed approaches for embedding graph structure within transformer architectures to reduce bias and improve local neighbourhood aggregation, particularly in task-oriented applications within computer vision (Senior *et al* 2024). A review highlighted an emerging concept in recommender systems called social recommender systems that has drawn attention, leading to a survey on GNN-oriented social recommendation (Sharma *et al* 2024). Furthermore, a study presented a comparative analysis of twelve different GNN explainers across six datasets for graph architecture and node classification, providing insights into the limitations, strengths, and applicability of each explainer (Longa *et al* 2024).

Huge GNNs are susceptible to unfairness due to their domain-specific data and aggregation mechanisms; consequently, different techniques have been proposed to address this issue. Techniques aimed at improving fairness during pre-processing, modelling, and deployment phases have been reviewed (Chen *et al* 2024). A tutorial discussing the basics of GNNs, including their variants, applications, datasets, and libraries, was presented in (Khemani *et al* 2024). Another survey focused on modelling epidemic spread using GNNs is provided in (Liu *et al* 2024). To enhance privacy, federated learning was combined with GNNs to create 'federated GNNs,' and a review examined how GNNs contribute to privacy-preserving training in federated learning applications is conducted (Liu *et al* 2024). Jin *et al* (2024) surveyed the use of GNNs for time series analysis, while Wang *et al* (2024) focussed on GNNs applications for text classification tasks. Additionally, Corso *et al* (2024) reviewed foundational concepts of GNNs and their applications in life sciences and physical sciences. Finally, a survey on 2D image understanding adopted GNN architectures for tasks such as visual question-answering, image captioning, and image retrieval (Senior *et al* 2024).

Another survey explored the development of GNN-based intrusion detection systems aimed at mitigating the increasing sophistication of cyber attacks, providing a framework to guide future research directions (Zhong *et al* 2024). Additionally, GNN model solutions addressing issues like imbalanced data, noisy data, out-of-distribution challenges, and privacy in real-world scenarios were reviewed (Ju *et al* 2024a). Approaches for summarizing graphs to reduce the complexity of huge graphs while preserving essential characteristics were reviewed (Shabani *et al* 2024). A survey by Ju *et al* (2024b) reviewed the fundamental components of deep graph representation learning and their practical applications. Lastly, counterfactual explainability methods for GNNs, including evaluation protocols, datasets, and metrics, were reviewed (Prado-Romero *et al* 2024).

5.6 Datasets suitable for graph neural networks

Datasets are critical for conducting research in ML. The data required by GNN to perform well has to be a graph dataset. So, the graph datasets suitable for GNN are presented in this section. Different scientific research areas investigate non-Euclidean space structure data. A typical example of such data are as follows: computational social sciences (social networks); communications (sensor networks); brain imaging (functional networks); genetics (regulatory networks) and computer graphics (meshed surfaces). In several applications, the dataset is large and complex such as geometric data and social network running into billions. Typically, such datasets are targeted for ML algorithms (Battaglia *et al* 2018). The presentation of data in the form of graphs has the benefit of modelling complex relationships, simplifying the modelling of complex problems, etc (Munikoti *et al* 2023). Different networks that create graph data are discussed in the next subsections. The datasets used to plot the figures in the next subsections indicating the number of edges and vertices for co-purchase network, web graph, citation network, temporal network, social network, telecommunications, autonomous graph and road networks were collected from Waikhom and Patgiri (2021).

5.6.1 Co-purchase networks

This type of network models the relationship that exists between products that are frequently purchased together at the same time by customers. In this situation, the product is representing the vertex and the purchase of two products frequently together forms a connection between the products. The connection between the products represents the edge. For example, say many customers frequently buy A and B together at the same time. Therefore, an edge exists between A and the B in the co-purchase network. The co-purchase network is very useful in understanding the behaviour of customers towards preferences and products of similarity and popularity (Prasad *et al* 2017). Amazon, one of the largest e-commerce platforms in the world, uses sales rank to estimate the popularity of products belonging to the same category. The Amazon sales-rank product prediction gives early insight on the popularity of products compared to the other products on the same Amazon platform. In the context of traditional methods for prediction, volume of reviews, text content reviews and so on are used for the prediction (Prasad *et al* 2017).

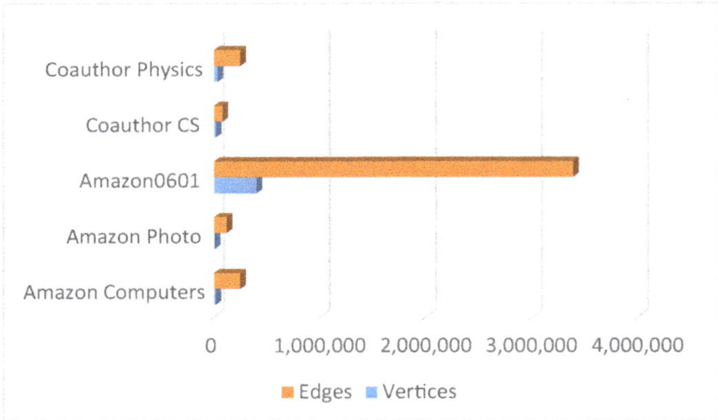

Figure 5.5. Graph data edges and vertices for different co-purchase networks.

E-commerce platforms like the Amazon can use the co-purchase network for the prediction of sales-ranking products. The co-purchase network can uncover communities of products belonging to the same sub-category or categories. Also, it can be used for the design of a cooperative buying program for the purchase of products together to reduce cost (Kunegis 2013, Shi *et al* 2017). Examples of co-purchase datasets include Amazon-created co-purchased network datasets such as Amazon Computers, Amazon Photo and Amazon0601 with vertex as the items and edges as the relationship of frequently purchased items. Co-author and Coauthor Physics are academic datasets based on Microsoft academic graph. The edges and vertex of the datasets are shown in figure 5.5 (Waikhom and Patgiri 2021).

5.6.2 Web graphs

The world wide web (www) commonly referred to as web sites is an information system that users depend on for accessing information on the internet. The www contains interlinked web pages running into billions and still growing on a daily basis. The www has spawn the sharing and dissemination of information on a large scale over the internet (Kumar *et al* 2000). The web graph is a directed graph that models the real-world large-scale www with billions of vertexes representing the html web pages and trillions of edges representing the hyperlinks. It typically exhibits inhomogeneity as such a developed community structure (Singh and Choudhury 2023). Examples of web graph datasets are Cornell, Texas and Washington datasets, containing web pages as the vertexes from Cornell University, Texas University and Washington University, respectively, with access on the web sites representing the edges. BerkStan, Google, Stanford and Notredame datasets of web pages are collected from various domains with large-scale vertices as the web pages and edges as the links (Waikhom and Patgiri 2021). Figure 5.6 indicates the number of edges and vertices for each of the datasets in this web graph category.

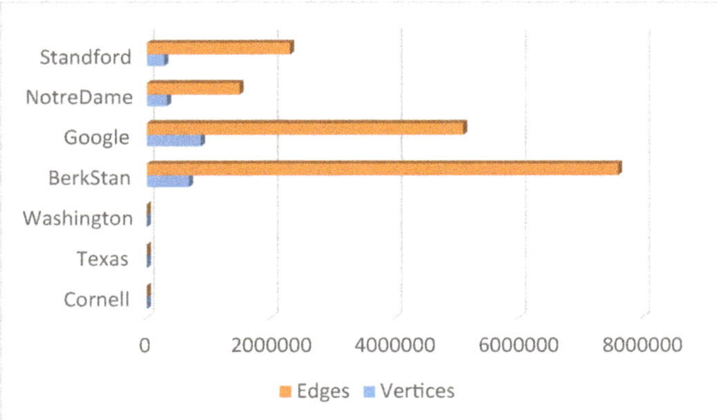

Figure 5.6. Web graphs with different numbers of edges and vertices.

5.6.3 Citation network

The citation network is the map of scientific directed graph structure of research publications belonging to a particular research area describing citations practice to the collection of documents from academic databases (academic databases are online search engines where abstract/indexed high quality collections of documents such as books, journals, conference proceedings, patents, magazines, etc from a particular research field or multiple research fields). The documents and the citations associated with each of the documents create a directed graph. Each document in the directed graph is the representation of the vertex while the edges directed from one document to another represent the citation. The examples of academic databases indexing collection of publications as provided in Waikhom and Patgiri (2021) include: DBLP computer science bibliography, PubMed, Patents, HepPhy, Cora and Citeseer. Each of these academic databases contain a large number of vertices (documents) and edges (citations), as shown in figure 5.7.

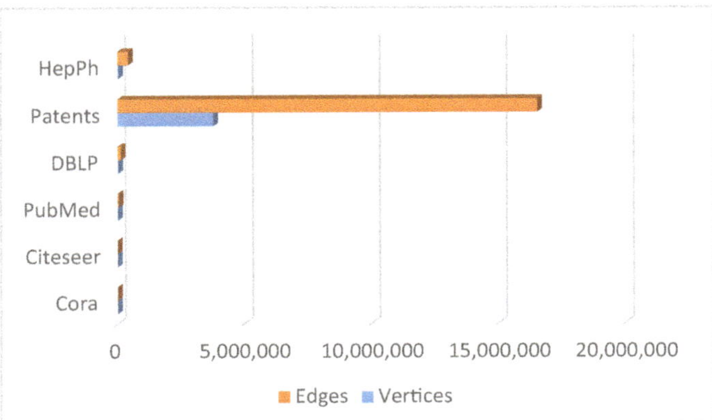

Figure 5.7. Indicating number of edges and vertices for different graph data.

5.6.4 Temporal networks

The temporal network referred to as the time-varying network is a type of network where the edges in the network are active temporarily. The information about the activeness of the edge in the network is carried with other corresponding characteristics including weight (Karsai *et al* 2014). Temporal networks are very useful in modelling systems where the interactions between vertices is dynamic but depends on event timing. A communication network is an example of temporal networks such as phone calls or email. These can be modelled as a temporal network in which the edge is the sequence of contacts that occurs between the two vertices. The temporal network can be used to study the flow of processes like the spreading of disease or information on the networks. The structure of the temporal network determines the speed, control and distance to be covered by the occurrence of an event (Eckmann *et al* 2004). The dynamics of neural networks and brain networks can be understood through temporal networkss especially in the situation where the neurons and brain region are time-correlated (Karsai *et al* 2014). The popular temporal networks are as follows: Stackoverflow, RedditHyperlinks, wiki-talk-temporal, mathoverflow, askubuntu, superuser and mooc, having thousands of vertices and edges, as can be seen in figure 5.8 (Waikhom and Patgiri 2021).

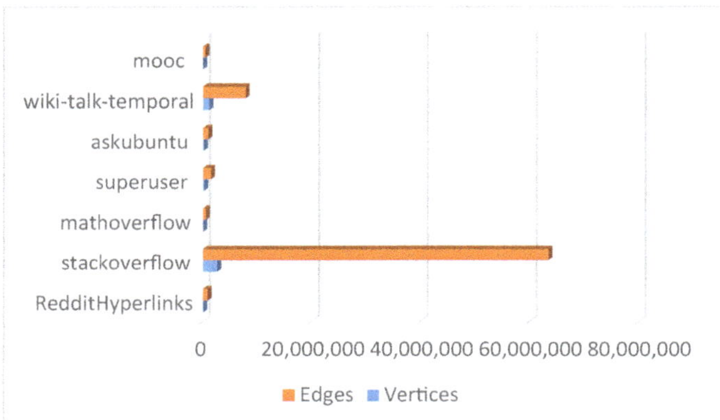

Figure 5.8. Edges and vertices for different temporal graphs.

5.6.5 Social networks

The idea of a social network is not totally new, as it has been in existence since 1954, the year Barnes introduced the concept as a social relationship in social situations (Mitchell 1974). Today, it is an online platform which allows people to build social relationships with people from different geographical locations who share similar content, background, activities or connections in the real physical world. The users of the platform generate and share videos, audios, images, posts, comments and many other happenings about people on the network virtually and in the real physical world. The content is typically generated by the social media users allowing the culture of participation (Chen *et al* 2023, Milroy and Llamas 2013). People form opinions about issues, create content and interact on the social media platforms (Taylor *et al* 2023). Presently, the online social networks platforms have billions of active users around the world. More than two thirds of internet users are on social media platforms with Facebook having the largest number of users (more than 2.4 billion). Other social networking site like YouTube and WhatsApp each have over a billion users (Ortiz-Ospina and Roser 2023). Social media forms graph data, for example, the Facebook dataset containing friends as nodes and interactions as the edges, the same as in YouTube. The Zachary karate club network dataset has social interaction among club members containing edges as the interaction between members and vertices as the club members. The Reddit dataset is a social media dataset with posts from the community. BlogCatalog dataset is the social network of bloggers from the Blogcatalog website. Flickr dataset is a social network generated from friend relationships where friends are the nodes and the edges are the status of the friends (Waikhom and Patgiri 2021). The edges and vertices for each of the social media graph data examples are depicted in figure 5.9.

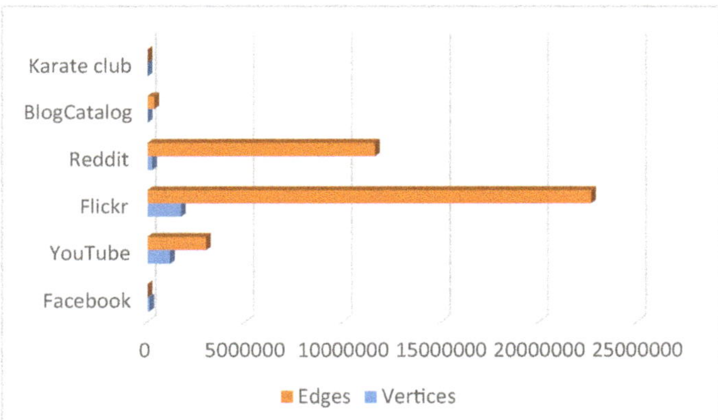

Figure 5.9. Social network graphs with different numbers of edges and vertices.

5.6.6 Communication networks

Networking and communication entail the design, analysis, implementation and the use of different networks such as the local area network, wider area network as well as mobile networks interconnecting computers. The internet is the network of networks making it feasible for computers to communicate globally. In a nutshell, a

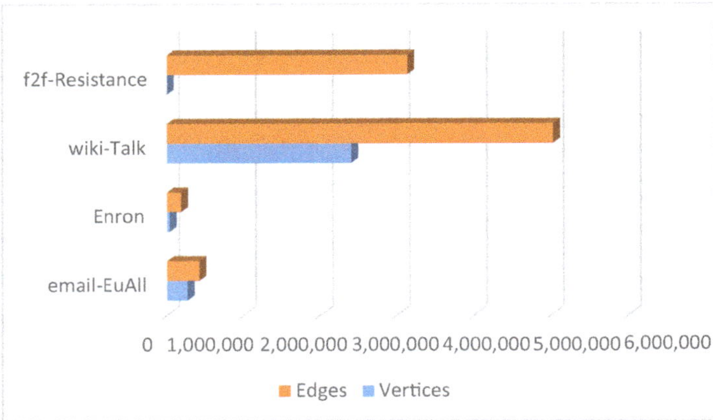

Figure 5.10. Number of edges and vertices for different communication network graphs.

communication network is the interconnection of systems that make it possible for sharing information and resources among users, teams and organizations (Leon-Garcia and Widjaja 2004, Monge and Contractor 2003). One of the widely used features of the internet is the email as it allows users to send and receive messages anywhere across the world (Dada *et al* 2019, Shafi *et al* 2017). Some available communication networks datasets are email-EuAll, Enron, wiki-Tal, and f2f-Resistance with thousands of vertices and edges, as shown in figure 5.10 (Waikhom and Patgiri 2021).

5.6.7 Road networks

A road network is used for the representation of road connectivity and structure within a particular area. Graphs with edges and vertices can be used for the modelling of road networks. The vertices represent locations like junctions or intersections, while the edges represent the road connections. The primal and dual are the two types of graphs that can be used for the representation of a road network where each vertex is a junction or intersection, whereas an edge is the segment of the road between the vertices. In dual graphs, the vertex represents a road or segment of the road and each of the vertices represent junctions or intersections between the two vertices. Attributes, e.g. name, type or length of road for vertex or edge, directions, e.g. direction of traffic flow or label and weights, e.g. speed limit, traffic volume and travel time, can add value to the graph. Applications of the road graph include traffic analysis, simulation, visualization, optimization and ML (Bachechi and Po 2022, He *et al* 2022, Jepsen *et al* 2019). The commonly used road network datasets are as follows: roadNet-CA, roadNet-PA, and roadNet-TX with data from California, Pennsylvania and Texas having vertices and edges as depicted in figure 5.11 (Waikhom and Patgiri 2021).

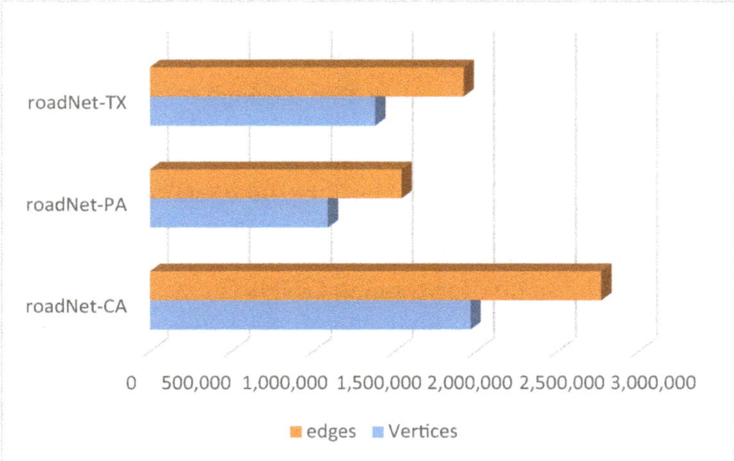

Figure 5.11. Indicating number of edges and vertices on road network graphs.

5.6.8 Autonomous systems graphs

The autonomous systems graph is an approach to modelling a network of routers that gives life to the internet. In the network, each router falls under a particular sub-network referred to as autonomous systems with an ID that is unique and capable of exchanging traffic with the autonomous system's peers. The communication between the autonomous systems create a connection. An autonomous system graph can be applied in studying structure and dynamics in the internet like connections, routing, resilience and traffic patterns (Leskovec *et al* 2005). The frequently used autonomous systems graph datasets are as follows: as-733, Skitter, Caida, Oregon-1, and Oregon-2 with vertices and edges as depicted in figure 5.12 (Waikhom and Patgiri 2021).

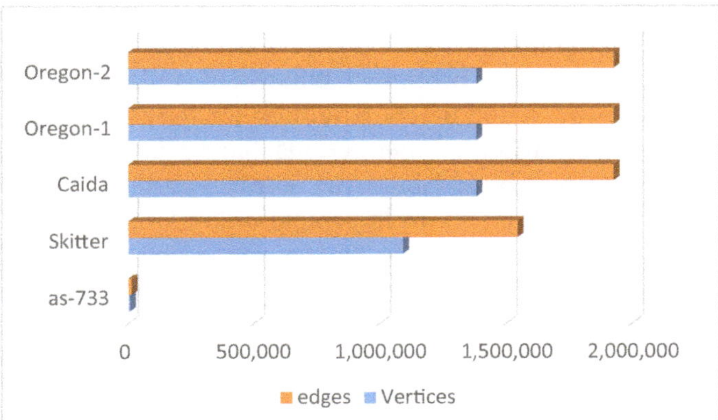

Figure 5.12. Edges and vertices for different autonomous system graphs.

5.7 Software platform for running graph neural networks

Many software platforms for running GNNs exist as both open source and subscription. The platforms discussed in this section is not exhaustive list but a representation of the platforms. A novice or early-career researcher or researcher willing to start work in this research field can easily locate the appropriate software platform to start running GNNs to understand its operations before proposing a new idea on the improvement of GNNs. The software platforms are as follows. *Pytorch-BigGraph* is an open-source large-scale graph framework of distributed systems developed by Facebook for training GNNs (Lerer *et al* 2019). *Deep Graph Library* is a Python library package that supports PyTorch, Tensorflow and Apache MXNet for executing deep learning on GNNs developed by Wang *et al* (2019), it is an open-source library. *NeuGraph* is a GNN platform that is subscription-based developed by the Microsoft researchers (Ma *et al* 2019). *FeatGraph* is a GNN platform that integrates variants of GNN frameworks for processing the workload of GNNs (Hu *et al* 2020). *AliGraph* it is an open-source platform referred to as graph-learn developed by the AliBaba group (Yang 2019). *FlexGraph*: is a system for scalable graph mining running on a distributed and parallel way on Apache Hadoop. The algorithms in FlexGraph include single source shortest path, weakly connected components, PageRank and random walk with restart (Wang *et al* 2021). *PyTorch Geometric*: The library of the Pytorch Geometric (PyG) is built on the PyTorch for easy writing and training of GNNs for use in different domains of applications with graph datasets. PyG is comprised of different methods for processing deep learning on graphs and geometric deep learning (Rozemberczki *et al* 2021).

5.8 Industrial applications

The major application of the GNN in industry is the recommender system, also referred to as the recommender engine. A lot of companies deploy GNN-based recommender systems for product suggestions as they are found to perform better than the stat-of-the-art algorithms.

Pharmaceutical companies are searching for a new and better means of discovering drugs. Fierce competition prompted billions of dollars to be pumping into research and development to find a new paradigm for drugs discovery. Graphs can be used for the representation of interactions happening at different scales in biology. Edges can represent bonds that exist between atoms at the molecular level or the amino-acid residues interactions in proteins. The complex nature of proteins, mRNA, or metabolites interactions can be represented by a graph. Subsequently, the graph can be used for targeting identification, predicting molecule property, screening of high-throughput, drugs design, engineering of proteins and the repurposing of drugs (Gaudelet *et al* 2021). The GNN is found to be useful for the discovery of drugs (Stokes *et al* 2020).

It is reported that giant companies like, but not limited to Google, Alibaba, Uber, Twitter and Pinterest have already shifted their base to the development of a GNN-based solution to their core products (Ramponi 2023), GNN product recommender system in Amazon e-commerce site (Hao *et al* 2020), GNN recommender system for recommending power content at Pinterest (Ying *et al* 2018). Uber Eats has already deployed GNNs for recommending dishes and restaurants to users (Huang *et al* 2020). GNNs are used in industry for design of physical layout of chip hardware (Mirhoseini *et al* 2021).

5.9 Case studies

The real-world scenario of the GNN application can make the reader value and appreciate GNNs. It also shows the bridge between theories and practice. Case studies on real-world applications of GNNs in different domains are presented below.

5.9.1 Google Maps

Typically, people use Google Maps for estimating time for a journey that covers a certain distance or when heading to an airport to catch a flight or trying to locate a new restaurant within a timeframe or arranging commuting in the morning. However, certain factors such as traffic congestion on the road and ongoing road maintenance work can hinder the success of these predictions. Thus, a team of researchers at Google applied GNNs to improve accuracy of the predictions and improve the possibility of arriving at the destination on time. A GNN was used because the local road networks were treated as a graph in which vertices were represented by each route segment and the consecutive segment or the segment of the road with intersections as a result of connection represented the edges of the graph. The GNN permitted the forecasting of road traffic ahead or behind the driver and surrounding cars and roads that intersected. The GNN solution has been deployed on Google Maps (Derrow-Pinion *et al* 2021).

5.9.2 Alibaba's e-commerce

A recommender system based on a GNN with billions of users and products was developed by a team of researchers at Alibaba group supporting different varieties of businesses, especially recommendation of products and the personalization of search. The recommender system has been deployed at the Alibaba e-commerce platform to support customer shopping such as the recommendation of content across multiple products that the customer may likely have interest in purchasing (Yang 2019).

5.9.3 Decathlon Canada

Developers developed a recommender system for an e-commerce site called Decathlon Canada that specializes in selling sports equipment. The developers used graphs to represent the information available like the users and the history of the sports equipment they purchased to apply GNNs for developing the recommender system. The developers used datasets for 50 weeks for training the GNN for the period of 14 days. The outcome indicated that the users were more likely to engage or interact with the items of the store than with the previous version of the recommender system where it recommends best-selling sport equipment of the previous two weeks to all the users. Unlike the previous version, the GNN-based recommender system tailored the relevant sports equipment based on individual preferences according to the past activities associated with the user. Therefore, the possibility of the users to click on the sports equipment suggested by the GNN recommender system was greater (Newton 2021).

5.9.4 Waymo driver

Waymo uses a GNN to improve an autonomous driving platform called Waymo driver. The GNN collects vector relationship information. On approaching an intersection or a pedestrian coming to a crosswalk, the GNN predicts the reaction of the other vehicles on the road or people walking on foot based on the information gathered by the GNN. Thus, this makes the vehicle easily take action that is appropriate for navigating traffic. The autonomous vehicle uses the data collected to give clues on the context of the surrounding environment. The performance of the GNN-based Waymo was found to be better than other types of ANN by 18% (Newton 2021).

5.10 Discussion

It has been established that this research area has attracted tremendous attention from the research community because of the high volume of reviews/surveys and tutorial publications available in different academic databases. Querying any of the academic databases with the keyword GNN returns a very large volume of documents with many reviews/surveys and tutorial papers. It is found that memory consumption by the GNN is a critical issue adding cost to the running of GNNs. Unfortunately, many researchers did not give adequate attention to this challenging issue. We recommend researchers to begin to report the amount of memory consumed in addition to accuracy and computational time. Clearly huge GNN is a trending topic in the field of AI, specifically ML. Figure 5.13 was created from the data extracted from section 5.6. Observing figure 5.13 indicates that publishing reviews/surveys and tutorial papers on GNN started in 2017 with only two reviews, followed by a slowdown in 2018 with just a single paper throughout the year, moving slowly to 2019 before witnessing a surge on reviews/surveys and tutorial papers in 2020 with eight published review/survey papers. The trends have continued growing continuously from 2020 with a little fluctuation in 2021 up to 2024, indicating that 2024 had the highest number of published reviews/surveys and tutorials on GNN.

This trend is expected to continue into the future because between 2020 and 2024 alone 55 reviews/surveys and tutorial papers on different perspectives of GNNs such as spatial–temporal GNN, graph convolutional neural network, GNN operators and quantum computing related to GNN have been published. In view of the fact that the GNN has been applied to solve ML problems in different domains of applications, a large number of reviews/surveys and tutorials were conducted with a focus on specific application domains such as recommender systems, traffic flow

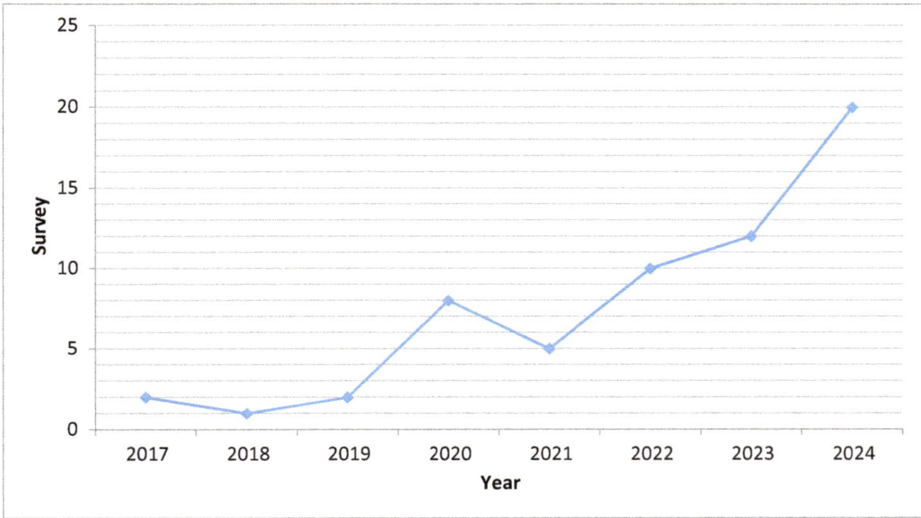

Figure 5.13. Trend of reviews/surveys and tutorials publications on GNNs from 2017 to 2024.

forecasting, neurological disorders and EEG. It is found that researchers heavily rely on GNNs for developing recommender systems, and as such, they received the highest attention from the research community. Other domains that received attention include social network, computer vision, natural language processing and pattern recognition. Apart from reviews, many tutorials have been published alongside reviews/surveys for beginners or researchers having interest with the intention to start research in the field of GNNs to have a grasp of the basic knowledge required to start work on the GNN field of research. Thus, both reviews/surveys and tutorials on GNNs were published. A review/survey and tutorial on GNNs is critical as it can pave the way for a massive improvement of GNNs, for which any additional improvement means rapid improvement across different domains of applications. It is evident from the surveys/reviews and tutorials that the GNN is a hot algorithm for solving real-world ML problems in different domains. Typically, surveys/reviews and tutorials on GNN have the potential to inspire novice and early-career researchers to begin work in the research field. On the other hand, it makes it easy for expert researchers to gain new ideas on the development of the GNN research area. Interestingly all the reviews/surveys and tutorials summarized in this chapter outlined and discussed challenges before pointing out opportunities for future research direction. The huge GNN can make contributions towards the realization of artificial general intelligence.

5.11 Limitations and future direction

The surveys/reviews and tutorials published in this research field are many, as shown in figure 5.14. Despite all the enormous reviews/surveys, there are many opportunities for conducting reviews/surveys in the field because some aspects of GNNs

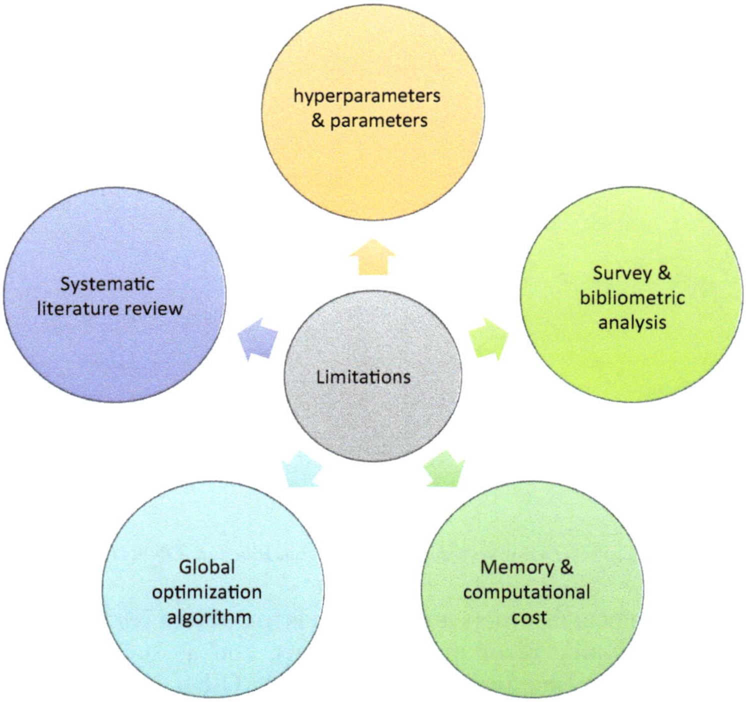

Figure 5.14. Visual representation of the already published surveys/review limitations as found in the study.

critical for their development were not covered, thus, creating gaps for future reviews/surveys to be conducted. A summary of the limitations found is represented in figure 5.14.

5.11.1 Hyper-parameters and parameters

The issue of pre-defining a GNN hyper-parameter is critical to the performance of the GNN in solving real-world complex problems as many hyper-parameters need to pre-set before running the GNN. Many combinations of factors (e.g. aggregator) are required for suitable architecture of the GNN to be tailored for solving problems in a particular domain. On the other hand, the GNN generates a lot of parameters from the training data running into millions or even billions in some cases. Considering the critical nature of the hyper-parameter settings and the model parameters, GNN surveys/reviews that focus mainly on hyper-parameters and parameters of GNNs are lacking in the literature. Therefore, we recommend the research community to conduct an extensive survey/review on GNN hyper-parameters, function combination and parameters.

5.11.2 Combining survey/review and bibliometric analysis

Typically, surveys/reviews should be combined with bibliometric analysis as agued by Donthu *et al* (2021) and practice by many researchers (e.g. Chiroma *et al* 2020,

Ezugwu *et al* 2021). Unfortunately, none of the GNN reviews/surveys published combine surveys/reviews with bibliometric analysis. The published surveys/reviews mainly focus on the survey/review aspect without bibliometric analysis or are focused on bibliometric analysis alone without survey/review, only one paper falls into this category. Therefore, it is recommended to the research community to include bibliometric analysis in any future GNN survey/review.

5.11.3 Cost of computational resources and memory consumption

The popularity of the huge GNN motivated the research community to apply it in solving real-world problems in which the size of the GNN is running into 100 million vertices and billions of edges. Unfortunately, the challenge of the huge GNN is its requirement for large-scale memory space, as such, most of the huge GNN cannot directly be applied to huge graph data (Hu *et al* 2020). The GNN computational cost and the use of memory increases as the size of the GNN increases. In a bid to reduce the learning task computational cost and the use of memory, graph sampling or sparsification is employed for the extraction of the graph sample from the large original graph, yet remains effective. This is signifying that the size of the GNN is directly proportional to the computational cost and usage of the memory space (Chen *et al* 2021). It is the activation that induces the memory usage. The consumption of memory by the GNN increases linearly with the GNN layers as most of the GNN requires the whole adjacency matrix to be stored in the memory. As the number of GNN layers keeps on increasing it can reach a stage where the computing system can run out of memory with the available hardware. This can make studying deeper huge GNNs impossible on the available hardware (Li *et al* 2021). Therefore, it creats both a computing memory consumption and computational cost challenge. As a result of the huge GNN challenges of memory and computational cost, many researchers proposed sampling strategies, e.g. layer and vertices sampling to reduce the size of the hug GNN. Therefore, it is recommended for researchers to conduct a comprehensive survey from the perspective of huge GNN memory consumption and computational cost. IEEE Computer Society (2023) suggested the development of special hardware as an accelerator with the capacity to accelerate running of the huge GNN.

5.11.4 Nature-inspired algorithm optimization of graph neural network

Searching for suitable GNN architecture and hyper-parameters has been a trial-and-error practice. Some researchers have proposed the use of global optimization algorithms for the automatic determination of the huge GNN architecture. For example, Shi *et al* (2022) automatically determined the optimal architecture of GNN-based on genetic algorithm from large search space. Yuan *et al* (2021) optimized the hyper-parameters of the GNN through genetic algorithms search. On the other hand, particle swarm optimization has been applied for the optimization of GNNs (Guo *et al* 2022, Hu *et al* 2023). Despite the published works on the automatic optimization of the GNN architecture and hyper-parameters, as yet no single review/survey has been conducted on the automatic optimization of GNN architecture using a global optimization algorithm like the genetic algorithm. A comprehensive review/survey on the automatic search of GNN architecture and hyper-parameters via global optimization algorithms should be conducted.

5.11.5 Systematic literature review

The reviews presented in this research field mostly ignored the standard procedure for conducting a systematic literature review. As a result, it will be difficult to understand the procedure used to avoid bias in the selection of the papers to include in a review and quality assessment. Highly limited papers attempted to follow the standard review methodology but the overwhelming majority of the papers ignore it. It is recommended that future reviews/surveys on GNNs should be conducted from the perspective of computer science systematic literature review procedure, as suggested by Chiroma and Abawjy (2023) and Weidt and Silva (2016).

5.12 Summary

This chapter introduced the fundamentals of graph and ANN as the requisite preliminary knowledge to make the reader easily understand the GNN concept of operations. Before the discussions on graphs and ANN, key terms such as features, vertex, edge, embedding and neighbourhood were defined. Basic theories and mathematical background of the graph, categories of graphs such as directed and undirected; static and dynamic; homogeneous and heterogeneous; bipartite graph, attributed and hypergraph were presented. The computational and mathematical description of the ANN is provided in the chapter. The GNN operation stages include pre-processing, feature vectors update and readout/output, GNN learning algorithms, hyper-parameters setting and learning task were discussed. The four major different architectures of the GNN were explained, namely, graph autoencoder, recurrent GNN, graph convolutional neural network and spatial–temporal graph neural network. Reviews of the GNN review papers (review of reviews) published in the literature from 2017 to 2023 from different perspectives of GNNs and domains of applications is contained in the chapter. The review papers were classified in different sections according to the period of publications. It is observed that the majority of GNN review papers were published between 2020 to 2023. This signifies that the GNN is enjoying tremendous attention from the research community in current times. This is expected to continue into the future, corroborating the prediction of IEEE computer society technology's prediction of 2023 that predicted the trending of GNNs in the future as a result of widespread adoption by academia and industry to solve problems related to graph data. Despite the large volume of reviews on GNN, it is found that there were still aspects of the GNN like its impact on memory consumption, hyper-parameter settings, computational cost, methodology, evolutionary optimization of hyper-parameter, integrating bibliometric analysis in survey that were not covered in the already published reviews.

References

Abadal S, Jain A, Guirado R, López-Alonso J and Alarcón E 2021 Computing graph neural networks: a survey from algorithms to accelerators *ACM Comput. Surv.* **54** 1–38

Adjeisah M, Zhu X, Xu H and Ayall T A 2023 Towards data augmentation in graph neural network: an overview and evaluation *Comp. Sci. Rev.* **47** 100527

Asratian A S, Denley T M and Häggkvist R 1998 *Bipartite Graphs and Their Applications* **vol 131** (Cambridge: Cambridge University Press)

Bachechi C and Po L 2022 Road network graph representation for traffic analysis and routing *European Conf. on Advances in Databases and Information Systems* (Cham: Springer) pp 75–89

Bai Y, Li C, Lin Z, Wu Y, Miao Y, Liu Y and Xu Y 2021 Efficient data loader for fast sampling-based gnn training on large graphs *IEEE Trans. Parallel Distrib. Syst.* **32** 2541–56

Battaglia P W, Hamrick J B, Bapst V, Sanchez-Gonzalez A, Zambaldi V, Malinowski M and Pascanu R 2018 Relational inductive biases, deep learning, and graph networks *arXiv preprint* arXiv:1806.01261

Belahcen A, Bianchini M and Scarselli F 2015 Web spam detection using transductive (inductive graph neural networks) *Advances in Neural Networks: Computational and Theoretical Issues* (Springer) pp 83–91

Bergstra J and Bengio Y 2012 Random search for hyper-parameter optimization *J. Mach. Learn. Res.* **13** 281–305

Bishop C M 1995 *Neural Networks for Pattern Recognition* (Oxford: Oxford University Press)

Bronstein M M, Bruna J, LeCun Y, Szlam A and Vandergheynst P 2017 Geometric deep learning: going beyond euclidean data *IEEE Signal Process Mag.* **34** 18–42

Bui K H N, Cho J and Yi H 2022 Spatial-temporal graph neural network for traffic forecasting: an overview and open research issues *Appl. Intell.* **52** 2763–74

Chami I, Abu-El-Haija S, Perozzi B, Ré C and Murphy K 2022 Machine learning on graphs: a model and comprehensive taxonomy *J. Mach. Learn. Res.* **23** 3840–903

Chen A, Rossi R A, Park N, Trivedi P, Wang Y, Yu T and Ahmed N K 2024 Fairness-aware graph neural networks: a survey *ACM Trans. Knowl. Discov. Data* **18** 1–23

Chen T, Sui Y, Chen X, Zhang A and Wang Z 2021 A unified lottery ticket hypothesis for graph neural networks *Int. Conf. on Machine Learning* (PMLR) pp 1695–706

Chen Y, Sherren K, Smit M and Lee K Y 2023 Using social media images as data in social science research *New Media Soc.* **25** 849–71

Chiroma H and Abawjy J H 2023 *Computing Research Survival Manual: A Practical Handbook for Beginners* (London: IOP Publishers)

Chiroma H, Ezugwu A E, Jauro F, Al-Garadi M A, Abdullahi I N and Shuib L 2020 Early survey with bibliometric analysis on machine learning approaches in controlling COVID-19 outbreaks *PeerJ Comput. Sci.* **6** e313

Choi J, Oh S and Kim J 2021 A tutorial on quantum graph recurrent neural network (QGRNN) *2021 Int. Conf. on Information Networking (ICOIN)* (Piscataway, NJ: IEEE) pp 46–9

Corso G, Stark H, Jegelka S, Jaakkola T and Barzilay R 2024 Graph neural networks *Nat. Rev. Methods Primers* **4** 17

Dada E G, Bassi J S, Chiroma H, Adetunmbi A O and Ajibuwa O E 2019 Machine learning for email spam filtering: review, approaches and open research problems *Heliyon* **5** e01802

Dai E, Zhao T, Zhu H, Xu J, Guo Z, Liu H and Wang S 2024 A comprehensive survey on trustworthy graph neural networks: privacy, robustness, fairness, and explainability *Mach. Intell. Res.* **21** 1011–61

Dai H, Kozareva Z, Dai B, Smola A and Song L 2018 Learning steady-states of iterative algorithms over graphs *Int. Conf. on Machine Learning* (PMLR) pp 1106–14

Derrow-Pinion A, She J, Wong D, Lange O, Hester T, Perez L and Velickovic P 2021 Eta prediction with graph neural networks in google maps *Proc. of the 30th ACM Int. Conf. on Information and Knowledge Management* pp 3767–76

Dong G, Tang M, Wang Z, Gao J, Guo S, Cai L and Boukhechba M 2023 Graph neural networks in IoT: a survey *ACM Trans. Sensor Netw.* **19** 1–50

Donthu N, Kumar S, Mukherjee D, Pandey N and Lim W M 2021 How to conduct a bibliometric analysis: an overview and guidelines *J. Bus. Res.* **133** 285–96

Dwivedi V P, Joshi C K, Luu A T, Laurent T, Bengio Y and Bresson X 2022 Benchmarking graph neural networks *J. Mach. Learn. Res.* **23** 1–48

Eckmann J P, Moses E and Sergi D 2004 Entropy of dialogues creates coherent structures in e-mail traffic *Proc. Natl. Acad. Sci.* **101** 14333–7

Ezugwu A E, Shukla A K, Nath R, Akinyelu A A, Agushaka J O, Chiroma H and Muhuri P K 2021 Metaheuristics: a comprehensive overview and classification along with bibliometric analysis *Artif. Intell. Rev.* **54** 4237–316

Gallicchio C and Micheli A 2010 Graph echo state networks *The 2010 Int. Joint Conf. on Neural Networks (IJCNN)* (Piscataway, NJ: IEEE) pp 1–8

Gao C, Zheng Y, Li N, Li Y, Qin Y, Piao J and Li Y 2023 A survey of graph neural networks for recommender systems: challenges, methods, and directions *ACM Trans. Recomm. Syst.* **1** 1–51

Gaudelet T, Day B, Jamasb A R, Soman J, Regep C, Liu G and Taylor-King J P 2021 Utilizing graph machine learning within drug discovery and development *Brief. Bioinform.* **22** bbab159

Goodrich M T, Tamassia R and Goldwasser M H 2014 *Data Structures and Algorithms in Java* (New York: Wiley)

Gori M, Monfardini G and Scarselli F 2005 A new model for learning in graph domains *Proc. 2005 IEEE Int. Joint Conf. on Neural Networks, 2005* vol 2 (Piscataway, NJ: IEEE) pp 729–34

Graña M and Morais-Quilez I 2023 A review of graph neural networks for electroencephalography data analysis *Neurocomputing* **562** 126901

Guan F, Zhu T, Zhou W and Choo K K R 2024 Graph neural networks: a survey on the links between privacy and security *Artif. Intell. Rev.* **57** 40

Guo K, Chen Z, Lin X, Wu L, Zhan Z H, Chen Y and Guo W 2022 Community detection based on multiobjective particle swarm optimization and graph attention variational autoencoder *IEEE Trans. Big Data* **9** 569–83

Hamilton W, Ying Z and Leskovec J 2017a Inductive representation learning on large graphs *NIPS'17: Proceedings of the 31st International Conference on Neural Information Processing Systems* **30**

Hamilton W L, Ying R and Leskovec J 2017b Representation learning on graphs: methods and applications *arXiv preprint* arXiv:1709.05584

Hao J, Zhao T, Li J, Dong X L, Faloutsos C, Sun Y and Wang W 2020 P-companion: a principled framework for diversified complementary product recommendation *Proc. of the 29th ACM Int. Conf. on Information and Knowledge Management* pp 2517–24

He Y, Garg R and Chowdhury A R 2022 TD-Road: top-down road network extraction with holistic graph construction *European Conf. on Computer Vision* (Cham: Springer Nature) pp 562–77

Hu L, Yang Y, Tang Z, He Y and Luo X 2023 FCAN-MOPSO: an improved fuzzy-based graph clustering algorithm for complex networks with multi-objective particle swarm optimization *IEEE Trans. Fuzzy Syst.* **31** 3470–84

Hu Y, Ye Z, Wang M, Yu J, Zheng D, Li M and Wang Y 2020 Featgraph: a flexible and efficient backend for graph neural network systems *SC20: Int. Conf. for High Performance Computing, Networking, Storage and Analysis* (Piscataway, NJ: IEEE) pp 1–13 https://github.com/amazon-science/FeatGraph

Hu Z, Dong Y, Wang K, Chang K W and Sun Y 2020 GPT-GNN: generative pre-training of graph neural networks *Proc. of the 26th ACM SIGKDD Int. Conf. on Knowledge Discovery and Data Mining* pp 1857–67

Huang B, Bi Y, Wu Z, Wang J and Xiao J 2020 Uber-GNN: a user-based embeddings recommendation based on graph neural networks *arXiv preprint* arXiv:2008.02546

Huang J 2022 Graph neural network in knowledge graph aided recommender systems *Proc. of the 2022 4th Int. Conf. on Robotics, Intelligent Control and Artificial Intelligence* pp 743–6

IEEE Computer Society 2023 *IEEE Computer Society Technology Prediction 2023* https://computer.org/2022-top-technology-predictions/ (accessed 20 January 2023)

Jepsen T S, Jensen C S and Nielsen T D 2019 Graph convolutional networks for road networks *Proc. of the 27th ACM SIGSPATIAL Int. Conf. on Advances in Geographic Information Systems* pp 460–3

Jia Y, Wang J, Shou W, Hosseini M R and Bai Y 2023 Graph neural networks for construction applications *Autom. Constr.* **154** 104984

Jiang W, Luo J, He M and Gu W 2023 Graph neural network for traffic forecasting: the research progress *ISPRS Int. J. Geo-Inform.* **12** 100

Jiang X, Jia T, Fang Y, Shi C, Lin Z and Wang H 2021 Pre-training on large-scale heterogeneous graph *Proc. of the 27th ACM SIGKDD Conf. on Knowledge Discovery and Data Mining* pp 756–66

Jin M, Koh H Y, Wen Q, Zambon D, Alippi C, Webb G I and Pan S 2024 A survey on graph neural networks for time series: forecasting, classification, imputation, and anomaly detection *IEEE Trans. Pattern Anal. Mach. Intell.* **46** 10466–85

Ju W, Fang Z, Gu Y, Liu Z, Long Q, Qiao Z and Zhang M 2024b A comprehensive survey on deep graph representation learning *Neural Netw.* **173** 106207

Ju W, Yi S, Wang Y, Xiao Z, Mao Z, Li H and Zhang M 2024a A survey of graph neural networks in real world: imbalance, noise, privacy and ood challenges *arXiv preprint* arXiv:2403.04468

Karsai M, Perra N and Vespignani A 2014 Time varying networks and the weakness of strong ties *Sci. Rep.* **4** 4001

Keramatfar A, Rafiee M and Amirkhani H 2022 Graph neural networks: a bibliometrics overview *Mach. Learn. Appl.* **10** 100401

Khemani B, Patil S, Kotecha K and Tanwar S 2024 A review of graph neural networks: concepts, architectures, techniques, challenges, datasets, applications, and future directions *J. Big Data* **11** 18

Khoshraftar S and An A 2024 A survey on graph representation learning methods *ACM Trans. Intell. Syst. Technol.* **15** 1–55

Kipf T N and Welling M 2016 Variational graph auto-encoders *arXiv preprint* arXiv:1611.07308

Kipf T N and Welling M 2016 Semi-supervised classification with graph convolutional networks *arXiv preprint* arXiv:1609.02907

Klepl D, Wu M and He F 2024 Graph neural network-based EEG classification: a survey *IEEE Trans. Neural Syst. Rehabil. Eng.* **32** 493–503

Kuhn M and Johnson K 2013 *Applied Predictive Modeling* **vol 26** (New York: Springer) p 13

Kumar R, Raghavan P, Rajagopalan S, Sivakumar D, Tompkins A and Upfal E 2000 The Web as a graph *Proc. of the 19th ACM SIGMOD-SIGACT-SIGART Symp. on Principles of Database Systems* pp 1–10

Kunegis J 2013 Konect: the koblenz network collection *Proc. of the 22nd Int. Conf. on World Wide Web* pp 1343–50

Lamb L C, Garcez A, Gori M, Prates M, Avelar P and and Vardi M 2020 Graph neural networks meet neural-symbolic computing: a survey and perspective *arXiv preprint* arXiv:2003.00330

Leon-Garcia A and Widjaja I 2004 *Communication Networks: Fundamental Concepts and Key Architectures* (New York: McGraw-Hill)

Lerer A, Wu L, Shen J, Lacroix T, Wehrstedt L, Bose A and Peysakhovich A 2019 Pytorch-biggraph: a large scale graph embedding system *Proc. Mach. Learn. Syst.* **1** 120–31 https://pypi.org/project/torchbiggraph/

Leskovec J, Kleinberg J and Faloutsos C 2005 Graphs over time: densification laws, shrinking diameters and possible explanations *Proc. of the 11th ACM SIGKDD Int. Conf. on Knowledge Discovery in Data Mining* pp 177–87

Li G, Müller M, Ghanem B and Koltun V 2021 Training graph neural networks with 1000 layers *Int. Conf. on Machine Learning* (PMLR) pp 6437–49

Li Y, Tarlow D, Brockschmidt M and Zemel R 2015 Gated graph sequence neural networks *arXiv preprint* arXiv:1511.05493

Li Y, Zhang G, Wang P, Yu Z G and Huang G 2022 Graph neural networks in biomedical data: a review *Curr. Bioinform.* **17** 483–92

Li Z, Cui Z, Wu S, Zhang X and Wang L 2019 Fi-gnn: modeling feature interactions via graph neural networks for ctr prediction *Proc. of the 28th ACM Int. Conf. on Information and Knowledge Management* pp 539–48

Liao S and Jia L 2007 Simultaneous tuning of hyperparameter and parameter for support vector machines *Proc. Advances in Knowledge Discovery and Data Mining: 11th Pacific-Asia Conf., PAKDD 2007 (Nanjing, China, May 22–25, 2007)* (Berlin: Springer) pp 162–72

Lin H, Yan M, Ye X, Fan D, Pan S, Chen W and Xie Y 2022 A comprehensive survey on distributed training of graph neural networks *arXiv preprint arXiv* **2211** 05368

Linmei H, Yang T, Shi C, Ji H and Li X 2019 Heterogeneous graph attention networks for semi-supervised short text classification *Proc. of the 2019 Conf. on Empirical Methods in Natural Language Processing and the 9th Int. Joint Conf. on Natural Language Processing (EMNLP-IJCNLP)* pp 4821–30

Liu C, Zhan Y, Wu J, Li C, Du B, Hu W and Tao D 2022 Graph pooling for graph neural networks: progress, challenges, and opportunities *arXiv preprint* arXiv:2204.07321

Liu R, Xing P, Deng Z, Li A, Guan C and Yu H 2024 Federated graph neural networks: overview, techniques, and challenges *IEEE Trans. Neural. Netw. Learn. Syst.* **36** 4279–95

Liu Z, Wan G, Prakash B A, Lau M S and Jin W 2024 A review of graph neural networks in epidemic modeling *Proc. of the 30th ACM SIGKDD Conf. on Knowledge Discovery and Data Mining* pp 6577–87

Longa A, Azzolin S, Santin G, Cencetti G, Liò P, Lepri B and Passerini A 2024 Explaining the explainers in graph neural networks: a comparative study *ACM Comput. Surv.* **57** 120

Ma L, Yang Z, Miao Y, Xue J, Wu M, Zhou L and Dai Y 2019 {NeuGraph}: parallel deep neural network computation on large graphs *2019 USENIX Annual Technical Conf. (USENIX ATC 19)* pp 443–58 https://neurograph.readthedocs.io/en/latest/install.html

McCulloch W S and Pitts W 1943 A logical calculus of the ideas immanent in nervous activity *Bull. Math. Biophys.* **5** 115–33

Milroy L and Llamas C 2013 Social networks *The Handbook of Language Variation and Change* (Blackwell) pp 407–27

Mirhoseini A, Goldie A, Yazgan M, Jiang J W, Songhori E, Wang S and Dean J 2021 A graph placement methodology for fast chip design *Nature* **594** 207–12

Mitchell J C 1974 Social networks *Annu. Rev. Anthropol.* **3** 279–99

Mohammadi A R 2023 Explainable graph neural network recommenders; challenges and opportunities *Proc. of the 17th ACM Conf. on Recommender Systems* pp 1318–24

Monge P R and Contractor N S 2003 *Theories of Communication Networks* (Oxford: Oxford University Press)

Munikoti S, Agarwal D, Das L, Halappanavar M and Natarajan B 2023 Challenges and opportunities in deep reinforcement learning with graph neural networks: a comprehensive review of algorithms and applications arXiv:2206.07922 https://doi.org/10.48550/arXiv.2206.07922

Newton E 2021 *Revolutionized* https://revolutionized.com/graph-neural-network/ (accessed 12 February 2023)

Nguyen H X, Zhu S and Liu M 2022 A survey on graph neural networks for microservice-based cloud applications *Sensors* **22** 9492

Ortiz-Ospina E and Roser M 2023 *The Rise of Social Media* (Oxford: Our World in Data)

Pareja A, Domeniconi G, Chen J, Ma T, Suzumura T, Kanezashi H and Leiserson C 2020 Evolvegcn: evolving graph convolutional networks for dynamic graphs *Proc. of the AAAI Conf. on Artificial Intelligence* vol 34 pp 5363–70

Phan H T, Nguyen N T and Hwang D 2023 Fake news detection: a survey of graph neural network methods *Appl. Soft Comput.* **139** 110235

Prado-Romero M A, Prenkaj B, Stilo G and Giannotti F 2024 A survey on graph counterfactual explanations: definitions, methods, evaluation, and research challenges *ACM Comput. Surv.* **56** 1–37

Prasad U, Kumari N, Ganguly N and Mukherjee A 2017 Analysis of the co-purchase network of products to predict amazon sales-rank *Proc. Big Data Analytics: 5th Int. Conf., BDA 2017 (Hyderabad, India, December 12–15, 2017)* (Springer) pp 197–214

Ramponi M 2023 *AI Trends in 2023: Graph Neural Networks* https://assemblyai.com/blog/ai-trends-graph-neural-networks/ (accessed 2 December 2023)

Rong Y, Xu T, Huang J, Huang W, Cheng H, Ma Y and Ma T 2020 Deep graph learning: foundations, advances and applications *Proc. of the 26th ACM SIGKDD Int. Conf. on Knowledge Discovery and Data Mining* pp 3555–6

Rossi A, Tiezzi M, Dimitri G M, Bianchini M, Maggini M and Scarselli F 2018 Inductive–transductive learning with graph neural networks *Artificial Neural Networks in Pattern Recognition: 8th IAPR TC3 Workshop, ANNPR 2018, Siena, Italy, September 19–21, 2018, Proc. 8* (Cham: Springer) pp 201–12

Rozemberczki B, Scherer P, He Y, Panagopoulos G, Riedel A, Astefanoaei M and Sarkar R 2021 Pytorch geometric temporal: spatiotemporal signal processing with neural machine learning models *Proc. of the 30th ACM Int. Conf. on Information and Knowledge Management* pp 4564–73 https://pytorch-geometric.readthedocs.io/en/latest/

Salha G, Hennequin R and Vazirgiannis M 2021 Simple and effective graph autoencoders with one-hop linear models *Proc. Machine Learning and Knowledge Discovery in Databases:*

European Conf., ECML PKDD 2020 (Ghent, Belgium, September 14–18, 2020) (Cham: Springer) pp 319–34

Sato R 2020 A survey on the expressive power of graph neural networks *arXiv preprint* arXiv:2003.04078

Scarselli F, Gori M, Tsoi A C, Hagenbuchner M and Monfardini G 2008 The graph neural network model *IEEE Trans. Neural Networks* **20** 61–80

Scarselli F, Yong S L, Gori M, Hagenbuchner M, Tsoi A C and Maggini M 2005 Graph neural networks for ranking web pages *The 2005 IEEE/WIC/ACM Int. Conf. on Web Intelligence (WI'05)* (Piscataway, NJ: IEEE) pp 666–72

Senior H, Slabaugh G, Yuan S and Rossi L 2024 Graph neural networks in vision-language image understanding: a survey *Vis. Comput.* **41** 491–516

Shabani N, Wu J, Beheshti A, Sheng Q Z, Foo J, Haghighi V and Shahabikargar M 2024 A comprehensive survey on graph summarization with graph neural networks *IEEE Trans. Artif. Intell.* **5** 3780–800

Shafi M A, Latiff M S A, Chiroma H, Osho O, Abdul-Salaam G, Abubakar A I and Herawan T 2017 A review on mobile SMS spam filtering techniques *IEEE Access* **5** 15650–66

Shao Y, Li H, Gu X, Yin H, Li Y, Miao X and Chen L 2024 Distributed graph neural network training: a survey *ACM Comput. Surv.* **56** 1–39

Sharma A, Singh S and Ratna S 2023 Graph neural network operators: a review *Multimedia Tools Appl.* **83** 23413–36

Sharma K, Lee Y C, Nambi S, Salian A, Shah S, Kim S W and Kumar S 2024 A survey of graph neural networks for social recommender systems *ACM Comput. Surv.* **56** 1–34

Shi F, Shi Y, Dokshin F A, Evans J A and Macy M W 2017 Millions of online book co-purchases reveal partisan differences in the consumption of science *Nat. Human Behav.* **1** 0079

Shi M, Tang Y, Zhu X, Huang Y, Wilson D, Zhuang Y and Liu J 2022 Genetic-GNN: evolutionary architecture search for graph neural networks *Knowl.-Based Syst.* **247** 108752

Shlomi J, Battaglia P and Vlimant J R 2020 Graph neural networks in particle physics *Mach. Learn.: Sci. Technol.* **2** 021001

Singh D K and Choudhury P 2023 Community detection in large-scale real-world networks *Adv. Comput.* **128** 329–52

Sperduti A and Starita A 1997 Supervised neural networks for the classification of structures *IEEE Trans. Neural Networks* **8** 714–35

Stokes J M, Yang K, Swanson K, Jin W, Cubillos-Ruiz A, Donghia N M and Collins J J 2020 A deep learning approach to antibiotic discovery *Cell* **180** 688–702

Taylor S J, Muchnik L, Kumar M and Aral S 2023 Identity effects in social media *Nat. Human Behav.* **7** 27–37

Veličković P 2023 Everything is connected: graph neural networks *Curr. Opin. Struct. Biol.* **79** 102538

Waikhom L and Patgiri R 2021 Graph neural networks: methods, applications, and opportunities *arXiv preprint* arXiv:2108.10733

Wang K, Ding Y and Han S C 2024 Graph neural networks for text classification: a survey *Artif. Intell. Rev.* **57** 190

Wang L, Yin Q, Tian C, Yang J, Chen R, Yu W and Zhou J 2021 FlexGraph: a flexible and efficient distributed framework for GNN training *Proc. of the Sixteenth European Conf. on Computer Systems* pp 67–82 https://github.com/snudatalab/FlexGraph

Wang M, Zheng D, Ye Z, Gan Q, Li M, Song X and Zhang Z 2019 Deep graph library: a graph-centric, highly-performant package for graph neural networks *arXiv preprint* arXiv:1909.01315 https://dgl.ai/

Wang Y 2021 Graph neural network in traffic forecasting: a review *2021 the 3rd Int. Conf. on Robotics Systems and Automation Engineering (RSAE)* pp 34–9

Wang Y, Zhang B, Ma J and Jin Q 2023 Artificial intelligence of things (AIoT) data acquisition based on graph neural networks: a systematical review *Concurr. Comput.: Pract. Exp.* **35** e7827

Ward I R, Joyner J, Lickfold C, Guo Y and Bennamoun M 2022 A practical tutorial on graph neural networks *ACM Comput. Surv. (CSUR)* **54** 1–35

Weidt F and Silva R 2016 Systematic literature review in computer science-a practical guide *RelatóriosTécnicos Do DCC/UFJF* **1** 1–7

Wu F, Souza A, Zhang T, Fifty C, Yu T and Weinberger K 2019 Simplifying graph convolutional networks *Int. Conf. on Machine Learning* (PMLR) pp 6861–71

Wu L, Cui P, Pei J, Zhao L and Guo X 2022 Graph neural networks: foundation, frontiers and applications *Proc. of the 28th ACM SIGKDD Conf. on Knowledge Discovery and Data Mining* pp 4840–1

Wu L, Cui P, Pei J, Zhao L and Song L 2022 *Graph Neural Networks* pp 27–37 (Singapore: Springer)

Wu S, Sun F, Zhang W, Xie X and Cui B 2022 Graph neural networks in recommender systems: a survey *ACM Comput. Surv.* **55** 1–37

Wu Z, Pan S, Chen F, Long G, Zhang C and Philip S Y 2020 A comprehensive survey on graph neural networks *IEEE Trans Neural Netw. Learn. Syst.* **32** 4–24

Wu Z, Song C, Chen Y and Li L 2021 A review of recommendation system research based on bipartite graph *MATEC Web of Conf.* 336 (EDP Sciences) p 05010

Xu K, Hu W, Leskovec J and Jegelka S 2018 How powerful are graph neural networks ? *arXiv preprint* arXiv:1810.00826

Xue R, Han H, Zhao T, Shah N, Tang J and Liu X 2023 Large-scale graph neural networks: the past and new frontiers *Proc. of the 29th ACM SIGKDD Conf. on Knowledge Discovery and Data Mining* pp 5835–6

Yang H 2019 Aligraph: a comprehensive graph neural network platform *Proc. of the 25th ACM SIGKDD Int. Conf. on Knowledge Discovery and Data Mining* pp 3165–6 https://github.com/alibaba/graph-learn

Ye Z, Kumar Y J, Sing G O, Song F and Wang J 2022 A comprehensive survey of graph neural networks for knowledge graphs *IEEE Access* **10** 75729–41

Ying R, He R, Chen K, Eksombatchai P, Hamilton W L and Leskovec J 2018 Graph convolutional neural networks for web-scale recommender systems *Proc. of the 24th ACM SIGKDD Int. Conf. on Knowledge Discovery and Data Mining* pp 974–83

Yuan Y, Wang W, Coghill G M and Pang W 2021 A novel genetic algorithm with hierarchical evaluation strategy for hyperparameter optimisation of graph neural networks *arXiv preprint* arXiv:2101.09300

Yuan Y, Wang W and Pang W 2021a Which hyperparameters to optimise? An investigation of evolutionary hyperparameter optimisation in graph neural network for molecular property prediction *Proc. of the Genetic and Evolutionary Computation Conf. Companion* pp 1403–4

Zhang S, Tong H, Xu J and Maciejewski R 2019 Graph convolutional networks: a comprehensive review *Comput. Soc. Netw.* **6** 1–23

Zhang S, Yang J, Zhang Y, Zhong J, Hu W, Li C and Jiang J 2023 The combination of a graph neural network technique and brain imaging to diagnose neurological disorders: a review and outlook *Brain Sci.* **13** 1462

Zhang Z, Cui P and Zhu W 2020 Deep learning on graphs: a survey *IEEE Trans. Knowl. Data Eng.* **34** 249–70

Zheng D, Ma C, Wang M, Zhou J, Su Q, Song X and Karypis G 2020 Distdgl: distributed graph neural network training for billion-scale graphs *2020 IEEE/ACM 10th Workshop on Irregular Applications: Architectures and Algorithms (IA3)* (Piscataway, NJ: IEEE) pp 36–44

Zhong M, Lin M, Zhang C and Xu Z 2024 A survey on graph neural networks for intrusion detection systems: methods, trends and challenges *Comput. Secur.* **141** 103821

Zhou J, Cui G, Hu S, Zhang Z, Yang C, Liu Z and Sun M 2020 Graph neural networks: a review of methods and applications *AI Open* **1** 57–81

IOP Publishing

Emerging Trends in Artificial Intelligence
Integrating theories and practice
Haruna Chiroma

Chapter 6

Brain–machine interface for autonomous robots control with feedback from augmented reality and its relevance to industry 4.0 and 5.0

The autonomous robot operates automatically without human intervention, whereas a brain–machine interface (BMI) is a direct means of communication between the brain and machines through electrophysiological signals. Augmented reality provides feedback in a BMI-controlled robot loop. This chapter covers as a tutorial the step-by-step procedure for designing and developing robots from the perspective of hardware and software. The chapter includes different types of autonomous robots such as autonomous vehicles, drones and autonomous underwater vehicles. Recent progress on the integration of BMI with augmented reality to control autonomous robots and their role in industry 4.0 and industry 5.0 for autonomous production are covered. Case studies where these technologies have been put into practice such as by Amazon, airports in Japan and the Netherlands, autonomous vehicle road trials, Onward Medical, and companies like Mercedes-Benz, Honda, Toyota, Volvo, Volkswagen, BMW, and Hyundai are outlined to help readers connect theory with practice.

6.1 Introduction

For decades, the inspiration for robotics systems originated from authors of science fiction and film directors (Saffari *et al* 2021). In 1942, the American writer, Isaac Asimov published *Runaround* as a short story. The story was about a robot built by engineers, named Gregory Powell and Mike Donavan. The robot story evolved around the threee laws of robots, as follows: First law: The robot is expected not to harm human beings. Second law: The robot is to operate based on human commands except in the situation where the commands contradict the first law. Third law: The robot is expected to compulsorily defend its own existence except in the situation where it contradicts the first law or second law. The work of Isaac

doi:10.1088/978-0-7503-6320-4ch6

Asimov motivated a lot of scientists to key into robotics, computer science and artificial intelligence (AI) (Haenlein and Kaplan 2019). In the 1960s, notable robot building efforts were traced to University of Edinburgh and the Stanford Research Institute, where they were attempting to integrate vision, planning and natural language capabilities into robots for effective operation (Haigh 2023).

Autonomous robots automatically perform tasks with minimal human intervention at the point of initiating action. They are in different categories such as spacecraft, unmanned surface vehicle (e.g. self-driving vehicles), unmanned aerial vehicle (e.g., drones). These autonomous systems deliberately interact with the environment autonomously through sensory motors to achieve their goals. Actions performed by robots triggered by specific objectives and justified by solid reasons with respect to the specific objectives are referred to as deliberation. Deliberation is thr computational function needed for acting deliberately. The interest for robotics is so much on the deliberation but more on acting deliberately, especially for autonomous robots. However, robots without autonomy are less concerned about deliberation. There are six different deliberation functions: planning, acting, observing, monitoring, goal reasoning and learning (Ingrand and Ghallab 2017). Autonomous robots perform functions similar to humans, with their processing unit serving as the 'robotic brain'. However, the robot 'brain' is incomparable to the human brain, falling far short of its complexity and sophistication. Attempts to simulate the advanced cognitive reasoning of the human brain in robots have proven extremely difficult and complex (Wahde 2012).

Developments in the field of BMI offer the potential impact for interfacing the human brain directly with the machine through non-invasive devices. The main motivation for the BMI is to resuscitate people with severe motor disabilities to gain independence. Studies have already proved the feasibility of integrating BMI with different types of assistive technologies specifically designed for restoration of effective communication or the control of robotics applications such as the drone, wheelchair, telepresence robots and robotic arms (Tonin *et al* 2021). Mostly, the research community focuses on the exploration of advanced algorithms with capacity to effectively decode the intention of the user from the brain's neural patterns, as well as focussing on improving BMI systems' reliability and robustness. However, the approaches to effectively capture the exact intention of the user for translation by the robot device into real-life actions is commonly ignored. This accounts largely for low transitional impact of BMI systems. This challenge is expected to be addressed by exploring new ways of human–robot interaction (HRI) theories and proposal of new solutions from different philosophical thinking. The integration of BMI with robotics is still at a very early stage of development, as such, its impact remains very low (Tonin *et al* 2021).

This chapter focusses on autonomous robots due to their rapid advancements and significant impact on both society and industry. Autonomous robots are predicted to dominate the future, penetrating almost every aspect of human and animal life. To stimulate the interest of postgraduate students and early-career researchers in autonomous robotics and BMI, and for expert researchers to stimulate their interest in integrating BMI into robots for interpreting human intentions, this chapter aims to provide insights in these areas. The concepts of autonomous robots and BMI are discussed, followed by a conceptual framework that explores the integration of BMI with autonomous robots to enable them to read human thoughts and perform actions.

6.2 Autonomous robots

Autonomous refers to the power of self-governance without external intervention (Antsaklis *et al* 1991). Do you remember watching sci-fi movies where robots operate without any human intervention? Well, it's no longer just movie magic—it has become a reality. We now have robots functioning in different real-world environments, from Roomba vacuums that clean rooms autonomously to drones making deliveries without a human pilot, and even self-driving cars navigating roads on their own. It's not just limited to gadgets; some robots explore outer space without needing humans to accompany them. These robots are described as 'autonomous,' meaning they operate without direct supervision from humans (Standard bot 2023). They're like the technological equivalent of growing up and leaving the nest. How did the world arrive at this era, and what do these robots offer? (Standard bot 2023). Don't worry—this chapter provides a step-by-step guide to understanding the basic information needed to grasp the stages involved in creating autonomous robots. For an easier understanding of the concept of robots, before we dive fully into them, let's first explore the similarities between animals, including humans, and robots. This is because the autonomous robot is inspired from animal behaviour. In this section, we will encounter technical terms like sensors, actuators, processors, etc, during the comparison between animals and robots. Don't worry about these terms; they will be thoroughly explained in the subsequent sections.

6.2.1 Inspiration

Animals possess the ability to respond swiftly to sudden changes in their environment to survive harsh conditions. For instance, it is common for animals to escape from predators, chase prey, forage, use tools, create nests, and breed, all depending on their ecological niches in resource-constrained situations (Fukuhara *et al* 2022). Figure 6.1 depicts images of humans, animals and a robot.

The behaviour of different types of animals across boundaries is dynamic, flexible, and robust. Let us assume that evolution is conservative in nature, implying the existence of a basic set of behavioural capabilities that are necessary and sufficient for producing adaptive, flexible, and robust behaviour. Identifying this set and its applicability in real-world practice is a significant milestone for many robotics applications, especially those involving uncertain environments or tasks that are independent and parallel (Hallam and Hayes 1992). Animals and robots both manipulate objects in the environment to achieve certain predefined goals. The environment is probed by the animals using senses such as vision, touch and smell. The information derived, in some instances, is also improved by the available information from internal states, and it could be short-term or long-term memory, the brain processes it before producing physical action using the animal's limbs.

Figure 6.1. Sample images of humans, animals and robot. (Left) this [Human shields greeted crossing border into Iraq] image has been obtained by the author from the Wikimedia website where it was made available by [Christiaan Briggs] under a CC BY-SA 3.0 licence. It is included within this book on that basis. It is attributed to [Christiaan Briggs]. (Middle) image credit: Samuel Howitt. (Right) this [NAO Robot] image has been obtained by the author from the Wikimedia website where it was made available by [Softbank Robotics Europe] under a CC BY-SA 4.0 licence. It is included within this book on that basis. It is attributed to [Softbank Robotics Europe].

In the case of robots, typically, they understand the information of their surrounding environment through sensors. The robot brain (or controller system) comprising a single or multiple number of processors processes the information from the sensors to create motor signals and transmit to actuators such as robot motors. The interaction of animals with the environment and adapting to changes is not perfect. The behaviour of an animal model at both the low-level models involves distinct neurons, whereas the high-level phenomenological model inspires the development of robot behaviour. In addition, animals have expertise in allocating optimal time to multi-tasking (e.g., sleeping, foraging, drinking, eating among others) intended to perform in different situations. The lesson regarding animal behaviour selection can provide significant inspiration for solving similar problems in robotics (Wahde 2012). Animals have inspired locomotion strategies in robots. However, the performance of robots is still far away from matching the inherent capabilities of animals. The difference in performance between robots and animals is due to factors such as agility, range, and robustness (Burden *et al* 2024).

6.2.2 Decision-making process

In general, animals including humans encounter the challenge of scarce resources, the ability for making optimal choices among the different activities is tied to survival completely. A typical example of a challenge is the optimal allocation of time across different basic activities while maintaining physiological variables such as but not limited to hunger, temperature and thirst between acceptable boundaries. Rational behaviour in animals is common, even in simple animals, despite the fact that the rational behaviour does not need rational thoughts. There are some rational behaviours in animals where the brain lacks the power to contemplate the sensory input on any level of details not to mention maintaining the internal state complexity. In this circumstance, rational decision-making takes place because of the animal's evolutionary design. It is worth noting that the rational behaviour of animals does not automatically imply intelligent behaviour. An agent is considered rational if it strives for the maximization of utility. However, intelligent behaviour occurs if the utility functions of the animal have been suitably shaped as a result of learning. The autonomous robot's decision-making process faces similar challenges to that of animals. Autonomous robots have to execute a complete task like delivering objects in a factory at the same time avoiding collision and maintaining enough battery charge for smooth operations. The quadratic costs have been used to model decision-making in robots using ethological results as the guiding principles based on optimization problems resulting in utility maximization or minimizing cost (Wahde 2012).

6.3 Robotics components

The autonomous robot comprises hardware and software components, however, this section mainly focusses on the major hardware components of the robot, as shown in figure 6.2 before delving into the software aspect. The hardware components in this section constitute the fundamental building blocks of any robot. However, robots can vary in shape, size, and function, with some possessing specialized features beyond the fundamental components. In addition, a number of the components can differ, for example, number of sensors or cameras can be 2, 3, 5, 6 or more depending on the type of robot. For anyone interested in building a robot, these fundamental building blocks are essential considerations.

The hardware is the physical components required for the construction of the robot's physical appearance. The major physical components of the robot are outlined as follows (Wahde 2012).

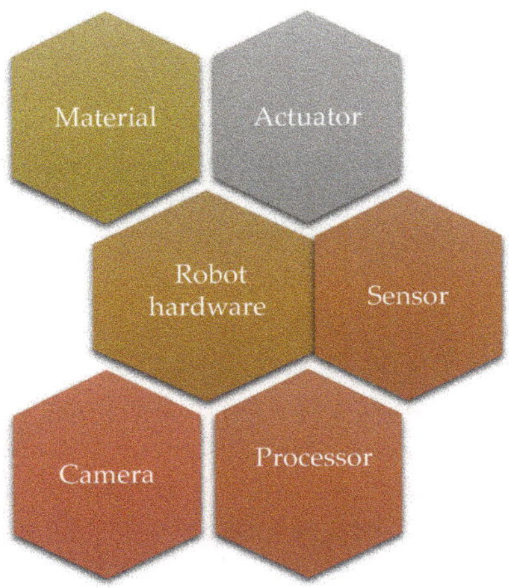

Figure 6.2. Hardware components of robot.

6.3.1 Material

The materials used for the construction of the actual robot frame are of different types including but not limited to aluminium, steel and different types of plastics, signifying that there are many options for the materials to be used for constructing the frame of the robot. However, the preferred material for robot construction should be light and sturdy, therefore, aluminium is the frequent chosen material as it possesses the required characteristics. However, aluminium is expensive, but it does have the combination of toughness with low weight close to the optima for small mobile robots at least.

6.3.2 Sensors

Sensors as shown in figure 6.3 are embedded in the robot for the purpose of measuring the physical characteristics of the robot such as acceleration or sensing the environment to detect intensity of light sources. In most cases, the raw data collected by the sensors has to be processed before forwarding to the robotic brain for use. Take for example, the possibility of infrared delivering voltage based on the distance between the sensor and the object as it is reading. Subsequently, it is converted to a distance using the available sensor characteristics obtained from data sheet.

Figure 6.3. Typical sensor. This [Sensor prinzip] image has been obtained by the author from the Wikimedia website, where it is stated to have been released into the public domain. It is included within this book on that basis.

6.3.3 Actuator

The robot produces physical action because of the presence of actuators to produce movement or manipulation of its surrounding environment in different ways. The actuators typically found in a robot are the motor and other types such as microphone for interaction between a human and the robot. The movement can be triggered with different techniques including electrical motors, pneumatic, direct current or a hydraulic system among many others. Figure 6.4 shows a pneumatic energized and actuated robot.

Figure 6.4. Pneumatic energized and actuated robotic. This [Pneumatically Energized and Actuated Robotic Leg (PEARL)] image has been obtained by the author from the Wikimedia website where it was made available by [AkshayP013] under a CC BY-SA 4.0 licence. It is included within this book on that basis. It is attributed to [AkshayP013].

Figure 6.5. Robot with two cameras as 'eyes' for visualization. Image by imjanuary from Pixabay

6.3.4 Cameras

The camera serves as the robotic eyes for visualization, as shown in figure 6.5. Mostly, two cameras are used on the robot to provide binocular vision so that the robot can have the capability to estimate distance of detected objects. Many robot cameras exist such as the CMUCam series among many others.

6.3.5 Processors

The robot manipulates its environment in different ways effectively and robustly as a result of sensors and actuators operations. The information received from the sensor is transmitted to the processor to be analyzed concerning the decision to make before transmitting the signal to the actuators to trigger action. It is common practice in autonomous robots to use multiple processors in the robotic brain. Figure 6.6 depicts the entire process from sensor information, analyzing the information and

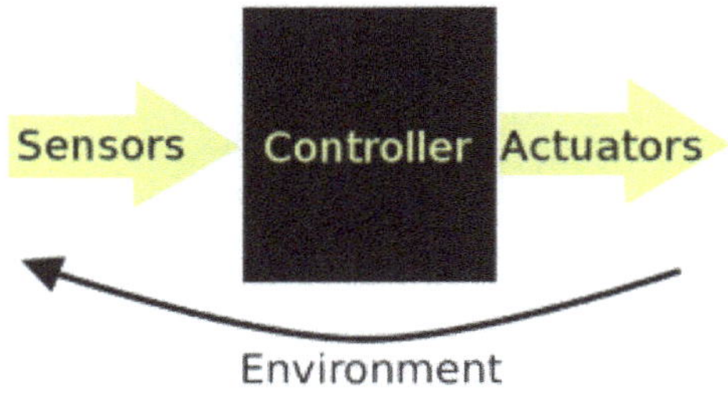

Figure 6.6. Example of sensors information processed and forwarded to actuators for a robot's perception of the environment. This [Sensors to actuators loop] image has been obtained by the authors from the Wikimedia website where it was made available by [JackPotte] under a CC BY-SA 3.0 licence. It is included within this book on that basis. It is attributed to [Cyberbotics Ltd].

transmitting it to actuators. The decision-making process involves the use of a standard PC mounted on the robot to execute high-level tasks, whereas the microcontrollers execute low-level tasks.

The autonomous controllers of the robot have the capacity and power of self-governance to perform control functions. The autonomous controller is made up of both hardware and software necessary to perform control functions without the need for intervention from external agents for a prolonged period of time. The autonomous control system should have the capability for tracking, monitoring, repair of faulty components, and self-regulation (Antsaklis *et al* 1991). The control systems of autonomous robots are designed to operate robustly under significant uncertainty conditions within the system and its surrounding environment for a prolonged time period. In addition, the control system must have the capability to recover from significant system failure without intervention from humans. The autonomy of an intelligent control system is achieved by adding an AI component to the conventional control system (Antsaklis *et al* 1991).

6.4 Robotic brain

The hardware components of robots remain static without undergoing any form of changed throughput the lifespan of the robot operations. On other hand, the brain of the robot, as shown in figure 6.7, is dynamic to handle different tasks at the appropriate times. The brain of the robot can be implemented in different ways, such as behaviour-based robotics and general-purpose robotic brain structure discussed as follows: behaviour-based robotics is developed from the set of basic behaviours, decision-making process and selecting appropriate behaviour at the right time. The general-purpose robotic brain structure uses a set of brain processes to develop in the robotic brain either robotic motor behaviour or cognitive processes. It typically allows the building of a complex robotics brain structure because it allows parallel execution of processes. General-purpose robotic brain structure transcends the behaviour-based robotics with its limited decisions (Wahde 2012).

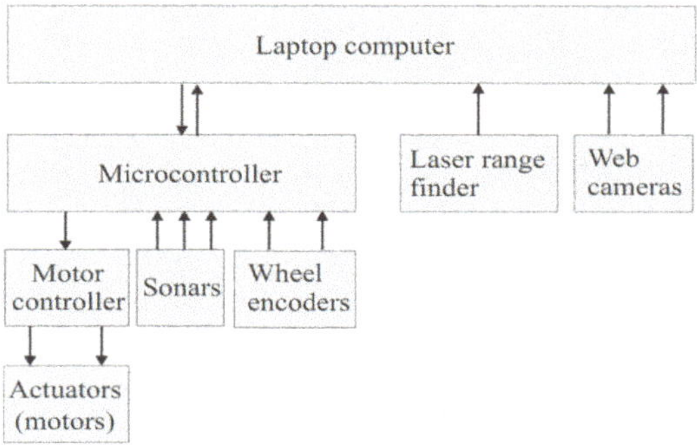

Figure 6.7. Typical architecture of a robotic brain. Reprinted with permission from Wahde (2012).

6.5 Robotics programming, modelling and simulation

Robots require software for smooth and coordinated operation, much like any other computing system. Numerous platforms are available for developing robotics applications/software, including modelling, simulation, and prototyping, before construction in a real-world environment. This section introduces some major robotics platforms suitable for beginners. First, a robot operating system (ROS) is a platform that provides an environment for developing robotics applications, it offers libraries, tools, drivers and algorithms required by developers to build robotic applications. It is an open-source platform compatible with major operating systems (OS) such as Windows, Mac and Ubuntu. Figure 6.8 presents a sample of library demonstrations from ROS (Open Robotics 2023).

Secondly, Webot is one of the reputable robotic platforms suitable for different types of robot modelling, simulation and prototype unlike the NVIDIA Developer that mainly focussed on autonomous vehicles providing software, hardware and workflow to support the end-to-end development of autonomous vehicle technologies. The other robotics platforms include Gazebo andRoboDKas, as summarized in table 6.1.

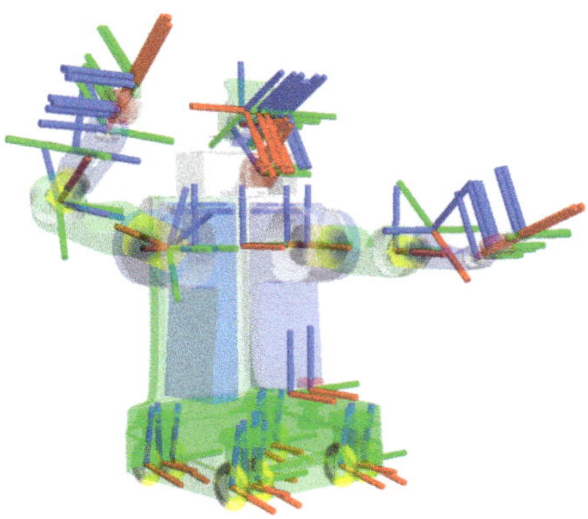

Figure 6.8. Sample library demonstration from ROS. This [ROS2 tf2 frames] image has been obtained by the author from the Wikimedia website where it was made available by [Croomfolk] under a CC BY 4.0 licence. It is included within this book on that basis. It is attributed to [kurshakuz].

Table 6.1. A summary of some major robotic simulators for building robots applications, modelling, simulation, prototype and deployment in the real world.

Simulator	Functions	Type	OS	User help manual	Link to platform
ROS	Platform for developing applications for robots. Libraries and tools are available to help build robotics application from research to prototype and real development.	Open source	Windows, Mac and Ubuntu	Getting started with tutorials	https://www.ros.org/
Webot	Provides an environment for modelling, programming and simulating robots.	Open source	Windows, Mac and Ubuntu	User guide and reference manual are available to help new user work-through	https://cyberbotics.com/
Gazebo	Toolbox to develop and simulate robots including library and cloud services.	Open source	Windows, Mac and Ubuntu	Getting start and tutorials are available	https://gazebosim.org
NVIDIA Developer	Mainly for software development and hardware design for autonomous vehicles.	Open source	Windows, Mac and Ubuntu	Tutorials and instructional materials	https://developer.nvidia.com
RoboDK	A platform with over 1000 robot arms. It provides tools for programming (online and offline) robots in a simulated environment.	Subscription but have 30 days trial version	Windows, Mac, Ubuntu, Raspberry Pi, Android and iPhone	Tips and tricks for getting started	https://robodk.com/

6.6 Deliberation function

The deliberation function is a key component in autonomous robots, as emphasized in the introduction section of this chapter. The types of deliberations in autonomous robotics, as depicted in figure 6.9, are explained as follows (Ingrand and Ghallab 2017).

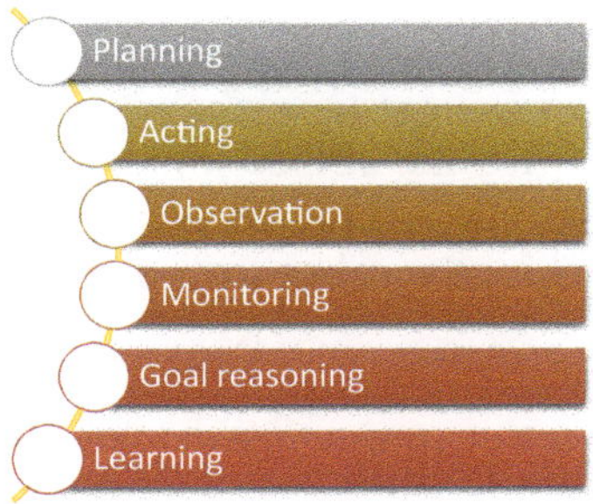

Figure 6.9. The six deliberation functions of autonomous robots.

6.6.1 Planning

The planning is used to achieve some purpose by combining prediction and search for synthetic trajectory in an abstract action space according to the environment predictive model and action that is considered feasible.

6.6.2 Acting

The planned action is refined into the appropriate commands based on the existing context and responds to events. Likely, the refinement and the reaction can depends on skills (i.e. collecting closed-loop functions). The sequence of stimulus input obtained from the sensors is processed by the skill before subsequently generating the output to be forwarded to the actuators to activate motor forces and control the selected action correctly.

6.6.3 Observation

Observation is the detection and recognition of features and relations that characterize the state of the environment, events, actions and plan for relevant task. Observing integrates processes bottom-up starting from the sensor to data that is meaningful, with the up-bottom approach activities like focussing on mechanism, sense action and plans for gathering information.

6.6.4 Monitoring

This is a comparative analysis of the predicted robot activities and real-world observations. It performs recovery actions when necessary after discrepancies are detected and interpreted through the diagnostic function.

6.6.5 Goal reasoning

This involves monitoring at the level of mission. The commitment and goals are kept in perspective. Their relevance is evaluated from the progress observed from new opportunities, failure or constraints. The results of the evaluation determine whether some commitments should be rejected and help decide the timing and approach for updating current goals.

6.6.6 Learning

This stage equips the robot with the ability to acquire knowledge through adaptability and improvement based on experience, which is essential for the deliberation process. Active learning provides the robot with opportunities to act deliberately to enhance its learning.

6.7 Types of autonomous robots

The evolution of robots has progressed from performing small, routine functions to becoming intelligent machines capable of various tasks across domains, such as surgery in healthcare, autonomous driving in transportation, human–robot interaction in daily activities, tutoring in education, surveillance in security, and guiding visitors in malls (Shamout *et al* 2022). As discussed in section 6.3, robots come in different types depending on their operational modes. For instance, robots that operate underwater without human intervention are known as autonomous underwater vehicles (AUVs), as illustrated in figure 6.10(e). If a robot operates autonomously on the Earth's surface, it is referred to as an unmanned surface vehicle (USV), such as the autonomous vehicle shown in figure 6.10(b), in contrast to the unmanned aerial vehicle (UAV) that operates in the atmosphere, like the drone shown in figure 6.10(a). Spacecraft, operating in space—e.g., deep space and cislunar space— are represented in figure 6.10(c).

One of the most widely used robots in industry is the robotic arm (figure 6.10(d)), frequently employed in autonomous manufacturing and production processes. Indoor mobile robots, such as the robot vacuum cleaner that autonomously navigates indoor spaces to keep them clean by removing dirt and debris, are typically compact, as shown in figure 6.10(h). Humanoid robots, depicted in figure 6.10(g), resemble human bodies and have been gaining popularity in recent years. Trans-medium vehicles, an emerging concept discussed by Chen *et al* (2024), are aircraft capable of autonomously operating in both air and water, creating an interface between the two mediums. The details of studies on different types of robots shown in figure 6.10 are presented in table 6.2.

Insect-inspired robots, which emulate the intelligent behaviours of insects, are designed for challenging tasks requiring limited computational and memory resources. These robots present an alternative approach to achieving AI in compact, mobile systems, resulting in small but powerful robots capable of handling complex tasks (De Croon *et al* 2022).

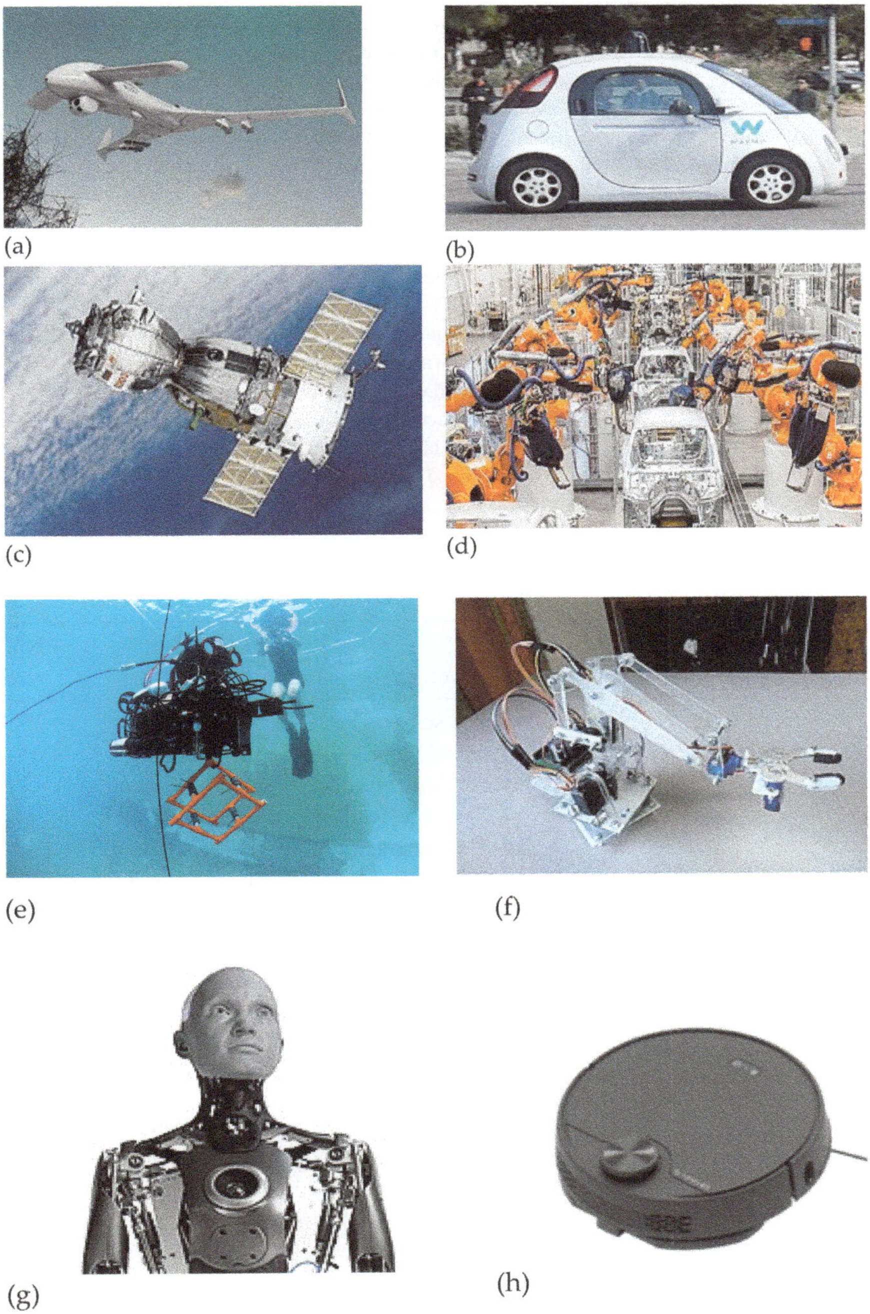

Figure 6.10. Samples of different types of autonomous robots: (a) drone, this [GIDS Shahpar 2 Drone] image has been obtained by the author from the Wikimedia website where it was made available by [IamMoaz] under a CC BY-SA 4.0 licence. It is included within this book on that basis. It is attributed to [Hezmok Media]. (b) self-driving car, this [Waymo self-driving car side view.gk] image has been obtained by the author from the

Wikimedia website where it was made available by [Grendelkhan] under a CC BY-SA 4.0 licence. It is included within this book on that basis. It is attributed to [Grendelkhan]. (c) Spacecraft, image credit: NASA. (d) Automotive robot, this [Robot-cong-nghiep-the-he-moi] image has been obtained by the author from the Wikimedia website where it was made available by [Haophuong21] under a CC BY-SA 4.0 licence. It is included within this book on that basis. It is attributed to [Haophuong21]. (e) Underwater autonomous vehicle, this [U.S. Navy Diver 2nd Class Andrew Bui, with Space and Naval Warfare Systems Center Pacific, recovers an autonomous underwater vehicle (AUV) built by students from Cornell University after navigating through an 130724-N-TM257-006] has been obtained by the author from the Wikimedia website, where it is stated to have been released into the public domain. It is included within this book on that basis. (f) Robotic arm, this [Braccio robotico con Arduino 01] image has been obtained by the author from the Wikimedia website where it was made available by [N.Bertucccioli] under a CC BY-SA 4.0 licence. It is included within this book on that basis. It is attributed to [Nicolò Bertuccioli]. (g) Humanoid, this [Ameca Generation 1] image has been obtained by the author from the Wikimedia website where it was made available by [Willy Jackson] under a CC BY-SA 4.0 licence. It is included within this book on that basis. It is attributed to [Willy Jackson]. (h) Robot vacuum cleaner, this [Somlos S1 Robot Vacuum Cleaner] image has been obtained by the author from the Wikimedia website where it was made available by [Ashledawn] under a CC BY-SA 4.0 licence. It is included within this book on that basis. It is attributed to [Ashledawn].

Table 6.2. The representative surveys on different types of autonomous robots.

References	Robot	Coverage	No. of references
Kangunde *et al* (2021)	Drone	The survey covered drone hardware, including sensors, controllers, microcontrollers, rotors, and more, as well as real-time operations, path planning, and applications across different domains. Also, the design of drone is covered by Hassanalian and Abdelkefi (2017).	150
Gidado *et al* (2020), Pali *et al* (2024), Betz *et al* (2022)	Self-driving vehicle	The steering control of autonomous vehicles, the deep learning algorithms adopted in different studies for steering angle prediction, and the platforms used for modelling self-driving vehicles were discussed. In addition, other surveys exist such as computing system of self-driving vehicles (Liu *et al* 2020), practice and emerging technologies (Yurtsever *et al* 2020) as well as self-driving in the context of cognitive science, psychology and neuroscience (Plebe *et al* 2024).	106
Martínez de Alegría, *et al* (2024)	AUV	This study covers different methods and technology for powering UUVs. Also,	254

		the operation of the UUV is provided by Waldner and Sadhu (2024) and Yuh (2000) survey covered the design and control of the UUV.	
Patidar and Tiwari (2016)	Robotic arm	Provides a survey on robotics arms technology covering 20 years. In addition, spatial robotic arm (Dai *et al* 2022), planning algorithms (Liu and Liu 2021) and robotic arm application (Jin and Han (2024) were surveyed.	43
Pandey *et al* (2014)	Robot vacuum cleaner	Provides a survey of technologies required for the design of autonomous home robots. The system design and hardware components were included.	13
Krejci and Lozano (2018)	Spacecraft	The technology for spacecraft propulsion is discussed. Also, a survey on relative spacecraft dynamic motion is covered by Sullivan *et al* (2017).	96

6.7.1 Autonomous underwater vehicle

The autonomous underwater vehicle (AUV) operates under the ocean autonomously without human intervention, as shown in figure 6.10(e). It is used for the development of ocean exploration, especially in deep underwater regions where it is impossible or dangerous for human access (Garcia *et al* 2018). Also, the AUV is expected to improve oceanic studies in the future. The effect of small AUVs on payload have an impact on trajectory, underwater attitude and safety of the AUV and payload (Chen *et al* 2024). The AUV coordinate systems and rotation transformation are shown in equations (6.1)–(6.7). The longitudinal plane of the AUV motion contains the coordinate system $A(O_A x_A y_A)$ and the coordinate origin. The body-fixed coordinate system $B(O_B x_B y_B)$ is at the centre of the AUV mass and is the origin of the separation tube-fixed coordinate system $C(O_C x_C y_C)$. The projection constituent of a given vector $\vec{v}$ is A, B and C systems are represented by markers v_A, v_B and v_C. Therefore, the transformation relationship satisfies the following expression (Chen *et al* 2024):

$$\begin{cases} v_A = T_{AB} v_B \\ v_B = T_{BC} v_C \\ v_A = T_{AC} v_C \end{cases} \tag{6.1}$$

where T_{AB}, T_{BC} and T_{AC} are defined as follows:

$$T_{AB} = \begin{pmatrix} \cos\delta & -\sin\delta \\ \sin\delta & \cos\delta \end{pmatrix} \tag{6.2}$$

$$T_{BC} = \begin{pmatrix} \cos\rho - \sin\rho \\ \sin\rho \quad \cos\rho \end{pmatrix} \tag{6.3}$$

$$T_{AC} = \left[\begin{pmatrix} \cos\delta - \sin\delta \\ \sin\delta \quad \cos\delta \end{pmatrix}\right]\left[\begin{pmatrix} \cos\rho - \sin\rho \\ \sin\rho \quad \cos\rho \end{pmatrix}\right] \tag{6.4}$$

where the $T_{AC} = [T_{AB}][T_{BC}]$ and pitching angle of the AUV is represented by δ and mounting angle of the separation tube is represented by ρ. Thus, a given constant parameter.

$$\frac{d\vec{v}_B}{dt} = \left(v_x^B, v_y^B\right)_B^T + \omega_B^{\times} \bullet \left(v_x^B, v_y^B\right)_B^T \tag{6.5}$$

The relative derivation is the first term in equation (6.5) and the second term is the implicated derivation. The coordinate system *B* pitching angle velocity tensor is expressed as (Chen *et al* 2024):

$$\omega_B^{\times} = T_{AB}{}^T T_{AB}$$

$$\omega_B^{\times} = \left[\begin{pmatrix} \cos\delta - \sin\delta \\ \sin\delta \quad \cos\delta \end{pmatrix}\right]^T \left[\begin{pmatrix} \cos\delta - \sin\delta \\ \sin\delta \quad \cos\delta \end{pmatrix}\right] \tag{6.6}$$

$$\omega_B^{\times} = \begin{pmatrix} 0 & -\rho \\ \rho & 0 \end{pmatrix} \tag{6.7}$$

6.7.2 Drone

The male honey bee is referred to as a drone according to the meaning in a dictionary. The sole responsibility of the honey bee drone is mating with the queen, then, the honey bee finishes its lifecycle with death. The same idea was adopted during World War II where remotely controlled autonomous pilotless aircraft were used to hit targets and destroy itself (Van der Merwe *et al* 2020). A drone is shown in figure 6.10(a). The main components of drones include sensor, camera, battery, GPS and controller (Chaudhary *et al* 2021). The drone flies autonomously but with control from a ground station to monitor and control its movement. Edge devices like a computer or laptop or smart tablet pre-installed with software providing necessary information (e.g., battery status, flight area on a map, movement and real-time images captured by the camera of the drone) are deployed in the ground station for the controlling the movement of the drone. Signals originating from the ground station remote control are translated to the motor speed (Juniper 2015). The drones are mainly classified into four, namely, fixed-wing, single rotor, hybrid and multi-rotor drones, depending on land topology, efficiency, flight time, endurance and energy efficiency (Vergouw *et al* 2016).

However, the commonly used drone is the quadcopter because of its simplicity and it provides a vehicle for autonomous flight by controlling the speed of the four propellers, enabling the quadcopter to roll, change yaw, pitch and accelerate. In a quadcopter, a brushless DC motor is used as the standard motor where the shaft is attached to the outside of the shell motor, whereas the motor axle is connected to the motor base firmly attached to the quadcopter frame. The shell outside typically spins around the axle. The torque of the quadcopter frame is decrease by the rotation of the motor. The magnitude of the torque generated is assumed to be proportional to the rotational speed squared with the constant k_1 proportionally, expressed as (Huang 2016):

$$\|\beth_i\| = \beta_1\theta_i^2 \tag{6.8}$$

The rotation of the motor shell is in the opposite direction to the torque induced by the rotation. Assumptions: We have four motors, 1, 2, 3 and 4. The motors' rotations are all positive in counterclockwise. When the rotations of all the motors are in positive direction, motor 1 and motor 3 rotors generate thrust force upward towards (+) y_3 direction positively. On the other hand, motor 2 and motor 4 rotors generate thrust force downward towards (−) y_3 direction. For suitable flying of the quadcopter, motor 2 and motor 4 must rotate clockwise while motor 1 and motor 3 must rotate anticlockwise to generate downward thrust. The magnitude of force generate by the rotors is proportional to the square of the rotational speed (θ_i^2) of every rotor expressed as follows with proportional constant (β_2) (Huang 2016):

$$\|F_i\| = \beta_2\theta_i^2 \tag{6.9}$$

By Newtonian setup, equations (6.8) and (6.9) represent the force and torque magnitude, whereas the direction of the force and torque need to be incorporated in equations (6.8) and (6.9). Thus,

$$\theta_i^2 = |\theta_i|\theta_i \tag{6.10}$$

Thus, equation (6.10) is the thrust force and motor torque direction to be determined. Equations (6.8) and (6.9) are reformulated for motors 1, 2, 3 and 4 as follows:

$$F_1 = \beta_2\ |\dot{\theta}_1|\dot{\theta}_1\hat{y}_3 \tag{6.11}$$

$$F_2 = -\beta_2\ |\dot{\theta}_2|\dot{\theta}_2\hat{y}_3 \tag{6.12}$$

$$F_3 = -\beta_2\ |\dot{\theta}_3|\dot{\theta}_3\hat{y}_3 \tag{6.13}$$

$$F_4 = -\beta_2\ |\dot{\theta}_4|\dot{\theta}_4\hat{y}_3 \tag{6.14}$$

$$\mu_1 = -\beta_1\ |\dot{\theta}_1|\dot{\theta}_1\hat{y}_3 \tag{6.15}$$

$$\mu_2 = -\beta_1\ |\dot{\theta}_2|\dot{\theta}_2\hat{y}_3 \tag{6.16}$$

$$\mu_3 = -\beta_1\ |\dot{\theta}_3|\dot{\theta}_3\hat{y}_3 \tag{6.17}$$

$$\mu_4 = -\beta_1 \, |\dot{\theta}_4|\dot{\theta}_4\hat{y}_3 \tag{6.18}$$

The cross product of $\mathbb{R}^3$ between forces and vector length for each of the arm frames is determined by the thrust forces inducing an additional set of torques for the quadcopter centre of mass. The length for each of the arm is represented by $\beth$, therefore, the expression for each of the induced torques is expressed as follows (Huang 2016):

$$\mu_{F_1} = -\beth\beta_2 \, |\dot{\theta}_1|\dot{\theta}_1\hat{y}_2 \tag{6.19}$$

$$\mu_{F_1} = -\beth(\beta_2 \, |\dot{\theta}_2|\dot{\theta}_2)\hat{y}_1 \tag{6.20}$$

$$\mu_{F_3} = -\beth\beta_2 \, |\dot{\theta}_3|\dot{\theta}_3\hat{y}_2 \tag{6.21}$$

$$\mu_{F_4} = -\beth(-\beta_2 \, |\dot{\theta}_4|\dot{\theta}_4)\hat{y}_1 . \tag{6.22}$$

6.7.3 Autonomous vehicles

The combination of many fields from computer science produces autonomous driving vehicles. The fields include AI, computer vision, automatic control systems, pattern recognition, among others. Autonomous vehicles use automation equipment in place of the manual systems in conventional vehicles to replace the human driver. The characteristics and functionality of the technologies illustrated in figure 6.11 required for the actualization of the autonomous vehicles are outlined and discussed as follows (Zhao *et al* 2018):

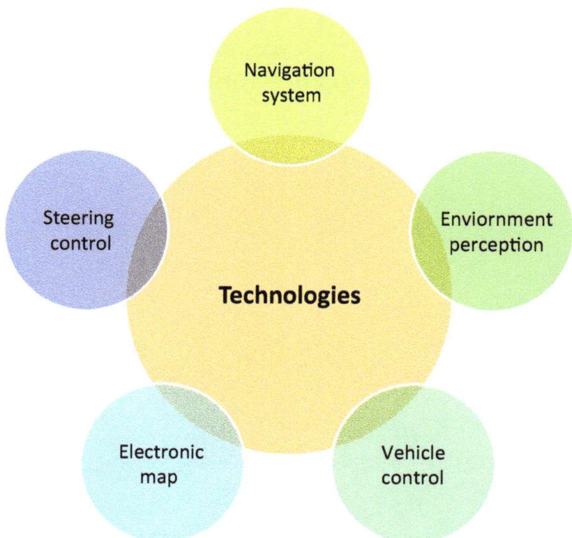

Figure 6.11. Main technologies involved in developing autonomous driving vehicles.

6.7.3.1 Navigation system

The current location of a car and the route it must follow to reach a desired destination are two key concerns that need to be settled. Solving these issues once required the expertise of a skilled human driver. In the case of an autonomous vehicle, however, the car must detect its location, plan its route, and drive to the destination entirely on its own, without human input. To achieve this, on-board navigation systems are installed in the vehicle. These systems rely on geographical information systems and global positioning systems to process location data from satellites (e.g., longitude, latitude). The map-matching model integrates data from the navigation system, location system, and digital map databases to inform intelligent path-planning algorithms, like Dijkstra's algorithm, which compute the optimal route. As a result, the vehicle can determine its position and, with both current and destination coordinates at hand, the path-planning model computes the best driving route from the current location to the destination.

6.7.3.2 Electronic map

The electronic map is a database that stores digital map information, including traffic data, buildings, geographical features, road infrastructure, and traffic signs, among other elements. Currently, most electronic maps used in autonomous vehicles are designed for human drivers. It is recommended that future electronic maps be specifically developed for autonomous vehicles, with the capability to automatically recognize road signs, facilitate inter-vehicle communication, and support other automated related functions. High-definition electronic maps for autonomous vehicles are already becoming available, offering significantly better coordinate accuracy compared to traditional maps.

6.7.3.3 Environment perception

The autonomous vehicle is equipped with an environment perception module. This module independently perceives the surrounding environment and provides the necessary data for the vehicle's control decision system. Environment perception is achieved through different methods, including laser, visual, and radar navigation. Multiple sensors, such as but not limited to laser sensors and radar sensors, are embedded in the vehicle to gather comprehensive information about the surroundings. The data from these sensors is then fused to create an accurate perception of the environment. Each sensor serves a specific function. For example, the laser sensor bridges real-world data with digital data, the radar sensor is used to detect distances, and the visual sensor recognizes traffic signs. The autonomous vehicle integrates the data generated by these sensors to process and generate a detailed perception of its surroundings, including the recognition of obstacles, road edges, road markings, and more.

6.7.3.4 Vehicle control

The major factors to control in a vehicle are speed and direction. Status perception and control development methods are the general functions of vehicle control. The computation of the vehicle's speed and direction is performed by the perception module, which receives data from different sources, including the vehicle's status, environmental perception, traffic regulations, driving knowledge, and desired driving behaviour. These data, provided by the electronic map, are processed by the perception module, allowing the vehicle control algorithm to compute the target control. These targets are then fed to the vehicle control system, which executes the commands to automatically control the vehicle's speed, direction, horn, lights, and more.

6.7.3.5 Steering control system

The design of an intelligent algorithm for controlling autonomous vehicles is a fundamental lateral task to control the vehicle. Humans achieved this mainly based on visual clues at an end-to-end approach (Eraqi *et al* 2017). The prediction of steering angle is critical for autonomous vehicle control (Gidado *et al* 2020). The emergence of autonomous vehicles prompted concern about the avoidance of collusion and stability in case of emergency circumstances. These emergency events occur unexpectedly within a short period of time and need large inputs from actuators along with highly nonlinear cornering of tyre response (He *et al* 2019). A path tracking system is critical in a steering control system as it controls the actuators based on the location of the vehicle from an inertia navigation system and the path planner provides the reference path. Path tracker and primitive driver are constituents of the steering control system. The modules in path tracker constitute velocity planning, path tracking and distance ahead decision. The required steering angle is generated by the path tracker after the goal point is selected on the reference path according to the look-ahead distance. The steering actuator is controlled by the steering controller to move towards the reference path (Park *et al* 2015).

Slipping and rolling over is prevented by velocity planning in running an autonomous vehicles system. It is the velocity planning module that uses path curvature, friction factor (f_f) and super-elevation to plan the velocity. Circular motion centripetal force is required for a vehicle to drive on a horizontal curve. The centrifugal force is applied through equation (6.23) depending on the horizontal curve radius, circular motion and speed (Park *et al* 2015):

$$f = \left[\frac{w}{g}\right] \times \left[\frac{v^2}{R}\right] \tag{6.23}$$

where v, g, R and w represent the velocity, gravitational force, horizontal curvature radius and weight of the vehicle, respectively.

Equation (6.24) is satisfied if f_f is for the lateral frictional force and safety of the vehicle.

$$(f \cos x - w \sin x) \leqslant f_f (f \sin x + w \cos x) \tag{6.24}$$

Where the bank angle is represented by x

$$\left[\frac{(f \cos x - w \sin x)}{\cos x}\right] \leqslant \left[\frac{f_f (f \sin x + w \cos x)}{\cos x}\right] \tag{6.25}$$

$$\left[\frac{f\cos x}{\cos x} - \frac{w\sin x}{\cos x}\right] \leqslant f_f\left[\frac{f\sin x}{\cos x} + \frac{w\cos x}{\cos x}\right] \tag{6.26}$$

where

$$\frac{\cos x}{\cos x} = 1, \quad \frac{\sin x}{\cos x} = \tan x \tag{6.27}$$

Substituting equation (6.27) in equation (6.26) we get equation (6.28)

$$(f - w\tan x) \leqslant f_f(f\tan x + w) \tag{6.28}$$

Based on super-elevation, taking $\tan x = i$

$$(f - wi) \leqslant f_f(fi + w) \tag{6.29}$$

We substitute equation (6.23) in equation (6.29) to get equation (6.30)

$$\left(\left[\frac{w}{g}\right] \times \left[\frac{v^2}{R}\right] - wi\right) \leqslant f_f\left(\left[\frac{w}{g}\right] \times \left[\frac{v^2}{R}\right](i) + w\right) \tag{6.30}$$

Simplifying equation (6.30) and dividing both sides by w

$$\left(\left[\frac{wv^2}{gR}\right] - wi\right) \leqslant f_f\left(\left[\frac{wv^2}{gR}\right]i + w\right)$$

$$\frac{1}{w}\left(\left[\frac{wv^2}{gR}\right] - wi\right) \leqslant f_f\left(\left[\frac{wv^2}{gR}\right]i + w\right)\frac{1}{w}$$

$$\left(\left[\frac{v^2}{gR}\right] - i\right) \leqslant f_f\left(\left[\frac{v^2}{gR}\right]i + 1\right) \tag{6.31}$$

Assuming the value of $f_f = 0$, then, equation (6.31) is expressed as:

$$\left(\left[\frac{v^2}{gR}\right] - i\right) \leqslant 0 \tag{6.32}$$

Simplifying equation (6.32) we get R expressed as:

$$R \geqslant \left[\frac{v^2}{g}\right]\left[\frac{1}{i + f_f}\right] \tag{6.33}$$

The velocity limit on the road that has a horizontal curve is computed by substituting $R = \frac{1}{k}$ where k is the road curvature.

$$\frac{1}{k} \geqslant \left[\frac{v^2}{g}\right]\left[\frac{1}{i + f_f}\right]$$

$$v \leqslant \sqrt{\frac{g(i + f_f)}{k}} \tag{6.34}$$

Finding the curvature of the road is computed by assuming that the path is curvy and assuming to be approximated by third degree polynomial. The curvature is determined after the desired path approximation with the third degree polynomial, thus, the curvature of the polynomial $y = x(t)$ is expressed as (Park *et al* 2015):

$$k = \frac{\frac{d^2y}{dx^2}}{\left(1 + \left(\frac{dy}{dx}\right)^2\right)^{\frac{3}{2}}}.$$

6.8 Brain–machine interface

It is understood that the most complex organ in the human body is the brain, whose main activity is managing all the other organs. The human brain is classified into two hemispheres, the left and right, which control the opposite sides of the body. Each hemisphere's cortex is divided into four lobes: temporal, frontal, parietal, and occipital, each responsible for different functions. The frontal lobes are responsible for reasoning, translating thoughts into words, planning, and shaping personality. The parietal lobes manage sensory perceptions such as taste, touch, temperature, and pain, as well as language comprehension and memory intervention. The occipital lobes decode visual information, including colours and shapes, and are involved in object recognition. Lastly, the temporal lobes process auditory stimuli and are involved in verbal memory (Kandel *et al* 2000). The human brain has approximately 86 billion neurons (8.6×10^{10}) with each of the neurons having the possibility of getting tens of thousands of synaptic connections. The neurons exchange information through the small conversation site. Hundreds of trillion synapses are estimated to exist in the human brain. Thus, recording simple binary information about synapses in a computer would need 100 terabytes. Therefore, the storage space required to store this simple information for one person per second for one day would need over 100 000 terabytes or 100 petabytes. The supercomputers of current times hold almost 10 petabytes without considering the dynamics in connectivity and positioning of the synapses over a period of time. The speed at which these connections changes leads to a very large amount of bytes. Counting the way the connections is transforming within a short period of time is amazing, let us say connection changes after a good night's sleep can lead to enormous amounts of bytes estimated at over 10^{80}, the amount of atoms in the universe (Goldin 2013).

Typically, the human communicates with external devices such as computers, robot arms, wheelchairs, etc through gestures, natural language or manipulating input devices like keyboards, mouse, touchscreens, etc, to command the computer to execute tasks. These have been the traditional way humans operate devices for a long time, until the emergence of BMI, where the human brain communicates directly with the

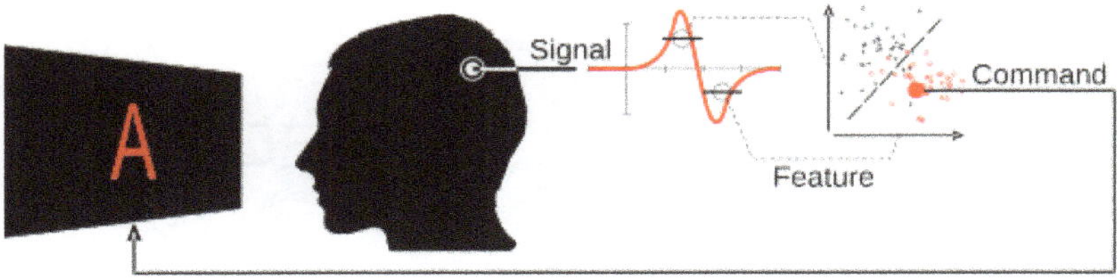

Figure 6.12. Brain–machine interface system direct communication. This [Brain-computer interface diagram] image has been obtained by the author from the Wikimedia website, where it is stated to have been released into the public domain. It is included within this book on that basis.

machine through electroencephalograph (EEG) or electrocorticogram (ECoG) signals without uttering words or making any body gestures, as illustrated in figure 6.12.

6.8.1 Electrophysiological signals

The BMI system can be controlled by any type of brain signal. However, the electrical signal mainly produced by the neuronal postsynaptic membrane polarity is the most commonly studied signal. It changes because of voltage activation gated or ion-gated channels (Berger 1929). The first non-invasive neuroimaging approach that emerged was EEG, typically used to measure the brain's electrical activities. In view of the fact that it is non-invasive, it doesn't require surgery incision into the human skull. This approach is globally accepted for use nowadays because of its operational simplicity, high temporal resolution and cost effectiveness (Teplan 2002). The ECoG is a neuroimaging method that uses electrodes directly placed on the human brain surface for recording electrical activities of the cerebral cortex, it is a popular invasive technique. The ECoG could be carried out during surgery in the operating room referred to as intraoperative ECoG, or outside the surgery procedure referred to as extraoperativeECoG. The electrode grid is required to be implanted in the human skull through surgery. Therefore, the ECoG procedure is referred to as invasive (Buzsáki *et al* 2012, Dubey and Ray 2019). EEG and ECoG are the popular techniques, however, other imaging techniques exist such as magnetic resonance imaging (MRI), functional magnetic resonance imaging (fMRI) and magnetoencephalography (MEG) (Babiloni *et al* 2009), as illustrated in figure 6.13.

The BMI offers another means of communication channels between the human brain and machines. Typically, the mental activities of the human brain are contained in the electrophysiological signals such as EEG or ECoG. The BMI system has the capacity to detect the dynamics in electrophysiological signals before transforming them into control signals. The control signals are subsequently used for manipulating objects, writing, opening doors, changing television channels or performing any other daily activities. The main goal of the BMI is to resuscitate humans with limited mobility or complete impairment due to neurocognitive disabilities to interact with the environment (McFarland and Wolpaw 2008). However, its application has been extended to different domains such as education (Wegemer 2019), entertainment (Martins and Teixeira 2024), animation (Sourina *et al* 2009), and games (Stein *et al* 2018). The BMI system should not be perceived as

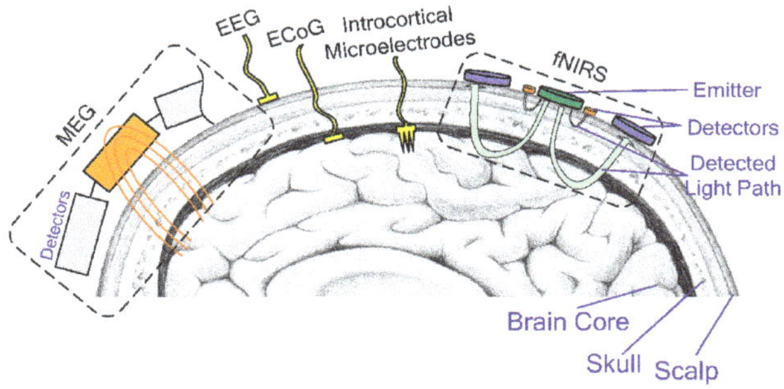

Figure 6.13. Types of the brain–machine interface device mounting: invasive, partially invasive and non-invasive. Reproduced from Peksa and Mamchur (2023), CC BY 4.0.

a device for reading the mind, this is incorrect because it is not possible to extract information or thoughts from a human unwillingly. Therefore, the BMI system allows humans to perform actions directly from brain activities only without engaging the muscles (Shih *et al* 2012).

6.8.2 Types of brain–machine interface devices

The brain signal (i.e. brain nerve cells' electrophysiological activities) is collected from the scalp surface or from the cortical surface directly. It is the fluctuation of a voltage generated by the neurons reflecting the dynamics of the current state of the human body (Collinger *et al* 2014). Different types of BMI for recording brain signals exist, as illustrated in figure 6.14. The types of BMI include the following. *Invasive BMI* (figure 6.14(A)): it is the device with the highest quality signal implanted directly into the brain to read the brain signal. It mainly focuses on the neural recordings. *Partially invasive BMI*: it is a brain signal reading process device

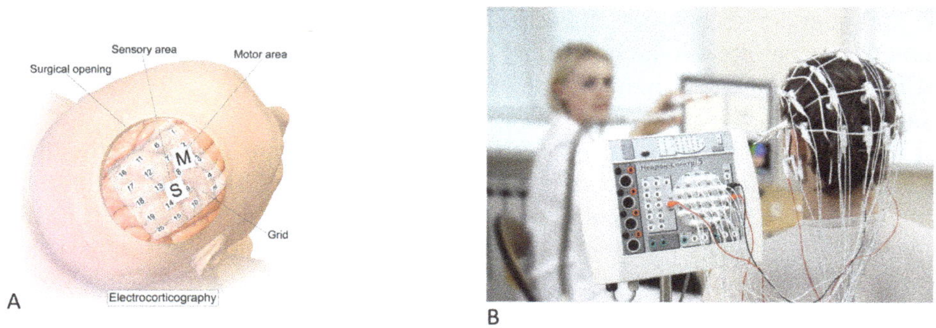

Figure 6.14. (A) *Invasive and partially invasive*: intracranial electrode grid for electrocorticogram (Blausen.com staff (2014). This [Intracranial electrode grid for electrocorticography] image has been obtained by the author from the Wikimedia website where it was made available by [Mikael Häggström] under a CC BY 3.0 licence. It is included within this book on that basis. It is attributed to [BruceBlaus]. (B) *Non-invasive*: electroencephalograph. This [Eeg registration] image has been obtained by the author from the Wikimedia website where it was made available by [Baburov] under a CC BY-SA 4.0 licence. It is included within this book on that basis. It is attributed to [Baburov].

implanted in the skull but outside the brain with the signal having weaker strength, e.g. ECoG. *Non- invasive BMI* figure 6.14(B): it is the device that has the lowest brain signal. However, it is the safest BMI device. The popular technique for the non-invasive device is the EEG providing brain signals with fine temporal resolutions. The non-invasive device is easier to use, cost-effective and portable compared to the invasive and partially invasive BMI devices. It is applied outside the skull, just on the scalp, it is regarded as the most useful neuron imaging technique (Edelman *et al* 2024, Zhang 2021).

6.8.3 Brain–machine interface system operation

The BMI system, showing its operational cycle in figure 6.15, operates in basically four stages, as depicted in figure 6.16. Typically, the operation begins by acquiring the brain signals, performing feature extraction before translating them into commands to be fed to the device output for desired action. A detailed discussion of the activities in each stage are as follows (Shih *et al* 2012).

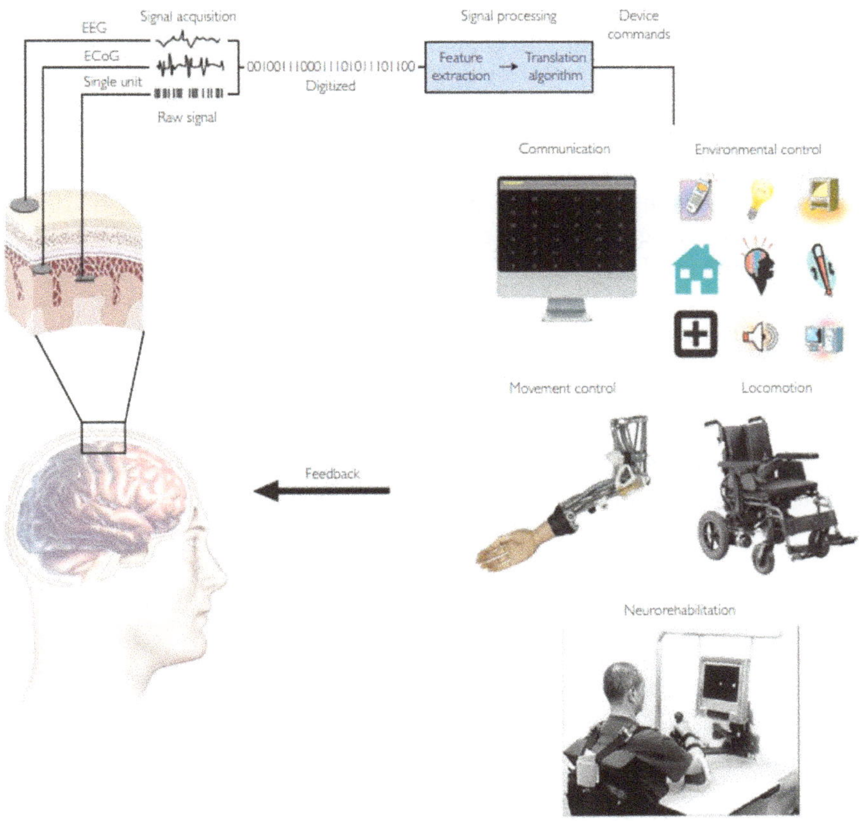

Figure 6.15. BMI system components and operations cycle. This [Wireless EEG Components] image has been obtained by the author from the Wikimedia website where it was made available by [RickLiang] under a CC BY-SA 4.0 licence. It is included within this book on that basis. It is attributed to [Vojkan Mihajlovi× c, Member, IEEE, Bernard Grundlehner, Member, IEEE, Ruud Vullers, Senior Member, IEEE, and Julien Penders].

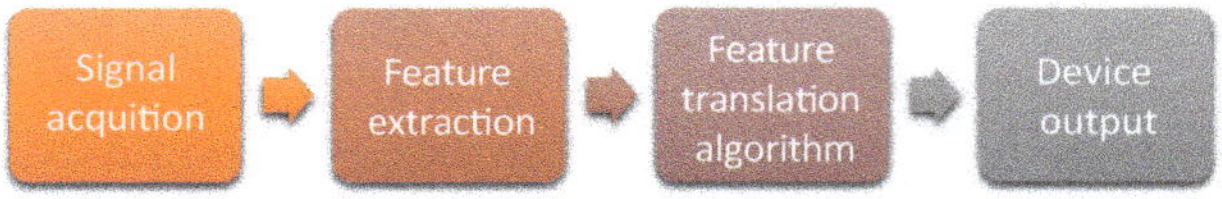

Figure 6.16. Major stages in BMI systems.

6.8.3.1 Acquisition of signal

Measuring the brain's neurophysiologic state is called signal acquisition. The recording interface in the BMI system operations tracks neural information that reflects the human intention contained in the current activities of the brain. The commonly used electrophysiological signals for BMI systems are EEG and ECoG as already discussed. However, the microelectrodes record local field potentials as well as the potential action of the neuron in the brain tissue. For operating the BMI system, the brain signal is acquired by the electrodes, amplified and digitized to simplify the signal processing activities, subsequently, easing feature extraction.

6.8.3.2 Feature extraction

This is the process of subjecting the digital signal to analysis to differentiate between signal features containing significant information about the person's intention and extraneous content before representing them in a suitable format for translating into output commands. The correlation between the extracted features and the intention of the user should be sufficiently strong in view of the fact that much of the relevant activities of the brain are either transient or oscillatory. The BMI system's commonly extracted signals falls into one of the following categories:

- (i) time-prompted EEG or ECoG response amplitudes and latencies;
- (ii) power specifically for frequency bands of EEG or ECoG; or
- (iii) the rate of firing of individual cortical neurons.

To ensure accuracy in measuring the brain signal features, environment artifacts and physiologic artifacts (e.g., electromyographic signals) are discarded or evaded. Bozhkov and Georgieva (2020) argued that the separation of noise from the main signals that emanate from the brain and finding of meaningful interpretation of the signal are the challenges facing the development of a non-invasive BMI system. Effective feature selection to select the significant spatio–temporal features of the EEG signals and selection of the suitable EEG frequency are crucial to foresee human intentions.

6.8.3.3 Feature translation algorithm

The collected signal features are fed to the feature translation algorithm responsible for converting the features into commands suitable for the output of the device, meaning the commands that prompt the execution of the user's intention. For instance, decreasing power in a given frequency band may mean the displacement of a cursor upward or the potential of P300 may mean selecting the letter invoking it. The feature translation algorithm should be adaptive enough to learn the changes occurring in the signal features as well as to ensure that the full range of the device control covers the possible feature values of the user.

6.8.3.4 Output from the device

The external device is operated based on commands received from the feature translation algorithm. The functions provided by the feature translation algorithm include letter selection, robotic arm operation, cursor control, and others. Feedback from the device's operations is transmitted to the user, thereby terminating the control loop.

6.9 Brain-controlled autonomous robot

The deployment of BMI to control robots is a significant area of research, where BMI technology is integrated with robots to enhance safety and enable real-time control through EEG signals, either via direct or shared control (Hu 2024). The BMI systems are mostly used to drive devices for navigation, for example, telepresence mobile robots (Tonin and Millán 2021). These systems provide a means of communication and control for different devices, ranging from domestic appliances to humanoid robots. Both low- and high-level commands are used exclusively by BMI systems to control these devices (Penaloza *et al* 2014).

It has been demonstrated that it is possible to transfer high fidelity information from the brain to machines to control cursors, robotic limbs and speech synthesizers via neuroprosthetics using 256 electrodes. The BMI has been in the forefront for helping to resuscitate people with speech impairment or requiring prostheses control, thereby, enabling them to interact with the environment with no intervention of the nerves and muscles using the control signal generated from EEG (Editorial 2021). The robot is comprised of two major mechanisms as follows: predict the thinking of the user and the mechanisms that enable the robot to present its own ideas in a human understandable format and easy to follow. These mechanisms are critical in the development of autonomous robots and HRI in society. Humans should be able to effectively operate and use autonomous robots if they are deigned to carry out instructions from humans to autonomously execute tasks (Sakai and Nagai 2022). The passive monitoring of human brain activity for the prediction of cognitive load, perceived error, level of attention and emotions were highlighted in the development of BMI and neurofeedback. The breakthrough in the extraction of such high-order information from the brain signal is view of a source of facilitating HRI. Passive BMI, especially in the area of robotics, offers a promising channel for the estimation of human cognitive and effective state of development for human adaptive interaction (Alimardani and Hiraki 2020). figure 6.17 illustrates a control loop and behavioural setup comprising a system for data acquisition, a linear model running in real time, the robot arm embedded with gripper and visualization monitor. The gripping force transducer is with the pole. The position of the robot is translated to the cursor position on the monitor and the gripping force feedback is delivered by the cursor size fluctuations (Lebedev *et al* 2005).

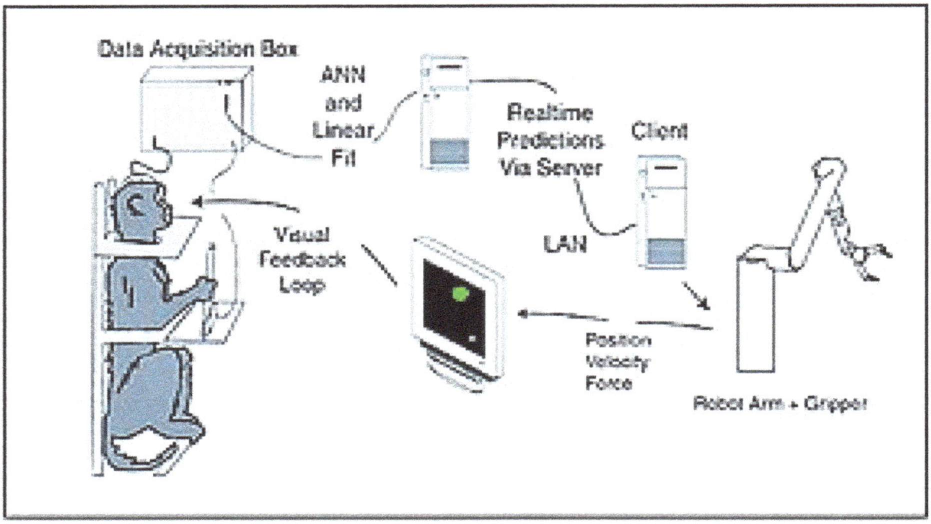

Figure 6.17. Controlling a robot arm through reading brain signals. Adapted from Carmena *et al* (2003) CC BY 4.0.

A BMI without requiring the use of a graphical user interface (GUI) for interaction has been developed where the robot uses a laser pointer to highlight objects in the environment. The goal of the user is decoded by prompting a response in the EEG. The BMI without the GUI allows room for more direct communication with the brain compared to the conventional BMI equipped with GUI. Eliminating the need for GUI implies little control over appearance of the stimulus for robots present in the stimuli environment (Kolkhorst *et al* 2020). Despite many daily tasks requiring the combination of multiple robotics devices, most of the BMI systems are designed for handling and controlling single-assistive technologies such as prosthetic limbs, wheelchairs or robotic arms. This motivated the authors to develop a hybrid of a BMI system based on EEG and electrooculogram for controlling multiple robotics device systems integrating wheelchairs and robotic arms. The user performs left/right hand motor imagery to turn the wheelchair left/right. Eye blinking and eyebrow movement generate the commands to control the wheelchair and the robotic arm. This BMI system has the potential to be applied to complex systems with multiple robotics devices (Huang *et al* 2019).

Ban *et al* (2024) use three signal modalities including steady-state visual-evoked potential, gyroscope and electrooculograph to develop a multimodal BMI multifunctional system for controlling a robot. The system succeeds in controlling the robot to perform multiple functions by receiving commands through the BMI-controlled device. A prototype of a steady-state visual-evoked potential system was developed for autonomous grasping and manipulation of objects controlled through visual overt attention (Reichert *et al* 2014). Karavas *et al* (2017) used brain signals during the process of imagining or actual limb movement, along with input from a joystick controller, to develop a hybrid BMI system. Subsequently, the system was used to control the overall behaviour of quadrotor swarm robots in real-time using brain signals.

6.10 Augmented reality

Integrating digital information into the user's environment in real time is referred to as augmented reality. Augmented reality superimposes digital content onto the real-world environment, enhancing the user's perception of reality rather than completely replacing it. Typically, augmented reality devices are embedded with sensors, a camera, and a display monitor. These devices can include tablets, smartphones, and wearable devices (e.g., smart headsets and glasses) to create a mobile augmented reality experience. The device captures the real physical world and integrates digital content generated by the computer, such as images, 3D models, or videos, into the scene—blending both the digital world and physical world. Augmented reality superimposes digital content onto the real world, allowing users to continue interacting with and seeing the physical world alongside supplementary digital information superimposed on their field of vision (Hayes and Downie 2024), as shown in figure 6.18(A).

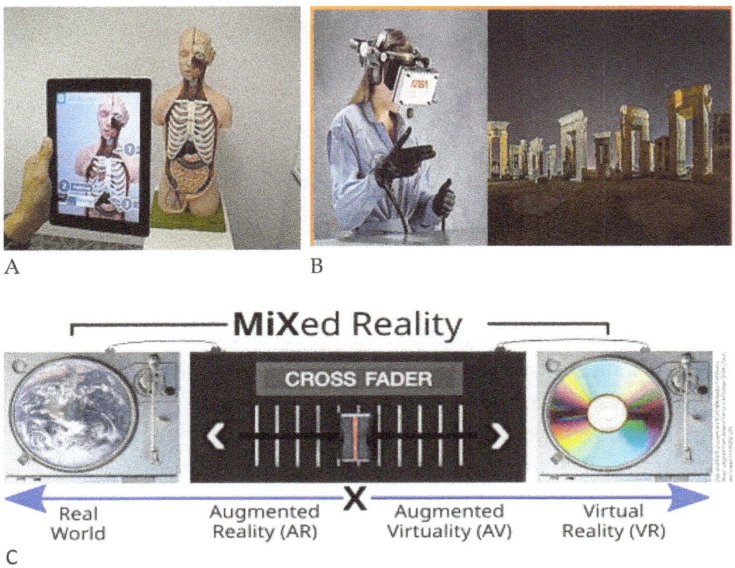

Figure 6.18. Metaverse technologies: (A) augmented reality of anatomy. This [Augmented-reality-1957411 1920] has been obtained by the author from the Wikimedia website, where it is stated to have been released into the public domain. It is included within this book on that basis. (B) Exploration of the univers in virtual reality. (Left) image credit: NASA, (right) this [Persepolis Panorama 360 Virtual Reality Tachar castle] image has been obtained by the author from the Wikimedia website where it was made available by [Mshayati] under a CC BY-SA 4.0 licence. It is included within this book on that basis. It is attributed to [Mshayati]. (C) Mixed reality. This [MixedReality DJ metaphor] image has been obtained by the author from the Wikimedia website where it was made available by [Glogger] under a CC BY-SA 4.0 licence. It is included within this book on that basis. It is attributed to [Glogger].

6.10.1 Augmented, virtual and mixed realities

Augmented reality should not be confused with virtual reality and mixed reality. For clarification purposes, the differences are explained as follows. Unlike augmented reality, virtual reality uses a virtual reality headset, mounted monitor display, or virtual reality goggles to immerse the user in a completely digital world, replacing the physical environment with a computer-generated one that provides a 360-degree view, as illustrated in figure 6.18(B). On the other hand, in mixed reality, the user can interact with both physical and virtual objects simultaneously, as shown in figure 6.18(C). This approach enhances augmented reality by blending virtual objects with the physical environment (Hayes and Downie 2024, Mann *et al* 2018).

6.10.2 Operation of augmented reality

The operation of augmented reality passes through three major stages: sensing, processing and display, as depicted in figure 6.19.

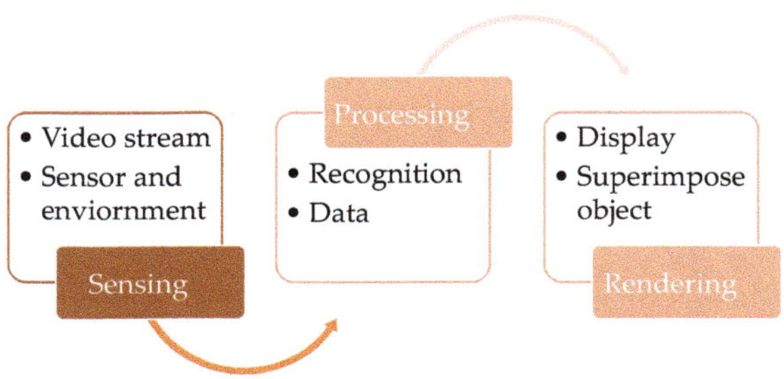

Figure 6.19. Standard stages involved in the operational process of augmented reality.

6.10.2.1 Sensing

Typically, the operation of augmented reality begins by accepting the content of the video stream from the user's field of vision. Sensors detect the environment and track the physical view of objects. It can likely involve data collection from different sources such as the global positioning system, accelerometers, gyroscopes, or lasers, combined with the video stream to track the position and orientation of the user (Hayes and Downie 2024).

6.10.2.2 Processing

In this stage, the environment is scanned and processed by the augmented reality software. This may means the connection of an object's digital twin (i.e. the object 3D copy stored in the cloud or the use of an intelligent algorithm to recognize the physical object). Subsequently, the information received is processed by augmented reality software to detect objects and features of the environment to be augmented. This can include sending of data by the sensor embedded on the physical object to a digital twin or the combination of tracking data and other information (Hayes and Downie 2024).

6.10.2.3 Rendering

The augmented reality device displays the information streamed from the augmented reality software, placed over the content generated by the computer onto the field vision of the user. The rendering of the generated content is typically in a perspective and orientation that is correct, displaying to the user to look as if the physical object is present in the arena. The user interacts with the object by given commands through the touchscreen using physical gestures or voice. The augmented reality software receives commands and displays the superimposed object for the user to manipulate (Hayes and Downie 2024).

6.10.3 Why combine augmented reality with BMI in robotics control?

The progress made in the adoption of BMI to control robotic devices was presented in the preceding section. However, despite the advancements achieved in controlling robots through BMI, lack of an information feedback mechanism in BMI presents significant challenges for the effective control of robotic devices. This limitation has motivated the integration of augmented reality with BMI, as shown in figure 6.20, and detailed operations are illustrated in figure 6.21, to enable more effective control of robotic devices with a high degree of freedom.

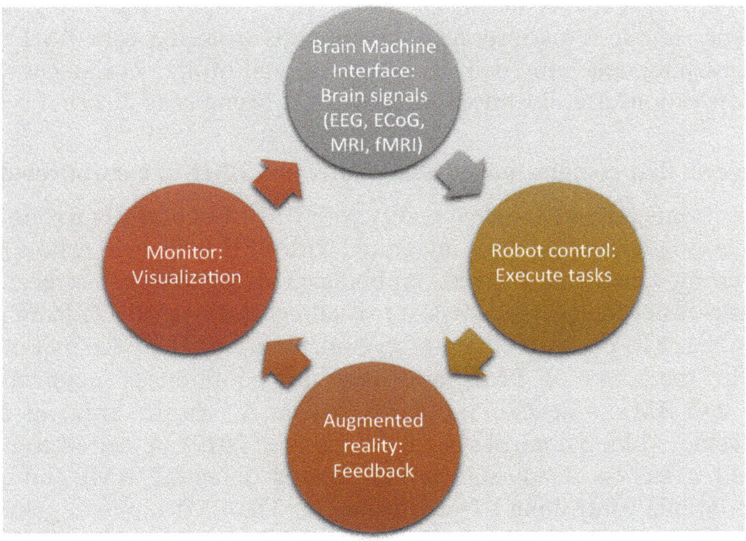

Figure 6.20. Closed-loop BMI with feedback from augmented reality to control robotics devices.

6.10.4 Operation of augmented reality with BMI to control robots

A subject chooses a segmented object through eye tracking and the BMI emits trigger commands for confirmation. The first command from the gaze through the BMI is applied to confirm the subject's selection of an object or prompt action to switch sequence or continue to control aperture gripper height at the course of

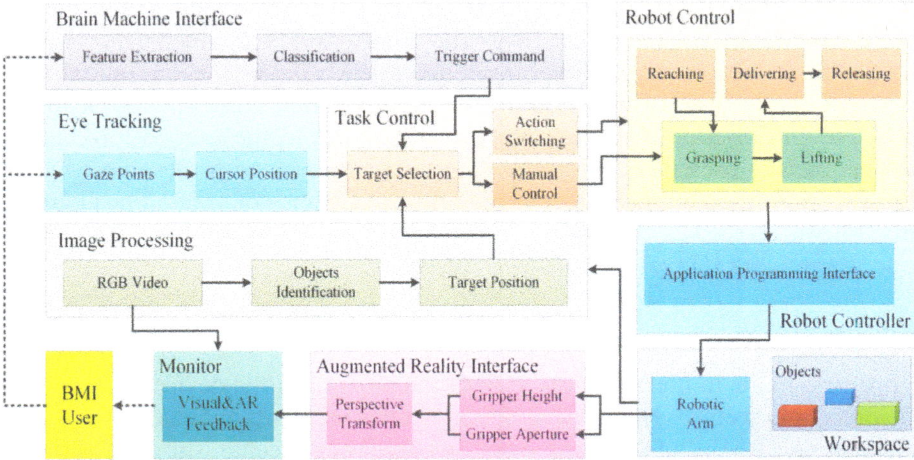

Figure 6.21. BMI robot control system with feedback from augmented reality. Reproduced from Zeng *et al* (2017) CC BY 4.0.

operation involving grasping and lifting. The user of the BMI receives feedback from the augmented reality during the process of grasping and lifting through the monitor. The robotic arms respond to commands from the gaze-BMI to perform tasks like grasping, reaching, delivery, releasing and lifting. The stages involved in the entire operations are illustrated in figure 6.21 (Zeng *et al* 2017).

6.10.5 Projects that combine augmented reality and BMI to control robots

Many projects integrate augmented reality with BMI for controlling robotic devices. For example, augmented reality is integrated with BMI to control robots involved in autonomous movement and object grabbing. This approach has been found to perform tasks faster than the steady-state visual-evoked potential (Zhang *et al* 2021). Lack of feedback to perform closed-loop control in a BMI device making grasping complex for the users of BMI motivated the adoption of augmented reality combined with BMI to develop a control system. A robotics arm was adopted to evaluate the closed-loop control system (Wang *et al* 2017). A shared control system is developed based on steady-state visual-evoked potential, BMI and augmented reality to continue controlling robot translation. The BMI inputs together with the data received from robot sensor continue predicting the object that the user has the intention to reach. Therefore, the shared BMI control system embedded with augmented reality can effectively control the robot (Kokorin *et al* 2024).

A robotic arm for pick-and-place tasks is used to evaluate the control system developed by coupling augmented reality and BMI. The signals generated from visual stimuli, specifically steady-state visual-evoked potentials, are processed by the BMI. Augmented reality is used to present the visual stimuli to the user (De Pace *et al* 2024). Another study, used steady-state visually evoked potentials driven by smart glasses for single-channel BMI to improve HRI. It was demonstrated that the stimulus signal could be generated with the smart glasses sufficient for stable frequency. The smart glasses Epson Moveriois were used for the augmented reality experiments (Angrisani *et al* 2018).

An approach that developed a robotic arm control system embedding BMI with augmented reality was proposed. The augmented reality served as guided assistance for providing improved feedback in a visual format. The feedback is conveyed to the user for closed-loop control combining both EEG and eye tracker to control robotic arms (Zeng *et al* 2017). A closed-loop BMI with augmented reality visual feedback was developed. The inputs of the BMI were EEG signals from multiple eye blinking. The augmented reality interface for the feedback is design for interactive path planning of the robot (Ji *et al* 2021). In a separate study, BMI based steady-state visual-evoked potential control system integrated with augmented reality was developed. The control system was deployed to control robotic arms allowing the user to select the intended target objects and more grasping of different objects was made with limited stimulus (Fang *et al* 2022). A study developed a robot control system that combined BMI with augmented reality. Trials indicated that the control system performed better than the conventional BMI without feedback from augmented reality in collaborative control of a robotic arm to perform the tasks of pick-and-place selection (Sanna *et al* 2022).

Another study, developed a control system for a robot arm integrating steady-state visual-evoked potential-based BMI, computer vision and augmented reality. The switching of attention between the robotic arm and the user is not required. The control system is able to effectively control the robotic arm in object selection tasks (Chen *et al* 2020). A device for controlling robots remotely through wearable BMI combined with augmented reality was developed to assist in rehabilitating children with attention disabilities. The flickering stimuli is generated by augmented reality glasses and a single-channel EEG BMI device detected the steady-state visual-evoked potential. Thus, allowing the viewing of the robot movement (Arpaia *et al* 2020). An asynchronous control system for robotic arm combining steady-state visual evoked potential-based BMI and augmented reality was developed. It is found that the robotic arm was controlled asynchronously through a high-frequency steady-state visual-evoked potential switching the system state (Chen *et al* 2021). Also, augmented reality and virtual reality were adopted to develop brain-controlled system. The control system was used to control robotic tasks (Hu 2024).

6.11 Autonomous robots, augmented reality and BMI in industry 4.0 and 5.0

This section presents the major roles of autonomous robots, augmented reality, and BMI in industry 4.0 and the emerging outlook of industry 5.0. It includes a brief overview of the industrial revolution from industry 1.0 to 5.0, highlighting the role of autonomous robots in autonomous production and the control of these robots via BMI for manufacturing processes. Lastly, it explores the integration of BMI with augmented reality to manage robotic tasks in industrial production.

6.11.1 Industrial revolution

Industry 4.0 represents the current industrial revolution, with origins tracing back to the first industrial revolution (industry 1.0) of 1784 over 230 years (Bahrin *et al* 2016). The subsequent revolutions in industry introduced manufacturing powered by water and steam, which later transitioned to electrical and digital production. This evolution made manufacturing processes more complex, automated, and sustainable, allowing operators to run machines with greater ease, efficiency, and determination (Qin *et al* 2016). The third industrial revolution (industry 3.0) adopted programmable logic controllers (PLCs) and IT systems to automate production processes. Industry 4.0 marks a new era in industrial automation and data exchange (Caiado *et al* 2021), focussing primarily on manufacturing's response to the growing interest in digitization and smart manufacturing. The key pillars of industry 4.0 include automation and industrial robotics, additive manufacturing, simulation and modelling, blockchain technology, augmented reality, the Internet of Things, cloud computing, cyber-physical systems, big data analytics, and AI (Bahrin *et al* 2016, Oztemel and Gursev 2020, Ryalat *et al* 2023). The progression from industry 1.0 to industry 5.0 is illustrated in figure 6.22.

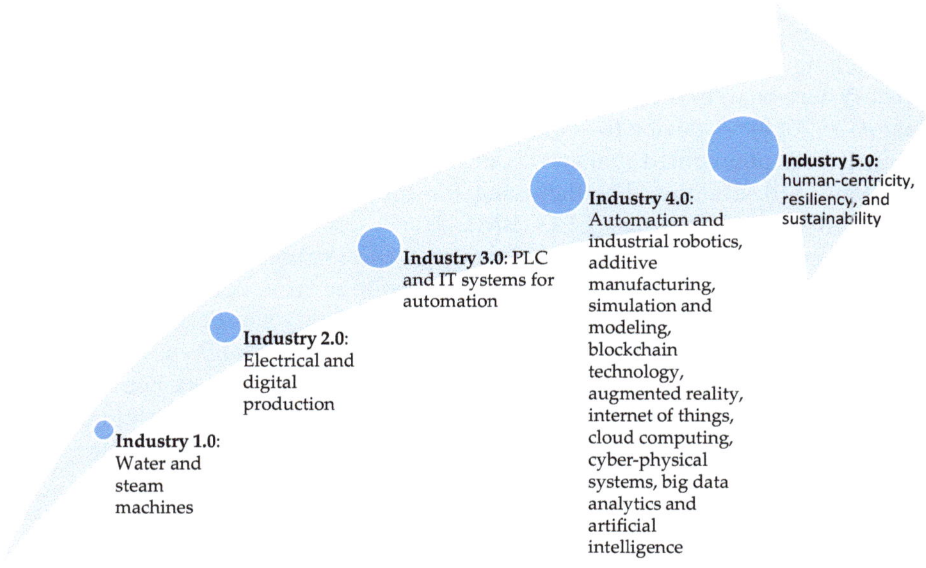

Figure 6.22. Industrial revolution from industry 1.0 to industry 5.0.

6.11.2 Autonomous production

As seen in figure 6.22, automation and industrial robots are one of the key indicators of industry 4.0. The example of different types of robots involved in the manufacturing process in the era of industry 4.0 includes mobile robot, collaborative robots, industrial manipulators among many other industrial applications. The advancement in robotics technology boosts productivity, versatility, adaptability, reconfiguration and ensures safety in automated manufacturing (Bahrin *et al* 2016). Autonomous robots are considered as one of key components contributing to the success of industry 4.0. The use of autonomous robots in production is found to increase production quality and reduce the cost of production. In many cases, autonomous robots are more practical compared to humans. The development in autonomous robots has transited from low-skill repetitive work to medium-skill repetitive work supporting the mass customization in the era of industry 4.0. Robotics advances have enabled the industrial system to learn from humans, perform work autonomously with context awareness and adapt to unexpected events (Bibby and Dehe 2018). The smart factory is a key aspect of industry 4.0 that mainly focussed on promoting smart production processes through the network of the manufacturing system as well as vertically integrating production process. The full deployment of cutting-edge technology to create smart factories made it possible for autonomous running of production processes to achieve performance on self-optimization, adapt to changing situations and learn from real-time activities. This enabled a high degree of flexibility, customization and efficiency (Ryalat *et al* 2023).

The goal of collaboration between robots and humans is to combine human intelligence with the capabilities of robots to enhance production capacity. In industrial human–robot collaboration, communication between robots and humans aims to foster a mutual understanding of each other's intentions for improved teamwork (Ji *et al* 2021).

It is believed that the fundamental component of industry 4.0 is the autonomous production process, driven by autonomous robots that intelligently execute tasks with an emphasis on safety, collaboration, flexibility, and versatility. Unlike in the past, isolating robots from the human working environment is no longer necessary; instead, robots are integrated into human workspaces to enhance both economic efficiency and productivity. This integration opens up many opportunities for industrial applications. Industrial robots are advancing and playing a key role in driving revolutionary changes, fuelled by ongoing technological innovations. The use of robots is no longer limited to replacing humans in simple, structured workflows within a closed loop. Instead, robots are expected to work collaboratively with humans in different ways within the industry 4.0 framework. The applications of industrial robots have extended beyond production to include logistics and office management, with integrated functions allowing remote control. This provides workers with the ability to operate robots from home using webcams linked to mobile phones to address issues, thus enabling continuous production without the immediate need for physical presence. Consequently, production can continue 24 h a day, while workers are only required to be on-site during standard working hours (Berger 2014).

A collaborative robot is embedded into industry 4.0 in four major ways. *Co-existing*: in this situation, both the robots and human operators share the same working environment without interactions among them. *Collaboration*: the robots and human operators perform the same job within the environment, the actions and activities of the two operators, robots and humans have correlation. *Cooperation*: both the robots and human operators share the same working environment simultaneously, whereas each is focusing on a different job. *Synchrony*: the operators, both human and robots, share the same working environment but at different periods of time (Müller *et al* 2017).

6.11.3 Augmented reality combined with a brain–machine interface to control robots

Augmented reality, when combined with robotics, is transforming industrial production by enabling human workers to perform their tasks faster, more efficiently, and with greater precision compared to conventional production processes (Spiess and Eckert 2022). Augmented reality improves HRI. The interaction of BMI with an augmented reality headset is effective, providing the experience of working with a 'thinking-mouse' as well as offering control of a system hands-free, giving room for the operator to perform tasks simultaneously (Angrisani *et al* 2018). Augmented reality has the ability to transmit much information to the user. For example, it can convey information about the status and intentions of collaborating robots or machines. The use of user interfaces, such as physical devices, voice, and gestures, may be prohibited in certain work settings, particularly industrial environments. However, a BMI integrated with an augmented reality device can provide an effective means of interaction with robots, offering technicians practical solutions (Sanna *et al* 2022).

6.11.4 Remote control of autonomous production: BMI, augmented reality and robot

A robotic arm in production can be remotely controlled by a human worker or operator through eye blinking, using a mobile phone connected to a webcam. This can be achieved by employing a BMI with augmented reality, which provides visual feedback through a monitor to the BMI. EEG signals generated by multiple eye blinks serve as inputs to the BMI, allowing the robotic arm to be controlled without the worker being physically present at the workplace. This approach can be extended to control multiple robotic devices by developing a hybrid BMI system based on multiple electrophysiological signals, enabling the management of a network of robotic systems that could include multiple robots such as robotic arms, robot vacuum cleaner and humanoid service robots simultaneously. This advancement can pave the way for a single operator or worker to remotely control a complex network of robots within an industrial environment for production purposes.

6.11.5 Industry 5.0

It is arguable that industry 5.0 will catch up with Industry 4.0 much more quickly than previous industrial revolutions transitions. Many researchers have already begun discussing the paradigm of industry 5.0. However, the framework that will shape the context of development for Industry 5.0 remains unclear (Baratta *et al* 2023). The prospects for industry 5.0 revolve around human-centricity, resilience, and sustainability, which are believed to be the pillars of this emerging industrial revolution (Akundi *et al* 2022, Huang *et al* 2022, Leng *et al* 2022). Unlike industry 4.0, which is heavily driven by technology, industry 5.0 is expected to be value-driven (Xu *et al* 2021), with human–robot co-working as a core component (Tiwari *et al* 2022).

6.12 Case study

It is critical to present case studies for readers to easily connect theories and real-world applications of research findings. Thus, this section presents relevant cases studies cutting across different domains.

6.12.1 Japan and Netherlands airports

It is expected that service robots will be actively engaged in public spaces for interactions with the general public, thereby bringing HRI into the limelight. Interactive strategies for the robot and the user within context are required for the service robot to achieve safety, trust, and acceptability from the general public. Examples of the deployment of robots in different application areas includes two stationary humanoid robots in train stations in Japan and a humanoid robot deployed in an airport to guide passengers to gates in the Netherlands (Babel *et al* 2022).

6.12.2 Deploying autonomous vehicles

Autonomous vehicles have been deployed in different parts of the world to drive innovations in the transportation systems of different countries. It is predicted that by 2035, 3.4 million fully autonomous vehicles will be operating on public roads in China (West 2016). Many autonomous vehicle technologies are currently either in laboratory testing, undergoing closed-track trials, or being tested on public roads. This progression facilitates the real-world application of autonomous vehicles (Ma *et al* 2020). Table 6.3 presents a summary of the real-world deployment of self-driving vehicles across different countries worldwide.

Table 6.3. Trials of autonomous vehicles in different countries across the world.

Country	Source of information	Developers/manufacturers	Pilot project	Month, year	City
South Africa	Engineering News	EasyMile	Trial	October 2017	Durban
Rwanda	MININFRA News	Volkswagen and Siemens	Trial	October 2019	Kigali
Saudi Arabia	Arab News	Navya	Trial	April 2023	Riyadh
Malaysia	Paultan News	NanoMalaysia	Trial	November 2021	Kuala Lumpur
Hong Kong	Hong Kong University of Science and Technology	Professor Ming Liu	Trial	October 2020	Hong Kong
Japan	Eastern Asia	Honda	Trial	March 2021	Tokyo
Australia	Keolis Downer latest News	Consortium	Trial	August 2017	Victoria
Singapore	Los Angeles Times	Google and Volvo	Trial	August 2016	Pittsburgh
Thailand	NSTDA	Public–private partnership	Trial	February 2020	SIRI VENTURES
China	Dayoo News	WeRide	Trial	August 2022	Guangzhou
China	Reuters	Baidu	Trial	December 2022	Beijing
China	China Daily	Baidu	Trial	July 2023	Shanghai
China	YouTube	Baidu	Trial	December 2017	Shenzhen
Kuwait	Kuwait Times	US Military	Trial	July 2023	Camp Buehrig
China	Mercedes-Benz group	Mercedes-Benz	Trial	December 2023	Beijing
USA	Automotive world	Volkswagen	Trial	July 2023	Texas
USA	Wusa9 News	Waymo	Trial	April 2024	Washington
USA	TechCrunch	Zoox	Trial	June 2023	Las Vegas
USA	Northern America	Tesla	Trial	October 2024	California
USA	Prof. ZetianMi website	Ford	Trial	November 2015	Michigan
USA	The Verge	Cruise	Trial	December 2020	San Francisco
USA	CNN Business	Mobileye	Trial	July 2021	New York

France	Simeon Foundation Automotive Museum	Renault	First Trial in history	Mid 1920s	Paris
Belgium	ADAS and Autonomous vehicle	Clevon	Trial	November 2022	Londerzeel
Norway	Forbes	Volvo	Trial	January 2021	Gjesdal
Portugal	Automotive Today	Continental	Trial	June 2022	Timisoara
Finland	Future mobility Finland	Sensible 4	Trial	December 2023	Tampere
Poland	Polish Science	PIMOT	Trial	December 2023	*X*
Turkey	OPINA project	OPINA	Platform	May 2024	Istanbul
France	Keolis Press release	Keolis	Trial	September 2016	Lyon
Sweden	Keolis Press release	Keolis	Trial	January 2021	Gothenburg
United Kingdom	Independent	Nissan	Trial	February 2023	London
Denmark	The Mayor	Holo	Trial	September 2019	Aalborg
Finland	Helsinki Times	Finferries and Roll Royce	Trial	December 2018	Turku
Austria	AVL website	AVL List GmbH	Trial	December 2016	Styria
Russia	The Verge	Yandex	Trial	February 2018	Moscow

6.12.3 Onward medical

A 40-year-old man named Gert-Jan Oskam was paralyzed after sustaining a spinal cord injury in a cycling accident, which interrupted communication between his brain and the spinal cord region responsible for walking. BMI technology was used to restore this communication by creating an interface between the spinal cord and the brain. Recording and stimulation systems were implanted to establish a link between cortical signals and the spinal cord, enabling him to stand and walk in a real-world environment. The BMI spinal cord device was developed by Onward Medical in the Netherlands (Lorach *et al* 2023).

6.12.4 Amazon

Amazon has adopted the use of drones to deliver items up to 5 lbs within 30 min. The company completed the delivery of 100 items in a small U.S. market, with plans to expand to Texas and California. Initially, Amazon aimed to deliver 10 000 items via drones but managed to deliver 100 due to restrictions imposed by aviation authorities (Tarasov 2023). Amazon has deployed over 750 000 autonomous amazon robots in its warehouses over the years to assist workers with tasks like item sorting and lifting to meet the high volume of daily orders (Amazon 2023).

6.12.5 Mercedes-Benz, Honda, Toyota, Volvo, Volkswagen, BMW, and Hyundai

The automotive industry has been adopting robots for a long time to facilitate task automation. General Motors is believed to be one of the earliest car manufacturers to implement robotics in automotive production, paving the way for other manufacturers. Robotic arms are the most widely used robots in automotive manufacturing. Car manufacturers—including, but not limited to, Mercedes-Benz, Honda, Toyota, Volvo, Volkswagen, BMW, and Hyundai—use robotic arms for various tasks, such as assembly operations like attaching doors, windshield wipers, engine hoods, tyre wheels, and hatches. Other tasks include painting the car, welding and fabrication, polishing car components, and conducting quality assessments.

6.12.6 Agriculture

Robotics and AI form the pillars for agriculture 5.0 expected to lead to autonomous agriculture where autonomous robots operate on the farm executing different tasks. This is expected to reduce cost of farm production, ease farm management and enhance smooth farming operations ubiquitously (Ghobadpour *et al* 2022). To facilitate the HRI, robots with 'emotions' and body posture have been generating interest (Arbib and Fellous 2004).

6.13 Summary

The demand for autonomous robots is increasing due to advancements in technology and their growing relevance in society and industry. Autonomous robots perform tasks independently with minimal human intervention. This chapter presents the major stages involved in the design and development of autonomous robots from both hardware and software perspectives. From a hardware perspective, the components required to construct the physical structure of robots include materials for building the frame, sensors for environmental perception and data collection, cameras for visualization, and a robotic brain for processing sensor data before passing decisions to the controller. The controller then activates actuators to trigger physical actions. Before the physical construction of robots, a prototype is programmed, designed, modelled, and simulated on platforms such as but not limited to Webots, Gazebo, ROS, RoboDK, and NVIDIA Developer. Autonomous robots can be classified into UAVs (e.g., drones), USVs (e.g., autonomous cars), AUVs (e.g., underwater autonomous vehicles), spacecraft and trans-medium vehicles—an emerging concept of autonomous vehicles that operate both underwater and above water or in the air.

Typically, humans communicate with external devices such as computers, robotic arms, and wheelchairs through gestures, natural language, or by manipulating input devices like keyboards, mouse, and touchscreens to command the computer to execute tasks. However, with the emergence of BMI, the human brain can communicate directly with machines using EEG or ECoG signals, without the need for speech or physical gestures. This development changes how humans interact with computing devices. While EEG and ECoG are the most popular techniques, other imaging methods such as MRI, fMRI, and MEG also exist. BMI can be integrated with robots to control their operations using EEG signals or other types of physiological signals. This chapter presents studies that have integrated BMI into robots for control via EEG signals. Additionally, the chapter covers the concept of augmented reality and its basic operations. To avoid confusion, especially for new readers, the chapter differentiates augmented reality from virtual reality and mixed reality.

The lack of a feedback mechanism in controlling robots via BMI has motivated many studies to incorporate augmented reality as a means to design closed-loop BMI-controlled robots, with augmented reality serving as the feedback mechanism. This feedback mechanism has been found to significantly improve the performance of closed-loop BMI-controlled robots. Among different types of robots, robotic arms have received the most attention for control through BMI integrated with augmented reality. Typically, BMIs have been used to control a single robotic device using a single brain signal. However, the concept of controlling multiple robotic devices with a combination of different brain signals is emerging, as demonstrated by recent studies.

The collaboration between humans and robots in Industry 4.0 aims to create a smooth autonomous production process. The goal is to combine human intelligence with robotic capabilities to enhance productivity. The main types of human–robot collaboration include collaboration, co-existence, and cooperation. This chapter explores the role of autonomous robots and the integration of BMI with augmented reality for controlling autonomous robotic operations in industry 4.0 from a remote location. Using a mobile phone connected to a webcam, workers can supervise autonomous production without being physically present at the industry site. While the concept of the industry 5.0 framework remains unclear to stakeholders, it is anticipated that industry 4.0 could evolve to align with industry 5.0. Factors such as human-centric approaches, resilience, and sustainability are expected to drive the development of industry 5.0. Case studies where these technologies have been put into practice such as Amazon, airports in Japan and the Netherlands, autonomous vehicle deployments, Onward Medical, and companies like Mercedes-Benz, Honda, Toyota, Volvo, Volkswagen, BMW, and Hyundai are outlined to help readers connect theory with practice.

References

Akundi A, Euresti D, Luna S, Ankobiah W, Lopes A and Edinbarough I 2022 State of Industry 5.0—analysis and identification of current research trends *Appl. Syst. Innov.* **5** 27

Alimardani M and Hiraki K 2020 Passive brain–computer interfaces for enhanced human–robot interaction *Front. Robot. AI* **7** 125

Amazon 2023 How Amazon deploys robots in its operations facilities (aboutamazon.com) https://aboutamazon.com/news/operations/how-amazon-deploys-robots-in-its-operations-facilities (accessed 28 October 2024)

Angrisani L, Arpaia P, Moccaldi N and Esposito A 2018 Wearable augmented reality and brain computer interface to improve human–robot interactions in smart industry: a feasibility study for SSVEP signals *2018 IEEE 4th Int. Forum on Research and Technology for Society and Industry (RTSI)* (Piscataway, NJ: IEEE) pp 1–5

Antsaklis P J, Passino K M and Wang S J 1991 An introduction to autonomous control systems *IEEE Control Syst. Mag.* **11** 5–13

Arbib M A and Fellous J M 2004 Emotions: from brain to robot *Trends Cogn. Sci.* **8** 554–61

Arpaia P, Duraccio L, Moccaldi N and Rossi S 2020 Wearable brain–computer interface instrumentation for robot-based rehabilitation by augmented reality *IEEE Trans. Instrum. Meas.* **69** 6362–71

Babel F, Kraus J and Baumann M 2022 Findings from a qualitative field study with an autonomous robot in public: exploration of user reactions and conflicts *Int. J. Soc. Robot.* **14** 1625–55

Babiloni C, Pizzella V, Del Gratta C, Ferretti A and Romani G L 2009 Fundamentals of electroencefalography, magnetoencefalography, and functional magnetic resonance imaging *Int. Rev. Neurobiol.* **86** 67–80

Bahrin M A K, Othman M F, Azli N H N and Talib M F 2016 Industry 4.0: a review on industrial automation and robotic *Jurnalteknologi* **78** 6–13

Ban N, Xie S, Qu C, Chen X and Pan J 2024 Multifunctional robot based on multimodal brain–machine interface *Biomed. Signal Process. Control* **91** 106063

Baratta A, Cimino A, Gnoni M G and Longo F 2023 Human robot collaboration in industry 4.0: a literature review *Procedia Comput. Sci.* **217** 1887–95

Berger H 1929 Über das elektroenkephalogramm des menschen *Arch. Psychiatr. Nervenkr.* **87** 527–70

Berger R 2014 INDUSTRY 4.0–The new industrial revolution| Maschinenbau| Engineered Products/High Tech| Branchenexpertise| Expertise| Roland Berger

Betz J, Zheng H, Liniger A, Rosolia U, Karle P, Behl M and Mangharam R 2022 Autonomous vehicles on the edge: a survey on autonomous vehicle racing *IEEE Open J. Intell. Transp. Syst.* **3** 458–88

Bibby L and Dehe B 2018 Defining and assessing industry 4.0 maturity levels—case of the defence sector *Product. Plan. Control* **29** 1030–43

Blausen.com staff 2014 Medical gallery of Blausen Medical 2014 *WikiJ. Med.* **1** 1–79

Bozhkov L and Georgieva P 2020 Deep learning models for brain machine interfaces *Ann. Math. Artif. Intell.* **88** 1175–90

Burden S A, Libby T, Jayaram K, Sponberg S and Donelan J M 2024 Why animals can outrun robots *Sci. Robot.* **9** eadi9754

Buzsáki G, Anastassiou C A and Koch C 2012 The origin of extracellular fields and currents—EEG, ECoG, LFP and spikes *Nat. Rev. Neurosci.* **13** 407–20

Caiado R G G, Scavarda L F, Gavião L O, Ivson P, de MattosNascimento D L and Garza-Reyes J A 2021 A fuzzy rule-based industry 4.0 maturity model for operations and supply chain management *Int. J. Prod. Econ.* **231** 107883

Carmena J M, Lebedev M A, Crist R E, O'Doherty J E, Santucci D M, Dimitrov D F, Patil P G, Henriquez C S and Nicolelis M A L 2003 Learning to control a brain–nachine interface for reaching and grasping by primates *PLoS Biol.* **1** e42

Chaudhary A, Singh R N, Rai V K, Dubey S K and Kumari K 2021 Introduction to drone technology for natural resource management in agriculture *Soil Science: Fundamentals to Recent Advances* (Springer) pp 553–79

Chen J, Han Y, Li R, Zhang Y and He Z 2024 Coupling dynamics study on multi-body separation process of underwater vehicles *Drones* **8** 533

Chen L, Chen P, Zhao S, Luo Z, Chen W, Pei Y and Yin E 2021 Adaptive asynchronous control system of robotic arm based on augmented reality-assisted brain–computer interface *J. Neural Eng.* **18** 066005

Chen X, Huang X, Wang Y and Gao X 2020 Combination of augmented reality based brain–computer interface and computer vision for high-level control of a robotic arm *IEEE Trans. Neural Syst. Rehabil. Eng.* **28** 3140–7

Collinger J L, Kryger M A, Barbara R, Betler T, Bowsher K, Brown E H and Boninger M L 2014 Collaborative approach in the development of high-performance brain–computer interfaces for a neuroprosthetic arm: translation from animal models to human control *Clin. Transl. Sci.* **7** 52–9

Dai Y, Xiang C, Zhang Y, Jiang Y, Qu W and Zhang Q 2022 A review of spatial robotic arm trajectory planning *Aerospace* **9** 361

De Croon G C, Dupeyroux J J G, Fuller S B and Marshall J A 2022 Insect-inspired AI for autonomous robots *Sci. Robot.* **67** eabl6334

De Pace F, Manuri F, Bosco M, Sanna A and Kaufmann H 2024 Supporting human–robot interaction by projected augmented reality and a brain interface *IEEE Trans. Human-Mach. Syst* **54** 599–608 .

Dubey A and Ray S 2019 Cortical electrocorticogram (ECoG) is a local signal *J. Neurosci.* **39** 4299–311

Edelman B J, Zhang S, Schalk G, Brunner P, Müller-Putz G, Guan C and He B 2024 Non-invasive brain–computer interfaces: state of the art and trends *IEEE Rev. Biomed. Eng.* **18** 26–49

Editorial 2021 Advances in the integration of brain-machine interfaces and robotic devices *Front. Robot. AI* **8** 653615

Eraqi H M, Moustafa M N and Honer J 2017 End-to-end deep learning for steering autonomous vehicles considering temporal dependencies *arXiv preprint* arXiv: 1710.03804

Fang B, Ding W, Sun F, Shan J, Wang X, Wang C and Zhang X 2022 Brain–computer interface integrated with augmented reality for human–robot interaction *IEEE Trans. Cogn. Develop. Syst.* **15** 1702–11

Fukuhara A, Gunji M and Masuda Y 2022 Comparative anatomy of quadruped robots and animals: a review *Adv. Robot.* **36** 612–30

Garcia F J C, Robb D A, Liu X, Laskov A, Patron P and Hastie H 2018 Explain yourself: a natural language interface for scrutable autonomous robots *arXiv preprint* arXiv: 1803.02088

Ghobadpour A, Monsalve G, Cardenas A and Mousazadeh H 2022 Off-road electric vehicles and autonomous robots in agricultural sector: trends, challenges, and opportunities *Vehicles* **4** 843–64

Gidado U M, Chiroma H, Aljojo N, Abubakar S, Popoola S I and Al-Garadi M A 2020 A survey on deep learning for steering angle prediction in autonomous vehicles *IEEE Access* **8** 163797–817

Goldin R 2013 Mind-boggling numbers: genetic expression in the human brain https://science20.com/rebecca_goldin/mindboggling_numbers_genetic_ expression_human_brain-109345 (accessed 15 October 2021)

Haenlein M and Kaplan A 2019 A brief history of artificial intelligence: on the past, present, and future of artificial intelligence *Calif. Manage. Rev.* **61** 5–14

Haigh T 2023 Conjoined twins: artificial intelligence and the invention of computer science *Commun. ACM* **66** 33–7

Hallam B and Hayes G M 1992 *Comparing Robot and Animal Behaviour* (University of Edinburgh, Department of Artificial Intelligence)

Hassanalian M and Abdelkefi A 2017 Classifications, applications, and design challenges of drones: a review *Prog. Aerosp. Sci.* **91** 99–131

Hayes M and Downie A 2024 What is augmented reality? | IBM. https://ibm.com/topics/augmented-reality (accessed 8 October 2024)

He X, Liu Y, Lv C, Ji X and Liu Y 2019 Emergency steering control of autonomous vehicle for collision avoidance and stabilisation *Vehicle Syst. Dynam.* **57** 1163–87

Hu J 2024 Augmented-reality based brain–computer interface of robot control *Heliyon* **10** e26255

Huang Q 2016 Mathematical modeling of quadcopter dynamics https://scholar.rose-hulman.edu/cgi/viewcontent.cgi? article = 1158and context = math_mstr accessed 10 October 2024)

Huang Q, Zhang Z, Yu T, He S and Li Y 2019 An EEG-/EOG-based hybrid brain–computer interface: application on controlling an integrated wheelchair robotic arm system *Front. Neurosci.* **13** 1243

Huang S, Wang B, Li X, Zheng P, Mourtzis D and Wang L 2022 Industry 5.0 and Society 5.0—comparison, complementation and co-evolution *J. Manuf. Syst.* **64** 424–8

Ingrand F and Ghallab M 2017 Deliberation for autonomous robots: a survey *Artif. Intell.* **247** 10–44

Ji Z, Liu Q, Xu W, Yao B, Liu J and Zhou Z 2021 A closed-loop brain–computer interface with augmented reality feedback for industrial human–robot collaboration *Int. J. Adv. Manuf. Technol.* **124** 3083–98

Jin T and Han X 2024 Robotic arms in precision agriculture: a comprehensive review of the technologies, applications, challenges, and future prospects *Comput. Electron. Agric.* **221** 108938

Juniper A 2015 *The Complete Guide to Drones Extended* 2nd edn (London: Hachette)

Kandel E R, Schwartz J H, Jessel T M, Siegelbaum S, Hudspeth A J and Mack S (ed) 2000 *Principles of Neural Science* **vol 4** (New York: McGraw-hill) pp 1227–46

Kangunde V, Jamisola Jr R S and Theophilus E K 2021 A review on drones controlled in real-time *Int. J. Dyn. Control* **9** 1832–46

Karavas G K, Larsson D T and Artemiadis P 2017 A hybrid BMI for control of robotic swarms: preliminary results *2017 IEEE/RSJ Int. Conf. on Intelligent Robots and Systems (IROS)* (Piscataway, NJ: IEEE) pp 5065–75

Kokorin K, Zehra S R, Mu J, Yoo P, Grayden D B and John S E 2024 Semi-autonomous continuous robotic arm control using an augmented reality brain–computer interface *IEEE Trans. Neural Syst. Rehab. Eng.* **32** 4098–108

Kolkhorst H, Veit J, Burgard W and Tangermann M 2020 A robust screen-free brain–computer interface for robotic object selection *Front. Robot. AI* **7** 38

Krejci D and Lozano P 2018 Space propulsion technology for small spacecraft *Proc. IEEE* **106** 362–78

Lebedev M A, Carmena J M, O'Doherty J E, Zacksenhouse M, Henriquez C S, Principe J C and Nicolelis M A 2005 Cortical ensemble adaptation to represent velocity of an artificial actuator controlled by a brain–machine interface *J. Neurosci.* **25** 4681–93

Leng J, Sha W, Wang B, Zheng P, Zhuang C, Liu Q and Wang L 2022 Industry 5.0: prospect and retrospect *J. Manuf. Syst.* **65** 279–95

Liu L, Lu S, Zhong R, Wu B, Yao Y, Zhang Q and Shi W 2020 Computing systems for autonomous driving: state of the art and challenges *IEEE Internet Things J.* **8** 6469–86

Liu S and Liu P 2021 A review of motion planning algorithms for robotic arm systems *RiTA 2020: Proc. of the 8th Int. Conf. on Robot Intelligence Technology and Applications* (Singapore: Springer) pp 56–66

Lorach H, Galvez A, Spagnolo V, Martel F, Karakas S, Intering N and Courtine G 2023 Walking naturally after spinal cord injury using a brain–spine interface *Nature* **618** 126–33

Ma Y, Wang Z, Yang H and Yang L 2020 Artificial intelligence applications in the development of autonomous vehicles: a survey *IEEE/CAA J. Autom. Sin.* **7** 315–29

Mann S, Furness T, Yuan Y, Iorio J and Wang Z 2018 All reality: virtual, augmented, mixed (x), mediated (x, y), and multimediated reality *arXiv preprint* arXiv:1804.08386

Martínez de Alegría I, RozasHolgado I, Ibarra E, Robles E and Martín J L 2024 Wireless power transfer for unmanned underwater vehicles: technologies, challenges and applications *Energies* **17** 2305

Martins B and Teixeira A R 2024 The influence of educational and entertainment videos on children's frontal EEG activity: a case study *Int. Conf. on Human–Computer Interaction* (Cham: Springer Nature) pp 68–76

McFarland D J and Wolpaw J R 2008 Brain–computer interface operation of robotic and prosthetic devices *Computer* **41** 52–6

Müller R, Vette M and Geenen A 2017 Skill-based dynamic task allocation in human–robot-cooperation with the example of welding application *Procedia Manuf.* **11** 13–21

Oztemel E and Gursev S 2020 Literature review of Industry 4.0 and related technologies *J. Intell. Manuf.* **31** 127–82

Pali I, Amin R and Abdussami M 2024 Autonomous vehicle security: current survey and future research challenges *Secur. Privacy* **7** e367

Pandey A, Kaushik A, Jha A K and Kapse G 2014 A technological survey on autonomous home cleaning robots *Int. J. Sci. Res. Publ.* **4** 1–7

Park M, Lee S and Han W 2015 Development of steering control system for autonomous vehicle using geometry-based path tracking algorithm *ETRI J.* **37** 617–25

Patidar V and Tiwari R 2016 Survey of robotic arm and parameters *2016 Int. Conf. on Computer Communication and Informatics (ICCCI)* (Piscataway, NJ: IEEE) pp 1–6

Peksa J and Mamchur D 2023 State-of-the-art on brain-computer interface technology *Sensors* **23** 6001

Penaloza C I, Mae Y, Kojima M and Arai T 2014 BMI-based framework for teaching and evaluating robot skills *2014 IEEE Int. Conf. on Robotics and Automation (ICRA)* (Piscataway, NJ: IEEE) pp 6040–6

Plebe A, Svensson H, Mahmoud S and Da Lio M 2024 Human-inspired autonomous driving: a survey *Cogn. Syst. Res.* **83** 101169

Qin J, Liu Y and Grosvenor R 2016 A categorical framework of manufacturing for industry 4.0 and beyond *Procedia Cirp* **52** 173–8

Reichert C, Kennel M, Kruse R and Hinrichs H 2014 An asynchronous BMI for autonomous robotic grasping based on SSVEF detection *Proc. of the 6th Brain–Computer Interface Conf. 2014*

Open Robotics 2023 Robot Operating System https://ros.org/ (accessed 24 September 2024)

Ryalat M, ElMoaqet H and AlFaouri M 2023 Design of a smart factory based on cyber-physical systems and Internet of Things towards Industry 4.0 *Appl. Sci.* **13** 2156

Saffari E, Hosseini S R, Taheri A and Meghdari A 2021 Does cinema form the future of robotics? A survey on fictional robots in sci-fi movies *SN Appl. Sci.* **3** 655

Sakai T and Nagai T 2022 Explainable autonomous robots: a survey and perspective *Adv. Robot.* **36** 219–38

Sanna A, Manuri F, Fiorenza J and De Pace F 2022 BARI: an affordable brain-augmented reality interface to support human–robot collaboration in assembly tasks *Information* **13** 460

Shamout M, Ben-Abdallah R, Alshurideh M, Alzoubi H, Kurdi B A and Hamadneh S 2022 A conceptual model for the adoption of autonomous robots in supply chain and logistics industry *Uncertain Supply Chain Manag.* **10** 577–92

Shih J J, Krusienski D J and Wolpaw J R 2012 Brain–computer interfaces in medicine *Mayo Clinic Proc.* **vol 87** (Amsterdam: Elsevier) pp 268–79

Sourina O, Sourin A and Kulish V 2009 EEG data driven animation and its application *Proc. Computer Vision/Computer Graphics CollaborationTechniques: 4th Int. Conf., MIRAGE 2009 (Rocquencourt, France, May 4–6, 2009)* (Berlin: Springer) pp 380–8

Spiess M and Eckert T 2022 *Augmented Reality Goes to Work on the Factory Floor* https://sap.com/blogs/augmented-reality-goes-to-work-on-the-factory-floor (accessed 9 October 2024)

Standard Bot 2023 What are autonomous robots? (Easy guide) *Standard Bots* https://standardbots.com/blog/autonomous-robots-101-what-are-autonomous-robots#:~:text=How%20Autonomous%20robots%20work.%20Autonomous%20robots%20can%20function (accessed 24 September 2024)

Stein A, Yotam Y, Puzis R, Shani G and Taieb-Maimon M 2018 EEG-triggered dynamic difficulty adjustment for multiplayer games *Entertain. Comput.* **25** 14–25

Sullivan J, Grimberg S and D'Amico S 2017 Comprehensive survey and assessment of spacecraft relative motion dynamics models *J. Guid. Control Dyn.* **40** 1837–59

Tarasov K 2023 Amazon's 100 drone deliveries puts prime air behind Google and Walmart CNBC News https://cnbc.com/2023/05/18/amazons-100-drone-deliveries-puts-prime-air-behind-google-and-walmart.html?msockid=153aa7a9f948691205cbb322f8416814 (accessed 28 November, 2024)

Teplan M 2002 Fundamentals of EEG measurement *Meas. Sci. Rev.* **2** 1–11

Tiwari S, Bahuguna P C and Walker J 2022 Industry 5.0: a macroperspective approach *Handbook of Research on Innovative Management Using AI in Industry 5.0* (London: IGI Global) pp 59–73

Tonin L, Menegatti E and Coyle D 2021 Advances in the integration of brain–machine interfaces and robotic devices *Front. Robotics AI* **8** 653615

Tonin L and Millán J D R 2021 Noninvasive brain–machine interfaces for robotic devices *Annu. Rev. Control Robot. Auton. Syst.* **4** 191–214

Van der Merwe D, Burchfield D R, Witt T D, Price K P, Sharda A, Mącik M, Gryta A, Frąc M, Dwivedi S L and Goldman I 2020 Drones in agriculture *Advances in Agronomy* **vol 162** (Elsevier) ch 1 pp 1–30

Vergouw B, Nagel H, Bondt G and Custers B 2016 Drone technology: types, payloads, applications, frequency spectrum issues and future developments *The Future of Drone Use: Oortunities and Threats from Ethical and Legal Perspectives* Information Technology and Law Series vol 27 *ed B Custers (Springer) pp 21–45*

Wahde M 2012 Introduction to autonomous robots *Lecture Notes from the Course Autonomous Agents, Chalmers University of Technology*

Waldner J F and Sadhu A 2024 A systematic literature review of unmanned underwater vehicle-based structural health monitoring technologies *J. Infrastruct. Intell. Resilience* **3** 100112

Wang Y, Zeng H, Song A, Xu B, Li H, Zhu L and Liu J 2017 Robotic arm control using hybrid brain–machine interface and augmented reality feedback *2017 8th Int. IEEE/EMBS Conf. on Neural Engineering (NER)* (Piscataway, NJ: IEEE) pp 411–4

Wegemer C 2019 Brain–computer interfaces and education: the state of technology and imperatives for the future *Int. J. Learn. Technol.* **14** 141–61

West D M 2016 *Moving Forward: Self-driving Vehicles in China, Europe, Japan, Korea, and the United States* (Washington, DC: Center for Technology Innovation at Brookings)

Xu X, Lu Y, Vogel-Heuser B and Wang L 2021 Industry 4.0 and industry 5.0—inception, conception and perception *J. Manuf. Syst.* **61** 530–5

Yuh J 2000 Design and control of autonomous underwater robots: a survey *Auton. Robots* **8** 7–24

Yurtsever E, Lambert J, Carballo A and Takeda K 2020 A survey of autonomous driving: common practices and emerging technologies *IEEE Access* **8** 58443–69

Zeng H, Wang Y, Wu C, Song A, Liu J, Ji P and Wen P 2017 Closed-loop hybrid gaze brain–machine interface based robotic arm control with augmented reality feedback *Front. Neurorobot.* **11** 60

Zhang D, Liu S, Wang K, Zhang J, Chen D, Zhang Y and Yan T 2021 Machine-vision fused brain machine interface based on dynamic augmented reality visual stimulation *J. Neural Eng.* **18** 056061

Zhang Y 2021 Invasive BCI and noninvasive BCI with VR/AR technology *Int. Conf. on Artificial Intelligence, Virtual Reality, and Visualization (AIVRV 2021)* vol 12153 (Bellingham, WA: SPIE) pp 186–92

Zhao J, Liang B and Chen Q 2018 The key technology toward the self-driving car *Int. J. Intell. Unmanned Syst.* **6** 2–20

Chapter 7

Recent developments in artificial intelligence and high-performance computing

This era of the artificial intelligence (AI) boom has sparked new concepts that were once thought to belong to science fiction. This chapter presents critical emerging concepts from diverse perspectives within AI across various domains. The chapter presents the status of fully autonomous robotic surgery. The state-of-the-art in high-performance computing systems is highlighted with exascale currently topping the performance chart. However, a zettascale supercomputer five-year project has been announced. Then, a quantum computing tutorial is presented before diving into how quantum computing is revolutionizing different fields in AI. The boom in large language models has seen a surge in high-energy demand by supercomputers at the data centres, as a result increasing carbon dioxide footprint as we find out in the chapter. However, the tech giants are making frantic efforts to make their data centres energy efficient. Lastly, decentralized blockchain technology is discussed, pointing out how accelerators influence crypto mining profits and outlining some recommended processors. It is found that many of the emerging applications remain at the concept, proof-of-concept, or trial stages, while others are ready for practice but have yet to be applied in real-world practice. Some AI applications are already in active use, albeit with unresolved challenges that are expected to be addressed in the future. Case studies are outlined to help readers appreciate the real-world operation of these emerging concepts.

7.1 Introduction

Arguably, AI is the most discussed scientific discipline in the world due to media hype and recent technological developments. The emergence of AI is penetrating different aspects of our daily lives, transforming workplaces and jobs, including tasks once thought impossible for machines to handle. Although many applications remain at the concept, proof-of-concept, or trial stage, some are ready for practice

doi:10.1088/978-0-7503-6320-4ch7

but not yet translated into real-world practice. Some AI applications are in active use, albeit with unresolved challenges that hope to be addressed in the future.

Many emerging AI application concepts are not new; they were conceived in the past but saw little progress and stagnation. Limited advancements in computing resources and power slowed the development of these ideas until recent breakthroughs in technology brought them back into the spotlight. For instance, the concept of autonomous robots is not entirely new, a test run of an autonomous vehicle took place on the streets of Paris, France, in the mid-1920s as revealed by Simeon Foundation Automotive Museum. Today, autonomous vehicles have gained widespread acceptance worldwide, with the goal of forming a significant part of the Internet of Vehicles.

Autonomous robots are gaining momentum in today's world, making inroads into medical practice. Significant efforts are underway to achieve fully autonomous surgery without human surgeon intervention, and notable progress has been made. Similarly, quantum computing, first conceived in the early 1980s, saw limited progress until recent technological advancements accelerated research and development, pushing the boundaries toward potential breakthroughs and real-world applications. Quantum computing is now coupled with AI to process large volumes of data. Rayhan and Rayhan (2023) explain that quantum computing is an emerging technology, with different organizations and institutions making concerted efforts to bring it into practical, real-world use.

High-performance computing has been around for decades, but recently it has seen massive improvements in both software and architecture, with supercomputers now operating at the exascale level. Recently, Japan announced plans for a zettascale supercomputer. Discussions around quantum supercomputers have also begun, with dedicated research centres focussing on their development. The proliferation of supercomputers, along with the modelling of large language models, has sparked increased interest in carbon-aware computing.

It is not feasible to cover all emerging AI applications in one chapter due to the rapidly expanding body of literature and the broad scope of the field, with new concepts continuously emerging. Therefore, this chapter aims to discuss major emerging applications of AI across different domains, focussing particularly on critical areas such as autonomous robotic surgery, exascale and zettascale supercomputers, carbon-aware computing, quantum computing, and decentralized blockchain technology.

7.2 Autonomous robotics surgery

The reader can refer to the full details of autonomous robots in chapter 6 as a prerequisite for understanding the concept of autonomous robotics surgery. In the medical field, most of the autonomous robots operate in a static environment with the use of solid bone structures and registration using fiduciary markers. The factors affecting the autonomy of robots includes environment, human independence and complexity of the goal to achieve (Moustris *et al* 2011). The use of robots in surgery date back to the mid-1980s; since then, engineers and researchers continue to put effort in autonomous robotics surgery. The use of autonomy in robotic surgery requires that the robot is safe and accurate in performing surgery similar to the requirements in conventional manual surgery. In addition, the autonomous robotic surgeon is expected to be equipped with the ability to adapt to patient and environmental dynamics to take suitable decisions (Yip and Das 2019). The prototype trial of robotic surgery performing endoscopy is shown in figure 7.1, and spinal cord surgery performed with the aid of a robot is shown in figure 7.2. Autonomous robotics surgery is expected to improve precision, safety and create new opportunities for deploying robust AI models, and to improve quality of imaging modalities and clinical outcomes (Han *et al* 2022).

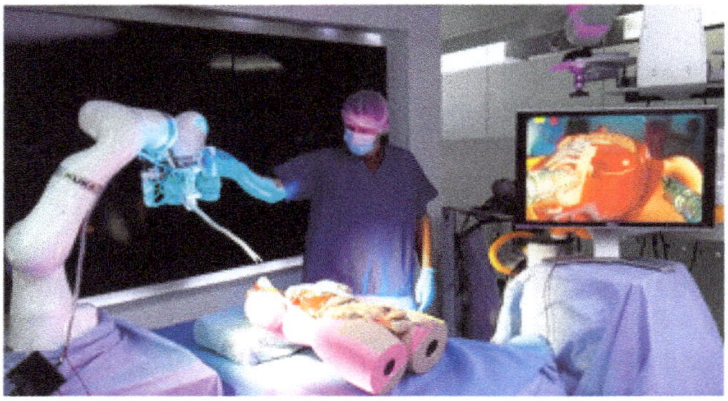

Figure 7.1. Prototype of robot performing endoscopic surgery. Reproduced from Berthet-Rayne *et al* (2018) CC BY 4.0.

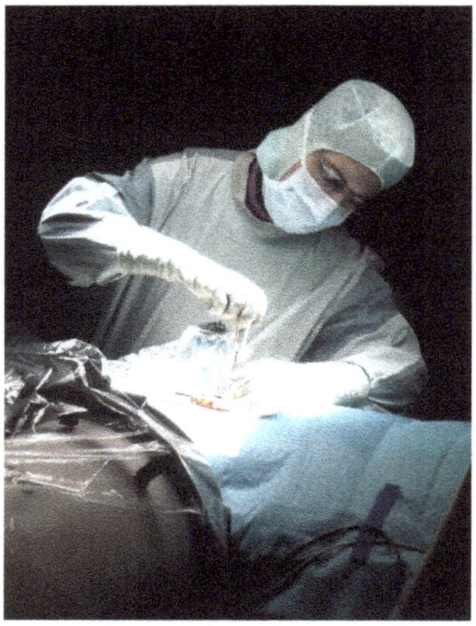

Figure 7.2. Performing spinal cord surgery with robot. This [Robotic Spinal Surgery] image has been obtained by the author from the Wikimedia website where it was made available by [Ap2296] under a CC BY-SA 3.0 licence. It is included within this book on that basis. It is attributed to [Ap2296].

Urology is believed to pioneer the emergence of new technologies and surgical techniques. In the last two decades, the medical domain witnessed advances in robotics surgery, and data from clinical trials of robotic-assisted surgery have been published. Currently, robotics surgery is strictly under the supervision of human surgeons (Connor *et al* 2020). For example, the skills and experience of human urological surgeons influence the operations of a robot surgeon directly (Khadhouri *et al* 2018). The use of robotics surgery is widely adopted in the UK with over 6000 operations performed by the robots on a yearly basis (Rassweiler *et al* 2017).

7.2.1 Level of autonomy in robotics surgery

The robotic arm is transforming clinical practice, particularly in the field of robotic surgery, which is known for employing techniques in minimally invasive surgery. Compared to traditional techniques, robotic surgery offers enhanced dexterity, reduction of tremor, and improved visualization. Autonomous tasks, such as suturing and tissue dissection, are a primary focus of robotic surgery to reduce the workload on surgeons and improve consistency (Iftikhar *et al* 2024). The use of autonomous robotic surgery is growing at an unprecedented rate in the medical device industry. However, barriers imposed by regulatory frameworks, particularly concerning ethical and legal issues, have prompted the consideration of different levels of robotic autonomy in surgery (Yang *et al* 2017), as shown in figure 7.3.

Figure 7.3 depicts the levels of surgical robotics autonomy, with each surgical robot categorized by its highest autonomy level, ranging from 0 (no autonomy) to 5 (full autonomy) (Lee *et al* 2024). The five levels of robotic autonomy in surgery, originally provided by Yang *et al* (2017) and Lee *et al* (2024), are presented in this

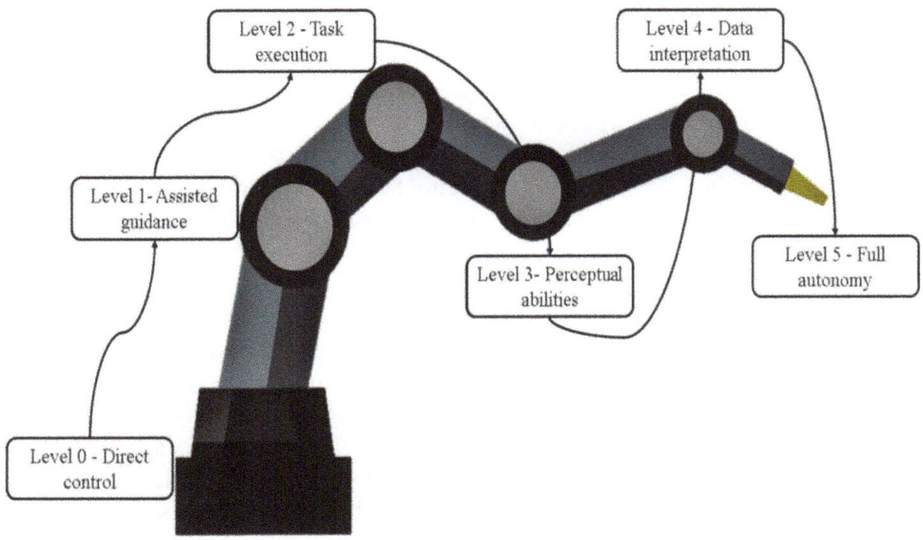

Figure 7.3. The level of robotic automation in surgery. Reproduced with permission from Iftikhar *et al* (2024), copyright 2024 The Authors.

chapter. The autonomy levels from both sources have been combined and are presented as follows.

7.2.1.1 Level 0: no autonomy

This level has no autonomy as tele-operated robots or prosthetic devices operate according to commands issued by the user. The output of surgical robots with motion scaling reflect the desired motion of the surgeon, therefore, surgical robots with motion scaling fall under this level of autonomy. The surgeon monitors all the surgical activities as well as generating, selecting and executing surgical actions. Performing surgery with the category of equipment in this level of autonomy is considered non-robotic procedure.

7.2.1.2 Level 1: robot assistance

Mechanical guidance or assistance are provided by robots during the process performing a task but the control of the system is managed by humans continuously. For instance, virtual fixtures with surgical robots and lower-limb equipment with balance control. In this level of autonomy, the surgical robot provides assistance to the surgeon to execute and monitor actions with support (passive) or guidance (active), whereas the surgeon generates, selects, executes and monitors surgical actions. The surgeon maintains free motion range in passive support while minor assistance without gross interference is provided to the surgeon by the surgical robot. Examples for passive support include tremor filtration, teleoperation, and tool tracking, whereas examples for active guidance include haptic feedback or motion constraints to influence the decisions or actions of the surgeon.

7.2.1.3 Level 2: task autonomy

At this level, the human surgeon initiates the robot to perform specific tasks autonomously. The control of the robot by the user is discrete, unlike the continuous control at level 1 autonomy. For example, a surgeon decides where a running suture is to be placed during surgical suturing, and the robot then performs the task autonomously under the surgeon's supervision, intervening when necessary. The surgeon defines the required parameters for the surgical robot to generate plans and take action; the robot itself has no capacity to independently define parameters. These actions reduce variability across procedures because they are predictable and designed for consistency.

7.2.1.4 Level 3: conditional autonomy

The different strategies for surgical procedure are generated by the surgical robot for a human surgeon to select the optimal strategy among the available strategies suggested by the surgical robot or the human surgeon can have the final decision in approving or disapproving or revising the strategy selected autonomously by the surgical robot. Then, the surgical robot autonomously performs actions based on the human surgeon's approved or revised strategy. The parameters used by the robot surgeon are extracted from the data streams uploaded such as preoperative patient scans. The surgical settings can be monitored through real-time intraoperative imaging for updating the strategies. Close monitoring of tasks perform by this kind of robot may not be required. Another example is that lower-limb prosthetic devices in active activity can sense the person wearing the lower-limb prosthetic device wishes to automatically adjust appropriately with no need for direct attention from the person wearing the prosthetic device.

7.2.1.5 Level 4: high autonomy

The robot surgeon generates and chooses the best surgical plans suitable for a specific patient to autonomously execute the surgical procedure after getting approval from the human surgeon or the robot surgeon to perform surgery under human surgeon supervision. The surgical environment is continuously monitored by the robot surgeon and autonomously makes minor adaptations to reflect changing surgical procedure plans as required. For safety purposes, in case of significant changes, the robot surgeon calls the attention of the human surgeon to intervene for the human surgeon to temporary take control of the surgery or provide additional inputs to the robot surgeon. This level of autonomy is a significant jump where robot surgeons have the capacity to interpret preoperative and intraoperative data to develop plans for intervention, execute and adapt to real-world environment dynamics. The potential examples include cancer surgery to remove tissue to minimize its damage in targeting areas affected by the cancer.

7.2.1.6 Level 5: full autonomy (no human required)

This is referred to as the level of fully autonomous 'robotic surgery' with general surgeon capabilities that perform surgery without humans in the loop from strategies preparation through the surgery procedure to the end of the surgery. However, this level of robotic surgery has not yet come to reality (Attanasio *et al* 2021, Iftikhar *et al* 2024, Saeidi *et al* 2022, Yang *et al* 2017); it remains as a concept in the realm of science fiction with the illusion of a surgery room, as shown in figure 7.4, without the presence of human surgeons. The robot surgeon generates and chooses the best surgical plans suitable for a specific patient to autonomously execute completely the surgical procedure without requiring prior approval from a human surgeon. However, the surgeon has an option of safety intervention and may decide to supervise the procedure at any stage. The robotics surgeon's capacity to respond to different types of sensor data will be required to be highly sophisticated for this level of autonomous surgery. The major requirement for the full autonomous technology is the replication of expert surgeon sensorimotor skills. The risk of malfunctioning with the potential to cause harm to the patient increases with drastic reduction of human supervision and growing robotic perception, decision-making process and actions. Issues of cybersecurity and privacy will form part of the sources of concern. In addition, as autonomy of the surgical devices increases, the regulatory framework will need to be changed. Iftikhar *et al* (2024) argued that the developments from level 1 through level 4 indicate significant progress toward achieving level 5, where a robotic surgeon can autonomously perform an entire surgical procedure. The future of autonomous robot surgery is bright and it is feasible that it will come to reality in clinical practice (figure 7.4).

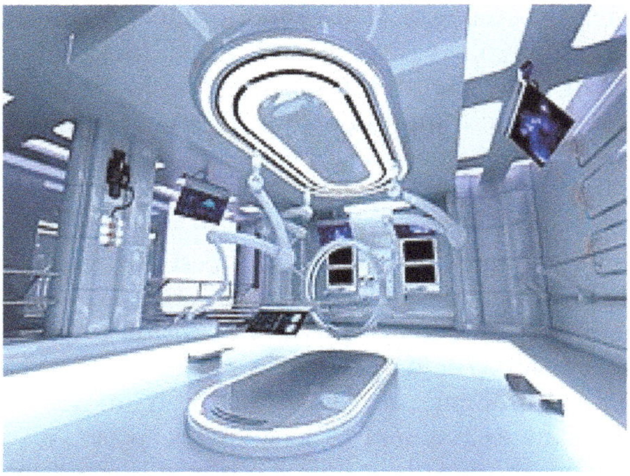

Figure 7.4. Robotics surgery room in science fiction at Level 5: perform complete surgical procedure autonomously without human surgeon in the loop. This [Science fiction surgery room] image has been obtained by the author from the Wikimedia website, where it is stated to have been released into the public domain. It is included within this book on that basis.

7.3 Readiness status levels of robotic autonomy surgery in clinical practice

Readiness for different levels of automation in surgery within clinical practice is depicted in figure 7.5, indicating the readiness of each technology and its practical applications. The data used to generate the figure is extracted from Attanasio *et al* (2021). It can be observed that levels 0 and 5 have no enabling technology and practical applications. This is because level 0 has no autonomy, and level 5 remains conceptual, without practical applications. As such, it has not translated into practice as pointed out by Iftikhar *et al* (2024). Robotic surgery requires parallel advancements in both the regulatory framework and surgical workflows at each level of automation. Recognizing automation at different levels in robotic surgery is significant for ensuring safety and facilitating its translation into clinical practice. However, since risk is specific to the procedure, the level of automation does not fully capture the classification of risk at each automation level (Lee *et al* 2024).

'Not ready' means that the technological equipment for the operation is not yet prepared to be translated into medical practice. In contrast, 'ready but unavailable' indicates that the technology is ready for clinical practice but is currently inaccessible. However, organ and tumour segmentation, assistive systems, and ablation are technologies that are already in use in clinical practice, albeit with unresolved challenges. For instance, assistive systems are employed in specific orthopaedic cases, such as the Stryker Mako system for replacing joints, but challenges remain for soft tissue surgeries. For ablation, treatment for benign prostatic hyperplasia has been effectively addressed, with platforms like PROCEPT BioRobotics' AquaBeam available for such procedures. However, ablation in endoscopic surgery remains an unresolved issue. Similarly, for organ and tumour segmentation, Brainlab is utilized to

Figure 7.5. Enabling technologies and practical applications readiness status for level 1: robot assistance, level 2: task automation, level 3: conditional automation, level 4: high automation and level 5: fully autonomous.

segment tumours from magnetic resonance imaging in neurosurgery. As yet, applications in thoracic and abdominal surgeries continue to face challenges (Attanasio *et al* 2021).

7.4 High-performance computing

Companies like Cray, Fujitsu, CDC, Thinking machine and NEC were the major players of high-performance systems designing scientific supercomputers between the periods of 1975 to 1995. The prices and performance of these scientific supercomputers were costly but effective in performance compared to the standard computers. The general-purpose computers with single chip designed in the 1970s struggled to hit the high-performance computing market in the 1980s. Building of cluster systems combining multiple numbers of standalone systems emerged and started competing in terms of performance in the 1990s. Presently, the market of high-performance computing has been revolutionalized by improvements leading to cost-effective and off-the-shelf computers with processors purposely designed as general-purpose computers not for scientific computing (Hager and Wellein 2010).

One of the most significant breakthroughs in this age is the development of supercomputing (figure 7.6). Supercomputing is refer to supercomputers with associated applications. The supercomputers have an impact on different domains from science to immediate practical applications. The supercomputer is experiencing unprecedented growth and impact more than any other technology in human history. It has played a significant role in the advancement of humanity, equipping humans with capabilities and provide better understanding of society including the environment. The supercomputer enables humans to perform computation in a magnitude of 10 trillion or 13 orders factor conservatively, a significant improvement from 1000 basic operations per second in the later 1940s (Sterling *et al* 2017).

The performance of the supercomputers in today's world exceeds 100 quadrillion floating-point operations per second (flops) (meaning more than 100 petaflops). Through steady improvement of programming, algorithms, technology, architecture, methods and operating system, the speed of the supercomputers has been improving with almost 200 times factor in each decade. High-performance computing is a term synonymous to supercomputing. Supercomputing provides the means for exploration to complement empirical methods and theoretical practice for the last four centuries. It has been a pillar for discoveries, inquiries, investigations, design, new techniques and new processes of operations (Sterling *et al* 2017).

Figure 7.6. Taiwania 3 supercomputer. This [Taiwania 3 Supercomputer] image has been obtained by the author from the Wikimedia website where it was made available by [Tony kang peppy] under a CC BY 4.0 licence. It is included within this book on that basis. It is attributed to [Focus Taiwan newsletter].

7.4.1 Supercomputers and application programs

High-performance computing is a field of study that relates to technology, methodology and applications required to achieve great capabilities in computing technology any time. High-performance computing encompasses supercomputers performing a wide range of computations to solve problems, possibly very fast. The act of executing applications in a supercomputer is referred to as supercomputing, which is synonymous with high-performance computing. The supercomputer today appears as multiple rows of racks occupying a large space of land spanning thousands of square feet requiring huge energy in megawatts of electric power for operations. Applications of supercomputers comprise both the problem to be solved and source code involved in the problem solving activities. The source code is the means where the user transmits to the supercomputer the instructions to perform computation to achieve the desired outcome as a solution to the problem (Sterling *et al* 2017). The supercomputer possesses essential functionality and sub-systems similar to a commonly used PC listed as follows (Sterling *et al* 2017):

1. transformation of input into output by operational functionalities;
2. internal memory for data storage;
3. communication channels for sub-systems and different components to communicate including data flow;
4. controllers coordinating interoperability of sub-systems;
5. mass storage space for storing operating systems, applications and data;
6. input/output channels and interface providing means of interaction between the system and user.

The software structure of the supercomputer serves a similar purpose to that of the commonly used PC or workstation such as interface, control, functionalities, operating systems (OS), compilers, file systems, software drivers, and much more (Sterling *et al* 2017).

7.4.2 Supercomputer operating systems

The controlling paradigm of a supercomputer is driven by the operating system (OS) and user interface. From the perspective of programmers, developers, users and administrators, the OS is the supercomputer. However, the evolution in physical structure of the supercomputer had an impact on the scalability, memory, heterogeneity and domain of applications, thus, prompting challenges to related software and OS support (Gerofi *et al* 2019). The supercomputer OS has been evolving to provide optimal capability to the hardware components distributed by means of applications. The issues faced by other domain OS is resolved in the supercomputer OS such as interacting with diverse devices, support to different level users and complex scheduling for a large number of applications, effectively coordinating system resources and users (Gerofi *et al* 2019).

Myriad developers of supercomputer OS are available in the market running different supercomputers. However, it has been established that Linux and Unix have dominated the supercomputer OS (Gerofi *et al* 2019). The supercomputer OS family includes Linux, Unix, Windows, BSD based, Mac and mixed. However, the top supercomputers OS system share and performance are illustrated in figures 7.7 and 7.8, respectively, generated from the TOP500 website with Linux OS dominating both the share and performance.

7.4.3 Cluster system

The switched network of several single-processor systems creating a high-performance computing environment installed with cluster OS (figure 7.9(B)) having load balancer and servers to operate in a coordinated manner to execute jobs for performance improvement is referred to as a cluster system (figure 7.9(A)).

The design and building of cluster systems was inspired by the cost of flops per dollar and unbelievable growing speed of graphic processing units (GPUs). The cluster of GPU systems with 30 GPU nodes was built to carry out high-performance scientific computing. A parallel flow simulation was developed to test the

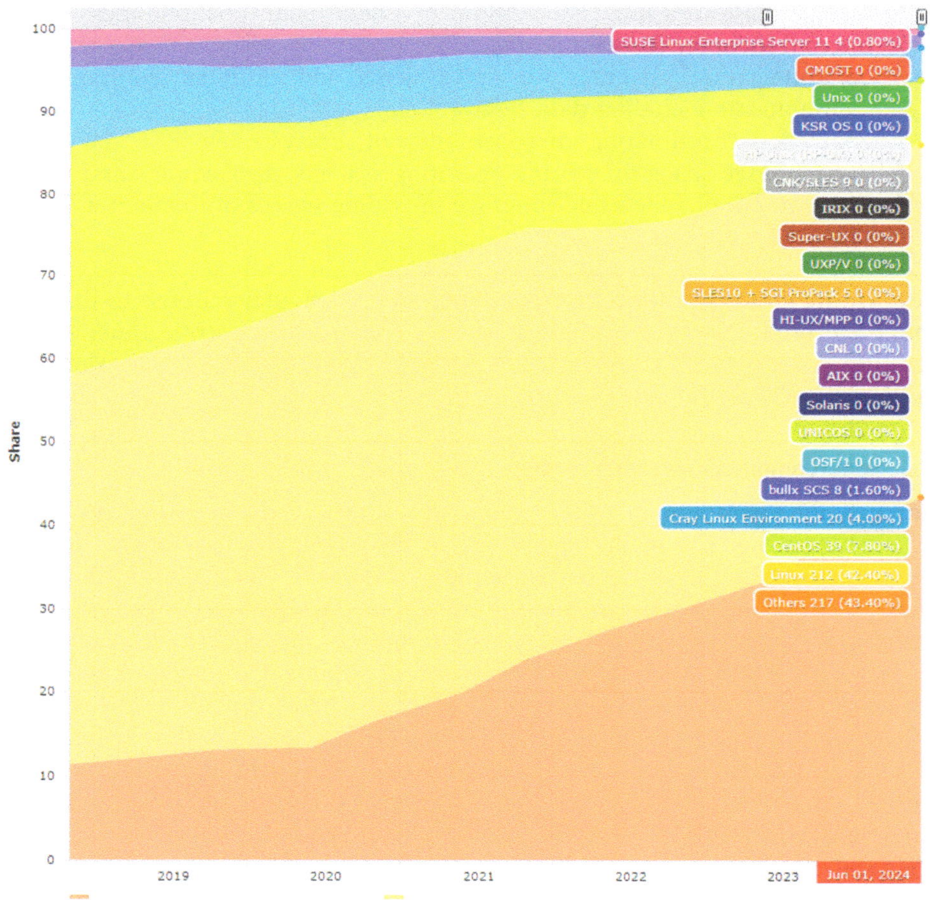

Figure 7.7. Top supercomputers OS share as at first June, 2024. Created using TOP500.

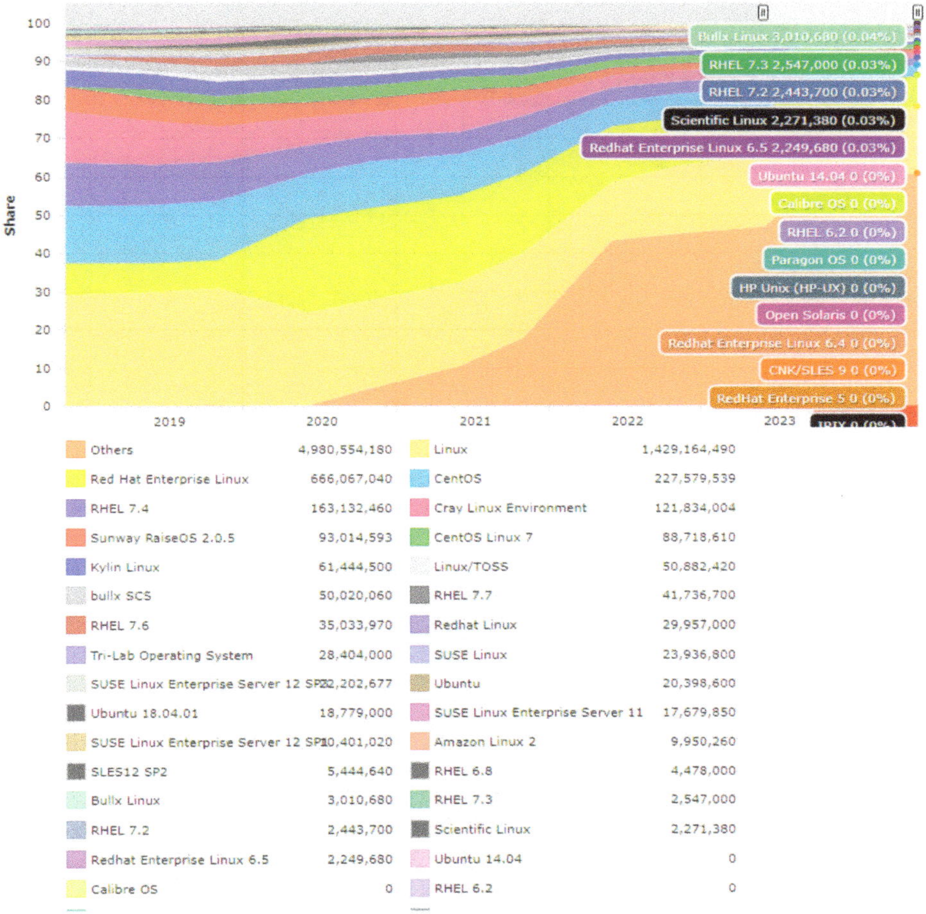

Figure 7.8. Top performing supercomputer OS as at first June, 2024. Created using TOP500.

effectiveness of the cluster system. The GPU cluster system was used to run the parallel flow simulation based on the lattice Boltzmann model. The dispersion of airborne pollution in New York City, Times Square, was simulated on the GPU cluster system. The GPU cluster system achieved the performance of 480 × 400 × 80 lBM within 0.31 s per step better than CPU cluster systems (Fan *et al* 2004). An example of a cluster system is shown in figure 7.10.

As at 2014, the petascale cluster system had become common and increased its dominance in TOP500 high-performance computing systems ranking (Meuer *et al* 2014). The cluster system evolved from a single-core processor system to platforms with multi-core and heterogeneous as witnessed in recent times (Rico-Gallego *et al* 2019). The June 2018 TOP500 list of powerful supercomputers indicated that among the 500 ranked high-performance computers, 437 were cluster systems (TOP500 2018).

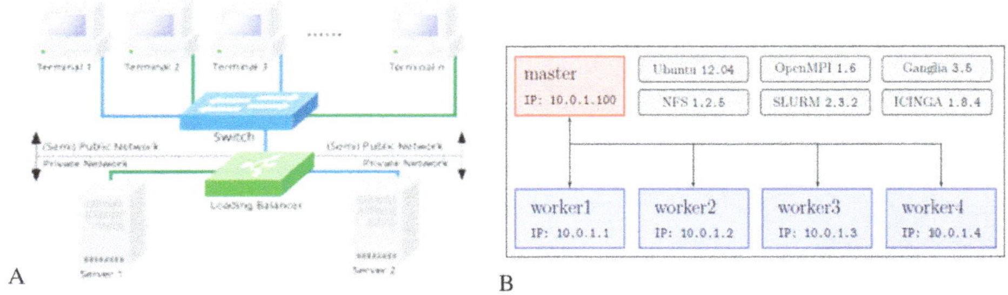

Figure 7.9. Cluster systems. (A) Cluster system with terminals, servers, load balancer and network. This [Load Balancing Cluster (NAT)] image has been obtained by the author from the Wikimedia website where it was made available by [HFWMan] under a CC BY-SA 4.0 licence. It is included within this book on that basis. It is attributed to [HFWMan]. (B) Cluster system Ubuntu operating system. This [Overview-cluster-software] image has been obtained by the author from the Wikimedia website where it was made available by [Informatikum] under a CC BY-SA 4.0 licence. It is included within this book on that basis. It is attributed to [Informatikum].

Figure 7.10. CSIRO graphic processing units cluster system. This [CSIRO ScienceImage 11313 The CSIRO GPU cluster at the data centre] image has been obtained by the author from the Wikimedia website where it was made available by [File Upload Bot] under a CC BY 3.0 licence. It is included within this book on that basis. It is attributed to [CSIRO].

7.4.3.1 Types of cluster system platforms

Typically, the system that comprises general-purpose central processing units (CPUs) and single or multiple GPUs is referred to as the general-purpose computing system with GPU. This type of system with both CPU and GPU is an example of heterogeneous computing systems (HCSs). The HCS is a computing environment consisting of different types of computational processing units such as multi-core GPUs, CPUs, application-specific integrated circuit, field-programmable gate array and demand-side platforms. Typically, computational processing unit of HCS are embedded with the CPU running the OS. Processors other than the general-purpose computational unit are referred to as accelerators because such processors assist

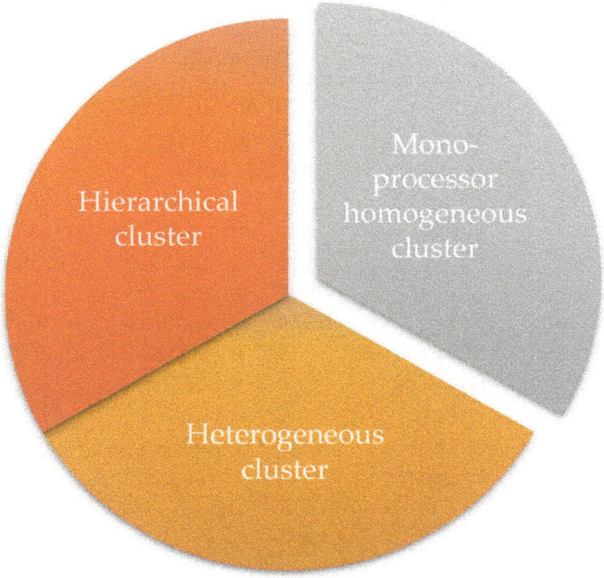

Figure 7.11. Standard types of cluster platforms.

the general-purpose processor in accelerating a specific computational task or job. They enable users of single-processor systems to gain additional performance to solve complex and difficult problems effectively (Vienne *et al* 2015).

The three major categories of cluster systems are shown in figure 7.11. Heterogeneous cluster is the type of cluster with a divers set of processors, communications channels and accelerators, whereas hierarchical cluster comprises the conventional multi-core processors with at least shared memory and network as communication channels (Rico-Gallego *et al* 2019). On the other hand, the mono-processor homogeneous cluster is a cluster with single type of processor in each of the nodes with uniform architecture and software on the network.

7.4.4 Performance metrics

The issue of performance in computing is subject to controversy as there is no universally accepted measure of performance that determines the operational performance of all supercomputing. The operational parameters of supercomputers that are observable and quantifiable are referred to as the metric. The characterizing of supercomputers from a multiple perspective are routinely applied to measure the capabilities and behavioural properties of a high-performance computing system. The fundamental measures typically used in isolation or combined to measure the quality of a supercomputer in different contexts are speed (time) and number of operations performed by the supercomputer under certain conditions. The performance metric widely used to measure the performance of high-performance computing system is flops. The floating-point operation refers to the addition or

Table 7.1. Summary of performance measurement scale of supercomputer computational power.

Metrics	Flops	Abbreviation	Description	Status
Kilo	Kiloflops	Kflops	10^3 or 1 thousand	The first breakthrough
Mega	Megaflops	Mflops	10^6 or 1 million	Available
Giga	Gigaflops	Gflops	10^9 or billion	Available
Tera	Teraflops	Tflops	10^{12} or trillion	Available
Peta	Petaflops	Pflops	10^{15} or quadrillion	Available
Exa	Exaflops	Eflops	10^{18} or quintillion	State-of-the-art
Zetta	Zetaflops	Zflops	10^{21} or sextillion	Concept
Yotta	Yottaflops	Yflops	10^{24} or septillion	Future
Bronto	Brontoflops	Bflops	10^{27} or octillion	Future
Geo	Geoflops	Geoflops	10^{30} or nonillion	Future
Zotza	Zotzaflops	Zoflops	10^{33} or decillion	Future
Nimc	Nimcflops	Nflops	10^{36} or undecillion	Future
Chams	Chams	Cflops	10^{39} or duodecillion	Future

multiplication of two floating-point numbers or real numbers suitable for manipulation and machine readability. The capabilities of supercomputers are described by Greek prefixes Kilo, Mega, etc similar to science and engineering (Sterling *et al* 2017) as presented in table 7.1.

The first supercomputers barely achieved 1 Kflop, but today's supercomputers operate at scales of 125 Tflops or more. A supercomputer is millions of times more powerful than a typical laptop, often measured in Gflops. A supercomputer's primary strength lies in solving real-world problems, such as simulating complex real-world phenomena. Flops measure a supercomputer's speed, but this metric doesn't apply universally, as problem complexity differs. High-performance computing communities have therefore adopted specific standardized problems, known as benchmarks, to measure performance. The benchmarks (e.g., Linpack, highly parallel Linpack and Time taken to solve a fix problem) provide the means for uniform evaluation of high-performance computing systems. The well-known Top 500 ranking organizations adopted highly parallel Linpack for ranking the performance of high-performance computing systems in the world (Sterling *et al* 2017). The supercomputers that operate at petaflops, exaflops, zettaflops etc are petascale supercomputers, exascale supercomputers, zettascale supercomputers etc, respectively.

7.4.5 Exascale supercomputers

Parallel computing applications and operations of a supercomputing centre are the major prerequisites that motivated the architectural development of exascale supercomputing. The scalability, efficiency of data flow and the use of supercomputers is faced with serious challenges. In the case of scalability, multiple-scale, multiple modal computation problems and complexity in task flow features require collaboration in the design of algorithms, applications and system architecture. It is absolutely required to collaborate for the purpose of building multiple-state and multiple-scale systems for mapping the sub-systems effectively with ease and understanding. This can ensure a high level of application efficiency as the scale of the system increases. In the case of data flow, the architectural design is facing a challenge in view of the dynamics and sparse features in some of the complex applications. In the situation where the problem to be solved scales up, data volume, accessing memory and volume of communication greatly increase and complexity in data interaction increases. To mitigate the memory access bandwidth challenge, it is imperative to revolutionize on-chip interconnection and on-chip cache. In addition, it is necessary to greatly improve the network performance of the supercomputer for solving the problem of irregular or abnormal communication. In the case of usability, developing exascale parallel applications is hitting the brick wall of tremendous difficulties. The issue of inconsistency existing between the supercomputer architectural high complexity and the application systems is triggering additional severity leading to an additional noticeable programming wall. In the case of availability, from the perspective of the hardware, failure emanating from any of the components such as the large number of processors, memory, power supply, networks and storage units can create challenges. From a software perspective, large-scale system software can create challenges through error to cause unavailability of the system. The issue of unavailability becomes hectic and seriously severe as the system is approaching operations at the level of exascale and large applications start utilizing millions of cores demanding a high level of system availability (Gao *et al* 2021).

The summary of the major challenges of the supercomputing architectural design are as follows: scalability—lack of robustness in handling operations as the systems scale up; energy consumption—high energy consumption at peak period and running time; movement of data—insufficient application efficiency because of the memory and communication limitations; programming—difficulties in transiting the state-of-the-art large-scale system and software system to an exascale system; availability—ensuring high level availability and stability of the exascale system is another troubling issue. These challenges were analyzed holistically by the team of engineers (hardware) and computer scientists (software) to carry out holistic customization and modification of a Sunway supercomputer at the level of processors, system software, design, parallel algorithms, infrastructure and assembly structure interconnected to perform computations at exascale. Thus, the architecture of the Sunway exascale supercomputer was proposed (Gao *et al* 2021). The supercomputer that operates at exascale is referred to as an exascale supercomputer.

The Fugaku exascale supercomputer claimed to be the world's first exascale supercomputer designed and developed by Riken Center for Computational Science and Fujitsu Ltd with contributions from almost all the stakeholders in high-performance computing communities in Japan. The project began in 2010, initiated at the final stage of producing the K Computer, the predecessor of Fugaku. The project lasted for almost seven years after the official commissioning on first of April 2014 and started production on 9 March 2021. The core components of the *Fugaku* exascale supercomputer are the arm processor perfectly compatible to Aarch64 configurations and innovative server arm general-purpose CPU w/7 nm (Matsuoka 2021). Similarly, the Aurora exascale supercomputer claimed to be the likely first supercomputer to operate at exascale running at one quintillion operations per second when powered. Aurora is 10 times the size of a tennis court. The Aurora is at the US Department of Energy, Argonne National Laboratory in Lemont. Aurora is expected to have twice the performance of the Fugaku supercomputer, the record holder at that time having the peak performance (Mann 2020).

7.4.6 Ranking the performance of supercomputers

The exascale supercomputers (figure 7.12) are currently the state-of-the-art supercomputers with promising performance and reliability in processing complex data and solving complex scientific simulation problems even when the system scales up. The first exascale supercomputer to be powered in the world is a subject of discussion because many high-performance computing centres claimed to be the first to power exascale supercomputers. At the moment many exascale supercomputers exist across different high-performance computing centres in the world with many of them in the Top 500 supercomputing ranking.

The ranking of the Top 500 supercomputers in terms of speed is depicted in figure 7.13, showing the top 10 list among the 500 ranked supercomputers. The Rmax is the maximum performance achieved on highly parallel Linpack, and Rpeak is the theoretical performance at peak. The data used to create figures 7.13–7.14 were collected from the TOP500 website (TOP500 2024).

The corresponding number of cores is depicted in figure 7.14. Cores is the amount of processors (e.g., GPUs, CPUs, TPUs) contained in the supercomputer.

Figure 7.12. Frontier exascale supercomputer with a performance of 1.206 exaflops. This [Frontier supercomputer (52280657003)] image has been obtained by the author from the Wikimedia website where it was made available by [Tm] under a CC BY 2.0 licence. It is included within this book on that basis. It is attributed to [Oak Ridge National Laboratory].

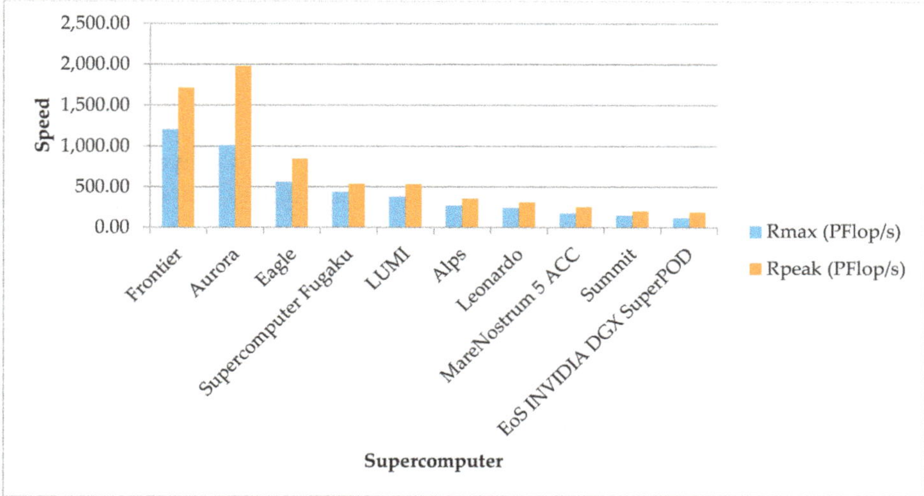

Figure 7.13. The performance achieved by each of the supercomputers on highly parallel Linpack and theoretical performance.

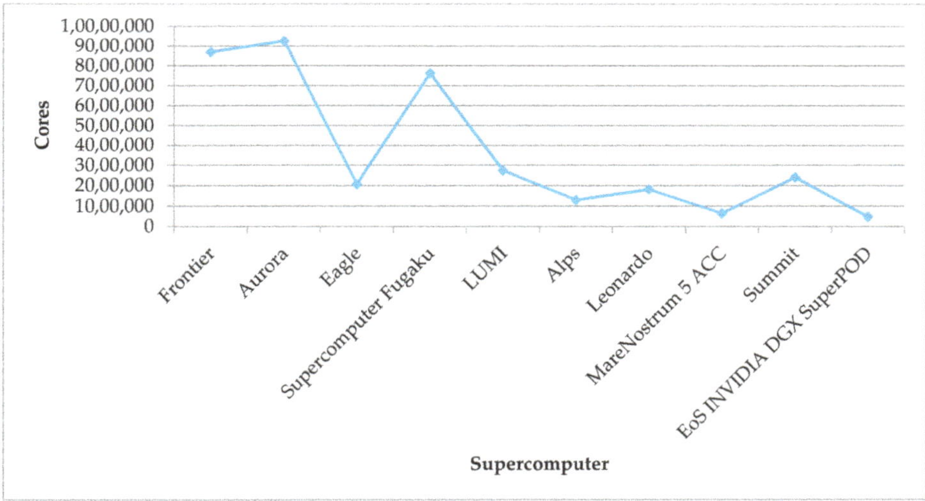

Figure 7.14. The number of cores for each of the supercomputers in the top 10 ranking list.

Figure 7.13 clearly indicates that Frontier is occupying the number one spot as the most powerful high-performance computing system in the world with a speed of 1.206 Eflops and number of cores combining both CPUs and GPUs of 8 699 904 (figure 7.14). The HPE Cray EX architecture of the Frontier is a combination of 3rd Gen AMD EPYC CPUs optimized for high-performance computing and AI accelerators (AMD Instinct MI250X).

7.4.7 Zettascale supercomputer and artificial intelligence evolution

Supercomputers are moving toward zettascale performance, a concept more powerful than today's exascale supercomputers, though it remains ambitious and is not yet realized. The zettascale supercomputer, anticipated to be the next goal of the high-performance computing community, will require significant hardware and software innovations, extensive co-design, and fabrication, as well as collaboration across diverse expert fields. It is not an easy project.

To keep in pace with the tremendous speed of AI evolution, Japan has announced a five-year plan to start the construction of zettascale supercomputers in 2025, projected to complete the project and aiming for full operation by 2030. The project is projected to cost over $750 million with a speed of zettascale never seen in the history of high-performance supercomputing. The zettascale supercomputer is expected to be 1000 times faster than the current world's most powerful exascale supercomputer (figure 7.12). The building of the zettascale supercomputer definitely is not a smooth road. It is expected to come with great challenges; first, to get such a powerful machine to run efficiently is an up-hill task. Secondly, experts have predicted that building a zettascale supercomputer by extending the current supercomputer technology could require energy equivalent to 21 nuclear power plants to run such a powerful machine (Baker 2024).

7.4.8 Supercomputers as platforms for large language models

The purpose of high-performance computing is to solve problems beyond the capabilities of the commonly used general-purpose computers. Supercomputers have been used for science and engineering, historically. The term third pillar of science has been used to refer to the methodology, complimentary experiments and theoretical mathematics. But the problems capable of being solved by supercomputers are beyond science and engineering. They include managing big data, machine learning, national security, socioeconomic and process control (Sterling *et al* 2017). Supercomputers are transient to machine learning modelling, big data analytics and cloud computing from the typical pure scientific simulation (Gerofi *et al* 2019).

Supercomputers or high-performance computing systems with hundreds of thousands or millions of GPUs or tensor processing units (TPUs) in data centres are typically used for developing large AI models and for inference to serve users. The number of large language models has increased significantly over the last two years. Currently, there are over one million large language models on Hugging Face, ranging from lightweight models with a small number of parameters to medium and heavyweight models with up to a trillion parameters. This growth indicates a rising demand and interest in developing large language models as a result of available resources like the supercomputers in data centres for training and inference.

For example, the pre-training of T5 with 1 terabyte of token data used 1024 TPU v3 units; BLOOM was pre-trained on 384 A100 GPUs over 105 days with 366 billion tokens; and AlexaTM was pre-trained with 1.3 trillion tokens on 128 A100 GPUs over 120 days (Zhao *et al* 2023).

For large language models to stay updated and remain relevant, they need to be pre-trained continuously with additional amounts of new data. Also, constant improvement is required to mitigate some of the current challenges militating against the effectiveness of the models such as hallucinations. The modifications of the models is required to increase their usability, for example, modifying from a unimodal model limited to text generation to a multimodal model with the capacity to produce multimodal output. These modifications and updates increase the size and complexity of the model, thus, increasing the resources required to cope with the growing demand of the model, especially pre-training and inference. Therefore, the model starts utilizing more cores, likely in the millions, not used in the previous versions, demanding a high level of supercomputing resources and availability. For example, it is reported by Todorović (2024) that the pre-training of GPT-3 with 175 billion parameters and GPT-4 with more than a trillion parameters took 34 days and 100 days, respectively. An increase of almost 70 days pre-training period were required to transform GTP-3 to GPT-4. It is the tremendous speed at which AI is evolving that motivated Japan to start the Zettascale supercomputer project. Refer to chapter 3 for a detailed tutorial on developing large language models from scratch.

7.5 Quantum theory

In the 20th century, quantum theory was recognized as one of the greatest scientific breakthroughs. It served as a springboard for the construction of many theories in modern physics. Quantum theory has been around for over 50 years before its adoption in computer science ushered another great intellectual breakthrough in the 20th century giving birth to quantum computing (Ying 2010). In addition to computer science and quantum theory, computer engineering is married to deal with the quantum hardware component (figure 7.15). To understand the discussion on quantum computing, pre-requisite ingredients are provided as follows.

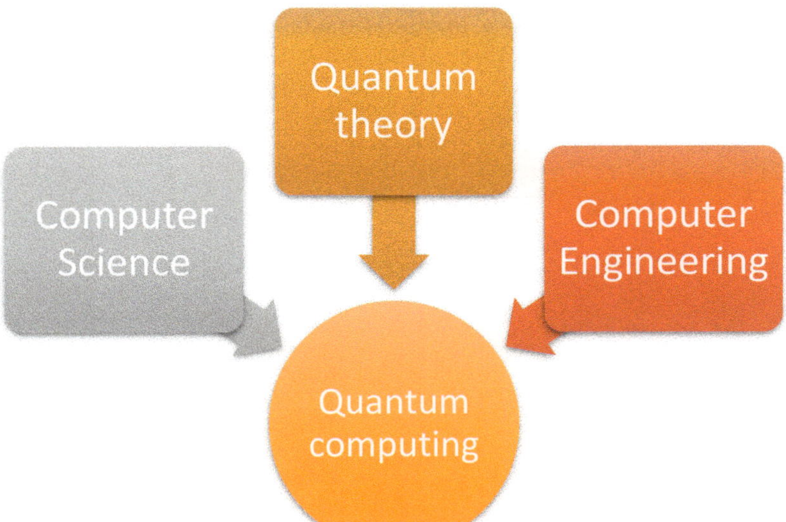

Figure 7.15. Quantum computing combining computer science, quantum theory and computer engineering.

7.5.1 Qubits

Qubit is the basic data unit in a quantum computer, obtained by two-level quantum mechanics. For example, the polarization of photons horizontally and vertically or the spin of one electron up and down. A unit vector in 2D complex Hilbert space is used to represent a qubit, mathematically expressed as (Ying 2010):

$$|\beta\rangle = \gamma_0\ |0\rangle + \gamma_1\ |1\rangle \tag{7.1}$$

where the two basis states are represented by $|0\rangle$ (qubits computational basis state corresponding to the state of classical bit) and $|1\rangle$ (qubits computational basis state corresponding to state of classical bit); the complex numbers are γ_0 and γ_1 with equation (7.2) expressed as:

$$|\gamma_0|^2 + |\gamma_1|^2 = 1 \tag{7.2}$$

The probability amplitudes of the state $|\beta\rangle$ are represented by γ_0 and γ_1. What differentiates qubits from classical bit is that qubits can be in *superposition* expressed as follows:

$$|-\rangle = \frac{1}{2}(|0\rangle - |1\rangle). \tag{7.3}$$

7.5.2 Quantum registers

Multiple qubits form a *quantum register*. The quantum register is created by joining together multiple qubits. Thus, n qubits is made up of a quantum register state expressed as:

$$|\beta\rangle = \sum_{\sigma\epsilon\{0,1\}^n} \gamma_\sigma\ |\sigma\rangle \tag{7.4}$$

$$|\beta\rangle = \sum_{\sigma_1,\sigma_2,\ldots\sigma_n\epsilon\{0.1\}} \gamma_1\gamma_2\cdot\cdot\cdot\gamma_n\ |\sigma_1, \sigma_2, \ldots, \sigma_n\rangle \tag{7.5}$$

$$|\beta\rangle = \sum_{\sigma\epsilon\{0,1\}^n} \gamma_\sigma\ |\sigma\rangle = \sum_{\sigma_1,\sigma_2,\ldots\sigma_n\epsilon\{0.1\}} \gamma_1\gamma_2\cdot\cdot\cdot\gamma_n\ |\sigma_1, \sigma_2, \ldots, \sigma_n\rangle \tag{7.6}$$

The normalization condition in equation (7.7) requires $\gamma_1, \gamma_2, .., \gamma_n$ complex numbers to be satisfied, expressed as:

$$\sum_{\sigma\epsilon\{0,1\}^n} |\gamma_\sigma|^2 = \sum_{\sigma_1,\sigma_2,\ldots\sigma_n\epsilon\{0.1\}} |\gamma_1\gamma_2\cdot\cdot\cdot\gamma_n|^2 = 1 \tag{7.7}$$

The $|\beta\rangle$ in equation (7.6) with $\sigma_1\sigma_2, \ldots, \sigma_n$ as probability amplitude is the superposition of computational states $|\sigma_1\sigma_2, \ldots, \sigma_n\rangle(\sigma_1, \sigma_2, \ldots, \sigma_n = 0, 1)$ for the quantum register also expressed as:

$$|\beta\rangle = \sum_{\sigma=1}^{2^n-1} \gamma_\sigma \, |\sigma\rangle. \tag{7.8}$$

7.5.3 Quantum gate

The computation in a quantum computer is performed by quantum circuits comprising of *quantum gates*. The description of discrete for quantum system time-step progression is performed by quantum gates and it is the gate that is acting on the quantum register with n qubits. This scenario can be expressed in the form of a unitary matrix: $2^n \times 2^n$, i.e., complex matrix U with UU^{T} as the identity matrix. The U^{T} represents the Hermitian conjugate of U where the entry (i,j) represents the complex conjugate entry (i,j) for U. If the quantum register current state is expressed as (Ying 2010):

$$|\beta\rangle = \begin{pmatrix} \gamma_1 \\ \vdots \\ \gamma_{2^n-1} \end{pmatrix} \tag{7.9}$$

$$\text{The quantum gate is } \bigcup = (u_{i,j})_{i,j=0}^{2^n-1} \tag{7.10}$$

Operating U on $|\beta\rangle$ produces the expression as follows:

$$|\delta\rangle = \begin{pmatrix} \theta_0 \\ \vdots \\ \theta_{2^n-1} \end{pmatrix} = U\,|\beta\rangle$$

where the $U\,|\beta\rangle$ is based on typical matrix multiplication, i.e.:

$$\theta_i = \sum_{j=0}^{2^n-1} u_{ij}\gamma_j$$

for $i = 0,1,\ldots, 2^n - 1$.

Hadamard gate is a single qubit, considered as one of the most useful gates.

$$H = \frac{1}{\sqrt{2}}\begin{pmatrix} 1 & 1 \\ 1 & -1 \end{pmatrix}$$

Assuming U_i is the gate operating on register ith for every $1 \leqslant i \leqslant x$. Subsequently, the gate acting on the big register is the tensor product of the $U_1, \ldots U_x$ created by x registers expressed as (Ying 2010):

$$\left(\bigotimes_{i=1}^{x} U_i\right)\left(\bigotimes_{i=1}^{x}|\beta_i\rangle\right) = \bigotimes_{i=1}^{x} U_i\,|\beta_i\rangle.$$

7.5.4 Quantum measurement

Measuring some quantum gates is needed for quantum computation to produce output. *Quantum measurement* is considered for the computational basis. Let us assume we have a register comprising qubits $q_1, \ldots, q_n$ *and* $q_{i1}, \ldots, q_{im}$ as posteriority of $q_1, \ldots, q_n$ (Ying 2010), where $m \leqslant n$ for every $\sigma \in \{0.1\}^n$. Let the restriction of σ on $q_{i1}, \ldots, q_{im}$ be defined as $\sigma | q_{i1}, \ldots, q_{im} = \sigma_{i1}, \ldots, \sigma_{im} \in \{0.1\}^m$. Assuming the quantum register is in the state of equation 7.4, let measurement operate on qubits $q_{i1}, \ldots, q_{im}$ for every $w_{im} \in \{0.1\}^m$, thus, output w associated with probability is expressed as (Ying 2010):

$$p(w) = \sum_{\sigma | q_{i1}, \ldots, q_{im} = w} |\gamma_\sigma|^2$$

And the quantum registers post-measurement state is expressed as (Ying 2010):

$$|\beta_w\rangle = \frac{1}{\sqrt{p(w)}} \sum_{\sigma | q_{i1}, \ldots, q_{im} = w} \gamma_\sigma \; |\sigma\rangle.$$

7.6 Quantum computing

The quantum computer can be described as a computing machine operating on the principles of quantum theory. It will likely be highly beneficial for many tasks with the hope of performing operations better than the top supercomputer of today with state-of-the-art performance. The quantum computer can be viewed as the co-processor of the classical computer similar to the case of GPUs in accelerating video games or pre-training of deep architecture of neural network. The classical computer handled the operation control by imposing the actual rate of the qubit operations to execute by the quantum gates simultaneously considering the quantum gate's computational time and the qubit's coherence time (i.e. total time taken for the qubits to remain in a state of superposition) (Zeguendry *et al* 2023).

Today's quantum computers (figure 7.16) are constructed based on the following key elements, atoms, electronics, or photons. Examples of the atoms used include cold atoms, nuclear magnetic resonance and trap ions. In the case of photons, an example is linear optics. Examples in the case of electronics include superconducting, topology and silicon. IBM, Google and D-Wave recorded significant success in building quantum computers, each with unique models. For instance, the IBM model is non-adiabatic, whereas the D-Wave model is developed based on quantum adiabatic with capacity to manage optimization or sampling probability (Zeguendry *et al* 2023).

The building blocks of quantum computers are similar to those of classical computers but operate differently. Key components in addition to those provided in section 7.5 include quantum memory, quantum CPUs, and quantum error correction (Gyongyosi and Imre 2019). Detailed explanations of each component can be found in Gyongyosi and Imre (2019). A summary of the differences between quantum computers and classical computers, as presented in table 7.2, was drawn from sources including Gyongyosi and Imre (2019), Jaeger (2007), Kitaev *et al* (2002), Steane (1998).

Figure 7.16. Intel quantum computer as a sample for visualization. This [Full wafer of Intel quantum computers] image has been obtained by the author from the Wikimedia website where it was made available by [Jacopo Werther] under a CC BY 2.0 licence. It is included within this book on that basis. It is attributed to [Steve Jurvetson].

Table 7.2. A summary of differences between quantum computers and classical computers.

	Quantum computer	Classical computers
Principle	Quantum mechanics in physics	Classical information
Storage pattern	Qubits—0, 1 or both	Bits, 0 or 1
Operations	Linear algebra and matrices handles qubits	Boolean algebra operate on 0 or 1
Scale	Exponential, as 0 and 1 can be stored simultaneously	Linear
Output	Possible output is link with a probability	The output is either 1 or 0
Circuit reversibility	Reversible quantum circuit is a must	Very few classical circuits are reversible, mostly are not reversible.
Copying data	The creation of unknown quantum state is impossible, thus, restrict copying of data	No restriction in copying data
Operation Condition	Lacks ability to operate at room temperature	Operate at room temperature
Scalability	The extreme sensitivity of qubits makes it unsuitable for scalability	Easily scalable at will

7.6.1 Layers of building a quantum computer

The building of a quantum computer can employ the divide-and-conquer approach where a large problem is broken down into small problems and each problem solved in isolation before combining the small solutions to make-up a complete solution to the large problem. In a similar approach, the quantum computer development can be broken down into five layers for simplifying work and control, as depicted in figure 7.17.

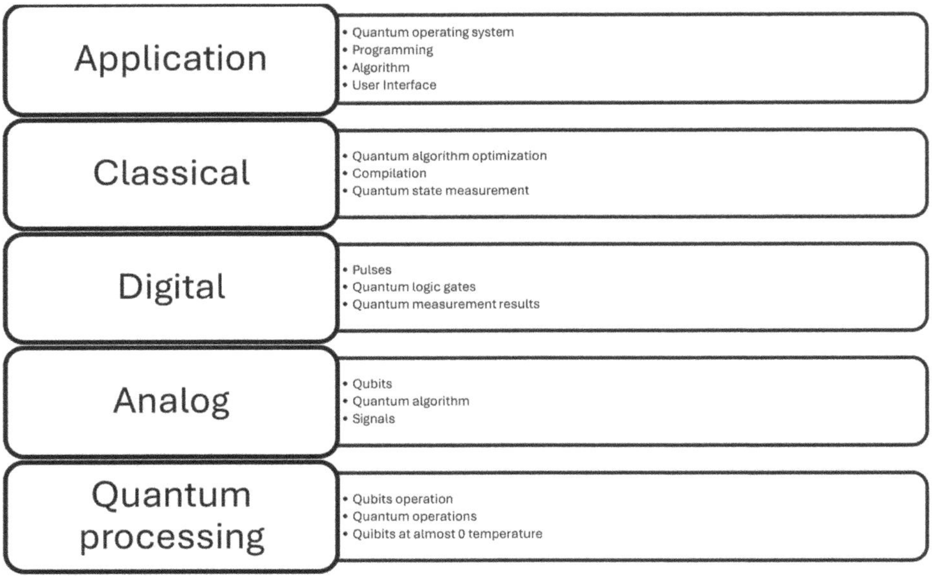

Figure 7.17. The five layers guiding the design and construction of a quantum computer.

These approaches are used by researchers in different tech giants such as IBM, Intel, Google, QuTech among others to build quantum computers, though other approaches exist elsewhere. The development of a quantum computer requires close teamwork because it involves different expertise to make the quantum computer become reality. Despite the split of the development into sub-layers, strong teamwork is required among the experts from different backgrounds such as programmers, quantum algorithm developers, chip designers, specialists in cryogenic-control, chip fabrication engineers, data engineers handling massive data and others (Versluis and Hagen 2020). The five processing layers are described in the following starting with the application before heading deep down to the quantum processing layer (Versluis and Hagen 2020).

7.6.1.1 Application layer

The first layer at the top of the quantum development layers is the application layer necessary for the overall systems. The layer comprised of the essential components and environment relevant to algorithms such as programming integrated development environment, quantum OS, user interface and others. The algorithm designed in this layer must be fully quantum with a combination of classical components, as such, combining both quantum and classical components. The application should be independent of hardware in the subsequent layers.

7.6.1.2 Classical layer

The classical layer is directly under the application layer with three major functions as follows: first, it is responsible for optimizing the quantum algorithm running, compiling and converting into micro-instructions similar to the process in a classical computer; secondly, it is responsible for processing the quantum state measurement that is returned by the hardware in the subsequent layers likely to feed back into the classical algorithm for final output; lastly, the calibration is processed by the classical layer and tuning to the subsequent layers.

7.6.1.3 Digital layer

This layer is responsible for the translation of micro-instructions into pulses, a signal suitable for qubit manipulation, enabling the signal to act as a logic gate for quantum computation. Specifically, the layer converts analogue pules to digital. The quantum processing unit in this layer generates the analogue pulses. Quantum computation measurement results are fed back to the classical layer for combination with results computed by the classical layer thus resulting in combined quantum and classical outputs. These tasks can be managed by PC or field-programmable gate arrays. Addition of an error correction tool at this layer makes it become more complex and sophisticated.

7.6.1.4 Analogue layer

Different types of signals are generated in this layer for sending to qubits in subsequent layers. Mostly, they are steps of voltage, sweeps and microwave burst pulses. The pulses are phase and amplitude for modulation to be executed by the suitable qubit operations. The qubits are connected together to create quantum logic gates for operations, subsequently, used to perform the whole computation based on running quantum algorithms. The signals transmitted to diverse qubits are required to be synchronized with picosecond timescales. For the signals to perform varying tasks, they have to be conveyed to different qubits.

7.6.1.5 Quantum-processing layer

This layer is the last layer under both the analogue and digital processing layers. It is the layer that holds the qubits at the temperature of almost zero. If the amount of qubits increases in the future, the cryogenic chip will have to integrate the three layers as a single package. Companies like Google, Intel and IBM have ventured into the production of systems with superconducting qubits having a few dozen qubits maximum with the capability to perform thousands of quantum operations.

7.6.2 Quantum computer simulators

Quantum computers are not yet commercially available in the market for users to purchase and use because they are still undergoing iteration of improvement and development in different laboratories across institutions, industries and organizations across the world. For now, quantum computers are mostly limited to laboratory environment (Gyongyosi and Imre 2019). The quantum simulators are software that allow the user to use classical computers in running quantum circuits to feel the experience of the quantum computer with the illusion of a real quantum computer. Many of the quantum simulators are available out there with five samples provided in table 7.3 (IonQ 2024) as a gateway to the world of quantum computing. Researchers, postgraduate students and newcomers into the world of quantum computing can start with the simulators provided.

Many organizations offer simulators for running quantum computers on the classical computers for the purpose of evaluating quantum source code before installation on quantum devices. The simulators are mostly limited to online availability through cloud services, run-it-yourself and other means locally or cloud-based. The simulators are not the true state of quantum because they run on a classical computer, however, they give an illusion as if the code is running on a true quantum computer and imitating noise of the quantum computer level of pulses, algorithm and circuits. This is useful for testing source code, flow and syntax. It also imitates the prediction of the reaction of qubits to diverse operations (Zeguendry *et al* 2023).

Table 7.3. List of simulators for experiencing the operations of quantum computers.

Simulator	Access	Link to simulator
IBM Quantum Simulator	Run-it-yourself	https://zenodo.org/records/2562111
Google Quantum AI	Run-it-yourself	https://quantumai.google/cirq/simulate/simulation
INVIDIA cuQuantum	Standalone	https://developer.nvidia.com/cuquantum-sdk
The IonQ Quantum Cloud	Cloud-based	https://ionq.com/resources ? type = docs#resourceArchive
Intel-QS	Standalone	https://github.com/intel/intel-qs

7.6.3 Quantum computing in artificial intelligence

Quantum computing has the potential to offer a valuable benefit to AI from different perspectives, especially processing voluminous data and handling the growing complexity of algorithms for better learning, understanding and reasoning. Machine learning and natural language processing stand to greatly benefit from the quantum computer. Recently, natural language processing has been run on quantum computers resulting in the 'meaningful aware' algorithm (Chambers-Jones 2021). Running machine learning models on quantum computers stands the chance of competing with humans in terms of learning, 'thinking' and data interpretation. Thus, with minimum instruction the model can learn new skills with limited and complex data (Chauhan *et al* 2022). A quantum computer is expected to run machine learning tasks with deep learning algorithms offering improved speed and accuracy over classical computers (Moin *et al* 2021). Already empirical evidence indicates the application of a classical–quantum deep learning framework in solving high-dimensional real-world problems (Benedetti *et al* 2018). An early work shows that Lemos *et al* (2014) developed a quantum recommender system and results indicate efficient recommendation from the system. The running of a quantum Boltzmann machine for sampling training has been demonstrated in (Amin *et al* 2018). Similarly, a five-qubit superconducting processor was used to solve an Oracle-based problem. It was found that the difference of query count in a classical computer and a quantum computer is large (Ristè *et al* 2017).

7.6.3.1 Quantum transformer

Typically, running complex machine learning problems on classical computers takes a long time to execute, even on supercomputers with hundreds or thousands of GPUs, especially training of large language models, which takes weeks or months to complete. With a quantum computer, the duration of running large language models will reduce significantly (Moin *et al* 2021). The transformer is the major building block of large language models, quantum algorithms are already making waves in transformers. For example, compound matrices are used to modify vision transformers to quantum vision transformers with quantum attention mechanisms built using shallow quantum circuits. This has proven to be effective on benchmarks (Cherrat *et al* 2024). A study proposed a transformer quantum error correction decoder to mitigate the local region and retraining required in classical algorithms. It was found to perform better than a non-decoder without requiring retraining (Wang *et al* 2023). Similarly, another study integrated quantum subroutines for the construction of significant transformer building blocks. The quantum algorithm run-time was determined and it indicated improved performance (Guo *et al* 2024). A survey on quantum transformers is covered by Chen *et al* (2024).

7.6.3.2 Quantum generative model

The quantum algorithm is making inroads into generative models, for example, a generative quantum algorithm was used to develop a quantum generative model. The content generated by the proposed quantum model indicated better probability distribution representation compared to the classical generative model with potential to improve pre-training computational speed and inference to serve users (Gao *et al* 2018). In addition, Ngo *et al* (2023) excellently covered a survey on quantum generative models. Significantly reducing the pre-training duration of the large language models with a quantum computer means the reduction of resources required to develop them. Therefore, the number of cores and energy consumption required at present to pre-train large language models and inferences to serve users will significantly reduce when run on quantum computers. The implication is that since the energy consumption is expected to reduce significantly, the carbon footprint currently experienced can drastically reduce, thus, contributing to sustainable AI solutions.

7.6.3.3 Quantum machine learning

Case studies illustrate the adaptation of standard algorithms to quantum versions, such as quantum convolutional neural networks versus traditional convolutional neural networks, quantum support vector machines versus support vector machines, and variational quantum classifiers versus support vector classifiers. Results show that quantum versions generally enhance performance (Zeguendry *et al* 2023). Surveys on quantum machine learning algorithms for solving problems from a computer science perspective are available in Peral-García *et al* (2024) and Zhang and Ni (2020). Another survey, focussing on quantum machine learning from a classical computing standpoint, is covered by Ciliberto *et al* (2018).

7.6.3.4 Quantum robotics

Quantum computing has the potential for applications in robotics science especially in the aspect of environment sensing such as perception, vision and data processing. In addition, it can be applied to kinematics and dynamic, 'thinking' ability and observations (Petschnigg *et al* 2019). A study of swarm robotics to establish the connection of each robot activity with the overall robotic swarm action was run on a quantum computer (Mannone *et al* 2022). A quantum-based path-planning algorithm for swarm robots was proposed. The logic gate is implemented using a quantum circuit as the Grover's search algorithm was run with a different quantum gate. The proposed swarm robots running on a quantum platform were deployed for search and rescue operations (Chella *et al* 2023). Another study designed quantum robots with quantum controller, quantum actuator and learning control algorithm for the quantum robots (Dong *et al* 2006). Surveys on quantum computing in robotics can be found in Haldorai (2024) and Petschnigg *et al* (2019).

7.6.3.5 Quantum brain–machine interface

Refer to chapter 6 for details about the brain–machine interface. Quantum computing is currently making waves in the area of the brain–machine interface similar to other topics in the area of AI. For example, quantum sensors are now used to solve the problem of brain metrology and this has been successful. Quantum technology is now the state-of-the-art direction aiming for practical technology to solve the limitations of the traditional brain–machine interface such as coding of electrophysiological signals in effective defining of the brain interface. Photons provide extraordinary resolution capabilities, non-invasive, multiplexed and spatio-temporal, to enhance the deeper penetration of the brain for more understanding of the neural and brain interfaces (Liao *et al* 2024). A quantum learning algorithm with different qubits and quantum circuits together with EEG signals has been deployed for the diagnose of schizophrenia. The quantum approach demonstrates superior performance and effectiveness (Aksoy *et al* 2024). The variational quantum circuit with features extraction and quantum genetic algorithm were used for the electro-encephalography-based motor imagery classification (Olvera *et al* 2024). For detailed information and more understanding of the integration of quantum computing and the brain–machine interface, refer to the discussion on quantum computing in neuroscience in Glisic and Lorenzo, (2024) and quantum sensing in (Liao *et al* 2024).

7.7 Decentralized blockchain technology

Often in some books, the distributed ledger technology is a synonymous term with blockchain. The distributed ledger technology is referred to the aspect of the blockchain technology that is distributed and decentralized. Distributed ledger technology enables secure maintenance of the ledger to depend on the computer network for authentication instead of relying on a centralized authority (e.g., a bank). In view of this broadcast, much of the transaction information can be in multiple systems with individuals or organizations but there exists no master copy of the transactions information with any central authority or individual (Michael *et al* 2018). The benefits of the blockchain are classified into decentralization, immutability, finality, smart contracts, provenance and consensus-driven approach, with the summarized main points as shown in figure 7.18.

The systematic collection of transactions is referred to as a ledger. Before the digital age, paper and pen had been the major means of keeping transaction records, known as a ledger, before its digitalization suitable for manipulation in a database. The database is typically owned, maintained and operated by central authorities as a third party on behalf of the users or customers community (Yaga *et al* 2019). The

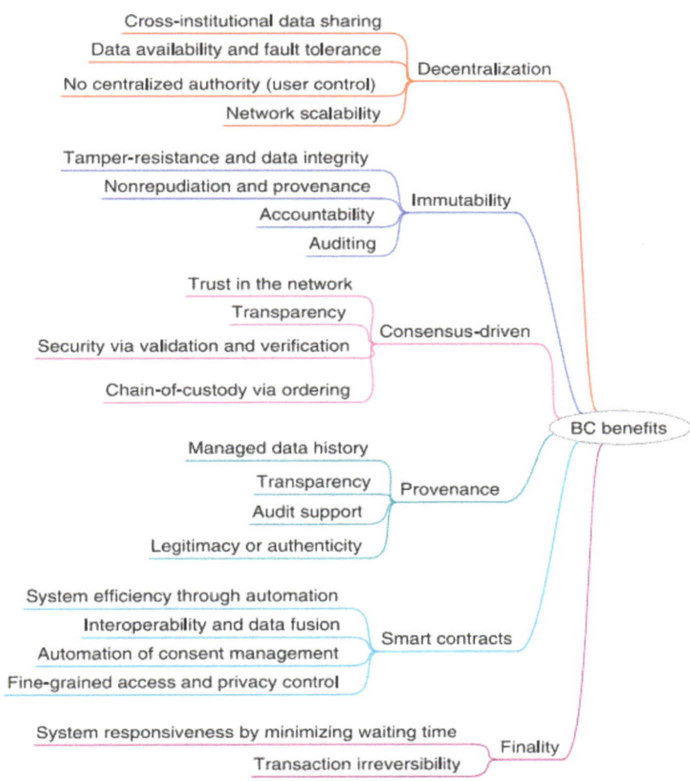

Figure 7.18. Visual representation of the benefits of blockchain technology. Reprinted from Marijan and Lal (2022), copyright (2022) with permission from Elsevier.

foundation of blockchain technology is the distributed ledger technology that provides a mechanism for consensus validation on the computer network to enable peer-to-peer transactions without requiring central or immediate authority to manage the transactions information generated. Each of the transactions is validated and added as a 'block' together with a group of validated transactions. The block is added as a new block in an existing transaction chain giving birth to the blockchain referring to the name of the technology. Generally, in this type of blockchain transactions, added transactions are immune to alteration or deletion, meaning no deletion or alteration after the transaction is completed and update is possible only with consensus (Michael *et al* 2018).

7.7.1 Flow of decentralized blockchain technology operation

The step-by-step operations of decentralized blockchain technology are outlined in simple terms to help readers understand how blockchain operates to achieve its goals. Figure 7.19 illustrates the entire operational process, making it easier to follow each stage alongside the corresponding textual description. The operation begins with block or transaction creation, followed by broadcasting, validation and verification, appending the block, competing to add the next block, creating a new block with a hash code, and finally, block alteration or deletion.

7.7.1.1 Block creation

A transaction or block is created by the buyer with detailed information about the business deal (Financial Times Report 2021). The block contains the following attributes, version of the block (rules to follow in validating the block), merkle tree root hash (transaction hash values in the block), Nonce (a field with 4 bits that typically begins with 0 and increases at every hash computation), parent block hash (the hash value with 256 bits pointing to the previous block), timestamp (current time at transaction period) and nBits (target of the hash in compact format) (Zheng *et al* 2018). Cryptography is the process of scrambling a message or data to make it

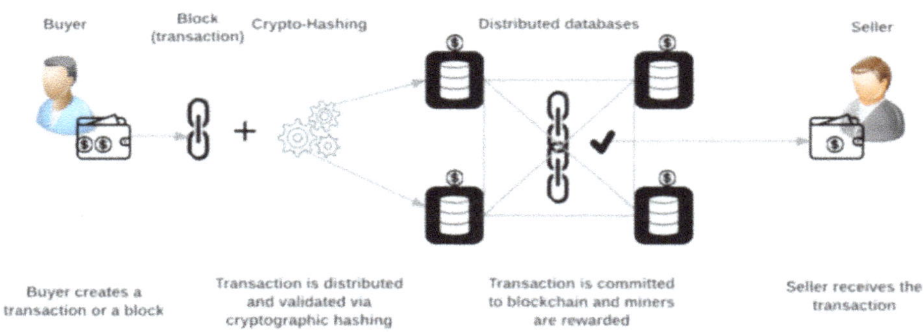

Figure 7.19. Stages involved in blockchain technology operational processes. This [Blockchain-Process] image has been obtained by the author from the Wikimedia website where it was made available by [B140970324] under a CC BY-SA 4.0 licence. It is included within this book on that basis. It is attributed to [B140970324].

appear meaningless, using cryptographic algorithms (e.g., transforming ‘I will send you money today’ into ‘zx569_^%#@!6tg/.,l;’[p]\’;.,”) as a way of protecting a message or data from unauthorized access. The cryptographic algorithm converts the data or message into an unreadable format during transmission over the network. At the receiving end, the scrambled message or data is converted back to its original form, making it understandable and accessible to the intended recipient.

7.7.1.2 Broadcast

Broadcasting communications allows the message sent to be received and kept by all the nodes on the network with the exception of the sending node. As a result of sending messages to all nodes, it generates high network traffic. A special address is used for receiving the broadcast message. However, it is not all the nodes on the network that may wish to receive the broadcast message and not all will be willing to broadcast especially sensitive messages. The broadcast could be sent to all nodes within the same network (limited broadcast) or small group of nodes on a network (directed broadcast) or nodes on small network having the same network address created on a large network (subnet broadcast). The nodes that received the message verify to ensure it matches their IP addresses, if yes the message is kept else discarded (Forouzan 2007, Tutorial 2023). In the blockchain operation, a record of the transaction is broadcast to the computers (nodes) on the peer-to-peer computer network (Financial Times Report 2021).

7.7.1.3 Validation and verification

Anonymity is one of the strong features of blockchain but also a weak point as regards trust. Can we 100% trust anonymous users for adding transactions to the ledger? In response to this concern, each transaction must be validated to ensure it is legitimate and free from double spending, malicious acts, etc before it is added to the block (Guo and Yu 2022). The process of the validation involves verifying the sender’s wallet address as well as checking the balance in the wallet to ensure sufficient funds for the intended transaction. Subsequently, the recipient address is verified to ensure its validity on the blockchain network. Also, a timestamp and other criteria may be added as means of validation (SoluLab 2024). The computers on the peer-to-peer network use the power of their computing capacity to validate a record of the transaction by running algorithms to solve cryptographic puzzles (Financial Times Report 2021).

7.7.1.4 Appending block

A validated transaction record is added to other records to generate a new block of data (Financial Times Report 2021). A consensus algorithm is typically applied to add a block to the blockchain through agreement. The consensus algorithm assumes that the majority of the users on the blockchain network are honest and willing to keep the sanctity of the blockchain. The heart-beat of the blockchain transactions is the consensus algorithm as it is used to build trust and store transactions on blocks (Guo and Yu 2022).

7.7.1.5 Competing to add the next block

All the computers or nodes on the network can access the information to start competing to be the next to validate the record of the new transaction before adding it to the block creating a chain of blocks (Financial Times Report 2021).

7.7.1.6 New block with hash code

The new block containing a hash as a unique code is added to the blockchain. The hash of the previous block in the chain is also contained in the new block. This is to prove that the chain is in the correct order and remains together (Financial Times Report 2021).

7.7.1.7 Block alteration or deletion

Attempts to alter or delete a block will trigger the block hash to change, therefore creating a difference with the hash held by the next block in the chain. This means that to maintain the chain intact all the successive hash codes need to be recomputed. This process requires extreme computational power. In practice, the blockchain is unchanged (i.e. it cannot be altered or deleted) (Financial Times Report 2021). This phonomemon is posing a challenge to increasing usage of blockchain and storage of dark data, thus, selective deletion is introduced to mitigate this challenge. The solution is devised by extending the funcitonality of the conensus algorithm to create the summary of previous chain data regularly and store again in a new block discarding irrelevant information. This process provides the opportunity for blocks to be deleted at the beginning of the blockchain (Hillmann *et al* 2020).

7.7.2 Types of blockchain networks

The operation of the blockchain discussed in the preceding section is categorized into permissionless (public blockchain network), permissioned (private blockchain network) strictly for a particular group of users and a consortium (private blockchain network) for certain organizations and individuals. Permissionless is like the internet where everyone with a device connected to the internet has access, and permissioned is similar to an intranet where access is restricted to members.

7.7.2.1 Permissionless blockchain network

This type of blockchain network is a decentralize network where anyone interested can publish a block without restriction or requesting for permission from any authority. It is open source software and freely available for download by anyone wishing to download. In view of the fact that anyone can publish a block it indicates that the blockchain can be read by anyone and anyone can create a transaction on the blockchain. The ledger can be read and written by any blockchain network user. As the permissionless blockchain is open to all, the chances of malicious user intrusion to compromise the blockchain exists. Therefore, a multi-party agreement where users are required to spend or maintain resources before publishing a block is used to mitigate the activities of malicious users (Kim *et al* 2020).

7.7.2.2 Permissioned blockchain network

The permissioned blockchain is restricted or permission is required by authorities either centralized or decentralized to be issued to the user before publishing blocks. Thus, issuing transactions or read access for maintaining the blockchain can be restricted to authorized users only or anyone deemed fit. Open source software or propriety software can be used to instantiate and maintain the permissioned blockchain network. Unlike the permissionless blockchain network, a permissioned blockchain doesn't require users to spend or maintain resources before publishing a block. Identity of the users of this type of blockchain is established as members, hence, creating a certain level of trust among the members (Kim *et al* 2020).

7.7.3 Cryptocurrency

Blockchain technology has applications in different areas such as but not limited to electronic voting, health, security and privacy, telecommunications, logistics and supply chain management, unmanned aerial vehicles and procurement process. However, this chapter focusses on the application of blockchain technology in currency because of its potential to democratize the distribution of wealth.

The founding application of the blockchain technology is the decentralized currency implemented with Bitcoin (figure 7.20). Cryptocurrencies are the currencies based on blockchain technology, classified into two major groups, namely, coins and tokens. The two differ in a such a way that the coins run on their own blockchain technology separately, whereas tokens run on blockchain technology that is already existing. For example, Ethereum has coins running on Ethereum blockchain technology. On the other hand, cryptocurrencies including Binance coin, Maker, Tether USD and basic attention are running on Ethereum blockchain technology already existing, as such, they are referred to as tokens. Coins serve the purpose of currency, whereas a token is typically a product asset, an investment, service, or rights representation. The value of cryptocurrency is directly proportional to the trust people have in the particular cryptocurrency (CoinMarketCap 2019).

The cryptocurrencies that are highly accepted are open source. A computational process is used to generate new coins through a consensus algorithm by the

Figure 7.20. Bitcoin BTC virtual currency. This [Bitcoin BTC Golden coins 8K wallpaper] image has been obtained by the author from the Wikimedia website where it was made available by [Satheesh Sankaran] under a CC BY-SA 2.0 licence. It is included within this book on that basis. It is attributed to [Satheesh Sankaran].

community of a particular cryptocurrency to form the immutable blockchain of the cryptocurrency. Thousands of cryptocurrencies are in circulation with many of them having over US $1 billion surpassing market capitalization (CoinMarketCap 2019).

7.7.3.1 Crypto mining, miners and the reward system

Mining is the process of finding correct proofs in solving functions of cryptography (in simple terms, mining refers to the verification of a block and adding the verified block to the blockchain). The computer (node) or participants involved in the process are called miners. Brute force is the only approach to solve the cryptographic function because of the one-way characteristics of cryptography. Therefore, the machine with the most powerful CPU has high chances of solving the function with the consensus algorithm, say, proof-of-work. An incentive in the form of a reward is awarded to the miner who solves the mathematical function using computational power and consumed electricity. The award is a newly minted coin also known as a block reward. The miners compete in finding the correct hash value through adjusting a difficult algorithm to ensure consistent block intervals. The difficulty in the proof-of-work algorithm adjustment is intentional as a form of security to prevent malicious users from flooding the network with messages and opens the opportunity for the convergence of honest nodes to a cohesive view (Kiayias and Panagiotakos 2015).

Miners play a significant role in many blockchain networks in the verification of transactions. In a multi-transactions block, a mining reward is awarded to the miner who verified a transaction successfully within the block. Cryptocurrencies such as Bitcoin, Ethereum, etc are the reward. The integrity of the blockchain network is maintain by the miners through mining to reward the miners for accurately validating transactions. In addition to minted coins, transactions fees or a combination of both can be the rewards (SoluLab 2024). The 21 million BTC is the maximum number of Bitcoins, if a miner finds the nonce value that correctly merges difficulty and the block accepted successfully, the miner is incentivized with US $24 and US $31 as transaction fees and 6.25 BTC as a mining reward (Guo and Yu 2022).

7.7.3.2 Crypto mining algorithms

A consensus protocol is the set of rules regulating the activities of the participants in view of the fact that there is no trusted third party. Thus, the consensus protocol is serving as the distributed consensus mechanism enforcing the protocol on all the users to agree on the current state of the blockchain. The consensus protocol is designed based on scarce resources, implying that the more the control over the scarce resources the more the control over the operations of the blockchain. Many consensus algorithms are in existence including but not limited to delegated proof-of-state, practical byzantine fault tolerance, proof-of-work, scalable byzantine, directed acyclic graph, proof of authority, proof of elapsed time, proof-of-state, tendermint, ripple, proof-of-importance and proof of capacity. However, proof-of-work, proof-of-state and delegated proof-of-state, are the most popular and common consensus algorithms (Guo and Yu 2022). The most popular among the three algorithms is the proof-of-work as it currently accounts for over 90% of the cryptocurrencies' total capitalization (Gervais *et al* 2016). Each consensus algorithm is suitable for a particular group of cryptocurrencies or a particular cryptocurrency, for example, proof-of-work (SHA-256) is suitable for mining Bitcoin, proof-of-work (Ethash) for Ethereum, proof-of-work (scrypt) for Litecoin, proof-of-work (SHA-256) for Bitcoin cash, proof-of-stake (Ouroboros algorithm) for Cardano (Kiayias and Panagiotakos 2015).

7.7.3.3 Maximizing crypto profits through accelerators

The emergence of mining kicked off slowly with a small number people mining crypto on systems equipped with CPUs. At that time, miners mainly relied on general-purpose CPUs for mining operations. The profits typically gained by miners started attracting new miners at an unprecedented speed to join the mining operations, prompting the mining operations to become complex, sophisticated and intricate. Therefore, demand for a system with better performance to cope with the increasing volume of mining operations and data increased significantly. As a result, the profits started to depend on the effectiveness and efficiency of the system used for the mining operations. Thus, miners begin to look for alternative processors to maximize profits. This led miners to find benefit in GPUs systems with superior mining power over CPUs, estimated to have nearly 30 times more mining power. This made the crypto miners abandon CPUs and switch en masse towards GPU systems prompting very high demand and pushing up the price. This motivated processor manufacturers to begin manufacturing processors suitable for mining operations offering better profits. As the mining operations kept on growing significantly, the GPU system started reaching its climax, demand reduced and prices fell back to normal market value. Field-programmable gate array emerged with superior mining power and profits better than with GPUs, thus attracting crypto miners to besiege field-programmable gate array as it provided $12 per day in profits. Another processor, AMD Zen 4 CPU become the darling of Qubic currency miners in view of the fact that it gave profits better than any other processor, driving the prices of the AMD Zen 4 CPU to go up outrageously, and subsequently it went out of stock. Similarly, CPU Ryzen 9 7950X is a darling processor among the miners because it gives $2 profits in a day, causing CPU Ryzen 9 7950X price to significantly shoot up beyond the reach of typical customers (Chiroma 2024).

A processor specifically designed for crypto mining known as application-specific integrated circuit targeting SHA-256 algorithm was suitable for mining Bitcoin and the Ethash algorithm was suitable for mining Ethereum. The application-specific integrated circuit is already a sought after processor among miners (Chiroma 2024). In another development, the AMD EPYC 9654 is a processor within the family of the fourth generation AMD EPYC with data centre-grade power. It is the current hottest processor profitable for mining Monero and other crypto using a RandomX algorithm costing about $5000. Despite the shift from mining with general-purpose CPUs mining, up to now there have been no cryptocurrencies using RandomX algorithm suitable for mining using CPUs such as Monero, Epic cash, quantum resistance ledger and Zephy (Wind 2024). Application-specific integrated circuits mine more efficiently than GPUs and CPUs because they are specifically designed to accelerate mining operations, unlike CPUs and GPUs, which are built to handle multiple tasks (Cointelegraphs 2024). At the time of writing this chapter, some of the best dedicated application-specific integrated circuits-based miners include the Antminer S19 Pro, costing between US $10 000 and $20 000; the AvalonMiner 1246, priced at a minimum of $5000; the AvalonMiner A1166 Pro, costing between US $2000 and $3000; the WhatsMiner M30S++, priced at US $10 000–$14000; the Ebang EBIT E11++, starting at US $2000; and the Bitmain Antminer S5, with a price tag of US $500. These powerful machines are highly profitable for Bitcoin mining (Beincrypto 2024). The mining activities contribute to heavy energy consumption as a result of the extreme computational power expended in cryptocurrency mining or the validation process. This therefore contributes to the carbon footprint.

7.8 Carbon-aware computing

Supercomputers consume enormous amounts of energy to power them (Mann 2020). The tremendous energy consumption has been the challenge in powering supercomputers in data centres expecting exascale supercomputers to need 10s of MGw electricity power (Gao *et al* 2021). The foundation for ensuring sustainable AI is gaining understanding of the cost related to the environment involved in developing AI models, especially in the pre-training phase. The pre-training of the large language models raises concern over green gas emissions with the danger of harming the environment caused by the pre-training phase of the model development. The emissions of carbon dioxide caused by the pre-training phase call for discussion to drive safe AI development (Liu and Yin 2024).

The resources required to drive research and practice in AI and support its operation have skyrocketed as a result of growing demand for AI (Zhao *et al* 2022). The energy demand for data centres is expected to increase to between 3% and 4% at the end of this decade against current data centres global power consumption of between 1% and 2%. It is forecasted that in Europe and USA, the growing demand for power will assist in generating power never emerging before. In view of the huge energy consumption, between 2022 and 2030, the data centres' carbon emissions (figure 7.20) may more than double. Despite the growing workload at data centres, for years the power consumption had been stable until the slow gain in power efficiency coupled with the AI boom that triggered unpreceded demands for power at the data centres, which is expected to increase by 160% by the year 2030. However, the computing speed can be boosted by some of the innovations in AI faster than the electricity consumption, though the increasing demand for AI products is directly proportional to the increase in power consumption by the technology. Generally, AI-driven power demand in data centres could reach 200 terawatt-hours (TWh) annually by 2030, with AI expected to account for almost 19% of data centre energy needs by 2028 (Goldman Sachs Research 2024). Similarly, Gordon (2024) estimates AI industries' energy use may grow by between 85 to 134 TWh per year starting in 2027. It is found that supercomputers can worsen carbon dioxide emission, especially in the city or region where the data centre is located (Yang and Wang 2023).

In 2020, Microsoft with heavy investment in OpenAI and offering generative AI products recently announced an increase in carbon dioxide footprint (figure 7.21) with an almost 30% surge as a result of expanding its data centre. In 2023, Google experienced an increase of 50% of carbon emission more than the 2019 fiscal year because of energy demand (Kemene *et al* 2024).

Figure 7.21. Carbon emission at industrial scale illustrating relationship with AI. This [Air Emissions and Pollutants - Mining Company (48659848652)] image has been obtained by the author from the Wikimedia website where it was made available by [Tony Webster] under a CC BY 2.0 licence. It is included within this book on that basis. It is attributed to [Tony Webster].

7.8.1 Large language model energy consumption and carbon footprint lifecycle

The carbon footprint of large language models arises from two main phases: operational and embodied. The operational carbon footprint results from energy consumed during hardware operations, while the embodied carbon footprint originates from the energy used in hardware manufacturing (Gupta *et al* 2021). The emission of carbon dioxide from every aspect of the lifecycle of large language models is significant. The carbon footprint cycle of the large language models, as shown in figure 7.22, indicates the different phases of the carbon emission footprint lifecycle. Even if the large language model is idle without any computing operations, it still emits carbon dioxide because of the hardware allocated to the model although

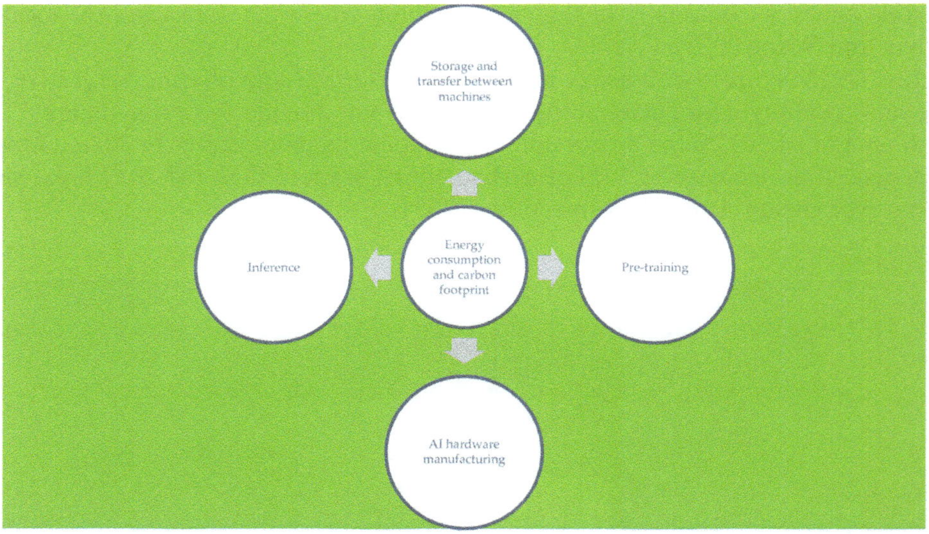

Figure 7.22. The lifecycle of large language model carbon footprint.

it is idle. It is estimated that the lifecycle of large language models contribute at least 24%–35% of the total carbon footprint (Faiz *et al* 2023).

7.8.1.1 Pre-training

The energy consumption needed for running a machine learning model is a function of the AI algorithm, the program executing it, the number of computational units running the program as well as the computational speed and power of the processors. In addition, the efficiency of the data centre in energy delivery, cooling of the computational processors and mixture of the energy sources such as but not limited to renewable, coal and gas, also contribute to energy required to run machine learning model (Patterson *et al* 2021). It is well known that machine learning consumes a significant amount of energy, especially when pre-training large language models, as it demands intensive resources. The pre-training of such models requires energy extensive processes, very high volume of data and often takes substantial time to complete on high-performance computing systems or supercomputers.

During the course of the pre-training period for a large language model, the CPUs and GPUs, data processing units continue running without a stop until they finish, consuming a significant amount of energy. For example, the pre-training of GPT-3 consumed electricity with the capacity of 1.3 GWh. As the model become more complex the energy consumption increased making the pre-training of GPT-4 consume 62.3 GWh of power (Todorović 2024).

The carbon emissions from machine learning modelling are a function of the time it takes to pre-train the model, type of the hardware, provider and the environment. The models emit different intensity of carbon because the modelling times differ depending on the time taken to pre-train the model and capacity of the model in parameters. It has been proven that models with different parameters emit different intensity of carbon dioxide and take different amounts of time to complete pre-training (Savci and Das 2023). The pre-training of the T5 large language model emits 40% more carbon dioxide than a return flight from San Francisco to New York (Faiz *et al* 2023).

7.8.1.2 Inference

The process where a user or customer prompts a generative model to generate content such as text, images, videos, voice, or multimodal outputs, is referred to as inference. Typically, inference starts after the foundation model has been fine-tuned into a chatbot and deployed to serve users or customers.

Every day, ChatGPT consumes 500 000 KWh of electricity in servicing almost 200 million requests. The daily use of power by ChatGPT is enough to power almost 180 000 households in USA (Gordon 2024). In a year, ChatGPT consumed 226.8 GWh of electricity to respond to 78 billion prompts. Each query in ChatGPT is estimated to consume electricity of 2.9 Wh almost 10 times that of the typical search in Google (Todorović 2024). This is a source of concern in view of the tremendous growing innovations in generative AI (refer to chapter 2 for details on generative AI) not from OpenAI alone but other technology giants or newcomers (e.g., Amazon, Microsoft, Nvidia, Anthropic and Cohere) (Gordon 2024). The large language model inference can emit more carbon dioxide compared to pre-training. The carbon footprint produced by GPT-4 inferences for 121 days equate to the carbon footprint emitted during the period of the GPT-4 pre-training (Achiam *et al* 2023). Most companies spend more energy on inference compared to pre-training. Both Nvidia and Amazon Web Services estimate that at least 80% of the workload for machine learning is on inference, indicating that the carbon footprint of inference is significant. The substantial role of inference triggers companies like Google, Nvidia, Alibaba and Amazon to design inference accelerators (Patterson *et al* 2021).

7.8.1.3 AI chip manufacturing

As a result of the AI boom, the demand for AI chips has significantly increased, leading to a rise in AI chip production, especially neural accelerators by different companies, including but not limited to Nvidia (GPUs), AMD (Ryzen AI), Intel (Neural processing unit), and Google (TPUs). For example, by 2027, Nvidia is expected to consume 85 to 134 TWh electricity for chip production (De Vries 2023). Consequently, energy consumption in these chip manufacturing companies has risen, contributing to higher carbon emissions.

The AI boom and demand for AI chips caused a surge in the market value of Nvidia never seen in the history of the company, and overtaking Amazon, with a market value of $1.78 trillion. It is the explosive demand for AI products that skyrocketed the demand for AI chips typically applied for AI applications to power large language models such as ChatGPT, robotics, metaverse, video analytics and medical imaging (Killa 2024). The production of AI chips involved procurement of raw materials, packaging, assembling and fabrication. All these stages consume energy (Gupta *et al* 2021). Carbon is emitted from fabrication of semiconductor parameters, consumption of energy per unit area at the course of production, the chemical used in the hardware manufacturing and sourcing for raw material for production (Faiz *et al* 2023).

7.8.1.4 Data storage and transfer between machines

Data storage consumes energy, the consumption of the energy is determined by the energy needed to power the disk for data storage and the energy consumed as a result of transferring the data between servers. The curated data comprised of pre-processed and raw data stored over a period of 6 months consumes 99 KWh of energy. The capacity of the bulk data is 210 TB stored for 24 h and consumed energy of 57 kWh. The bulk data becomes 25 TB after processing and storage for 6 months, consuming 1.3 MWh of power. The Noor model weights are 5.7 TB consuming energy of 0.3 MWh. 25 TB of data was transferred to a specific machine for archiving and transfer to a supercomputer for pre-training. The 5.7 TB Noor model was moved out of the supercomputer one time. Energy consumption from these processes resulted in a carbon footprint, with storage and transfer contributing 12% (Lakim *et al* 2022).

7.8.2 Sustainable supercomputing

The objective of green supercomputing is to address the high energy demands of supercomputers while enhancing performance and reliability by designing eco-friendly software, chips, and hardware. This approach introduces a multi-objective optimization challenge: maximizing performance while minimizing energy consumption to reduce environmental impact and carbon footprint.

Regulators are beginning to impose requirements for energy efficient systems to mitigate the surge in energy consumption. Development in technology is expected to reduce the extensive AI energy demand by improving the energy efficiency of workloads for AI applications. New accelerators and 3D chips are specialized hardware designed by researchers to improve performance and energy efficiency (Kemene *et al* 2024). The Superchip designed by Nvidia improved performance by 30 times when running generative AI tasks and consumed 25% less energy. The data centres are making efforts to become energy efficient. Also, alternative technologies for cooling systems, sites with better computation and cheap power as well as sustainability are explored to improve energy efficiency (Kemene *et al* 2024).

Many companies are actively working to incorporate renewable energy sources to help reduce their carbon footprint. The data centres are making frantic efforts to move to renewable energy sources. For example, the Meta Data Center is running on 97% renewable energy sources (Wu *et al* 2022). In another development, Google, Amazon and Microsoft are routing for nuclear, solar and wind with heavy investment as alternative sources of energy expected to start operations in 2030 (The Batch 2024). To encourage energy efficiency for supercomputers in data centres, supercomputers with top energy efficiency are ranked on a regular basis by Green Top 500. Figure 7.23 presents the top 10 green supercomputers representing those with the best energy efficiency in the list of green top 500 for the month of June 2024 with

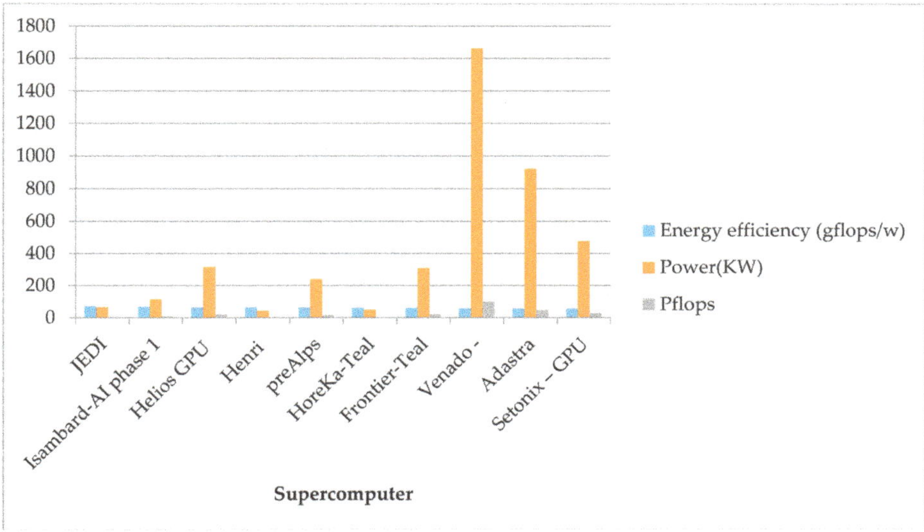

Figure 7.23. Ranking of supercomputers top 10 out of green TOP500 with JEDI topping the list and Setonix-GPU at number 10.

the JEDI at the number one spot and descending down to Setonix-GPU at number 10. Data was collected from the TOP500 website (TOP500 2024).

7.9 Case study

Case studies where these technologies are in practice in the real world are outlined. The case studies connect theory and practice for the reader to appreciate the role of the emerging technologies in human transformation.

7.9.1 OpenAI, Nvidia, Google and Meta

Supercomputers are distributed across various high-performance computers and data centres worldwide, supporting a range of operations and applications. Companies like OpenAI (ChatGPT-4), Google (Gemini), Meta (LLaMA 2), and Nvidia (NeMo) utilize supercomputers to pre-train their large language models before deploying these models to data centres for inference to serve users. The ChatGPT model you query or prompt to generate output is already operating on a supercomputer. Similarly, some of the noticeable high-performance computing centres include Oak ridge National Laboratory housing the Frontiers supercomputer, USA; Argonne National Laboratory with Aurora, USA; Microsoft Azure with the Eagle supercomputer, USA; EuroHPC/CSC housing the LUMI supercomputer, Finland; RIKEN Center for Computational Science housing the supercomputer Fugaku, Japan.

7.9.2 Clemenceau Medical Center Hospital, Dubai

At the Clemenceau Medical Center Hospital in Dubai, the Davinci XI robotic system is available for performing surgery. The medical team uses the robot to perform general surgery like robotic gastric and oesophageal operations, including solid organ robotic surgery. The Davinci XI robotic surgery platform is also used for performing gynaecologist operations for women to remove uterus and fibroid (CMCH 2024).

7.9.3 Marathon digital holding and core scientific

Many companies are dedicated to mining Bitcoin, using powerful machines with high computing capabilities that consume substantial amounts of energy for mining operations. These companies invest heavily in infrastructure, hardware, and energy. Marathon Digital Holdings, with a hash rate of 29.9 EH/s, is considered one of the largest crypto mining companies in the world. Core Scientific is another major crypto mining company with significant investments in hardware and energy for Bitcoin mining. Both Core Scientific and Marathon Digital Holdings are located in the USA.

7.9.4 Quantum computer projects

Quantum computers exist mostly at the industrial scale with the giant technology companies at the forefront of the development. Quantum computers are currently under improvement and development at IBM International, Invidia, Intel, Google and QuTech.

7.10 Summary

This chapter provided insights into emerging AI applications in high-risk domains like medical technology and high-performance computing, including quantum computing, carbon-aware computing, fully autonomous robotic surgery, quantum supercomputing, and blockchain technology. It began by examining the use of autonomous robots in surgery, highlighting levels of autonomy from level 1 to level 5, with level 5 representing fully autonomous surgery. While full autonomy in robotic surgery remains conceptual, significant progress has been made toward achieving level 5 fully autonomous capabilities. Robotic surgery enabling technologies and practical applications readiness status for level 1–5 autonomy are summarized in the chapter.

Quantum computing utilizes qubits (0, 1, or both) for computation. The quantum computer is the combination of classical computing and quantum computation. The five layers of quantum computers include applications, classical, digital, analogue and quantum processing. They have already started penetrating AI with many applications from different perspectives such as quantum generative model, quantum transformer, quantum robotics, quantum machine learning, etc.

Blockchain technology is covered in a summarized form for quick understanding of the processes involved. The operation of the blockchain network is provided from block creation to block alteration or deletion. The applications of blockchain in currency leading to cryptocurrency are discussed including cryptocurrency mining, miners, the reward system, mining algorithms and maximizing cryptocurrency profits through accelerators.

This chapter covers high-performance computing systems at the exascale level (i.e., exascale supercomputers operating at exaflops), including cluster systems and platforms, to help readers understand the importance of high-performance computing in the AI boom. An overview of supercomputer OS highlights the dominance of Linux and Unix in both performance and system share. The top scale of supercomputers remains the exascale with the Frontier supercomputer occupying the number one spot on the TOP500 ranking as of June 2024, but Japan has announced a five-year plan for a zettascale supercomputer project to be completed in 2030. The substantial energy demand to power supercomputers for AI models, such as large language models, sparks discussions on carbon-aware computing. The carbon footprint lifecycle of large language models include the following phases: pre-training, inference, data storage and movement, and AI chip manufacturing.

Many of the emerging technologies remain at the concept, proof-of-concept, or trial stages, while others are ready for practice but have yet to be applied in real-world practice. Some AI applications are already in active use but associated with unresolved challenges that are expected to be addressed in the future.

References

Achiam J, Adler S, Agarwal S, Ahmad L, Akkaya I, Aleman F L and McGrew B 2023 Gpt-4 technical report *arXiv preprint* arXiv:2303.08774 (accessed 2 November 2024)

Aksoy G, Cattan G, Chakraborty S and Karabatak M 2024 Quantum machine-based decision support system for the detection of schizophrenia from EEG records *J. Med. Syst.* **48** 29

Amin M H, Andriyash E, Rolfe J, Kulchytskyy B and Melko R 2018 Quantum boltzmann machine *Phys. Rev.* **8** 021050

Attanasio A, Scaglioni B, De Momi E, Fiorini P and Valdastri P 2021 Autonomy in surgical robotics *Annu. Rev. Control Robot. Auton. Syst.* **4** 651–79

Baker H 2024 Japan to start building 1st 'zeta-class' supercomputer in 2025, 1,000 times more powerful than today's fastest machines *Live Sci.* https://livescience.com/technology/computing/japan-to-start-building-1st-zeta-class-supercomputer-in-2025-1000-times-more-powerful-than-todays-fastest-machines (accessed 2 November 2024)

Beincrypto 2024 The 7 Best Cryptocurrency Mining Hardware for 2024 https://beincrypto.com/learn/best-cryptocurrency-mining-hardware/ (accessed 9 November 2024)

Benedetti M, Realpe-Gómez J and Perdomo-Ortiz A 2018 Quantum-assisted Helmholtz machines: a quantum–classical deep learning framework for industrial datasets in near-term devices *Quantum Sci. Technol.* **3** 034007

Berthet-Rayne P, Gras G, Leibrandt K, Wisanuvej P, Schmitz A, Seneci C A and Yang G-Z 2018 The i^2*Snake* robotic platform for endoscopic surgery *Ann. Biomed. Eng.* **46** 1663–75

Chambers-Jones C 2021 AI, big data, quantum computing, and financial exclusion: tempering enthusiasm and offering a human-centric approach to policy *FinTech, Artificial Intelligence and the Law* (Routledge) pp 193–210

Chauhan V, Negi S, Jain D, Singh P, Sagar A K and Sharma A K 2022 Quantum computers: a review on how quantum computing can boom AI *2022 2nd Int. Conf. on Advance Computing and Innovative Technologies in Engineering (ICACITE)* (Piscataway, NJ: IEEE) pp 559–63

Chella A, Gaglio S, Mannone M, Pilato G, Seidita V, Vella F and Zammuto S 2023 Quantum planning for swarm robotics *Rob. Autom. Syst.* **161** 104362

Chen I C, Singh H, Anukruti V L, Quanz B and Yogaraj K 2024 A survey of classical and quantum sequence models *2024 16th Int. Conf. on COMmunication Systems and NETworkS (COMSNETS)* (Piscataway, NJ: IEEE) pp 1006–11

Cherrat E A, Kerenidis I, Mathur N, Landman J, Strahm M and Li Y Y 2024 Quantum vision transformers *Quantum* **8** 1265

Chiroma H 2024 Influence of Computer Processor on maximizing crypto mining profits *Daily Trust* https://dailytrust.com/influence-of-computer-processor-on-maximizing-crypto-mining-profits/ (accessed 6 November 2024)

Ciliberto C, Herbster M, Ialongo A D, Pontil M, Rocchetto A, Severini S and Wossnig L 2018 Quantum machine learning: a classical perspective *Proc. R. Soc. A: Math., Phys. Eng. Sci.* **474** 20170551

Clemenceau Medical Center Hospital (CMCH) 2024 Robotics Center of Excellence https://cmcdubai.ae/ (accessed 10 November 2024)

CoinMarketCap 2019 https://coinmarketcap.com. (accessed 10 November 2024)

Cointelegraphs 2024 ASICs vs. Quantum Rigs: The Future of Cryptocurrency Mining https://cointelegraph.com/learn/asics-vs-quantum-rigs-evolution-in-mining-hardware (accessed 9 November 2024)

Connor M J, Dasgupta P, Ahmed H U and Raza A 2020 Autonomous surgery in the era of robotic urology: friend or foe of the future surgeon ? *Nat. Rev. Urol.* **17** 643–9

De Vries A 2023 The growing energy footprint of artificial intelligence *Joule* **7** 2191–4

Dong D, Chen C, Zhang C and Chen Z 2006 Quantum robot: structure, algorithms and applications *Robotica* **24** 513–21

Faiz A, Kaneda S, Wang R, Osi R, Sharma P, Chen F and Jiang L 2023 Llmcarbon: Modeling the end-to-end carbon footprint of large language models *arXiv preprint* arXiv:2309.14393

Fan Z, Qiu F, Kaufman A and Yoakum-Stover S 2004 GPU cluster for high performance computing *SC'04: Proc. of the 2004 ACM/IEEE conference on Supercomputing* (Piscataway, NJ: IEEE) pp 47–7

Financial Times Report 2021 Blockchain: A Clickable Guide https://ft.com/content/52c98479-e50a-4cb0–9f88-a427f1818e28 (accessed 7 December 2024)

Forouzan B A 2007 *Data Communications and Networking* (Huga Media)

Gao J, Zheng F, Qi F, Ding Y, Li H, Lu H and You H 2021 Sunway supercomputer architecture towards exascale computing: analysis and practice *Sci. China Inform. Sci.* **64** 141101

Gao X, Zhang Z Y and Duan L M 2018 A quantum machine learning algorithm based on generative models *Sci. Adv.* **4** eaat9004

Gerofi B, Ishikawa Y, Riesen R and Wisniewski R W (ed) 2019 *Operating Systems for Supercomputers and High Performance Computing* (Singapore: Springer)

Gervais A, Karame G O, Wüst K, Glykantzis V, Ritzdorf H and Capkun S 2016 On the security and performance of proof of work blockchains *Proc. of the 2016 ACM SIGSAC Conference on Computer and Communications Security* pp 3–16

Glisic S and Lorenzo B 2024 Quantum computing and neuroscience for 6G/7G networks: survey *Intell. Syst. Appl.* **23** 200346

Goldman Sachs Research 2024 AI is poised to drive 160% increase in data center power demand *Goldman Sachs* https://goldmansachs.com/insights/articles/AI-poised-to-drive-160-increase-in-power-demand (accessed 1 November 2024)

Gordon C 2024 ChatGPT and generative AI innovations are creating sustainability Havoc *Forbes Magazine* https://forbes.com/sites/cindygordon/2024/03/12/chatgpt-and-generative-ai-innovations-are-creating-sustainability-havoc/ (accessed 1 November 2024)

Guo H and Yu X 2022 A survey on blockchain technology and its security *Blockchain: Res. Appl.* **3** 100067

Guo N, Yu Z, Agrawal A and Rebentrost P 2024 Quantum linear algebra is all you need for transformer architectures *arXiv preprint* arXiv:2402.16714

Gupta U, Kim Y G, Lee S, Tse J, Lee H H S, Wei G Y and Wu C J 2021 Chasing carbon: the elusive environmental footprint of computing *2021 IEEE Int. Symp. on High-Performance Computer Architecture (HPCA)* (Piscataway, NJ: IEEE) pp 854–67

Gyongyosi L and Imre S 2019 A survey on quantum computing technology *Comput. Sci. Rev.* **31** 51–71

Hager G and Wellein G 2010 *Introduction to High Performance Computing for Scientists and Engineers* (Boca Raton, FL: CRC Press)

Haldorai A 2024 Advancements and applications of quantum computing in robotics *J. Comput. Natur. Sci.* **2** 53–63

Han J, Davids J, Ashrafian H, Darzi A, Elson D S and Sodergren M 2022 A systematic review of robotic surgery: From supervised paradigms to fully autonomous robotic approaches *Int. J. Med. Robot. Comput. Assist. Surg.* **18** e2358

Hillmann P, Knüpfer M, Heiland E and Karcher A 2020 Selective deletion in a blockchain *2020 IEEE 40th Int. Conf. on Distributed Computing Systems (ICDCS)* (Piscataway, NJ: IEEE) pp 1249–56

Iftikhar M, Saqib M, Zareen M and Mumtaz H 2024 Artificial intelligence: revolutionizing robotic surgery *Ann. Med. Surg.* **86** 5401–9

IonQ 2024 The Value of Classical Quantum Simulators https://ionq.com/resources/the-value-of-classical-quantum-simulators#:~:text=Quantum%20simulators%E2%80%94software%20programs%20that,the%20world%20of%20quantum%20computing (accessed 7 November 2024)

Jaeger G 2007 Classical and quantum computing *Quantum Information: and overview* (Springer) pp 203–17

Kemene E, Valkhof B and Tiadi T 2024 AI and Energy: Will AI Help Reduce Emissions or Increase Demand? Here's What to Know https://weforum.org/stories/2024/07/generative-ai-energy-emissions/ (accessed 1 November 2024)

Khadhouri S *et al* 2018 The British Association of Urological Surgeons (BAUS) radical prostatectomy audit 2014/2015—an update on current practice and outcomes by centre and surgeon case-volume *BJU Int* **121** 886–92

Kiayias A and Panagiotakos G 2015 *Speed-Security Tradeoffs in Blockchain Protocols* (Cryptology ePrint Archive)

Killa S 2024 Nvidia Overtakes Amazon in Market Value: ETFs to Tap https://finance.yahoo.com/news (accessed 1 November 2024)

Kim H M, Turesson H, Laskowski M and Bahreini A F 2020 Permissionless and permissioned, technology-focused and business needs-driven: understanding the hybrid opportunity in blockchain through a case study of insolar *IEEE Trans. Eng. Manage.* **69** 776–91

Kitaev A Y, Shen A and Vyalyi M N 2002 *Classical and Quantum Computation* (Providence, RI: American Mathematical Society) (No. 47)

Lakim I, Almazrouei E, Abualhaol I, Debbah M and Launay J 2022 A holistic assessment of the carbon footprint of noor, a very large Arabic language model *Proc. of BigScience Episode# 5 —Workshop on Challenges and Perspectives in Creating Large Language Models* pp 84–94

Lee A, Baker T S, Bederson J B and Rapoport B I 2024 Levels of autonomy in FDA-cleared surgical robots: a systematic review *NPJ Digital Med.* **7** 103

Lemos G B, Borish V, Cole G D, Ramelow S, Lapkiewicz R and Zeilinger A 2014 Quantum imaging with undetected photons *Nature* **512** 409–12

Liao K, Yang Z, Tao D, Zhao L, Pires N, Dorao C A and Jiang Z 2024 Exploring the intersection of brain–computer interfaces and quantum sensing: a review of research progress and future trends *Adv. Quantum Technol.* **7** 2300185

Liu V and Yin Y 2024 Green AI: exploring carbon footprints, mitigation strategies, and trade offs in large language model training *Disc. Artif. Intell.* **4** 49

Mann A 2020 Nascent exascale supercomputers offer promise, present challenges *Proc. Natl. Acad. Sci.* **117** 22623–5

Mannone M, Seidita V and Chella A 2022 Categories, quantum computing, and swarm robotics: a case study *Mathematics* **10** 372

Marijan D and Lal C 2022 Blockchain verification and validation: techniques, challenges, and research directions *Comput. Sci. Rev.* **45** 100492

Matsuoka S 2021 Fugaku and A64FX: the first exascale supercomputer and its innovative arm CPU *2021 Symp. on VLSI Circuits* (Piscataway, NJ: IEEE) pp 1–3

Meuer H, Strohmaier E, Dongarra J *et al* 2014 Top 500 supercomputer sites http://top500.org/

Michael J, Cohn A L A N and Butcher J R 2018 Blockchain technology *Journal* **1** 1–11

Moustris G P, Hiridis S C, Deliparaschos K M and Konstantinidis K M 2011 Evolution of autonomous and semi-autonomous robotic surgical systems: a review of the literature *Int. J. Med. Robot. Comp. Assist. Surg* **7** 375–92

Ngo T A, Nguyen T and Thang T C 2023 A survey of recent advances in quantum generative adversarial networks *Electronics* **12** 856

Olvera C, Ross O M and Rubio Y 2024 EEG-based motor imagery classification with quantum algorithms *Expert Syst. Appl.* **247** 123354

Patterson D, Gonzalez J, Le Q, Liang C, Munguia L M, Rothchild D and Dean J 2021 Carbon emissions and large neural network training *arXiv preprint* arXiv:2104.10350

Peral-García D, Cruz-Benito J and García-Peñalvo F J 2024 Systematic literature review: quantum machine learning and its applications *Comput. Sci. Rev.* **51** 100619

Petschnigg C, Brandstötter M, Pichler H, Hofbaur M and Dieber B 2019 Quantum computation in robotic science and applications *2019 Int. Conf. on Robotics and Automation (ICRA)* (Piscataway, NJ: IEEE) pp 803–10

Rassweiler J J, Autorino R, Klein J, Mottrie A, Goezen A S, Stolzenburg J U and Liatsikos E 2017 Future of robotic surgery in urology *BJU Int.* **120** 822–41

Rayhan A and Rayhan S 2023 Quantum computing and AI: a quantum leap in intelligence *AI Odyssey: Unraveling the Past, Mastering the Present, and Charting the Future of Artificial Intelligence* (NotunKhabar)

Rico-Gallego J A, Díaz-Martín J C, Manumachu R R and Lastovetsky A L 2019 A survey of communication performance models for high-performance computing *ACM Comput. Surv. (CSUR)* **51** 1–36

Ristè D, Da Silva M P, Ryan C A, Cross A W, Córcoles A D, Smolin J A and Johnson B R 2017 Demonstration of quantum advantage in machine learning *npj Quantum Inform.* **3** 16

Saeidi H, Opfermann J D, Kam M, Wei S, Léonard S, Hsieh M H and Krieger A 2022 Autonomous robotic laparoscopic surgery for intestinal anastomosis *Sci. Robot.* **7** eabj2908

Savci P and Das B 2023 Comparison of pre-trained language models in terms of carbon emissions, time and accuracy in multi-label text classification using AutoML *Heliyon* **9** e15670

SoluLab 2024 Blockchain Verification Process: Ensuring Data Integrity https://solulab.com (accessed 9 November 2024)

Steane A 1998 Quantum computing *Rep. Prog. Phys.* **61** 117

Sterling T, Brodowicz M and Anderson M 2017 *High Performance Computing: Modern Systems and Practices* (San Mateo, CA: Morgan Kaufmann Publishers)

The Batch 2024 Amazon, Google, and Microsoft Bet on Nuclear Power to Meet AI Energy Demands (deeplearning.ai) https://deeplearning.ai/the-batch/amazon-google-and-microsoft-bet-on-nuclear-power-to-meet-ai-energy-demands/ (accessed 2 November 2024)

Todorović I 2024 ChatGPT Consumes Enough Power in One Year to Charge Over Three Million Electric Cars https://balkangreenenergynews.com/chatgpt-consumes-enough-power-in-one-year-to-charge-over-three-million-electric-cars/ (accessed 2 November 2024)

TOP500 2018 TOP500—The List https://top500.org/lists/2018/06/ (accessed 15 December 2024)

TOP500 2024 Top 500 list https://top500.org/ (accessed 3 November 2024)

Tutorial 2023 What is broadcasting in computer network? *GeeksforGeeks* https://geeksforgeeks.org/what-is-broadcasting-in-computer-network/ (accessed 9 December 2024)

Versluis R and Hagen C 2020 Quantum computers scale up: constructing a universal quantum computer with a large number of qubits will be hard but not impossible *IEEE Spectr.* **57** 24–9

Vienne J, Rosales C, Milfield K, Jeffers J and Reinders J (ed) 2015 Heterogeneous computing with MPI *High Performance Parallelism Pearls, Volume Two: Multicore and Many-Core Programming Approaches* (San Mateo, CA: Morgan Kaufmann Publishers) ch 13

Wang H, Liu P, Shao K, Li D, Gu J, Pan D Z and Han S 2023 Transformer-qec: Quantum error correction code decoding with transferable transformers (2023) *arXiv preprint* arXiv:2311.16082

Wind P 2024 5 Best CPUs for mining crypto in 2024 *CoinCodex* https://coincodex.com/article/45283/best-cpu-for-mining/ (accessed 7 December 2024)

Wu C J, Raghavendra R, Gupta U, Acun B, Ardalani N, Maeng K and Hazelwood K 2022 Sustainable AI: environmental implications, challenges and opportunities *Proc. Mach. Learn. Syst.* **4** 795–813

Yaga D, Mell P, Roby N and Scarfone K 2019 Blockchain technology overview *arXiv preprint* arXiv:1906.11078

Yang G Z, Cambias J, Cleary K, Daimler E, Drake J, Dupont P E and Taylor R H 2017 Medical robotics—regulatory, ethical, and legal considerations for increasing levels of autonomy *Sci. Robot.* **2** eaam8638

Yang H and Wang G 2023 The impact of computing infrastructure on carbon emissions: an empirical study based on China National Supercomputing Center *Environ. Res. Commun.* **5** 095015

Ying M 2010 Quantum computation, quantum theory and AI *Artif. Intell.* **174** 162–76

Yip M and Das N 2019 Robot autonomy for surgery *The Encyclopedia of MEDICAL ROBOTICS, Volume 1: Minimally Invasive Surgical Robotics* (World Scientific Publishing) pp 281–313

Zeguendry A, Jarir Z and Quafafou M 2023 Quantum machine learning: a review and case studies *Entropy* **25** 287

Zhang Y and Ni Q 2020 Recent advances in quantum machine learning *Quantum Eng.* **2** e34

Zhao D, Frey N C, McDonald J, Hubbell M, Bestor D, Jones M and Samsi S 2022 A green (er) world for AI *2022 IEEE Int. Parallel and Distributed Processing Symp. Workshops (IPDPSW)* (Piscataway, NJ: IEEE) pp 742–50

Zhao W X, Zhou K, Li J, Tang T, Wang X, Hou Y and Wen J R 2023 A survey of large language models *arXiv preprint* arXiv:2303.18223

Zheng Z, Xie S, Dai H N, Chen X and Wang H 2018 Blockchain challenges and opportunities: a survey *Int. J. Web Grid Serv.* **14** 352–75

Chapter 8

Explainable artificial intelligence tailored to emerging concepts linking human acceptability

The black-box nature of artificial intelligence (AI) models has motivated a growing interest in explainable AI (XIA), especially in recent times. At least 100 survey papers have been published from different perspectives of XAI, indicating the significant attention the field has generated. This chapter covers the procedure for the integration of XAI into AI-based models at different stages, including pre-modelling, modelling, and deployment. The chapter explores XAI tailored to generative AI, multimodal model, graph neural networks, large language models (LLMs), autonomous robots (autonomous vehicles and drones), brain–machine interfaces, and AI-assisted development and operations linking to human acceptability. Additionally, the chapter highlights industrial applications of XAI and presents relevant case studies (e.g., PayPal, MasterCard, LinkedIn, IBM). This XAI coverage can offer valuable insights for academic research and motivate practical AI model adoption in the real-world environment, as such, improving human acceptability.

8.1 Introduction

The goal of AI is to steer the fundamental theories for machine learning (ML) in developing autonomous software with the capability to learn from experience autonomously without human intervention in the loop (Shahriari *et al* 2015). AI has its foundation from computer science, a subset of computing before extending to include many other fields such as but not limited to physics, social science, linguistics, chemistry and philosophy. The emergence of XAI resulted from lack of explainability of ML complex black-box models. The root of XAI is from AI itself, the relationship among the major fields from computing to XAI is depicted in figure 8.1 for easy understanding.

doi:10.1088/978-0-7503-6320-4ch8

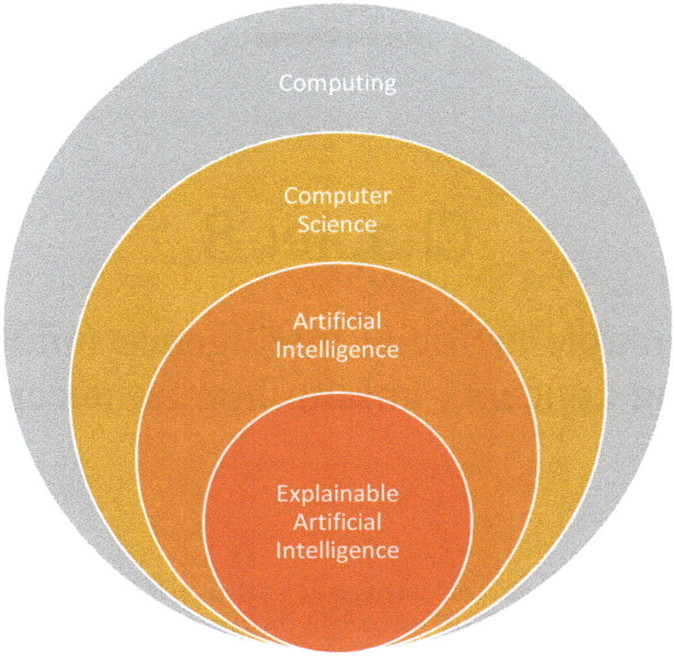

Figure 8.1. The relationship among computing, computer science, AI and XAI.

The fundamental problems related to explainability can be traced to the origin of AI itself. Despite the fact that the practical applications of AI play a critical role in different domains, the effectiveness of the applications remain limited because of the lack of an explainable module to explain the reasons behind the decision-making process in an understandable manner (Core *et al* 2006). AI projects for many decades depended on the reliability of human experts mixed with the knowledge of engineers. Both of them made the project clearly designed and easily understood by stakeholders. Take expert systems that are frequently based on decision trees, they are models for human decision-making, giving the opportunity for stakeholders to naturally understand (Yampolskiy 2019).

In recent times, XAI has been developed to mitigate the lack of explanation, transparency, and interpretation limitations of the conventional AI. Although AI has recorded a lot of success in different domains of applications, previously listed limitations on the processes used by AI models to reach certain decision remain a challenge. In resolving the challenges, AI is embedded with perceived ability, learning within a particular context, reasoning, and ability to have an abstract view to develop XAI. One of the AI algorithms that has received serious backlash for its black-box nature is the artificial neural networks and their variants with the new generation referred to as deep learning. With the advent of XAI, it is now possible to extract a relational explanation for deep learning, as evident in Townsend *et al* (2019), thereby allowing naïve people and developers to understand the internal working of the deep learning algorithm (Mankodiya *et al* 2022).

Montavon *et al* (2018) present instances of the problems surrounding the concept of interpretation in a learned deep learning algorithm. The neurons at the top layer of the network can represent the learned concept to be interpreted. The top layer neurons are not perceived by humans and they are abstract. However, both images and text as the input domain of the network are always interpretable (Montavon *et al* 2018). The training of deep learning algorithms on complex data is extremely difficult to interpret. This is because of the brute force interpolation on voluminous data instead of through high-level generalizable rule extraction (Elton 2020). The mathematical background of the model if understood, is intricate and it is impossible to explain how the internal working mechanism of the model operates to arrive at certain decisions (Holzinger *et al* 2017). As such XAI has been gaining enormous interest from academia and industry from different domains such as medical (Biffi *et al* 2020), engineering design (Sasaki *et al* 2021), the Choquet integral (Murray *et al* 2020), autonomous vehicles (Lu *et al* 2024), etc. The growing interest motivated the efforts in integrating explainability in deep learning networks, particularly in the domain of medicine and autonomous vehicles, areas considered high risk. The explanability can be useful for ensuring that the deep learning network operates with known rules and during recovering from failures (Elton 2020). The black-box nature of AI models is only addressed implicitly despite the tremendous interest generated by XAI (Holzinger *et al* 2017).

The field of XAI is rapidly growing at an unprecedented rate, with an influx of original research and survey articles (Holzinger *et al* 2017). At least 100 survey papers on different aspects of XAI have been published in the literature. This trend is expected to continue growing in the future due to the increasing interest in adopting intelligent systems in nearly all areas of society, coupled with the current AI boom and rapid adoption by industry, as well as the increasing need for AI-based system explainability by stakeholders.

In light of the significant interest in XAI from academia, industry, and developers, this chapter aims to discuss the concept of XAI, the procedures for developing AI models with explainability and interpretation, the relevant stakeholders, and many case studies. Mostly, XAI methods do not come as one solution to fit all but tailored in the context of each individual unique application requirement (Jiménez-Luna *et al* 2020). Therefore, the chapter explores XAI within the context of each individual emerging AI concept such as generative AI, graph neural networks (GNNs), autonomous robots, AI-assisted development and operations (AI-DevOps) and brain–machine interfaces (BMIs), providing readers with an opportunity to view XAI from a broad perspective within the framework of cutting-edge technologies.

8.1.1 Terminologies

The definitions of some important terminology (see figure 8.2) in the context of XAI as a prerequisite for better understanding the content of this chapter are explained as follows. **Interpretability**: this is the understanding of how the AI model operates to achieve its goal. **Explainability:** this refers to the explanation of the choices made by the model for different consumers. **Transparency**: this refers to the assessment of the

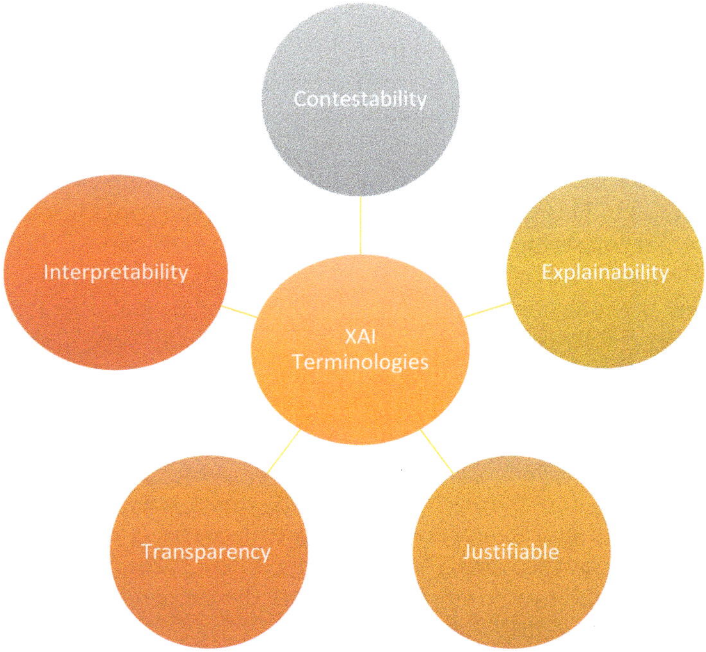

Figure 8.2. Explainable artificial intelligence terminologies.

model level of availability. **Justifiability**: the facts supporting the final decision made by the model. **Contestability**: this shows the way the model judgement can be challenged by the consumers (Saraswat *et al* 2022). The difference between the *explainability* and *interpretability* is that the former gives understanding to the relevant stakeholders to meet a criterion, whereas the latter is the level to which the insight provided by the explainability makes sense to the stakeholders' domain knowledge (Saeed and Omlin 2023).

8.2 Why explainable artificial intelligence?

The ability to provide clear explanations justifying the reasons behind decisions is a significant aspect of human intelligence, especially in social interactions. A person making decisions without explaining the rationale behind them may be seen as strange. This aspect of human intelligence extends to education, where it is critical, as learners seek to understand the reasons behind a teacher's decisions. Providing explanations is a prerequisite for establishing trust among people. For example, explanations given by medical doctors to patients regarding therapy decisions enhance trust (Xu *et al* 2019).

In the context of AI, explainability is crucial for understanding the internal workings of the AI model's decision-making process and for explaining the model's final decisions to users to build trust between the model and its stakeholders. Human acceptance and confidence on AI models is tied to understanding, interpretation,

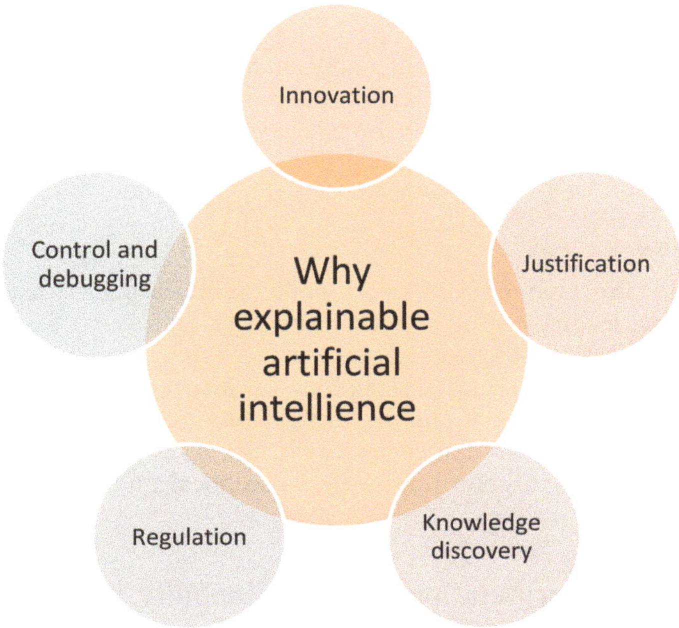

Figure 8.3. Reasons behind XAI.

and explainability of the model. The reasons for XAI as shown in figure 8.3 cut across different perspectives outlined as follows:

8.2.1 Justification

This is to explain the rationale behind the decisions made by the model, especially when the model produces significant or seemingly strange decisions. Providing such explanations helps improve confidence in the operations of the model (Adadi and Berrada 2018).

8.2.2 Control and debugging

Controlling the model enables the prevention of risks it might generate. An in-depth understanding of the model can increase visibility of unknown flaws that have the potential to harm the model or its users. Additionally, increased visibility facilitates the timely tracing of errors and debugging (Adadi and Berrada 2018).

8.2.3 Innovation

Gaining understanding of the deep neural network internal structure and working mechanism can give insight to stakeholders at the understanding stage to produce new architecture leading to innovations in the field of explainable deep neural networks (Pezzotti *et al* 2017).

8.2.4 Knowledge discovery

Visualization of the model output with understanding why the output appears as it is can lead to new knowledge. Likewise, humans can possibly learn new skills from the model by observing and understanding the behaviour of the model, especially in the case of games (Adadi and Berrada 2018).

8.2.5 Regulation

The demand for the responsible use of AI models is increasing, especially in this era of the AI boom, leading to the establishment of regulatory bodies to oversee AI adoption and mitigate misuse. Regulators and users cannot trust black-box models that provide decisions without explanations or interpretations of their internal workings. To meet regulatory criteria, explainable and interpretable models are required for deployment. No matter how sophisticated or accurate a model is, if it functions as a black-box, companies may be sceptical about adopting it due to regulatory concerns.

8.3 Integrating interpretation and explainability into machine learning models

The reason why many ML models face the problem of black-box is because the models are developed by pre-training of the algorithm directly from the dataset. In such a situation, the developers of the model cannot provide an explanation of how the model with complex functions of variables operates to achieve its goal (e.g., prediction) despite the fact that the input variables are available. Construction of interpretable models at the early phase of the modelling process can help prevent the black-box problem (Minh *et al* 2022). Figure 8.4 depicts the pipeline for developing black-box ML models without explainability. However, figure 8.5 presents a modified version of the stages involved in developing ML models integrating explainability and interpretation. The integration of XAI into an ML model for explainability is performed at three different levels: pre-modelling, modelling and deployment phases.

8.3.1 The pre-modelling phase

This phase mainly focusses on the dataset as data is the backbone of an ML model, without data no ML. The pre-modelling explainability is the activities at data pre-processing methods adopted to improve the understanding of the collected data to be used for training the ML models. The data is analyzed before the training through set of techniques to get a summary of the statistical information about the data including feature engineering, standard deviation, mean, range of the data as well as missing points (Minh *et al* 2022). The explainability of the data can be categorized into three, namely, data transformation, summarization and analysis.

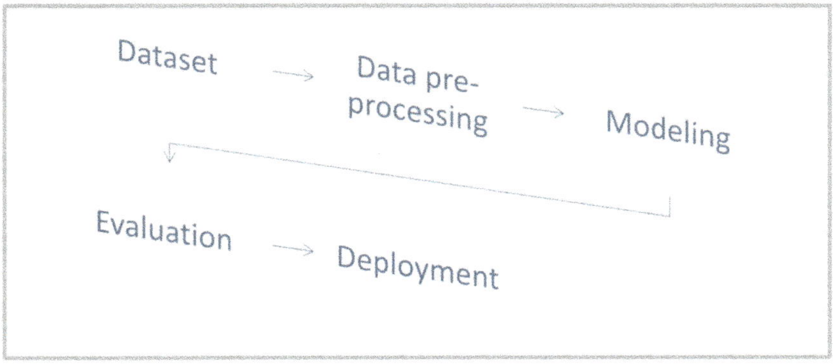

Figure 8.4. Pipeline for developing a black-box ML model without explainability. The process begins with the collection of relevant data, followed by pre-processing to improve data quality. The pre-processed data is then fed into the ML algorithm to develop a model for performing tasks such as prediction or classification. The model is validated by evaluating its performance using relevant metrics to ensure its effectiveness and efficiency in solving the prediction or classification problem. If the model satisfies the performance criteria, it is deployed in a real-world environment for users to start utilizing it. If the model fails to meet the performance criteria, adjustments are made at various stages, and the modelling process is repeated. This is an iterative process. The final model can have the capacity to provide accurate decision but lacks explainability and interpretation.

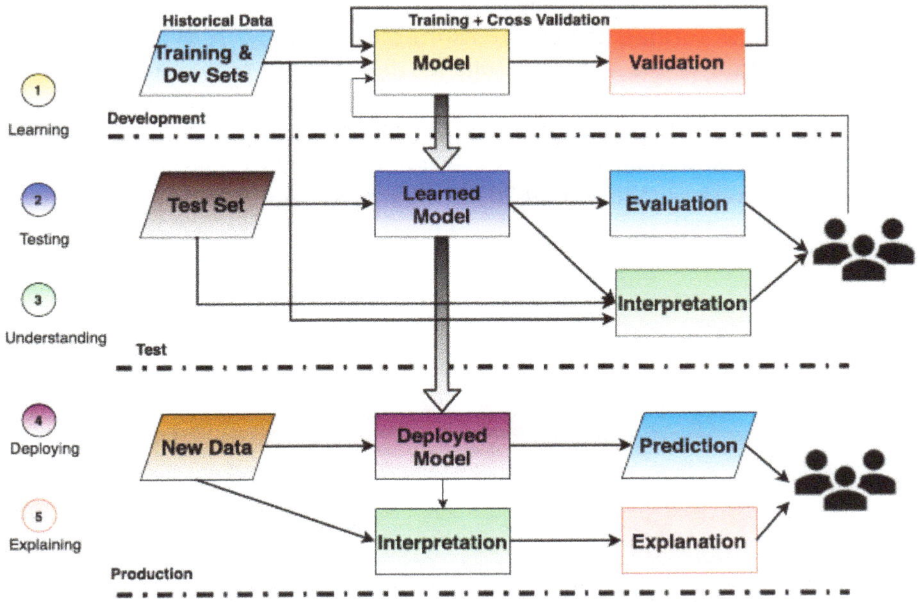

Figure 8.5. Phases involved in developing an ML model with explainability and interpretation. Reprinted with permission from Dwivedi *et al* (2023).

8.3.1.1 Data analysis

This involves the stages required for data extraction, transformation, loading and modelling of the data for features selection to select required features needed to model the ML algorithm to make decisions. The four major elements of data analysis typically encountered in data science are depicted in figure 8.6.

For example, Wang *et al* (2022) adopted descriptive analysis to analyze the evolution of National Basketball Association (NBA) games using clustering and principle component analysis. Subsequently, they developed an ML model based on an interpretable model-agnostic explanation approach for predicting NBA games results with interpretation.

8.3.1.2 Data summarization

This involves the process of generating an informative and concise summary of the original data both structured and unstructured. Typically, unstructured data are voluminous collections of data in plain text, numerical values, dates and punctuations. Thus, before conducting pre-training, the summarization of the textual data is a fundamental process of pre-processing. Structured data shows any data in an organized manner in rows and columns in matrix form, typically in spreadsheets and relational databases (Minh *et al* 2022).

8.3.1.3 Data transformation

This is a data processing approach based on rules applied for mapping the structure of data source to target format of the structure, subsequently, making the data have similar content and format, therefore ensuring consistency. A typical example of data transformation is the names of clients that can be represented in different formats. The different components of the client names that includes title, first name, middle name can be parsed to organize the components into a rule based representation. This standardized representation facilitates easy manipulation of data from other sources (Minh *et al* 2022) (figures 8.4 and 8.5).

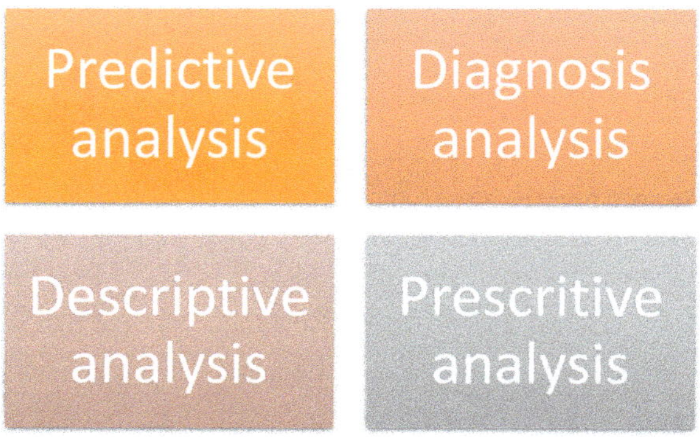

Figure 8.6. The four major data analysis at data pre-processing stage for explainability.

8.3.2 Modelling phase

The learning process of the model is infused with the knowledge of the domain expert to effectively capture patterns in the data. This is because the process used by the domain expert in capturing an image's exact region of interest can be mimicked by the model to help develop new architecture of the model mimicking the domain expert processes to arrive at informed decisions (Messina *et al* 2022). In addition, the use of domain technical terms enhances interpretable and informative explanation (Zhang *et al* 2021). For example, a deep neural network was adopted for the classification of lung nodule with explanations. The data used for the modelling were labelled by clinicians based on both severity and five visual attributes (Shen *et al* 2019).

Design is critical in developing explainable models (Mohseni *et al* 2021). Thus, it is significant to communicate varying data quality tailored to different types of users at the design stage. The performance and explainability of an ML model can deteriorate with the quality of the data, as the performance of the explainable model is correlated to the quality of the training data. This means that low quality data reduces the performance and explainability of the model resulting in unfair decisions, whereas high-quality data improves the explainability and performance of the model. This shows the significance of communicating high-quality data to users through practical and measurable means (Saeed and Omlin 2023). Unfortunately, no universally agreed definition of explainability and interpretation, as such, poses a challenge on the adoption of uniform metrics to measure explainability or interpretation between a proposed explainable ML model and the baseline explainable ML model. Therefore, it is extremely difficult to measure level of quality for explainability and interpretation through comparative analysis (Saeed and Omlin 2023). The evaluation metrics have the ability for measuring the extent of different explainability characteristics. Here are a few examples of metrics for measuring explainability: pixel flipping, insertion/deletion, pointing game, stability, sparseness, effective complexity, cascading randomization, completeness and sensitivity (Akhtar 2023). Most research on XAI tends to reach biased conclusions regarding the performance of explainable models, and in some cases, the evaluation procedures are questionable. This raises concerns that, in the long-run, these issues could undermine the credibility of the XAI field and hinder its success (Hedström *et al* 2023).

The responsibilities of stakeholders at this phase include iteratively evaluating the model until it meets the intended requirements and ensuring it can operate in a real-world environment. Critical activities during this phase include debugging and enhancing the model, detecting bias, improving scientific understanding, and building a robust model (Dwivedi *et al* 2023). The final model is typically evaluated by the stakeholders to ensure accuracy and potential to operate accurately in a real-world environment. This stage involves the interpretation of significant features including their interaction, interpreting the behaviour of the pre-trained model and analysis of bias in the data to ensure it is not captured by the model (Dwivedi *et al* 2023). For example, Pezzotti *et al* (2017) developed a visual system called DeepEyes to support the analysis of deep neural networks at the phase of the training process. DeepEyes has the capabilities of detecting unstable layers, pointing out worthless degenerated filters, identifying unprocessed inputs neglected by the filters in the network, providing reasons for the network layers and determining additional layers if needed or removing unwanted layers (Pezzotti *et al* 2017).

8.3.3 Deployment phase

The explainable stage involves the deployment of the model in a real-world environment and utilization of the model by users. This stage aims at interpreting how the model arrives at its decision by providing a human readable explanation to the users in a real-world environment using real-life data, especially in critical applications (Dwivedi *et al* 2023). Explainability at the deployment phase improves black-box models' explainability through different methods inspired by the way humans interpret a system and the system's processes. The methods include visualization, text-based justification, simplification, and techniques for determining the relevance of features. Each of the methods requires unique data for its operation, though some methods from different categories can perform well on other types of data (Minh *et al* 2022).

The different phases involved in communicating the explanation to users are as follows (Neerincx *et al* 2018). *Generating explanation*: when the model produces an action or decision, this module generates an explanation to justify the reason behind the action or decision. Implementation of this explanation generation module is determined by the AI model. Examples of the explanation generation process include desires, goals and emotions. *Communicating the explanation*: once the explanation is generated from the first module, this stage communicates the explanation to the user, determining exactly what explanation to be given and the way the explanation should be presented. *Explanation reception*: the best way humans can understand the explanation is to study in this module to ease human comprehension. Assessing this involves research on user studies and subjective evaluation. Meaningful metrics are devised for evaluation of the explanation to understand explanation reception.

The explanation provided by the explainable model should be tailored to different stakeholders. The explainable model should generate different types of explanation for understanding and diversity (Saeed and Omlin 2023). The different types of explanation are as follows (Mankodiya *et al* 2022). *Global explanation*: this type of explanation uses visual charts, images, or graphs to illustrate how the model operates to predict outcomes or make suggestions. The global explanation typically provides elaborate explanation. *Contrastive explanation*: this type of explanation highlights the 'why' and 'why not' behind the model's predictions and behaviour. The minimal changes in the inputs that can affect the overall prediction result are determined by the contrastive explanations. *Local explanation*: this mainly focusses on explainability of specific model attributes, making the local explanation completely different from the global explanation. *What-if explanation:* this explanation is for understanding the attributes and predictions of the model. *Counterfactual explanation*: responding to the question of 'how to' take informed decisions. *Example-based explanation:* this type of explanation uses a small sample of data for explaining the model computational output as a prelude to explaining the large-scale data distribution (Mankodiya *et al* 2022). Providing only an explanation by the model to the user without the opportunity for interactive conversation between the user and the model doesn't guarantee understanding. For that reason, it is better to provide an opportunity for interaction between the model and different categories of users for better understanding of the explanation offered by a model (Saeed and Omlin 2023).

8.4 Stakeholders

A stakeholder can be an individual, neighbourhood, group of people, organization, or institution with an interest in related activities, decisions, or the final outcome of a project, innovation, or institution. Typically, the end-product or performance of an entity has a direct impact on them. They are affected by the achievements of the organization or institution (Benn *et al* 2016). This is a general explanation of stakeholders, although different versions of the definition of stakeholder exist, as evident in Benn *et al* (2016). This section discusses stakeholders in the context of XAI. The growing impact of AI-based systems has triggered an increasing need for explainability, as many of these systems are operated by humans or influence human lives. This indicates that numerous groups of people have an interest in the explainability of AI-based systems. These systems are used and improved by people, who are also affected by decisions made based on the system's outputs, their deployment for daily use, and the formulation of regulatory frameworks for responsible application. As such, these individuals are stakeholders due to their significant interest in explainable AI systems (Langer *et al* 2021). The decision-making process of an AI-based system can be contested by stakeholders. Figure 8.7 depicted the structural representation of XAI stakeholders followed by discussion on each of the class of stakeholders.

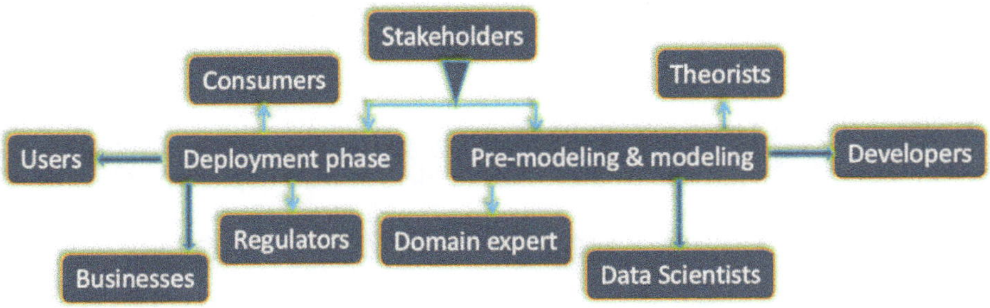

Figure 8.7. Taxonomy of explainable AI stakeholders.

8.4.1 Stakeholders at pre-modelling and modelling phase

The stakeholders in phases ensure that the model is evaluated to produce an accurate model in both the simulation and the real-world environments based on requirements. Refer to section 8.3 for the role of the stakeholders in the pre-modelling and modelling phases. With the exception of the domain expert, the discussion of the stakeholders in these phases were originally presented in Dwivedi *et al* (2023) and are explained below.

8.4.1.1 Developers

The developers are saddled with the responsibility of developing the AI applications. Quality assurance is the primary purpose of seeking the explainability of the model. This is expected to help the smooth testing of the system, evaluation, debugging and enhance the robustness of the applications.

8.4.1.2 Theorists

The theorist mainly understands and improves AI theories. They aim to enhance the understanding of deep neural network fundamental properties in which it derives a multi-disciplined research field called artificial neuroscience. The membership of the theorists group is overlapping with that of the developers. For example, an industrial researcher that works on theoretical aspects of a deep neural network as a theorist can use the deep neural network to develop the system as a developer.

8.4.1.3 Data scientists

The data scientist is expected to have a clear understanding of every component of the AI-based system, from data collection and pre-processing to pre-training, deployment, and explaining the prediction results produced by the system. Any errors generated by the AI-based system should be addressed by the data scientist.

8.4.1.4 Domain experts

This refers to someone with in-depth knowledge and significant experience in a particular domain (e.g., medical, finance, agriculture). The development of an AI model requires the expertise of domain specialists for data interpretation and guidance. For example, a clinician interpreting the severity of malaria for the purpose of developing an AI model to detect malaria and explain the level of severity with justification.

8.4.2 Stakeholders at the deployment phase

Refer to section 8.3 for the role of stakeholders in the deployment phase. This section presents the stakeholders involved in the deployment phase of XAI in the ML model process (Dwivedi *et al* 2023).

8.4.2.1 Users

These are people who utilize AI-based systems. This category of users requires explanations about the system to assist them in making decisions based on the system's output and to justify the system's behaviour. For example, an insurance company may deploy an AI-based system to help make informed decisions on the cost of selling policies to clients. Members of this user community include the company directors, system end-users, and clients.

8.4.2.2 Consumers

The end-products and services generated by AI-based systems are consumed by consumers. Therefore, explanations must be clear and simple to comprehend, allowing users with minimal understanding to utilize the information without needing to seek help elsewhere. A system with such explainability characteristics enhances its trustworthiness and transparency.

8.4.2.3 Businesses

This type of stakeholder is any person who is willing to deploy AI-based systems in their own products. Members of the business stakeholder community include, but are not limited to, government officials, judges, police, bank associates, and doctors. It is critical for these stakeholders to understand the model's decision-making process to ensure fairness and protect users from faulty decisions made by the model.

8.4.2.4 Regulators

Regulators consistently monitor and audit AI-based systems to ensure compliance. In cases where the intelligent system produces faulty decisions, regulators or experts follow the decision trail. Their responsibilities include ensuring continuous model training with new data at regular intervals to update the AI-based system's knowledge (Dwivedi *et al* 2023). Additionally, regulators are made up of ethicists, lawyers, and politicians. It is mandatory for these groups to know how to evaluate, control, and regulate AI-based systems (Langer *et al* 2021).

8.5 Explainable artificial intelligence methods

Many methods for integrating explainability and interpretation of complex black-box model predictions (e.g., deep neural networks) have been developed by the research community over the years. XAI methods span a wide range of categories. Seventeen popular XAI methods were covered in Holzinger *et al* (2022), primarily focused on neural networks, likely because neural networks have faced the greatest criticism for their black-box nature (Townsend *et al* 2019). In this section, six of the popular XAI methods are discussed, as a comprehensive review of all methods is beyond the scope of this chapter. For more in-depth coverage of XAI methods, interested readers can refer to Holzinger *et al* (2022), Dwivedi *et al* (2023) and Islam *et al* (2021).

8.5.1 Explainable graph neural networks

Refer to chapter 5 for details on huge GNNs. Understanding the prediction results of GNNs is critical because it increases trust and transparency in decision-critical applications (Doshi-Velez and Kim 2017). Explainable GNN is developed for the purpose of explaining graph classification tasks. The graphs produced are believed to be the best representative of the GNN decision. The graphs typically have specific in-built property to ease the validation of the graphs. The explainable GNN is the only approach that offers a level explanation of a model for GNN topologies. Searching for sufficient graphs is driven by the use of reinforcement learning because searching for an explainable graph is a non-differentiable problem. The reinforcement learning doesn't only rely on performance, it includes credibility and validation of the graph produced. In view of the fact that the GNN training stages include aggregations and combinations, this is an efficient procedure to deviate from the problem of non-differentiability. The explanation is believed to be effective on large-scale data where human lacks the previous time to sequentially peruse every example's explanation (Holzinger *et al* 2022). Many existing methods focussing on GNN explainability are covered by Yuan *et al* (2022). GNNExplainer is developed based on agnostic methods to provide interpretation of a GNN prediction explanation. Compact subgraph structure and nodes with significant information that contribute to the prediction can be identified by the GNNExplainer. In addition, the GNNExplainer can consistently generate and summarize the explanation of the whole class (Ying *et al* 2019). The applicability of the GNNExplainer in drugs discovery is discussed in (Jiménez-Luna *et al* 2020). Explainable GNN has been applied in different domains such as medical (Hu *et al* 2024, Teng *et al* 2020), cybersecurity (Lo *et al* 2023, Xu *et al* 2021) and agriculture (Chhetri *et al* 2023).

8.5.2 Textual explanations of visual models

Textual generation of image description has been addressed by many ML models comprising algorithms that process the image, typically convolutional neural networks and the components that learn the textual sequence, typically recurrent neural networks. The two algorithms operate in a coordinated manner to generate a textual description of an image indicating successful completion of a classification task. The textual description of image content is different from the explanation of the reason (decision taken process of the neural network) behind the decision taken by the neural network model. The sentence produced can be considered class relevant when it contains the unique features of the image that significantly contribute to the image classification task, thus differentiating between classes of images. The main goal of this method is to search for the discriminative characteristics for the reason that the discriminative characteristics were used by the neural network to solve the classification problem. The textual explanation generated should contain this information (Holzinger *et al* 2022). The textual explanations of visual models has been applied in autonomous driving vehicles (Kim *et al* 2018), multimodality (Park *et al* 2018) and recommendations (Wu *et al* 2020).

8.5.3 Local interpretable model-agnostic explanations

Model-agnostic differentiates between the explanation and the ML model given room for compatibility of the explanation method with different models. Distinguishing between the two has the advantage of the interpretation to work with different ML models, offering a variety of explanation in the form of visualizing significant features and linear formula for a specific ML model as well as allowing flexibility in representation such as text classifier using abstract words embedded in classification. However, actual words are used for the explanation. Examples of the model-agnostic interpretation methods include local surrogate (local interpretable model-agnostic explanations (LIME)), Shapley values (SHAP), accumulation local effects plot, feature interaction and importance, partial dependence plot, global surrogate and individual conditional expectation (Islam *et al* 2021). LIME is explained, but for a detailed discussion of the other examples of the model-agnostic interpretation methods readers can refer to Islam *et al* (2021).

The model-agnostic explanation approaches only focus on the model output without treating the ML model black-box functions. The methods don't require any information about the internal operation of the models, for example, let us consider a neural network. The approaches don't care about the architecture of the neural network (e.g., layers, neurons), parameters (e.g., weights, biases) and activation values, therefore, the approaches become flexible and generally applicable. The major goal of LIME is the explainability of complex model prediction such as a deep neural network. This is achieved by fitting a local surrogate, where the predictions can be more easily explained. LIME has many successful applications across domains demonstrating the popularity of the agnostic method (Holzinger *et al* 2022). Broad studies of the agnostic method are published in the literature (e.g., Natesan Ramamurthy *et al* 2020, Palatnik de Sousa *et al* 2019, Ribeiro *et al* 2018, Zafar and Khan 2021, Zolanvari *et al* 2021).

8.5.4 Anchors

Anchors are derived from the individual prediction that explained the finding of a decision rule anchoring the prediction. IF–THEN statements that defined regions in feature space result from explainability of the decision rule. The predictions are static or 'anchored' in these regions to the data point class to be explained. No matter the extent to which the values of the other features in the data not belonging to the anchor were altered, the classifications remain the same. The anchors are independent of the model and compatible to different modalities like tabular data, textual and images content, depending on the strategy of the perturbation (Holzinger *et al* 2022).

8.5.5 Asymmetric Shapley values

The values of SHAP are symmetric, meaning that for one model's behaviour (e.g. because the variables have the same values) with two variables having the same effect on the model, the two variables will receive the same attribution. However, this property is not always required. In the case where it is known that one of the variables can have an impact on the other variable, at that point it is more sensible to assign the whole attribution to the source variable. A causal graph for variables is required for the use of asymmetric Shapley values. Typically, the graph is generated according to the domain knowledge. For example, the inclusion of applications in bioinformatics that signal a pathway data where the causal structure is verified experimentally or in social science where expert knowledge (e.g., age affecting income instead of income affecting age) determine the direction of the relationship (Holzinger *et al* 2022).

8.5.6 Explainable neural-symbolic learning

In recent decades, the neural-symbolic systems research field became very active (D'AvilaGarcez *et al* 2009). The lack of reasoning and cognition in a neural system motivated the combination of neural and symbolic systems for a neural-symbolic learning system with powerful perception and cognition to emerge (Yu *et al* 2023). Symbolic AI contributes to the field of XAI. The explainable neural-symbolic learning method provides explainability by design, meaning that at every pre-training stage, the end result is ensured to be interpretable. The method is not ad hoc and training has a loss for guiding neural networks on explainability with structure similar to that of human experts (Holzinger *et al* 2022). The integration of connectionist and symbolic paradigms is believed to be the best approach to generate explanations to naïve users (Bennetot *et al* 2019). Neural-symbolic can be used to improve interpretation of deep neural networks with the concept of reason (Barbiero *et al* 2023).

8.6 Emerging concept linking to human acceptability

Explainability of AI models facilitates human acceptability (Islam *et al* 2022) and trustworthiness (Panagoulias *et al* 2024). A research model has been developed for researchers to adopt for qualitative, quantitative or mixed-mode study on how explainable systems relate to the satisfaction of stakeholders (Langer *et al* 2021). Emerging technology acceptability in respect to explainability and interpretation tailored to different models is discussed as follows.

8.6.1 Large language models

Despite the impressive performance displayed by LLMs in natural language processing, the internal working mechanism is still not clear, as such, lacking transparency, thus posing an undesirable risk especially for the downstream applications. Because of that, the LLM itself needs to be understandable and explainable to understand the LLM limitations, behaviour and social impact (Zhao *et al* 2024). The integration of different AI tasks and adaptation to different use cases by LLMs gives them a robust solution that can improve the deployment of XAI and reduce cost of operations (Ali and Kostakos 2023). The development of LLMs is mainly divided into two stages. The first is pre-training the transformer with large-scale volume of textual data to gain general knowledge of language representations. The second stage involves aligning the model through fine-tuning with supervised and reinforcement learning for unambiguous tasks and preferences for users. Refer to chapter 3 for detailed information about the development of LLMs from scratch. Integrating explainability into LLMs focusses on whether it would be predominantly from the first stage or at the second stage of the LLMs' development stage. How to enhance the LLMs' performance interpretation is determined by the understanding of the model source of knowledge (Zhao *et al* 2024).

The introduction of textual explanations in LLMs' in-context learning has been shown to extract strong reasoning with a suitable explanation, reasonably (Li *et al* 2022). Skills in AI systems are critical but commonsense reasoning in a computer is a difficult task. The skills in AI can improve the explanation of AI models by allowing the AI models to provide explanation to decisions similar to the human explanations. It was demonstrated that ChatGPT poses the capability to reason with common sense, achieving an accuracy that ranges between 56%–93% on different questions and answers tasks outperforming human accuracy. In terms of XAI, ChatGPT offers good explanation about its numerous decisions (Krause and Stolzenburg 2023).

The prompting paradigm in LLMs involves the use of prompts (e.g., sentences written in natural language) with empty space for the LLMs to complete, to allow zero-short or few short learning without the need to add a training dataset. Typically, the goal of foundation or base model explanation is to understand the processes used by the model to learn pre-trained knowledge in responding to prompts (Zhao *et al* 2024). A massive increase in LLM scale, reasoning abilities and processes of prompting-based models are too complex, making the conventional explainability methods unfit to introduce explainability in LLMs. Therefore, the emergence of a novel technique was triggered for introducing an explanation specifically for the prompting paradigm. There are a few examples. Understanding and explaining the actions of an LLM based on prompting can be accomplished by an XAI approach called chain-of-thought explanations. Also, the prominence of the approach that mainly focusses on the identification of significant features contributing to predictions is growing. The understanding of the features in the dataset with varying significance can improve the understanding of the composition in the datasets. The traditional fine-tuning paradigm uses a global explanation approach in an LLM based on prompting. These approaches have the capability to impart high-level explanations (e.g., concept- and module-based explanations) (Zhao *et al* 2024).

Explaining medium-sized language models' (MSLMs') fine-tuning mainly focusses on two perspectives, namely, understanding and analysis. First, understanding: this is the understanding of how adaptive pre-training allows the MSLM to learn foundational understanding of language including semantics, context and syntax. Secondly, analysis of how the fine-tuning processes built the capacity of the models through pre-training to solve downstream tasks effectively (Zhao *et al* 2024). Yue *et al* (2023) was able to leverage XAI on ChatGPT to explain intricate financial principles to users outside the financial community.

8.6.2 Role of an explainable model in artificial intelligence-assisted DevOps

Refer to chapter 4 for detailed information about the role of code generators in an AI-DevOps cycle. Industries are sceptical in the adoption of software analytics because of lack of trust resulting from lack of transparency. Without understanding the predictions made by the model, software practitioners cannot trust the predictions blindly without explanation justifying the prediction or deployment efforts, time and resources on the predicted outcome. Some level of trust can be accorded to the model if the performance of the prediction during test phase is high. However, the performance exhibited by the model at the testing phase may not be necessary be the same when the model is deployed in the real-world environment, as such, making the prediction model less effective. When the model produces a prediction different from the expectations of the practitioners, it begins to put doubt in the mind of the practitioners about the model, thus, trust is crucial. An example is when the model generates alerts for the segment of the source code that the software developers expected to be free from any error. Therefore, explainability is the prerequisite for trust, with explainability the practitioners can have trust and prompt new understanding in the practitioner's mind (e.g., software developer may like to understand the reason why the model predicts the existence of a defect so as to give clue to the developer for debugging. It is not sufficient for a model to just predict defects without explanation). Tracing error and justification for the traces are both required by the developers to embark on effective debugging (Dam *et al* 2018).

A code generation model developed with a deep learning algorithm have shown the potential to help software developers in programming with accuracy competing at the level of human (Chen *et al* 2024). Explainable deep learning-based code generation, code named DeciX, was developed by constructing a causal inference dependence graph to measure the contribution of each edge in the graph to the prediction outcome. The succinctness, correctness, overhead and stability of DeciX indicate significant better performance compared to the baseline methods. DeciXwas deployed in a real-world environment for practical applications. It was found that DeciX ca be used in practice without the need for deep learning-based code generation knowledge explanation (Chen *et al* 2024).

CodeT5 and CodeGPT are the pre-trained language models recently adopted for automatic generation of code, repairs and translation. The program for automatic generation of source code leverages language models for analysis and imitates the pattern distribution of the code and text, thus, allowing new source code to be generated. A model-agnostic XAI method was employed to create an explainable language model for generating source code with capability to explain and justify suggestions. It was observed that the explainable language model mainly focusses attention on the programming language keywords and identifiers compared to separators and operators, indicating that language models have the capacity for recognizing source code grammar and information about the structure. It is the explainability that helps the understanding of the model inference behaviours and the learning capabilities of the code generation program behaviours. It has been established that the XAI methods are effective and promising in analysis or enhancing a language model code generator's reliability. However, the removal of token decreases the performance of the language model indicating lack of robustness (Liu *et al* 2024).

The need to understand user's explainability need for a language model code generator motivated researchers to organize nine workshops with 43 software engineer participants using three use cases of code generators, namely, code translation, natural language to source code and automatic code completion. Eleven categories of user's explainability need in the context of a code generative model were identified as follows: examples and tutorials, software engineering capabilities, model performance, output code quality and utility, supported languages and frameworks, data, control, deployment requirements and platform, model explanations, usage right, intended usage and lastly, optimal and poor conditions (Sun *et al* 2022).

8.6.3 Explainability in autonomous robots

The increasing penetration of robots into nearly every aspect of daily life is driven by the growing capabilities of intelligent systems (Das *et al* 2021). The study of human–robot interaction, particularly in the context of explainability, is known as explainable robotics. This field focusses on developing new computational models, approaches, and algorithms that enable robots to generate explanations. This process allows robots to provide explanations at different levels of autonomy, communicating with humans in a friendly and trustworthy manner. During interactions between humans and robots, users may require explanations for various reasons, depending on the context and the individuals involved (Setchi *et al* 2020). Trust calibration in robotic systems is crucial for effective human–robot team performance. This can be achieved by explaining the robot's behaviour, which enhances human trust in the robot by clarifying the robot's purpose, processes, and performance. Both global-level and local-level (functional specificity) trust should be appropriately calibrated (Sanneman and Shah 2020). Refer to chapter 6 for information about autonomous robots; as an example, the following sections discuss explainability in autonomous vehicles and drones.

8.6.3.1 Autonomous vehicles

The major stakeholders in the realm of autonomous vehicles include the end-users, software engineers and data scientists (Mankodiya *et al* 2022). Autonomous vehicles have the capability to perform various computational functions, such as vision recognition and intrusion detection. The ability of an autonomous vehicle to provide explanations for these computational decisions can instill trust in humans from ethical, moral, and legal perspectives. It is expected that passengers in autonomous vehicles should trust the vehicle while it is driving autonomously. Without human trust in the autonomous vehicle, travelling becomes unsafe and can be perceived as dangerous by passengers due to a lack of confidence in the vehicle's decisions (Madhav and Tyagi 2022).

In a study conducted, XAI is integrated onto autonomous vehicle semantic segmentation for the classification of objects on the road to be justified by the explainability. Semantic segmentation was used for the classification of the road and surroundings, whereas XAI analyzed the decision of the segmentation to improve the interpretability of the segmentation. It provides a user with an advantage for easy understanding of the decisions made by the autonomous vehicle and for the developer, it provides details on the black-box module complex internal operations. A beneficial example of integrating XAI into autonomous vehicles to stakeholders, in traffic accident situations, without XAI, the user would be unable to understand the decision-making process of the autonomous vehicle. Additionally, the developer would struggle to anticipate potential threats, as the black-box nature of deep learning algorithms lacks transparency. On the other hand, by integrating an XAI module, the user can access real-time explanations of the decisions made by the autonomous vehicle, enabling them to take control if need be. Meanwhile, the developer would have the necessary information to predict the deep learning algorithm's decision-making process, allowing for quick identification and resolution of any flaws in the autonomous vehicle (Mankodiya *et al* 2022).

The task of computer vision in autonomous vehicles goes beyond merely detecting objects; it involves identifying objects with the potential to cause hazards to the vehicle and generating explanations for all predicted actions. These explanations, tailored to the specific object triggering the action, are more effective and easier to generate than generic explanations in a standard computer vision environment. Research has shown that adding explanations enhances the accuracy of action prediction in autonomous vehicles (Xu *et al* 2020).

8.6.3.2 Autonomous drones

The popularity of deploying unmanned aerial vehicles (UAVs) is increasing at a fast rate (Kim *et al* 2015), such as drone deployment for searching (Andersen and Michaelsen 2023). The management model for managing UAVs for safety and efficient operation in the airspace especially at low altitude is scarce (Kim *et al* 2015). However, the management of UAV operation in the airspace is critical for safety, efficiency and optimal resources allocation by the airspace system (Alharbi *et al* 2023). In the expanding field of drone applications, designers encounter different difficulties related to weather conditions and decision-making during flight operations. As a result, XAI could play a crucial role in improving the operations of UAV (Banimelhem and Al-khateeb 2023).

The effective use of drones in society can be significantly enhanced by integrating XAI into different drone operations. This explainability empowers developers and users to deploy drones more efficiently and effectively across a wide range of tasks, including healthcare delivery, rescue operations, agricultural activities, surveillance, environmental monitoring, reforestation efforts, mining operations, and more. Common grounded learning explanation is an XAI system tailored for autonomous drones to deliver supplies in mountainous areas with field units (Stefik *et al* 2021). A hybrid XAI machine learning model is used to manage UAV demand and management services. The model's functions include trajectory allocation, optimal capacity utilization, and flight planning. It has been found to minimize costs of operations while simultaneously maintaining traffic flow density within the threshold of urban airspace (Alharbi *et al* 2023).

Tethered drones represent the future of the drone industry, expected to provide next-generation ad hoc wireless networks (Lim *et al* 2022). Currently, tethered drones are widely used for applications such as surveillance, monitoring of traffic, and establishing ad hoc communication networks. While most commercial tethered drones hover in a fixed position, control becomes difficult when movement of the robot on ground or station is needed. In this situation, the drone must manage its movement with the moving ground vehicle to prevent the tether from disrupting the drone. The issues raised are addressed by utilizing passive or force-based control, where the tension in the tether guides the drone's movements. Fuzzy logic is employed to implement this force-based controller as a module for XAI (Barawkar and Kumar 2024).

8.6.4 Brain–machine interface

This section presents a discussion on the integration of XAI into BMIs for readers to understand the significant of XAI in the field of BMI.

The contemporary movement of the integration of symbolic and numerical AI triggered the emergence of XAI into BMI (XAI4BCI) (Rajpura *et al* 2024). XAI can provide a feasible approach to the investigation of functional brain development as suggested by the developmental cognitive neuroscience framework (Kiani *et al* 2022). Deep understanding of physiological processes is required for the design and development of BMI, requiring the integration of XAI to provide explanation on the behaviour of the models typically used in the applications (Hashem *et al* 2023). BMI utilizes the prediction power of models for the interpretation of an electroencephalogram (EEG) brain signal for different high-stake applications. Despite the significant of explainability in such a complex predictive model, integrating explainability onto the model is a challenging task in view of the fact that it decreases accuracy. Achieving trust in these models requires the incorporation of reasoning or a causal relationship emanating from the domain expert. The acceptability of BMI by large users depends on the brain signal interpretation to detect behaviour, pattern for diagnosis and prediction of anticipated actions (Rajpura *et al* 2024).

EEG-based BMI requires deep understanding of interpretability to display numerous features in the EEG influencing the behaviour of the ML model. That is why the sensitivity of various features involved in the classification process is needed for the explainability of ML models (Ieracitano *et al* 2022). Therefore, analyzing these diverse features to identify the most significant ones for solving classification problems is crucial in developing explainable ML models. Mastering the interpretation of EEG-based BMIs can reveal how various factors in the EEG influence the behaviour of the ML model (Islam *et al* 2022). Feature extraction from diverse and complex EEG signals offers researchers and clinicians the opportunity to develop effective motor prognosis systems capable of providing personalized rehabilitation treatments (Lin *et al* 2024). Explainable deep learning architecture was employed in understanding multi-state EEG signals for the most significant regions and bands that contribute to post-stroke motor gains (Lin *et al* 2024). Research shows that explainable BMI recognizes the deflection of P300 in single-trial EEG more accurately compared to the state-of-the-art accuracy (Leoni *et al* 2022). In addition, explainable deep learning architecture in combination with Fourier transform has been improving visual interpretation of BMI (Salami *et al* 2022).

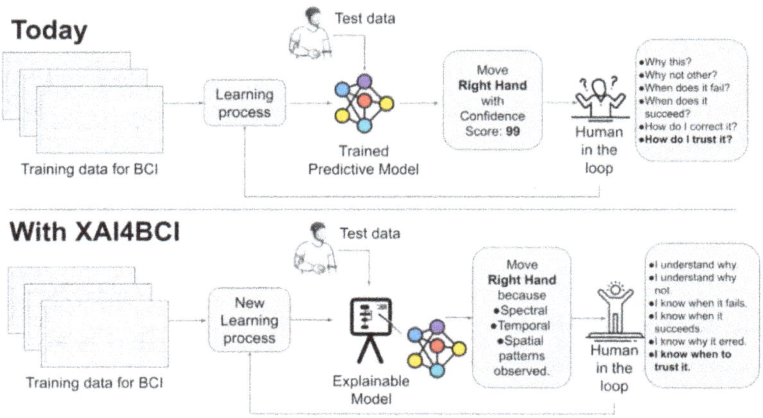

Figure 8.8. The flow of integrating XAI into BMIs to explain decision to humans. Reproduced from Rajpura *et al* (2024),

The aim of XAI is to instill trust typically in the decisions of black-box models, thus making stakeholders such as developers, researchers and policymakers continuously discuss the definition and necessity of explainability in BMI. As shown in figure 8.8, the main purpose of introducing XAI into BMI is to help the stakeholders in the loop. The traditional BMI without explainability makes it less transparent and unreliable because of the black-box nature of the complex predictive model. The stakeholders may require one or more explanations for the reasons needed to validate the adoption of BMI. Stakeholders involving end user, domain experts, researchers, regulatory agencies, industry, managers, executives, developers and designers drive the demand for the interpretation of predictive models and generate relevant explanation in the design space of XAI4BCI (Rajpura *et al* 2024). The integration of explainability in BMI shouldn't be restricted to the software perspective alone, hardware issues should be explainable because it is critical, especially when the BMI is deployed in the real-world environment, clinic or home (Rajpura *et al* 2024).

8.6.5 Multimodal model

Visual question-answering (VQA) for visual-language tasks involves responding to questions about images. Multiple skills are needed for effective answers, including visual perception, textual understanding, and multimodal reasoning across both visual and natural language domains. Providing explanations for responses in natural language offers a better understanding of the reasoning involved in answering the questions, adding transparency to the process (Salewski *et al* 2020). Figure 8.9 depicted examples of answers and explanation for multimodal in both natural language and visualization.

Counterfactual explanations can be used to provide multimodal explanation in deep learning. The thinking in humans is in the form of cause and effect as human thinking is both contrastive and causal. Humans often question why a specific

VQA-X
Question: Does this scene look like it could be from the early 1950s?

e-SNLI-VE
Hypothesis: A woman is holding a child.

CLEVR-X
Question: There is a purple metallic ball; what number of cyan objects are right of it?

Answer | Explanation:
Yes | The photo is in black and white and the cars are all classic designs from the 1950s

Answer | Explanation:
Entailment | If a woman holds a child she is holding a child.

Answer | Explanation:
1 | There is a cyan cylinder which is on the right side of the purple metallic ball.

Figure 8.9. Typical example of answer and explanation involving natural language and visualization. Reproduced from Salewski *et al* (2020) CC BY 4.0.

decision is taken, say *X*, or why not take decision *Y* in place of decision *X*. Take, for example, a particular application that a loan is rejected. In this situation, the applicant is interested in measuring and minimizing changes to be performed to improve the chance of the application and be accepted in the next round of applications. The multimodal explanation based on counterfactual explanation can offer a suggestion that gives actionable insight and recourse (Karimi *et al* 2021).

8.7 Industry applications and case studies

The applications of XAI in industry and case studies where these technologies are currently under operations are outlined and discussed as follows.

8.7.1 Industry

The field of XAI is progressing due to significant investments in research and development, with tech giants at the forefront. This indicates ongoing efforts in XAI innovations aimed at promoting transparency and interpretability (Silicon Valley Information Center 2024). The market value of XAI is expected to grow from US $8.07 billion in 2023 to US $36.42 billion by 2032, with North America holding the largest share and Asia Pacific being the fastest-growing market. This growth spans various XAI segments, including components (e.g., solutions, services), deployment (e.g., cloud, on-premises), applications (e.g., fraud and anomaly detection, predictive maintenance), and end-use industries (e.g., healthcare, automotive, retail, and e-commerce). Key companies in the XAI market include Amelia US LLC, BuildGroup, DataRobot Inc., Ditto.ai, DarwinAI, Factmata, Google LLC, IBM Corporation, Kyndi, and Microsoft Corporation (Precedence Research 2023).

The adoption of XAI across industries is already ongoing, particularly in sectors that handle sensitive information and depend on trust, such as finance, healthcare, self-driving vehicles, and law (Inspire X 2023), e.g. model interpretation of legal judgement suggestion (Zhong *et al* 2020). Other industries investing in XAI to enhance transparency and trust include, but are not limited to, automotive, information technology, retail, energy, and manufacturing (Silicon Valley Information Center 2024). For example, XAI is deployed in finance for credit rating, in healthcare to improve trust and understanding of the AI system's decision-making process (e.g., diagnoses, prognosis) by medical professionals, in law to enhance case analysis, and in self-driving vehicles to provide justification and transparency in decision-making (Inspire X 2023). Table 8.1 presents the summarized representative of XAI platforms developed by different companies.

Despite the fact that the XAI is still evolving, the risks associated with its adoption are eclipsed by its benefits, especially in industries where trust and transparency are paramount. Transparency not only fosters stronger relationships with customers but also provides businesses that embrace XAI with a competitive edge. Furthermore, early adoption enables businesses to shape the evolution of XAI, ensuring its maturation aligns with their operational requirements (Silicon Valley Information Center 2024). The significance of XAI has driven industries to rely on it as a new layer of interpretability, particularly in critical sectors like surgery or autonomous driving, where detailed explanations of procedures are essential (VentureRadar 2019).

Table 8.1. Explainable AI case studies summary.

Explainable platform	Description	Website
IBM OpenScale service	Developed for enterprise XAI applications to provide transparent and explainable decisions free from bias allowing businesses to operate	https://www.ibm.com/
Google cloud XAI	Tool designed for data scientists to understand AI models decision-making process to provide insight, making it more accessible to users	
Flowcast	Developed ML model for credit-risk to provide simple English explanation on credit-risk decisions	https://flowcast.ai
Logical Glue	This is an explainable model banking software solution to provide insight into automated decision-making process	http://www.logicalglue.com/
Imandra	Cloud-based service platform with reasoning, it is safe, explainable and fair	https://www.imandra.ai/
Z advance computing	Is a cognitive explainable model for search and 3D image recognition	https://www.zadvancedcomputing.com/
DarwinAI	Explainable platform that allows developers and data scientists the understanding, interpretation and justifyication of the internal mechanism decision-making process of a deep neural network	http://darwinai.ca
Factmata	Automated fact-check platform with explainability for checking fake and misinformation spreading online	http://factmata.com/

8.7.2 Case studies

This section provides case studies of companies where XAI has been adopted and put into practice in real-world environments. Representative leading companies utilizing XAI to improve understanding and transparency across different operations, thereby enhancing human acceptance of emerging technologies, are depicted in figure 8.10.

The goal is to bridge the gap between XAI theories and industry practices, helping readers appreciate its real-world applications. In turn, improving human acceptability. The discussion on the role of XAI across different companies is as follows.

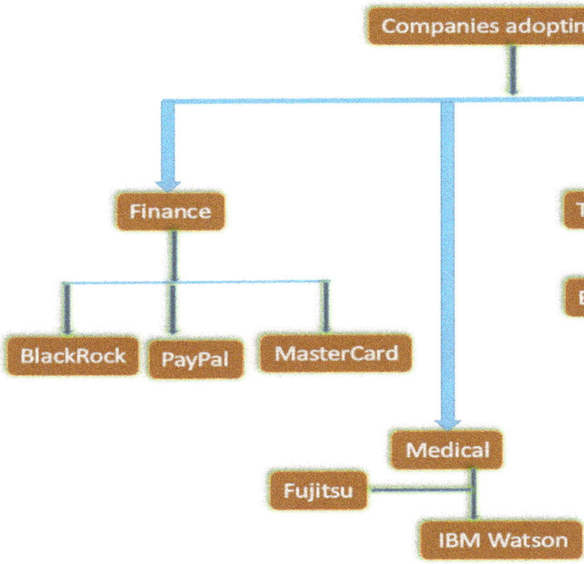

Figure 8.10. Companies adopting explainable ML models in their operations.

8.7.2.1 PayPal

PayPal has adopted an explainable ML model for detecting fraudulent transactions on its platform. The platform processes millions of real-time transactions, and the model monitors these transactions to identify any that are suspected to be fraudulent. Thanks to the explainable ML model, PayPal can understand why a transaction is flagged as suspicious and, if necessary, subject it to human review for further judgement (Inspire X 2023).

8.7.2.2 MasterCard

This company deployed an explainable ML model to improve transparency leading to explaining the rationale behind the decision-making process of the model financial transactions. Decline in volume of transactions can be addressed with the model transparency as transparency is critical for addressing such issues. When the model flagged transactions, justification was provided for the reason behind the decisions, especially detecting fraudulent transaction or evaluation of credit risk. MasterCard aims to win the trust of the users, meet the requirement of regulatory agencies and ensure responsible use of the ML model by deploying an explainable ML model for monitoring transactions. Finally, it provides additional security and reliability to the transaction platform (Silicon Valley Information Center 2024).

8.7.2.3 IBM Watson

IBM's Watson analyzes health data to support diagnoses, treatment and management of patients in a personalized manner. It also analyzes large-scale medical literature and information of the patient to suggest options for treatment of particular diseases and provide the explanation of the reason behind the suggestions to medical practitioners (Inspire X 2023).

8.7.2.4 Ericsson

To improve the adoption of an AI model for optimization of a network in communication service providers, Ericsson adopted an explainable ML model in a cognitive software portfolio to offer transparency by explainable decisions. The explanation can help the communication service providers easily understand the cause of the network problem and suggest ways to handle the problem. Ericsson adopted an explainable ML model on its large-scale data for improving Radio Access Network efficiency to ensure faster time to value. The additional capabilities brought by the explainable model in communication service providers has already demonstrated improved performance for network operators such as Robi Axiata and Bouygues Telecom (Silicon Valley Information Center 2024).

8.7.2.5 BlackRock

BlackRock, a leading asset management company, has deployed an explainable ML model to enhance its investment strategies. The company handles a voluminous amount of asset management data, and the ML model analyzes this data to identify opportunities for investment. In view of the fact that the ML model is explainable, it allows investors and clients to transparently understand why the model makes certain decisions (Inspire X 2023).

8.7.2.6 Fujitsu

The developed explainable ML model for cancer treatment and genomics. The model achieved leading accuracy in the world in detecting different types of cancer and chances of breast cancer survival. The ML model combined different formats of diverse data into knowledge graphs, improved transparency and diagnosed reliability. Fujitsu intended to deploy the model on a portal to be accessible to users by the end of 2024 (Silicon Valley Information Center 2024).

8.7.2.7 LinkedIn

The popular social media platform, LinkedIn integrated an explainable ML model into its platform for strengthening the sales business team, the model explains its decisions to users resulting in an 8% increase in subscription revenue generation. This is achieved by predicting the clients at risk of cancelling their subscription with justifiable reasons for reaching the conclusion (Dave 2022).

8.8 Summary

It is critical for AI-based systems to integrate XAI to enhance interpretation, understanding, transparency, explainability, and trustworthiness. XAI is not a standalone field; it collaborates with other AI domains because systems or models can be derived from different areas, including, but not limited to, computational linguistics, artificial neural networks, natural language processing, BMI, robotics, computer vision, generative AI, ML, and artificial general intelligence. XAI is not a new concept—it has been around for decades. However, the field has recently garnered significant attention from both the research community and industry. This surge in interest is likely due to the rapid penetration of AI-based systems into nearly every aspect of society at an unprecedented speed in the history of computing. As AI adoption increases, so does the demand from stakeholders for interpretation, explanation, and understanding of how these models or systems function to achieve their goals. This has resulted in a current boom in the development of explainable models. The prerequisite for the wide adoption of AI models or AI-based systems heavily depends on their explainability. Many stakeholders remain sceptical of adopting these models due to concerns about explainability. In summary, human acceptance of AI models is highly dependent on their explainability and interpretability.

The procedure for integrating explainability into ML models consists of three phases: pre-modelling, modelling, and deployment. This chapter comprehensively covers each phase, allowing readers to understand the activities involved in developing explainable ML models. The three key stages in communicating model explanations to users include generating the explanation, conveying the explanation, and the reception of the explanation. Different types of explanations are tailored to suit different stakeholders. The five types of explanations are: contrastive explanation, global explanation, local explanation, example-based explanation, and counterfactual explanation.

Stakeholders can be categorized into two groups: those involved in the pre-modelling and modelling phases: developers, theorists, domain experts, and data scientists—and those involved in the deployment phase: users, consumers, businesses, and regulators. A deeper understanding of the model by stakeholders at the pre-modelling and modelling stages can lead to the emergence of new model architectures with improved performance, credibility, and validity. On the other hand, better comprehension of model explanations by stakeholders at the deployment phase can result in broader acceptance and massive adoption of the models. There are many methods for integrating explainability into models, depending on the stage or target stakeholders. No single method fits all types of explainability, leading to the development of different XAI methods suited to different needs. Popular methods, such as LIME, textual explanations of visual models, explainable

GNNs, explainable neural-symbolic learning, asymmetric Shapley values, and anchors, are discussed.

As explainability is typically tailored to different models based on their unique characteristics, the link between explainability and human acceptability is discussed in the context of emerging concepts. The concepts covered include BMI, autonomous robots (self-driving vehicles and drones), LLMs, multimodal models, AI-DevOps, and GNNs. Additionally, the industrial applications of XAI are explored through case studies of companies where XAI has been adopted and implemented in real-world environments. Leading companies utilizing XAI in their operations across health, finance, telecommunications, and social media domains include MasterCard, PayPal, Ericsson, IBM, LinkedIn, BlackRock, and Fujitsu. The goal is to bridge the gap between XAI theories and industry practices, helping readers appreciate its real-world applications.

References

Adadi A and Berrada M 2018 Peeking inside the black-box: a survey on explainable artificial intelligence (XAI) *IEEE Access* **6** 52138–60

Akhtar N 2023 A survey of explainable ai in deep visual modeling: methods and metrics *arXiv preprint* arXiv:2301.13445

Alharbi A, Petrunin I and Panagiotakopoulos D 2023 Assuring safe and efficient operation of UAV using explainable machine learning *Drones* **7** 327

Ali T and Kostakos P 2023 HuntGPT: integrating machine learning-based anomaly detection and explainable AI with large language models (LLMs) *arXiv preprint* arXiv:2309.16021

Andersen A S and Michaelsen P 2023 Explainable alerts for drone swarm-based search and rescue: how information detail impacts performance *Master's Thesis* Aalborg University

Banimelhem O and Al-khateeb B 2023 Explainable artificial intelligence in drones: a brief review *2023 14th Int. Conf. on Information and Communication Systems (ICICS)* (Piscataway, NJ: IEEE) pp 1–5

Barawkar S and Kumar M 2024 Active manipulation of a tethered drone using explainable AI *Complex Eng. Syst.* **4** 6

Barbiero P, Ciravegna G, Giannini F, Zarlenga M E, Magister L C, Tonda A and Marra G 2023 Interpretable neural-symbolic concept reasoning *Int. Conf. on Machine Learning* (PMLR) pp 1801–25

Benn S, Abratt R and O'Leary B 2016 Defining and identifying stakeholders: views from management and stakeholders *S. Afr. J. Bus. Manag.* **47** 1–11

Bennetot A, Laurent J L, Chatila R and Díaz-Rodríguez N 2019 Towards explainable neural-symbolic visual reasoning *arXiv preprint* arXiv:1909.09065

Biffi C, Cerrolaza J J, Tarroni G, Bai W, De Marvao A, Oktay O and Rueckert D 2020 Explainable anatomical shape analysis through deep hierarchical generative models *IEEE Trans. Med. Imaging* **39** 2088–99

Chen S, Li Z, Yang W and Liu C 2024 DeciX: explain deep learning based code generation applications *Proc. ACM Softw. Eng.* **1** 2424–46

Chhetri T R, Hohenegger A, Fensel A, Kasali M A and Adekunle A A 2023 Towards improving prediction accuracy and user-level explainability using deep learning and knowledge graphs: a study on cassava disease *Expert Syst. Appl.* **233** 120955

Core M G, Lane H C, Van Lent M, Gomboc D, Solomon S and Rosenberg M 2006 Building explainable artificial intelligence systems *AAAI* pp 1766–73

Dam H K, Tran T and Ghose A 2018 Explainable software analytics *Proc. of the 40th Int. Conf. on Software Engineering: New Ideas and Emerging Results* pp 53–6

Das D, Banerjee S and Chernova S 2021 Explainable AI for robot failures: generating explanations that improve user assistance in fault recovery *Proc. of the 2021 ACM/IEEE Int. Conf. on Human–Robot Interaction* pp 351–60

Dave P 2022 AI is explaining itself to humans. And it's paying off *Reuters* [Online] https://reuters.com/technology/ai-is-explaining-itself-humans-its-paying-off-2022-04-06/ (accessed 17 September 2024)

D'AvilaGarcez A S, Lamb L C and Gabbay D M 2009 *Neural-Symbolic Learning Systems* (Berlin: Springer) pp 35–54

Doshi-Velez F and Kim B 2017 Towards a rigorous science of interpretable machine learning *arXiv preprint* arXiv:1702.08608

Dwivedi R, Dave D, Naik H, Singhal S, Omer R, Patel P and Ranjan R 2023 Explainable AI (XAI): core ideas, techniques, and solutions *ACM Comput. Surv.* **55** 1–33

Elton D C 2020 Self-explaining AI as an alternative to interpretable AI *Proc. Artificial General Intelligence: 13th Int. Conf., AGI 2020 (St. Petersburg, Russia, September 16–19, 2020)* (Cham: Springer International Publishing) pp 95–106

Hashem H A, Abdulazeem Y, Labib L M, Elhosseini M A and Shehata M 2023 An integrated machine learning-based brain–computer interface to classify diverse limb motor tasks: explainable model *Sensors* **23** 3171

Hedström A, Weber L, Krakowczyk D, Bareeva D, Motzkus F, Samek W and Höhne M M C 2023 Quantus: an explainable AI toolkit for responsible evaluation of neural network explanations and beyond *J. Mach. Lea rn. Res.* **24** 1–11

Holzinger A, Biemann C, Pattichis C S and Kell D B 2017 What do we need to build explainable AI systems for the medical domain? *arXiv preprint* arXiv:1712.09923

Holzinger A, Saranti A, Molnar C, Biecek P and Samek W 2022 Explainable AI methods—a brief overview *Int. Workshop on Extending Explainable AI Beyond Deep Models and Classifiers* (Cham: Springer) pp 13–38

Hu X, Sun Z, Nian Y, Wang Y, Dang Y, Li F and Tao C 2024 Self-explainable graph neural network for Alzheimer disease and related dementias risk prediction: algorithm development and validation study *JMIR Aging* **7** e54748

Ieracitano C, Mammone N, Hussain A and Morabito F C 2022 A novel explainable machine learning approach for EEG-based brain–computer interface systems *Neural Comput. Appl.* **34** 11347–60

Inspire X 2023 Use cases of explainable AI (XAI) across various sectors *Medium* https://medium.com/@inspirexnewsletter/use-cases-of-explainable-ai-xai-across-various-sectors-ffa7d7fa1778 (accessed 15 September 2024)

Islam M R, Ahmed M U, Barua S and Begum S 2022 A systematic review of explainable artificial int elligence in terms of different application domains and tasks *Appl. Sci.* **12** 1353

Islam R, Andreev A V, Shusharina N N and Hramov A E 2022 Explainable machine learning methods for classification of brain states during visual perception *Mathematics* **10** 2819

Islam S R, Eberle W, Ghafoor S K and Ahmed M 2021 Explainable artificial intelligence approaches: a survey *arXiv preprint* arXiv:2101.09429

Jiménez-Luna J, Grisoni F and Schneider G 2020 Drug discovery with explainable artificial intelligence *Nat. Mach. Intell.* **2** 573–84

Karimi A H, Schölkopf B and Valera I 2021 Algorithmic recourse: from counterfactual explanations to interventions *Proc. of the 2021 ACM Conference on Fairness, Accountability, and Transparency* pp 353–62

Kiani M, Andreu-Perez J, Hagras H, Rigato S and Filippetti M L 2022 Towards understanding human functional brain development with explainable artificial intelligence: challenges and perspectives *IEEE Comput. Intell. Mag.* **17** 16–33

Kim J, Rohrbach A, Darrell T, Canny J and Akata Z 2018 Textual explanations for self-driving vehicles *Proc. of the European Conf. on Computer Vision (ECCV)* pp 563–78

Kim Y, Jo J and Shaw M 2015 A lightweight communication architecture for small UAS Traffic Management (SUTM) *2015 Integrated Communication, Navigation and Surveillance Conf. (ICNS)* (Piscataway, NJ: IEEE) pp T4–1

Krause S and Stolzenburg F 2023 Commonsense reasoning and explainable artificial intelligence using large language models *European Conf. on Artificial Intelligence* (Cham: Springer Nature) pp 302–19

Langer M, Oster D, Speith T, Hermanns H, Kästner L, Schmidt E and Baum K 2021 What do we want from Explainable Artificial Intelligence (XAI)? A stakeholder perspective on XAI and a conceptual model guiding interdisciplinary XAI research *Artif. Intell.* **296** 103473

Leoni J, Strada S C, Tanelli M, Brusa A and Proverbio A M 2022 Single-trial stimuli classification from detected P300 for augmented brain–computer interface: a deep learning approach *Mach. Learn. Appl.* **9** 100393

Li S, Chen J, Shen Y, Chen Z, Zhang X, Li Z and Yan X 2022 Explanations from large language models make small reasoners better *arXiv preprint* arXiv:2210.06726

Lim S, Yu H and Lee H 2022 Optimal tethered-UAV deployment in A2G communication networks: multi-agent Q-learning approach *IEEE Internet Things J.* **9** 18539–49

Lin P J, Li W, Zhai X, Li Z, Sun J, Xu Q and Li C 2024 Explainable deep-learning prediction for brain–computer interfaces supported lower extremity motor gains based on multi-state fusion *IEEE Trans. Neural Syst. Rehabil. Eng.* **32** 1546–55

Liu Y, Tantithamthavorn C, Liu Y and Li L 2024 On the reliability and explainability of language models for program generation *ACM Trans. Softw. Eng. Methodol.* **33** 1–26

Lo W W, Kulatilleke G, Sarhan M, Layeghy S and Portmann M 2023 XG-BoT: an explainable deep graph neural network for botnet detection and forensics *Internet Things* **22** 100747

Lu H, Liu Y, Zhu M, Lu C, Yang H and Wang Y 2024 Enhancing interpretability of autonomous driving via human-like cognitive maps: a case study on lane change *IEEE Trans. Intell. Veh.* https://ieeexplore.ieee.org/document/10416370

Madhav A S and Tyagi A K 2022 Explainable Artificial Intelligence (XAI): connecting artificial decision-making and human trust in autonomous vehicles *Proc. of the 3rd Int. Conf. on Computing, Communications, and Cyber-Security: IC4S 2021* (Singapore: Springer) pp 123–36

Mankodiya H, Jadav D, Gupta R, Tanwar S, Hong W C and Sharma R 2022 Odxai: explainable ai-based semantic object detection for autonomous vehicles *Appl. Sci.* **12** 5310

Messina P, Pino P, Parra D, Soto A, Besa C, Uribe S and Capurro D 2022 A survey on deep learning and explainability for automatic report generation from medical images *ACM Comput. Surv.* **54** 1–40

Minh D, Wang H X, Li Y F and Nguyen T N 2022 Explainable artificial intelligence: a comprehensive review *Artif. Intell. Rev.* **55** 3503–68

Mohseni S, Zarei N and Ragan E D 2021 A multidisciplinary survey and framework for design and evaluation of explainable AI systems *ACM Trans. Interact. Intell. Syst.* **11** 1–45
Montavon G, Samek W and Müller K R 2018 Methods for interpreting and understanding deep neural networks *Digital Signal Process.* **73** 1–15
Murray B J, Islam M A, Pinar A J, Anderson D T, Scott G J, Havens T C and Keller J M 2020 Explainable ai for the choquet integral *IEEE Trans. Emerg. Top. Comput. Intell.* **5** 520–9
Natesan Ramamurthy K, Vinzamuri B, Zhang Y and Dhurandhar A 2020 Model agnostic multilevel explanations *Adv. Neural Inf. Process. Syst.* **33** 5968–79
Neerincx M A, van der Waa J, Kaptein F and van Diggelen J 2018 Using perceptual and cognitive explanations for enhanced human-agent team performance *Proc. Engineering Psychology and Cognitive Ergonomics: 15th Int. Conf., EPCE 2018, Held as Part of HCI Int. 2018 (Las Vegas, NV, July 15–20, 2018)* (Cham: Springer) pp 204–14
Palatnik de Sousa I, Maria BernardesRebuzziVellasco M and Costa da Silva E 2019 Local interpretable model-agnostic explanations for classification of lymph node metastases *Sensors* **19** 2969
Panagoulias D P, Virvou M and Tsihrintzis G A 2024 A novel framework for artificial intelligence explainability via the technology acceptance model and rapid estimate of adult literacy in medicine using machine learning *Expert Syst. Appl.* **248** 123375
Park D H, Hendricks L A, Akata Z, Rohrbach A, Schiele B, Darrell T and Rohrbach M 2018 Multimodal explanations: justifying decisions and pointing to the evidence *Proc. of the IEEE Conf. on Computer Vision and Pattern Recognition* pp 8779–88
Pezzotti N, Höllt T, Van Gemert J, Lelieveldt B P, Eisemann E and Vilanova A 2017 Deepeyes: progressive visual analytics for designing deep neural networks *IEEE Trans. Visual Comput. Graph.* **24** 98–108
Precedence Research 2023 *Explainable AI Market Size to Hit USD 36.42 Billion by 2032* https://precedenceresearch.com/explainable-ai-market#:~:text=The%20global%20explainable%20AI%20market%20size%20accounted%20for,during%20the%20forecast%20period%20from%202023%20to%202032 accessed 15 September 2024)
Rajpura P, Cecotti H and Meena Y K 2024 Explainable artificial intelligence approaches for brain–computer interfaces: a review and design space *J. Neural Eng.* **21** 014003
Ribeiro M T, Singh S and Guestrin C 2018 Anchors: high-precision model-agnostic explanations *Proc. of the AAAI Conference on Artificial Intelligence* 32
Saeed W and Omlin C 2023 Explainable AI (XAI): a systematic meta-survey of current challenges and future opportunities *Knowl.-Based Syst.* **263** 110273
Salami A, Andreu-Perez J and Gillmeister H 2022 EEG-ITNet: an explainable inception temporal convolutional network for motor imagery classification *IEEE Access* **10** 36672–85
Salewski L, Koepke A S, Lensch H P and Akata Z 2020 Clevr-*x*: a visual reasoning dataset for natural language explanations *Int. Workshop on Extending Explainable AI Beyond Deep Models and Classifiers* (Cham: Springer) pp 69–88
Sanneman L and Shah J A 2020 Trust considerations for explainable robots: a human factors perspective *arXiv preprint* arXiv:2005.05940
Saraswat D, Bhattacharya P, Verma A, Prasad V K, Tanwar S, Sharma G and Sharma R 2022 Explainable AI for healthcare 5.0: opportunities and challenges *IEEE Access* **10** 84486–517
Sasaki H, Hidaka Y and Igarashi H 2021 Explainable deep neural network for design of electric motors *IEEE Trans. Magn.* **57** 1–4

Setchi R, Dehkordi M B and Khan J S 2020 Explainable robotics in human-robot interactions *Procedia Comput. Sci.* **176** 3057–66
Shahriari B, Swersky K, Wang Z, Adams R P and De Freitas N 2015 Taking the human out of the loop: a review of Bayesian optimization *Proc. IEEE* **104** 148–75
Shen S, Han S X, Aberle D R, Bui A A and Hsu W 2019 An interpretable deep hierarchical semantic convolutional neural network for lung nodule malignancy classification *Expert Syst. Appl.* **128** 84–95
Silicon Valley Information Center 2024 *The Role of Explainable AI in 2024* https://svicenter.com/blog/the-role-of-explainable-ai-in-2024 (accessed 15 September 2024)
Stefik M, Youngblood M, Pirolli P, Lebiere C, Thomson R, Price R and Schooler J 2021 Explaining autonomous drones: an XAI journey *Appl. AI Lett.* **2** e54
Sun J, Liao Q V, Muller M, Agarwal M, Houde S, Talamadupula K and Weisz J D 2022 Investigating explainability of generative AI for code through scenario-based design *Proc. of the 27th Int. Conf. on Intelligent User Interfaces* pp 212–28
Teng F, Yang W, Chen L, Huang L and Xu Q 2020 Explainable prediction of medical codes with knowledge graphs *Front. Bioeng. Biotechnol.* **8** 867
Townsend J, Chaton T and Monteiro J M 2019 Extracting relational explanations from deep neural networks: a survey from a neural-symbolic perspective *IEEE Trans. Neural. Netw. Learn. Syst.* **31** 3456–70
VentureRadar 2019 *Explainable AI and the Companies Leading the Way* https://blog.ventureradar.com/2019/08/19/explainable-ai-and-the-companies-leading-the-way/(accessed 15 September 2024)
Wang Y, Liu W and Liu X 2022 Explainable AI techniques with application to NBA gameplay prediction *Neurocomputing* **483** 59–71
Wu Q, Zhao P and Cui Z 2020 Visual and textual jointly enhanced interpretable fashion recommendation *IEEE Access* **8** 68736–46
Xu F, Uszkoreit H, Du Y, Fan W, Zhao D and Zhu J 2019 Explainable AI: a brief survey on history, research areas, approaches and challenges *Proc., Part II 8 Natural Language Processing and Chinese Computing: 8th CCF Int. Conf., NLPCC 2019 (Dunhuang, China, October 9–14, 2019)* (Cham: Springer International Publishing) pp 563–74
Xu J, Xue M and Picek S 2021 Explainability-based backdoor attacks against graph neural networks *Proc. of the 3rd ACM Workshop on Wireless Security and Machine Learning* pp 31–6
Xu Y, Yang X, Gong L, Lin H C, Wu T Y, Li Y and Vasconcelos N 2020 Explainable object-induced action decision for autonomous vehicles *Proc. of the IEEE/CVF Conf. on Computer Vision and Pattern Recognition* pp 9523–32
Yampolskiy R V 2019 Unexplainability and incomprehensibility of artificial intelligence *arXiv preprint* arXiv:1907.03869
Ying Z, Bourgeois D, You J, Zitnik M and Leskovec J 2019 GNNExplainer: generating explanations for graph neural networks *Adv. Neural Inform. Process. Syst.* **32** 9240–51
Yu D, Yang B, Liu D, Wang H and Pan S 2023 A survey on neural-symbolic learning systems *Neural Netw.* **166** 105–26
Yuan H, Yu H, Gui S and Ji S 2022 Explainability in graph neural networks: a taxonomic survey *IEEE Trans. Pattern Anal. Mach. Intell.* **45** 5782–99
Yue T, Au D, Au C C and Iu K Y 2023 Democratizing financial knowledge with ChatGPT by OpenAI: unleashing the power of technology *SSRN* 4346152
Zafar M R and Khan N 2021 Deterministic local interpretable model-agnostic explanations for stable explainability *Mach. Learn. Knowl. Extract.* **3** 525–41

Zhang Y, Tiňo P, Leonardis A and Tang K 2021 A survey on neural network interpretability *IEEE Trans. Emerg. Top. Comput. Intell.* **5** 726–42

Zhao H, Chen H, Yang F, Liu N, Deng H, Cai H and Du M 2024 Explainability for large language models: a survey *ACM Trans. Intell. Syst. Technol.* **15** 1–38

Zhong H, Wang Y, Tu C, Zhang T, Liu Z and Sun M 2020 Iteratively questioning and answering for interpretable legal judgment prediction *Proc. of the AAAI Conf. on Artificial Intelligence* 34 pp 1250–7

Zolanvari M, Yang Z, Khan K, Jain R and Meskin N 2021 Trust XAI: model-agnostic explanations for AI with a case study on iiot security *IEEE Internet Things J.* **10** 2967–78

Chapter 9

Proposed bibliometric methods for artificial intelligence domain and bibliometric analysis on artificial intelligence for over six decades

Bibliometric analysis explores and provides analysis of large-scale scientific data to increase public awareness about a specific field of study, promotes the development of the field and serves policymakers. In this chapter, the strong theoretical foundation of bibliometric analysis including mathematical fundamentals is discussed. Bibliometric analysis methodology is proposed for the artificial intelligence (AI) research community to adopt in the domain of AI. To the best of the author's knowledge, no bibliometric analysis conducted for AI covers up to six decades. Thus, this chapter presents a comprehensive bibliometric analysis on the development of AI for over six decades, showing the performance analysis and science mapping. Bibliometric analysis of top AI literature sources, disciplines, prolific countries in AI, prolific authors, trending topics, authorship, impact, author-keywords and co-keywords were analyzed. The current trending topics includes transformers, robotics surgery, machine learning, control and fuzzy systems. China is ahead of the United States of America in AI research. Industrial applications and case studies where bibliometric analysis is in practice are outlined. We believe that readers including organizations across the world can use the bibliometric analysis to identify relevant information in the area of AI.

9.1 Introduction

AI has been gradually developing for a long period of time, mainly from the early 1920s. Many people outside the mainstream AI community view AI as a new technology penetrating every aspect of society, making transformation and changing the way citizens interact with the environment. However, AI is not a new concept—it has been around for over 100 years, developing gradually. The first major breakthrough in AI mimicking the human brain was the discovery of artificial

doi:10.1088/978-0-7503-6320-4ch9

neural networks (ANNs) in 1943 by Warren McCulloch and Walter Pitts, who proposed that ANNs can learn if the network is well-defined (refer to chapter 1 for details about historical development of AI). The journey of AI was not a smooth road; its progress witnessed hitches along the line of development, especially in the 1970s. However, development in AI in recent times has been dramatically accelerated because of the availability of high-performance computing machines, a voluminous amount of data generated from different sources at a very high speed and significant breakthroughs in AI.

AI has attracted the attention of the media and society in general in recent times with many welcoming the development, while some are calling for caution about the continued training of AI systems because of potential dangers associated with intelligent systems. In addition, privacy concern is raised about the use of intelligent systems. Generally, mixed reactions and feelings are trailing the development of AI because of it is double-edged sword nature—negative and positive implications. AI systems have been used for deepfake (creating fake images, videos and audios), job replacement and spreading distorted information in society. On the other hand, AI has been deployed in many positive aspects such as generating revenue, improving systems performance in different domains including healthcare and maximizing the utilization of scarce resources in cities. AI is expected to play a critical role in the emerging fourth industrial revolution as the future reality of industry.

It was found in the literature that papers reporting bibliometric analysis on AI from different points of view exist. The rigorous method of exploring and analyzing a very large-scale volume of scientific data is referred to as bibliometric analysis or scientometrics, and it is highly popular. It provides the opportunity to unravel evolutionary hints of a particular research area and point out the direction of emerging subfields within the research field (Donthu *et al* 2021). Bibliometric analysis is one of the widely recognized standard methods for quantitative and statistics analysis of publication venues or articles to establish structure of knowledge that is useful. It can be used to find the growing structure, quantity of articles, structure and citation accumulation of a publication venue, e.g. a journal. Bibliometric analysis can provide the opportunity for the reader to identify the strength and limitations of research, prolific authors, country performance regarding the research area, etc (Du and Teixeira 2012).

AI is receiving massive public attention, and it is believed that it is the most discussed scientific subject in recent times (China Report 2018). As a result of that, the AI community is flooding the literature with the publications of high-quality new findings emanating from different AI projects. The originality of those findings has been peer reviewed and standardized by top academic journals. Yet, the application of bibliometric analysis in AI is an emerging area under development based on evidence from the literature. Bibliometric analysis is well established, tracing back to the 1920s. However, in the context of AI it is at the infant stage.

To the best of the author's knowledge based on research conducted in several reputable academic databases such as Web of Science, Scopus, DBLP computer science bibliography, ACM Digital Library and Google Scholar, it was found that no AI bibliometric analysis covers up to six decades despite the fact that bibliometric analysis is a well-established area of study, as reported in Godin (2006).

Thus, this chapter presents a comprehensive bibliometric analysis on the development of AI for over six decades showing performance analysis and mapping. Secondly, we propose a comprehensive bibliometric analysis methodology to be adopted by the AI research community. This is intended to provide broad understanding of the research area, indicating the direction of emerging areas within AI and identifying relevant information on AI to the reader.

9.2 Bibliometric analysis theoretical background

The advent of the term bibliometric analysis relegated statistical analysis of scientific literature's almost 50 years' dominance. Alfred J Lotka in 1926 pioneered the publication of '*The frequency distribution of scientific productivity determined from a decennial index*' from 1907 to 1916 (Glanzel 2003). It was reported that the editor of *Science* from 1895 to 1944, James McKeen Cattell, founded a systematic collection of scientific statistics on science that produced bibliometrics as a field of study (Godin 2006). After the advent of bibliometrics as a research field, bibliometricians begin to expand the research area by conducting massive research to develop and evaluate research indicators for impact of the research such as the impact factor of a journal and h-index. The bibliometric method for data visualization was used to visualize the structural relationship that exists among researchers or items of research. Bibliometrics has since developed into the broad field of information systems. It has been adopted in different research fields from different disciplines (Ninkov *et al* 2022).

Bibliometrics and scientometrics were introduced to the literature at the same period in 1969 by Pritchard, and Nalimov and Mulchenko, respectively. Pritchard defined bibliometrics as the act of applying a mathematical and statistical approach to communication media such as books, whereas Nalimov and Mulchenko defined scientometrics as the use of those quantitative methods tackling analysis of science as information processing. The two explanations of the terms bibliometrics and scientometrics limited scientometrics to the measurement of communication in science, whereas bibliometrics deals with information processing in general. The borderline that restricted each of the terms to its boundary has been almost removed completely in the last 30 years. In recent times, both bibliometrics and scientometrics have been used interchangeably as synonymous terms (Gorkova 1988).

Most journals are recording an increasing number of manuscript submissions globally because of the ease of communication via the internet revolution that facilitated international collaboration. Researchers are currently confronted with the challenge of meaningful synthesis of the large-scale volume of scientific data via analytical methods immune from the researcher's own bias in addition to the challenge of a novel conceptual theoretical framework and its validation empirically. Bibliometric analysis is believed to be one of the trusted, reliable and unbiased methods of synthesizing the large-scale volume of published literature (Baker *et al* 2020). Publication of research output is one of the most significant measures for a researcher. Therefore, bibliometric analysis is the basic tool required to assess and analyze scientific research output that contributes to the body of scientific knowledge advancement from different perspectives. The assessment criteria in bibliometrics for measuring performance are quality and productivity of research published by researchers is objective. The scientific outputs are mined and analyzed using scientific mapping (Donthu *et al* 2021). In summary, bibliometric analysis combines both performance analysis and mapping for quantifying of the research area, detecting subfields as revealed by clusters and the evolution of the research area (Cobo *et al* 2011).

9.3 Theories of scientific change

Many theories of scientific change exist in the literature. However, this section provides the major theories of scientific change, as shown in figure 9.1, as representative to suit the discussion on scientific research relating to science mapping.

Theories of scientific change were established in the literature and are widely known by the research community. For example, establishing a new scientific research area is highly close to the relationship that exists in the forming of a research network. The process of forming the research network creates a cycle of three stages, namely, exploration, unification and diminishing/displacement. Each of the stages in the cycle is characterized by the number of relationships of intellectual

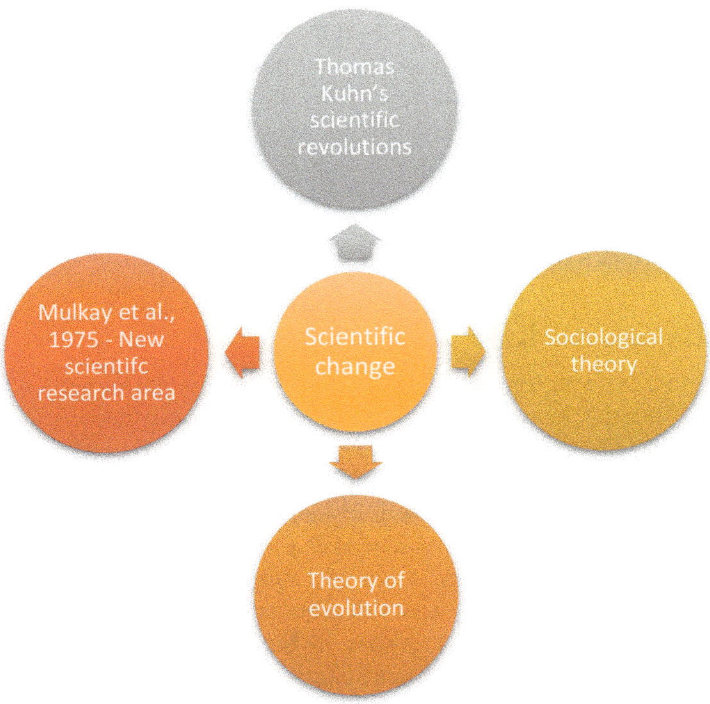

Figure 9.1. Theories of scientific change.

and social growth. The factors responsible for the establishment of the new scientific research area become stable in the second stage of the cycle like the forming of an intellectual framework and standards for cognitive and technical issues, creation of research groups, setting of the recruitment mechanism and research funding, establishing a journal that is specialized in content, considering small number of research publication to be recognized as paradigmatic and researches that cite the published works frequently, monitoring the growing amount of research activities in the new research area and practitioners associated with the new area (Mulkay *et al* 1975).

The sociological theory of scientific change was established in 1993. It repelled the Kuhnian paradigm shift model for exaggerating the simplicity of complexity in reality. Thus, it argued that sociological reasons such as competing for recognition and reputation among scientists within entities drives the technological advancement of science (Fuchs 1993). Thomas Kuhn's *The Structure of Scientific Revolutions* was published in 1962 by Thomas Kuhn. It explained that the development of science is an iterative process of revolution whereby the scientific paradigms predominant position is based on competition (Kuhn 1962). Another theory is the theory of evolution of scientific discipline established in 2009, relatively new compared to the well-established theories of scientific change like Thomas Kuhn's scientific revolutions. The evolution of scientific discipline theory has four stages, as follows: conceptualization stage for new discipline or research specialty where the research object is established like in science mapping the scientific knowledge domain is the object; the second stage involved the development of research tools to be used for investigating the phenomena in consideration; in stage three, the research question formulated by the support of newly established methods for research is investigated. Subsequently, new findings are established and new research specialties emerge; the fourth stage involves the characterization of knowledge transfer for the specialty through authoring comprehensive textbooks. The knowledge accumulated in the research domain is summarized, analyzed, synthesized and presented to beginners and expert researchers of the specialty (Shneider 2009).

9.4 Performance analysis

Performance analysis is the act of measuring the performance of individuals, countries and institutions regarding their respective contributions to a particular field of research. Development trends of a research field and prolific authors, journals, institutions and countries are studied by performance analysis (Donthu *et al* 2021). The nature of performance analysis from bibliometric data is descriptive. It is embedded in most literature review at the minimal in the situation where the mapping was not conducted in view of the fact that it is a global standard practice to include performance analysis of the research entities of the research field in a standard literature review. This is similar to the profiles or background study of participants typically found in empirical studies. The main performance measures typically measured in performance analysis include citation per year or citation per publication, and number of publications. The productivity is measured by the

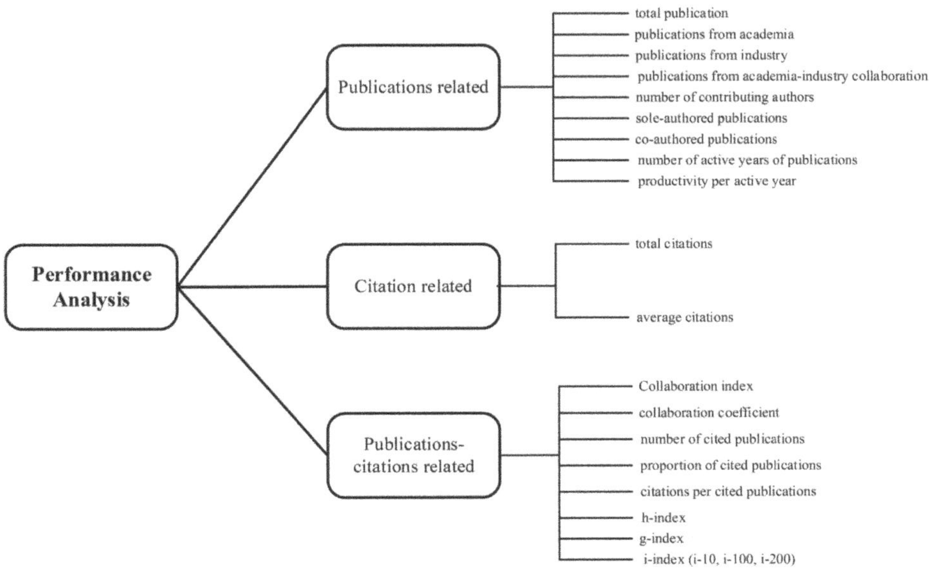

Figure 9.2. Bibliometric performance analysis metrics.

number of publications, whereas the impact and influence are measured by the citations. The research constituents performance like the h-index and citation/publication is measured by both citations and publications. The significance of the different research constituents is recognized by the performance analysis despite the fact that the analysis is descriptive in nature (Ramos-Rodríguez and Ruíz-Navarro 2004).

The metrics typically used in performance analysis metrics, as shown figure 9.2, for publication-related metrics includes total publication, publications from academia, publications from industry, publications from academia–industry collaboration, number of contributing authors, sole-authored publications, co-authored publications, number of active years of publications and productivity per active year of publications. On the other hand, citation-related metrics includes: total citations and average citations. Publications—citations-related metrics include: collaboration index, collaboration coefficient, number of cited publications, proportion of cited publications, citations per cited publications, h-index, g-index, m-index (Ahmi 2022) and i-index (i-10, i-100, i-200) (Donthu *et al* 2021).

9.5 Science mapping

Scientific mapping is the technique of studying the intellectual interactions and structural connections that exist among the entities of the research. Scientific mapping involves citation analysis, bibliographical coupling, co-words, analysis of co-citation and analysis of co-authorship. Combining the techniques with the

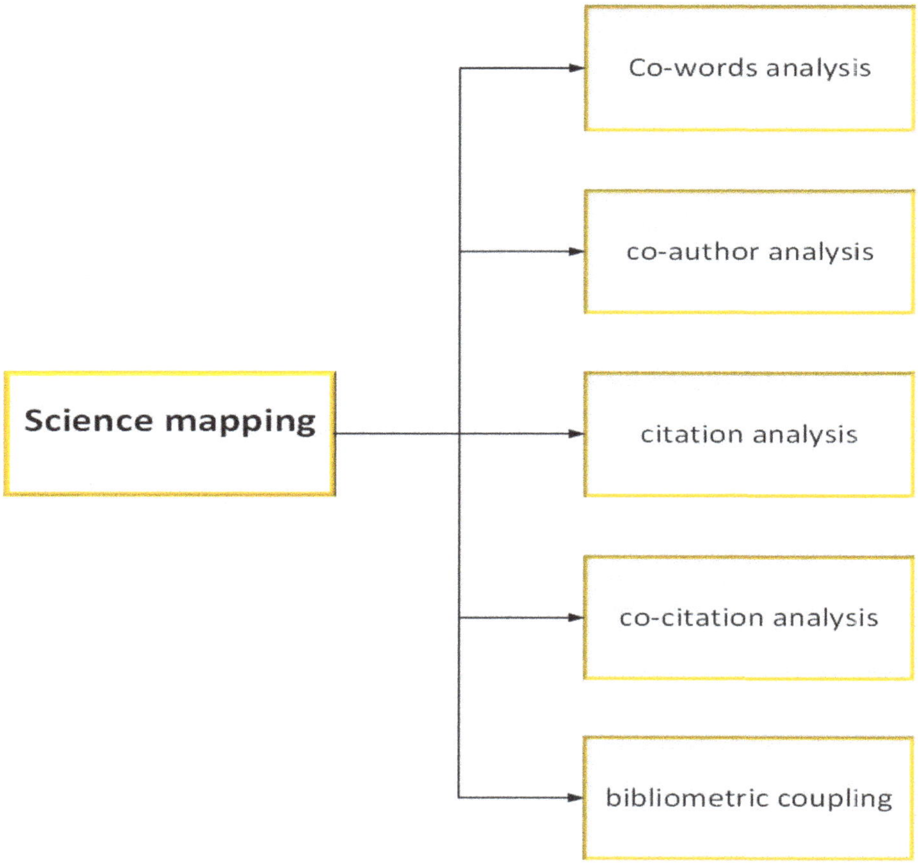

Figure 9.3. Bibliometric science mapping metrics.

network analysis produces bibliometric structure and intellectual structure of the research area (Tunger and Eulerich 2018) (figure 9.3).

Science mapping is a general process of analyzing a domain and visualizing it. The science mapping scope can be limited to scientific discipline, research area or area of a topic with the concern about answering certain research questions. The scope is required to contain the main relevant subjects critical to the research problem. Possible revolutionary and constant changes can be experienced in the structure of the domain. Many components are involved in the science mapping study; major ones include body of scientific literature, scientometric sets and analytical tools for visualization, metrics/indicators to show patterns and trends significantly, and scientific change theories guiding exploring and the visual structure interpretation as well as the interpretation of dynamic patterns. The scientific change theories include scientific revolutions views that are paradigmatic, development of science is determined by competing scientists and the scientific discipline evolutionary stages (Chen 2017).

9.6 Bradford law

If scientific journals are arranged according to productivity in descending order for a particular subject area, the journals can be classified into periodic nucleus based on subject areas in different groups, with each zone having a group of articles with the same number in the nucleus. The periodicals in a nucleus in the zone will be 1: n: n^2... driving the publications to be the same size can be expressed as (Bailón-Moreno *et al* 2005):

$$R(r) = iy_o \tag{9.1}$$

where the accumulated journals for a particular field are represented by R, accumulated articles for a particular field are represented by $R(r)$, the number of zones referred to as the Bradford is i and the nucleus of the journals productivity is represented by y_o. The r as the number of the periodicals is expressed as:

$$r = (1 + k + k^2 + k^{i-1})r_o \tag{9.2}$$

Where the Bradford multiplier is represented by k and nucleus accumulated journals for a particular field is r_o the typical representation of equation (9.2) is expressed as:

$$r = r_o + kr_o + k^2r_o + k^{i-1}r_o \tag{9.3}$$

The Bradford has a logarithmic as the second component with expression of the linear fraction expressed as:

$$R(r) = \alpha \log\left(\frac{r}{\theta}\right) \tag{9.4}$$

Where the slope of the fraction is represented by α and parameter of the Brookes is θ. For θ formal issues when $\theta < 1$ the equation of Brookes may not necessarily be the best, therefore, the following expression is used:

$$R(r) = \alpha \log\left(\frac{r}{x_1}\right) + \quad y_1 \tag{9.5}$$

where the coordinate of the straight fraction points are represented by x_1 and y_1. For direct fit to the straight fraction with c as the ordinate the origin of the following expression is deemed fit:

$$R(r) = \alpha \log r + c \tag{9.6}$$

Equation (9.6) has been proven to be effective in journal nucleus evaluation of publish works and c is expressed as (Bailón-Moreno *et al* 2005):

$$c = \alpha \log \theta. \tag{9.7}$$

9.7 Previously published bibliometric analysis

In this section, previously published bibliometric analyses on AI are presented to show the difference between the current bibliometric study on AI and the ones already discussed in the literature. China Report (2018) presents a bibliometric analysis of the development of AI mainly focusing on China compared to the development of AI across the world. The study was conducted to increase the awareness of AI development to the public, to promote industrial development of AI and serve policymakers with sufficient information to take decisions in China. Similarly, another bibliometric study conducted on the applications of AI in sustainability to give the picture of future sustainability in the context of AI was put forward. It was found in the study that the major theme published in the literature includes energy consumption efficiency, smart grid and renewable energy. The study uncovered the research trends and proffered a direction for solving the research challenges identified in the literature (Bracarense *et al* 2022). The bibliometric analysis of the supply chain in the context of AI to cope with the increasing complex nature of supply chain has been presented. It is found that the AI technologies such as machine learning, robotics, natural language processing transformed the approach to supply chain. The study has been conducted from the perspective of processes (Riahi *et al* 2021).

Yu *et al* (2019) studied bibliometrics with the focus on the journal *Applied Intelligence* with the first set of publications in 1991. It is considered as one of the influential journals in the field of computer science. The study investigated the evolution of the journal, structure and citation landscape based on data from Web of Science. Bibliometric performance analysis and science mapping were conducted to reveal a comprehensive view of the journal over decades. In another study, a bibliometric analysis on AI applications for a period of one decade was conducted. The study used Web of Science to retrieve information about the applications of AI in different domains of applications. Performance analysis and science mapping were conducted. The attractive research areas receiving attention from the research community were uncovered in the study, which include perception intelligence, simulated human mind, machine learning, bio-inspired algorithms and big-data intelligence. The study revealed the trends in AI development (Gao *et al* 2021). Ezugwu *et al* (2021) present an extensive literature survey and bibliometric analysis for Nature-inspired meta-heuristic algorithms. The study covered more than 300 global optimization algorithms inspired from different natural intelligent agents spanning over 30 years.

A similarly study presented a bibliometric analysis study that covered 10 years from 2011 to 2021 to examine the trends in the publications of AI research related to the COVID-19 pandemic. Both performance analysis and science mapping were conducted to provide the trend and emerging areas in AI publications. Image processing, deep learning and machine learning were found to be the common AI technology applied to the healthcare domain (Suhail *et al* 2022). Bibliometric raw data from 1988 to 2018 were collected from Web of Science and Scopus about engineering applications of *The AI Journal*, one of the prestigious journals in the domain of AI. The citation structure such as distribution of the citations, yearly citations, trending themes and impelling factors of the journal were analyzed. A co-authorship map and geographical issues were analyzed quantitatively, and performance analysis was included in the bibliometric study (Shukla *et al* 2019). Lei and Liu (2019) presented bibliometric analysis on the growth of AI from 2007 to 2016 spanning 10 years, analyzing performance such as the prolific countries, institutions, authors, etc. The study retrieved information from Web of Science. A valuable reference for the development of AI was provided to the research community in the study. Chiroma *et al* (2024) have presented both performance analysis and mapping of the research progress in the applications of AI in Internet of Medical Things. The bibliometric analysis covered the period between 2016 and 2023. The study established that security and privacy were the major concerns in the adoption of AI Internet of Medical Things.

9.8 Methodology

This section proposes a bibliometric analysis methodology for researchers in the domain of AI to adopt for conducting bibliometric analysis from different perspectives of AI (e.g. generative AI, robotics, brain–machine interface). The methodology of bibliometric analysis encapsulates its applications including both performance analysis and science mapping. The complete stages of the methodology are provided in figure 9.4.

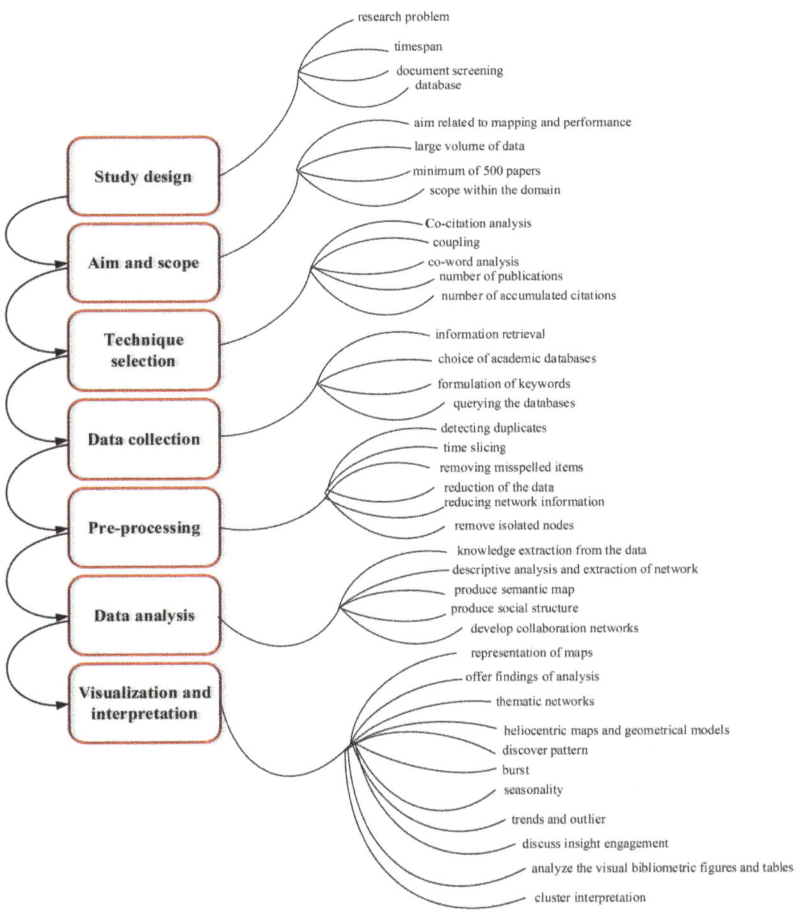

Figure 9.4. Proposed procedure for conducting bibliometric analysis in the AI domain.

9.8.1 Study design

Study design is critical in bibliometric analysis (Leydesdorff 1987). It is in the study design that a researcher is expected to formulate research questions and select the appropriate technique that can adequately respond to the formulated research question. There are generally three categories of questions that can be answered in science mapping, including: (1) intellectual structure of the knowledge-based research area or subject identification; (2) observing the conceptual structure of the research area; and (3) the structure of social networks of the scientific research community for the research field (Aria and Cuccurullo 2017). In addition to the formulation of research questions pertaining to performance analysis are prolific authors, countries, institutions, journals, etc.

Aria and Cuccurullo (2017) argued that one of the critical issues in the design of the study is the choice of timespan or taken decision in dividing the timespan into different slices by the researcher. Typically, bibliometric study is conducted within a certain period of time to represent the static nature of the research area within the period under consideration. The timespan can be sliced to capture the progress achieved in the research area at different periods of time. Researchers can choose the appropriate databases for the collection of bibliometric data, screen the main documents and export the bibliometric data for the study to be performed (Waltman 2016). The chosen database for data collection is Scopus within a timespan of 1960–2023 for the first phase and the second phase 1960–2024. The study includes data analysis using software tools (Aria and Cuccurullo 2017). The research question is formulated based on the proposed study objectives, thus, different studies can have different research questions. In this study, the main research questions are as follows:

- (i) What country, institution, funding agency, conference proceedings, authors and journals are the most prolific in the field of AI?
- (ii) What is the pattern of publications and citation trends in AI for over six decades from 1960?
- (iii) What are the trending research topics in the AI domain?
- (iv) What are the co-words in the AI domain?
- (v) Who are the top leading authors in AI research?

9.8.2 Aims and scope

It is required in the bibliometric analysis for the researcher to define the aim and scope of the bibliometric study because it plays a role in the selection of the techniques to be used for the bibliometric study and data collection. Selecting bibliometric analysis techniques without properly defining the aim and scope of the study can pose a challenge to the bibliometric analysis by making the whole process unworkable. Thus, a lot of time, efforts and resources could be wasted that could have been used in in improving the bibliometric study if the study was properly planned. The aim of the study is expected to relate to the science mapping and performance analysis of the bibliometric study. In performance analysis, the study can seek to uncover prolific institutions, authors, journals and countries. Science mapping is typically designed to uncover the underlying intellectual structure found in clusters created by the network. A large volume of data is required for bibliometric analysis, thus, a large volume of the bibliometric data should be in the scope set for the bibliometric study. The volume of bibliometric data considered to be enough for the study is benchmarked at the minimum of 500 published papers in the research area as suggested. However, a research field with few papers such as 50, or tens, or between 100–300 is not suitable for bibliometric analysis (Donthu *et al* 2021). For example, the study aims to establish the most prolific institution, journal, authors, conference proceedings, country, funding agency, publication and citation trend as well as uncover patterns in the intellectual and scientific structures of networks in the field of AI. The scope of the study is core AI covering different aspects. AI is a very hot research area, currently the most discussed science subject in the world, experiencing a boom never previously seen in history. The number of documents returned after a search in Scopus is in the millions as AI is a broad area coupled with the current boom.

9.8.3 Bibliometric analysis technique selection

To meet the aim and scope of the bibliometric study as outlined in the aim and scope section, the technique for the bibliometric analysis should be chosen properly. The common issue typically confronting researchers at this stage is the decision to select the technique before data retrieval or collect the data before choosing a suitable technique. It is recommended to researchers to choose the technique first based on the bibliometric data intended to be collected. Subsequently, one can prepare the data reflecting the technique selected. This is because if the data is collected first before the technique is selected it can limit the choice of the technique to be used by the researcher. In addition, the bibliometric study data is frequently being retrieved in a format that is raw. Thus, the researcher will be required to preprocess the raw data based on the format that can suit the selected bibliometric technique. Therefore, the recommendation put forward can give researchers ample opportunity to choose the bibliometric analysis technique among alternatives instead of limiting the choices. For instance, if bibliometric analysis proposed to review the past, current and the future of certain research area using voluminous bibliometric corpus, the combination of co-citation representing the past, bibliographical coupling representing the present and the co-word analysis showing notable words for the future research direction and implications can be chosen for the study. On the other hand, if the bibliometric study proposes to uncover general themes within a specified period of time, co-word analysis can be used with author keywords in conjunction to improve the analysis of the co-citations and coupling. The bibliometric performance analysis is just similar to the participants profile in empirical published works, as such, number of publications, number of accumulated citations, etc can be chosen, analyzed and discussed in a descriptive manner (Donthu *et al* 2021). In this study, in view of the research questions, aims and scope of the study outlined in the preceding sections, both performance analysis and science mapping are selected for illustration. This allows the chapter to demonstrate to readers how to conduct both techniques, especially early career researchers and expert researchers willing to start including bibliometric analysis in their survey papers.

9.8.4 Data collection

Many online bibliographical and abstracting databases indexing scientific literature and the accumulated citations exist in today's research world. The majority of the scientific field literature can be found in the databases allowing the search and retrieval of information in a particular scientific area. Despite the fact that many academic databases exist, the following databases are undoubtedly considered the most significant academic databases: Web of Science, Scopus, Google scholar and MEDLINE. These databases cover journals in the scientific field using different approached as proved by different studies. The use of Google scholar to download a large volume of data is difficult and the dump containing the complete data is unavailable. Other than the academic databases outlined in the previous section, the following databases for indexing scientific literature can be used for the retrieval of scientific information: DBLP computer science bibliography, arXiv, SAO/NASA Astrophysics Data System, CiteSeerX and Science Direct (Cobo *et al* 2011).

The different databases have different bibliometric data formats, and researchers can decide to use multiple numbers of academic databases for bibliometric analysis, for example to use Scopus and Web of Science. As a result of that, extra effort is required to merge the documents into one compatible format. It is suggested for researchers to use only one academic database for bibliometric analysis to avoid the need to merge two databases. Merging multiple databases is vulnerable to errors, therefore, settling on one database for the study can minimize human efforts and eliminate the potential of introducing errors in the bibliometric datasets (Donthu *et al* 2021). Collection of data involves a series of activities such as the data retrieval from the academic databases to get the complete bibliometric data. A database such as Web of Science is queried to retrieve the required information. An API can be used to assist researchers automatically retrieving the meta-data about the scientific publications of the scholars list. To query the database, keywords need to be formulated specifying language of the publication and timespan, e.g. 1985–2015, required for the bibliometric study (Aria and Cuccurullo 2017). Before querying the database to retrieve data, keywords are formulated. Considering the scope of the study as already discussed in the scope section, the following keywords were used: artificial intelligence, robots, transformer, natural language processing, machine learning, generative models, artificial neural networks, artificial general intelligence, deep learning, expert system, fuzzy system, brain–machine interface, graph neural network, robotics, and explainable artificial intelligence. Scopus database was queried using the keywords for the collection of data to retrieve meta-data about the scientific publications in the field of AI. The study choosing a single database avoids the possibility of introducing error that typically arises from merging multiple databases. The data were collected on the 16th of November, 2024, from the period 1960 to 2024. The total number of documents retrieved amounted to 2 716 683. To have a clue on the distribution of languages typically used for publications in AI, the study included languages in the data collection.

9.8.5 Data pre-processing

Datasets for research need to be prepared to be suitable for the research under consideration. Collecting data typically comes with issues that need to be tackled before processing the data to get the desired output. This is true especially if the data is voluminous because it will come with irrelevant and redundant attributes. These unwanted attributes need to be removed before presenting the data for analysis. It is suggested that high-quality research outcome emanates from high-quality data, on the other hand, poor quality data produces poor findings regardless of the methodology (Chiroma and Abawjy 2023). Typically, the data retrieved from academic bibliographical sources comes with errors. Thus, to have quality data, a pre-processing stage is required to be applied to the data for cleaning. In performing a bibliometric study, pre-processing of the data is required to have quality results as it is a significant stage for quality outcome (Cobo *et al* 2012). The data for bibliometrics has to be cleaned in view of the fact that the academic databases were never designed mainly for conducting bibliometric studies. Allowing the erroneous items in the data without pre-processing to clean the data may lead to erroneous findings of the research area (Donthu *et al* 2021).

Data pre-processing involves different stages such as detecting duplicates, time-slicing, items that were misspelled, reduction of the data based on productivity, impact or any other journal metrics, because it is very difficult for voluminous data to produce a good outcome. In addition, reducing network information can be applied to the raw data retrieved from the academic databases. This is performed by carefully examining the entire raw data. This pre-processing stage improves the quality of the raw data. The de-duplicating process is performed before the reduction of the data to get only the representative of the entire data for analysis. If duplicate items are found only one is maintained in the data while the other item is removed. However, if both items in the databases represent the same entity, the content of the two entities can be merged together. The network can be processed by selecting the most significant vertices on the network structure of the relationship that exists between the analysis units based on different criteria (e.g., removal of isolated vertexes and insignificant links connecting the vertexes) (Cobo *et al* 2012). A subfield in a research field can be identified using data reduction techniques. Examples of the data dimension reduction techniques include multiple correspondence, clustering algorithms, principal component analysis and multi-dimensional scaling (Aria and Cuccurullo 2017, Klavans and Boyack 2017). In this study, the data collected underwent a thorough data pre-processing stage, in the case of duplicate data, one item was removed and only one maintained, multiple entries with different numbers of items were found and merged. For example, multiple entries of *LeCun Y* were found and merged together, items without any meaning, e.g., undefined and isolated vertices, were removed. To demonstrate data reduction because of the high volume of data, the data were reduced based on impact and 10 000 articles were obtained (the 10 000 top-cited articles).

9.8.6 Data analysis

This stage involves descriptive analysis and extraction of the network. There are different methods for the extraction of the network such as co-word analysis that uses keywords or significant words in the documents published in the research area to conceptualize the research area structure. This approach uses the content of the document for the construction of similarity measures unlike other methods that establish relationship in the document through citations which are indirect. The semantic map of the research area is produced by the co-words analysis to help in comprehending the cognitive structure. Keywords, full text or abstracts can be used for the co-word analysis. Unit analysis is typically not a document, journal or author but a concept or keyword. Another approach is the co-author analysis that investigates the authors and corresponding affiliations for the study of the social structure including collaboration networks. Similarly, citation analysis is another approach that is common, the analysis method is used in accumulated citations to measure the similarities among documents, journals and authors. The citation analysis comprises coupling and co-citation analysis such as the journal co-citations, author coupling, journal citation and author citation. The coupling relationship is established by the authors that publishes the articles and detects research groups connections, whereas the authors citing the analyzed documents form the co-citation connections. The co-citation analysis detects paradigm shifts and schools of thought in a research field when it is observed over a period of time. All these different approaches to the bibliometric analysis are available alternatives to researchers to choose the required technique to apply in the study depending on the objectives of the bibliometric study. For example, to perform mapping of old papers, co-citation can be employed. It is suggested to be performed within different slices of time. On the other hand, the mapping of current published papers is performed by coupling. It is recommended that the use of direct citations to represent a current research front is better compared to the coupling and co-citation. Normalized process can be performed on the edges between the vertices if the network is developed. The normalization is performed using similarity measures including Jaccard's coefficient, correlation coefficient and Salton's cosine (Aria and Cuccurullo 2017, Klavans and Boyack 2017).

Publication analysis determines productivity and identifies social dominance. Citation analysis determines the impact and identifies social dominance. Hybrid analysis determines impact related to productivity and identifies social impact (Mukherjee *et al* 2022). The bibliometric analysis is run using a bibliometric software tool (section 9.9) and the structure is created from running the software tool after the data is uploaded. Theoretically, running the bibliometric analysis and the bibliometric review writing are considered as two distinct stages. However, in practice, the two are joined together because both activities go side by side. For instance, the situation where the network is divided into clusters and the visual representation of the network summaries is generated directly, determine the paper writing. As such, the writing and running of the bibliometric analysis to generate the finding summaries are considered as single content. The writing style is considered an important component, thus, the writing style depends on the target journal and research area where the bibliometric analysis is performed. For example, a journal that focusses on theory may give priority to the theoretical part of the study and no limit to number of words. Another journal may give high priority to findings established in the study such as the journals that have stringent limitations on the number of words allowed in a paper. In this case, it is recommended for researchers to visit the target journal to download previously published a bibliometric analysis paper, study it and follow a similar pattern of writing (Donthu *et al* 2021). In this study, the chapter extracts the following descriptive: article publications trend, institutional, funding agencies, languages, conference proceedings, countries, authors and journals productivity. Subsequently, citation analysis is conducted. Co-words, co-authorship collaboration and keywords are analyzed. For the descriptive analysis the complete data was used for the analysis, whereas for the citation analysis and mapping, the 10 000 articles filtered based on citations were used.

9.8.7 Data visualization and interpretation

The data analysis stage entails knowledge extraction from the data to depict it via intuitive visualization or a map such as the bi-dimensional maps, social networks and dendrograms. Network analysis gives room to researchers to conduct statistical analysis from generated maps for the purpose of indicating different measures of the complete network or relationship or detecting the overlapping of clusters. The visual techniques are tools typically used for the representation of science maps and offer the findings of different analysis. For example, thematic networks, heliocentric maps and geometrical models, can be used for the representation of networks or maps in which the distance that exists between the items represents similarity. Conceptual, intellectual or social evolution of a research area can be indicated by temporal analysis. It can discover patterns, bursts, seasonality, trends and outliers in a research field. The features with high intensity over periods of time are identified by a temporal analysis. Cluster string and thematic areas are used for the demonstration of research field evolution over different periods of time. Where an event occurred and the impact of the event on the neighbouring field can be discovered using geospatial analysis (Aria and Cuccurullo 2017). After that, the researcher has to interpret the findings and the maps based on knowledge and experience of the researcher to discover new knowledge.

Researchers drafting bibliometric paper for publication are enjoined to discuss insight engagement directly with the observed trends and the corresponding rationale instead of presenting a summary report of the bibliometric corpus. Thus, researchers are encouraged to analyze the visual bibliometric figures and tables for the analytical discussion rather than presenting descriptive discussions. The content and context of the concept should be appropriately explained. The content of every thematic cluster and the meaning of the publications topics within the cluster should be interpreted from the bibliometric analysis findings. It is significant to observe the contextual meaning of the entities rationale that characterizes the content to have a great understanding of the content itself. For example, researchers with different cluster words can be found from the co-word analysis. Researchers can depend on the wordings that appear frequently in the cluster to understand the content of the words. For instance, words that were connected more than others, however, the way the words were connected together must be reviewed to interpret the context of each cluster, for example, studies where the words appear (Donthu *et al* 2021). The visualization and interpretation of the results for the current study are presented and discussed in section 9.10.

9.9 Bibliometric software tools

Software tools developed for the purpose of bibliometric analysis are available. To ease the work of researchers in finding suitable tools for bibliometric analysis, this section presents ten different bibliometric analysis software tools suitable for the analysis of scientific documents through science mapping. Each of these are briefly explained in this section for the reader to get insight on the functionality of each. The choice of the software tool for bibliometric study depends on the nature of the study and objectives. Researchers are recommended to chose a suitable software tool based on the objectives and nature of the study. For example, a study that requires patent information from Derwent Innovations Index can chose CiteSpace. As each of the software tools has its own unique weakness and strength, multiples of the software tool can be used in combination to complement each other in case the use of one software tool is not sufficient. In the current study, VOSViewer is adopted with biblioshiny to compliment the VOSViewer, which is suitable and sufficient to perform the analysis based on the research questions and aim of the study. A schematic of the software tools is depicted in figure 9.5.

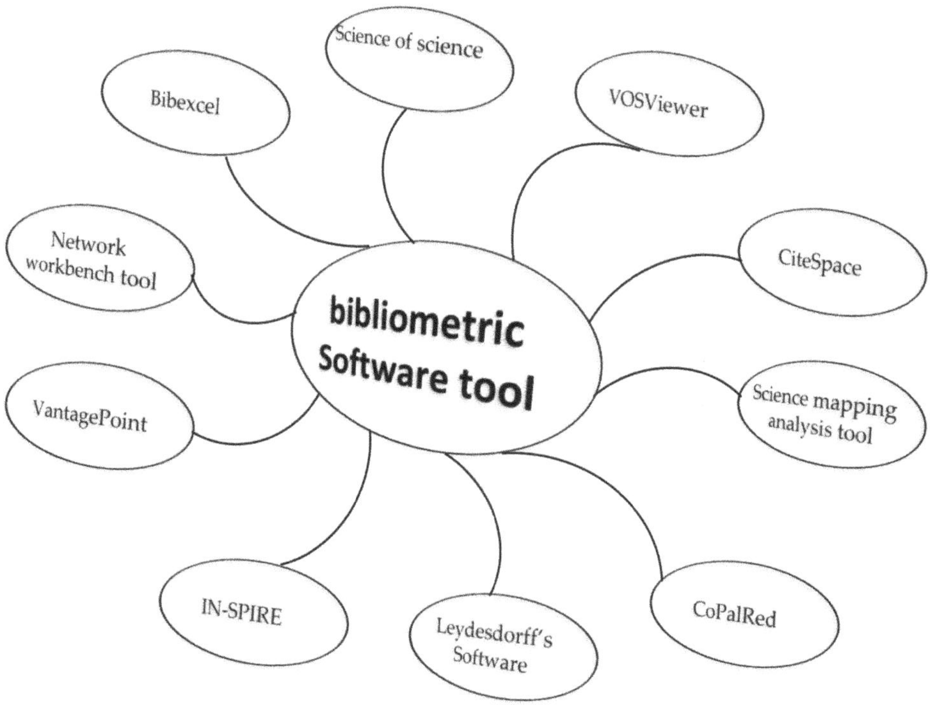

Figure 9.5. Bibliometric software tools.

9.9.1 Science mapping analysis tool

The science mapping analysis tool (SciMAT) is a bibliometric software tool developed for the purpose of performing science mapping within the framework of longitude. The software offers different modules of workflow for conducting science mapping. The features that make SciMAT unique from other bibliometric analysis software include a powerful module dedicated for pre-processing the raw bibliometric data to clean and make it suitable for the analysis. Another interesting feature is the application of bibliometric measures for studying the impact of each of the elements being studied and lastly, a module that can automatically configure the analysis (Cobo *et al* 2012).

9.9.2 VOSViewer

VOSViewer is one of the established bibliometric software tools widely accepted in the bibliometric research community, developed by Centre for Science and Technology Studies at Leiden University. VOSViewer is designed and developed purposely for the construction and visualization of bibliometric maps with a remarkable feature for graphically representing maps. VOSViewer uses functionalities such as zoom, special labelling algorithms and density metaphors for the representation of big maps. It is open source software freely available to the research community. The software doesn't support co-occurrence matrix from the data to extract and build. However, it supports the construction and visualization of bibliometric maps for any type of co-occurrence data (Van Eck and Waltman 2010).

9.9.3 IN-SPIRE

IN-SPIRE is a bibliometric software tool mainly for performing bibliometric analysis whereby the software has the capability of uncovering relationships, trends and hidden themes in data to uncover new knowledge and insights. The relationship among documents and a set of very similar documents can be uncovered easily by IN-SPIRE using a landscape metaphor. IN-SPIRE characterizes documents in its context based on statistical word patterns (Hetzler and Turner 2004).

9.9.4 CiteSpace

This is a bibliometric software tool developed for the detection, analysis and visualization of patterns and trends in scientific publications. The software was designed and developed by Drexel University, it is open source software freely available for download by the research community. Its main purpose is to enhance emerging trends in a knowledge domain. CiteSpace has the ability to be compatible with different bibliometric sources formats like Web of Science, PubMed, arXiv and SAO/NASA Astrophysics Data System. In addition, it can read grant information and patent information from Derwent Innovations Index (Chen 2006, 2014).

9.9.5 CoPalRed

This is a bibliometric analysis software tool developed mainly for performing co-word analysis based on the keywords extracted from scientific publications. The software is commercial, designed and developed by the University of Granada research group EC3. It is best described as a knowledge system that retrieves information from databases to discover new knowledge. The CoPalRed support csv file is generated from reference management software (Cobo *et al* 2011).

9.9.6 VantagePoint

VantagePoint is a commercial software tool that deals with text-mining, developed by Search Technology Inc. The tool is used for discovering new knowledge from search data retrieved from academic databases or general structured text and patents. It has the capacity to handle a large volume of structured text to analyze, to uncover patterns and relationships. Researchers have used VantagePoint to conduct bibliometric science mapping studies. The import filters of the tool are 180, allowing the user to retrieve data from virtually any academic database that has indexed/abstract publications and databases that warehouse patents. In addition, it is compatible with the filters for loading data from Excel, Access, XML file format2 and filters defined by the user (Oliveira *et al* 2015).

9.9.7 Leydesdorff's software

This is a science mapping software application that uses a command line interface program with a variety of functionality for performing analysis. The Leydesdorff's software was designed and developed at the University of Amsterdam. It is open source software freely available for the research community to download and use. The analysis to be performed by Leydesdorff's software includes co-word, author coupling, co-authorship, journal coupling and author co-citation (Leydesdorff 2005).

9.9.8 Network workbench tool

This is bibliometric analysis software designed and developed at the Indiana University for network analysis, visualization and modelling mainly for the domain of physics, social science and biomedical. The network workbench software tool is freely available for the research community to access. The tool is encoded with specific algorithms for constructing and analyzing networks and maps from data obtained from literature. It has a support for different bibliometric data export formats including Web of Science, Scopus, EndNote and Bibtex. Funding information can be extracted using the software tool in csv file format (NWB Team 2006).

9.9.9 Science of science

This is open source software mainly designed and developed by Indiana University dedicated to perform science study. This software supports the visual representation of data at micro—individual, meso—local and global—macro levels and supports network analysis, temporal, geospatial and topical analysis (Garfield 2009).

9.9.10 Bibexcel

The bibliometric software tool was developed at the University of Umeå mainly focussing on the management of bibliometric data to build maps. The Bibexcel software is open source freely available to the research community for research purposes only and not for profit making. It supports different file formats from different bibliometric sources such as Web of Science and Scopus (Persson *et al* 2009).

9.10 Results and discussion

In this section, visualization of network structure and results are presented, interpreted and discussed. The discussion should not be just providing a summary of bibliometric data and presentation of visuals. Insightful and analytical discussion including rationale is expected from the researcher. The contextual meaning of the major clusters in the different networks generated in the course of the study is expected to be explained clearly for easy understanding of the findings. The discussion should be strictly based on the results within the current study. For example, the publication trend observed in the study should be discussed strictly based on the trends.

In this chapter, the performance analysis and science mapping for the AI subject area mainly focus on the AI topics covered in the book as already listed as keywords in the methodology section. The bibliometric analysis relies on descriptive analyses and mapping analysis—networks. The descriptive analysis includes trend of publications from 1960 to 2024, authorship, language, collaboration, source titles and productivity. Also, it includes citation analysis, collaboration, keywords and co-words.

9.10.1 Annual artificial intelligence publications trend

Figure 9.6 illustrates the annual trend in AI publications, clearly indicating a steady increase in the number of publications in most of the period studied, from 1960 to 2024. The growth in AI literature has been generally consistent, with only minor fluctuations over time. The trend shows that between 1960 and 1981, the number of publications remained at a low level, likely due to limited interest and a lack of groundbreaking technological advancements during this early period. Another likely reason is the discouragement and slow pace of work on neural networks in the 1970s because Minskey and Papert published a paper indicating that neural networks have a parity problem. Another likely reason is the suspension of AI funding in most of the British Universities in the 1970s because of the Lighthill report that pointed out disappointment and criticized AI for lack of impact as expected. Observing the trend more closely, there is a noticeable increase in publications from 1999 to 2003 compared to previous years. An unprecedented surge in AI publications begins around 2009, accelerating significantly from 2012/2013 to the present. This rapid

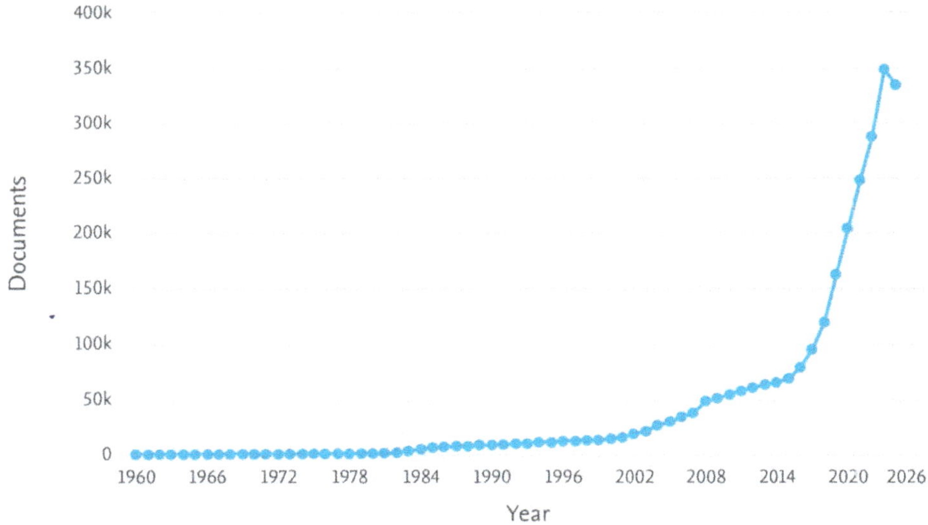

Figure 9.6. Publications trend covering the period from 1960–2023 on yearly bases.

growth can likely be attributed to the AI boom, fuelled by extensive mainstream and social media attention, coupled with the availability of voluminous datasets and high-performance computing systems that support ongoing innovations in AI.

9.10.2 Top prolific countries in artificial intelligence research

Figure 9.7 illustrates the top 10 most prolific countries contributing to AI research. Authors from China lead in AI publications, contributing more articles than authors from any other country. This is followed by United States of America, highlighting

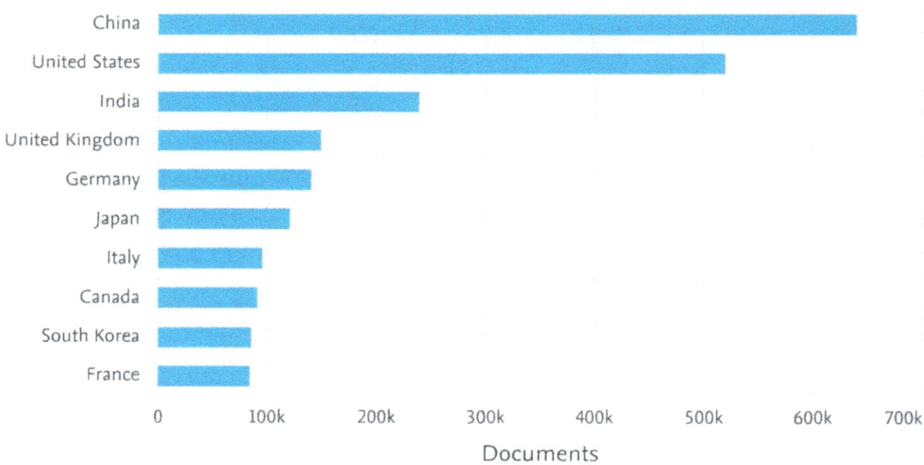

Figure 9.7. Countries' productivity on publications.

the significant roles both countries play in AI research and development, likely due to substantial investment in AI by government and private sectors in both countries. India ranks third, followed by the United Kingdom and Germany in fourth and fifth place, respectively. It is further observed that the gap between China and United States of America is relatively small, whereas the difference between United States of America and India in the third position is quite large, as shown in figure 9.7. Although no European country appears in the top three, most of the countries represented in the top 10 are from Europe and Asia indicating a strong presence of European and Asian authors in AI research.

9.10.3 Prolific institutions in artificial intelligence

Figure 9.8 depicts the most prolific institutions with publication contributions in the area of AI. It is indicated that authors from China Academic Science have the highest contributions of articles followed by authors from Ministry of Education of the People's Republic of China before authors from Tsinghua University at the third spot. It is observed that most of the institutions in the Top 10 ranked institutions are dominated by institutions from China. This is indicating the role played by authors from these institutions contributing a significant number of articles in the field of AI. This pattern is not surprising considering the fact that China is the most prolific country contributing the highest number of articles in AI, globally.

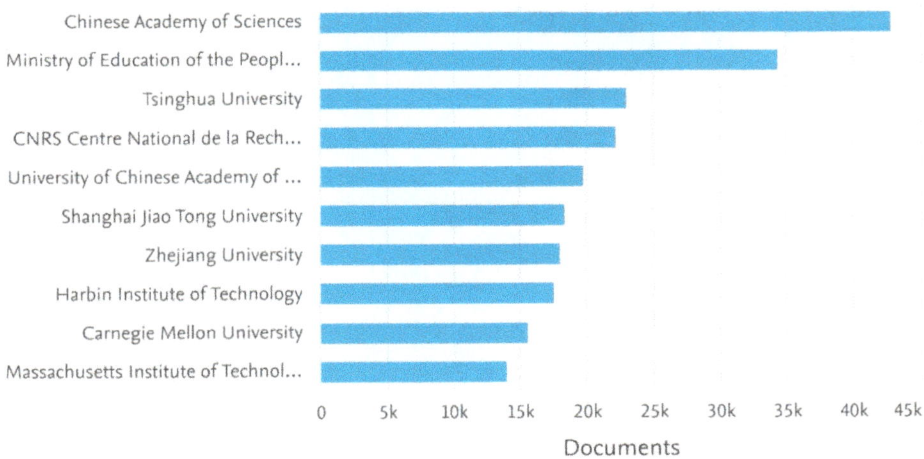

Figure 9.8. Productivity of institutions base on contributions.

9.10.4 Prolific source title in artificial intelligence

Figure 9.9 presents the source titles that publish the highest number of articles in the field of AI. The top publishing source is *Lecture Notes in Computer Science*, including its subseries *Lecture Notes in Artificial Intelligence* and *Lecture Notes in Bioinformatics*, contributing the highest number of articles from 1960 to 2024.

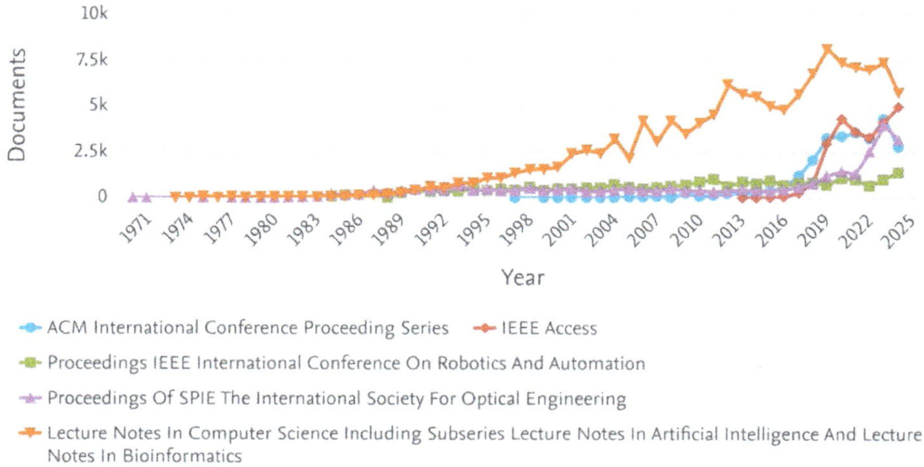

Figure 9.9. Top 5 ranked source titles in AI.

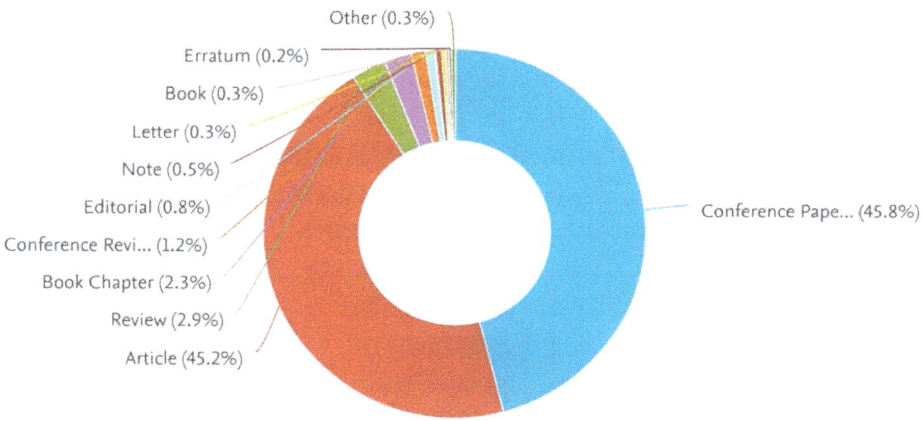

Figure 9.10. Type of AI publications sources.

Observing the figure reveals that the top sources are primarily AI-focused journals and conference proceedings.

Comparing figure 9.9 and figure 9.10 clearly shows that the AI research community heavily relied on journals and conference proceedings for publishing research findings, with conference proceedings holding the majority share (figure 9.10), while other sources played little role. One likely reason authors prefer conference proceedings is because of AI's rapid evolution, where timely publication is essential to avoid findings becoming outdated or superseded by newer research findings. Publications in conference proceedings are typically much faster than those in journals, particularly those with subscription models or authored books.

9.10.5 The most prolific authors based on productivity

Figure 9.11 depicts the top 10 prolific authors with the highest number of contributions in the field of AI. As evident from the bars, Anon has the longest bar indicating over 2000 articles in the field of AI publishing do not mention the author, followed by Fukuda T publishing over 1000 articles and Ishiguro H at the third position with more than 750 articles.

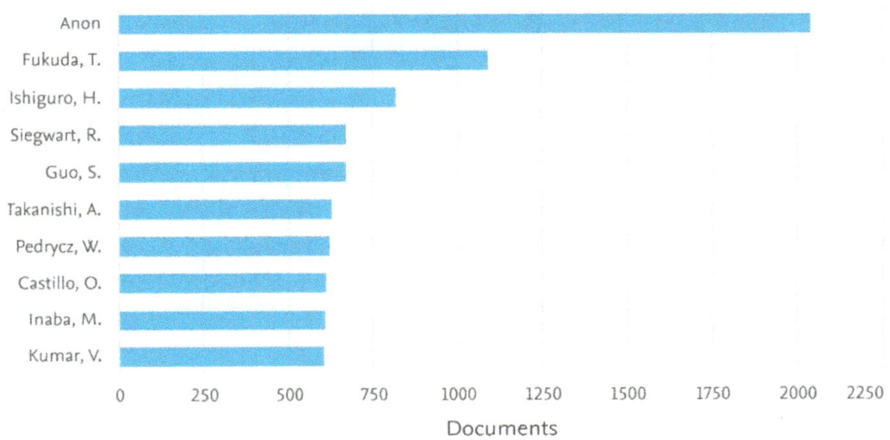

Figure 9.11. The 10 most prolific authors in the field of AI.

9.10.6 Top organizations funding artificial intelligence research and development

Figure 9.12 shows the top 10 funding agencies ranked based on the number of AI researches funded by each of the funding agencies. It shows funding agencies from

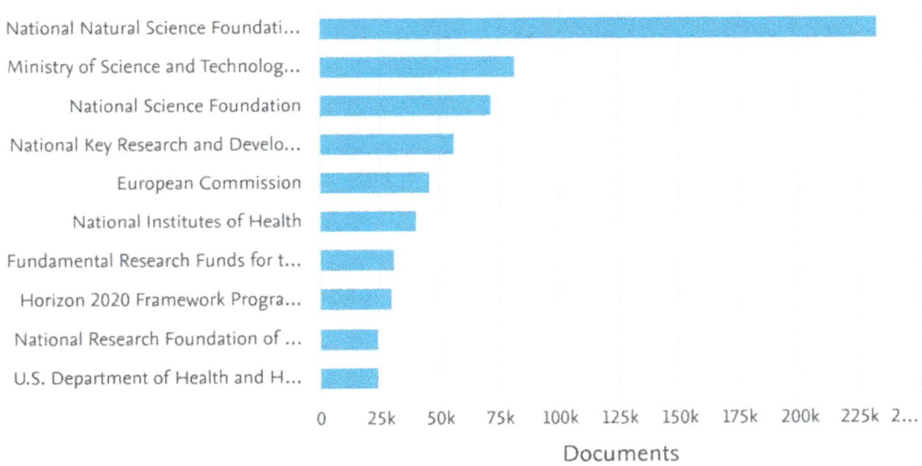

Figure 9.12. Prolific organizations in funding AI research.

different countries sponsoring research in the field of AI. The top AI funding agency is the *National Natural Science Foundation of China*, holding the largest share of funding, followed by the *Ministry of Science and Technology, Taiwan and National Science Foundation* of the United States in third and second places, respectively. The prominence of the funding agencies from China and America are not surprising given the productivity and significant contributions of both countries to AI research. These funding agencies are likely investing heavily to gain a competitive edge in driving AI innovations and the race for leadership in the field of AI. Surprisingly, Taiwan at the second position in funding AI research did not post highly in the competition of the top 10 most prolific institutions.

9.10.7 Language for publishing artificial intelligence research

The distribution of the languages used for the publication of AI research findings is depicted in figure 9.13, indicating the number of articles published in each of the languages. Out of the 10 different languages, English language is top with over 2.6 million articles and the second place Chinese with less than 100 000 articles. This is indicating that English language is the official language of research in AI because of its global acceptability as a medium of research in AI.

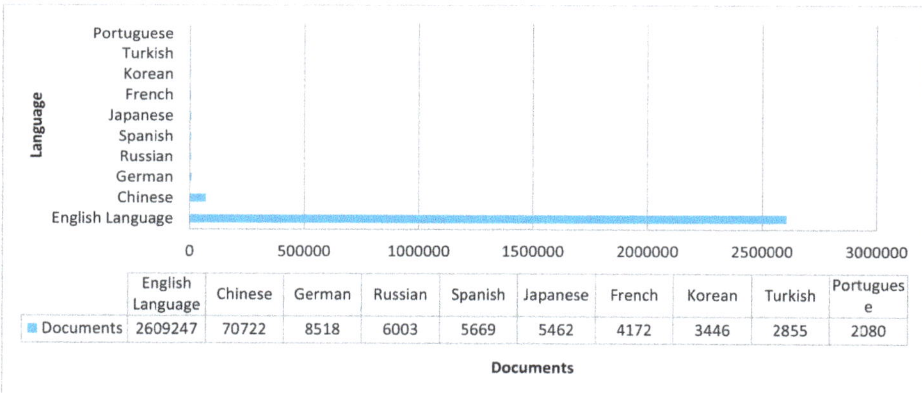

	English Language	Chinese	German	Russian	Spanish	Japanese	French	Korean	Turkish	Portugues e
Documents	2609247	70722	8518	6003	5669	5462	4172	3446	2855	2080

Figure 9.13. Top 10 languages used for the publication of AI research output.

9.10.8 Citation analysis and mapping

This section presents citation analysis results and a mapping network. The results in this section are based on the 10 000 articles filtered by citations. The top 10 000 most cited articles in the area of AI are used.

9.10.8.1 Average citation per year

Figure 9.14 depicts the trend of the average citations per year in the field of AI from 1960 to 2024. Based on the trend the citations maintain consistent growth with small fluctuations along the line, which is normal and expected. The citations have been

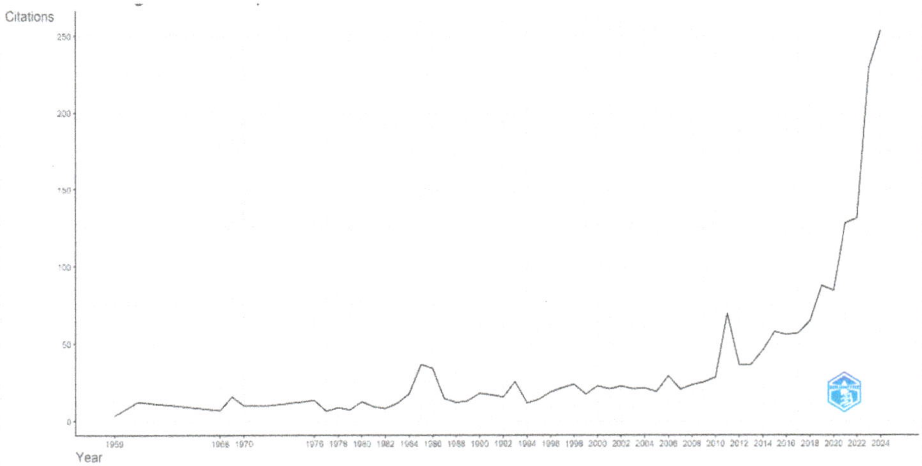

Figure 9.14. Average citations per year from 1960 to 2024.

growing at a normal pace until an unprecedented growing of the citations begins around 2018 and maintains the growth to date with average citations of 333 per document. This clearly indicates that the growth of AI is not limited to the growing number of publications over time but the publication impact grows along with the publications. This is likely because of the attention the field of AI has been generating over time, the unprecedented citations growth notice from 2018 is likely due to the boom in AI as a result of innovations in transformers that led to the development of large language models attracting unprecedented attention, prompting many researchers to switch to AI. In addition, the penetration of AI in almost every field of study is likely a factor that contributes to the growing number of citations as almost every discipline wants to interconnect with AI technology.

9.10.8.2 Top production sources among the 10 000 articles filtered based on citations

Figure 9.15 depicts the trend of top five prolific article production venues productivity-wise per year. The highest publishing venue with the articles with top citations is *IEEE Transactions on Pattern Analysis and Machine Intelligence* followed by *Lecture Notes in Computer Science*, including its subseries *Lecture Notes in Artificial Intelligence* and *Lecture Notes in Bioinformatics.* This is interesting as the growing number of publications from *Lecture Notes in Computer Science*, including its subseries *Lecture Notes in Artificial Intelligence* and *Lecture Notes in Bioinformatics* grows with the impact as evident in comparing figure 9.15 and figure 9.9. It is observed that the top two sources come from journals and conferences, this concurs with the findings showing an overwhelming majority of AI share of publications is from conferences and journals. These are highly reputable venues in the field of AI ranking on top in Web of Science—Clarivate Analytics, Scopus and Australian Business Deans Council. A closer observation

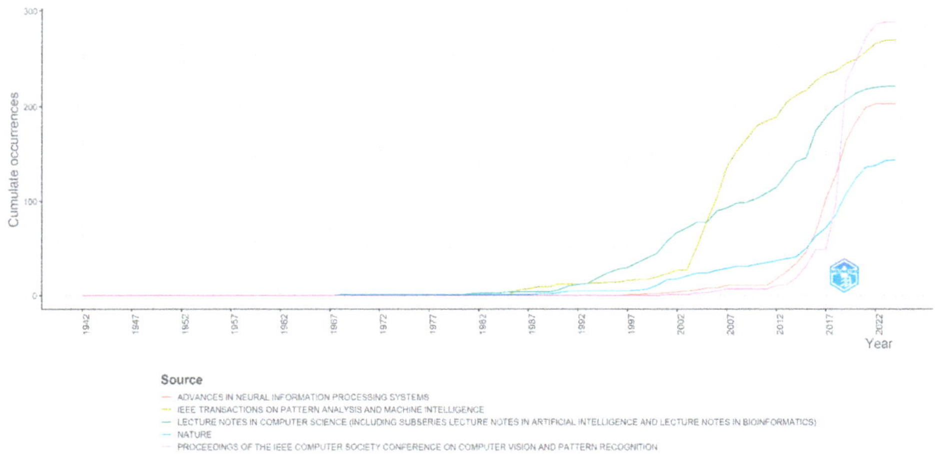

Figure 9.15. Top five production sources of AI literature.

reveals that four out of the five venues are strong AI focus venues with the trend of publications increasing consistently for all the five venues indicating interest in the area of AI.

9.10.8.3 Highly cited artificial intelligence publication venues

Figure 9.16 Illustrates the top-cited venues in the field of AI. *Advances in Neural Information Processing Systems* has the highest impact with 371 196 citations, followed by *IEEE Transactions on Pattern Analysis and Machine Intelligence* with 350 342 citations, both venues are among the top five article production sources, as revealed in figure 9.15. The likely reason why these venues accumulated high citations is because of their prestige, long history of reputation and ranking at the

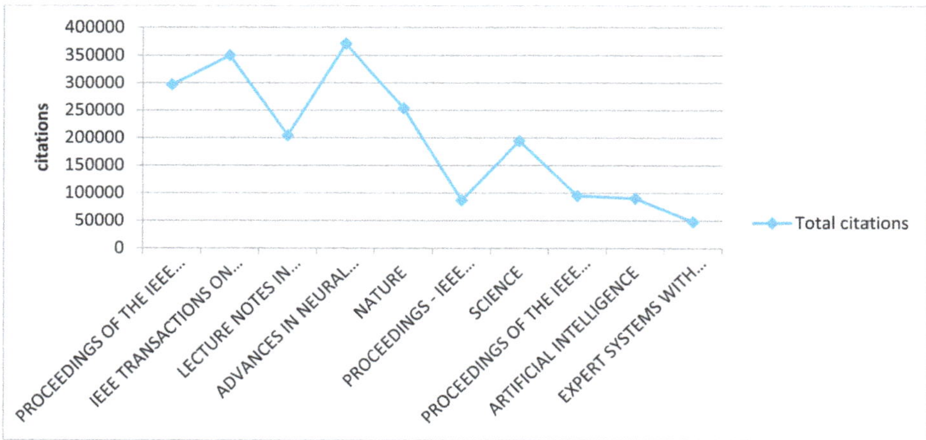

Figure 9.16. Top-cited AI journals and conference proceedings.

top of journal/conference ranking bodies. All the top-cited journals are ranked in the first quarter of Web of Science journal citations reports. These have shown the tremendous impact of these production venues in the field of AI.

9.10.8.4 Top AI journals and conference proceedings h-index, g-index and m-index

Figure 9.17 presents the h-index, g-index, and m-index of top AI publication venues. The *Proceedings of the IEEE Computer Society Conference on Computer Vision and Pattern Recognition* has the highest h-index of 288, meaning that the conference proceedings have published 288 articles, each cited at least 288 times. The g-index is 288, indicating that the top 288 articles have at least 82 944 cumulative citations. The m-index is 12, demonstrating an exceptionally high citation rate. Clearly, these proceedings have an outstanding research impact in the field of AI.

In terms of journals, *IEEE Transactions on Pattern Analysis and Machine Intelligence* has the highest h-index among journals, with a value of 269, meaning it has published 269 articles with at least 269 citations each. The g-index is 269, indicating that the top 269 articles have accumulated at least 72 361 citations. The m-index is 6.405, reflecting an exceptionally high citation rate. This journal also has an outstanding research impact in the field of AI.

Both the conference proceedings and the journal attract a high volume of submissions from leading AI researchers and have very high rejection rates.

Figure 9.18 indicates the top cited authors with high impact in the field of AI. It is indicated that *LeCun Y* is the most cited author with total citations of 101 479 citations among the top cited authors. He is followed by *Breiman L, Hochreiters S, and Vaswani A* with 89 219, 72 098, and 69 157 total citations, respectively.

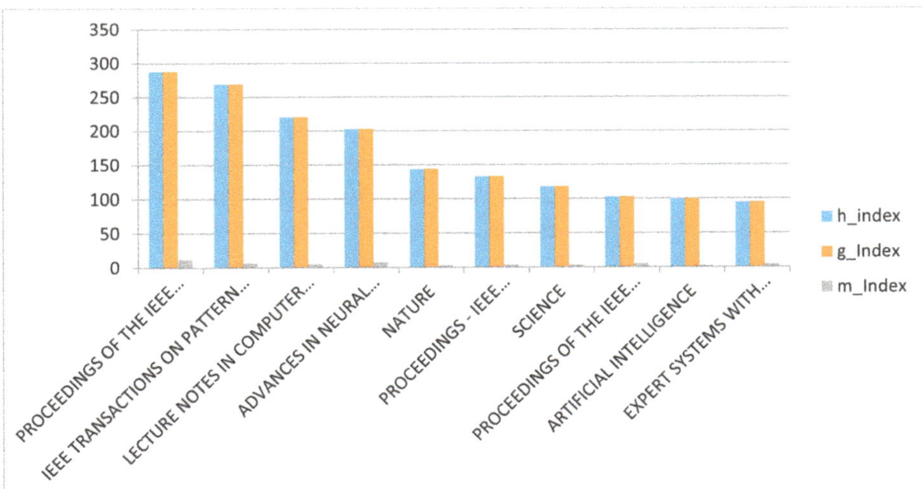

Figure 9.17. Journals and conference proceedings with top h-index, g-index and m-index.

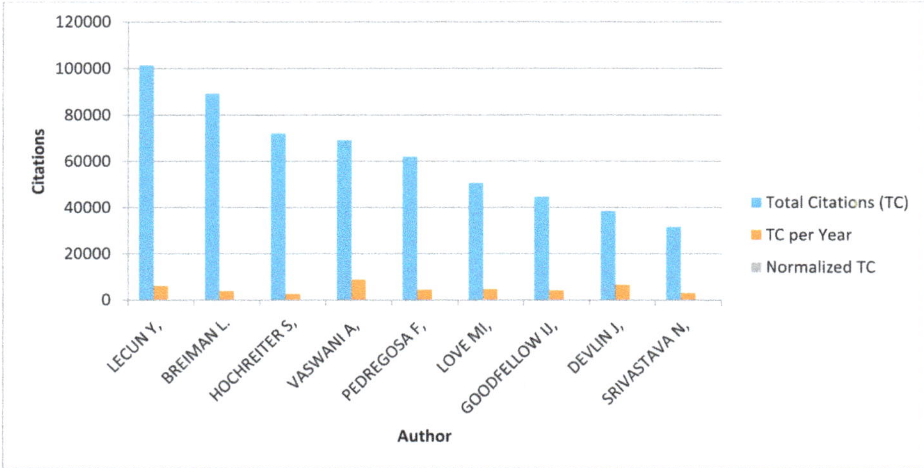

Figure 9.18. The most prolific authors citation-wise impact measure.

A closer look at the top cited authors shows that Vaswani A has the highest total citation average per year with 8644.63 citations followed by Devlin J with 6431.67. In regards to normalized total citations, Vaswani A has the highest with 67.43 followed by *Breiman L* with 58.35. This has shown the impact of these authors in the field of AI. *Lecun Y* is the world-leading researcher in AI. Comparing figure 9.18 side by side with figure 9.11 indicates that highly cited and top productivity authors are different on the two ranking lists. This shows that becoming a highly productive author doesn't automatically translate to being a highly cited author. An author can be highly productive with low impact or low productivity with high impact or both.

9.10.8.5 Authorship keywords

Figure 9.19 provides the network of authorship keywords occurrences displaying the visualization of the dominant keywords in the domain of AI research. The thickness of a keyword vertex is directly proportional to the intensity of the keyword. Meaning that the more the thickness of the vertex the more the intensity of the keyword. Because of that, the prominent keywords include machine learning, human, algorithms and computer simulation as identified from the network map. The number of main clusters created on the network is five. The first cluster has machine learning as the prominent keyword, the second cluster has robotics, the third cluster has computer simulation and robots, the fourth cluster has human and the fifth cluster has male, treatment outcome and clinical study. With machine learning having more prominence than any other keywords indicates the high level of research going on towards developing machine learning models or devices such as large language models.

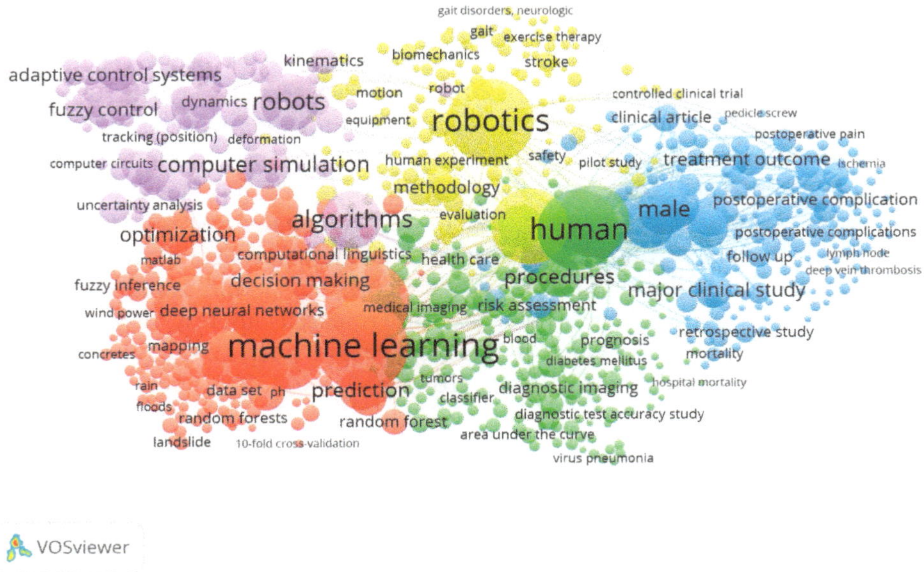

Figure 9.19. The authorship keywords occurrence.

9.10.8.6 Co-words

Figure 9.20 is the visualization of co-words with vertex represented as the occurrence of the keyword, whereas the thickness of the vertex is indicating the magnitude of the keywords' occurrences. So the bigger the vertex the more the magnitude of the keyword occurrences. The co-occurrences is the edge connecting the keywords

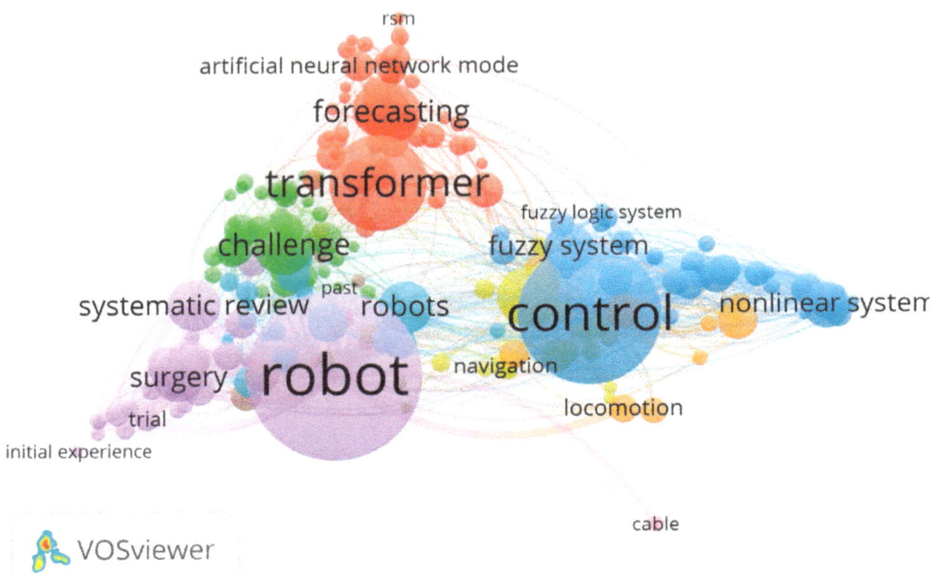

Figure 9.20. Keywords co-occurrence (co-words).

together and the thicker the edge, the more the occurrences of the co-occurrences of the keywords meaning the number of times the keywords occur together. The colours accumulated in different parts of the network represent clusters explaining coverage of the vertex and the edge connecting them together within the cluster. The major clusters identified in the network are three, the first cluster indicates the frequent co-occurrences between 'robot, trial and surgery' but the co-occurrence is more between robot and trial; and 'surgery and systematic review'. In the second cluster 'transformer, artificial neural network and forecasting' have frequent co-occurrences. In the third cluster, 'fuzzy system, control and nonlinear systems'. These keywords co-occurrences indicate the research interest in transformers applications such as large language models, image and video task. Likewise, interest in robotics surgery with clinical trials is growing.

9.10.8.7 Collaborations

Figure 9.21 presents the visualization of the co-authorship collaboration network presenting the relationship between the authors publishing in the field of AI. The vertex in the network is representing the authors, whereas the edge connecting the authors together is indicating the collaboration relationship between the authors. Similarly, the thickness of the edge indicates the intensity of the collaboration, thus, the thicker the edge the more the intensity of the collaboration and vice versa. With regard to vertex, a larger vertex shows higher publication volume by the author. The major clusters created by the co-authorship collaboration network are as follows: Liu Y and Chen Y are the key authors in cluster 1. In cluster 2: Zhang Y and Wang Y are the major authors in the cluster, whereas cluster 3 has Wang W and Wang S as the main authors. The varying edge thickness within clusters highlights the strength of intra-cluster collaborations. Thicker edges between certain authors suggest strong, perhaps long-term partnerships, while thinner edges may indicate occasional or emerging collaborations. Overall, the network suggests that impactful research in AI is being driven by a few highly productive and well-connected authors within a tightly integrated collaborative cluster. Encouraging inter-cluster collaborations could potentially foster more interdisciplinary innovation and knowledge exchange across the broader AI research landscape.

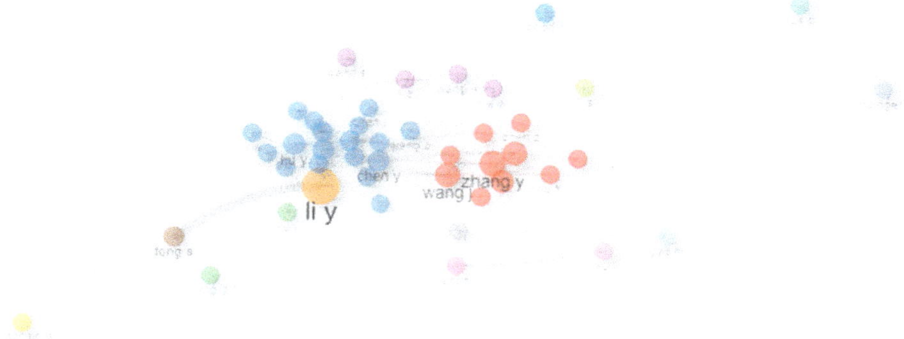

Figure 9.21. Co-authorship collaboration network.

9.10.9 Discussions including implication for theory and practice

Descriptive analysis, citation analysis, and mapping were conducted and discussed. The analysis reveals that China and the United States are the two leading countries in AI research and development, followed by Europe as a whole. The productivity of China and the United States can be linked to substantial research funding, as both countries are home to some of the top AI research funding agencies, which likely supports the high levels of productivity observed. The trending research areas in AI include transformers, robotic surgery, robotics, control systems, and algorithms.

The field of AI will continue to expand, becoming increasingly relevant across nearly every discipline. AI's impact will grow as emerging concepts (e.g., robotic surgery) mature and public awareness of AI increases daily. As various disciplines adopt AI, its influence will rise alongside productivity, balancing both quantity and quality. Countries worldwide can use this bibliometric study to assess areas of strength and weakness, aiming to improve and maintain their current milestones in AI. For countries considering new funding in AI research, this study can serve as a valuable guide to inform funding priorities. Policymakers can leverage the study to uncover insights and extract valuable knowledge about AI for decisions-making process.

This chapter contributes to the body of literature in several ways: it highlights the development of AI in terms of productivity and impact, alongside contributions from different entities; it identifies key areas of current research focus within AI; and it outlines thematic clusters within the field.

9.10.10 Limitations and recommendations to the artificial intelligence research community

In this study, only the Scopus database was used to retrieve data. This may exclude many reputable, emerging AI publication venues not yet indexed in Scopus, as numerous AI-focused journals and conferences are entering the field due to the AI boom. Many of these reputable, emerging AI publications cannot be indexed directly in Scopus and typically appear first in the DBLP Computer Science Bibliography. It is recommended that future bibliometric analyses in AI topics include DBLP as a secondary database, regardless of the primary databases chosen for conducting the study.

This study is to demonstrate its feasibility to the AI community especially new researchers without knowledge of bibliometric analysis. Therefore, many of the analysis were not captured such as academia–industry collaboration, institutional collaborations, single authorship analysis, etc. Refer to the methodology section for other analysis not captured. It will be interesting to capture those analysis in the future.

It is unrealistic to conduct a bibliometric analysis in the field of AI as it is challenging due to the very large scale of articles in this domain, which number in the millions. Sampling, as recommended, may not be sufficient to provide an accurate representation of the rapidly growing volume of AI-related publications. Additionally, the analysis may become skewed toward particular subfields within AI. For instance, if the data is filtered, reduced, or selected based on impact due to the high volume, fields with lower impact could be underrepresented. Similarly, if data is screened based on productivity, emerging areas within AI might not be adequately captured, especially with such large-scale datasets like those seen in AI research. Therefore, it is recommended that bibliometric analysis in AI should focus on a specific research area within the AI. For example, the analysis could be limited to subfields (e.g., robotics, generative AI).

It has been noted that there is a rapidly growing number of literature reviews and surveys in the field of AI. For example, between 2017 and the present, at least 55 survey papers have been published in the subfield of graph neural networks alone (chapter 5). Additionally, over 100 survey papers have been published in the area of explainable AI (chapter 8), and this trend is expected to continue. Despite the increasing interest in publishing survey papers in AI, it is extremely difficult to find a survey paper in the domain of AI that is combined with bibliometric analysis. However, embedding bibliometric analysis within survey papers, even if limited to performance analysis, is a standard global practice, as emphasized by Ramos-Rodríguez and Ruíz-Navarro (2004). Future surveys in AI should incorporate bibliometric analysis to present a comprehensive view of the past, present, and emerging trends in the subfield.

The language barrier in the field of AI is evident; English is the dominant language of AI. Conducting research in AI requires scholars to be proficient in English, placing those who are not fluent at a disadvantage. Those who only understand languages other than English are effectively shut-out from the field of AI. It is recommended that researchers begin developing models to accommodate multiple languages in AI top literature databases.

9.11 Industrial applications and case studies

The industry typically uses bibliometric analysis to scout for trending innovations and identifies the major actors driving these developments. Tracking patent filings and the publication outputs of competitors can help companies monitor their rivals' innovation levels. A company that develops a product will aim to target markets where the product can be sold to customers. Bibliometric analysis can assist companies in analyzing market trends, providing insights on how to tailor products to align with these trends. AI companies, in particular, can use bibliometric analysis to identify leading expert researchers in the field. This can help them scout for talent for hiring, collaboration, or consultation on specific areas of need, ultimately enhancing their products and competitive edge. For example, Google, OpenAI and Microsoft can use bibliometric analysis to monitor innovations in the field of AI.

One of the best venues to identify those talents involved in trending innovations is through bibliometric analysis. Individual talent can be identified from bibliometric analysis and targeted for possible recruitment in a frontline AI company. For example, in an effort to win the leadership race in AI, it has been reported that the CEO of Meta Mark Zuckerberg was personally writing emails to leading AI researchers at Google DeepMind with the intention of enticing them to switch to Meta by hiring them (Huang and Victor 2024). It is not clear in the report how the CEO identified the top AI researchers at Google.

9.12 Summary

For understanding of the field of bibliometric analysis, establish theories forming the fundamentals of the bibliometric analysis including theory of scientific change such as Thomas Kuhn's scientific revolution, Mulkay *et al*'s scientific research area, theory of evolution and sociological theory were outlined and discussed. The Bradford law is discussed including mathematical background.

The bibliometric analysis comprises performance analysis and scientific mapping. The metrics typically used for performance analysis is classified into two major classes, namely, publication-related metrics and citations related metrics. Publication metrics are as follows: total number of publications, publications from academia and industry including academia–industry collaboration, contributing authors, sole-authored articles, co-authored articles and productivity per year. Citation-related metrics are as follows: total citations and average citations, publications citations, index and coefficient of collaboration, proportion of publications citations, citations per article, h-index, i-index (i-10, i-100, i-200), g-index and m-index. Mapping includes collaborations, co-words and keywords.

The chapter presented the bibliometric studies conducted in the field of AI to show the difference between the current work and the already published work paving the way in this chapter. A comprehensive methodology encouraging the AI community to adopt it as the standard protocol for bibliometric analysis in the field of AI is presented. The stages involved in the methodology include study design, aim and scope, bibliometric analysis selection technique, data collection, data pre-processing, data analysis, selection of bibliometric software tools, data visualization and interpretation.

As an example to demonstrate the proposed bibliometric analysis procedure potential applicability in the domain of AI in addition to already existing studies, empirical study is covered. The chapter performed bibliometric analysis based on mostly chapters topics covered in the book like generative AI, artificial general intelligence, huge graph neural network, robotics, brain–machine interface, explainable AI and others. The results of the study relied on descriptive analyses and mapping analysis—networks with visualization and discussion. The trend of publications in AI over the years has been growing together with the impact. In a nutshell, the domain of AI is dominated by China and United States of America. There is stiff competition for leadership in the field of AI between the two countries. Lastly, implication of the bibliometric analysis for theory and practice in AI research was discussed, including limitations and suggestions for future work.

References

Ahmi A 2022 Bibliometric analysis using R for non-coders *J. Family Bus. Manag.* **12** 67–89

Aria M and Cuccurullo C 2017 bibliometrix: an R-tool for comprehensive science mapping analysis *J. Informetr.* **11** 959–75

Bailón-Moreno R, Jurado-Alameda E, Ruiz-Baños R and Courtial J P 2005 Bibliometric laws: empirical flaws of fit *Scientometrics* **63** 209–29

Baker H K, Kumar S and Pattnaik D 2020 Twenty-five years of review of financial economics: a bibliometric overview *Rev. Financ. Econ.* **38** 3–23

Bracarense N, Bawack R E, FossoWamba S and Carillo K D A 2022 Artificial intelligence and sustainability: a bibliometric analysis and future research directions *Pacific Asia J. Assoc. Inform. Syst.* **14** 9

Chen C 2006 CiteSpace II: detecting and visualizing emerging trends and transient patterns in scientific literature *J. Am. Soc. Inform. Sci. Technol.* **57** 359–77

Chen C 2014 The citespace manual *College Comput. Inform.* **1** 1–84

Chen C 2017 Science mapping: a systematic review of the literature *J. Data Inform. Sci.* **2** 1–40

China Report 2018 *China AI Development Report* (China Institute of Science and Technology Policy at Tsingua University) https://docslib.org/doc/5431286/china-ai-development-report-2018 (accessed 23 of September 2023)

Chiroma H and Abawjy J H 2023 *Computing Research Survival Manual: A Practical Handbook for Beginners* (Bristol: IOP Publishing)

Chiroma H, Hashem I A and Maray M 2024 Bibliometric analysis for artificial intelligence in internet of medical things: mapping and performance analysis *Front. Artif. Intell.* **7** 1347815

Cobo M J, López-Herrera A G, Herrera-Viedma E and Herrera F 2011 Science mapping software tools: review, analysis, and cooperative study among tools *J. Am. Soc. Inform. Sci. Technol.* **62** 1382–402

Cobo M J, López-Herrera A G, Herrera-Viedma E and Herrera F 2012 SciMAT: a new science mapping analysis software tool *J. Am. Soc. Inform. Sci. Technol.* **63** 1609–30

Donthu N, Kumar S, Mukherjee D, Pandey N and Lim W M 2021 How to conduct a bibliometric analysis? An overview and guidelines *J. Bus. Res.* **133** 285–96

Donthu N, Kumar S, Pandey N, Pandey N and Mishra A 2021 Mapping the electronic word-of-mouth (eWOM) research: a systematic review and bibliometric analysis *J. Bus. Res.* **135** 758–73

Du Y and Teixeira A A 2012 A bibliometric account of Chinese economics research through the lens of the China Economic Review *China Econ. Rev.* **23** 743–62

Van Eck N and Waltman L 2010 Software survey: VOSviewer, a computer program for bibliometric mapping *Scientometrics* **84** 523–38

Ezugwu A E, Shukla A K, Nath R, Akinyelu A A, Agushaka J O, Chiroma H and Muhuri P K 2021 Metaheuristics: a comprehensive overview and classification along with bibliometric analysis *Artif. Intell. Rev.* **54** 4237–316

Fuchs S 1993 A sociological theory of scientific change *Soc. Forces* **71** 933–53

Gao F, Jia X, Zhao Z, Chen C C, Xu F, Geng Z and Song X 2021 Bibliometric analysis on tendency and topics of artificial intelligence over last decade *Microsyst. Technol.* **27** 1545–57

Garfield E 2009 From the science of science to Scientometrics visualizing the history of science with HistCite software *J. Informetr.* **3** 173–9

Glanzel W 2003 Bibliometrics as a research field a course on theory and application of bibliometric indicators (course handout) https://www.cin.ufpe.br/~ajhol/futuro/references/01%23_Bibliometrics_Module_KUL_BIBLIOMETRICS%20AS%20A%20RESEARCH%20FIELD.pdf

Godin B 2006 On the origins of bibliometrics *Scientometrics* **68** 109–33

Gorkova V I 1988 *Informatics* (Moscow: *VINITI*)

Hetzler E and Turner A 2004 Analysis experiences using information visualization *IEEE Comput. Graphics Appl.* **24** 22–6

Huang K and Victor J 2024 Meta pursues AI talent with quick offers, emails from Zuckerberg *The Information* https://theinformation.com/articles/meta-joins-the-ai-talent-war-with-quick-offers-emails-from-zuckerberg (accessed 20 November 2024)

Klavans R and Boyack K W 2017 Which type of citation analysis generates the most accurate taxonomy of scientific and technical knowledge? *J. Assoc. Inform. Sci. Technol.* **68** 984–98

Kuhn T S 1962 *The Structure of Scientific Revolutions* (Chicago, IL: University of Chicago Press)

Lei Y and Liu Z 2019 The development of artificial intelligence: a bibliometric analysis, 2007–2016 *J. Phys.: Conf. Ser.* **1168** 022027

Leydesdorff L 1987 Various methods for the mapping of science *Scientometrics* **11** 295–324

Leydesdorff L 2005 Similarity measures, author cocitation analysis, and information theory *J. Am. Soc. Inform. Sci. Technol.* **56** 769–72

Mukherjee D, Lim W M, Kumar S and Donthu N 2022 Guidelines for advancing theory and practice through bibliometric research *J. Bus. Res.* **148** 101–15

Mulkay M J, Gilbert G N and Woolgar S 1975 Problem areas and research networks in science *Sociology* **9** 187–203

Ninkov A, Frank J R and Maggio L A 2022 Bibliometrics: methods for studying academic publishing *Persp. Med. Educ.* **11** 173–6

NWB Team 2006 *Network Workbench Tool* (Indiana University, Northeastern University, and University of Michigan)

Oliveira M G, Mendes G H and Rozenfeld H 2015 Bibliometric analysis of the product-service system research field *Procedia Cirp* **30** 114–9

Persson O, Danell R and Schneider J W 2009 How to use Bibexcel for various types of bibliometric analysis *Celeb. Scholar. Commun. Stud.* **5** 9–24

Ramos-Rodríguez A R and Ruíz-Navarro J 2004 Changes in the intellectual structure of strategic management research: a bibliometric study of the Strategic Management Journal, 1980–2000 *Strateg. Manag. J.* **25** 981–1004

Riahi Y, Saikouk T, Gunasekaran A and Badraoui I 2021 Artificial intelligence applications in supply chain: a descriptive bibliometric analysis and future research directions *Expert Syst. Appl.* **173** 114702

Shneider A M 2009 Four stages of a scientific discipline: four types of scientists *Trends Biochem. Sci.* **34** 217–23

Shukla A K, Janmaijaya M, Abraham A and Muhuri P K 2019 Engineering applications of artificial intelligence: a bibliometric analysis of 30 years (1988–2018) *Eng. Appl. Artif. Intell.* **85** 517–32

Suhail F, Adel M, Al-Emran M and Shaalan K 2022 A bibliometric analysis on the role of artificial intelligence in healthcare *Augmented Intelligence in Healthcare: A Pragmatic and Integrated Analysis* (Springer) pp 1–14

Tunger D and Eulerich M 2018 Bibliometric analysis of corporate governance research in German-speaking countries: applying bibliometrics to business research using a custom-made database *Scientometrics* **117** 2041–59

Waltman L 2016 A review of the literature on citation impact indicators *J. Informetr.* **10** 365–91

Yu D, Xu Z and Fujita H 2019 Bibliometric analysis on the evolution of applied intelligence *Appl. Intell.* **49** 449–62

www.ingramcontent.com/pod-product-compliance
Ingram Content Group UK Ltd.
Pitfield, Milton Keynes, MK11 3LW, UK
UKHW051906100926
8556IPUK00005B/785

9 780750 3631